한국의 토익 수험자 여러분께,

토익 시험은 세계적인 직무 영어능력 평가 시험으로, 지난 40여 년간 비즈니스 현장에서 필요한 영어능력 평가의 기준을 제시해 왔습니다. 토익 시험 및 토익스피킹, 토익라이팅 시험은 세계에서 가장 널리 통용되는 영어능력 검증 시험으로, 160여 개국 14,000여 기관이 토익 성적을 의사결정에 활용하고 있습니다.

YBM은 한국의 토익 시험을 주관하는 ETS 독점 계약사입니다.

ETS는 한국 수험자들의 효과적인 토익 학습을 돕고자 YBM을 통하여 'ETS 토익 공식 교재'를 독점 출간하고 있습니다. 또한 'ETS 토익 공식 교재' 시리즈에 기출문항을 제공해 한국의 다른 교재들에 수록된 기출을 복제하거나 변형한 문항으로 인하여 발생할 수 있는 수험자들의 혼동을 방지하고 있습니다.

복제 및 변형 문항들은 토익 시험의 출제의도를 벗어날 수 있기 때문에 기출문항을 수록한 'ETS 토익 공식 교재'만큼 시험에 잘 대비할 수 없습니다.

'ETS 토익 공식 교재'를 통하여 수험자 여러분의 영어 소통을 위한 노력에 큰 성취가 있기를 바랍니다.

감사합니다.

Dear TOEIC Test Takers in Korea,

The TOEIC program is the global leader in English-language assessment for the workplace. It has set the standard for assessing English-language skills needed in the workplace for more than 40 years. The TOEIC tests are the most widely used English language assessments around the world, with 14,000+ organizations across more than 160 countries trusting TOEIC scores to make decisions.

YBM is the ETS Country Master Distributor for the TOEIC program in Korea and so is the exclusive distributor for TOEIC Korea.

To support effective learning for TOEIC test-takers in Korea, ETS has authorized YBM to publish the only Official TOEIC prep books in Korea. These books contain actual TOEIC items to help prevent confusion among Korean test-takers that might be caused by other prep book publishers' use of reproduced or paraphrased items.

Reproduced or paraphrased items may fail to reflect the intent of actual TOEIC items and so will not prepare test-takers as well as the actual items contained in the ETS TOEIC Official prep books published by YBM.

We hope that these ETS TOEIC Official prep books enable you, as test-takers, to achieve great success in your efforts to communicate effectively in English.

Thank you.

입문부터 실전까지 수준별 학습을 통해 최단기 목표점수 달성!

ETS TOEIC® 공식수험서
스마트 학습 지원

www.ybmbooks.com에서도 무료 MP3를 다운로드 받을 수 있습니다.

ETS 토익 모바일 학습 플랫폼!

ETS 토익기출 수험서 [어플]

구글플레이　앱스토어

교재 학습 지원
- 교재 해설 강의
- LC 음원 MP3
- 교재/부록 모의고사 채점 분석
- 단어 암기장

부가 서비스
- 데일리 학습(토익 기출문제 풀이)
- 토익 최신 경향 무료 특강
- 토익 타이머

모의고사 결과 분석
- 파트별/문항별 정답률
- 파트별/유형별 취약점 리포트
- 전체 응시자 점수 분포도

ETS 토익 학습 전용 온라인 커뮤니티!

ETS TOEIC® Book [공식카페]

etstoeicbook.co.kr

강사진의 학습 지원　토익 대표강사들의 학습 지원과 멘토링

교재 학습관 운영　교재별 학습게시판을 통해 무료 동영상
　　　　　　　　　　강의 등 학습 지원

학습 콘텐츠 제공　토익 학습 콘텐츠와 정기시험
　　　　　　　　　　예비특강 업데이트

ETS 토익®
단기공략
950[+]

LC

RC

기출
모의고사
3회

ETS 토익 단기공략
950+

발행인	허문호
발행처	YBM

편집	이태경, 박효민, 오유진, 이주명
디자인	김현경, 정규리
마케팅	정연철, 박천산, 고영노, 김동진, 박찬경, 김윤하

초판발행	2024년 10월 1일
2쇄인쇄	2024년 11월 1일

신고일자	1964년 3월 28일
신고번호	제 1964-000003호
주소	서울시 종로구 종로 104
전화	(02) 2000-0515 [구입문의] / (02) 2000-0429 [내용문의]
팩스	(02) 2285-1523
홈페이지	www.ybmbooks.com

ISBN	978-89-17-23961-4

ETS 토익®
단기공략
950⁺

LC

RC

기출
모의고사
3회

PREFACE

Dear test taker,

The purpose of this book is to help you prepare for success on the TOEIC Listening and Reading Test. A good TOEIC score is a valuable asset for demonstrating your English communication proficiency to colleagues and clients in Korea and globally. Now more than ever, English proficiency is a tool that can yield great professional rewards.

This book provides practical steps that you can use right now, in a two-week or four-week program of study for the TOEIC test. Use your TOEIC test score as a respected professional credential and a sign that you are ready to take your career to the next level. Your TOEIC score is recognized globally as evidence of your English-language proficiency.

With 〈ETS 토익 단기공략 950+〉, you can make sure you have the best and most thorough preparation for the TOEIC test. This book contains key study points that will familiarize you with the test format and content, and you will be able to practice at your own pace. The test questions are created by the same test specialists who develop the TOEIC test itself, and the book contains questions taken from actual TOEIC tests.

Here are some features of 〈ETS 토익 단기공략 950+〉.

> · This book features carefully selected questions from actual TOEIC tests, chosen specifically for their advanced level of difficulty, and contains three full-length actual TOEIC tests.
> · All TOEIC Listening and Reading test content is included in one book that is suitable for two-week or four-week short-term study plans.
> · You will hear the same voice actors that are used for the actual TOEIC Test.
> · Key study points are provided to help you achieve your target score with the least amount of time and effort.

In preparing for the TOEIC test with 〈ETS 토익 단기공략 950+〉, you can be confident that you have a solid resource at hand and are taking the best approach to maximizing your TOEIC test score. Use 〈ETS 토익 단기공략 950+〉 to become familiar with the test, including actual test tasks, content, and format. You will be well prepared to show the world what you know by taking the test and receiving your score report.

We hope that you will find this high-quality resource to be of the utmost use, and we wish you all the very best success.

출제기관이 만든 점수대별
단기 완성 전략서!

⊙ 고난도 전략과 최신 기출 모의고사 3회 수록
최신 기출 문항으로 고난도 전략을 학습한 후 실제 시험에 출제된 최신 기출 모의고사 3회로 마무리하는, 전략과 실전을 한 번에 해결하는 고품질 단기 완성 교재이다.

⊙ 단기 목표 달성에 최적화된 구성
고득점 달성을 위한 LC, RC의 핵심 내용과 실전 감각을 익힐 수 있는 최신 기출 모의고사 3회까지 알차게 수록하여 학습 부담을 최소화하였다.

⊙ 정기시험과 동일한 성우 음원
토익 정기시험 성우가 실제 시험과 동일한 속도와 발음으로 직접 녹음하였으므로 실전에 완벽하게 대비할 수 있다.

⊙ ETS만이 제시할 수 있는 체계적인 공략법과 실전 대비
토익 각 파트의 고득점 달성을 위한 체계적인 공략법을 제시하고, 기출 모의고사 3회로 실전까지 완벽하게 대비한다.

⊙ 토익 최신 경향을 반영한 명쾌한 분석과 해설
이 책의 모든 토익 문항은 최신 출제 경향을 완벽하게 분석하고 반영하여 고득점을 달성하게 해줄 해법을 낱낱이 제시하고 있다.

CONTENTS

LC

TOEIC 소개

» TOEIC

Test of English for International Communication(국제적 의사소통을 위한 영어 시험)의 약자로, 영어가 모국어가 아닌 사람들이 일상생활 또는 비즈니스 현장에서 꼭 필요한 실용적 영어 구사 능력을 갖추었는가를 평가하는 시험이다.

» 시험 구성

구성	PART		유형	문항 수	시간	배점
Listening	Part 1		사진 묘사	6	45분	495점
	Part 2		질의 응답	25		
	Part 3		짧은 대화	39		
	Part 4		짧은 담화	30		
Reading	Part 5		단문 빈칸 채우기	30	75분	495점
	Part 6		장문 빈칸 채우기	16		
	Part 7	독해	단일 지문	29		
			이중 지문	10		
			삼중 지문	15		
Total	**7 Parts**			**200문항**	**120분**	**990점**

» 평가 항목

LC	RC
단문을 듣고 이해하는 능력	읽은 글을 통해 추론해 생각할 수 있는 능력
짧은 대화체 문장을 듣고 이해하는 능력	장문에서 특정한 정보를 찾을 수 있는 능력
비교적 긴 대화체에서 주고받은 내용을 파악할 수 있는 능력	글의 목적, 주제, 의도 등을 파악하는 능력
장문에서 핵심이 되는 정보를 파악할 수 있는 능력	뜻이 유사한 단어들의 정확한 용례를 파악하는 능력
구나 문장에서 화자의 목적이나 함축된 의미를 이해하는 능력	문장 구조를 제대로 파악하는지, 문장에서 필요한 품사, 어구 등을 찾는 능력

※ 성적표에는 전체 수험자의 평균과 해당 수험자가 받은 성적이 백분율로 표기되어 있다.

수험 정보

» **시험 접수 방법**
한국 토익 위원회 사이트(www.toeic.co.kr)에서 시험일 약 2개월 전부터
온라인으로 접수 가능

» **시험장 준비물**

신분증	규정 신분증만 가능 (주민등록증, 운전면허증, 기간 만료 전의 여권, 공무원증)
필기구	연필, 지우개 (볼펜이나 사인펜은 사용 금지)

» **시험 진행 시간**

09:20	입실 (9:50 이후 입실 불가)
09:30 ~ 09:45	답안지 작성에 관한 오리엔테이션
09:45 ~ 09:50	휴식
09:50 ~ 10:05	신분증 확인
10:05 ~ 10:10	문제지 배부 및 파본 확인
10:10 ~ 10:55	듣기 평가 (LISTENING TEST)
10:55 ~ 12:10	독해 평가 (READING TEST)

» **토익 성적 확인**
시험일로부터 약 10~11일 후, 인터넷 홈페이지와 어플리케이션을 통해 성적을 확인할 수 있다.
TOEIC 성적표는 우편이나 온라인으로 발급받을 수 있다(시험 접수 시 양자택일).
우편으로 발급받을 경우는 성적 발표 후 대략 일주일이 소요되며, 온라인 발급을 선택하면
유효기간 내에 홈페이지에서 본인이 직접 1회에 한해 무료 출력할 수 있다. TOEIC 성적은
시험일로부터 2년간 유효하다.

» **토익 점수**
TOEIC 점수는 듣기 영역(LC)과 읽기 영역(RC)을 합계한 점수로 5점 단위로 구성되며
총점은 990점이다. TOEIC 성적은 각 문제 유형의 난이도에 따른 점수 환산표에 의해
결정된다.

LC 출제 경향 분석

PART 1

문제 유형 및 출제 비율
(평균 문항 수)

사람을 주어로 하는 사람 묘사 문제가 가장 많은 비중을 차지하며 사람/사물 혼합 문제, 사물/풍경 묘사 문제가 각각 그 다음을 이룬다.

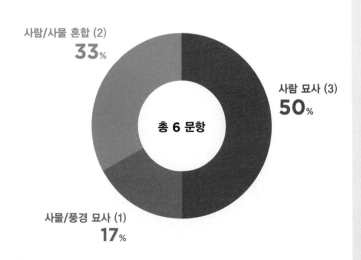

사람/사물 혼합 (2)
33%

사람 묘사 (3)
50%

총 6 문항

사물/풍경 묘사 (1)
17%

PART 2

문제 유형 및 출제 비율
(평균 문항 수)

의문사 의문문이 거의 절반 가량을 차지하며 일반 의문문과 평서문이 그 다음을 이룬다. 부가/부정/선택 의문문은 평균 2문항씩 출제되며 간접 의문문은 간혹 1문제 출제된다.

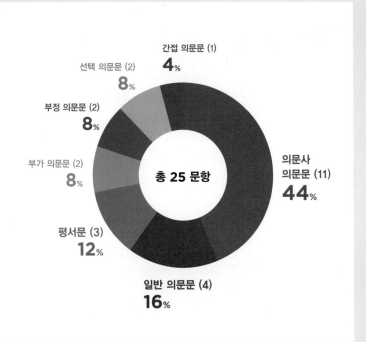

간접 의문문 (1)
4%

선택 의문문 (2)
8%

부정 의문문 (2)
8%

부가 의문문 (2)
8%

의문사
의문문 (11)
44%

총 25 문항

평서문 (3)
12%

일반 의문문 (4)
16%

PART 3

문제 유형 및 출제 비율
(평균 문항 수)

세부 사항을 묻는 문제가 가장 많은 비중을 차지하며 화자/장소, 제안/요청, 다음에 할 일, 주제/목적 문제가 그 다음을 차지한다. 문제점 및 걱정거리 문제는 출제 빈도가 다소 낮다. 의도 파악 문제와 시각 정보 연계 문제는 각각 2문항, 3문항의 고정 비율로 출제된다.

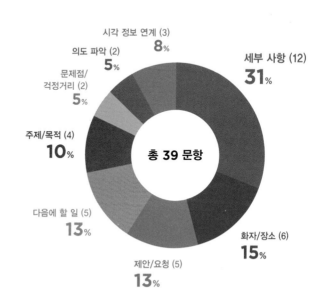

시각 정보 연계 (3)
8%

의도 파악 (2)
5%

문제점/
걱정거리 (2)
5%

주제/목적 (4)
10%

다음에 할 일 (5)
13%

제안/요청 (5)
13%

총 39 문항

세부 사항 (12)
31%

화자/장소 (6)
15%

PART 4

지문 유형 및 출제 비율
(평균 지문 수)

전화 메시지와 공지, 안내, 회의 발췌록이 가장 많이 출제된다. 광고, 방송, 보도가 그 다음을 차지하며 여행, 견학, 관람, 인물, 강연, 설명은 출제 빈도가 다소 낮다.

인물/강연/설명 (1)
10%

여행/견학/관람 (1)
10%

방송/광고 (2)
20%

총 10 지문

전화 메시지 (3)
30%

공지/안내/회의 (3)
30%

RC 출제 경향 분석

PART 5

문법 문제 유형 및 출제 비율
(평균 문항 수)

전치사와 접속사를 구분하는 문제와
동사 문제, 품사 문제 출제 비중이
가장 높다. 기타 문법에서는 준동사가
1~2문항, 관계사가 매회 거의
1문항씩 출제된다.

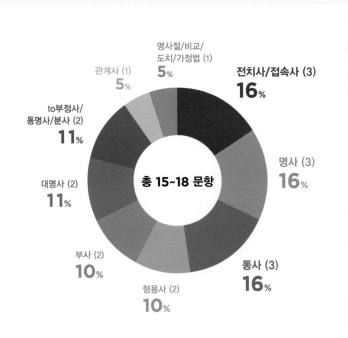

- 명사절/비교/도치/가정법 (1) 5%
- 관계사 (1) 5%
- to부정사/동명사/분사 (2) 11%
- 전치사/접속사 (3) 16%
- 명사 (3) 16%
- 대명사 (2) 11%
- 부사 (2) 10%
- 형용사 (2) 10%
- 동사 (3) 16%

총 15~18 문항

PART 5

어휘 문제 유형 및 출제 비율
(평균 문항 수)

전치사, 명사, 부사 어휘 문제가 가장
많이 출제되며 형용사, 동사 어휘가
그 뒤를 잇는다.

- 접속사 어휘 (1) 6%
- 동사 어휘 (2) 14%
- 전치사 어휘 (3) 22%
- 형용사 어휘 (2) 14%
- 명사 어휘 (3) 22%
- 부사 어휘 (3) 22%

총 12~15 문항

PART 6

문제 유형 및 출제 비율
(평균 문항 수)

문법과 어휘 비중이 비슷하게
출제되며 접속부사는 1~2문항
출제된다. 문장 고르기 문제는 4문항
고정 비율로 출제된다.

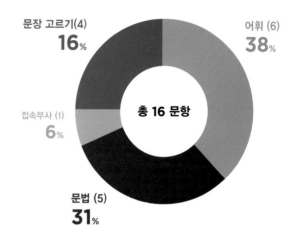

문장 고르기(4)
16%

어휘 (6)
38%

접속부사 (1)
6%

문법 (5)
31%

총 16 문항

PART 7

문제 유형 및 출제 비율
(평균 문항 수)

세부 사항 문제가 가장 높은 비율을
차지하며 추론/암시 문제와 (NOT)
mention/true 문제가 그 다음으로
출제율이 높다. 주어진 문장 넣기와
의도 파악 문제는 각각 2문항씩
고정 비율로 출제된다. 이중, 삼중
지문에서는 연계 문제가 8문항 정도
출제된다.

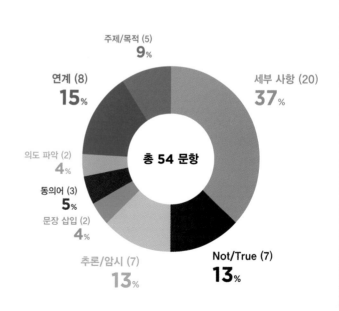

주제/목적 (5)
9%

연계 (8)
15%

세부 사항 (20)
37%

의도 파악 (2)
4%

동의어 (3)
5%

문장 삽입 (2)
4%

추론/암시 (7)
13%

Not/True (7)
13%

총 54 문항

점수 환산표

LISTENING Raw Score (맞은 개수)	LISTENING Scaled Score (환산 점수)	READING Raw Score (맞은 개수)	READING Scaled Score (환산 점수)
96-100	475-495	96-100	460-495
91-95	435-495	91-95	425-490
86-90	405-470	86-90	400-465
81-85	370-450	81-85	375-440
76-80	345-420	76-80	340-415
71-75	320-390	71-75	310-390
66-70	290-360	66-70	285-370
61-65	265-335	61-65	255-340
56-60	240-310	56-60	230-310
51-55	215-280	51-55	200-275
46-50	190-225	46-50	170-245
41-45	160-230	41-45	140-215
36-40	130-205	36-40	115-180
31-35	105-175	31-35	95-150
26-30	85-145	26-30	75-120
21-25	60-115	21-25	60-95
16-20	30-90	16-20	45-75
11-15	5-70	11-15	30-55
6-10	5-60	6-10	10-40
1-5	5-50	1-5	5-30
0	5-35	0	5-15

*이 환산표는 본 교재에 수록된 'ETS 기출 모의고사'용으로 개발된 것이다. 이 표를 사용하여 자신의 실제 점수를 환산 점수로 전환하도록 한다. 즉, 예를 들어 Listening Test의 실제 정답 수가 61~65개이면 환산 점수는 265점에서 335점 사이가 된다. 여기서 실제 정답 수가 61개이면 환산 점수가 265점이고, 65개이면 환산 점수가 335점임을 의미하는 것은 아니다. 본 책의 'ETS 기출 모의고사'를 위해 작성된 이 점수 환산표가 자신의 영어 실력이 어느 정도인지 대략적으로 파악하는 데 도움이 되긴 하지만, 이 표가 실제 TOEIC 성적 산출에 그대로 사용된 적은 없다는 사실을 밝혀 둔다.

학습 플랜

2주 완성

초단기에 고득점을 달성하고자 하는 중·고급 수험생을 위한 2주 완성 플랜

DAY 1	DAY 2	DAY 3	DAY 4	DAY 5
LC UNIT 1 **RC** UNIT 5	**LC** UNIT 2 **RC** UNIT 6	**LC** UNIT 3 **RC** UNIT 7	**LC** UNIT 4 **RC** UNIT 8	ETS 기출 모의고사 1회
DAY 6	**DAY 7**	**DAY 8**	**DAY 9**	**DAY 10**
ETS 기출 모의고사 1회 REVIEW	ETS 기출 모의고사 2회	ETS 기출 모의고사 2회 REVIEW	ETS 기출 모의고사 3회	ETS 기출 모의고사 3회 REVIEW

4주 완성

짧은 기간 차근차근 고득점을 달성하고자 하는 중·고급 수험생을 위한 4주 완성 플랜

DAY 1	DAY 2	DAY 3	DAY 4	DAY 5
LC UNIT 1	**RC** UNIT 5	**LC** UNIT 2	**RC** UNIT 6	**LC** UNIT 3
DAY 6	**DAY 7**	**DAY 8**	**DAY 9**	**DAY 10**
RC UNIT 7	**LC** UNIT 4	**RC** UNIT 8	ETS 기출 모의고사 1회 **LC**	ETS 기출 모의고사 1회 **LC** REVIEW
DAY 11	**DAY 12**	**DAY 13**	**DAY 14**	**DAY 15**
ETS 기출 모의고사 1회 **RC**	ETS 기출 모의고사 1회 **RC** REVIEW	ETS 기출 모의고사 2회 **LC**	ETS 기출 모의고사 2회 **LC** REVIEW	ETS 기출 모의고사 2회 **RC**
DAY 16	**DAY 17**	**DAY 18**	**DAY 19**	**DAY 20**
ETS 기출 모의고사 2회 **RC** REVIEW	ETS 기출 모의고사 3회 **LC**	ETS 기출 모의고사 3회 **LC** REVIEW	ETS 기출 모의고사 3회 **RC**	ETS 기출 모의고사 3회 **RC** REVIEW

PART

1

UNIT 1 사진 묘사

PART 1 만점 전략

PART 1은 주어진 사진을 가장 적절하게 묘사한 보기를 선택하는 유형으로, 사람 및 사물의 동작이나 상태, 풍경 등을 묘사하는 문장이 제시된다. PART 1에 자주 등장하는 빈출 표현들을 정리하여 암기하고, 오답 유형을 익혀 소거하는 연습을 반복 훈련한다.

빈출 오답 유형

❶ 사진에 없는 사람이나 사물을 언급하는 오답

오답 He's sweeping **a chimney**.
남자가 굴뚝을 청소하고 있다.
▶ 사진에 굴뚝(a chimney)이 보이지 않으므로 오답

정답 He's using a brush to clean a roof.
남자가 지붕을 청소하기 위해 솔을 사용하고 있다.

❷ 혼동되는 상태 동사와 동작 동사를 이용한 오답

오답 A woman is **putting on** a safety helmet.
여자가 안전모를 쓰고 있다.
▶ 여자가 안전모를 쓰고 있는 동작(putting on)이 아니라
상태(wearing)이므로 오답

정답 A woman is riding a bicycle.
여자가 자전거를 타고 있다.

❸ 혼동되는 유사 발음 어휘를 이용한 오답

오답 The man is making a pot of **coffee**.
남자가 커피를 끓이고 있다.
▶ 사진에서 연상되는 어휘 copy와 발음이 유사한 coffee를 이용한 오답

정답 The man is operating a machine.
남자가 기계를 작동하고 있다.

❹ 잘못된 위치를 묘사하는 오답

오답 A bag has been placed **on a chair**.
가방이 의자 위에 놓여 있다.
▶ 가방이 의자 위(on a chair)에 놓여 있지 않으므로 오답

정답 One of the men is looking into a bag.
남자들 중 한 명이 가방 속을 들여다보고 있다.

01 인물 등장 사진

인물 등장 사진에서는 주로 사람의 손, 발 동작 및 자세나 시선을 묘사하는 문제가 출제된다. 그러나 사진 속에 사람이 있더라도 주변 사물이나 풍경을 묘사하는 선택지가 정답으로 제시되기도 하므로 유의한다.

❶ 인물 중심 사진

사람의 동작이나 상태를 나타내는 동사에 집중해서 듣고, 동작 묘사와 상태 묘사를 구분해야 한다.

■ 사람의 동작/상태를 묘사하는 「사람 주어+be -ing」
The man **is adjusting** his glasses. (O) 남자가 안경을 고쳐 쓰고 있다.
The man **is reaching** for some tools. (X) 남자가 도구를 향해 손을 뻗고 있다.

■ 동작과 상태의 구분
The man is **wearing** overalls. (O) 남자가 작업복을 입고 있다. [상태]
The man **is tying** his shoelaces. (X) 남자가 신발끈을 묶고 있다. [동작]

만점 TIP

사람의 동작과 상태 표현으로 혼동을 주는 문제가 종종 출제되므로 유의한다.

동작	상태
be putting on protective gear 보호 장비를 착용하고 있다	**be wearing** headphones 헤드폰을 끼고 있다
be picking up a broom 빗자루를 집어 들고 있다	**be grasping** a railing 난간을 잡고 있다
be boarding a train 열차를 타고 있다	**be riding** a motorcycle 오토바이를 타고 있다

❷ 인물+사물 혼합 사진

사람의 동작이나 상태뿐 아니라 인물 주변 사물의 위치와 상태도 파악한다. 사물 주어와 현재진행 수동태(be being p.p.)로 사람의 행동을 묘사할 수 있는 데 유의한다.

■ 사람의 행동을 묘사하는 「사물 주어+be being p.p.」
The car **is being washed** on the street. (O) 차가 길에서 세차되고 있다.
cf. A man **is washing** the front of a car. (O) 남자가 차 앞면을 세차하고 있다.

■ 주변 사물/풍경을 묘사하는 「사물 주어+be p.p/have been p.p.」
Cars **are parked** on the road. (O) 차들이 길에 주차되어 있다.
Some trees **have been planted** on a street. (O) 나무들이 길에 심어져 있다.

☑ 만점 기출 표현 – 인물의 동작/상태 묘사

손 동작

be typing on a laptop 노트북에 타자를 치고 있다

be tying a rope to a fence 울타리에 밧줄을 묶고 있다

be reaching for a purse 지갑에 손을 뻗고 있다

be adjusting some equipment 장비를 조정하고 있다

be pruning some branches 가지치기를 하고 있다

be raking some leaves 나뭇잎을 긁어 모으고 있다

be trimming some bushes 덤불을 다듬고 있다

be stacking some plates 접시를 쌓고 있다

be stocking some shelves 선반을 채우고 있다

be waving to a friend 친구에게 손을 흔들고 있다

be shaking hands 악수를 하고 있다

be loading bags into a car 차에 가방을 싣고 있다

be unloading boxes from a van
밴에서 상자를 내리고 있다

be hanging a coat on a rack
옷걸이에 코트를 걸고 있다

be gripping the handle of a suitcase
여행 가방 손잡이를 잡고 있다

be inserting a key into the lock
자물쇠에 열쇠를 넣고 있다

be attaching a name tag to a gift
선물에 이름표를 붙이고 있다

발 동작

be descending some stairs 계단을 내려가고 있다

be strolling on a pier 부두에서 산책하고 있다

be approaching a fountain in the park
공원에 있는 분수대에 다가가고 있다

자세

be leaning over/against a column
기둥에 기대고 있다

be bending over the canvas
캔버스 위로 몸을 굽히고 있다

be crouching down near a bench
벤치 근처에 웅크리고 있다

be kneeling down in front of a counter
카운터 앞에 무릎을 꿇고 있다

시선

be glancing at a monitor 모니터를 보고 있다

be facing the chalkboard 칠판을 마주 보고 있다

be studying a document 문서를 보고 있다

be inspecting machinery 기계를 점검하고 있다

be examining some artworks
예술 작품을 살펴보고 있다

be browsing through a magazine
잡지를 훑어보고 있다

ETS 기출 유형연습

🎧 950_U1_01 정답과 해설 p.002

1.

(A)   (B)   (C)   (D)

2.

(A)   (B)   (C)   (D)

사물/풍경 사진에서는 사물의 위치나 상태, 공간 사용 여부를 다양한 동사 형태로 묘사하는 선택지가 제시된다. 사진 속 다양한 사물이 주어로 나오며 사진에 없는 사물을 언급하는 오답에 유의한다.

❶ 사물 사진

사물의 위치나 상태를 묘사하는 다양한 동사 형태를 익혀 두고, 사람의 행동을 묘사하는 be being p.p.가 포함된 선택지는 소거한다.

■ **사물의 위치/상태를 묘사하는 다양한 동사 형태:**
  be p.p., have been p.p., be -ing, There be＋명사

Some books **are placed/have been placed** on shelves. (O)
책들이 선반에 놓여 있다.

Some decorations **are hanging** on a wall. (O) 장식들이 벽에 걸려 있다.

There are some tables and chairs near book shelves. (O)
책장 근처에 테이블과 의자들이 있다.

Some chairs **are being stacked** in a corner. (X)
의자들이 구석에 쌓이고 있다.

> **만점 TIP**
>
> 사진에 사람이 없어도 be being p.p.가 정답이 될 수 있는 예외적인 동사 display, cast, grow 등을 암기해 두자.
>
> Some clothing **is being displayed** on the racks. 의류가 선반에 진열되어 있다.
> Shadows **are being cast** along a walkway. 보도를 따라 그림자가 드리워져 있다.
> Some flowers **are being grown** on balconies. 꽃들이 발코니에서 자라고 있다.

❷ 풍경 사진

전체적인 풍경과 눈에 띄는 사물의 구도를 파악하고, 수동태 표현뿐 아니라 능동태 현재형과 현재진행형도 풍경을 묘사할 수 있는 데 유의한다.

■ **풍경을 묘사하는 현재형과 현재진행형**

Some trees **surround** a bulletin board. (O)
나무들이 게시판을 둘러싸고 있다.

A fence **is standing** in a wooded area. (O)
울타리가 숲이 우거진 지역에 있다.

Leaves **are covering** the bench. (X) 나뭇잎이 벤치를 덮고 있다.

> **만점 TIP**
>
> 공간의 사용 여부를 묘사하는 occupied와 unoccupied의 발음이 유사하므로 주의 깊게 듣는다.
>
> A wooden bench is **unoccupied**. 나무 벤치가 비어 있다. [사람이 없는 경우]
> An outdoor dining area is **occupied**. 야외 식사 공간이 사용 중이다. [사람이 있는 경우]

✅ 만점 기출 표현 – 사물 및 풍경 묘사

overlook 내려다보다	lead to ~으로 이어지다	line ~을 따라 늘어서 있다
cast a shadow 그림자를 드리우다	be laid 놓여[깔려] 있다	be lying (바닥에) 놓여 있다
be stacked 쌓여 있다	be stocked with ~으로 채워져 있다	be scattered 흩어져 있다
be erected 세워져 있다	be unattended 방치되어 있다	be mounted 고정되어 있다
be situated 놓여 있다	be propped against ~에 받쳐져 있다	be suspended from ~에 매달려 있다

There is a balcony **overlooking** a beach. 해변이 내려다보이는 발코니가 있다.

A staircase **leads to** an entrance. 계단이 입구로 이어져 있다.

Streetlights **line** the avenues. 가로등이 도로를 따라 늘어서 있다.

Some buildings **are casting a shadow** on the park. 건물들이 공원에 그림자를 드리우고 있다.

A tablecloth **is laid** out on the dining table. 식탁보가 식탁 위에 깔려 있다.

A hat **is lying** on the sandy shore. 모자가 모래사장에 놓여 있다.

Wooden crates **have been stacked** on the floor. 나무 상자들이 바닥에 쌓여 있다.

Closet **is stocked with** winter coats. 옷장이 겨울 외투로 채워져 있다.

Some paperwork **has been scattered** on a desktop. 서류들이 책상에 흩어져 있다.

Some scaffolding **has been erected** along the wooden fence. 비계가 나무 울타리를 따라 세워져 있다.

Some files **have been left unattended** on the desk. 파일들이 책상 위에 방치되어 있다.

A television **has been mounted** on the wall. TV가 벽에 고정되어 있다.

A lamppost **is situated** at the corner of the street. 가로등 기둥이 길 모퉁이에 있다.

A skateboard **is propped against** the garage door. 스케이트보드가 차고 문에 기대어져 있다.

A curtain **has suspended** from the curtain rod. 커튼이 커튼봉에 매달려 있다.

ETS 기출 유형연습

🎧 950_U1_02 정답과 해설 p.002

 1.

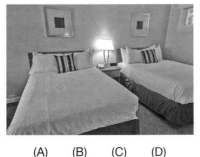

(A)　　(B)　　(C)　　(D)

2.

(A)　　(B)　　(C)　　(D)

1.

(A)　　(B)　　(C)　　(D)

2.

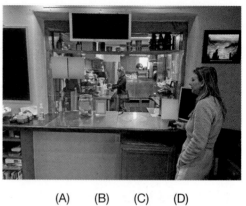

(A)　　(B)　　(C)　　(D)

3.

(A)　　(B)　　(C)　　(D)

4.

(A)　　(B)　　(C)　　(D)

5.

(A) (B) (C) (D)

6.

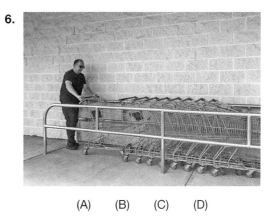

(A) (B) (C) (D)

7.

(A) (B) (C) (D)

8.

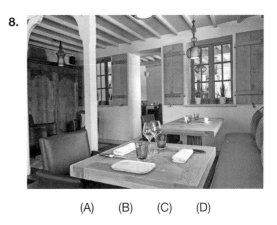

(A) (B) (C) (D)

1.

(A)   (B)   (C)   (D)

2.

(A)   (B)   (C)   (D)

3.

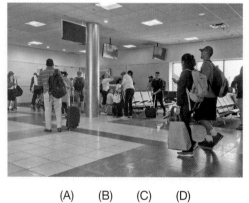

(A)   (B)   (C)   (D)

4.

(A)   (B)   (C)   (D)

5.

(A) (B) (C) (D)

6.

(A) (B) (C) (D)

7.

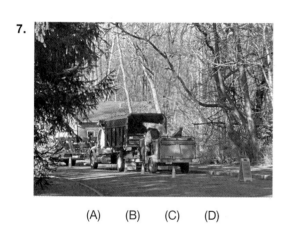

(A) (B) (C) (D)

8.

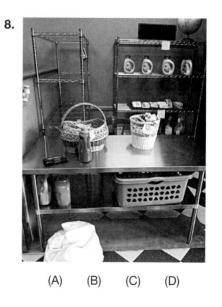

(A) (B) (C) (D)

PART 2

UNIT 2 질의 응답

PART 2 만점 전략

PART 2는 질문에 직접적인 답변을 하는 경우보다 우회적인 답변을 하는 비중이 증가하여 난이도가 높아지고 있다. 이런 경우 오답을 하나씩 지워 나가는 소거법을 이용하여 정답을 선별하는 것이 효과적이다. 따라서 고난도 응답 유형과 빈출 오답 유형을 미리 익혀 두면 고득점을 달성할 수 있다.

빈출 오답 유형

❶ 의문사 의문문에 Yes/No로 답하는 오답
Yes, Okay와 같은 긍정 응답이나 No, Not at all 같은 부정 응답은 의문사가 없는 질문에만 사용할 수 있다.

Q	**When** will the new shipment of shoes arrive?	새로 배송한 신발은 언제 도착하나요?
오답	**Yes**, we've ordered more stock.	네, 재고를 더 주문했습니다.
정답	The delivery company hasn't given us a confirmed date yet.	배송 업체에서 아직 확정 날짜를 알려주지 않았습니다.

❷ 의문사를 혼동하는 오답
질문에 사용된 의문사 대신 다른 의문사가 들어갔다면 정답이 될 수 있는 보기가 오답으로 나오기도 한다.

Q	**Where** are we hosting the annual conference?	연례 콘퍼런스는 어디에서 개최되나요?
오답	At the end of the month.	이달 말입니다. [의문사 When에 대한 응답]
정답	The venue's still being decided.	장소는 아직 결정 중입니다.

❸ 연상 어휘를 이용한 오답
질문에 나온 어휘에서 연상할 수 있는 어휘를 활용한 오답이 자주 등장한다.

Q	Who's picking up our guests from the **airport**?	공항에서 누가 손님을 픽업하나요?
오답	From the international terminal.	국제선 터미널에서요.
정답	We've arranged for a car service.	차량 서비스를 준비했어요.

❹ 유사 발음/파생어/반복 어휘를 이용한 오답
질문에서 들린 어휘와 동일한 어휘나 발음이 유사한 어휘, 혹은 파생어가 포함된 보기는 오답일 가능성이 높다.

Q	The **launch** event for the new product line was canceled, wasn't it?	새로운 제품 라인의 출시 행사가 취소되었죠, 그렇지 않나요?
오답	A reservation for **lunch** on Saturday.	토요일 점심 예약입니다.
정답	I haven't heard anything about that.	저는 그런 이야기 못 들었어요.

PART2 질문에 직접적인 답을 하지 않고 간접적으로 답하거나, 잘 모르겠다는 답변 등 다양한 응답이 정답으로 출제된다.
우회적인 답변들을 살펴본 후 미리 알아두는 것이 중요하다.

❶ 돌려서 말하는 간접 답변

Q Our training session is at four o'clock, isn't it? 우리 교육 세션은 4시에 시작하죠. 그렇지 않나요?

A1 **The meeting doesn't end till five.** 회의가 5시는 되어야 끝나요.

A2 **It was rescheduled two days ago.** 이틀 전에 일정이 변경됐어요.

❷ 잘 모르겠다/결정되지 않았다는 답변

Q Don't we have an employee discount program? 직원 할인 프로그램은 없나요?

A1 **I just started working here.** 여기서 일하기 시작한 지 얼마 안 됐어요. [잘 모르겠다는 답변]

A2 **That idea's only been proposed.** 그 아이디어는 제안된 것일 뿐이에요. [결정되지 않았다는 답변]

❸ 다른 사람에게 물어보라는 답변

Q I don't know which document I need to review first. 어떤 문서를 먼저 검토해야 할지 모르겠어요.

A1 **Ask the project coordinator.** 프로젝트 담당자에게 문의하세요.

A2 **You should talk to Lisa.** 리사에게 이야기해 보세요.

❹ 되묻는 답변

Q Why was the meeting rescheduled at the last minute? 회의 일정이 왜 막바지에 변경되었나요?

A1 **Didn't you see the explanation in the e-mail?** 이메일에 있는 설명 못 보셨나요?

A2 **Do you think it's related to the recent road construction?** 최근 도로 공사와 관련이 있다고 생각하시나요?

ETS 기출 유형연습　　　　🎧 950_U2_01　정답과 해설 p.007

1. Mark your answer.　　　(A)　(B)　(C)

2. Mark your answer.　　　(A)　(B)　(C)

3. Mark your answer.　　　(A)　(B)　(C)

4. Mark your answer.　　　(A)　(B)　(C)

5. Mark your answer.　　　(A)　(B)　(C)

의문사 의문문

의문사 의문문은 PART 2에서 가장 많은 부분을 차지하는 유형으로 When, Where, Who, What, Which, Why, How 의문사에 대한 답변을 찾는 문제이다. 기본 응답 유형 이외에 다양한 응답 유형에도 익숙해지는 훈련을 해야 한다.

❶ When/Where/Who 의문문

When 의문문은 시간/시점, Where 의문문은 위치/장소/출처, Who 의문문은 사람 이름/직책/부서명이 기본 응답이 되지만, 고난도 유형으로 자주 출제되는 이외의 응답에 유의해야 한다.

■ **When 의문문에서 불확실한 시점을 부사구나 부사절로 나타내는 고난도 시점 표현에 주의한다.**

Q **When** do you plan to finalize the project proposal? 프로젝트 제안서를 언제 마무리할 계획인가요?

A1 **Not until** the end of the week. 이번 주말은 되어야 해요.

A2 **No later than** Monday morning. 늦어도 월요일 아침까지요.

Q **When** will the new safety procedures be implemented? 새로운 안전 절차는 언제 시행되나요?

A1 **Sometime** after the committee's review. 위원회의 검토 후 언젠가요.

A2 **As soon as** the necessary training is completed. 필요한 교육이 완료되는 대로요.

■ **Where 의문문에서 사람 이름이나 부서명으로, Who 의문문에서 장소나 위치로 응답할 수 있다.**

Q **Where** can I find the employee handbook? 직원 안내서는 어디에서 찾을 수 있나요?

A1 **John** usually keeps copies in his office. 보통 존이 사무실에 사본을 보관해요.

A2 Please contact **the human resources department**. 인사부에 문의하시기 바랍니다.

Q **Who** has the key to the storage room? 창고 열쇠는 누가 가지고 있나요?

A1 It's usually kept **in the manager's office**. 보통 관리자 사무실에 보관되어 있어요.

A2 Try looking for it **in the file cabinet**. 파일 캐비닛에서 찾아보세요.

■ **Who 의문문에서는 직책, 직업, 부서명이나 부정대명사를 이용한 응답이 자주 출제된다.**

Q **Who** is in charge of the software development project?
소프트웨어 개발 프로젝트는 누가 담당하나요?

A1 **The senior software engineer.** 선임 소프트웨어 엔지니어요.

A2 **The project manager in the IT department.** IT 부서의 프로젝트 매니저요.

Q **Who** can access the confidential files? 기밀 파일에 누가 접근할 수 있나요?

A1 **No one** on our team. 우리 팀에는 아무도 없어요.

A2 **Anyone** among the senior staff members. 고위 직원 누구나 가능해요.

② What/Which 의문문

What, Which 의문문은 시간, 주제, 방법 등 다양한 정보를 묻는 질문으로, 의문사 뒤에 나오는 부분을 특히 집중해서 들어야 한다.

■ **What/Which 의문문은 의문사 뒤에 나오는 명사나 동사에 따라 정답이 결정된다.**

Q **What time** do we have to reserve the meeting room for? 회의실을 몇 시까지 예약해야 하나요?

A1 We need to book it for 3 P.M. 오후 3시까지 잡아야 합니다.

A2 Let's discuss that after lunch. 점심시간 이후에 논의해 봅시다.

Q **What** should I **include** in the project proposal? 프로젝트 제안서에 무엇을 포함해야 하나요?

A1 A detailed timeline would be helpful. 자세한 일정이 도움이 될 거예요.

A2 Shouldn't you incorporate a budget estimate? 예산 견적을 포함해야 하지 않나요?

Q **Which candidate** has the most experience with this type of work?
어느 지원자가 이 유형의 업무에 가장 많은 경험을 가졌나요?

A1 Sarah, with over ten years in the field. 이 분야에서 10년 이상 경력을 쌓은 사람요.

A2 Perhaps we need to consider someone with a fresh perspective.
새로운 시각을 가진 사람을 고려해야 할 것 같아요.

③ Why/How 의문문

Why 의문문은 because 이외에도 다양한 표현을 이용하여 답할 수 있고, 직접적인 단서 표현이 생략된 정답도 자주 등장한다. How와 「How+형용사/부사」 의문문은 뒤에 연결되는 키워드에 따라 다양한 질문이 가능하다.

■ **Why 의문문은 because 뿐만 아니라 because of, to부정사구, 전치사구 등으로 답할 수 있다.**

Q **Why** did the committee propose these policy changes?
위원회에서 왜 이러한 정책 변경을 제안했나요?

A1 Because of the upcoming security audit. 다가오는 보안 감사 때문에요.

A2 To stay in line with industry standards. 업계 표준을 준수하기 위해서요.

A3 For employee's safety. 직원들의 안전을 위해서요.

만점 TIP

Why don't you[we] ~?는 주로 제안의 의미를 나타내지만, 간혹 이유를 묻는 질문으로 출제되어 Because로 답하는 문장도 정답이 될 수 있으므로 유의한다.

Q **Why don't we** provide printed materials at the presentation?
우리는 왜 발표용 출력 자료를 제공하지 않나요?

A **Because** attendees can access them digitally later.
참석자가 나중에 디지털로 액세스할 수 있기 때문이에요.

■ **How**가 단독으로 쓰이면 방법이나 의견, 「**How+형용사/부사**」는 수량, 가격, 기간, 빈도 등을 묻는다.

Q   **How** can I improve my gardening skills? 원예 기술을 향상시키려면 어떻게 해야 하나요? [방법]

A1 **Through** gardening workshops at the community center.
커뮤니티 센터에서 열리는 원예 워크숍을 통해서요.

A2 **By reading** the gardening blogs and online forums. 원예 블로그와 온라인 포럼을 읽어서요.

Q   **How** would you rate the company's latest smartphone model? [의견]
회사의 최신 스마트폰 모델에 대해 어떻게 평가하시나요?

A1 Most users find its features quite impressive. 대부분의 사용자가 기능들이 매우 인상적이라고 생각합니다.

A2 It's hard to say without trying it out firsthand. 직접 사용해 보지 않고는 말하기 어렵습니다.

Q   **How many** seats are available for the seminar? 세미나에 몇 개의 좌석이 준비되어 있나요? [수량]

A1 There are fifty seats available in total. 총 50석이 준비되어 있습니다.

A2 I'll need to check on that. 확인해 봐야겠어요.

Q   **How often** should I replace the air filter? 에어 필터는 얼마나 자주 교체해야 하나요? [빈도]

A1 About once every three months. 3개월에 한 번 정도요.

A2 There's a manual in the drawer. 서랍에 설명서가 있어요.

ETS 기출 유형연습   🎧 950_U2_02 정답과 해설 p.008

1. Mark your answer.   (A)   (B)   (C)

2. Mark your answer.   (A)   (B)   (C)

3. Mark your answer.   (A)   (B)   (C)

4. Mark your answer.   (A)   (B)   (C)

5. Mark your answer.   (A)   (B)   (C)

일반/부정/부가 의문문

일반/부정/부가 의문문은 비의문사 의문문으로, 동사와 주어를 정확하게 듣고 문장 전체를 이해해야 풀 수 있다. 문제 유형에 따른 정답과 오답을 확실하게 알아두는 것이 필요하다.

❶ 일반 의문문

일반 의문문은 보통 Yes나 No로 시작하는 답변이 자주 나오지만, Yes나 No가 없어도 정답이 될 수 있는 응답도 종종 출제된다. 그리고 간접 의문문의 형태와 이에 대한 응답도 같이 익혀두어야 한다.

■ Yes나 No가 함축된 응답을 이해할 수 있어야 한다.

Q **Has** the research project been approved? 연구 프로젝트가 승인되었나요?

A1 (Yes,) The director said she loves the idea! (네,) 부장님이 아이디어가 맘에 든다고 하셨어요!

A2 (No,) It's still being reviewed. (아니요,) 아직 검토 중입니다.

Q **Did** you see the announcement about Zack's promotion? 잭의 승진 발표를 보셨나요?

A1 (Yes,) I read it earlier today. (네,) 오늘 아침에 봤어요.

A2 (No,) I've been busy all morning. (아니요,) 오전 내내 바빴어요.

■ 간접 의문문은 문장 중간에 나오는 의문사에 대한 적절한 응답을 골라야 한다.

Q Could you tell me **where** the health clinic is? 진료소가 어디 있는지 알려주실 수 있나요?

A1 It's across the street from the public library. 공공 도서관 맞은편에 있습니다.

A2 Actually, I'm headed over there right now. 실은 지금 그곳에 가는 중이에요.

Q Do you know **whose glasses** those are in the break room? 휴게실에 있는 저 안경이 누구의 것인지 아시나요?

A1 Aren't they Ms. Watson's? 왓슨 씨 안경 아닌가요?

A2 A few people have ones like those. 그런 안경을 가진 사람이 몇 명 있어요.

❷ 부정/부가 의문문

부정 의문문과 부가 의문문은 둘 다 사실을 확인하거나 동의를 구할 때 주로 사용된다. Yes/No로 응답하는 경우, 이어지는 내용이 Yes/No와 일치하는지 파악하고, Yes/No를 생략하고 응답하는 경우에는 함축된 의미를 이해할 수 있어야 한다.

■ 부정 의문문은 부정어에 상관없이 답변이 긍정이면 Yes, 부정이면 No로 대답한다.

Q **Isn't** the company retreat taking place outdoors?
회사 야유회는 야외에서 진행되지 않나요? ▶ 야외에서 진행되면 Yes, 그렇지 않으면 No

A1 **Yes,** we'll be doing outdoor team-builing activities. 네, 야외 팀워크 활동을 진행할 예정입니다.

A2 **No,** it will be held indoors due to weather concerns. 아니요, 날씨 문제로 실내에서 진행됩니다.

A3 The schedule's on your desk. 당신 책상에 일정이 있어요.

■ 부가 의문문은 앞에 나온 평서문의 내용에 집중하고, **not**이 있어도 답변이 긍정이면 **Yes**, 부정이면 **No**로 대답한다.

Q The train schedule will be adjusted for the holiday season, **won't it**?
휴가철을 맞아 열차 운행 일정이 조정될 거죠, 그렇지 않나요?

A1 **Yes,** they'll be adding extra trains. 네, 열차가 추가 운행될 예정입니다.

A2 **No,** there won't be any changes. 아니요, 변경 사항은 없습니다.

A3 Check for updates closer to the holidays. 연휴가 가까워지면 업데이트를 확인하세요.

■ 일반/부정/부가 의문문에서만 정답이 될 수 있는 표현들이 있다.

Q **Are** we allowed to bring carry-on luggage on the flight to Paris?
파리행 항공편에 기내 수하물을 반입할 수 있나요?

A1 (Yes,) **I think so.** 그렇게 생각해요. (반입할 수 있다고 생각함)

A2 (No,) **I don't think so.** 그렇게 생각하지 않아요. (반입할 수 없다고 생각함)

Q **Didn't** we finalize the details for the client presentation?
고객 프레젠테이션에 대한 세부 사항을 확정하지 않았나요?

A1 (Yes,) **I believe so.** 그런 것 같아요. (확정한 것으로 알고 있음)

A2 (No,) **I don't believe so.** 그런 것 같지 않아요. (확정하지 않은 것으로 알고 있음)

Q Julian purchased a watch from that antique store, **didn't he**?
줄리안은 골동품 가게에서 시계를 구입했죠, 그렇지 않나요?

A1 **That's what I heard.** 저는 그렇게 들었어요.

A2 **Not that I know of.** 제가 알기론 아니에요.

UNIT 2

ETS 기출 유형연습 　　　　　　　　　　　950_U2_03　정답과 해설 p.009

1. Mark your answer. (A) (B) (C)

2. Mark your answer. (A) (B) (C)

3. Mark your answer. (A) (B) (C)

4. Mark your answer. (A) (B) (C)

5. Mark your answer. (A) (B) (C)

04 기타 의문문/평서문

선택 의문문과 제안/요청 의문문, 그리고 평서문은 오답률이 가장 높은 유형으로, 각각의 특징을 파악하고 고난도 유형으로 출제되는 우회적 답변에 대비해야 한다.

❶ 선택 의문문

선택 의문문은 A와 B 둘 중에 하나를 선택하는 응답이 자주 출제되지만, 이외에도 다양한 응답이 출제될 수 있다.

■ 둘 다 선택하거나 둘 다 선택하지 않는 응답, 또는 제3의 선택 사항에 대한 응답, 선택 사항과 관련 없는 응답 등 다양한 응답이 정답으로 출제될 수 있다.

Q Are you going to **submit a report** or **give a presentation** to your manager?
관리자에게 보고서를 제출할 예정인가요, 아니면 발표할 예정인가요?

A1 I'll be handing in a detailed report. 자세한 보고서를 제출할 예정입니다. [둘 중 하나 선택]

A2 I'll probably do **both**. 둘 다 할 것 같습니다. [둘 다 선택]

A3 I'm waiting for instructions. 지침을 기다리는 중입니다. [선택 사항과 관련 없는 응답]

Q Would you like to schedule **a face-to-face meeting** or **a video conference**?
대면 회의를 하고 싶으신가요, 아니면 화상 회의를 하고 싶으신가요?

A1 **Either** one is fine. 어느 쪽이든 괜찮습니다. [둘 다 상관 없음]

A2 **Neither**—I'm really busy these days. 둘 다 안 돼요. 요즘 너무 바빠서요. [둘 다 선택하지 않음]

A3 Actually, I'd prefer e-mail. 사실 저는 이메일을 선호합니다. [제3의 선택 사항]

> **만점 TIP**
>
> 선택 의문문에 Yes나 No로 대답하는 경우는 오답일 확률이 높다.
>
> **Q** Would you prefer to go to **the restaurant on Forbes Avenue** or **the one on Main Street**?
> 포브스 가에 있는 식당에 가는 게 좋으신가요, 아니면 메인 가에 있는 식당에 가는 게 좋으신가요?
>
> 오답 **No**, I don't mind. 아니요, 상관없습니다.
>
> 정답 I prefer whichever one has the most diverse menu. 저는 메뉴가 가장 다양한 곳을 선호해요.

❷ 제안/요청 의문문

제안/요청 의문문은 무언가를 제안하거나 부탁할 때 사용하는 의문문이다. 따라서 수락하거나 거절하는 응답을 익혀두는 것이 중요하다.

■ 상대방의 제안/요청에 대해 수락 또는 거절하는 응답이 주로 정답이다.

Q **Would you like** to subscribe to our online newsletter? 저희 온라인 소식지를 구독하시겠습니까? [제안]

A1 Sure, I'd love to. 네, 그러고 싶어요. [수락]

A2 I already get too much e-mail. 이미 이메일이 너무 많이 와요. [거절]

Q **Could you** help organize the company picnic next month? [요청]

다음 달에 있을 회사 야유회 준비를 도와 주실 수 있나요?

A1 I'd be happy to get involved. 기꺼이 참여할게요. [수락]

A2 I'm not sure I can take on any more tasks right now. [거절]

지금은 더 이상 업무를 맡을 수 있을지 모르겠습니다.

❸ 평서문

평서문은 정보 전달이나 상황 설명, 의견 제시, 문제 제기, 제안/요청 등 다양한 의도를 가지고 상대방의 응답을 요구한다. 다른 의문문과 달리 정해진 응답 패턴이 없어 문장 전체를 이해해야 정답을 고를 수 있는 고난도 유형이다.

■ **동의/반대, 의견/해결책 제시, 수락/거절, 되묻기 등의 응답이 정답으로 제시된다.**

Q I think we should hire some temporary staff. 임시 직원을 고용해야 할 것 같아요. [의견 제시]

A1 It could improve our efficiency. 효율성을 향상시킬 수 있겠네요. [동의]

A2 I'm not convinced that's necessary. 꼭 필요한지 잘 모르겠어요. [반대]

Q The projector in the meeting room isn't working. 회의실에 있는 프로젝터가 작동하지 않습니다. [문제 제기]

A1 I'll see if it's a problem with the connections. 연결에 문제가 있는지 확인해 보겠습니다. [해결책 제시]

A2 Did you try restarting it? 재작동해 보셨나요? [되묻기]

Q I'd like you to proofread this document. 이 문서를 교정해 주셨으면 합니다. [요청]

A1 I'll take a look at it as soon as I can. 가능한 한 빨리 검토해 보겠습니다. [수락]

A2 I'm currently busy with another assignment. 현재 다른 작업으로 바빠요. [거절]

ETS 기출 유형연습　　　　🎧 950_U2_04　정답과 해설 p.010

1. Mark your answer.　　　　(A)　(B)　(C)

2. Mark your answer.　　　　(A)　(B)　(C)

3. Mark your answer.　　　　(A)　(B)　(C)

4. Mark your answer.　　　　(A)　(B)　(C)

5. Mark your answer.　　　　(A)　(B)　(C)

1. Mark your answer.   (A)   (B)   (C)

2. Mark your answer.   (A)   (B)   (C)

3. Mark your answer.   (A)   (B)   (C)

4. Mark your answer.   (A)   (B)   (C)

5. Mark your answer.   (A)   (B)   (C)

6. Mark your answer.   (A)   (B)   (C)

7. Mark your answer.   (A)   (B)   (C)

8. Mark your answer.   (A)   (B)   (C)

9. Mark your answer.   (A)   (B)   (C)

10. Mark your answer.   (A)   (B)   (C)

11. Mark your answer.   (A)   (B)   (C)

12. Mark your answer.   (A)   (B)   (C)

13. Mark your answer.   (A)   (B)   (C)

14. Mark your answer.   (A)   (B)   (C)

15. Mark your answer.   (A)   (B)   (C)

16. Mark your answer.   (A)   (B)   (C)

17. Mark your answer.   (A)   (B)   (C)

18. Mark your answer.   (A)   (B)   (C)

19. Mark your answer.   (A)   (B)   (C)

20. Mark your answer.   (A)   (B)   (C)

PART 2

UNIT 2

1. Mark your answer.   (A)   (B)   (C)

2. Mark your answer.   (A)   (B)   (C)

3. Mark your answer.   (A)   (B)   (C)

4. Mark your answer.   (A)   (B)   (C)

5. Mark your answer.   (A)   (B)   (C)

6. Mark your answer.   (A)   (B)   (C)

7. Mark your answer.   (A)   (B)   (C)

8. Mark your answer.   (A)   (B)   (C)

9. Mark your answer.   (A)   (B)   (C)

10. Mark your answer.   (A)   (B)   (C)

11. Mark your answer.   (A)   (B)   (C)

12. Mark your answer.   (A)   (B)   (C)

13. Mark your answer.   (A)   (B)   (C)

14. Mark your answer.   (A)   (B)   (C)

15. Mark your answer.   (A)   (B)   (C)

16. Mark your answer.   (A)   (B)   (C)

17. Mark your answer.   (A)   (B)   (C)

18. Mark your answer.   (A)   (B)   (C)

19. Mark your answer.   (A)   (B)   (C)

20. Mark your answer.   (A)   (B)   (C)

PART 2

UNIT 2

PART 3&4

PART 3&4 빈출 유형 만점 전략

PART 3와 PART 4는 각각 대화와 담화를 들으면서 관련된 세 개의 문제를 풀어야 하는 파트로, 청취력과 독해력이 동시에 요구된다. 문제와 선택지의 키워드를 미리 파악해 놓는 것이 중요하며, 보통 문제 순서대로 대화나 담화에서 정답 단서가 제시되므로 집중력을 놓치지 않도록 한다. 또한 대화나 담화에 나온 표현이 선택지에 패러프레이징 (paraphrasing)되어 제시되는 경우가 많으므로, 고득점을 위해서는 대표적인 패러프레이징 유형과 표현을 학습해 두는 것이 필수이다.

패러프레이징 유형

❶ 상위 개념 어휘 사용

W	Unfortunately, boarding for this flight has been delayed because of **storms** passing through the area.	Q	What has caused a delay?
		A	**Bad weather**
여	안타깝게도 해당 지역을 통과하는 폭풍우로 인해 항공편의 탑승이 지연되고 있습니다.	질문	지연된 이유는 무엇인가?
		정답	기상 악화

❷ 동의어, 유사 표현 활용

M	This coat's one of our best sellers. And it's a great time to buy it. We're having a discount sale—25 percent off **purchases** of 100 dollars or more.	Q	According to the man, how can the woman receive a discount?
		A	By **spending** $100.
남	이 코트는 우리 베스트셀러 중 하나입니다. 지금이 구매하기 좋은 시기입니다. 100달러 이상 구매 시 25퍼센트 할인 판매 중입니다.	질문	남자에 따르면, 여자는 어떻게 할인을 받을 수 있는가?
		정답	100달러를 소비해서

❸ 내용 축약

W	I'm calling because **my credit card has been rejected by stores and restaurants recently.**	Q	What problem does the woman mention?
		A	**A credit card is not working.**
여	최근 상점과 식당에서 신용 카드 결제가 거부되어 전화했습니다.	질문	여자는 어떤 문제를 언급하는가?
		정답	신용 카드를 사용할 수 없다.

01 주제/목적, 직업/장소

① 주제/목적 문제

🎧 950_U3_01 정답과 해설 p.019

대화나 담화의 중심 내용이나 목적을 묻는 유형으로, 주로 초반부에 단서가 언급되지만, 간혹 중반부까지 들어야 정답을 알 수 있는 경우도 있으므로 유의한다.

빈출 문제 유형

What are the speakers **mainly discussing**?
What is the conversation **mainly about**?
What is the main **topic** of the talk?

Why is the man **calling**?
Why does the man **call** the woman?
What is the **purpose** of the advertisement?

정답 단서 패턴

❶ 화두를 꺼내는 **Let's talk about ~, Do you think ~?** 등의 문장과 원하는 것을 이야기하는 **want to, need to, would like to** 등의 표현 뒤를 집중해서 듣는다.

M1 We **need to pick a story to run on the front page of tomorrow's newspaper**. Hiroshi, what are your thoughts? **M2** I think we should cover the expansion of the zoo. It's going to finish soon, and the zoo is one of the most-visited sites in town.	**Q** **What** are the speakers **mainly discussing**? **A** Selecting a newspaper article

❷ 전화/방문의 이유나 목적은 **I'm calling to, I'm here to** 등의 표현 뒤에 나온다.

W Hello, everyone. As you know, **we're here** from our company's quality assurance department **to perform our annual safety inspection** of this factory.	**Q** **What** is the **purpose** of the speaker's **visit**? **A** To conduct an inspection (Paraphrasing) 담화의 perform our ~ inspection → 정답의 conduct an inspection

② 직업/장소 문제

🎧 950_U3_02 정답과 해설 p.019

대화나 담화에서 직업이나 장소를 직접적으로 언급하지 않는 경우가 많으므로 관련 어휘를 듣고 내용을 종합하여 판단하는 것이 중요하다.

빈출 문제 유형

Who most likely is the woman?
What field[industry] does the speaker **work in**?
Where do the listeners most likely **work**?

Where is the conversation **taking place**?
Where is the announcement **being made**?
Where most likely are the speakers?

정답 단서 패턴

❶ 직업, 업종과 관련된 어휘나 상황을 종합하여 정답을 유추한다.

W Great job so far on your training, Andrey. You'll be able to **fix cars** on your own soon.	**Q** **Who** most likely are the speakers?
	A Automobile mechanics
M Thanks, Silvia. I'm looking forward to the next stage. I'll be learning about **sports car repairs** today, right?	(Paraphrasing) 대화의 cars ➝ 정답의 Automobile

❷ 장소를 유추할 수 있는 키워드를 듣고 내용을 종합하여 정답을 찾는다.

W Good evening, **passengers**. This is the **preboarding announcement** for **Greenway Airlines flight 59** from London to Madrid.	**Q** **Where** most likely are the listeners?
	A At an airport

ETS 기출 유형연습

🎧 950_U3_03   정답과 해설 p.020

주제 / 목적

1. Why is the man calling?

(A) To discuss a contract
(B) To request a letter of reference
(C) To confirm a conference schedule
(D) To organize a marketing campaign

2. Why do the speakers think a product will be successful?

(A) An idea is original.
(B) Similar products are popular.
(C) Market tests have been positive.
(D) Advance orders are higher than anticipated.

3. What task does the woman say will take extra time?

(A) Correcting some errors in a draft
(B) Choosing a graphic designer
(C) Gathering input from professionals
(D) Visiting a location

직업 / 장소

4. Where does Joshua Lee work?

(A) At a car manufacturer
(B) At a university laboratory
(C) At a nature preserve
(D) At a power station

5. What did Joshua Lee receive an award for?

(A) A journal article
(B) A machine design
(C) A management plan
(D) A volunteer project

6. What will Joshua Lee most likely talk about next?

(A) His future plans
(B) His research experience
(C) His daily responsibilities
(D) His educational background

02 문제점/걱정거리, 세부 사항

❶ 문제점/걱정거리 문제

🎧 950_U3_04 정답과 해설 p.021

주로 대화 초반부에 단서가 나오고 선택지가 문장으로 제시되는 경우가 많으므로 미리 읽어두는 것이 좋다. 문제점이나 걱정거리를 직접적으로 나타내는 표현이 나오기도 하지만, 종종 반전을 나타내는 표현이 등장하는 경우도 있으므로 유의한다.

빈출 문제 유형

What is the (woman's) **problem**?
What problem do the speakers **have**?
What problem does the man **mention**?

What is the woman **concerned about**?
Why does the speaker say **she is concerned**?
Why is the man **concerned**?

정답 단서 패턴

❶ 문제점이나 걱정을 표현하는 **I'm concerned/worried** 또는 **trouble, problem, difficulty** 등이 언급된 다음을 집중해서 듣는다.

W I'm glad your ticket office is open early so I can get a ticket to today's performance. **I had so many problems with your Web site** earlier today. M Sorry about that—there's **something wrong with the Web site**.	Q **What problem** do the speakers **discuss**? A A Web site is not working.

❷ 대조나 반전을 나타내는 **but, however, unfortunately, actually** 등의 표현이나 **부정어** 뒤에 정답의 단서가 나올 수 있다.

W Hi, Doo-Jae. I want to make sure we have enough filling for the pillows we're planning to produce this quarter. M We just got a delivery of feather and polyester filling, **but the delivery of the foam filling has been delayed**.	Q **What problem** does the man **mention**? A A shipment is late. (Paraphrasing) 대화의 the delivery ~ has been delayed ➡ 정답의 A shipment is late.

❷ 세부 사항 문제

🎧 950_U3_05 정답과 해설 p.021

화자가 특정 대상에 대해 언급한 내용을 묻거나 What, Why, How 등 의문사로 다양한 세부 정보를 묻는 문제이다. 대화나 담화에 나오는 어휘가 정답에 그대로 제시되기보다는 패러프레이징되는 경우가 많다.

빈출 문제 유형

According to the man, **what** caused a delay?
What does the man **say[mention] about** a hotel?
What is mentioned about the owner?

How can the listeners receive a gift?
Why does the speaker apologize?
When will the service be updated?

정답 단서 패턴

❶ 문제에 나온 시점, 장소, 인물 등과 관련된 키워드를 집중해서 듣는다.

W Hi, everyone. Thanks for coming in. I **sprained my wrist** while playing tennis **last weekend**. It's nothing serious, but it does mean that I won't be able to operate on my patients for the next two weeks, at least.	**Q** **What happened** to the speaker **last weekend**? **A** She injured her wrist. (Paraphrasing) 담화의 sprained my wrist → 정답의 injured her wrist

❷ 문제의 키워드가 패러프레이징되어 대화에 등장할 수도 있으므로 유의해서 듣는다.

W Orders for our custom-designed dresses have really gone up this month. **M** I know. It's great. But since **all of our clothing items are handmade**, it's almost too much for us to handle.	**Q** What does the man say about **some products**? **A** They are handmade. (Paraphrasing) 대화의 all of our clothing items → 정답의 some products

ETS 기출 유형연습

🎧 950_U3_06　정답과 해설 p.021

1. What is the conversation mainly about?

(A) Choosing a retail space
(B) Reviewing some job applications
(C) Selecting an interior designer
(D) Testing a new product line

[세부 사항]

2. What do the women say is a priority?

(A) To create innovative ideas
(B) To employ sustainable practices
(C) To follow an efficient business model
(D) To interact with the community

[문제점 / 걱정거리]

3. What problem does the man mention?

(A) A fee will be higher than expected.
(B) Some renovations will be needed.
(C) A market is extremely competitive.
(D) Some materials are unavailable.

4. Where is the tour most likely taking place?

(A) At an automobile museum
(B) At a car factory
(C) At a post office
(D) At a construction site

[세부 사항]

5. What advantage of a machine does the speaker mention?

(A) It is easy to maintain.
(B) It is lightweight.
(C) It is efficient.
(D) It can be operated remotely.

[세부 사항]

6. According to the speaker, what will Kavi talk about?

(A) Paint colors
(B) Maintenance schedules
(C) Operating permits
(D) Insurance options

03 제안/요청, 다음에 할 일

① 제안/요청 문제

🎧 950_U3_07 정답과 해설 p.023

정답의 단서가 주로 후반부에 등장하며, 요청하는 사람과 받는 사람의 성별을 정확히 구분해야 한다. 요청/제안과 관련된 표현들을 미리 알아두는 것이 좋다.

빈출 문제 유형

What does the woman **ask** the man **to do**?
What is the man **asked to do**?
What does the speaker **ask** listeners **to do**?

What does the speaker **suggest[recommend]**?
What are the listeners **advised to do**?
What does the man **offer to do**?

정답 단서 패턴

❶ 제안 사항은 **Why don't you/we ~?, I recommend/suggest/propose, You should, You'd better, Let's** 등의 표현 뒷부분을 들으면서 정답의 단서를 파악한다.

M	I only found this coat in large, and I wear a medium. Do you have other sizes in the back?	Q	**What** does the woman **suggest** the man **do**?
W	We don't. But **I'd recommend buying the large coat** because you'll probably want to wear more layers underneath it.	A	Buy a large size

❷ 요청 사항은 **Please, Make sure, Can/Could you ~?, I'd like you to, I was wondering if** 등이 언급된 다음을 주의 깊게 듣는다.

W	**Please have your boarding passes out** for verification so we can begin screening passengers. Thank you for your patience. We appreciate your business.	Q	**What** does the speaker **ask** the listeners **to do**?
		A	Present boarding passes

② 다음에 할 일 문제

🎧 950_U3_08 정답과 해설 p.023

세 문제 중 보통 마지막 문제로 출제되며, 미래를 나타내는 표현뿐만 아니라 제안/요청하는 표현에도 집중한다.

빈출 문제 유형

What will the woman most likely **do next**?
What are the speakers **going to do next**?
What does the man say he **will do** in June?

What will happen next Tuesday?
What is scheduled to do later today?
What will take place on August 8?

정답 단서 패턴

❶ 미래를 나타내는 **will, be going to, be supposed to** 등의 표현이 포함된 문장을 집중해서 듣는다.

W Well, I didn't see any information about lunch hours posted on the door.	**Q** **What** does the man say **he will do**?
	A Make sure a sign is in place
M Thanks for letting me know. We had the windows cleaned yesterday. Someone may have moved the business hours sign. **I'll hang it back up.**	(Paraphrasing) 대화의 hang it back up → 정답의 Make sure a sign is in place

❷ **Let me, I can, You can** 등의 표현 또는 **제안/요청 표현** 뒤에서 정답의 단서를 말해줄 확률이 높다.

W I sold some pedestals just last month that would be perfect for you. **Let me check** my computer to see **if I have any in stock**.	**Q** **What will** the woman **do next**?
	A Check inventory
	(Paraphrasing) 대화의 any in stock → 정답의 inventory

PART 3&4 UNIT 3

ETS 기출 유형연습

🎧 950_U3_09   정답과 해설 p.023

1. Where do the speakers most likely work?

(A) At a library
(B) At a museum
(C) At a farmers market
(D) At a city office

제안 / 요청

2. What does the woman propose?

(A) Building a community garden
(B) Organizing a charity walk
(C) Expanding a parking area
(D) Offering weekend classes

3. What will the man do tomorrow?

(A) Write a review
(B) Conduct an interview
(C) Attend a meeting
(D) Place an advertisement

4. Where does the speaker most likely work?

(A) At a clothing manufacturer
(B) At a museum gift shop
(C) At an art supply store
(D) At a software company

5. What is the speaker excited about?

(A) Hiring more staff
(B) Advertising online
(C) Selling specialty items
(D) Attending a celebration

다음에 할 일

6. What will the speaker do next?

(A) Show some images
(B) Present some statistics
(C) Distribute refreshments
(D) Collect feedback

1. Where most likely are the speakers?

   (A) At a grocery store
   (B) At a conference center
   (C) At a laboratory
   (D) At a warehouse

2. What industry does the woman work in?

   (A) Construction
   (B) Education
   (C) Medical research
   (D) Food packaging

3. Why does the man want to arrange a meeting with the woman?

   (A) To introduce her to some industry contacts
   (B) To discuss investing in her company
   (C) To interview her for an article
   (D) To offer some business advice

4. What most likely is the man's job?

   (A) Lawyer
   (B) Sales representative
   (C) Repair technician
   (D) Financial adviser

5. What does the man ask the woman to do?

   (A) Attend a meeting
   (B) Update some software
   (C) Postpone an appointment
   (D) Create some training materials

6. What does the man offer to do?

   (A) E-mail an agenda
   (B) Prepare a presentation
   (C) Provide transportation
   (D) Copy some documents

7. Where does the conversation take place?

   (A) At a travel agency
   (B) At a local market
   (C) On a boat
   (D) On an airplane

8. Who are the men?

   (A) Restaurant chefs
   (B) Marine biologists
   (C) Tour guides
   (D) Safety inspectors

9. What does the woman say she will do?

   (A) Buy some equipment
   (B) Go to a library
   (C) Take a vacation
   (D) Write an article

10. Where is the announcement being given?

(A) At an airport
(B) At a bus terminal
(C) At a train station
(D) At a ferry terminal

11. What does the speaker say about passenger belongings?

(A) They should not be left unattended.
(B) They should have an identification tag.
(C) They should not be placed on seats.
(D) They should be stored in a locker.

12. How can some of the listeners save on the purchase of an item?

(A) By showing a ticket
(B) By downloading a mobile application
(C) By posting a review
(D) By applying for a discount card

13. What is the speaker discussing?

(A) Cameras
(B) Laptop computers
(C) Outdoor lights
(D) Suitcases

14. What problem does the speaker mention about a product?

(A) It is expensive.
(B) It is heavy.
(C) It is complicated to use.
(D) It is unattractive.

15. What does the speaker mean when he says, "it's a very popular model"?

(A) Replacement parts are widely available.
(B) A product may not be reliable.
(C) Many people agree with an opinion.
(D) A product might sell out quickly.

16. According to the speaker, why was product testing behind schedule?

(A) A testing area was closed.
(B) A delivery was delayed.
(C) Some software was updated.
(D) Some equipment was broken.

17. What does the speaker say will happen next week?

(A) Some products will be compared.
(B) Some employees will be on vacation.
(C) A press release will be drafted.
(D) A manufacturer will be contacted.

18. What will the listeners most likely do next?

(A) Watch a safety video
(B) Review a report
(C) Take a break
(D) Look at some logos

PART 3&4 UNIT 3

49

1. Where are the speakers?

(A) At an appliance store
(B) At an auto body shop
(C) At an art school
(D) At a paint store

2. What will the man do today?

(A) Organize a storage area
(B) Clean a work space
(C) Learn a new skill
(D) Review an updated policy

3. What does the woman remind the man about?

(A) A job opportunity
(B) A safety guideline
(C) A supply delivery
(D) A work schedule

4. What types of products are the speakers discussing?

(A) Patterned textiles
(B) Machine parts
(C) Kitchen appliances
(D) Cleaning supplies

5. What will the man do for the women's company?

(A) Secure its databases
(B) Increase its international market share
(C) Help develop sustainable products
(D) Improve staff morale

6. What will the women most likely do next?

(A) Schedule some catering
(B) Collect some data
(C) Place a supply order
(D) Prepare for a presentation

7. What is the purpose of the conversation?

(A) To address a staffing shortage
(B) To negotiate a project budget
(C) To approve a press release
(D) To discuss a service disruption

8. What does the man say he will do?

(A) Determine a new route
(B) Hire a contractor
(C) Change a supply order
(D) Revise a project deadline

9. What does the woman plan to do?

(A) Assign tasks to some employees
(B) Prepare for a press conference
(C) Make some information public
(D) Inform bus drivers of a policy change

10. What news does the speaker share?

(A) Business hours have been extended.
(B) A new location will open.
(C) A business will be reviewed.
(D) A staff member has been promoted.

11. Why does the speaker apologize?

(A) Table assignments have been reduced.
(B) A parking area is being repaired.
(C) An event has been postponed.
(D) Paychecks have been slightly delayed.

12. What are the listeners asked to memorize?

(A) A password
(B) A greeting
(C) A guest list
(D) A menu

13. What is being advertised?

(A) A sporting event
(B) A local parade
(C) An indoor market
(D) A cooking demonstration

14. What will some attendees receive?

(A) Discount coupons
(B) Product samples
(C) Free parking
(D) T-shirts

15. What can the listeners do on a Web site?

(A) Sign up for a contest
(B) Find driving directions
(C) Download a schedule
(D) Reserve a booth

16. Why does the speaker say, "Adeola was in charge of researching that product"?

(A) To justify a decision
(B) To correct a misunderstanding
(C) To praise a colleague
(D) To explain a manufacturing delay

17. According to the speaker, what is the focus of the meeting?

(A) Creating a budget
(B) Responding to clients
(C) Discussing sales approaches
(D) Generating ideas

18. What does the speaker want more details about?

(A) A timeline
(B) A vendor
(C) Costs
(D) Staffing

PART 3&4

UNIT 4 대화/담화 고난도 유형

PART 3&4 고난도 유형 만점 전략

화자의 숨은 의도를 파악하는 의도 파악 문제와 대화나 담화를 들으면서 단서를 찾아 그래프, 지도 등의 시각 정보에 대입하여 정답을 찾아야 하는 시각 정보 연계 문제는 청취력과 추론 능력이 동시에 요구되어 LC 문제 중 난이도가 높은 유형에 속한다. 매회 출제되는 이 유형들을 놓치지 않기 위해서는 문제 유형과 정답 단서 패턴을 미리 익혀 두고 접근하는 것이 중요하다.

PART 3&4 고난도 유형 공략법

❶ 의도 파악 문제는 제시된 문장의 표면적 의미만 생각하고 정답을 고르면 안 된다.

M Well, I'm relocating and looking forward to all the cultural activities your city has. **What do employees do in their free time after work?**

W I have a long commute so I don't really do much socially after work. But there's a concert hall just around the corner.

Q Why does the woman say, "there's a concert hall just around the corner"?

오답 To give directions
정답 To suggest an activity

남 저는 이사를 왔고 이 도시의 모든 문화 활동이 기대돼요. 직원들은 퇴근 후 여가 시간에 무엇을 하나요?

여 저는 출퇴근 시간이 길어서 퇴근 후 사교 활동을 많이 하지는 않아요. 하지만 모퉁이를 돌면 바로 콘서트홀이 있어요.

질문 여자는 왜 "모퉁이를 돌면 바로 콘서트홀이 있어요"라고 말하는가?

오답 길을 알려주려고
정답 활동을 제안하려고

❷ 시각 정보 연계 문제는 대화나 담화에서 정답을 직접적으로 언급하지 않는다.

M I'll change **Ms. Becker's song** in the program. Any other changes?

W No. Just a reminder that all employees will be meeting at two o'clock today to go over last-minute details.

Song	Musician
"Thunder Nights"	Klaus Mayer
"Warm Rain"	Haru Itu
"Lilies in Bloom"	Polina Becker
Intermission	
"Thoughts for Tomorrow"	Taro Wakabayashi

Q Look at the graphic. Which song title will be changed in the program?
A **"Lilies in Bloom"**

남 행사 계획표에서 베커 씨의 노래를 변경하겠습니다. 다른 변경 사항은 없나요?

여 없습니다. 오늘 2시에 전 직원이 모여 최종 세부 사항을 검토할 예정임을 다시 한번 알려 드립니다.

질문 시각 정보에 따르면, 행사 계획표에서 어떤 노래 제목이 변경될 것인가?

정답 〈꽃이 핀 백합〉

01 의도 파악

제시된 문장은 문맥에 따라 의미가 달라질 수 있으므로 대화의 흐름을 파악하여 정답을 고른다. 특히 제시된 문장의 주변 대사를 반드시 이해해야 하며, 난이도가 높은 유형은 전반적인 맥락을 이해해야 풀 수 있다.

빈출 문제 유형

🎧 **950_U4_01** 정답과 해설 p.032

Why does the speaker **say**, "~"?　　　　**What** does the speaker **mean[imply]** when he says, "~"?

정답 단서 패턴

❶ 제시된 문장의 앞이나 뒤 문장에 정답의 단서가 있는 경우가 대부분이다.

M　Hi. **I just read in the newspaper that your library is organizing a free photography class next week. I was hoping to sign up**. W　Let me look. Hmm—our computer system is down again. **Could you call back in an hour or so?**	Q　**What** does the woman **imply** when she says, "our computer system is down again"? A　She is unable to fulfill the man's request.
W　Unfortunately, the introduction of these trains will be delayed by approximately six months. **Now, many residents have contacted our department asking for a faster timeline.** However, Kolwenski Manufacturing controls production.	Q　**Why** does the speaker **say**, "Kolwenski Manufacturing controls production"? A　To correct a misunderstanding

❷ 전체 흐름을 파악해야 풀 수 있는 문제에 유의해야 한다.

M　Jessica, I just got a call from a production company in Korea. W　Someone wants me to make a film there? M　Actually, **they're interested in buying the rights to *Blue Sand* to remake it with a Korean cast.** W　Wow! **Well, I'd want to have the final OK on the director and cast that they choose.** Can that all be written into the contract? I've never had to negotiate one of these before. M　As your agent, I'll be taking care of all of that for you. **You won't sign anything until you've seen the profiles of everyone involved.** W　OK. **I'm afraid I'm quite busy this month.** M　Oh, they haven't sent us any names yet.	Q　**Why** does the man **say**, "they haven't sent us any names yet"? A　To assure the woman that a task is not urgent

W Good morning, everyone. As you remember, **one of our current projects is inserting an advertisement on the company Web site** for the new line of running shoes that'll be released next month. Well, I finally received the product photos, so **we should have everything we need to finish that Web page**. But since **the photos arrived later than expected, we're behind schedule. I know you all have other projects going on in addition to working on this page**, but this will launch on Friday.

Q **What** does the speaker **imply** when she says, "this will launch on Friday"?

A A project needs to be completed soon.

---

1. Where is the conversation most likely taking place?
   (A) At a garden center
   (B) At a furniture outlet
   (C) At a construction site
   (D) At a real estate agency

   의도 파악
2. What does the woman mean when she says, "That workshop was very popular"?
   (A) A workshop now attracts fewer participants.
   (B) A workshop should be offered again.
   (C) An instructor should be congratulated.
   (D) Some materials will not need to be reprinted.

3. What does the man offer to create?
   (A) A list
   (B) A map
   (C) A presentation
   (D) A schedule

4. What is the speaker discussing?
   (A) A celebrity appearance
   (B) A video game release
   (C) A music concert
   (D) A book signing

   의도 파악
5. What does the speaker imply when she says, "people have been lined up for over two hours"?
   (A) More employees are needed.
   (B) A product is very popular.
   (C) A parking lot is full.
   (D) An event has been delayed.

6. According to the speaker, how can the listeners get more information?
   (A) By clicking on a link
   (B) By going to a store
   (C) By contacting a ticket office
   (D) By reading a pamphlet

02 시각 정보 연계

시각 정보 연계 문제에서는 목록, 지도, 그래프 등 다양한 유형의 시각 정보가 등장한다. 시각 정보에서 보기와 상응하는 부분이나 질문의 키워드가 대화나 담화 내에 단서로 등장할 수 있다.

❶ 목록(List) / 표(Table)

🎧 950_U4_03 정답과 해설 p.034

가장 많이 출제되는 유형으로, 일정표를 비롯해 다양한 형식의 목록과 표가 출제된다. 보기와 상응하는 정보를 눈여겨보면서 듣는 것이 중요하다.

W The first group will be all of you who are in the first two scenes. We can rehearse in the main room. The second group, those of you in scene three, **Travel to the Past**, will have to go talk to the playwright. She just made substantial revisions to that scene, so you'll have to go over it again.

Pages	Scene
1–10	Opening Scene
11–15	In the Garden
16–20	Travel to the Past
21–28	The Ordeal
29–32	Conclusion

Q **Look at the graphic.** Which pages in the script have been revised?

A **16–20**

☑ 만점 기출 표현

overdue balance 연체 잔액	travel itinerary 여행 일정	inventory 재고 (목록)
extension number 내선 번호	webinar 웨비나(온라인 세미나)	markdown 가격 인하
price quote[estimate] 가격 견적(서)	shareholders' meeting 주주 회의	baggage claim (공항의) 수하물 찾는 곳

❷ 지도(Map) / 평면도(Floor plan)

🎧 950_U4_04 정답과 해설 p.034

지도, 평면도, 좌석 배치도 등의 시각 정보가 출제된다. 주로 위치를 설명하는 내용이 나오므로 위치나 방향 관련 전치사 표현들을 익혀 둔다.

M I'm calling with some information about your photo shoot next week. I found a great location for your professional photos—it's a little garden that's **between the public library and the courthouse**. It'll be the perfect place to take your photos—I'm sure they'll look great on your Web site and business cards.

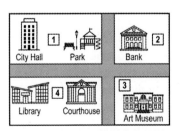

Q **Look at the graphic.** Which location does the speaker mention?

A Location 4

☑ 만점 기출 표현

across from the fuel station 주유소 맞은편에

on the other side of the aisle 통로 반대편에

on the corner of Willow Street and Poll Avenue 윌로우 가와 폴 가의 모퉁이에 있는

closest to the stairs 계단에서 가장 가까운

beside the entrance 입구 옆에

at the entrance outside of the gallery 갤러리 외부 입구에서

ETS 기출 유형연습 1 🎧 950_U4_05 정답과 해설 p.034

Number of Bedrooms	Parking	Price per Month
1 Bedroom	Outdoor	$850
2 Bedrooms	Outdoor	$950
3 Bedrooms	Garage	$1,200
4 Bedrooms	Garage	$1,450

1. What did the woman do yesterday?

(A) She signed a lease.

(B) She moved some furniture.

(C) She purchased a vehicle from the man.

(D) She visited the man's business.

시각 정보 연계

2. Look at the graphic. How much will the woman pay?

(A) $850

(B) $950

(C) $1,200

(D) $1,450

3. What does the man ask the woman to do?

(A) Take some measurements

(B) Choose a location

(C) Supply payment information

(D) Send some references

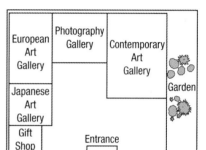

4. What good news does the speaker share?

(A) A fund-raiser was successful.

(B) A contract has been finalized.

(C) A new exhibit has opened.

(D) Ticket sales have increased.

시각 정보 연계

5. Look at the graphic. Where will a project begin?

(A) In the European Art Gallery

(B) In the Photography Gallery

(C) In the Contemporary Art Gallery

(D) In the Japanese Art Gallery

6. What does the speaker reassure the listeners about?

(A) A project will not be delayed.

(B) Noise will not be a problem.

(C) Flowers will be sold in a gift shop.

(D) A gallery will be open in the evening.

PART 3&4

UNIT 4

❸ 그래프(Graph)

🎧 950_U4_06 정답과 해설 p.036

막대 그래프, 원 그래프, 선 그래프 등의 형태로 출제되며, 시장 점유율, 수익이나 매출, 설문 조사 결과 등을 보여준다.
최상급 표현과 증감을 나타내는 숫자 표현에 주목한다.

M The training will include a demonstration of how these robots differ from our old ones. With the upgrade, we are projecting an increase in production. In fact, next quarter, we're expecting to **surpass 1,000 units for the first time**.	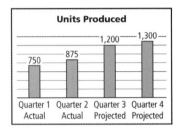

Q **Look at the graphic.** Which quarter does the speaker refer to?

A Quarter 3

☑ 만점 기출 표현

the highest sales numbers 가장 높은 판매량	profit margin 이익률
the next highest category 다음으로 높은 카테고리	rapid growth 빠른 성장
the lowest price 가장 낮은 금액	cost breakdown 비용 내역
the second lowest figure 두 번째로 낮은 수치	customer satisfaction ratings 고객 만족도

❹ 기타

🎧 950_U4_07 정답과 해설 p.036

쿠폰, 티켓, 웹페이지, 휴대폰 화면 등과 같이 다양한 시각 정보가 출제된다. 시각 정보를 전반적으로 살피는 것이 중요하며
숫자, 날짜, 이름 등에 유의하여 들어야 한다.

W I like both Fresh Linen and Lavender Field, but **Fresh Linen is definitely my favorite**. **M** That's my preference too. It's not cheap, but we want a distinctive room fragrance to help establish more uniformity across our hotel chain. **W** Right. The fragrance will be one of the first things our guests experience when they enter one of our hotels, so let's make it a good one.	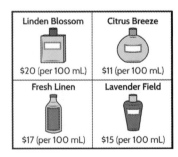

Q **Look at the graphic.** How much does the speakers' preferred product cost?

A $17

current balance 현재 잔액	store credit 상점 내 마일리지	under warranty 보증 기간 중인
expiration date 만료일	proof of purchase 구매 증거	amount due 지불해야 할 금액
debit card 직불 카드	pull up the website 웹사이트를 열다	valid in-store only 매장에서만 유효한
gift certificate 상품권		

ETS 기출 유형연습 2

🎧 950_U4_08　정답과 해설 p.036

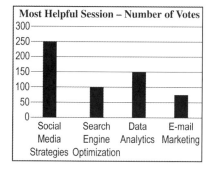

Most Helpful Session – Number of Votes

Candidates for Song of the Year	
Polina Evans	Raquel Clement
⭐	⭐
"Here and There"	"The Promise"
Asako Shimizu	Emily Molina
⭐	⭐
"Changing Times"	"Beyond the City"

시각 정보 연계

1. Look at the graphic. Which presentation did the man give?

(A) Social Media Strategies
(B) Search Engine Optimization
(C) Data Analytics
(D) E-mail Marketing

2. What problem does the woman mention?

(A) A guest speaker was late.
(B) There was not enough food.
(C) The air conditioning was not working.
(D) The Internet connection was unreliable.

3. What does the woman say the conference attendees received?

(A) A partial refund
(B) Free parking
(C) Meal vouchers
(D) Promotional materials

시각 정보 연계

4. Look at the graphic. Who is giving the speech?

(A) Polina Evans
(B) Raquel Clement
(C) Asako Shimizu
(D) Emily Molina

5. What does the speaker say inspired her career?

(A) Taking music lessons
(B) Being given a guitar
(C) Attending a concert
(D) Watching a particular music video

6. What does the speaker explain about her songs?

(A) They take a long time to write.
(B) They have been used in movies.
(C) They reveal a lot about her.
(D) They are usually recorded in a local studio.

PART 3&4

UNIT 4

1. Who most likely is the woman?

(A) A physician
(B) A lawyer
(C) A professional athlete
(D) A pharmacist

2. Why does the man say, "it's true I don't know much about fitness routines"?

(A) To clarify a misunderstanding
(B) To complain about a decision
(C) To recommend a more qualified candidate
(D) To agree with a suggestion

3. What will the man do next?

(A) Fill out a form
(B) Meet with a specialist
(C) Make a phone call
(D) Pay a bill

4. What does the man want to discuss?

(A) Customer complaints
(B) Pay increases
(C) Operating hours
(D) Dining options

5. What does the woman suggest?

(A) Getting customer feedback
(B) Changing ticket prices
(C) Booking local entertainers
(D) Sponsoring a community event

6. What does the woman mean when she says, "It wouldn't take long to create a draft"?

(A) She can meet with the man soon.
(B) She is willing to complete a task.
(C) Some volunteers are needed.
(D) A document is almost finished.

7. Where does the speaker work?

(A) At a real estate agency
(B) At a law office
(C) At an architecture firm
(D) At a medical clinic

8. What information does the speaker ask new clients to provide?

(A) Who they were referred by
(B) How they would like to pay
(C) When they are available to meet
(D) How they can be contacted

9. What does the speaker imply when he says, "our office building is undergoing renovations"?

(A) A service is no longer being offered.
(B) Hours of operation have been extended.
(C) An office may be hard to find.
(D) A business has opened a new location.

10. What is the podcast mainly about?

(A) Company start-ups
(B) Financial management
(C) Exercise habits
(D) Publishing tips

11. Why does the speaker say, "they haven't read Ms. Aslan's book"?

(A) To apologize for a delay
(B) To express disappointment
(C) To challenge an opinion
(D) To explain a decision

12. What does the speaker say is available on a Web site?

(A) A product link
(B) A discount code
(C) Some survey results
(D) Some customer reviews

Total Imports by Mode of Transport

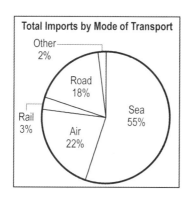

Video	Length
Proper Tomato Plant Care	13:55
How to Prune Basil	5:30
Preparing a Raised-Bed Garden	17:45
Avoid Mistakes with Watering	11:20

13. Who most likely is the woman?

(A) A pilot
(B) A journalist
(C) A government official
(D) A travel agent

14. Look at the graphic. Which percentage is the woman trying to verify?

(A) 2%
(B) 18%
(C) 22%
(D) 55%

15. Why will the man have to call the woman back?

(A) He needs to check a corporate policy.
(B) He cannot find some documents.
(C) There is a lot of background noise.
(D) There are people waiting to speak to him.

16. Look at the graphic. How long is the video that the speaker recommends?

(A) 13:55
(B) 5:30
(C) 17:45
(D) 11:20

17. Why does the speaker thank Kevin Graham?

(A) For creating some graphics
(B) For providing a work space
(C) For supplying materials
(D) For writing a video script

18. What will the speaker learn this summer?

(A) Fly fishing
(B) Traditional dancing
(C) Portrait painting
(D) Mountain climbing

PART 3&4 UNIT 4

61

1. What has especially impressed the man about the woman?

   (A) She has a strong educational background.
   (B) She is willing to take risks.
   (C) She has a positive attitude.
   (D) She has good problem-solving skills.

2. What does the man ask the woman about?

   (A) Her references
   (B) Her professional goals
   (C) Her vacation plans
   (D) Her preferred work location

3. What does the man imply when he says, "Alberto's about to retire"?

   (A) The man is planning a party.
   (B) A team should finish a project quickly.
   (C) A job opportunity will be available.
   (D) An office will be repurposed.

4. Who most likely is the woman?

   (A) An engineer
   (B) A university professor
   (C) A financial adviser
   (D) A retail associate

5. Why is the man calling the woman?

   (A) To ask for her opinion
   (B) To share some news
   (C) To collaborate on a project
   (D) To cancel a meeting

6. Why does the man say, "we're meeting with another group on Friday"?

   (A) To express gratitude
   (B) To complain about a schedule
   (C) To disagree with a policy
   (D) To recommend waiting

7. Who most likely is the speaker?

   (A) An accountant
   (B) A software engineer
   (C) A construction worker
   (D) A delivery driver

8. What does the speaker imply when he says, "this is her first month on the job"?

   (A) He is impressed with an employee's work.
   (B) He has not met an employee yet.
   (C) An employee needs additional training.
   (D) An employee has a reduced workload.

9. According to the speaker, what will be in a newsletter?

   (A) Photos from a company event
   (B) Directions to a location
   (C) A list of new employees
   (D) Details about a team's project

10. According to the speaker, what did the listener request?

    (A) A client list
    (B) A cost estimate
    (C) Some digital images
    (D) A property deed

11. According to the speaker, what does the listener need to do next?

    (A) Arrange for a soil assessment
    (B) Order a septic pump
    (C) Apply for a permit
    (D) Provide a credit card number

12. Why does the speaker say, "our team can't dig once the weather gets cold"?

    (A) To recommend another company
    (B) To explain a cost increase
    (C) To express urgency
    (D) To change a plan

**Baja's Grocers
Weekly Specials**

Save $3 on $25 or more!

Save $5 on $40 or more!

Save $7 on $60 or more!

Save $9 on $75 or more!

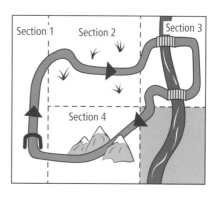

13. What did the store do last week?

(A) It updated its Web site.
(B) It expanded its online offerings.
(C) It started a delivery service.
(D) It launched a mobile application.

14. Look at the graphic. How much will the woman save?

(A) $3
(B) $5
(C) $7
(D) $9

15. What will the woman most likely do next?

(A) Return an item
(B) Go to the bakery department
(C) Answer some survey questions
(D) Leave the store

16. According to the speaker, what is special about this year's race?

(A) It is longer than usual.
(B) It has more runners.
(C) Prizes will be given.
(D) Children can participate.

17. Look at the graphic. Which section of the race does the speaker mention?

(A) Section 1
(B) Section 2
(C) Section 3
(D) Section 4

18. What will the listeners do next?

(A) Sign a waiver
(B) Gather supplies
(C) Take photos
(D) Form a line

PART 3&4

UNIT 4

PART
5&6

UNIT 5 문법 빈출 유형

PART 5&6 빈출 유형 만점 전략

품사 자리와 문장 구성 요소를 묻는 문제들은 Part 5&6에서 가장 빈출도가 높은 유형으로 난도는 비교적 평이한 편이다. 기본적으로 출제되는 명사, 동사, 형용사, 부사 자리를 익혀 두고, 다른 문법 포인트가 복합되는 고득점 포인트에 유의한다.

빈출 유형 공략법

❶ 품사 문제

한 단어의 네 가지 형태가 보기로 주어지는 문제이다. 빈칸이 주어, 동사, 목적어, 보어, 수식어 중에 어떤 자리인지를 파악해서 알맞은 품사나 형태를 고른다.

Q Accepting a job in a foreign country was a ------- decision, but Mr. Angelo said he enjoyed the experience of living abroad.

(A) risk   (B) risky
(C) risked   (D) risking

앞에 부정관사 a, 뒤에 명사 decision이 있으므로 보기에서 decision과 어울리는 형용사를 찾아야 한다. 형용사 (B) risky(무모한, 위험한)와 분사 (C) risked(위태롭게 된), (D) risking(~을 위태롭게 하는)이 명사를 수식할 수 있는데, 문맥상 '무모한 결정'이라는 의미가 되어야 하므로 (B) risky가 답이 된다.

외국에 있는 일자리를 수락한 것은 무모한 결정이었지만 안젤로 씨는 해외에 사는 경험이 즐거웠다고 말했다.   **정답 (B)**

❷ 동사 문제

선택지가 모두 한 동사의 다양한 형태로 제시된다. 본동사와 준동사의 구별, 자·타동사의 구별, 주어와의 수 일치/시제/태를 동시에 따져 알맞은 동사의 형태를 고르는 문제가 출제된다.

Q This coming week, Jones' Bookstore ------- up to 50 percent discount on all their children's books.

(A) was offered   (B) offered
(C) will offer   (D) has been offering

보기에 시제와 태가 다른 동사 어형들이 제시되어 있으므로, 시제와 태를 구분 짓는 단서를 찾아야 한다. 미래 시제 부사인 This coming week와 빈칸 뒤 목적어 up to 50 percent discount가 있으므로 미래 시제이며 능동형인 (C)가 답이 된다.

이번 주 존스 서점에서는 모든 아동 도서에 최대 50퍼센트 할인을 제공합니다.   **정답 (C)**

❸ 전치사 vs. 부사절 접속사 문제

접속사, 전치사, 부사 등이 선택지에 같이 나오는 문제 유형이다. 먼저 문장 구조를 파악해 구와 절을 구별해야 하며, 빈칸 앞뒤를 이어주는 모습에 따라 전치사와 접속사, 수식어인 부사를 선택한다.

Q ------- lengthy negotiations, Mr. Wooten finally signed the contract with the South Australia football team.

(A) On   (B) Thereafter
(C) In that   (D) Following

빈칸이 문장 맨 앞에 위치하고, 콤마와 완전한 절이 뒤 따르면 빈칸은 전치사 또는 부사절 접속사 자리이다. 빈칸 뒤에 명사구 lengthy negotiations가 있으므로 전치사 자리이며, '긴 협상 후에 마침내 계약했다'라는 의미가 되어야 하므로 (D) Following(~ 후에)이 답이다.

오랜 협상 후에 우튼 씨는 마침내 사우스 오스트레일리아 축구팀과 계약을 체결했다.   **정답 (D)**

명사/대명사/형용사/부사

기본 품사 문제는 빈칸에 알맞은 품사를 고르는 유형으로 난도가 낮은 편에 속한다. 하지만 빈칸에 들어갈 수 있는 품사를 두 개 이상 출제해 혼동을 주는 경우가 있으므로 유의한다.

❶ 명사

> 명사는 주어, 목적어, 보어 역할을 하며 한정사인 관사, 소유격 대명사, 형용사/분사 뒤에 나온다.
>
> • 관사 + 명사   **The** project timeline requires modification.   프로젝트 일정은 수정이 필요하다.
> • 소유격 + 명사   The CEO will announce **his** resignation soon.   대표 이사가 곧 사임을 발표할 것이다.
> • 형용사/분사 + 명사   The warranty is valid only on **authentic** products from **certified** retailers.
>   보증은 인증된 판매점에서 구입한 정품에만 유효합니다.

■ 가산 / 불가산명사와 한정사

보기에 명사가 두 개 이상인 경우 한정사가 문제 해결의 중요한 단서가 된다. 가산 단수명사는 반드시 한정사가 있어야 하지만, 가산 복수명사나 불가산명사는 한정사 없이 쓸 수 있다.

> **고난도 유형 1**   가산명사 vs. 불가산명사
>
> Contact technical support for [**assistance** / ~~assistant~~].   도움 요청은 기술 지원팀에 문의하세요.
> → 사람명사 assistant는 가산명사이므로 앞에 한정사가 있거나 복수형이어야 한다.

빈출 가산명사 vs. 불가산명사			
an approach 접근	— access 접근	a package 소포, 우편물	— packaging 포장재
an attendee 참가자	— attendance 참석(률)	a plan 계획	— planning 기획
funds 자금	— funding 재정 지원	a process 처리, 과정	— processing 처리
furnishings 가구	— furniture 가구	a survey 설문 조사	— research 조사

■ 복합명사

주로 앞 명사 자리는 형용사/분사, 뒤 명사 자리는 부사 또는 분사가 함정으로 제시되며, 수 일치 여부를 판단해야 하는 문제나 어휘 관련 문제가 고난도 문제로 출제된다.   ▶ p.96 명사+명사 참조

> **고난도 유형 1**   명사 + 명사
>
> Following [**security** / ~~secure~~] **policies** helps prevent unauthorized access.
> 보안 정책을 준수하는 것은 승인받지 않은 접근을 방지하는 데 도움이 된다.

> **고난도 유형 2**   명사 + 명사
>
> The staff update each log once **a work** [~~periodically~~ / **period**].   직원은 작업 기간에 한 번씩 일지를 업데이트한다.
> → work는 불가산명사로 관사 a와 어울리지 않으므로 가산명사를 이루는 복합명사 자리이다.

빈출 복합명사		
staffing plan 인력 배치 계획	mail receptacle 우편물 수신함	target audience 목표 대상
property boundary 소유지 경계(선)	color scheme 색감	insurance coverage 보험 보장 (범위)
security policy 보안 정책	housing allowance 주거 수당	language proficiency 언어 숙련도

■ **명사와 동명사 구별**

보기에 명사와 동명사가 함께 나오면 한정사와 목적어의 유무로 판단한다. 명사는 한정사/형용사의 수식을 받지만, 동명사는 부사가 수식한다. 빈칸 뒤에 목적어가 있으면 동명사, 없으면 주로 명사가 답이 된다.

고난도 유형 1 명사 vs. 동명사

[~~Accessing~~ / **Access**] **to** the restricted area is granted only to maintenance staff.

제한 구역 출입은 유지 관리 직원에게만 허가된다.

→ access는 동사로 쓰이는 경우 타동사이므로 동명사 accessing 뒤에는 목적어가 필요하다.

② 대명사

대명사에는 인칭/지시/부정대명사가 있으며 모두 주어, 목적어, 보어 자리에 들어갈 수 있다. Part 5에서 대명사 문제는 문장 내에 대명사가 가리키는 명사가 있어야 한다는 점에 유의한다.

- **인칭대명사** **All employees** submitted **their** timesheets. 전 직원이 그들의 근무 시간표를 제출했다.
- **지시대명사** **This** is **a reminder** that your lease will end soon. 이것은 곧 있을 임대 종료를 알리는 통지입니다.
- **부정대명사** Check **all** of **the items** below applicable to you.
  귀하에게 해당되는 아래의 모든 항목에 표시하세요.

■ **인칭대명사 / 소유대명사 / 재귀대명사**

단순히 인칭대명사의 격을 묻는 문제 이외에 소유대명사, 재귀대명사, 관계사/접속사가 생략된 절의 주어로 쓰인 주격 인칭대명사 등이 고난도 문제로 출제된다.

고난도 유형 1 인칭대명사 vs. 소유대명사

The architects claimed that [~~they~~ / **theirs**] was the most sustainable building design.

건축가들은 자신들의 건축물이 가장 지속 가능한 건축물 디자인이라고 주장했다.

고난도 유형 2 명사(+ 목적격 관계사) + 주격 대명사 + 동사

Researchers are encouraged to explore **any topics** [**they** / ~~themselves~~] **find** interesting.

연구원들은 그들이 흥미롭다고 생각하는 어떠한 주제라도 탐구하도록 권장된다.

■ **지시대명사 that / those**

that과 those는 이미 언급된 명사를 대신하거나 특정 대상을 나타낸다. 또한 those는 뒤에 who 관계사절, 분사구, 전치사구 등의 수식어를 동반하여 '~한 사람들'이라는 의미로도 쓰인다.

고난도 유형 1 those + 수식어: ~한 사람들

Ms. Kim emerged as the most qualified candidate among [**those** / ~~them~~] **with credentials**.

김 씨는 자격이 있는 지원자들 중 가장 자격이 뛰어난 후보로 떠올랐다.

고난도 유형 2 비교 상황의 that vs. those

The **specifications** of the recent model are **superior to** [~~that~~ / **those**] of its predecessors.

최신 모델의 사양은 이전 모델에 비해 월등히 뛰어나다.

▶비교급, 원급 비교, comparable to(~에 맞먹는), equivalent to(~와 동일한), indistinguishable from(~와 구분이 안 되는) 등의 비교 표현과 자주 출제된다.

■ 부정대명사

부정대명사는 의미뿐 아니라 대명사가 가리키는 명사를 찾아 수 일치를 확인해야 한다. 「부정대명사+of the/소유격+명사」 구문 또한 수 일치가 정해져 있으므로 암기해 둔다.

one / each / either / neither	of the items 복수명사	is on sale. 단수동사
(a) few / many / several / both	of the items 복수명사	are on sale. 복수동사
(a) little / much	of the merchandise 불가산명사	is on sale. 단수동사
all / some / most / any / none	of the items 복수명사 of the merchandise 불가산명사	are on sale. 복수동사 is on sale. 단수동사

▶ neither는 복수동사와도 쓰인다.

고난도 유형 1 부정대명사의 수 일치

Among **the complaints**, [few / ~~much~~] concerned our service. 민원들 중 우리 서비스에 관한 것은 거의 없었다.
→ few는 가산 복수명사, little은 불가산명사를 대신한다.

고난도 유형 2 「부정대명사 + of the/소유격 + 명사」의 수 일치

Since [~~every~~ / some] **of the attendees** have scheduling conflicts, the meeting will be rescheduled. 참석자 중 일부의 일정이 겹치기 때문에 회의 일정은 변경될 것이다.
→ every와 other는 대명사가 아닌 형용사이므로 주어나 목적어 자리에 올 수 없다.

> **만점 TIP**
>
> **-thing, -one, -body로 끝나는 부정대명사는 「of the/소유격+명사」의 수식을 받지 못한다.**
>
> [Any / ~~Anyone~~] **of the candidates** could potentially be selected for the position.
> 후보자들 중 누구라도 그 직책에 선발될 가능성이 있습니다.

③ 형용사

> 형용사는 명사 앞/뒤에서 명사를 수식하거나 문장에서 주어/목적어를 보충 설명하는 보어 역할을 한다.
>
> • **명사 수식**   LB Ltd. develops **interactive programs appropriate** for children.
>   LB 사는 어린이에게 적합한 대화형 프로그램을 개발한다.
> • **보어 자리**   The court **found** him **liable** for embezzlement. 법원은 그가 횡령에 책임이 있다고 판단했다.

■ 형용사 자리

주로 명사 수식 관련이거나 2형식/5형식 동사 뒤 보어 자리를 묻는 문제가 출제된다. 명사를 뒤에서 수식하거나 혼동하기 쉬운 형용사를 구분하는 문제 등이 고난도 유형으로 출제된다.

고난도 유형 1 명사 뒤 형용사 vs. 부사

The college provides transition programs for overseas **students** [new / ~~newly~~] **to the country**.
대학교는 이 나라에 처음 온 해외 유학생을 위한 적응 프로그램을 제공한다.

고난도 유형 2 보어 자리의 형용사 vs. 부사

The team **considered** revising the agenda [**necessary** / ~~necessarily~~]. 팀은 안건을 수정할 필요가 있다고 생각했다.
→ consider를 3형식 동사로 본다면, 부사 necessarily가 동사 consider를 수식하게 되므로 문맥상 오답이다.

고난도 유형 3 혼동하기 쉬운 형용사

The magazine article mentioned that the artist's latest exhibition was [~~impressed~~ / **impressive**].

잡지 기사는 그 예술가의 최신 전시회가 인상적이었다고 언급했다.

→ impressed 감명받은 / impressive 인상적인

혼동하기 쉬운 형용사

extensive 광범위한	extended 연장된	confident 자신 있는	confidential 기밀의
considerable 상당한	considerate 사려 깊은	advisory 자문의	advisable 바람직한
exhaustive 철저한	exhausting 진을 빼는	complimentary 무료의	complementary 보완적인

■ 수량형용사

수식하는 명사와의 수 일치에 유의해야 한다.

one / each / every / another / either / neither	device 단수명사
(a) few / many / several / both / a number of / a majority of	devices 복수명사
(a) little / much / a large amount of	equipment 불가산명사
all / some / other / more / most / a lot of / plenty of	devices/equipment 복수명사/불가산명사

▶ any는 가산 단/복수명사와 불가산명사, 즉 모든 명사와 어울린다.

고난도 유형 1 수량형용사의 수 일치

The discount applies to [**any** / ~~every~~] **merchandise** in the store. 할인은 매장 내 어떤 상품에도 적용됩니다.

→ every는 가산 단수명사를 수식하므로 불가산명사 merchandise와 함께 쓰일 수 없다.

❹ 부사

> 부사는 동사, 형용사, 부사, 문장 전체를 수식할 수 있으며 보통 수식하는 말 앞에 위치한다.
>
> • **동사(구) 수식**   Make sure your seat belt **is securely** fastened. 안전벨트가 단단히 매어져 있는지 확인하세요.
>
> • **형용사/부사 수식**   Job opportunities are **widely** available in hospitality.
> 호텔 산업에는 많은 일자리 기회가 있다.
>
> • **완전한 문장 수식**   **Consequently, the proposal was rejected.** 결과적으로 그 제안서는 받아들여지지 않았다.

■ 부사 자리

동사 외에도 to부정사, 동명사, 분사 등 준동사를 수식하는 부사와 전치사구, 접속사절 앞 부사 자리가 출제된다.

고난도 유형 1 부사 + 동명사

The manager thanked us for [~~brief~~ / **briefly**] **explaining** the project goals.

매니저는 프로젝트 목표를 간단히 설명해 준 것에 대해 우리에게 감사했다.

고난도 유형 2 부사 + 부사절 접속사

The manager will review the sales figures [~~immediate~~ / **immediately**] **after** the store closes.

매니저는 매장이 문을 닫은 직후에 판매 수치를 검토할 것이다.

▶ immediately/directly/shortly/soon + after/before: 직후에/직전에

■ 특정 표현과 어울리는 부사

수식하는 대상의 특징에 따라 함께 쓰이는 부사를 묻는 문제가 고난도 유형으로 출제된다.

고난도 유형 1 증감동사 수식 부사 vs. 형용사/부사 수식 부사

The profits [**drastically** / ~~highly~~] **increased** last year, surpassing all expectations.
지난해 수익이 모든 기대를 뛰어넘으며 급격히 증가했다.

→ highly(매우)는 동사를 수식하지 않는다. (단, recommend(추천하다), value(평가하다) 등은 예외)

증감동사를 수식하는 부사	significantly/considerably/substantially 상당히 steadily 꾸준히 gradually 점진적으로 remarkably/noticeably 눈에 띄게 drastically/dramatically 급격히
형용사/부사만 수식하는 부사	very/pretty/highly 매우 quite/fairly 꽤 extremely 매우, 극도로 relatively 비교적

고난도 유형 2 특정 시제와 어울리는 부사

The library [~~recently~~ / **regularly**] updates its collection with new books and resources.
도서관은 새로운 도서와 자료로 소장품을 정기적으로 업데이트한다.

과거 시제 부사	recently 최근에 once 한때 previously/formerly 이전에 originally 원래
현재 시제 부사	regularly/periodically 정기적으로 ordinarily/usually 보통 typically 일반적으로
미래 시제 부사	potentially 가능성 있게, 잠재적으로 soon 곧, 이내 shortly/momentarily 곧

ETS 기출 유형연습

정답과 해설 p.046

1. Road ------- in Hampton caused minor delays in computer shipments from the main warehouse this week.

   (A) repaired   (B) repairer   (C) repairs   (D) repairable

2. Nova Feast Catering is looking for ------- who are willing to commit to creating catchy social media posts on a weekly basis.

   (A) those   (B) them   (C) someone   (D) anyone

3. Portfolio managers who were hired ------- are reminded to attend the advanced training session tomorrow in conference room A.

   (A) soon   (B) recently   (C) often   (D) yet

4. Some hardware stores rent large, ------- items, such as snowblowers and power washers, by the hour.

   (A) cost   (B) costing   (C) costs   (D) costly

02 동사

단순히 동사 자리를 묻는 문제뿐 아니라 선택지가 모두 동사 형태로 구성된 문제도 출제된다. 또한, 어휘 문제처럼 보이는 동사 문제는 자·타동사의 구분이나 특정 구조와 어울리는 동사의 용법을 묻는 유형으로 난도가 높다.

① 동사

> 동사는 크게 목적어가 필요 없는 자동사와 목적어가 필요한 타동사로 나뉜다. 자동사는 1·2형식 문장을, 타동사는 3·4·5형식 문장을 만든다.
>
> • **자동사** Spectators laughed loudly at the commentary. 관중들은 해설에 크게 웃었다.
> • **타동사** The two parties reached a compromise on the contract. 양측이 계약에 대한 타협점을 찾았다.

■ 자동사와 타동사

자동사는 전치사구나 부사가 뒤따를 수 있고, 타동사는 명사(구), 준동사구, 명사절 형태의 목적어를 동반한다.

고난도 유형 1 자동사 vs. 타동사

The team will [~~act~~ / conduct] a survey on the new product. 팀에서 신제품에 대한 설문 조사를 실시할 것이다.
→ 목적어(a survey)가 있으므로 타동사 conduct가 정답. act는 자동사

The recent market shift [accounts / ~~explains~~] for the decline in our revenues.
최근 시장의 변화가 수익 감소를 설명한다. → 뒤에 전치사 for가 있으므로 자동사 account가 정답. explain은 타동사

혼동하기 쉬운 자동사와 타동사

참여하다	participate in	attend	준수하다	comply with	observe
설명하다	account for	explain	반대하다	object to	oppose
고려하다	think about/on	consider	방해하다	interfere with	interrupt

■ 3형식 / 4형식 / 5형식 동사

목적어를 하나만 취하는 3형식 동사와 직접/간접목적어 2개를 취하는 4형식 동사의 구분에 유의한다.

고난도 유형 1 3형식 동사 vs. 4형식 동사

The company [provides / ~~offers~~] its employees with substantial benefits.
회사는 직원들에게 상당한 혜택을 제공한다. → 「간접목적어 + with 명사」의 구조가 뒤따르므로 3형식 동사 provide가 정답. offer는 4형식 동사

고난도 유형 2 3형식 동사 + that절 vs. 4형식 동사 + 사람 목적어 + that절

We [~~announced~~ / informed] our customers that the delivery schedule has changed.
우리는 고객들에게 배송 일정이 변경되었음을 알렸다.
→ 사람 목적어와 that절이 뒤따르므로 4형식 동사 inform이 정답. announce는 3형식 동사

동사+사람 목적어+that절/of+명사/to부정사

inform/notify 알려주다 assure/convince 확신시키다 remind 상기시키다	clients 고객들에게	that the price policy has been revised. 가격 정책이 바뀌었다고 of the revised price policy. 변경된 가격 정책에 대해 *to renew their subscriptions. 구독을 갱신하라고

*사람 목적어를 취하는 동사 뒤에 to부정사가 오면 목적격 보어로 5형식 구문이 된다.

3형식 동사 vs. 5형식 동사

The manager [~~understood~~ / **considered**] **the new policy** somewhat **difficult** to implement.
매니저는 새 정책이 시행하기에 다소 어렵다고 여겼다.

→ 「목적어＋형용사」의 구조가 나왔으므로 5형식 동사 consider가 정답. understand는 that절을 목적어로 취한다.

② 동사의 수/태/시제 일치

동사는 주어와의 수 일치, 목적어 유무에 따른 능·수동태, 시제를 종합적으로 확인한다.

①**Merchandise** crafted by local artists ③**typically** provides ②**income** for the community.

지역 예술가들이 제작한 상품은 보통 그 지역 사회에 수입원이 된다.

① 주어가 단수이므로 단수, ② 목적어가 있으므로 능동, ③ 빈도부사와 어울리는 현재 시제 ▶ **provides**

■ 동사의 수 일치

주어를 수식하는 전치사구, 준동사구, 관계사절은 수 일치에 영향을 주지 않는다는 점에 유의한다. 또한 동명사구 주어는 단수 취급하므로, 주어 자리에 -ing가 오면 동명사인지 분사인지 살펴봐야 한다.

주어 + 수식어구/절 + 동사

The unique flora and fauna on the island [~~attracts~~ / **attract**] tourists.
섬의 독특한 동식물이 관광객을 끌어들인다.

The employee who achieves the highest sales figures [~~receive~~ / **will receive**] a prize.
최고의 판매 실적을 달성한 직원은 상을 받을 것이다.

→ 주어가 단수이므로 복수동사 receive는 답이 되지 않는다.

주어 자리의 「동명사＋명사」 vs. 「분사＋명사」

[**Coordinating** / ~~Coordinated~~] schedules **involves** communicating with various departments.
일정을 조율하는 것은 여러 부서와 소통하는 일을 포함한다.

→ Coordinated가 오면 schedules가 주어가 되는데 문장의 동사인 involves와 수 일치가 되지 않는다.

Rising **prices** for fuel [~~is~~ / **are**] affecting transportation costs.
상승하는 연료 가격이 운송 비용에 영향을 미치고 있다.

→ Rising은 prices를 수식하는 현재분사로 복수명사 prices가 주어

■ 동사의 태

수동태는 능동태의 목적어가 주어가 되는 것이므로 타동사만 가능하다. 수동태 뒤에는 주로 부사나 전치사구가 오지만, 명사가 올 수 있는 4형식과 명사, 형용사, to부정사 등이 올 수 있는 5형식 동사의 수동태가 고난도 유형으로 출제된다.

4형식 동사의 수동태

The passengers will be [~~sending~~ / **sent**] **confirmation** of their booking upon receipt of payment.
승객들은 결제 즉시 예약 확인서를 받게 된다.

→ 승객은 예약 확인서를 '받는' 입장이므로 문맥상 sent가 정답. sending(주고 있는)은 주어와 어울리지 않아 오답.

5형식 동사의 수동태

Peggy's Cove [**has been voted** / ~~voted~~] **Halifax's most popular attraction.**
페기스코브는 핼리팩스의 가장 인기 있는 관광지로 선정되었다.

Candidates **are** [**encouraged** / ~~encouraging~~] **to demonstrate** their talents.
지원자들은 자신의 재능을 발휘할 수 있도록 격려된다. → 「encourage+목적어+to부정사」 구문의 수동태

■ 동사의 시제 일치

시제 일치 문제는 단서가 되는 시간 표현이 주어지므로 관련 부사, 전치사, 접속사 등을 파악해 문제를 해결한다. 또한 시제
일치가 적용되지 않는 예외 구문에 주의한다.

고난도 유형 1   **단순 시제 vs. 완료 시제**

On arrival at our facility, packages [**are** / ~~have been~~] processed by the shipping department.
공장에 도착 시, 배송 부서가 소포를 처리한다. → 「on+(동)명사」(~할 때, ~하자마자)와 같이 특정 시점 표현은 단순 시제와 쓰인다.

고난도 유형 2   **과거완료 vs. 미래완료**

By the time we complete this study, we [~~had furthered~~ / **will have furthered**] our understanding
of biodiversity. 우리가 이 연구를 완료할 때 즈음이면, 생물의 다양성에 대한 우리의 이해가 증진될 것이다.
→ By the time+주어+현재 시제, 주어+will have p.p. / By the time+주어+과거 시제, 주어+had p.p.

고난도 유형 3   **시제 일치의 예외**

Unless the furniture delivery [**arrives** / ~~will arrive~~] on time, the office renovation **will be delayed**.
가구 배송이 제때 도착하지 않으면 사무실 개보수는 지연될 것이다 → 시간/조건의 부사절에서는 현재(완료)가 미래(완료)를 대신한다.

The manager **demanded** that the project deadline [~~was extended~~ / **be extended**].
관리자는 프로젝트 마감일을 연장해야 한다고 요구했다.
→ 주장, 제안, 요청의 동사와 당위성을 나타내는 형용사 뒤 that절에는 should가 생략된 동사원형이 온다.

ETS 기출 유형연습   정답과 해설 p.046

1. The Bradford is our narrowest display case, ideal for stores that ------- limited space for
   products.
   (A) has been   (B) has   (C) have   (D) have been

2. Please ------- the written report short and avoid including any irrelevant data.
   (A) maintain   (B) keep   (C) allow   (D) retain

3. All appliances sold during Zhao Kitchen Supply's sale next month ------- a money-back
   guarantee.
   (A) includes   (B) will include   (C) including   (D) will be included

03 전치사와 부사절 접속사

전치사, 접속사, 접속부사를 구분하는 문제는 거의 매회 출제된다. Part 5에서는 전치사와 접속사 중 적절한 품사를 선택하는 문제가, Part 6에서는 접속부사를 이용한 어휘 문제가 자주 출제된다.

❶ 전치사와 부사절 접속사

전치사 뒤에는 명사(구)나 동명사구가 나오고, 접속사 뒤에는 주어와 동사가 있는 완전한 절이 나온다.

- **전치사+명사(구)** Due to **low registration**, the event has been canceled.
  낮은 등록률 때문에 행사는 취소되었다.

- **접속사+주어+동사** Access to the building is restricted **because it is being renovated**.
  보수 공사 중이어서 건물 출입이 통제된다.

■ 전치사 vs. 부사절 접속사
유사한 의미의 전치사와 부사절 접속사를 구분하는 문제가 자주 출제되므로, 의미와 품사를 정확히 익혀 둔다.

의미		전치사	부사절 접속사
시간	~할 때, ~하자마자	on[upon]	when, as soon as
	~ 후에 / ~ 전에	after, following / before, prior to	after / before
	~ 동안	for+기간(숫자), during+특정 기간(명사)	while
	~ 까지	by (완료), until (계속)	by the time, until
양보	~에도 불구하고, ~일지라도	despite, in spite of, notwithstanding	although, even though[if]
조건	~이 라면, ~한 경우를 대비하여	in case of, in the event of	if, provided (that), in case (that)
이유	~ 때문에	because of, due to, attributed to	because, as, since, now that

고난도 유형 1 전치사 vs. 부사절 접속사

The presentation was well-received, [**in spite of** / ~~even if~~] **technical difficulties** with the equipment.
장비의 기술적인 어려움에도 불구하고 발표는 좋은 평가를 받았다. ➡ 전치사+명사구

Have a backup plan [~~in the event of~~ / **in case**] **your first one falls through**.
첫 계획이 실패할 경우를 대비해 대안을 세우세요. ➡ 접속사+주어+동사

■ 주의해야 할 전치사
시점/기간을 나타내는 표현과 어울리는 전치사를 구분하는 문제가 자주 출제된다. 전치사처럼 보이지 않는 분사형 전치사와 구전치사 또한 유의한다.

고난도 유형 1 시점 전치사 vs. 기간 전치사

The main entrance gate will be closed [**in** / ~~until~~] **10 minutes**. 주 출입구는 10분 후에 닫힐 것입니다.
➡ 기간(10 minutes) 표현과 함께 '~ 후에'라는 의미의 in이 정답. until은 시점 표현과 쓰인다.

고난도 유형 2 분사형 전치사와 구전치사

[**Given** / ~~Apart from~~] **the large scale of the project**, the deadline should be extended.
프로젝트의 큰 규모를 고려하면 기한이 연장되어야 한다.

빈출 분사형 전치사/구전치사		
regarding, concerning ~에 관한	regardless of ~와 상관없이	according to ~에 따르면
except (for). apart from ~을 제외하고	instead of, in place of ~ 대신에	such as ~와 같은
given, in light[view] of ~을 고려하면	in addition to, besides ~에 더하여	as of ~부로, ~부터

■ 주의해야 할 부사절 접속사

시간/조건의 부사절에서 현재(완료)가 미래(완료)를 대신하는 시제 일치 예외 사항은 접속사 어휘 문제에서 중요한 단서가 되기도 한다. 또한, 부사절에서 주어와 be동사를 생략하여 접속사 뒤에 분사가 올 수 있다.

고난도 유형 1 시간/조건의 부사절 접속사

[~~Although~~ / **As soon as**] the loan **has been approved**, the funds **will be deposited in your account**. 대출이 승인되는 즉시, 자금이 고객님의 계좌로 입금될 것입니다.

고난도 유형 2 「부사절 접속사＋현재분사」 vs. 「전치사＋동명사」

[**While** / ~~During~~] **being interviewed**, Mr. Choi expressed great enthusiasm.
면접이 진행되는 동안, 최 씨는 대단한 열정을 보여주었다.
→ 접속사 while과 being interviewed가 분사구문을 이룬다. 전치사 during은 동명사를 목적어로 취하지 않는다.

② 접속부사

접속부사는 접속사가 아닌 부사로, 접속사처럼 단독으로 두 개의 절을 연결하여 한 문장으로 만들 수 없다.

Pay the invoice by the due date; **otherwise**, there will be a late fee.
기한 내에 송장을 지불하십시오, 그렇지 않으면 연체료가 부과될 것입니다.

접속부사는 Part 6에서 앞뒤 문장의 문맥을 연결하는 어휘 문제로 자주 출제되며, Part 5에서는 문장 중간에 위치해 부사의 수식 기능을 묻는 유형으로 출제되기도 한다.

고난도 유형 1 접속사 vs. 접속부사

TEC, Inc., adopted the latest technology early, and [~~unless~~ / **therefore**] became a market leader.
TEC 주식회사는 최신 기술을 일찍 도입하여 그 결과 시장 선도 기업이 되었다.

빈출 접속부사

meanwhile 그동안에   therefore 그러므로   however 그러나   likewise 마찬가지로   if so 그렇다면
afterwards/thereafter 그 후에   nevertheless/even so 그럼에도 불구하고   if not/otherwise/or else 그렇지 않다면

ETS 기출 유형연습
정답과 해설 p.047

1. ------- sending correspondence to customers, be sure to use the association's revised letterhead.

   (A) When   (B) During   (C) Meanwhile   (D) Yet

2. Conference attendees must check in ------- 8:30 A.M. if they wish to participate in the first session.

   (A) by   (B) until   (C) since   (D) within

3. ------- our artist revised the logo for the Cooke account, the client is still not satisfied.

   (A) As long as   (B) Even so   (C) Although   (D) Nonetheless

1. ------- among cable TV providers has led to lower prices for residential subscribers.

   (A) Competition　(B) Competitive
   (C) Competitor　(D) Competes

2. The latest marketing survey indicates that the price of Cinabyte's action-adventure games is too -------.

   (A) high　(B) higher
   (C) highest　(D) highly

3. ------- sales revenue grew 22 percent last quarter, there is more money available for employee training.

   (A) Due to　(B) Since
   (C) Like　(D) Thus

4. Only authorized employees ------- access to patient records.

   (A) is granting　(B) are granted
   (C) has been granting　(D) to be granted

5. The lead ------- at the interior design conference will discuss innovations in lighting systems.

   (A) speaker　(B) spoke
   (C) speaks　(D) spoken

6. ------- purchasing fifteen or more tickets, contact the theater box office regarding group discounts and seating arrangements.

   (A) Otherwise　(B) Whatever
   (C) Although　(D) Before

7. To receive a full refund, hair-care products must be returned unopened ------- 30 days of purchase.

   (A) about　(B) within
   (C) during　(D) except

8. For a low annual fee, Platinum Trinidad's Web site ------- templates for many common business tasks.

   (A) provides　(B) belongs
   (C) remembers　(D) notifies

9. If enough team members ------- interest in a conference call by Monday, Mr. Mayer will set it up.

   (A) express　(B) expressed
   (C) expressing　(D) will express

10. Ricksby Publishing offers textbooks covering ------- different topics.

    (A) any　(B) others
    (C) several　(D) something

11. The new accounting system will make buying office supplies more -------.

    (A) convenience　(B) convenient
    (C) conveniently　(D) conveniences

12. With proper training and online tools, remote workers can collaborate ------- on most advertising campaigns.

    (A) product　(B) productive
    (C) productively　(D) productivity

13. Employees who report to ------- appreciate the exceptional career guidance provided by Ms. Carbone and Mr. Lee.

(A) they
(B) their
(C) theirs
(D) them

14. ------- will be asked to rank the effectiveness of ten advertisements during tomorrow's focus-group meeting.

(A) Attendance
(B) Attending
(C) Attendant
(D) Attendees

Questions 15-18 refer to the following package insert.

Thank you for purchasing a water ------- system installed by Fluxopure, a world leader

15.

in innovative water filtration. The product you have purchased, the Pichet II, employs Fluxopure's proprietary, redesigned filter. ------- . To fill the jug, simply screw the filter into the

16.

lid, run tap water into the convenient funnel-shaped entry port, and wait for the water to pass

------- the filter. Then you can drink and cook with water that is free of common contaminants

17.

that spoil its ------- . Before you use the Pichet II for the first time, please read the enclosed

18.

illustrated booklet of directions.

15. (A) purify
(B) pure
(C) purification
(D) purer

17. (A) through
(B) toward
(C) plus
(D) along

16. (A) Furthermore, the Pichet II can be found in all Home Values stores.
(B) Pichet II's two-liter jug is made from food-grade recycled plastic.
(C) Using recycled plastic for the Pichet II helps the environment.
(D) No other firm can match the low price of the Pichet II.

18. (A) flavorful
(B) flavorless
(C) flavored
(D) flavor

1. Clients ------- to manage their accounts through our online banking service.

   (A) are encouraged   (B) are encouraging
   (C) will encourage   (D) encourage

2. Increasing subscriber ------- is a top priority for our sales team in the coming year.

   (A) engages   (B) engaged
   (C) engage   (D) engagement

3. The product development team hopes its plant-based water bottle will ------- reduce plastic waste.

   (A) extremely   (B) fairly
   (C) seldom   (D) significantly

4. The vans have been retrofitted to enable the technicians to find the tools ------- need more easily.

   (A) themselves   (B) what
   (C) few   (D) they

5. Windsor Apartment Complex residents may bring guests to the on-site pool ------- the hosts remain with the guests.

   (A) in view of   (B) instead
   (C) as long as   (D) whether

6. Ms. Angelo found ------- unable to predict Whiffley Manufacturing's next-quarter sales.

   (A) she   (B) herself
   (C) myself   (D) hers

7. Ticket holders will be allowed ------- into Cedar Lane Stadium at 5:00 P.M.

   (A) enter   (B) entry
   (C) entering   (D) entered

8. Radbord Technologies has long ------- a premier employer for engineers in multiple fields.

   (A) been   (B) thought
   (C) granted   (D) created

9. The new department store will ------- open on February 15, though construction delays would require extending that start date.

   (A) equally   (B) considerably
   (C) formerly   (D) potentially

10. Purchase a large coffee and get half off ------- food item at Brown's Coffeehouse this week.

    (A) great   (B) filled
    (C) any   (D) whole

11. Conference attendees were ------- that lunch boxes would be distributed in the check-in area.

    (A) provided   (B) engaged
    (C) elected   (D) reminded

12. Through September 30, all Rodon Auto service stations are offering ------- brake inspections.

    (A) compliment   (B) complimented
    (C) complimenting   (D) complimentary

13. ------- being Penny Footwear's busiest store, the Lakewood Mall branch reported a decrease in sales this quarter.

(A) Unless (B) Despite
(C) Otherwise (D) Yet

14. It is advised that any customer requiring assistance after business hours ------- a message at our emergency number.

(A) leave (B) leaves
(C) left (D) to leave

Questions 15-18 refer to the following e-mail.

To: GT Ink Customer Service
From: Georgette Simpson
Date: May 14
Subject: Account OS-1147

Good morning,

I want to upgrade my ink delivery plan as of June 1. I have reviewed my monthly ink order and have found that I use more ink than I ------- thought. Please change my account from the
15.
standard plan to the ------- one that includes enough ink to print up to 350 pages per month.
16.
I will need a high-capacity black ink cartridge and a standard color ink cartridge with each

delivery. ------- . You may consider ------- my authorization to bill my account accordingly.
17. **18.**

Thank you,

Georgette Simpson

15. (A) eventually
(B) separately
(C) suddenly
(D) previously

16. (A) limited
(B) smallest
(C) premium
(D) functional

17. (A) The inkjet printer is on back order and will arrive shortly.
(B) Thank you for returning my call in a timely manner.
(C) Also, discontinue my subscription to your service effective immediately.
(D) As I understand it, my monthly cost will increase by $20.

18. (A) those
(B) either
(C) this
(D) he

PART
5&6

UNIT 6 문법 고난도 유형

PART 5&6 고난도 유형 만점 전략

준동사와 명사절, 관계사절, 비교, 도치 관련 문제들은 출제 빈도가 낮은 편이지만, 오답률이 높아 고득점을 위해서는 학습이 필요한 필수 유형이다. 다소 복잡해 보이는 문장들로 문장 구성의 정확한 이해와 분석이 필요하다.

고난도 유형 공략법

❶ 준동사의 용법 문제

본동사와 비교되는 준동사의 기능과 능·수동 형태를 구분하는 문제가 자주 출제된다.

Q All items ------- in to the lost-and-found desk will be kept until the end of the current calendar year.

(A) are turned   (B) turned
(C) turning   (D) to turn

본동사 will be kept가 있으므로, 빈칸은 All items를 수식하는 분사 자리이다. 구동사 turn in은 '~을 제출하다'라는 의미의 타동사로 뒤에 전치사 to가 있으므로, '제출된'이라는 수동의 의미가 되어야 자연스럽다. 따라서 과거분사 (B)가 정답이다.

분실물 보관소에 제출된 모든 물품은 당해 말까지 보관됩니다.   정답 (B)

❷ 종속절 접속사의 자리 비교 문제

문장 구조와 주절과의 상관관계에 따른 명사절, 형용사절, 부사절 접속사의 자리 비교 문제가 출제된다. 각 종속절은 명사, 형용사, 부사 역할을 하므로 자리가 이들 품사와 같다는 점에 유의한다.

Q The manufacturer's specifications state ------- the television stand can support up to 50 kilograms.

(A) what   (B) whose
(C) that   (D) unless

보기가 모두 접속사이므로 빈칸 앞뒤 구조를 확인한다. 앞에 동사 state가 있고 뒤에 완전한 절이 있으므로 명사절 접속사가 필요하다. 보기 중 that이 완전한 절을 취하는 명사절 접속사이므로 (C)가 답이 된다.

제조업체의 사양에는 TV 스탠드가 최대 50킬로그램까지 지지할 수 있다고 명시되어 있다.   정답 (C)

❸ 비교급/최상급 관련 문제

비교급과 최상급 문제는 각각 잘 쓰이는 어구와 함께 출제되므로 표현 중심으로 학습한다. 형용사와 부사의 품사 구분 문제도 비교급, 최상급 관련으로 출제되므로, 문장 구조를 꼼꼼히 파악해야 한다.

Q The public reacted to the newly announced government healthcare system much ------- than expected.

(A) more strongly   (B) too strong
(C) most strongly   (D) far stronger

빈칸 뒤에 than, 앞에 비교급 강조 부사 much(훨씬)가 보이므로 보기에서 비교급을 찾는다. (A)와 (D) 중 이미 비교급 강조 부사 far(훨씬)가 포함된 (D)는 제외되므로 (A) more strongly가 답이 된다.

대중은 새로 발표된 정부의 의료 보험 제도에 예상보다 훨씬 더 강하게 반응했다.   정답 (A)

01 to부정사/동명사, 분사와 분사구문

to부정사, 동명사, 분사는 동사의 성질을 가진 준동사로 쓰임에 따라 문장에서 명사, 형용사, 부사 역할을 한다. to부정사나 동명사와 어울리는 표현, 명사를 수식하는 분사, 분사구문 관련 문제 등이 고난도 유형으로 출제된다.

❶ to부정사와 동명사

미래의 의미를 함축하고 있는 to부정사는 명사, 형용사, 부사 역할을 하고, 동명사는 명사 역할을 한다.

• **to부정사** The company reduced expenses **to increase** profits. 회사는 수익을 늘리기 위해 경비를 줄였다.

• **동명사**   **Delegating** tasks is helpful in managing workloads. 업무를 위임하는 것은 작업량 관리에 도움이 된다.

토익에서 to부정사와 동명사 문제는 잘 쓰이는 표현들이 단서가 되어 출제되므로 관용 표현처럼 익혀 둔다.

고난도 유형 1 to부정사 vs. 동명사

The HR department is [**planning** / ~~suggesting~~] **to implement** a new performance review system.
인사부는 새로운 성과 검토 제도를 시행할 계획 중이다.

to부정사를 목적어로 취하는 동사		동명사를 목적어로 취하는 동사	
aim to do ~을 목표로 하다	deserve to do ~할 자격이 있다	risk -ing ~을 감행하다	oppose -ing ~을 반대하다
intend to do ~할 작정이다	agree to do ~하기로 합의하다	consider -ing ~을 고려하다	postpone -ing ~을 연기하다
wish to do ~하기를 바라다	manage to do 가까스로 ~하다	include -ing ~을 포함하다	suggest -ing ~을 제안하다

고난도 유형 2 to부정사를 목적격 보어로 취하는 동사

The incentive program **motivated** employees [~~participated~~ / **to participate**] in the initiative.
인센티브 프로그램은 직원들이 그 계획에 참여하도록 동기를 부여했다.

This app will **help** you [**form** / ~~forming~~] healthy habits. 이 앱은 여러분이 건강한 습관을 형성하는 데 도움을 줄 것입니다.
→ help는 목적어와 목적격 보어로 to부정사와 원형부정사를 모두 취할 수 있다.

to부정사를 목적격 보어로 취하는 동사		
allow 명사 to do ~하도록 허락하다	require 명사 to do ~하라고 요구하다	encourage 명사 to do ~하라고 격려하다
advise 명사 to do ~하도록 권고하다	instruct 명사 to do ~하라고 지시하다	convince 명사 to do ~하라고 설득하다
invite 명사 to do ~하도록 권유하다	enable 명사 to do ~할 수 있게 하다	urge 명사 to do ~하라고 촉구하다

고난도 유형 3 to부정사 vs. 전치사 to

Sensitive information **is vulnerable to** [**being** / ~~be~~] leaked online.
민감한 정보는 온라인에서 유출되기 쉽다. → vulnerable 뒤 to는 전치사 to이므로 동명사가 와야 한다.

be+형용사+to부정사	be+형용사+전치사 to
be likely to ~할 가능성이 높다	be subject to ~의 대상이다, ~될 수 있다
be reluctant/hesitant to ~하기를 꺼리다	be vulnerable to ~에 취약하다, 피해를 입기 쉽다
be pleased/delighted/honored to ~하게 되어 기쁘다	be committed/dedicated/devoted to ~에 전념[헌신]하다

고난도 유형 4 명사를 수식하는 to부정사 vs. 현재분사

The proposal [**to develop** / ~~developing~~] the district has been approved. 그 지구를 개발할 제안이 승인되었다.
→ 미래 계획을 나타내는 proposal은 to부정사와 어울린다.

② 분사와 분사구문

분사는 형용사 역할을 하며 수식하는 명사와 능동 관계이면 현재분사, 수동 관계이면 과거분사를 쓴다.

- **현재분사** HR conducts exit interviews with **departing employees**.
  인사부는 퇴사하는 직원과 퇴직 면담을 진행한다.

- **과거분사** We offer **services tailored** to your needs. 저희는 고객의 요구에 맞춘 서비스를 제공합니다.

■ 분사

명사 앞에서 수식하는 분사는 해석으로, 명사 뒤에서 수식하는 분사는 목적어 유무로 판단한다. 목적어가 있으면 현재분사, 없으면 과거분사를 쓴다. 단, 자동사가 분사가 되는 경우 현재분사로만 쓰이는 데 유의한다.

고난도 유형 1 분사 + 명사

The [~~presenting~~ / **presented**] **reports** can also be found on our Web site.
발표된 보고서는 자사 웹사이트에서도 확인할 수 있습니다. ➜ 보고서는 발표되는 대상, 즉 수동 관계이므로 과거분사

고난도 유형 2 명사 + 분사

The area [**surrounding** / ~~surrounded~~] **the hotel** gets a lot of foot traffic.
그 호텔을 둘러싼 지역은 유동 인구가 많다.

We still have **one task** [**remaining** / ~~remained~~] **for** the project. 아직 프로젝트에 남겨진 작업이 하나 있다.
➜ 자동사인 remain은 수동의 과거분사를 쓰지 않으므로 현재분사만이 명사를 수식한다.

■ 분사구문

「접속사+주어+동사」의 부사절에서 접속사와 주어를 생략하고 동사를 -ing나 (being) -ed의 분사구로 바꾼 구문이다. 분사 자리에 현재분사 또는 과거분사를 고르는 문제나, 접속사를 생략하지 않은 분사구문 문제가 출제된다.

고난도 유형 1 부사절 접속사 + 분사

As unanimously [~~agreeing~~ / **agreed**] **upon**, the terms are final. 만장일치로 합의된 대로 이 약관은 최종입니다.
➜ 접속사 as는 과거분사와 함께 '~된 대로'라는 의미로 자주 출제된다. ⓔ as stated(명시된 대로), as advertised(광고된 대로)

만점 TIP

분사구문에서 be동사는 주로 생략하므로 보어로 쓰인 형용사나 명사가 남아 분사구문을 이끌 수도 있다.

[**Distinct** / ~~Distinction~~] from its competitors, our product comes with a lifetime warranty.
경쟁 상품들과는 확연히 다르게, 우리 제품은 평생 보증을 제공합니다.

ETS 기출 유형연습
정답과 해설 p.051

1. Magic Clear spray is specially formulated ------- streaks on glass surfaces.

   (A) prevented　　　(B) to prevent　　　(C) prevention　　　(D) will prevent

2. The new accounting software will make it easier to generate ------- financial reports.

   (A) customs　　　(B) customized　　　(C) customizing　　　(D) customize

3. Members of the demolition team must be cautious when ------- the deteriorated building.

   (A) entrance　　　(B) entered　　　(C) entering　　　(D) to enter

명사절과 관계사절

명사절과 형용사절인 관계사절을 포함해 종속절은 접속사와 문장 구조, 주절과의 상관관계 관련 문제가 출제된다.

① 명사절

> 명사절은 문장에서 주어, 목적어, 보어 역할을 하며 that, whether/if, 의문사, 복합관계대명사 등이 명사절을 이끈다.
>
> **Whether the initiative will attract investors** is yet to be seen.
> 그 계획이 투자자들을 끌어들일지는 아직 미지수다.
>
> The clinical results suggest **that the intervention is effective.** 임상 결과는 개입이 효과적임을 시사한다.

명사절을 이끄는 접속사 뒤에 이어지는 문장의 구조와 접속사의 쓰임을 확실하게 익혀 두도록 한다.

that / whether / 의문부사 when, where, how, why	+ 완전한 절
의문대명사 what, who, which / 의문형용사 which, whose + 명사 / 복합관계대명사 whoever, whatever, whichever	+ 불완전한 절

*whichever/whatever는 명사를 수식하는 복합관계형용사 역할도 할 수 있다.

고난도 유형 1 **that** vs. **what**

Evidence [that / ~~what~~] the product is environmentally friendly will appeal to consumers.
제품이 환경 친화적이라는 증명은 소비자의 관심을 끌 것이다. → what 뒤에는 불완전한 절이 온다.

that절을 취하는 동사, 형용사, 명사		
동사 + that	**형용사 + that**	**명사 + that(동격)**
ensure/make sure 확실히 하다	positive/convinced 확신하는	idea 아이디어 fact 사실
observe 유의하다 agree 동의하다	aware/conscious 알고 있는	opinion 견해 news 뉴스
suggest 시사하다 assume 추정하다	hopeful 낙관하는 likely ~할 것 같은	evidence 증거 story 이야기

고난도 유형 2 **that** vs. **whether**

The employee **asked** [~~that~~ / whether] he was eligible for the benefits.
직원은 자신이 혜택을 받을 자격이 되는지 물었다. → 동사 ask(묻다)는 '~인지 아닌지'라는 미정 사실과 어울리므로 whether

고난도 유형 3 **의문부사** vs. **의문형용사**

The consultant advised us on [which / ~~how~~] **plan** would yield the best results.
컨설턴트는 우리에게 어떤 전략이 최상의 결과를 가져올 수 있는지 조언해 주었다.
→ plan은 단수 가산명사이지만 앞에 한정사가 없다. 따라서 완전한 절과 쓰이는 의문부사 how는 오답이다.

고난도 유형 4 **복합관계대명사** vs. **의문대명사**

[Whoever / ~~Who~~] **is hired** will be in charge of accounting. 채용된 사람 누구든 회계를 담당하게 될 것이다.
→ 문맥상 anyone who의 의미를 나타내야 하므로 복합관계대명사 whoever

고난도 유형 5 **명사를 수식하는 whichever**

Visit the appetizers table, and try [whichever / ~~whose~~] **ones** you want.
에피타이저 테이블에 오셔서 원하는 것은 무엇이든 드셔 보세요.

② 관계사절

> 관계사절은 선행사(명사)를 수식하는 형용사절이다. 관계대명사 뒤에는 불완전한 절, 관계부사 뒤에는 완전한 절이 온다.
>
> • **관계대명사** **Anyone** who works in this area is welcome to join. 이 분야에 종사하는 누구나 참여 가능합니다.
>
> • **관계부사** London is **the city** where the next convention will happen. 런던이 다음 컨벤션이 열릴 도시이다.

문장 구조에 알맞은 관계사를 선택하는 유형으로, 보기에 접속사, 대명사 등이 함께 제시되기도 한다. 관계대명사와 관계부사의 구분, 목적격/소유격 관계대명사의 구분, 「전치사/수량 표현 of+목적격 관계대명사」 관련 문제가 고난도로 출제된다.

고난도 유형 1 관계대명사 vs. 관계부사

A tour of **a hydroelectric plant** [~~which~~ / **where**] **they generate electricity from water** is available. 물로 전기를 생산하는 수력 발전소 견학이 가능하다. → 선행사가 장소 명사이고 뒤에 완전한 절이 이어지므로 관계부사 where

고난도 유형 2 소유격 관계대명사 vs. 목적격 관계대명사

The smartphone, [~~which~~ / **whose**] **features** include a high-resolution camera, was just released. 고해상도 카메라 기능을 탑재한 스마트폰이 막 출시되었다. → 뒤에 명사와 함께 동사와 목적어가 이어지므로 소유격 관계대명사 whose

고난도 유형 3 전치사/수량 표현 of + 목적격 관계대명사

The company will host **a workshop**, **during** [**which** / ~~whom~~ / ~~that~~] new strategies will be introduced. 회사는 워크숍을 개최할 예정인데, 그 워크숍 동안 새로운 전략이 소개될 것이다.
→ 선행사가 사물인 a workshop이므로 which. 관계대명사 that은 콤마나 전치사 뒤에 쓸 수 없다.

The programs benefit **interns**, **most of** [~~them~~ / **whom**] look to gain industry experience. 프로그램은 인턴에게 도움이 되며, 그들 대부분은 업계 경험을 쌓고자 한다. → 두 문장을 연결하는 접속사가 없으므로 them은 오답

③ 명사절/형용사절/부사절의 자리 비교

종속절은 문장에서 명사, 형용사, 부사의 역할을 하므로 자리가 이들 품사의 위치와 같다.

고난도 유형 1 명사절 vs. 형용사절 vs. 부사절

The promotion ends at 6 P.M. or when supplies run out, [~~what~~ / ~~whose~~ / **whichever**] happens first. 프로모션은 6시에 끝나거나 재고 소진 시까지 유효하며, 둘 중 먼저 발생하는 것에 따릅니다.
→ 콤마 앞 완전한 문장의 주절을 수식해야 하므로 부사절 접속사 whichever. 복합관계대명사는 명사절뿐 아니라 부사절을 이끌 수도 있다.

ETS 기출 유형연습 정답과 해설 p.052

1. Ms. Hong needs to know ------- bus routes run during off-peak hours.

    (A) this   (B) which   (C) either   (D) until

2. ------- replaces Dr. Chang must be available one evening each week for patient appointments.

    (A) Whose   (B) Whoever   (C) Anyone   (D) Anything

3. Before they are released to clients, contracts should be read carefully for language ------- might be misleading.

    (A) that   (B) in that   (C) what   (D) whose

비교/도치 구문, 병렬 구조

비교 구문은 각 비교급과 잘 쓰이는 표현 중심으로 익혀 두어야 하고, 앞뒤 동일한 구조가 오는 병렬 구조는 품사의 자리 문제에서 활용도가 높다. 도치 구문은 출제 빈도가 낮지만 오답률이 높은 유형으로 고득점을 위해서는 각 패턴을 학습해 두어야 한다.

① 비교 구문

> 「as+원급+as」, 「비교급+than」, 「the/소유격+최상급」의 형태로 둘 또는 그 이상의 대상을 비교한다.
>
> • **원급** Our goal is to operate **as profitably as** possible. 우리의 목표는 최대한 수익성 있게 운영하는 것이다.
> • **비교급** The event attracted **fewer** attendees **than** expected. 이번 행사는 예상보다 적은 참석자를 유치했다.
> • **최상급** Coffee is one of **the most consumed** beverages. 커피는 가장 많이 소비되는 음료 중 하나이다.

비교급과 최상급을 수식하는 부사 관련 문제와 관용 표현이 고난도 유형으로 출제된다.

고난도 유형 1 비교급 vs. 최상급 수식 부사

The installation of ramps made the facilities [**far** / ~~by far~~] **more accessible** for those with wheelchairs. 경사로 설치로 휠체어 이용객의 시설 접근성이 훨씬 더 높아졌다.

The renovation project turned out to be **the** [~~costly~~ / **costliest**] **ever**. 보수 공사는 역대 가장 많은 비용이 들었다.

비교급을 수식하는 부사	최상급을 수식하는 부사
a lot/much/even/far/still better 훨씬 더 나은 **considerably/significantly/substantially** more 상당히 더 **marginally/slightly** less 약간 덜	**by far** the best 역대 최고 the best **ever/yet** 역대 최고 the **very** best 단연코 최고 the best **possible** 가능한 최고 **easily/quite** the best 단연코 최고

고난도 유형 2 비교 구문 관용 표현

A majority of shoppers still tend to buy groceries at a store [~~better~~ / **rather**] **than** online.
여전히 대다수의 쇼핑객은 온라인보다는 실제 매장에서 식료품을 구매하는 경향이 있다.

빈출 비교 관용 표현			
no later than 늦어도 ~까지	no sooner than ~ 이후에야	no longer 더 이상 ~않다	other than ~ 이외에
rather than ~보다는	at the latest 늦어도	nearly[almost] as ~ as 거의 ~만큼 ···한/하게	

② 도치 구문

> 강조하려는 말을 문장 앞으로 보냈을 때 주어와 동사의 어순이 바뀌는 도치가 일어난다.
>
> • **부정어 도치** Never **do we compromise** on product quality. 자사는 제품 품질에 대해 절대 타협하지 않습니다.
> • **가정법 도치** Should **you have** any inquires, feel free to contact us. 문의 사항이 있으면, 저희에게 연락 주세요.

부정어, only+부사(구/절), 보어 등이 문장 맨 앞으로 나오거나 가정법의 if가 생략되면 도치가 일어난다.

고난도 유형 1 부정어 도치

[**Little** / ~~Ever~~] **did they know** their investment would yield such high returns.
그들은 투자가 이처럼 높은 수익을 낼 줄은 거의 알지 못했다.

고난도 유형 2   only + 부사(구/절) 도치

Only when the conditions are favorable [~~we will~~ / **will we**] proceed.   조건이 양호한 경우에만 진행합니다.

고난도 유형 3   보어 도치

[~~Enclosure~~ / **Enclosed**] **is the money order** for the subscription renewal.

구독 갱신을 위한 우편환이 동봉되어 있습니다.

고난도 유형 4   가정법 도치

[**Had** / ~~Should~~] **it** not **been** for the extra support, the project **would have failed**.

추가적인 지원이 없었다면 프로젝트는 실패했을 것이다. → 가정법 과거완료 도치: Had+주어+p.p., 주어+would have p.p.

③ 병렬 구조

> 등위접속사나 상관접속사로 연결된 단어, 구, 절 등이 동일한 문법적 역할을 하는 구조를 뜻한다.
>
> • **단어+단어**   Kim is in charge of **both** event planning **and** marketing.
>   김은 이벤트 기획과 마케팅 모두 담당하고 있다.
>
> • **구+구**   Cancellation requests must be received **either** by mail **or** by fax.
>   취소 요청은 우편이나 팩스로 받아야 합니다.
>
> • **절+절**   The proposal is due tomorrow, **so** review it carefully.
>   제안서는 내일까지이므로 신중하게 검토하십시오.

등위접속사와 상관접속사는 동일한 품사와 구조를 연결한다. 이는 품사 문제에서 단서가 되기도 한다.

고난도 유형 1   병렬 구조

The instructions were **brief yet** remarkably [~~detail~~ / **detailed**].   설명서는 간단하면서도 매우 상세했다.

To submit your application and [**schedule** / ~~schedules~~] an interview, please visit our Web site.

지원서를 제출하고 면접 일정을 잡으려면 웹사이트를 방문하세요.

→ to부정사구가 병렬 연결될 때 두 번째 나오는 to는 생략할 수 있다.

ETS 기출 유형연습
정답과 해설 p.052

1. Colleagues of Mr. Groh said that no one is ------- of the award than he is.

    (A) worth   (B) worthy   (C) worthier   (D) worthiest

2. The respected literary magazine *Laguna Review* proudly features both established and ------- writers.

    (A) emerge   (B) emerging   (C) emerges   (D) to emerge

3. ------- in the appliance's user manual is there information about a blinking orange light.

    (A) Someone   (B) Either   (C) While   (D) Nowhere

1. Through his vivid oil paintings, Korean artist Kyung-Jin Bae offers fresh ways of ------- color and light.

   (A) appreciate　　(B) appreciative
   (C) appreciating　(D) appreciation

2. City council recently approved a set of guidelines that businesses wishing ------- solar panels must follow.

   (A) install　　(B) to install
   (C) installing　(D) installed

3. Purchase an annual membership to the Patchville Swim Club and ------- the indoor pool year-round.

   (A) enjoy　　(B) enjoyed
   (C) enjoying　(D) to enjoy

4. According to the publisher, the updated algebra textbook makes the subject ------- easier to understand.

   (A) any　　(B) further
   (C) much　(D) been

5. When ------- work tasks, a manager should balance the needs of the firm with the interests of the employee.

   (A) assign　　(B) assigner
   (C) assigning　(D) to assign

6. Clear Shoot digital cameras have autofocus turned on by default, ------- most other brands force users to open a menu.

   (A) themselves　(B) whatever
   (C) elsewhere　(D) whereas

7. Lynder Company is looking for a graphic designer ------- its marketing team.

   (A) joining　　(B) to join
   (C) joined　　(D) will join

8. Westlee washing machines clean clothes using ------- water than other brands do.

   (A) less　　(B) inferior
   (C) little　　(D) much

9. Besides Ms. Perloff, ------- joined us last month, the members of the pilot project team were all recruited in June.

   (A) personally　(B) herself
   (C) alone　　(D) who

10. Gedge Printing Ltd. utilizes ------- materials throughout the company's global operations.

    (A) recycle　　(B) of recycling
    (C) to recycle　(D) recycled

11. The leadership team will do ------- is needed to retain employees, including offering bonuses for long-term service.

    (A) whatever　(B) whoever
    (C) everything　(D) another

12. Sign up ------- for Spee-D Delivery Service and receive your earnings as a daily deposit to your debit card account.

    (A) driver　　(B) to drive
    (C) driving　　(D) to be driven

13. Please let Ms. Kamida in human resources know ------- you can help plan Mr. Jino's retirement party.

(A) while   (B) what

(C) whose   (D) whether

14. Shivari Home Furnishings has just opened two new locations, ------- it an exception to the city's shrinking retail sector.

(A) make   (B) making

(C) has made   (D) to be made

Questions 15-18 refer to the following blog post.

It's not just potatoes that can be made into treats. Lots of vegetables and legumes are easily transformed into crispy ------- . Chickpeas, for example, can be seasoned and dried by
15.
roasting them in a single layer on a baking sheet until crispy. ------- . Eggplant is another
16.
good choice. It can be ------- sliced and baked into something that tastes a bit like beef jerky.
17.
When ------- with oil and seasoning and baked for 20 minutes, kale leaves develop a texture
18.
akin to potato chips.

15. (A) meals

(B) snacks

(C) bars

(D) dips

16. (A) Countless recipes for main courses can be found online.

(B) It is easier to control calorie intake when cooking at home.

(C) The resulting batch of crunchy balls is packed with protein and fiber.

(D) The newer oven models include bake, convection, and air-fry settings.

17. (A) thinly

(B) thinner

(C) thinnest

(D) thinning

18. (A) mixed

(B) mixing

(C) are mixing

(D) having mixed

PART 5&6   UNIT 6

1. Please move the tables as quietly as possible so as not ------- the meeting next door.

   (A) to be disrupted   (B) disrupting
   (C) to disrupt   (D) having disrupted

2. Mr. Han was surprised to learn that having the old refrigerator repaired is ------- as expensive as buying a brand-new one.

   (A) mutually   (B) nearly
   (C) closely   (D) substantially

3. The phones at the store have been ringing all day with customers ------- information about the annual sale.

   (A) to request   (B) requested
   (C) requesting   (D) requests

4. Stirling Music is honored to be among the half-dozen record labels ------- revenues surpassed £30 million last year.

   (A) which   (B) in which
   (C) whose   (D) until

5. The organization's finance committee strongly opposes ------- any potential risky investments this year.

   (A) making   (B) is making
   (C) to make   (D) make

6. The factory's new automated system ------- the company to produce more garments in less time.

   (A) enables   (B) notifies
   (C) offers   (D) ensures

7. Mortgage rates hit a five-year low, which helps ------- the sharp rise in home sales.

   (A) explain   (B) explaining
   (C) explained (D) explanation

8. Chef Amina Diallo's cookbook has recipes for Senegalese dishes, most ------- are simple to prepare.

   (A) which   (B) of what
   (C) of which (D) in that

9. The ------- board of the Montserrat Historical Society has approved the new budget.

   (A) governed   (B) governing
   (C) govern   (D) governs

10. ------- from previous models, the newly redesigned FZ-550 motorcycle is more powerful yet lighter in weight

    (A) Differs   (B) Differently
    (C) Difference (D) Different

11. Should you ------- unsatisfied with your purchase, place the item in its original packaging and return it to us within fourteen days.

    (A) have   (B) be
    (C) are   (D) been

12. The contractor estimated ------- it would take three hours to replace the broken tiles in the lobby.

    (A) because of   (B) in which
    (C) that   (D) what

13. ------- installing keyless-entry pads on tenants' doors, the landlord has saved at least $500 on lock repairs and replacements.

(A) Once (B) Since
(C) From (D) With

14. ------- receives the second highest number of votes will be named vice president of the stamp club.

(A) Whom (B) Whose
(C) Whoever (D) Who

Questions 15-18 refer to the following article.

KOBE (18 May)—Tasty Smoothie is testing automated smoothie kiosks in select locations here in Kobe. The kiosks ------- six smoothie choices with additional customized options. The
15.
drinks are selected via a touch screen, and the machine then prepares the order. No workers need to be present. However, a team of employees monitors each kiosk's ingredient usage ------- , and stockers are dispatched to refill the machines as needed.
16.

------- . If the test machines continue to be popular, Tasty Smoothie will install more kiosks
17.
nationwide. These will allow the company to sell its products in places ------- there is no
18.
space for a traditional smoothie shop.

15. (A) provide
(B) provided
(C) must provide
(D) were providing

16. (A) conditionally
(B) abruptly
(C) distinctly
(D) remotely

17. (A) Tasty Smoothie expects to hire more employees to maintain the kiosks.
(B) To date, the company has reported only positive customer feedback.
(C) As long as ingredients are available, customer choices will not be affected.
(D) Fortunately, the kiosks are located on university campuses.

18. (A) as
(B) that
(C) where
(D) though

Reading Comprehension

PART
5&6

UNIT 7 어휘 Collocation

PART 5&6 어휘 만점 전략

어휘 문제는 핵심 요소를 빠르게 해석하여 문맥에 맞는 어휘를 찾는 것이 중요하다. 단순 어휘 문제도 있지만, 문법 요소가 복합되어 빈칸 앞뒤 구성 요소가 단서가 되는 경우도 있고, 서로 짝을 이루는 연어(collocation)가 출제되기도 한다. 단순히 우리말 의미에 의존하는 것보다 단어의 성질과 쓰이는 상황, 용법 등을 알아두어야 고득점 획득에 유리하다.

빈출 유형 공략법

❶ 단순 어휘 문제
단순 어휘 문제는 최소한의 핵심 요소만 빠르게 해석하는 것이 중요하다.

Q Palomino Bistro boasts ------- views of the Detroit River.

(A) amusing   (B) accomplished
(C) impressive   (D) excessive

빈칸이 명사를 수식하는 형용사 자리이며 보기가 모두 형용사 어휘임을 확인한다. 명사 view와 어울려 '인상적인 전망'이라는 의미가 자연스러운 (C) impressive가 답이 된다. 참고로, (A) amusing은 재미있고 유쾌한 상황을 묘사할 때 쓰이므로 view와 어울리지 않는다.

팔로미노 비스트로는 디트로이트강의 인상적인 전망을 자랑한다.   **정답 (C)**

---

❷ 어법과 복합된 어휘 문제
동사의 자동사와 타동사 구분, 특정 단어와 함께 쓰이는 전치사 등의 암기가 필수이다.

Q The outdoor concert ------- as scheduled despite the bad weather.

(A) conducted   (B) took
(C) established   (D) proceeded

동사 어휘 문제로 빈칸 뒤에 분사구문의 접속사 as가 있는 것으로 보아 자동사가 필요함을 확인한다. '콘서트가 예정대로 진행되었다'는 의미가 되어야 하므로 (D) proceeded가 답이 된다. 나머지 보기의 동사들은 모두 타동사로 목적어가 필요하다.

악천후에도 불구하고 야외 콘서트는 예정대로 진행되었다.   **정답 (D)**

---

❸ 서로 짝을 이루어 쓰이는 어휘 문제
단어의 의미 못지않게 중요한 것이 용법이다. 서로 짝을 이루는 연어(collocation)는 물론 쓰이는 상황까지 익혀 두어야 고득점에 대비할 수 있다.

Q The play scripted by Nick LaChapelle has a reputation for being entertaining and full of engaging -------.

(A) characters   (B) spaces
(C) notes   (D) ways

주어가 연극(The play)이므로, 빈칸 앞 형용사 engaging과 짝을 이루어 극이나 소설 등의 등장인물 묘사 시 자주 사용되는 engaging characters(매력적인 등장인물)를 떠올릴 수 있다. 따라서 (A)가 정답이다.

닉 라샤펠이 대본을 쓴 연극은 재미있고 매력적인 등장인물이 가득하다는 평을 듣는다.   **정답 (A)**

동사＋명사, 동사＋전치사

동사의 어휘 문제는 의미뿐 아니라 타동사와 자동사의 용법을 묻는 유형이 주를 이룬다. 타동사는 자주 쓰이는 목적어를 함께 외우고, 자동사의 경우 자주 동반되는 전치사를 함께 암기해 두어야 한다.

❶ 동사＋명사

address an inquiry	문의 사항을 해결하다	hit a new low	최저치를 갱신하다
archive records	기록을 (기록실에) 보관하다	extend a welcome to	~을 환영하다
retrieve data	데이터를 복구하다	carry raw materials	원자재를 취급하다
extend an offer	권유[제안]하다	make an exception for	~을 예외로 하다
issue a refund	환불해 주다	observe an anniversary	기념하다
construct a facility	공장[시설]을 짓다	report record revenue	기록적인 수익을 내다
take measures	조치를 취하다	oversee production	생산을 감독하다
pay a visit	방문하다	plant a garden	정원을 조성하다
determine the cause	원인을 규명하다	raise awareness of	~에 대한 의식을 높이다
streamline procedures	절차를 간소화하다	devise a strategy	전략을 세우다
draw comparison	비교하다	reschedule a conference	회의 일정을 변경하다
exercise[use] caution	주의하다	assume responsibility	책임을 맡다
expedite a process	과정을 신속히 처리하다	scout locations	장소를 물색하다
establish an environment	환경을 구축하다	evacuate a building	건물에서 대피시키다
face opposition	반대에 직면하다	initiate a plan	계획을 추진하다
feature artwork	예술품을 선보이다	take initiative	솔선수범하다
fill a prescription	처방약을 조제하다	undergo renovations	보수 공사를 진행하다
exceed expectations	기대[예상]를 넘어서다	waive a fee	수수료를 면제해 주다
observe a policy	정책을 준수하다	yield results	결과를 산출하다
lift sanctions	제재를 풀다[철회하다]	obey regulations	규정을 따르다
discuss an issue	문제를 논의하다	delegate authority	권한을 위임하다
moderate a debate	토론의 사회를 보다	negotiate terms	약관[조항]을 협상하다
generate publicity	홍보 효과를 창출하다	secure funding	자금을 확보하다
prioritize tasks	작업의 우선 순위를 정하다	offset the shortfall	부족량을 상쇄하다
reimburse expenses	비용을 상환하다	reach a compromise	타협에 이르다
decline an offer	제안을 거절하다	cover expenses	비용을 충당하다

② 동사＋전치사

coincide with	~와 일치하다	register for	~에 등록하다
persist in	~을 고집하다, 지속하다	apply to	~에 적용되다
persevere in	(인내심을 갖고) 계속 ~하다	adhere to	~을 지키다
result in	결과적으로 ~이 되다	evolve from	~으로부터 발전하다, 진화하다
withdraw from	~에서 철수[탈퇴]하다	allow for	~을 감안하다; 허용하다
contribute to	~에 기여하다	cope with	~에 대처하다; 감당하다
specialize in	~을 전문으로 하다	work alongside	~와 함께 일하다
proceed with	~을 계속하다	extend beyond	~ 너머까지 미치다
get through	~을 마치다, ~을 통과하다	interfere with	~을 방해하다
correspond with	~와 부합하다	consult with	~와 협의하다
originate from	~에서 기인하다	come up with	~을 생각해 내다
derive from	~에서 유래[파생]되다	refer to	~을 참고하다; 언급하다
belong to	~에 속하다	vary depending on	~에 따라 다양하다
watch out for	~을 조심[주의]하다	refrain from	~을 삼가다
fall within	~의 범위에 속하다	succeed in	~에 성공하다
comply with	~을 준수하다	decide on	~에 관련된 결정을 하다
profit[benefit] from	~에서 이익[혜택]을 얻다	comment on	~에 대해 논평하다
appeal to	~의 관심을 끌다	lead to	~으로 이어지다
account for	~을 설명하다; (비율) 차지하다	opt for	~을 선택하다
inquire about	~에 대해 문의하다	serve on	~의 일원으로 활약하다
insist on	~을 주장하다	look into	~을 조사하다
collaborate on/with	~에 대해/~와 협력하다	dispose of	~을 버리다

ETS 기출 유형연습

정답과 해설 p.057

1. Finn Architectural Associates has been ------- locations for a new office in the greater Vancouver area.

   (A) scouting　　(B) looking　　(C) watching　　(D) transmitting

2. Yesterday's Internet problems ------- from the use of outdated software.

   (A) interpreted　　(B) acknowledged　　(C) originated　　(D) determined

명사+명사, 명사+전치사/전치사+명사

복합명사 문제는 형용사나 그 밖의 다른 품사가 함정으로 출제되지만 문법적인 특징보다 어휘에 초점을 맞추어 학습해 두어야 한다. 명사에 동반되는 전치사 또한 다소 까다로운 유형으로 고득점을 위해 대비해 두어야 한다.

① 명사+명사

data entry	데이터 입력	payroll department	급여 부서
copyright infringement	저작권 침해	budget surplus	예산 초과액
cash flow	현금 흐름	product launch	제품 출시
tax evasion	탈세	account balance	은행 잔고[잔액]
expense report	비용 보고서	career path	직업 경로
distribution center	물류 센터	sales associate	영업 사원
customer satisfaction	고객 만족도	exit strategy	출구 전략
employee productivity	직원 생산성	capital investment	자본 투자
supply chain	공급망	compliance audit	규정 준수 감사
production stage	생산 단계	job opportunity	일자리 기회
travel itinerary	여행 일정(표)	cost estimate	가격 견적서
workplace safety	작업장 안전	earnings yield	(증권) 이율
assembly line	(공장의) 조립 라인	inventory control	재고 관리
benefits package	근로 복지, 복리 후생	labor cost	인건비
contingency plan	긴급 사태 대책	logistics manager	물류 관리자
customer loyalty	고객 충성도	employee retention	인재 유지, 직원 보유
plant specimen	식물 표본	search committee	인사 위원회, 조사 위원회
speaking engagement	연설 약속	text alert	재난 문자, 문자 경고
safety procedure	안전 절차	performance appraisal	업무 성과 평가
maternity leave	출산 휴가	guest waiver	배상 책임 면책 서약서
insurance premium	보험료	contest entry	대회 참가(자)
risk assessment	위험성 평가	hiring policy	채용 정책
credit limit	(신용카드의) 이용 한도	working conditions	근무 조건
end user	실수요자, 최종 사용자	deposit slip	입금 전표
field representative	현장 담당자	market share	시장 점유율
workplace culture	직장 문화	inventory turnover rate	재고 회전율

② 명사＋전치사/전치사＋명사

enrollment in	~에 등록	in an orderly fashion	순서대로, 질서 정연하게
dispute over	~에 대한 논쟁	with accuracy	정확하게
objection to	~에 대한 반대	at full capacity	전면 가동으로
contrast to	~와의 대조	until further notice	추후 공지까지
response to	~에 대한 응답	beyond[past] repair	수리가 불가능한
admittance to	~에의 입장	upon[on] arrival	도착 즉시
complaint about	~에 관한 불만[민원]	at stake	위기에 처한
discount on	~에 대한 할인	after much deliberation	심사숙고 끝에
lack of	~의 부족[결핍]	in mint condition	새것이나 다름없는
demand for	~에 대한 수요	for business purposes	영업용으로
commitment to	~에 대한 전념[헌신]	under warranty	보증 기간 중인
feedback on	~에 관한 (개선) 의견	at random	무작위로
impact[influence] on	~에 대한 영향	in effect	시행 중인; 사실상
proximity to	~에 근접함	at hand	가까이에; 머지않아
downturn in	(경기)의 침체, 하락	on call	당직인
request for	~에 대한 요청	in person	대면으로, 직접
substitute for	~의 대체품	for some reason(s)	어떤 이유에서인지
outlet for	(감정, 표현)의 발산 수단	on a regular basis	정기적으로
revision to	~의 수정[개정]	by proxy	대리인을 통해
an excess of	과도한	in a fraction of the time	순식간에
an assortment of	모둠의, 다양한	without prior consent	사전 동의 없이
a wealth of	풍부한	within a week of receipt	수령 후 일주일 이내에

ETS 기출 유형연습

정답과 해설 p.057

1. All briefcases and packages will be scanned at the front desk ------- arrival.

   (A) by   (B) to   (C) in   (D) upon

2. Harwich Publishing's search ------- will begin interviewing candidates for the senior editor position next week.

   (A) society   (B) process   (C) solution   (D) committee

03 형용사+명사, 형용사+전치사

형용사는 수식 받는 명사에 따라 쓰임이 결정되므로 어울리는 명사와 함께 익혀야 한다. 짝을 이루는 형용사와 전치사 또한 빈출 유형이므로 하나의 조합으로 외워 두도록 한다.

① 형용사+명사

영어	한국어	영어	한국어
advanced degree	(석·박사 등의) 고급 학위	generic drug	(상표 미등록) 약, 복제약
captivating architecture	매혹적인 건축물	impending storms	임박한 폭풍
strong work credentials	탄탄한 업무 자격	key factor	주요 요인
customized furniture	주문 제작 가구	monthly allowance	월 수당[용돈]
designated driver	지명[대리] 운전자	discontinued model	단종된 모델
detailed description	자세한 설명	qualifying examination	자격 시험
determining factor	결정적인 요소	permanent position	정규직
participating nation	참가국	perishable food	상하기 쉬운 음식
enclosed courtyard	건물로 둘러싸인 안뜰	exhaustive research	철저한 조사
preventive medicine	예방 의학	prestigious award	권위[명망] 있는 상
excess inventory	과잉 재고	engaging characters	매력적인 등장인물
processed dairy product	가공 유제품	primary concern	최대[주요] 관심사
physical exertion	격렬한 신체 운동	ergonomic design	인체 공학적 디자인
extended warranty	연장 보증 (기간)	proven track record	검증된 실적
favorable effect	긍정적인[유리한] 효과	primary source	(논문의) 1차 인용 자료
flat rate[fee]	정액 요금[수수료]	exclusive access	독점적인 접근
sustainable business	지속 가능한 사업	projected sales figures	예상 매출액
flexible scheduling	유연한 일정 관리	certified instructor	공인[검증]된 강사
formal attire	정장, 격식을 갖춘 복장	rigorous inspection	엄격한 검사
surrounding areas	주변 지역	sensible solution	합리적인 방안[해결책]
groundbreaking device	획기적인 장비	incremental improvement	점진적 개선
hearty dish	푸짐한 요리	unexpected circumstances	예상치 못한 상황
sluggish sales	부진한 판매	free quote	무료 견적
intriguing theory	흥미로운 이론	synthetic materials	합성 소재
outstanding amount	미지급 금액, 미납액	unique perspective	독특한 관점
conservative estimate	보수적인[낮춰 잡은] 추산	prefabricated house	조립식 주택
moving story	감동적인 이야기	user-friendly design	사용자 친화적인 디자인

② 형용사＋전치사

be apprehensive about	~에 대해 걱정하다	be accompanied by	~을 동반하다
be appropriate for	~에 적합하다	be due by	~까지가 기한이다
be attentive to	~에 주의를 기울이다	be liable for	~에 (법적인) 책임이 있다
be based in	~에 근거지[기반]를 두다	be affiliated with	~에 소속되다; 관련되다
be commensurate with	~와 상응[비례]하다	be aimed at	~을 대상으로 하다
be engaged in	~에 (열심히) 참여하다	be credited with	~한 공적을 인정받다
be identical to	~와 동일하다	be permitted in	~에 출입이 허용되다
be contaminated with	~으로 오염[감염]되다	be entitled to[for]	~에 대한 자격이 되다
be designed for	~을 의도하여 만들어지다	be enthusiastic about	~에 열광하다
be accountable for	~에 책임이 있다	be compatible with	~와 호환되다
be equivalent to	~와 동등하다	be equipped with	~이 구비되어 있다
be helpful in	~하는 데 도움이 되다	be exempt from	~을 면제받다
be irrelevant to	~와 무관하다	be factored into	~에 반영[고려]되다
be preoccupied with	~에 골몰하다[사로잡히다]	be deducted from	~에서 공제되다
be reflective of	~을 반영하다	be grateful for	~을 고맙게 여기다
be reliant on	~에 달려 있다	be interchangeable with	~와 바꿔 쓸 수 있다
be skeptical of	~에 대해 회의적이다	be restricted to	~에 국한되다
be transferable to	~에게 양도 가능하다	be contingent on	~에 달려 있다
be useful for	~에 유용하다	be suspended until	~까지 중단되다
be valid until	~까지 유효하다	be comparable to	~에 필적하다, 비슷하다
be fond of	~을 좋아하다	be short of	~이 부족하다
be vulnerable to	~에 취약하다	be mindful of	~을 유념하다

ETS 기출 유형연습

정답과 해설 p.057

1. The Top Training app connects gyms with ------- instructors who can teach a wide variety of fitness classes.

   (A) identical   (B) certified   (C) defensive   (D) academic

2. Hearten Theater has begun a series of preshow workshops ------- at families.

   (A) aimed   (B) designed   (C) looked   (D) acted

04 부사+동사, 부사+형용사

부사 어휘 문제는 논란을 자주 일으키는 유형 중 하나로, 우리말 의미는 적절해 보여도 용법에 어긋나 답이 안 되는 경우가 많다. 부사의 성격과 수식 대상과의 관계를 이해하고 자주 함께 쓰이는 표현 위주로 외워 두어야 한다.

1 부사+동사

closely monitor	면밀히 감시하다	act accordingly	그에 따라 행동하다
cordially invite	정중하게 초대하다	donate anonymously	익명으로 기부하다
badly deteriorate	몹시 악화되다	diminish gradually	서서히 줄어들다
gingerly approach	조심해서 접근하다	listen intently	열심히 경청하다
briefly welcome	잠시 동안 환영하다	take seriously	중요하게 여기다
highly value	(가치를) 높이 평가하다	articulate clearly	명확히 말로 설명하다
completely demolish	완전히 철거하다	display chronologically	연대순으로 진열하다
markedly increase	눈에 띄게 증가하다	send directly	바로 보내다
mutually agree	공동으로 합의하다	work closely	밀접하게 일하다
deliberately ignore	고의적으로 무시하다	function properly	제대로 작동하다
barely manage	간신히 해내다	fit perfectly	완벽하게 맞다
evenly divide	균등하게 나누다	integrate seamlessly	매끄럽게 통합하다
enthusiastically await	열렬히[손꼽아] 기다리다	work remotely	원격으로 일하다
eagerly participate	열심히 참여하다	thrive economically	경제적으로 호황을 누리다
carefully consider	신중하게 고려하다	go smoothly	원활히 진행하다
accurately assess	정확하게 평가하다	arise spontaneously	저절로 발생하다
confidently introduce	자신 있게 소개하다	implement companywide	회사 전반에 걸쳐 시행하다
heavily invest	많은 투자를 하다	operate profitably	수익성 있게 운영하다
significantly reduce	상당히 줄이다	respond promptly	신속히 응대하다
sincerely thank	진심으로 감사하다	benefit immensely	대단히 큰 이익을 누리다
ultimately decide	마침내 결정하다	vote unanimously	만장일치로 표결하다
regularly update	정기적으로 업데이트하다	rise quickly	고속 승진하다
strictly observe	엄격히 준수하다	happen swiftly	신속하게 이루어지다
efficiently organize	효율적으로 정리하다	inspect thoroughly	철저히 검사하다
easily identify	쉽게 식별하다	attach securely	단단히 부착하다
widely vary	매우 다양하다	run year-round	일년 내내 운영하다

② 부사+형용사

architecturally sound	구조적으로 견고한	partially completed	부분적으로 완료된
automatically prompted	(컴퓨터) 창이 자동으로 뜨는	nearly finished	거의 끝난
clearly listed	(목록으로) 명확히 기재된	highly critical	매우 비판적인; 중대한
poorly written	형편없게 작성된	readily available	쉽게 이용 가능한
mutually beneficial	상호 이득이 되는	perfectly aligned	완벽하게 정렬을 맞춘
directly opposite	정반대의, 바로 맞은편의	recently adopted	최근에 채택된
profoundly grateful	깊이[크게] 감사하는	soundly based	근거가 타당한[탄탄한]
entirely different	완전히 다른	firmly established	확고하게 확립된
severely criticized	심한 혹평을 받은	temporarily halted	일시적으로 중단된
fully booked	예약이 꽉 찬	highly likely	매우 일어날 만한
currently unavailable	현재 구할 수 없는	tentatively scheduled	잠정적으로 일정이 잡힌
highly contagious	전염성이 매우 강한	unseasonably cold	계절에 맞지 않게 추운
overly complicated	지나치게 복잡한	fully aware	완전히 인지하고 있는
potentially problematic	잠재적으로 문제가 많은	virtually all	거의 모든
generally accepted	일반적으로 인정되는	moderately successful	적당히 성공적인
widely acclaimed	널리 인정받는	barely noticeable	거의 눈에 띄지 않는
increasingly competitive	점점 경쟁이 심해지는	strictly enforced	엄격하게 시행되는
reasonably priced	합리적으로 가격이 매겨진	closely related	밀접하게 관련된
particularly well-suited	특히 잘 어울리는	internationally renowned	세계적으로 유명한
somewhat vague	다소 애매모호한	environmentally conscious	(사람이) 환경을 생각하는
deeply involved	깊이 관여된	densely populated	인구가 밀집한
relatively minor	비교적 사소한	technically proficient	기술적으로 숙달된

ETS 기출 유형연습

정답과 해설 p.058

1. Dance patrons are ------- awaiting the premiere of choreographer Jean Wall's new ballet *Midnight Moon*.

    (A) deliberately   (B) enthusiastically   (C) sympathetically   (D) courageously

2. Ms. Baek's essay in *Miners Weekly* is generating some ------- critical feedback from readers.

    (A) nicely   (B) closely   (C) neatly   (D) highly

1. Following his graduation, Mr. Olujimi decided to seek a job ------- at a firm in his hometown of Ingawa.

   (A) growth   (B) candidate
   (C) opportunity   (D) security

2. All Grenman Café employees are ------- to one new uniform a year at no charge.

   (A) deserved   (B) permitted
   (C) allowed   (D) entitled

3. The Mechanical Engineers Association is looking for ------- on its recent conference in Seoul.

   (A) quality   (B) feedback
   (C) statement   (D) conduct

4. A reception will take place in the foyer ------- following the presentation by Ms. Schriver.

   (A) immediately   (B) mutually
   (C) lately   (D) suddenly

5. Speedstrom Technologies will ------- the cash register with one that processes transactions twice as fast.

   (A) repair   (B) replace
   (C) lock   (D) purchase

6. Because of scheduling issues, this Friday's seminar will be held virtually rather than -------.

   (A) on time   (B) after all
   (C) in person   (D) for certain

7. Jung Shipyards is constructing a new boatbuilding ------- on the North Bay waterfront.

   (A) plan   (B) qualification
   (C) announcement   (D) facility

8. Arlene's Ceramics Studio is ------- renovations and is expected to reopen on October 1.

   (A) undergoing   (B) establishing
   (C) describing   (D) forming

9. All reservation changes should be sent ------- to Ms. Ishida, the head of customer service.

   (A) distinctly   (B) curiously
   (C) directly   (D) reasonably

10. Proxy ballots are due from shareholders ------- noon on September 6.

    (A) in   (B) by
    (C) to   (D) of

11. Landscape paintings by artist Joshua Luben are ------- in a new exhibit at the Granidos Museum of Art.

    (A) featured   (B) spread
    (C) broadcast   (D) demonstrated

12. When the highways are completed, drivers will be able to travel quickly to ------- urban areas.

    (A) surrounding   (B) perfunctory
    (C) pleased   (D) short

13. The benefits of working at Kamlo Industries are ------- listed on the company's Web site.

(A) clearly
(B) considerably
(C) highly
(D) eagerly

14. Mission Pharmaceuticals offers a ------- variety of educational opportunities to its employees.

(A) long
(B) wide
(C) excited
(D) very

Questions 15-18 refer to the following article.

City Names Firm to Design New Municipal Center Wing

LOCH HAVEN (June 9)—The Loch Haven City Council has approved the hiring of Leplatt Architectural Associates to design a new wing for the existing municipal center. ------- .
15.
The new wing ------- the mayor's office, the controller's office, and the parks and utilities
16.
departments. Other ------- could include office space for the Loch Haven Historical Society
17.
and a small café.

"The final configuration of the new wing is going to depend on both the cost and the attractiveness of the proposed design," said Ivan Hensdale, president of the Loch Haven City Council. "We are eager to see what Leplatt comes up with in its ------- design."
18.

---

15. (A) The decision was made at the council's most recent monthly meeting.
(B) The council consists of seven members who are elected to two-year terms.
(C) The next council meeting will be held on July 23.
(D) Many architects have been invited to apply for the job.

16. (A) houses
(B) will house
(C) is housing
(D) has housed

17. (A) sites
(B) images
(C) examples
(D) uses

18. (A) alternate
(B) competitive
(C) balanced
(D) initial

PART 5&6 UNIT 7

1. The Sheehan Art Museum has invested
------- in software programs to create more
interactive exhibitions.

(A) randomly　　　(B) instantly
(C) roughly　　　　(D) heavily

2. Because the negotiations took longer than
expected, Ms. Lucas had to ------- her
departure by one day.

(A) postpone　　　(B) contract
(C) cancel　　　　(D) compromise

3. The proposed development faced
substantial ------- from local residents.

(A) condition　　　(B) opposition
(C) prediction　　 (D) deduction

4. Roscoe Dry Cleaners will ------- its five-year
anniversary by hosting a party for staff and
giving discounts to customers.

(A) observe　　　 (B) examine
(C) invite　　　　 (D) contain

5. The newest factory built by Tramovidan
Motors, Inc., has the ------- to produce 900
vehicles per day.

(A) capacity　　　(B) judgment
(C) association　　(D) contraction

6. To the untrained eye, a simulated gemstone
appears ------- to a natural gemstone from
a mine.

(A) identical　　　(B) positive
(C) suitable　　　 (D) convenient

7. Ms. Roja is the strongest of the job
candidates because she has a proven track
------- of generating sales.

(A) retort　　　　(B) regard
(C) record　　　　(D) report

8. Ms. Nishikawa's transition to vice president
of the research department happened more
------- than had been anticipated.

(A) partially　　　(B) ultimately
(C) adequately　　(D) swiftly

9. Chabot Hospital's accounting department
can ------- your billing-related questions.

(A) address　　　(B) respond
(C) attend　　　　(D) appeal

10. According to surveys, many people are
taking up baking as an -------
for expressing their creativity.

(A) entry　　　　(B) outcome
(C) outlet　　　　(D) obstacle

11. Today's conference call with the buyers
in Singapore will be ------- for Thursday
morning.

(A) planned　　　(B) maintained
(C) heard　　　　(D) rescheduled

12. Employees are not permitted ------- the
warehouse without the proper safety gear.

(A) from　　　　(B) to
(C) for　　　　　(D) in

13. Despite a ------- in the economy, the electronics industry realized a 24 percent growth in profits this year.

(A) protocol
(B) longevity
(C) drawback
(D) downturn

14. Howth Laboratory benefits ------- from staff scientists who have interdisciplinary training.

(A) jointly
(B) immensely
(C) evenly
(D) impulsively

Questions 15-18 refer to the following announcement.

To Our Valued Customers:

We are happy to announce that after ten wonderful years on West Grove Street, Terry's Grocery Mart is moving to the Vale Shopping Center. We will be taking over the space ------- occupied by Bennett's Department Store. ------- . Our new grocery store will offer **15.** **16.** a less crowded experience, with a lot more space to display special goods. Customers will have access to an ample parking lot and a bus stop next to the shopping center. What's more, a sunny café will be featured at the front of the store. The grand opening ------- for **17.** 10 September. ------- , we apologize for any disruption in service. **18.**

15. (A) barely
(B) once
(C) highly
(D) further

17. (A) plan
(B) planned
(C) is planned
(D) was planned

16. (A) The larger building will help us serve you better.
(B) The search for a new location is ongoing.
(C) The store is now under new management.
(D) Company leaders agree that the merger was a good idea.

18. (A) Similarly
(B) Nearby
(C) In the meantime
(D) On the contrary

PART 7

PART 7 독해 만점 전략

PART 7은 평균적으로 한 문항당 50초에서 1분 사이를 넘기지 않아야 하며, 정답의 근거를 확인하며 풀어야 한다. 대체로 문제의 순서는 지문의 흐름을 따르므로, 독해에 앞서 해당 문항의 문제를 미리 파악하고 접근하면 지문의 흐름을 유추할 수 있어 시간 관리에 도움이 된다.

패러프레이징 유형

❶ 동의어/유사 표현

I think we should look at costs and consider just postponing **the luncheon** if it's going to be more expensive to hold it somewhere else.

비용을 살펴보고 다른 곳에서 개최하는 것이 더 비싸다면 오찬을 연기하는 것을 고려해야 한다고 생각합니다.

Q What does Ms. Boland suggest they do?

A **Move** the event to a later date

질문 볼란드 씨는 무엇을 하라고 제안하는가?

정답 행사를 후일로 변경

❷ 포괄적 상위어 표현

You may send a technician to my home **to check the connection both on the keyboard and on my computer**.

키보드와 컴퓨터의 연결을 확인하기 위해 기사를 집으로 보내 주셔도 됩니다.

Q Why does Ms. Davis suggest that a technician visit her home?

A **To ensure that** all her devices **are working correctly**

질문 데이비스 씨는 왜 기사 방문을 제안하는가?

정답 그녀의 모든 장치가 올바르게 작동하는 것을 확실히 하기 위해

❸ 축약 표현

The transport associate transfers books and other merchandise **from the company warehouse in Eustis to all seven store locations**.

운송 직원은 유스티스에 있는 회사 창고에서 책과 기타 상품을 일곱 곳의 모든 매장으로 옮깁니다.

Q What does the job advertisement indicate about Tattered Page Books?

A It has **multiple locations**.

질문 구인 광고에서 태터드 페이지 북스에 대해 명시된 것은?

정답 여러 곳에 지점이 있다.

❹ 풀어 쓰는 표현

I am **booked all day**, unfortunately.

안타깝게도 하루 종일 일정이 잡혀 있어요.

Q What does Ms. Reitz indicate about herself?

A She is **very busy**.

질문 라이츠 씨가 자신에 대해 명시하는 것은?

정답 그녀는 매우 바쁘다.

지문 유형

❶ 이메일 / 편지

이메일/편지는 수신자와 발신자, 제목 등을 보고 누가 누구에게 무슨 목적으로 보내는지 파악한 후 내용의 흐름을 놓치지 않는 것이 중요하다.

TIP 이메일의 수신자(From) & 발신자(To) 도메인은 둘의 관계와 대략적인 내용을 파악하는 데 도움이 된다.

도메인	관계	주요 내용
info@회사명.com ➜ -mail.com	업체 → 개인	구독 연장, 문의 답변, 상품 소개, 주문, 구인
-mail.com ➜ info@회사명.com	개인 → 업체	불만 제기, 상품/서비스/행사 문의, 주문, 구직
같은 회사명 도메인	동료 → 동료	업무 보고/지시, 일정 확인, 협조 요청

❷ 공지 / 회람

회사가 직원에게, 공동주택 관리자가 입주민들에게, 행정기관에서 시민들에게 공지하는 내용이 대부분이고, 정책 소개 및 변경, 정비, 보수, 행사 안내 등의 내용이 주를 이룬다. 주로 초반에 주제/목적이 드러나고 요청 또는 당부 사항으로 마무리되는 경우가 많다.

❸ 기사

인물 소개, 업체 및 상품 홍보, 공공시설물의 개장 및 보수 등의 내용이 다뤄진다. 제목과 도입부에 주제가 언급되며, 기사의 발행일과 지역 또한 문제 풀이의 단서가 되기도 한다.

TIP 기사는 매체 기자가 작성하는 article과 자사 홍보를 주 내용으로 하는 press release로 나뉜다.

종류	예시	주요 내용
Article	**DALEMONT MARKET REOPENING** FULTON CITY (December 19)—Following extensive remodeling, the **Dalemont Market** on Ashland Boulevard **celebrated a reopening** with a ceremony last Friday.	인물/회사 소개, 시설물의 개장/이용 안내, 지역 사회 소식/행사, 시장 동향/소비 패턴 등
Press release	**FOR IMMEDIATE RELEASE** **Contact:** Petra Delaurier, pdelaurier@heskinsshops.co.uk LONDON (2 September) **Heskin's Shops**, the takeaway shops where busy consumers go to pick up soup, baked goods, and freshly made sandwiches, **is now providing catering throughout the London metropolitan area**.	자사 상품 홍보, 신상품 출시 발표, 회사의 사업 계획 홍보, 신임 임원 소개 등

❹ 광고

상품, 서비스 및 구인 광고가 출제되며 제목과 머리말에 주제가 드러난다. 후반부에 구매 정보, 할인 행사, 지원 방법, 연락처 등이 등장한다.

⑤ 문자 메시지/온라인 채팅

직장 동료 간의 업무 관련 대화가 주를 이루고, 기타 비즈니스 관계자 간의 대화나 지인 간의 일상생활 관련 대화 등이 출제된다. 평균 2지문이 출제되며, 의도 파악 문제가 항상 포함되어 있다. 여러 명이 참여하는 다인 대화의 경우, 문맥이 순서대로 연결되지 않을 수도 있다는 점에 유의하여 대화 주도자를 찾아 흐름을 파악한다.

TIP 의도 파악 문제의 빈출 표현

동의, 수락	거절, 부정
Couldn't be better. 더 좋을 순 없어요.	No way. / Not a chance. 그럴 일 없습니다.
Make sense. 일리 있네요.	I doubt it. 아닐걸요.
I'm on it. / I'll get right on it. 바로 처리하겠습니다.	Don't bother. 신경 쓰지 마세요.
I'd say so. 그런 것 같아요.	That won't work. 소용없을 거예요.
Absolutely. / Sure thing. 물론이죠.	I don't think I can make it. 못 갈 것 같아요.
Good call. 좋은 결정이에요.	Don't get your hopes up. 너무 기대하지 마세요.

⑥ 웹페이지

회사나 기관의 소개, 연혁, 행사 안내, 이용 후기 등이 자주 출제되고, 웹페이지 탭에서 주제가 파악되기도 한다.

TIP 주소의 마지막 부분과 탭에서 글의 종류와 흐름을 예측할 수 있다.

⑦ 기타 양식

주문서, 영수증, 일정표 등의 양식은 날짜, 수량, 가격, 시간, 장소 등의 단편 정보로 구성되는 것이 보편적이다. 별표(*), 비고(Notes), 추가 의견(Comments)이 있으면 문제로 출제될 확률이 높으므로 유의한다.

주제/목적, 세부 사항

① 주제/목적

지문 도입부에서 파악되는 것이 일반적이지만 간혹 중반부 또는 후반부에 나오거나 전체 내용을 포괄하는 경우도 있으므로 유의한다.

빈출 문제 유형

What is **the (main) purpose** of the e-mail?
What is **one purpose** of the memo?

What is the article **mainly about**?
Why was this letter **written**?

기출 대표 예제 | The question refers to the following e-mail.   정답과 해설 p.062

Hello, Ms. Kim,

I've just been informed that I will be taking a group of visiting dignitaries to South Canyon tomorrow morning. Please arrange for Mr. McNeil to lead the 8:00 A.M. activity originally assigned to me. Thank you.

Incidentally, **are you aware that the path to the lake is partially blocked by a couple of fallen branches? These could pose a tripping hazard.**

Q **What** is **one purpose** of the e-mail?
(A) To move the South Canyon tour time
(B) To inform Ms. Kim about a safety problem

(Paraphrasing) 지문의 a tripping hazard
→ 정답의 a safety problem

② 세부 사항

가장 많은 비중을 차지하는 유형으로 육하원칙의 의문사를 이용해 구체적인 정보를 묻는다. 대체로 문제에 고유명사, 숫자, 장소 등의 키워드가 주어지므로 본문에서 관련 내용을 찾아 접근하는 것이 문제 풀이에 수월하다.

빈출 문제 유형

What impressed Mr. Kim?
Why did Ms. Yi mention the Web site?

Where does the shuttle pick up passengers?
How will people apply for the position?

기출 대표 예제 | The question refers to the following advertisement.   정답과 해설 p.062

COMING SOON!

Our *Next Flight* is not a typical love story. Actors Julianna Burns and David Owolabi star as travelers who meet by accident at an airport in Hanoi.

Streaming on the Tencast app starts on Friday, April 10. Subscribers can **get a sneak peek by watching film highlights at www.tencastnow. com/ournextflight**.

Q According to the advertisement, **what** can be found on a Web site?
(A) Subscription information
(B) A preview of parts of a film

(Paraphrasing) 지문의 a sneak peek by watching film highlights → 정답의 A preview of parts of a film

Questions 1-3 refer to the following announcement.

https://www.sanburyfarmersmarket.net/announcements

| Who Are We? | **Announcements** | Products | Vendor Survey |

For the past five years, vendors at Sanbury Farmers Market have offered a wide selection of high-quality fruits, vegetables, prepared foods, and sweets. With our new season off to a strong start, we are seeking additional vendors. If you think your food products would be a good fit, we encourage you to complete our questionnaire for prospective vendors by visiting the "Vendor Survey" page on this Web site. Once we have reviewed your information, we may contact you to discuss your products and your possible participation in the market. If applicable, please include a description of your farming methods—for example, "All our soils are organic"—in the section at the end of the survey.

Sanbury Farmers Market is on the first floor of the Town Plaza Building on Henry Street, just south of Route 7. This convenient location, which is in the heart of Sanbury's architectural heritage district, has heavy foot traffic. Our season runs from early May to late October. The market is open from 11:00 A.M. to 8:00 P.M. on Fridays and Saturdays. And this season, by popular demand, we have made a special arrangement for our largest vendor, Carrie's Grocery, to be open on Thursdays as well—from 9:00 A.M. to 3:00 P.M.

주제 / 목적

1. What is one purpose of the announcement?

   (A) To give updates on some renovations
   (B) To publicize a community celebration
   (C) To recruit some new food sellers
   (D) To mark the anniversary of a business

2. What is indicated about Sanbury Farmers Market?

   (A) It occupies two floors of a building.
   (B) It has been operating for over a decade.
   (C) It sells only organically grown foods.
   (D) It is located in a historic district.

세부 사항

3. What change did Sanbury Farmers Market make recently?

   (A) It expanded the parking areas for its shoppers.
   (B) It increased the operating hours of one of its stores.
   (C) It lengthened its seasonal schedule.
   (D) It published data from a previous customer survey.

PART 7

UNIT 8

111

Questions 4-7 refer to the following Web page.

https://www.bartrumcity.gov/BCHC/home

Established 30 years ago, the Bartrum City Historical Commission (BCHC) is a city-run body whose mission is to preserve the unique character of Bartrum City's historical district. The commission's responsibilities include ensuring that any redevelopment project conducted within the district is in keeping with this special character. Permission is required for any modification to structures overseen by the BCHC, including the 150-year-old residences located within the district.

Building modification proposals must be submitted to the BCHC's Architectural Heritage Committee for review. The review process can take up to 60 days. If the remodeling project is approved, a building permit will be issued for a fee of $400. A list of area contractors specializing in the refurbishment of historical structures can also be requested.

Individuals considering submitting a building modification request are strongly encouraged to contact our historical preservation architect, Ms. Beth Pataki. She can offer guidance and directives to the project team before and during the implementation of the project. She can be reached by e-mail at patakib@bartrumcity.gov.

Upon completion of the project, a site inspection will be conducted. If the inspection result is satisfactory, a Certificate of Validation will be issued, stating that the modification project was performed in full accordance with BCHC guidelines.

4. What is one purpose of the Web page?

   (A) To explain the significance of Bartrum City's historical district
   (B) To give details about an organization's duties
   (C) To explain changes in an application process
   (D) To provide an update on a project

5. What is mentioned about the Bartrum City Historical Commission?

   (A) It oversees 150 historical buildings.
   (B) It is made up solely of architects.
   (C) It is operated by the government.
   (D) It is seeking 30 volunteers.

6. Why should building owners in Bartrum City's historical district contact Ms. Pataki?

   (A) To obtain a map of the district
   (B) To compare bids from contractors
   (C) To get recommendations for remodeling changes
   (D) To learn about the history of Bartrum City

7. What is indicated about the Certificate of Validation?

   (A) It requires an additional fee.
   (B) It takes up to 60 days to obtain.
   (C) It is signed by Ms. Pataki.
   (D) It is presented if a project passes inspection.

PART 7

UNIT 8

02 Not / True, 추론 / 암시

① Not / True

Not/True 문제는 지문과 내용이 일치하거나 일치하지 않는 보기를 찾는 유형이다. 같은 내용을 다르게 나타낸 패러프레이징 표현을 빨리 이해해야 하며, 지문에 있는 단어나 표현이 반복적으로 보이는 보기는 함정일 수 있으므로 유의한다.

빈출 문제 유형

What is **NOT mentioned** as the qualifications?
What is **NOT included** in the invoice?

What is **indicated** about the service?
What is **true** about the production facility?

기출 대표 예제 | The question refers to the following Web page.   정답과 해설 p.064

---

https://www.hotelverra.co.uk

Guests are welcome to share their experiences at Hotel Verra. All feedback posted by guests is read by hotel management. **Comments are directly addressed here by management as needed.**

Q **What** is **true** about the Web page?

   (A) It requires reviewers to create an account.

   (B) Managers may respond to comments on it.

(Paraphrasing) 지문의 Comments ~ as needed
→ 정답의 Managers may respond ~ on it

---

② 추론 / 암시

지문에 제시된 단서를 근거로 유추 가능한 사실을 묻는 유형으로, 세부 사항 추론과 전체 정보 추론 문제로 구분된다. 반드시 지문 내의 정보만을 근거로 유추하여 답을 찾아야 한다.

빈출 문제 유형

For whom is the notice **most likely intended**?
Where would the sign **most likely** be found?

What is **suggested** about Mr. Chandler?
What does the article **indicate** about the map?

기출 대표 예제 | The question refers to the following notice.   정답과 해설 p.064

As a registered Cesito guitar owner, you will have all the information you need regarding instrument care, repairs, and accessories right at your fingertips.

All registered Cesito guitar owners in the United States and Canada receive a complimentary subscription to our magazine, *Guitar Universe*, which includes album reviews, interviews with musicians, and all the latest news about our new products.

Q **For whom** is the notice **most likely intended**?

   (A) Sellers of musical instruments

   (B) Cesito Guitars customers

(Paraphrasing) 지문의 a registered Cesito guitar owner → 정답의 Cesito Guitars customers

---

Questions 1-3 refer to the following article.

Green Spaces to Grow Freely

ELK (July 12)—Randolph County officials have announced plans to fundamentally change the way roadside green spaces are managed.

Under the new plan, the grass in most areas will be cut only once per year. In some areas, trees and wildflowers will be planted. These spaces include areas along freeways and between streets and sidewalks in urban districts. These spaces have historically been planted with grass that must be mowed two or three times a month.

According to Dawn Liu, spokesperson for Randolph County, the change is being made primarily to improve habitats for wildlife, although it has the added benefit of improving drainage during rainstorms. It will also allow the county to divert portions of the road-maintenance budget to other needs. Commuters are advised that traffic flow along some roadways may be affected while trees and wildflowers are being planted.

1. What is the purpose of the article?

(A) To announce the opening of a recreation space

(B) To argue against reducing the county budget

(C) To describe a policy that will soon be implemented

(D) To promote tourism in Randolph County

2. According to the article, what is one change that will take place?

(A) More parking spaces will be created.

(B) Grass near roadsides will be cut less often.

(C) Several county roads will be widened.

(D) Land will be set aside for community vegetable gardens.

[Not / True]

3. What is NOT mentioned as an expected result of the changes?

(A) Improved habitats for wild animals

(B) Reduced risk of flooding

(C) Increased funding for other projects

(D) Increased property values for Homeowners

Businesses See a Future in Podcasts

SYDNEY (9 May)—The rising number of podcasts is presenting small companies with more opportunities to reel in new customers. One approach being employed is to pay a sponsorship fee to a podcast's producer in exchange for advertising time and endorsements.

"Obviously, we don't reach as many people as we could with TV or radio advertisements," said Vito Regalado, owner of Regalado Flowers in Wollombi, which opened less than a year ago. "But podcast listeners are a particularly attentive audience."

Leora Tremper, who teaches a course in advertising at Baines Technical Academy, agrees. "Listeners seem to remember details about any business that sponsors their favourite podcast," she says.

A benefit of sponsorship is illustrated by *Continental Table,* the Sydney-based podcast hosted by chef Tina Longo. Each week, Ms. Longo describes how to prepare a dish from a different region of Australia. One of the podcast's sponsors, Spice Life, experienced a 25 percent growth in online sales after just two episodes.

"Unlike most of our orders, these were from people outside Sydney," said Yuukou Iwase, owner of Spice Life. "Ms. Longo likes our line of spices and promotes it during her show, which gives her fans enough confidence to take a chance on a new business like ours."

4. What is the purpose of the article?

(A) To describe an emerging trend in advertising

(B) To highlight the content of some new podcasts

(C) To analyze promotional expenditures by small businesses

(D) To compare different forms of broadcast media

Not / True

5. What is true about both Mr. Regalado and Mr. Iwase?

(A) They attended Baines Technical Academy.

(B) They advertise on the same television show.

(C) They run businesses that are relatively new.

(D) They have been guests on *Continental Table*.

6. What is the topic of Ms. Longo's podcast?

(A) Travel

(B) Cooking

(C) Interior design

(D) Australian history

추론 / 암시

7. What is suggested about some listeners of Ms. Longo's podcast?

(A) They started their own podcasts.

(B) They buy fresh flowers once a week.

(C) They recommend topics to Ms. Longo.

(D) They ordered products from Mr. Iwase's company.

03 의도 파악, 동의어, 문장 삽입

① 의도 파악

문자 메시지와 온라인 채팅에서 각각 1문항씩 출제된다. 문제에서 묻는 표현은 주로 앞 내용에 대한 응답이므로 앞뒤 대화 흐름에 주목한다. 여럿이 등장하는 온라인 채팅에서는 메시지를 보낸 화자를 찾아 흐름을 파악해야 한다.

빈출 문제 유형

At 7:26 P.M., what does Mr. Wilson **mean[imply]** when he writes, "**I'd say so**"?

기출 대표 예제 | The question refers to the following online chat discussion. 정답과 해설 p.066

Marisa Coari (10:45 A.M.)
Good morning, everyone. What are your thoughts about **where we should hold the employee appreciation luncheon?**

Susie Boland (10:47 A.M.)
I didn't know you were planning that already.

Tyler Lemkuhl (10:49 A.M.)
What's wrong with the place we always use?

Marisa Coari (10:51 A.M.)
Candicci's Kitchen is under renovation right now. It won't be open again until July, and we always have the event in June.

Q At 10:49 A.M., what does Mr. Lemkuhl **imply** when he writes, "**What's wrong with the place we always use**"?

(A) He did not realize an event was canceled.

(B) He thinks they should use Candicci's Kitchen.

---

② 동의어

여러 의미를 지닌 다의어가 자주 출제되므로, 지문의 문맥을 통해 대체 가능한 동의어를 골라야 한다.

빈출 문제 유형

The word "incorporated" in paragraph 2, line 3, is **closest in meaning to**

기출 대표 예제 | The question refers to the following article. 정답과 해설 p.066

Aside from the residential sector, Loxby stands out by having an above-average percentage of businesses with storage needs. One facility, Yarnell Storage, **draws** nearly all of **its customer base** from commercial enterprises in the neighboring industrial park.

Q The word "draws" in paragraph 3, line 4, is **closest in meaning to**

(A) sketches

(B) attracts

(Synonym) draw 끌어들이다 ➜ attract
　　　　　 선화를 그리다 ➜ sketch

---

③ 문장 삽입

지문에 할당된 문제 중 마지막에 배치되므로 순서대로 문제를 풀면 처음부터 지문을 다시 읽어야 할 수도 있다. 따라서 문장 삽입 문제의 주어진 문장을 가장 먼저 읽고, 앞의 다른 문제를 풀면서 빈칸에 문장을 대입해 접근하면 시간 절약에 도움이 된다. 또한 대명사와 정관사, 접속부사, 시간 순서 표현은 중요한 단서가 된다.

빈출 문제 유형

In which of the positions marked [1], [2], [3], and [4] does the following sentence best belong?
"Then, we will sit down and address the issue."

기출 대표 예제 | The question refers to the following Web page.   정답과 해설 p.067

---

https://www.landmersupply.com

| Shop | Customize | About Us | Contact |

Landmer Supply, headquartered in Vancouver, British Columbia, manufactures pocket-size paper notebooks, memo books, and travel journals.

In today's increasingly paperless world, where many people document their lives using mobile phones, **paper products** can still be as relevant as ever. — [1] —. **That** is why photographers and international travelers tell us that they rely on our memo books for jotting down notes during their explorations. Our loyal customers have helped keep our business growing in the digital era. — [2] —. Last year, our sales volume was the highest it has ever been!

Q **In which of the positions marked [1] and [2] does the following sentence best belong?**

"**They** will never let you down with dead batteries or weak Internet connections."

(A) [1]

(B) [2]

Clue

문제의 They → 지문의 paper products
지문의 That → 문제의 They will ~ Internet connections.

PART 7

UNIT 8

Questions 1-2 refer to the following text-message chain.

> **Juan Rosas (7:38 P.M.)**
> Hi. Are you still at work? I need a favor.
>
> **Ranish Douglass (7:44 P.M.)**
> I am. How can I help?
>
> **Juan Rosas (7:46 P.M.)**
> Please go into my office. Text me when you get there.
>
> **Ranish Douglass (7:54 P.M.)**
> OK. I am here.
>
> **Juan Rosas (7:55 P.M.)**
> See the blue timer on my lab desk? What time is it set for?
>
> **Ranish Douglass (7:56 P.M.)**
> 3:45 A.M.
>
> **Juan Rosas (7:58 P.M.)**
> Could you reset the timer? I reviewed the data when I got home, and I think we'll get better results if the machine starts at 5:45 in the morning.
>
> **Ranish Douglass (8:00 P.M.)**
> Done.
>
> **Juan Rosas (8:01 P.M.)**
> I owe you, Ranish. See you tomorrow!

1. What will happen at 5:45 A.M.?

   (A) Mr. Rosas will reset a timer.
   (B) The office door will be unlocked.
   (C) Mr. Douglass will be awakened by an alarm clock.
   (D) Some equipment will turn on automatically.

의도 파악

2. At 8:01 P.M., what does Mr. Rosas most likely mean when he writes, "I owe you, Ranish"?

   (A) He is grateful for Mr. Douglass' help.
   (B) He regrets making a mistake.
   (C) He intends to repay a loan promptly.
   (D) He will analyze the results of an experiment.

Questions 3-5 refer to the following information.

Money River Referral Program

As a Money River app user, you already know how easy it is to make everyday financial transactions safely and securely. But did you know that you can extend the same convenience to a friend or family member while earning a bonus payment for yourself? Whenever someone you have referred makes their first purchase, you will each earn five dollars! Here is a quick look at our terms.

• Refer someone directly by using the Money River phone app or by visiting our Web site at www.moneyriver.com/referral.

• Refer up to ten individuals within one year.

• Offer is limited to users in the United States and Canada.

• Bonus rewards typically appear in users' Money River accounts within ten business days.

Take full advantage of the Money River program by making your first referral now!

---

3. What is the Money River app designed to help users do?

(A) Chat with friends
(B) Make travel arrangements
(C) Start a business
(D) Make simple purchases

동의어

4. The word "extend" in paragraph 1, line 2, is closest in meaning to

(A) offer
(B) restore
(C) prolong
(D) accelerate

5. What is indicated about the Money River referral program?

(A) It can be used anywhere in the world.
(B) It credits bonuses to users' accounts within 24 hours.
(C) It allows for a maximum of ten referrals annually.
(D) It can be initiated through the app only.

FOR IMMEDIATE RELEASE

Contact: Yvonne Stepanian, ystepanian@skarnov.ca

TORONTO (21 August)—The Skarnov Company, a leading manufacturer of health-promoting energy drinks, will soon introduce its popular Vigorate brand energy drink in 500-millilitre aluminum bottles. This larger bottle will appear on store shelves alongside the standard 250-millilitre bottle size within the next few weeks. Like the smaller bottles, the 500-millilitre bottles are reusable and fully recyclable. — [1] —.

Skarnov introduced its Vigorate energy drink ten years ago to meet consumer demand for healthier beverages. Vigorate is available in three delicious, 100 percent natural flavours—strawberry, peach, and lemon. — [2] —. The company expects to add two more flavours to the product line next year.

Vigorate products are currently sold in most supermarkets, and the company hopes that the larger bottle option will increase the brand's visibility. — [3] —. The energy drinks can also be purchased at many restaurants, fitness centres, and hotels.

Skarnov has recently launched a marketing push through various social media platforms and health and fitness podcasts. — [4] —. More information can be found at www.skarnov.ca/vigorate.

문장 삽입

6. What is suggested about the 250-milliliter bottles of Vigorate?

   (A) They are available in a variety of places.
   (B) They were previously made of glass.
   (C) They will soon replace the 500-milliliter bottles.
   (D) They will be sold in yellow containers.

7. According to the press release, what did the Skarnov Company do recently?

   (A) It changed the ingredients of a drink.
   (B) It opened a new production facility.
   (C) It stopped selling in supermarkets.
   (D) It increased its advertising efforts.

8. In which of the positions marked [1], [2], [3], and [4] does the following sentence best belong?

   "This ensures that the Vigorate brand is eco-friendly."

   (A) [1]
   (B) [2]
   (C) [3]
   (D) [4]

연계 문제

연계 문제는 특정 사실에 대한 단서를 2~3개의 지문에서 찾아야 하는 유형으로, 주로 숫자나 날짜, 인물, 지명과 같은 세부 정보에 관해 추론하는 문제가 출제된다. 특히 목록, 양식, 표 등이 지문 중 하나로 제시되면 연계 문제의 단서 지문일 확률이 높다. 대체로 이중 지문에서 1-2문항, 삼중 지문에서 2문항 정도가 출제된다.

빈출 문제 유형

What can be concluded about Mr. Choi?

What vehicle did Ms. Oh use during her trip?

Where will the reception **most likely** be held?

How far did Mr. Kim travel for his appointment?

기출 대표 예제 │ The question refers to the following job advertisement and schedule.

정답과 해설 p.069

job advertisement

App Developers Needed

Gamesake, a recently formed software start-up based in Bangalore, seeks full-time app developers to help build our team. Candidates must have experience with the latest app-development tools, understand the needs of online consumers, and be available to work on-site full-time. Working remotely two or three days a week is negotiable after an initial six months of employment.

If you would like more information, please attend one of our free live webinars. For dates and a link to sign up, e-mail your résumé to **our vice president, Vin Misra**, at vmisra@gamesake.co.in. Write "Project 8900" in the subject line.

---

schedule

Project 8900 Webinars		
Leader	**Date, Time**	**Session**
Mr. Rian Sanyal	11 November, 10:00 A.M.	202
Ms. Sita Tipani	12 November, 2:00 P.M.	203
Ms. Vin Misra	**13 November**, 12:30 P.M.	204
Mr. Rian Sanyal	14 November, 8:00 P.M.	205

Q **What can be concluded** about the vice president of Gamesake?

(A) She will lead a webinar on November 13.

(B) She created a tool for developing virtual reality apps.

(Problem Solving)

① 문제의 **vice president of Gamesake** 단서 찾기

② job advertisement의
첫 번째 단락 첫 번째 문장, **Gamesake**
두 번째 단락 두 번째 문장, **our vice president,**
                                    Vin Misra

③ schedule의 다섯 번째 칸
Leader: Ms. Vin Misra
Date, Time: **13 November**, 12:30 P.M.

PART 7

UNIT 8

Questions 1-5 refer to the following advertisement and article.

Musical Production International Tour

Orpheus Revisited is the electrifying new musical based on the myth of Orpheus and Eurydice. It's a feast for the eyes and ears! Written by award-winning composer Adrien Ansari, *Orpheus Revisited* is sure to delight all viewers. The touring schedule includes performances in four European capital cities.

Previews:

9–28 April: Wordwright Theatre (Eastbourne, England)

Touring Schedule:

4–15 May: Pinnacle Theatre (London, England)

18–29 May: Centre Musique (Paris, France)

1–12 June: Ravenstein Hall (Brussels, Belgium)

15–26 June: The Diamant (Amsterdam, Netherlands)

Theatre Renovations Finished

by Reese Kaneko

EASTBOURNE (10 March)—On 9 April, the acclaimed Wordwright Theatre will reopen its doors after a major renovation project. The 1950s-era building was closed four years ago owing to structural damage caused by a broken water main. Patrons feared it might never open again as the theatre's board of directors struggled with costly repairs.

Cristela Marmor, a member of the theatre's board for twenty years, was appointed as the new chairperson last March. "Seeing the renovations to completion these past twelve months has been one of the largest challenges I've faced, but it is such a gift to be able to bring this important building back for the benefit of the community," said Ms. Marmor.

Work on the building has included repair to the foundations, restoration of detailed plaster decorations, installation of a new heating and air-conditioning system, and upgrades to the theatre's seating and stage technology.

Local audiences are thrilled at the prospect of seeing the debut of Adrien Ansari's new musical version of an ancient myth. The director, Seema Kumhar, is an Eastbourne native who helped raise funds for the Wordwright's reconstruction. Her efforts were vital in bringing the show here.

1. What does the advertisement indicate about the international tour for *Orpheus Revisited*?

(A) It will include four different countries.
(B) It will receive funding from investors.
(C) It will hold previews in May.
(D) It will feature lectures by Mr. Ansari.

2. Why did the Wordwright Theatre undergo renovations?

(A) The patrons requested more comfortable seating.
(B) The stage was too small for modern productions.
(C) The building suffered water damage.
(D) Ms. Kumhar offered to pay for improvements.

3. How long has Ms. Marmor been chairperson of the theater's board of directors?

(A) One year
(B) Two years
(C) Twelve years
(D) Twenty years

연계

4. What is suggested about *Orpheus Revisited*?

(A) It was written in the 1950s.
(B) It uses specialized technology.
(C) It was written by a native of Eastbourne.
(D) It will be the first production for the reopened theater.

5. In the article, the word "vital" in paragraph 4, line 7, is closest in meaning to

(A) essential
(B) refreshing
(C) athletic
(D) productive

PART 7

UNIT 8

125

Come to the Callan Summer Fair—Fun for All!

The annual Callan Summer Fair will be held this year from 11 July to 14 July (rain dates: 25 July to 28 July) on the fairgrounds just south of the city. The fair will be open each day from 9:00 A.M. to 9:00 P.M. The summer fair has been a tradition for over a hundred years! Visit www.callansummerfair.ie to read more about the history and to see ticket information and a schedule of this year's entertainment.

As always, the fair will feature dozens of vendors, food stalls, performances, and more. If you would like to be a vendor or performer, please e-mail Damien Dougherty at ddougherty@callansummerfair.ie. Also, we still need volunteers to assist us with this year's event. If you are interested, please contact Aislinn Maloney at amaloney@callansummerfair.ie.

E-mail

To:	Jonas Skerla <jskerla@callancitycouncil.ie>
From:	Aislinn Maloney <amaloney@callansummerfair.ie>
Date:	19 July
Subject:	Preparations

Dear Mr. Skerla:

I wanted to check with you to ensure everything is ready for the fair next week, as we were rained out on our original dates. Have the grounds crews and maintenance workers been notified? The fairgrounds should be freshly mowed before 25 July, and cleanup crews will be needed to remove rubbish during the fair and after the last day. As no sporting events are happening next week, we may see a larger crowd than initially anticipated. We can always use more volunteers to work with the maintenance staff. They will, of course, receive complimentary admission to the fair. With luck, the weather will be more pleasant this time!

Sincerely,

Aislinn Maloney
Planning Director, Callan Summer Fair

```
https://www.callansummerfair.ie/comments
```

As part of my studies this past year, I worked in the Callan city council office. At Mr. Skerla's suggestion, I volunteered to help the maintenance crew prepare for the summer fair. Then I attended the fair on 26 July, and it was so much fun! The food, music, and demonstrations were wonderful, and everything was well organised. If I can return to Ireland in the future, I hope to attend the fair again.

—Soon-Hee Oh (Seoul, South Korea)

6. What does the notice indicate about the fair?

(A) It is open to city residents only.
(B) It has occurred annually for more than a century.
(C) Its history will be compiled by researchers soon.
(D) It is held in a different location each year.

연계

7. Why are readers advised to contact the planning director?

(A) To rent a food stall
(B) To sign up to give a performance
(C) To receive an updated schedule of events
(D) To volunteer to help at the fair

8. What does Ms. Maloney mention in her e-mail to Mr. Skerla?

(A) She hired people to mow the fairgrounds.
(B) The fair will include a sporting event.
(C) The fair was rescheduled because of rainy weather.
(D) The cost for a vendor to rent a food stall has increased.

9. Why did Ms. Oh post a comment on the fair's Web site?

(A) To ask about ticket prices for the fair
(B) To find out when the fair will be held
(C) To describe her experience at the fair
(D) To make a suggestion about future fairs

연계

10. What is most likely true about Ms. Oh?

(A) She currently works for Mr. Skerla.
(B) She attended the fair for free.
(C) She will be studying in Ireland next year.
(D) She helped plan the food and music for the fair.

PART 7

UNIT 8

Questions 1-3 refer to the following instructions.

Safespray Upholstery Protector—Instructions for Use

Safespray Upholstery Protector is an environmentally friendly fabric treatment that helps prevent stains caused by liquids such as tea or juice. Free from harmful chemicals, Safespray produces a liquid-repelling microlayer on cloth surfaces. It's an easy-to-use product with a light, fresh scent that keeps moisture from damaging fabric-covered chairs and other soft furnishings.

To use Safespray, shake the bottle well and hold it six inches away from the fabric to be treated. Then spray the surface in a sweeping motion. Do not use too much: the fabric should not be saturated. Let the material dry completely. For maximum protection, reapply every few months.

---

1. What is indicated about Safespray Upholstery Protector?

　(A) It has no detectable fragrance.
　(B) It is made with nontoxic ingredients.
　(C) It might damage hard surfaces.
　(D) It should be used only once per year.

2. According to the instructions, what should a person do before using the product?

　(A) Open a window for fresh air
　(B) Add water to the bottle
　(C) Shake the bottle thoroughly
　(D) Clean the area to be treated

3. The word "saturated" in paragraph 2, line 3, is closest in meaning to

　(A) soaked
　(B) satisfied
　(C) intense
　(D) pure

Questions 4-6 refer to the following advertisement.

Modern Photography Museum—Educational Workshops

Founded by the city's Association for Visual Artists, the Modern Photography Museum aims to raise interest in photography as an art form. — [1] —. Free and open to the public, the museum showcases an array of contemporary photographs in its main gallery. It also features exhibits of vintage cameras, accessories, film rolls, and other related objects of historical interest.

To share the museum staff's enthusiasm for photography, we offer free educational workshops focusing on photography as a means of creative expression. — [2] —. No previous photography experience is necessary, and participants of all skill levels are welcome.

This month's workshop, titled "Capturing Architecture," will take place at Central City Plaza on Saturday, April 13, between 3:30 P.M. and 6:00 P.M. The class will begin with an informative lesson by instructor Brian Campos, a noted urban photographer. — [3] —. Ample time will then be provided to explore the plaza area and take photographs of it. All types of cameras are suitable for this class.

The session is limited to ten participants, and online registration via the museum's Web site is required. The group will assemble in the picnic area alongside the plaza, next to the Central City Business Hotel. In the event of bad weather, the class will be rescheduled for another time. — [4] —.

---

4. What is indicated in the advertisement about the museum?

(A) It charges a small admission fee.
(B) It is noted for its modern exterior.
(C) It displays old photographic equipment.
(D) It was founded by a group of educators.

5. What is indicated about the "Capturing Architecture" workshop?

(A) It will be offered twice in one month.
(B) It does not require a specific type of camera.
(C) It will be held indoors if the weather is bad.
(D) It includes complimentary snacks in the picnic area.

6. In which of the positions marked [1], [2], [3], and [4] does the following sentence best belong?

"Attendees will receive his expert advice on techniques for photographing buildings."

(A) [1]
(B) [2]
(C) [3]
(D) [4]

Questions 7-10 refer to the following text-message chain.

Richard Cohen (3:42 P.M.) Hello, everyone. I wanted to check in regarding our monthly meeting, verify the assigned reading, and welcome our newest club member, Karima Alaoui!

Karima Alaoui (3:45 P.M.) Thank you, Richard. It's so nice to find a group of like-minded people in the San Francisco Bay area. You are the first people that I've met since moving here.

Enzo Tomasso (3:47 P.M.) Welcome to the group, Karima! Richard was also my first connection here when I moved from Salinas. His life mission seems to be connecting avid readers.

Richard Cohen (3:49 P.M.) It's my pleasure. This month we'll be reading William Shields's *Bound for the Gulf of Mexico*. It's a memoir chronicling his steamboat journey down the Mississippi River. Has everyone been able to pick up a copy?

Karima Alaoui (3:52 P.M.) Yes. I bought one from the Bradley & Newell shop near my apartment in San Bruno. A used paperback copy was less than ten dollars.

Sarah Morita (3:56 P.M.) I'll have to check that out. I love supporting small businesses, but I must admit that I buy from Atacama more often than I'd like. They have a huge selection and make it so easy to browse for books to buy online.

Richard Cohen (3:59 P.M.) OK. Then it seems like everyone should be ready. See everyone at 11 A.M. on May 28 at the Berlin Café in Mission Bay.

Karima Alaoui (4:00 P.M.) Before we meet, I need some advice from you. I don't have a car, and I'm a little uncertain about finding my way around the city.

Sarah Morita (4:02 P.M.) From San Bruno, it's a quick trip on the L train. I live in Millbrae, and that's not too far from you. I find that public transit is incredibly convenient for getting around the city.

7. Who most likely are the writers?

   (A) Publishing company employees
   (B) Members of a book club
   (C) Authors of historical fiction
   (D) Bookstore owners

8. At 3:49 P.M., what does Mr. Cohen most likely mean when he writes, "It's my pleasure"?

   (A) He likes living in San Francisco.
   (B) He is happy to share his opinion on
       a topic.
   (C) He enjoys organizing the group.
   (D) He appreciates feedback from readers.

9. What type of business most likely is Atacama?

   (A) An office supply store
   (B) A private library
   (C) A publishing house
   (D) An online store

10. Where will the writers meet in person?

    (A) In Salinas
    (B) In San Bruno
    (C) In Mission Bay
    (D) In Millbrae

Questions 11-15 refer to the following e-mail and receipt.

To:	Marketing Team
From:	Shane Holliday
Date:	6 May
Subject:	Tomorrow's meeting

Good morning, team,

Our meeting tomorrow will focus on upcoming marketing efforts. Expanding into North America last year has allowed us to redesign some of our most popular products and to launch some new ones.

The meeting is currently scheduled to be held in the Oak Conference Room from 2:30 P.M. to 5:00 P.M. In the event that the meeting runs long, a meal will be provided. Please make every effort to attend, as necessary information will be discussed and decisions that require team input will be taken. We will address our plans to rebrand our line of women's running shoes, which has seen a slowdown in sales, especially in Europe. Arthur Greene from Product Development will be there to show some mock-ups of new designs and colours. We must ensure these shoes regain their place in the market.

Sincerely,

Shane Holliday
Vice President of Marketing, Soft Sprint Shoes

Eloise's Eatery

11 Keeling Road
Perivale
UB6 7JB
www.eloiseseatery.co.uk

Date:	7 May	Order received: 4:00 P.M.
Customer:	Shane Holliday	sholliday@softsprintshoes.co.uk
Delivery address:	Soft Sprint Shoes Wadsworth Business Centre Bonham Road Perivale HA0 1BW	

Order:		
	1 large tray fish and chips	£125
	1 large tray pasta with Italian tomato sauce	£ 80
	1 mixed greens salad (10 servings, Italian dressing)	£ 40
	5 one-litre bottles sparkling water	£ 9
	Cutlery No **Napkins** Yes	
	TOTAL	£254

11. What is suggested in the e-mail about Soft Sprint Shoes?

(A) It is in the process of hiring product designers.

(B) It recently began selling shoes in a new market.

(C) It plans to open a new production center in North America.

(D) It significantly increased its revenue over the last year.

12. What problem does Mr. Holliday mention in the e-mail?

(A) A product is no longer selling well.

(B) Production of a new item has been delayed.

(C) Some staff members have resigned.

(D) Product reviews have been negative.

13. What can be concluded about the marketing meeting?

(A) It ended after 5:00 P.M.

(B) It was poorly attended.

(C) It was held in a restaurant.

(D) It featured a speech from the company president.

14. In the e-mail, the word "line" in paragraph 2, line 5, is closest in meaning to

(A) row

(B) route

(C) border

(D) collection

15. According to the receipt, what was NOT included in Mr. Holliday's order?

(A) Napkins

(B) A salad

(C) A dessert

(D) A beverage

Questions 1-4 refer to the following letter.

European Titanium Congress

28 June

Lizette Ozols
Rue Belliard 1365
Bruxelles, BE 1000

Dear Ms. Ozols,

Thank you for joining the European Titanium Congress (ETC), the international trade group for the titanium metal industry. The ETC is dedicated to educating engineers and business professionals on the unique properties of titanium and its crucial role in modern manufacturing. — [1] —.

As an ETC member, you have access to our technical literature and support from our team of experts. — [2] —. You may attend our annual European Titanium Exposition and periodic workshops on topics pertinent to the titanium industry.

Titanium's usefulness in manufacturing increases every year. — [3] —. Titanium's low weight, superior strength, and flexibility, as well as its resistance to rust and other forms of corrosion, make it an excellent alternative to iron and steel in many applications. — [4] —. I look forward to seeing you at our future events.

Sincerely,

Sigurd Vinje

Sigurd Vinje
Executive Secretary
European Titanium Congress

---

1. Why did Mr. Vinje write the letter to Ms. Ozols?

   (A) To welcome her into a professional organization
   (B) To offer her a job in the titanium industry
   (C) To negotiate a purchase of titanium from her firm
   (D) To invite her to speak at a trade conference

2. What is mentioned about the ETC?

   (A) It manufactures and sells titanium.
   (B) It funds academic research.
   (C) It helps governments resolve titanium trade issues.
   (D) It provides access to technical specialists.

3. What is NOT mentioned as a reason that titanium is a good substitute for iron and steel?

   (A) It is inexpensive.
   (B) It is lightweight.
   (C) It is flexible.
   (D) It is strong.

4. In which of the positions marked [1], [2], [3], and [4] does the following sentence best belong?

   "This growth is being driven by high demand in the aerospace and medical industries."

   (A) [1]
   (B) [2]
   (C) [3]
   (D) [4]

Questions 5-6 refer to the following text-message chain.

Lena Henderson (9:29 A.M.)
This is Lena from Amara Bake Shop. I'm parked at your back door and am ready to unload your delivery.

Joe Nakamura (9:30 A.M.)
Hello, Lena. My kitchen staff expected you to arrive 45 minutes ago!

Lena Henderson (9:31 A.M.)
I know. We were short-staffed, so baking the bread and dinner rolls took longer than usual.

Joe Nakamura (9:32 A.M.)
I wish you had let me know sooner. My catering team has already packed up the truck with the rest of the food. We are expected to arrive at the banquet hall at 10:30 A.M., so we need to load your products on our truck immediately.

Lena Henderson (9:33 A.M.)
My apologies. I'll be sure to give you some notice if it happens again.

Joe Nakamura (9:34 A.M.)
At least one hour in advance. One of our team members will meet you at the loading dock door right now.

PART 7

UNIT 8

5. Where most likely is Ms. Henderson?

(A) In a vehicle
(B) In a kitchen
(C) At a bakery
(D) At a banquet hall

6. At 9:34 A.M., what does Mr. Nakamura mean when he writes, "At least one hour in advance"?

(A) He expects a loading job to take an hour.
(B) He believes a drive will take more than an hour.
(C) He wants to be alerted sooner.
(D) He hopes Ms. Henderson will meet some team members soon.

Whangarei Utility Company • 166 Northern Crescent • Whangarei 0112

2 April

Dear Valued Customer:

Do we have your correct telephone number on file? These days, nearly everyone has a mobile phone. In fact, you may be one of the millions of New Zealanders who gave up a landline in favour of using a mobile phone exclusively. Without your current phone number on file, Whangarei Utility Company cannot recognise you when you call. This may affect how quickly we respond when you need us.

We use your phone number in several ways. When you call or text to report a problem, our automated system instantly associates your number with your home address. This enables us to respond to your issue more quickly. And if you call our customer care centre regarding your account, we use your phone number to verify that we are speaking with the customer of record.

When we schedule temporary outages to upgrade lines and equipment, we call the phone number on file to inform you in advance. Advance notification can lessen the inconvenience of a break in service and allow you to plan ahead.

To check or update your phone number, log in to your account through either the Whangarei Utility Company Web site or mobile app or call (09) 429 9755. If you pay your bills by mail, write the number on the back of your bill.

Thank you for helping us serve you better.

Sincerely,

Whangarei Utility Company Customer Care Team

---

7. What is the purpose of the letter?

(A) To announce an update to a mobile app
(B) To encourage customers to keep a piece of information updated
(C) To tell customers about an upcoming maintenance project
(D) To explain a recent change in utility rates

8. What is one way Whangarei Utility Company uses customers' telephone numbers?

(A) To send payment reminders
(B) To promote community outreach activities
(C) To identify the customers who use the most power
(D) To link callers to their service locations

9. The word "break" in paragraph 3, line 3, is closest in meaning to

(A) escape
(B) opening
(C) interruption
(D) opportunity

10. What communication method is NOT mentioned in the letter?

(A) E-mail
(B) Telephone call
(C) Postal service
(D) Smartphone app

Rock-E and His Rocks

By Carolee Spangler

LIVERPOOL (4 March)—Some celebrities like to collect objects such as sports memorabilia or art pieces; others acquire less ordinary items. One unusual collection is kept by reggae music superstar Rock-E, who is originally from Kingston, Jamaica.

As a child, Rock-E (whose birth name is Erwin Tufton) learned a lot about earth minerals, particularly rocks, from his father, a geologist. In primary school, it was all he wanted to talk about. Soon, his schoolmates nicknamed him Rock-E. He would go on to adopt that as his stage name.

Rock-E never outgrew his geological fascination. Over his twenty-year career, he has picked up a rock in every city where he has played. Each one has been engraved with the name of the city and the performance date. The stones are arranged in a special garden at his Manchester home.

When Rock-E shows his rock collection to visitors, they are often shocked by his technical knowledge of the mineral composition and geological origins of each piece. His new manager, Preeti Maraj, remarked, "The wealth of information that Rock-E has about these rocks is astounding. Plus, they add great value to Rock-E's brand."

To:	Rock-E <rock_e@dandeliondance.co.uk>
From:	Preeti Maraj <preeti.maraj@nightglitz.co.uk>
Date:	9 March
Subject:	Your input requested

Dear Rock-E,

Thanks for inviting me to the social gathering at your house last week. It was a special treat to see the members of the band Greenfast there. You may not be aware, but my connection with them goes back fifteen years when they hired me as their agent. I had just launched my career here in Liverpool, and they were my very first clients.

Needless to say, I also enjoyed seeing your rock collection in person. I must confess I was initially surprised at the idea, but the more I reflected on it, the more sense it made. Those rocks, like photographs, tell the story of your career.

For your upcoming tour in Australia, it occurred to me that perhaps we could add a merchandising item: a rock with the tour logo, city, and concert date imprinted on it. We could sell these commemorative rocks online alongside your T-shirts and other items.

I have already researched some companies that do such work. However, before exploring this further, I'd like to know if the idea appeals to you. Please let me know what you think.

Sincerely,

Preeti Maraj
Owner, Nightglitz Talent Agency

11. What is NOT mentioned about Rock-E in the article?

(A) He learned about geology from his father.
(B) He turned his childhood nickname into his professional name.
(C) He went to a university in Jamaica before becoming a performer.
(D) He displays his rock collection for guests to see.

12. What is indicated about the rocks in Rock-E's collection?

(A) They were given to him by his fans.
(B) They remind him of the home he grew up in.
(C) They will be featured in a documentary about him.
(D) They bear the names of cities where he has performed.

13. What is one reason that Ms. Maraj e-mailed Rock-E?

(A) To inquire about his background
(B) To promote a marketing idea
(C) To introduce him to other clients of hers
(D) To invite him to a celebration in Liverpool

14. What is most likely true about Ms. Maraj?

(A) She recently was in Manchester.
(B) She used to be a professional musician.
(C) She has been Rock-E's only publicity agent.
(D) She was gifted a rock from Rock-E's collection.

15. What is suggested about the members of the band Greenfast?

(A) They are currently touring in Australia.
(B) They collect items that are considered unusual.
(C) They have been together for at least fifteen years.
(D) They have added new members to the group.

Questions 16-20 refer to the following advertisement, e-mail, and review.

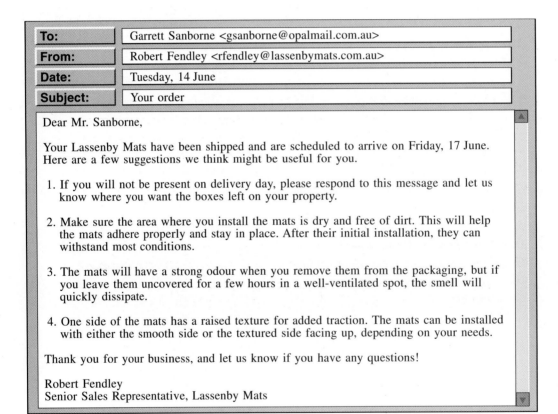

You Can Rely on Lassenby Mats

Lassenby Mats has been Australia's largest manufacturer of recycled rubber floor mats for more than 40 years. We keep millions of car tyres out of incinerators and landfills every year, transforming them into durable, customisable mats that have a wide variety of applications.

We primarily serve agriculture, marine, and forestry clients, but we have also supplied our mats to schools around the country. Contact us at (03) 5550 0821 to speak with a sales representative who can answer questions about our product line, assist you with direct orders, or provide information about our distribution partners and retailers. For a complete list of our products and where they can be purchased, visit our Web site at www.lassenbymats.com.au.

To:	Garrett Sanborne <gsanborne@opalmail.com.au>
From:	Robert Fendley <rfendley@lassenbymats.com.au>
Date:	Tuesday, 14 June
Subject:	Your order

Dear Mr. Sanborne,

Your Lassenby Mats have been shipped and are scheduled to arrive on Friday, 17 June. Here are a few suggestions we think might be useful for you.

1. If you will not be present on delivery day, please respond to this message and let us know where you want the boxes left on your property.

2. Make sure the area where you install the mats is dry and free of dirt. This will help the mats adhere properly and stay in place. After their initial installation, they can withstand most conditions.

3. The mats will have a strong odour when you remove them from the packaging, but if you leave them uncovered for a few hours in a well-ventilated spot, the smell will quickly dissipate.

4. One side of the mats has a raised texture for added traction. The mats can be installed with either the smooth side or the textured side facing up, depending on your needs.

Thank you for your business, and let us know if you have any questions!

Robert Fendley
Senior Sales Representative, Lassenby Mats

Excellent product!

I operate a commercial fishing boat, and I found Lassenby Mats when researching slip-resistant mats. When I spoke with Robert Fendley, a sales representative, I was impressed with his expertise and quick grasp of my particular needs. For my boat, we installed the mats with the bumpy side up, and that has been ideal for us, since the crew operates in wet conditions that can make the boat's deck dangerous. I highly recommend this company and its products.

—Garrett Sanborne

16. What does the advertisement suggest about Lassenby Mats?

(A) It recently changed its manufacturing formula.
(B) It sells a portion of its products through other companies.
(C) It provides free installation for certain clients.
(D) It donates a percentage of its profits to educational institutions.

17. What does the e-mail indicate about the mats?

(A) They will perform better if placed on a clean surface.
(B) They should be returned if they become damaged.
(C) They require special equipment to install.
(D) They are available in a range of colors.

18. According to the review, what impressed Mr. Sanborne?

(A) An employee's knowledge
(B) A product demonstration
(C) A customer's testimonial
(D) A marketing video

19. What can be concluded about Mr. Sanborne?

(A) He was referred to Lassenby Mats by one of his crew members.
(B) He works in one of the main industries served by Lassenby Mats.
(C) He will apply for a job at Lassenby Mats.
(D) He has ordered from Lassenby Mats in the past.

20. What suggestion from Mr. Fendley did Mr. Sanborne most likely apply?

(A) Suggestion 1
(B) Suggestion 2
(C) Suggestion 3
(D) Suggestion 4

PART 7

UNIT 8

ETS
기출 모의고사

1 회

⏱ **시험 시간: 120분**

	맞은 개수	환산 점수대
LISTENING TEST		
READING TEST		
총점		

*14쪽의 점수 환산표 및 산출법을 참조하세요.

LISTENING TEST

In the Listening test, you will be asked to demonstrate how well you understand spoken English. The entire Listening test will last approximately 45 minutes. There are four parts, and directions are given for each part. You must mark your answers on the separate answer sheet. Do not write your answers in your test book.

PART 1

Directions: For each question in this part, you will hear four statements about a picture in your test book. When you hear the statements, you must select the one statement that best describes what you see in the picture. Then find the number of the question on your answer sheet and mark your answer. The statements will not be printed in your test book and will be spoken only one time.

Statement (C), "They're sitting at a table," is the best description of the picture, so you should select answer (C) and mark it on your answer sheet.

1.

2.

GO ON TO THE NEXT PAGE

3.

4.

5.

6.

GO ON TO THE NEXT PAGE

PART 2

Directions: You will hear a question or statement and three responses spoken in English. They will not be printed in your test book and will be spoken only one time. Select the best response to the question or statement and mark the letter (A), (B), or (C) on your answer sheet.

7. Mark your answer on your answer sheet.

8. Mark your answer on your answer sheet.

9. Mark your answer on your answer sheet.

10. Mark your answer on your answer sheet.

11. Mark your answer on your answer sheet.

12. Mark your answer on your answer sheet.

13. Mark your answer on your answer sheet.

14. Mark your answer on your answer sheet.

15. Mark your answer on your answer sheet.

16. Mark your answer on your answer sheet.

17. Mark your answer on your answer sheet.

18. Mark your answer on your answer sheet.

19. Mark your answer on your answer sheet.

20. Mark your answer on your answer sheet.

21. Mark your answer on your answer sheet.

22. Mark your answer on your answer sheet.

23. Mark your answer on your answer sheet.

24. Mark your answer on your answer sheet.

25. Mark your answer on your answer sheet.

26. Mark your answer on your answer sheet.

27. Mark your answer on your answer sheet.

28. Mark your answer on your answer sheet.

29. Mark your answer on your answer sheet.

30. Mark your answer on your answer sheet.

31. Mark your answer on your answer sheet.

PART 3

Directions: You will hear some conversations between two or more people. You will be asked to answer three questions about what the speakers say in each conversation. Select the best response to each question and mark the letter (A), (B), (C), or (D) on your answer sheet. The conversations will not be printed in your test book and will be spoken only one time.

32. What are the speakers preparing for?

(A) A company retreat
(B) A sports competition
(C) A team meeting
(D) A trade show

33. What did the man just do?

(A) He made a reservation.
(B) He printed out a product description.
(C) He ordered some supplies.
(D) He e-mailed some information.

34. According to the woman, why should the man participate in an event?

(A) To socialize with his coworkers
(B) To improve his computer skills
(C) To meet potential clients
(D) To raise money for charity

35. Why is the man calling?

(A) To extend a car rental period
(B) To report that a rental car has broken down
(C) To inquire about charges for a rental car
(D) To ask about returning a rental car in a different city

36. What does the woman warn the man about?

(A) A road closure
(B) A weather forecast
(C) A policy change
(D) A business closing time

37. What will the man most likely do next?

(A) Check a flight schedule
(B) Make a payment
(C) Update a calendar
(D) Call another rental office

38. Where most likely are the speakers?

(A) At a hotel
(B) At a fitness center
(C) At a museum
(D) At a bus terminal

39. According to the woman, what can be found in the city center?

(A) Dining options
(B) Indoor activities
(C) Parking garages
(D) A walking path

40. What does the man say he will look into?

(A) Age requirements
(B) Driving directions
(C) Available discounts
(D) Operating hours

41. What is the conversation about?

(A) A billing error
(B) A delayed shipment
(C) A misplaced invoice
(D) A damaged product

42. What does the man offer?

(A) A substitute item
(B) A full refund
(C) Discounted installation
(D) Overnight delivery

43. Why will the woman visit the store?

(A) To make a complaint
(B) To return an appliance
(C) To pick up an order
(D) To view a product

GO ON TO THE NEXT PAGE

44. What are the speakers organizing?

(A) A company celebration
(B) A product launch
(C) A business course
(D) An internship program

45. What does the woman offer to do?

(A) Run a workshop
(B) Make some assignments
(C) Send an invitation
(D) Contact a supervisor

46. What information will the man gather?

(A) Cost estimates
(B) Policy updates
(C) Staff availability
(D) Seating preferences

47. Where do the speakers most likely work?

(A) At a garden center
(B) At a food processing plant
(C) At an appliance store
(D) At a restaurant

48. What does the man explain how to do?

(A) Replace a machine part
(B) Organize some receipts
(C) Clean an appliance
(D) Set up a display

49. What does the man hand to the woman?

(A) A checklist
(B) Safety gloves
(C) A work schedule
(D) Order forms

50. What industry does the woman most likely work in?

(A) Manufacturing
(B) Technology
(C) Shipping
(D) Television

51. What document is the woman asked to sign?

(A) A rental agreement
(B) A photo release form
(C) An itemized receipt
(D) An employee contract

52. What will be the focus of the interview?

(A) Community outreach efforts
(B) Workplace safety
(C) Environmentally friendly policies
(D) Employee retention strategies

53. What does the woman say she would like to do?

(A) Organize a business convention
(B) Design a new product line
(C) Expand a customer base
(D) Start a membership program

54. Why does the man say, "I've done a lot of research in this area"?

(A) To offer reassurance
(B) To make a correction
(C) To disagree with a suggestion
(D) To explain a decision

55. According to the man, what should be the focus of a plan?

(A) Process efficiency
(B) Customer rewards
(C) Product quality
(D) Social media

56. Where most likely are the speakers?

(A) At a photography studio
(B) At a medical office
(C) At a sports arena
(D) At a fitness center

57. What does the woman display on a computer screen?

(A) A schedule
(B) A contract
(C) Some prices
(D) Some results

58. What does the woman want to do next?

(A) Discuss a portfolio
(B) Check a policy
(C) Perform an evaluation
(D) Revise a schedule

59. What type of products does the man's company sell?

(A) Children's clothing
(B) Shipping boxes
(C) Kitchen supplies
(D) Frozen foods

60. What is the woman being sent in a text message?

(A) A passcode
(B) A hyperlink
(C) A virtual ticket
(D) A photo

61. Why does the man say, "We'd like to supply our own models"?

(A) To decline an offer
(B) To express surprise
(C) To ask for an address
(D) To defend a product's quality

Investment Options	Useful Apps
Government bonds	Reliad
Real estate	Foundations
Large-scale stocks	Moonshot
Small-scale stocks	Paise

62. Where did the speakers meet?

(A) At university
(B) At a conference
(C) At an airport
(D) At a job interview

63. Why is the man calling?

(A) To remind the woman of a deadline
(B) To offer the woman a job opportunity
(C) To follow up on a request
(D) To help finalize an agenda

64. Look at the graphic. Which application did the woman download?

(A) Reliad
(B) Foundations
(C) Moonshot
(D) Paise

GO ON TO THE NEXT PAGE

Pool Weekend Schedule		
Classes	Day	Time
Water aerobics	Saturday	9:00 A.M.
Beginner swimming	Saturday	1:00 P.M.
Scuba diving	Sunday	8:00 A.M.
Lifeguard training	Sunday	2:00 P.M.

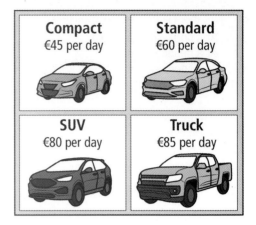

65. What does the woman ask the man to do?

(A) Clean a pool
(B) Open a workout area
(C) Review some information
(D) Check a member list

66. Look at the graphic. Which class will be canceled?

(A) Water aerobics
(B) Beginner swimming
(C) Scuba diving
(D) Lifeguard training

67. What will the speakers most likely do next?

(A) Contact a team coach
(B) Post some pool rules
(C) Teach a class
(D) Prepare some badges

68. What industry do the speakers most likely work in?

(A) Real estate
(B) Catering
(C) Tourism
(D) Film

69. Look at the graphic. What rate will the speakers pay to rent a vehicle?

(A) €45 per day
(B) €60 per day
(C) €80 per day
(D) €85 per day

70. What will the man most likely do next?

(A) Send some photographs
(B) Download a mobile application
(C) Contact a colleague
(D) Print a map

PART 4

Directions: You will hear some talks given by a single speaker. You will be asked to answer three questions about what the speaker says in each talk. Select the best response to each question and mark the letter (A), (B), (C), or (D) on your answer sheet. The talks will not be printed in your test book and will be spoken only one time.

71. Who is the speaker?

(A) A salesperson
(B) A board member
(C) A product developer
(D) A data analyst

72. What feature does the speaker mention?

(A) A shatterproof glass screen
(B) An advanced camera
(C) Extended battery life
(D) Satellite messaging

73. What does the speaker say she expects to happen?

(A) Job applications will increase.
(B) Demand will be high.
(C) Manufacturing will be delayed.
(D) Product reviews will be favorable.

74. Where is the speaker?

(A) At a recording studio
(B) At a convention center
(C) At an airport
(D) At a train station

75. What has caused a problem?

(A) Bad weather
(B) A staff shortage
(C) Overbooking
(D) A computer malfunction

76. What does the speaker say he has tried to do?

(A) Replace some equipment
(B) Contact an official
(C) Complete an assignment
(D) Change a reservation

77. What type of event is taking place?

(A) An anniversary celebration
(B) A product launch
(C) A retirement party
(D) A grand opening

78. What has the speaker helped the company with?

(A) Training executives
(B) Ensuring safety
(C) Increasing sales
(D) Designing displays

79. What is on the speaker's wall?

(A) A signed photograph
(B) An industry award
(C) A handmade clock
(D) A welcome note

80. Why does the speaker want to hold an event?

(A) To support a charity
(B) To thank some employees
(C) To welcome a new company executive
(D) To announce a company award

81. Why does the speaker say, "the forecast is calling for rain"?

(A) To acknowledge a mistake
(B) To complain about a venue
(C) To suggest postponing an event
(D) To justify a request

82. What does the speaker say he would like to do by the end of the week?

(A) Send out invitations
(B) Confirm a catering order
(C) Buy decorations
(D) Print some certificates

GO ON TO THE NEXT PAGE

83. Who is Claudia Tong?

(A) A journalist
(B) An environmental activist
(C) A company president
(D) A research scientist

84. What topic will tomorrow's broadcast focus on?

(A) Developing an alternative energy source
(B) Improving science education
(C) Regulating new technologies
(D) Making scientific advances safer

85. What does the speaker invite the listeners to do on social media?

(A) Suggest topics for future broadcasts
(B) Listen to previous broadcasts
(C) Post questions for a guest
(D) Access additional information on a topic

86. Why is the speaker in Hamburg?

(A) To meet some clients
(B) To train some employees
(C) To visit some relatives
(D) To appoint a branch manager

87. Which department does the speaker work in?

(A) Sales
(B) Information Technology
(C) Human Resources
(D) Community Outreach

88. Why does the speaker say, "it's been a bit cold here"?

(A) To disagree with a report
(B) To correct some information
(C) To explain a delay
(D) To offer advice

89. What does the speaker say took place last night?

(A) A sporting event
(B) A city council meeting
(C) A business convention
(D) A shopping mall opening

90. According to the speaker, what addition is being made to an airport?

(A) A shuttle station
(B) A hotel
(C) A food court
(D) An indoor garden

91. What will the listeners hear next?

(A) A stock market update
(B) An advertisement
(C) A weather report
(D) A traffic report

92. Who most likely is the speaker?

(A) An apartment complex manager
(B) A parking area attendant
(C) A commercial painter
(D) A real estate agent

93. What does the speaker mean when she says, "it's across the highway"?

(A) A shopping center is easy to find.
(B) A restaurant is worth visiting.
(C) A location is inconvenient.
(D) A suggestion is being considered.

94. What does the speaker ask Silvia to do?

(A) Call a contractor
(B) Hang signs
(C) Move a vehicle
(D) Purchase paint

Market Sectors

Hotels 15%
Hospitals 5%
Hair Salons 20%
Department Stores 60%

Vegetable Type	Unit Price
Cabbage	$15
Onion	$20
Tomato	$23
Spinach	$25

95. What type of product does the speaker's company sell?

(A) Hair care products
(B) Flavored teas
(C) Decorative candles
(D) Laundry detergent

96. Look at the graphic. Which market sector does the speaker want to focus on?

(A) Hospitals
(B) Department stores
(C) Hair salons
(D) Hotels

97. What new marketing feature does the speaker want to offer?

(A) Bulk discounts
(B) A variety of product sizes
(C) Different scents
(D) An e-newsletter

98. What is the purpose of the telephone call?

(A) To request a refund
(B) To update a delivery schedule
(C) To make a complaint
(D) To change an address

99. Look at the graphic. Which unit price has recently increased?

(A) $15
(B) $20
(C) $23
(D) $25

100. Who most likely is the speaker?

(A) A supermarket manager
(B) A restaurant owner
(C) A delivery driver
(D) A farmer

This is the end of the Listening test. Turn to Part 5 in your test book.

GO ON TO THE NEXT PAGE

ETS 기출
모의고사 1회

READING TEST

In the Reading test, you will read a variety of texts and answer several different types of reading comprehension questions. The entire Reading test will last 75 minutes. There are three parts, and directions are given for each part. You are encouraged to answer as many questions as possible within the time allowed.

You must mark your answers on the separate answer sheet. Do not write your answers in your test book.

PART 5

Directions: A word or phrase is missing in each of the sentences below. Four answer choices are given below each sentence. Select the best answer to complete the sentence. Then mark the letter (A), (B), (C), or (D) on your answer sheet.

101. Known for ------- outdoor sculptures, Irina Reyes also creates artwork on paper.

(A) her
(B) she
(C) hers
(D) herself

102. Dr. Ko ------- his partners have a special interest in rehabilitative medicine.

(A) and
(B) but
(C) so
(D) both

103. Freshly made sandwiches can be purchased from the food truck ------- the rear of the parking lot.

(A) even
(B) do
(C) get
(D) at

104. Customers who wish to return an ------- to the Grover Garden Center are required to present a receipt.

(A) item
(B) items
(C) itemize
(D) itemized

105. The Mildorn Processing Plant ------- Nelson City upgraded its equipment for faster production.

(A) for
(B) in
(C) as
(D) to

106. City officials reported that the renovations to the public library have progressed -------.

(A) steadiest
(B) steadiness
(C) steady
(D) steadily

107. The Delfin Naval Museum is open from 10:00 A.M. ------- 5:30 P.M. Monday through Friday.

(A) since
(B) until
(C) during
(D) except

108. Amber Kitchen Supply ------- a one-year warranty on all its products.

(A) provider
(B) provides
(C) provide
(D) providing

109. The Blainesville Downtown Amphitheater hosts many events that are ------- with the city's residents.
(A) popular
(B) careful
(C) happy
(D) helpful

110. Bestform Stationery now sells quality paper goods through the mail, online, and in retail -------.
(A) store
(B) stored
(C) storing
(D) stores

111. New residents should contact the Ewing Water Department ------- by e-mail or phone to activate their account.
(A) than
(B) either
(C) besides
(D) as if

112. Applications for the software engineer position ------- online at vntsystems.net.
(A) submitted
(B) are submitting
(C) must submit
(D) must be submitted

113. The board of directors is seeking new members, ------- individuals with experience in the technology sector.
(A) especially
(B) sincerely
(C) positively
(D) seriously

114. Akemi's Café is looking forward to welcoming back customers ------- a two-month renovation project.
(A) because of
(B) now that
(C) after
(D) when

115. Following an ------- break of ten years, the band The Myth Riders will resume its live shows.
(A) extend
(B) extended
(C) extension
(D) extending

116. Travelers should ensure they have all required documents before ------- home.
(A) expanding
(B) leaving
(C) allowing
(D) managing

117. Quailux Depot has the right facilities for all your ------- storage needs at affordable rates.
(A) residing
(B) to reside
(C) residential
(D) resides

118. Following a review of the strongest résumés, Mr. Eiji Arakaki was ------- the most qualified individual for the position.
(A) neutrally
(B) clearly
(C) usually
(D) very

119. A motorcycle dealership is opening a few blocks from where the old ------- used to be.
(A) me
(B) us
(C) one
(D) other

120. Mr. Bajaj, a robotics expert, ------- provides consultation services to companies interested in industrial automation.
(A) highly
(B) comparably
(C) frequently
(D) deeply

GO ON TO THE NEXT PAGE ➤

121. The marketing team made a ------- decision to keep conducting customer surveys.
    (A) collect
    (B) collects
    (C) collective
    (D) collectively

122. Each Chefware pan ------- with a twelve-year customer satisfaction guarantee.
    (A) includes
    (B) serves
    (C) adjusts
    (D) comes

123. The delivery company has ------- experienced delays when transporting goods from the factory in Newcastle.
    (A) occasioned
    (B) occasional
    (C) occasionally
    (D) occasioning

124. The contract will be awarded ------- all required documents are received.
    (A) yet
    (B) instead
    (C) similarly
    (D) once

125. The operations manual states which equipment parts must be lubricated at the ------- of the shift.
    (A) start
    (B) day
    (C) place
    (D) side

126. The manager of Lucky Bridge Restaurant asked ------- willing to work overtime to write their name on a sign-up sheet.
    (A) those
    (B) which
    (C) who
    (D) yours

127. As expected, the internal audit ------- that the company had overpaid for travel expenses by a small amount.
    (A) having revealed
    (B) revealing
    (C) to reveal
    (D) revealed

128. The latest ------- of decorations in stock indicates that Festal Seasons Ltd. is well prepared for the holiday rush.
    (A) proposal
    (B) inventory
    (C) consideration
    (D) commitment

129. Frinson Technologies' online catalog contains detailed ------- of its software products.
    (A) computers
    (B) salespeople
    (C) predictions
    (D) descriptions

130. All bank transfers are ------- to review and could be delayed if an issue is identified.
    (A) required
    (B) imaginary
    (C) conscious
    (D) subject

PART 6

Directions: Read the texts that follow. A word, phrase, or sentence is missing in parts of each text. Four answer choices for each question are given below the text. Select the best answer to complete the text. Then mark the letter (A), (B), (C), or (D) on your answer sheet.

Questions 131-134 refer to the following article.

Norlich Agricultural Brands Opens New Frozen Vegetable Plant

Norlich Agricultural Brands has completed construction of its new vegetable-processing plant in Eamley. It replaces an outdated ------- located nearby. The new plant can process 10 million kilos
                                131.
of corn, peas, and beans annually. ------- . The new plant will ------- use 25 percent less water per
                                    132.   133.
kilo of product.

The vegetables processed at the new site will come from regional growers. Norlich works closely with its local network of suppliers ------- that vegetables are picked and processed when they are
                                              134.
ripest.

131. (A) shop
     (B) facility
     (C) machine
     (D) monument

132. (A) This figure represents a 20 percent
         increase over the old plant.
     (B) Norlich has been a part of the local
         economy for more than 50 years.
     (C) Some local families have worked at
         Norlich for generations.
     (D) A plant-based diet can be a healthy
         alternative.

133. (A) therefore
     (B) instead
     (C) quite
     (D) also

134. (A) ensured
     (B) to ensure
     (C) ensures
     (D) will ensure

GO ON TO THE NEXT PAGE

Questions 135-138 refer to the following e-mail.

To: Greater Metro Bank
From: Joe Michaelson
Date: December 2
Subject: Loan request
Attachment: Business plan

Dear Sir or Madam,

I own and operate a local bakery, Joe's Breads and Treats. It has become increasingly ------- **135.**
over the past five years. ------- , my bakery is doing so well that I am planning to open a coffee **136.**
shop, which will also sell some of my baked goods. I plan to locate this new business on the
north side of town so I can serve new customers. To make my plan a reality, though, I need to
request a loan. ------- . **137.**

I have attached my business plan to this e-mail so you can see precisely ------- I plan to use the **138.**
loan. Once you have read it over, I hope you will contact me regarding the next steps.

Thank you,

Joe Michaelson

135. (A) important
(B) necessary
(C) affordable
(D) successful

136. (A) In fact
(B) Of course
(C) In addition
(D) On the contrary

137. (A) I will renovate my bakery as soon as I save enough money.
(B) I also required a loan to start my first business.
(C) My customers highly recommend my products.
(D) I hope your bank can provide me with this loan.

138. (A) for
(B) that
(C) how
(D) much

Questions 139-142 refer to the following letter.

October 10

Julia Souza Gomes
Burlama Farms, Inc.
548 Burke Road
Melbourne
Victoria 3126

Dear Ms. Gomes:

Thank you for offering me the opportunity ------- as a mechanical engineer at Burlama Farms. I
                                          139.
thoroughly enjoyed meeting you and the other technicians during my ------- last month. However,
                                                                    140.
I have already taken a similar position at Sugo Agroindustrial. The company is closer to my

home, and working there will allow me more time with my family. ------- . I hope to see you -------
                                                                141.   **142.**
at a future conference or other agricultural event.

Sincerely,

Leonard Hale

---

139. (A) to work
(B) works
(C) that worked
(D) working

140. (A) show
(B) vacation
(C) interview
(D) presentation

141. (A) Sugo Agroindustrial is certainly an
impressive company.
(B) I would be happy to provide you with
additional references.
(C) I can recommend a good friend for the
job.
(D) The decision was very difficult given my
interest in your products.

142. (A) too
(B) then
(C) there
(D) again

Questions 143-146 refer to the following notice.

Notice of Public Meeting

The Sulbury Town Council will hold a public meeting on Tuesday, October 3, at 7:30 P.M. The purpose of the meeting is to discuss the plan for ------- Clifton Road. The primary goal is to make
143.
the road safer for pedestrians and bicyclists. A secondary aim of the ------- is to reduce traffic
144.
jams. Any modifications ------- must allow easy access to shops, offices, homes, and businesses.
145.
For this reason, existing sidewalks are expected to be extended and new traffic lights installed
where needed. ------- . Members of the public are encouraged to review all available information
146.
about the plan before attending the meeting.

---

143. (A) using
 (B) closing
 (C) widening
 (D) renaming

144. (A) crew
 (B) project
 (C) signage
 (D) gathering

145. (A) prior to
 (B) as of
 (C) having set
 (D) made

146. (A) Store owners must take care to keep sidewalks clear of obstructions.
 (B) We are now accepting proposals from urban-planning firms.
 (C) Several residents asked whether traffic studies had been commissioned.
 (D) Details of the proposed plan can be found on the Sulbury municipal Web site.

PART 7

Directions: In this part you will read a selection of texts, such as magazine and newspaper articles, e-mails, and instant messages. Each text or set of texts is followed by several questions. Select the best answer for each question and mark the letter (A), (B), (C), or (D) on your answer sheet.

Questions 147-148 refer to the following e-mail.

To:	Ticket Holders
From:	Magenta Theater
Date:	November 12
Subject:	Chloe Chang concert

Dear Ticket Holder:

We regret to inform you that tomorrow's 8:00 P.M. performance by Chloe Chang has been postponed because the singer is ill. We apologize for any disappointment or inconvenience this situation causes. We ask that you please retain your tickets while we work to reschedule the performance. No other action is needed on your part at the moment. Details about the rescheduled performance date will be e-mailed to you as soon as they are available.

For any questions, contact the Magenta Theater box office at 555-0112. Again, we sincerely apologize for the inconvenience.

Kind regards,

Magenta Theater Staff

147. What is the purpose of the e-mail?

(A) To explain a new procedure for purchasing tickets
(B) To announce a change to a performance
(C) To offer patrons discounted tickets for a performance
(D) To promote an upcoming concert tour

148. What are ticket holders advised to do?

(A) Save their tickets
(B) Send an e-mail to Ms. Chang
(C) Call the box office immediately
(D) Arrive at the theater by 8:00 P.M.

GO ON TO THE NEXT PAGE

Questions 149-150 refer to the following notice.

Upcoming Bolano Lunch

It is time for a favourite annual tradition! Bolano, one of our most popular restaurant partners, is once again providing a free lunch on 2 June for the entire Kiyoti Event Planning staff in honour of our continued business collaboration. As everyone who has worked on an event with Bolano knows, their food is delicious. Please speak with the receptionist to register for the lunch by 31 May. We want to ensure that there is enough food for everyone.

The lunch will be served buffet style in our cafeteria starting at noon. Beverages will also be provided, so there is no need for you to prepare anything for the event. We will be circulating a thank-you card for Bolano's staff, so please make sure to add your signature by 1 June. We look forward to seeing everyone there.

---

149. Why is Bolano providing lunch for Kiyoti Event Planning staff?

(A) To celebrate Kiyoti Event Planning's anniversary
(B) To share samples of new menu items
(C) To express appreciation for a business partnership
(D) To demonstrate a new catering process

150. What are staff members asked to do before the event?

(A) Sign a card
(B) Make a payment
(C) Visit a restaurant
(D) Prepare some decorations

Questions 151-152 refer to the following advertisement.

Pamela's Clothes for Kids—shop now!

Playtime clothes for children shouldn't be boring or trite! At Pamela's Clothes for Kids, we believe children's clothing should be comfortable, affordable, and stylish. This is why we use only quality materials and thoughtful designs across our entire line of clothing for children.

Plus, moms and dads demand that the clothes kids play in must be sturdy and easy to launder. Our jeans, overalls, T-shirts, shoes, swimwear, chinos, shorts, and sweaters are all machine washable, stain resistant, and quick drying.

Make a clothing playdate today for your youngsters at one of our fifteen retail locations! Or check us out online at https://pamelasclothesforkids.com.

151. What is being advertised?
    (A) A new brand
    (B) A fashion show
    (C) A clothing store
    (D) A children's gathering

152. What is indicated about the line of clothing for children?
    (A) It includes clothing that can be easily cleaned.
    (B) It is approved by school officials.
    (C) It was created by a famous fashion designer.
    (D) It will soon be available in retail stores.

GO ON TO THE NEXT PAGE

Questions 153-154 refer to the following text-message chain.

Luis Olivera (8:10 A.M.)
I am confirming our 2:00 P.M. meeting today to discuss which engineers we want to hire for the Harland City water pipeline project. We interviewed five engineers, and we have two positions to fill.

Suzanne Arnold (8:12 A.M.)
Yes, I'll be there. I have another meeting scheduled until 2:00 P.M., so I might be a few minutes late. Why don't I text you when I am on my way?

Luis Olivera (8:15 A.M.)
That makes sense. I also want to show you the design plans. Will Samantha Martinez from human resources be joining us for the meeting?

Suzanne Arnold (8:17 A.M.)
She's away at a conference this week, but she e-mailed the hiring guidelines to me. She wants our final determination by Monday.

Luis Olivera (8:20 A.M.)
OK. See you this afternoon.

153. At 8:15 A.M., what does Mr. Olivera most likely mean when he writes, "That makes sense"?

(A) He is in favor of the pipeline design plans.
(B) He agrees with Ms. Arnold's offer to send a notification.
(C) He would prefer to meet Ms. Arnold on another day.
(D) He understands that more engineers will probably be needed.

154. What do Ms. Arnold and Mr. Olivera need to do by Monday?

(A) Interview some job candidates
(B) Prepare a conference presentation
(C) Decide who will be hired
(D) Edit the guidelines Ms. Martinez sent

Questions 155-157 refer to the following Web page.

https://www.taoblar.com/features

| History | **Features** | Shop | Contact Us |

A well-designed desk lamp is vital for any workspace, whether at home or in the office. Yet people tend to buy lamps without much thought, and some will undoubtedly settle on a less-than-ideal lighting solution. We think that with a bit of planning, however, consumers can avoid wasting their money and being disappointed with poor products.

Every product manufactured by Taoblar, Inc., is fully adjustable to direct light where needed. The Model TT-1, for example, is our most compact lamp and is designed specifically for small or narrow computer desks. It has a very focused light, while Models TT-2 and TT-3 are intended for larger workspaces and thus cast a wider beam. Furthermore, all Taoblar, Inc., lamps are dimmable and have a simple knob for controlling the lamp's brightness to whatever degree the user wishes. This helps avoid eyestrain and fatigue.

Our lamps have become mainstays in all types of workplaces. Recently, a panel of top design specialists examined the features of our product line and concluded that Taoblar, Inc., was worthy of their Excellence in Design award. To view all our offerings, visit our Shop page.

ETS 기출

모의고사 1회

155. What does the Web page describe?

(A) Assembly instructions for computer workstations
(B) An awards celebration for industrial design
(C) The desirable aspects of Taoblar, Inc., products
(D) The process Taoblar, Inc., uses to manufacture its products

156. What is suggested about the Model TT-1 ?

(A) It is based on a well-known work of art.
(B) It is currently out of stock.
(C) It is the company's best-selling product.
(D) It is the smallest model the company makes.

157. What is indicated about Taoblar, Inc.?

(A) Its products have earned industry recognition.
(B) Its products are known for their durability.
(C) It recently redesigned an important lighting component.
(D) It plans to open more stores in other regions.

GO ON TO THE NEXT PAGE

Questions 158-160 refer to the following e-mail.

```
╔══════════════════════ *E-mail* ══════════════════════╗

   To:        Sue Koh <sue_koh@swipemail.com>

   From:      Customer relations <customer_relations@harborhopferries.ca>

   Date:      24 July

   Subject:   Your recent trip

   Dear Ms. Koh,

   Thank you for using Harborhop Ferries on 7 July to go to Galiano Island and on 12 July
   to return from it. We hope you were pleased with our service.

   For 50 years now, Harborhop Ferries has helped to support and strengthen the economy
   of Galiano Island, bringing visitors to the area to enjoy its spectacular beaches, scenic
   biking and hiking trails, shops, and restaurants. While our role in boosting the island's
   economy might be small, we nevertheless take it very seriously. Therefore, so as to keep
   improving our service to the public, we invite you to take a few minutes to answer
   some questions about your experience with us. You can complete the survey on our Web
   site at www.harborhopferries.ca/survey.

   As a thank-you gift, we will send you a 20 percent discount voucher that you can apply
   toward the cost of your next trip with us. It is good for up to six months after the date
   of issue.

   Thank you for your time, and we look forward to seeing you again.

   Sincerely,

   Customer Relations, Harborhop Ferries
```

158. What is suggested about Ms. Koh?

(A) She brought her bicycle on the boat.
(B) She often uses Harborhop Ferries.
(C) She usually visits Galiano Island in July.
(D) She spent several nights on Galiano Island.

159. What is indicated about Harborhop Ferries?

(A) Its boats have onboard restaurants.
(B) It has been in business for fifty years.
(C) It offers service to Galiano Island several times a day.
(D) It will stop service to Galiano Island in six months.

160. What is the purpose of the e-mail?

(A) To confirm a ferry reservation
(B) To announce changes to a ferry service
(C) To ask for feedback on a service provided
(D) To report on the economic growth of an island

To:	Angelina Noboa
From:	Oliver Robinson
Subject:	Information
Date:	1 October
Attachment:	🔗 Robinson book 1

Dear Angelina,

As a member of the Employee Wellness Committee, you know that we recently started a walking club here at Walbourne Manufacturing. You will be pleased to know that 32 employees have already signed up! — [1] —. A group walk is planned for 16 October, and we might get even more walkers to join before then. — [2] —. The group is planning to meet in the cafeteria as the starting point for the walk.

Since you were unable to attend the last meeting, I also wanted to let you know that the committee has decided to create a cookbook containing healthy recipes submitted by employees. The recipes could be collected on an internal Web site. — [3] —. Alternatively, we could have the recipes printed and bound as a book, which we could then sell as a fund-raiser. — [4] —. I've attached a proposal to send to managers for approval. Let me know what you think!

Sincerely,

Oliver

161. Why did Mr. Robinson send the e-mail to Ms. Noboa?

(A) To ask her to join a club
(B) To invite her to attend a fund-raiser
(C) To provide an update on committee activities
(D) To inform her that she has won a contest

162. What is scheduled to take place on October 16 ?

(A) A book reading
(B) An online party
(C) An exercise event
(D) A planning meeting

163. In which of the positions marked [1], [2], [3], and [4] does the following sentence best belong?

"Books always make great gifts for friends and family."

(A) [1]
(B) [2]
(C) [3]
(D) [4]

GO ON TO THE NEXT PAGE

Questions 164-167 refer to the following e-mail.

To:	Film Chat Distribution List
From:	<newsletter@filmchat.ca>
Date:	October 17
Subject:	Daily film chat

Dear Film Chat Friends,

Today's spotlight is on an early Peter Kucharsky film. In the past decade, Kucharsky has directed intense action films such as *Billion Dollar Rescue* and *Far Space Adventure*. These successes have established Kucharsky's reputation. But before directing blockbusters, Kucharsky explored other film genres.

His first film from fifteen years ago, *Snow Song*, is a family drama. It tells the story of an older shop owner, played by Anna Bednarska, who lives with her bright and creative grandson, portrayed by actor and musician Bratan Malinowski. One day, while reading a book, the grandson comes across a poem that has a profound effect on him. In fact, it transforms both his and his grandmother's lives.

The subject matter is completely different from that of Kucharsky's later films. And yet, we can already see Kucharsky's talent for making films that evoke emotion. Grandmother and grandson have occasional misunderstandings, but these are offset with moments of obvious love and devotion. Also noticeable is the director's ability to bring a touch of humor to all situations.

To view this softer side of Kucharsky, be sure to check out a special matinee of *Snow Song* at the Bijou Film Festival this coming Saturday at 12 noon.

164. According to the e-mail, what is Peter Kucharsky known for?

(A) Acting in plays
(B) Directing movies
(C) Composing music
(D) Publishing journalism

165. In the film *Snow Song*, what causes a change in the main characters' lives?

(A) A business failure
(B) A family celebration
(C) A work of literature
(D) A misunderstanding

166. Who is Bratan Malinowski?

(A) A performer
(B) A newsletter subscriber
(C) A boy's grandfather
(D) A shop's owner

167. The word "softer" in paragraph 4, line 1, is closest in meaning to

(A) newer
(B) smoother
(C) quieter
(D) gentler

Questions 168-171 refer to the following memo.

MEMO

To: All Nanvero Employees
From: Clive Bataya, President
Date: April 18
Subject: New sabbatical-leave benefit

Nanvero is pleased to introduce our new sabbatical-leave program. Employees become eligible after ten years of service and can apply for up to six weeks of leave. Nanvero is offering staff members 50 percent of their usual salary while taking sabbatical.

Sabbaticals free employees to engage in activities they normally would be unable to pursue. — [1] —. These may include traveling, especially overseas; volunteering, especially on extended projects or in another country; researching topics of interest or relevance to their careers; studying or training to advance or change careers; or pursuing arts-related activities, such as writing or painting.

— [2] —. Advance requests will enable your supervisor to arrange coverage for your job while you are away. You may use available Paid Time Off (PTO) days to extend your sabbatical.

We sincerely hope this new benefit will show our appreciation for our veteran employees. — [3] —. Visit the Human Resources tab of the Nanvero employee intranet for a complete set of rules and to access the sabbatical request form. The form must be completed online and submitted electronically. — [4] —.

168. What is one expectation of staff who ask to take sabbatical leave?

(A) They should be willing to receive reduced pay during this period.
(B) They should agree not to work for any other company while on leave.
(C) They should submit a report when they return from their sabbatical.
(D) They should occasionally check in with management while out on leave.

169. What is NOT mentioned as a reason for a sabbatical request?

(A) Conducting research
(B) Traveling internationally
(C) Advancing professional skills
(D) Spending time with family members

170. According to the memo, why is Nanvero implementing the new policy?

(A) To reduce employee turnover
(B) To attract potential employees
(C) To reward long-term employees
(D) To save money on employee salaries

171. In which of the positions marked [1], [2], [3], and [4] does the following sentence best belong?

"Sabbatical leave must be requested at least three months prior to the desired start date."

(A) [1]
(B) [2]
(C) [3]
(D) [4]

GO ON TO THE NEXT PAGE

Questions 172-175 refer to the following online chat discussion.

Anne Wymer (11:21 A.M.)
Good morning, everyone. I want to make certain everything is set for the trade show next week. It's such an important event for us, and I'll be away at my cousin's wedding.

Larry Bonnet (11:22 A.M.)
The event coordinator has confirmed that our booth is ready. She also assured me that we'll have access to electrical outlets, wireless Internet, and space for demonstrations.

Hae-Jin Sung (11:25 A.M.)
I have the posters and brochures. The photos are stunning! We also have videos to play in the booth. Some show us putting in counters, floors, and appliances, others show our projects in a before-and-after format, and one highlights our total redesign of the cooking area at the Marlton house. Our intern Jacob has been handling the social media. He'll be live streaming our event demonstrations on our Web site.

Larry Bonnet (11:26 A.M.)
We really lucked out when we found Jacob!

Hae-Jin Sung (11:27 A.M.)
There's no question about it! So, yes, the materials and media are all set.

Martha Varela (11:28 A.M.)
I'll be here handling in-home estimates and sales. I want to point out that if this quarter continues the way it's begun, our sales figures will be higher than they've ever been.

Anne Wymer (11:30 A.M.)
Wonderful! OK, let's have a quick meeting on Thursday morning, but please let me know before that if any problems arise.

172. Where do the writers most likely work?

(A) At a photography studio
(B) At an electrical-supply shop
(C) At an event-planning company
(D) At a kitchen-remodeling business

173. Why does Ms. Wymer mention her cousin's wedding?

(A) To explain why she will miss the trade show
(B) To inform her colleagues of a change in the trade show's schedule
(C) To suggest that she might arrive late to the trade show
(D) To compare the trade show to a different type of event

174. At 11:27 A.M., what does Ms. Sung most likely mean when she writes, "There's no question about it"?

(A) She agrees that an intern has done good work.
(B) She thinks that a live streamed event was successful.
(C) She can confirm that some items were delivered.
(D) She believes that using social media is important.

175. What does Ms. Varela indicate?

(A) That an appointment had to be rescheduled
(B) That sales have been increasing at a favorable rate
(C) That the quarter began more slowly than expected
(D) That she may be late for a sales meeting

GO ON TO THE NEXT PAGE

Vroman Manufacturing
Workplace Safety Inspection Checklist   Date completed: April 11
Inspector: Tamar Nuriya, Operations Department

Area	Tasks	Time Completed
Workshop	• Verify that safety glasses are available in the entryway. • Ensure that tools are in good condition. • Check all electrical cords for damage and fraying. • Inspect workstations for debris or hazards. • Take inventory of the first aid kit and replace any used and expired supplies.	9:00 a.m.
Storeroom	• Make sure aisles are clear of hazardous obstructions. • Confirm that shelving and stacks of boxes are stable.	10:15 a.m.
Offices	• Inspect each office and cubicle to verify that no electric heaters or other heat-producing devices are present. • Examine extension cords to make sure only one device is plugged into each cord.	11:00 a.m.
Lunchroom	• Confirm that refrigerator temperature is between 3 and 5 degrees Celsius.	11:45 a.m.

Workplace Safety Compliance Report

Filed by: Tamar Nuriya

Report date: April 11

While performing the safety inspection for this month, I observed the following instances of noncompliance.

In the workshop, a table saw at workstation 7 had a dull, rusty blade, which can prevent the saw from moving smoothly. I tagged the saw so that it would not be used until after repairs are made.

In the storeroom, I found boxes stacked in an aisle where they were a tripping hazard. I told the manager they needed to be placed on the shelves.

In office 114, I found an electric coffeepot in use. I advised the occupant to unplug and remove the item and stated that I would make an unannounced follow-up inspection.

176. According to the checklist, when was the first aid kit restocked?

(A) At 9:00 A.M.
(B) At 10:15 A.M.
(C) At 11:00 A.M.
(D) At 11:45 A.M.

177. How often is the checklist used?

(A) Daily
(B) Weekly
(C) Monthly
(D) Annually

178. Where did Ms. Nuriya notice an obstruction?

(A) In the offices
(B) In the workshop
(C) In the lunchroom
(D) In the storeroom

179. In the report, the word "placed" in paragraph 3, line 2, is closest in meaning to

(A) put
(B) given
(C) ranked
(D) identified

180. What does Ms. Nuriya indicate she will do?

(A) Repair a tool
(B) Revisit an office
(C) Label some boxes
(D) File an additional report

GO ON TO THE NEXT PAGE

Long Road Productions

Movie Title: *Anchored Ascent*
Director: Lee Jiang
Target Audience: 18 to 30 year olds; adventure-story enthusiasts

PRODUCTION SCHEDULE OVERVIEW (tentative)

Preproduction: January
- 25 January – Financial projection report to investors
- Finalise cast contracts – Vernon Scafidi, Jenn Ahn
- Secure filming location permits and contracts

Production: February–May
- Principal filming
- 28 February and 25 May – Interim finance reports to investors

Postproduction: June–August
- Finalise edits to the film

Promotional campaign and launch: September–October
- 15 September: Premiere film at Pinelands Film Festival
- 1 October: General distribution to cinemas
- Weekly revenue report to investors

Director Lee Jiang Discusses
Anchored Ascent

GALWAY (15 October)—After a month's delay, *Anchored Ascent* premiered at the Pinelands Film Festival this week. This film tells the true story of acclaimed mountain climber Quinn Deacon.

According to the director, Lee Jiang, the film crew endured several production setbacks that caused concern among investors. First, lengthy negotiations with actor Vernon Scafidi ultimately fell through when his salary demands could not be met. "Luckily, Mark Tobel was available to take on the role, and he joined our cast right at the beginning of February," Mr. Jiang explained, "so we still could have met our production deadlines. However, filming of outdoor scenes was postponed for six weeks due to an unusually heavy snow season and impassable roads."

The delay in outdoor camerawork meant Long Road Productions had to pay for an extension to their filming permit. "In the end, though, starting a month later meant longer daylight hours, helping us make up some of the lost time." If the audience response at the Pinelands Film Festival is any indication, the movie's financial backers will be quite pleased with their return on investment.

Anchored Ascent is now set for general distribution to cinemas on 1 November.

181. According to the production schedule, what is true about the investors?

(A) They are between the ages of 18 and 30.
(B) They selected filming locations.
(C) They attended the Pinelands Film Festival.
(D) They received several financial updates.

182. What is the purpose of the article?

(A) To describe the difficulties encountered while making a film
(B) To tell the true story that inspired a movie
(C) To provide details about Mr. Jiang's career
(D) To explain how filming permits are obtained

183. What caused the interruption in filming *Anchored Ascent*?

(A) Observance of a national holiday
(B) A change in the film's director
(C) Poor weather conditions
(D) The need to pay for a new location

184. During which phase of the production schedule did Mr. Tobel become involved with the film?

(A) Production
(B) Preproduction
(C) Postproduction
(D) Promotional campaign and launch

185. Based on the article, what is mentioned about the audience at the Pinelands Film Festival?

(A) They expected Mr. Scafidi to be in the film.
(B) They enjoyed the film.
(C) They watched the film in September.
(D) They paid extra for tickets.

To:	Harris Nofrim
From:	Sal Pollestro
Date:	September 10
Subject:	Cleaning service for Safferton Museum

Hello, Harris,

As you probably know, our cleaning service comes to the museum once a week on the day it is closed to the public. When the cleaners come on September 15, please let them in when they arrive at 8:00 a.m. Also, please make sure they wash the large windows in the pottery gallery. The windows there are frequently missed by cleaning crews because of the heavy curtains that often hide them.

If you have any questions, please give me a call, or you can just ask me at tomorrow's staff meeting.

Thank you,

Sal

Video Viewing Area: Desert Week Films

Wednesday, Sept. 16	*Desert Colors*	10 A.M. and 2 P.M.
Wednesday, Sept. 16	*The Art of the Southwest*	Noon and 4 P.M.
Thursday, Sept. 17	*The Paintings of Lizzie McPhree*	10 A.M. and 2 P.M.
Thursday, Sept. 17	*Natural Gems of the Desert West*	Noon and 4 P.M.

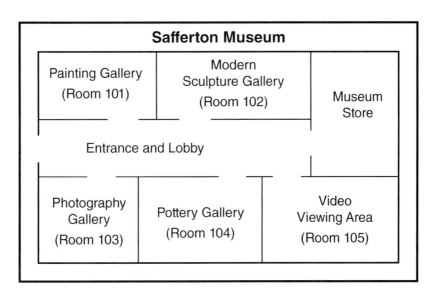

Safferton Museum

Painting Gallery (Room 101)	Modern Sculpture Gallery (Room 102)	Museum Store

Entrance and Lobby

Photography Gallery (Room 103)	Pottery Gallery (Room 104)	Video Viewing Area (Room 105)

186. Who most likely is Mr. Nofrim?

(A) A pottery artist
(B) A museum employee
(C) A cleaning professional
(D) An art collector

187. On what day of the week is the Safferton Museum closed?

(A) On Monday
(B) On Tuesday
(C) On Wednesday
(D) On Thursday

188. According to the schedule, what video will be shown on September 17 at noon?

(A) *Desert Colors*
(B) *The Art of the Southwest*
(C) *The Paintings of Lizzie McPhree*
(D) *Natural Gems of the Desert West*

189. In what room does Mr. Pollestro want the windows cleaned?

(A) In room 102
(B) In room 103
(C) In room 104
(D) In room 105

190. According to the map, where is the museum store located?

(A) Adjacent to the painting gallery
(B) Between the pottery gallery and the video viewing area
(C) Next to the modern sculpture gallery
(D) Directly across from the photography gallery

GO ON TO THE NEXT PAGE

From:	m.carmen@olive.com
To:	customerservice@valliegrocery.com
Date:	April 1
Subject:	Curbside pickup

Dear Vallie Grocery Customer Service,

I moved to Langley City last month and find that prices at your store are very competitive. However, I was surprised to learn that curbside pickup is not available. As a busy professional, I would find it extremely convenient to select and pay for groceries online, then pick everything up on my way home from work. I would even be willing to pay a small fee for this service.

Would you consider offering curbside pickup? Doing so would provide an added incentive for me to patronize Vallie Grocery instead of the Foodmore located down the street from you.

Kind regards,

Mary Carmen

E-Mail Message

From:	tenyuu.sakai@valliegrocery.com
To:	lien.cheng@valliegrocery.com
Date:	June 15
Subject:	Curbside Pickup

Dear Ms. Cheng,

I am writing to let you know that every week at least two or three customers ask me why our store does not offer curbside pickup. I explain that our staff is too small and that our Web site is not set up for this service. I am increasingly concerned that we are losing customers to our closest competitor, which has been offering curbside pickup for several years. Since I have the technical skills to update our Web site to process online orders, I could update the Web site by the end of June, and if we hire one or more additional workers, I believe we could increase our store's profits and customer base.

Sincerely,

Tenyuu Sakai
Customer Service Manager

Vallie Grocery Employee News
July Issue

Curbside pickup to begin on August 1

Vallie Grocery is implementing curbside pickup. Here is how it will work:

1. Customers place and pay for their orders online.

2. A team member collects and bags the groceries, then texts the customer.

3. Customers wait in a designated parking space and reply to the text with their space number.

4. A team member brings the groceries to the customer's vehicle.

Let's work together to make this new program a success!

---

191. What does Ms. Carmen suggest in the first e-mail?

(A) Vallie Grocery is located between her home and her workplace.
(B) She has lived in Langley City for many years.
(C) Curbside pickup is no longer offered at Foodmore.
(D) Foodmore's prices are lower than Vallie Grocery's.

192. What can be concluded about Ms. Carmen?

(A) She was recently interviewed by Ms. Cheng.
(B) She is one of many shoppers who requested curbside pickup.
(C) She is employed in the food-services industry.
(D) She believes that curbside pickup should be free.

193. What is the purpose of the second e-mail?

(A) To suggest longer store hours
(B) To schedule a meeting
(C) To recommend a new service
(D) To discuss a projected budget

194. In the second e-mail, what does Mr. Sakai offer to do?

(A) Post a help-wanted sign in his store
(B) Reassign some members of his team
(C) Expand the customer complaint department
(D) Add an enhancement to his employer's Web site

195. What can be concluded about Vallie Grocery?

(A) It earned more profits from its delivery service than expected.
(B) It requires customers to bring their own shopping bags.
(C) It does not allow its employees to accept tips from customers.
(D) It will have a larger staff in August than it did in April.

GO ON TO THE NEXT PAGE

Questions 196-200 refer to the following report introduction, e-mail, and note.

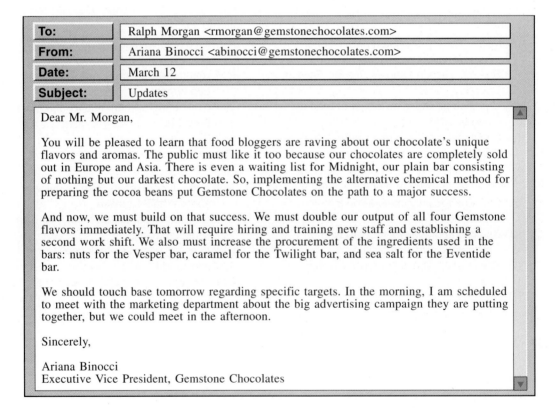

Introduction: An Alternative Technique for Processing Cocoa Beans

Our study focused on the processing of cocoa beans for the purpose of making chocolate. In the traditional method, cocoa beans are harvested and, before they are used to make chocolate, they are spread out and covered for a few days to ferment. The covering most favored is banana peels. During this time, microbes go to work reducing the beans' bitterness and enhancing certain flavors and aromas that are later experienced by consumers of the chocolate.

In this research, our team evaluated an alternative process called moist incubation. The raw cocoa beans were dried and then rehydrated and heated for 72 hours in a special liquid. They were then redried and used to make chocolate bars. This process, which relies on an artificial chemical reaction rather than natural microbes, was significantly faster than the traditional method and produced much more predictable results. The team also found a notable increase, under controlled circumstances, of more complex and intriguing flavor profiles; the incubated chocolate had higher levels of chemical compounds that deliver aromas and flavors that are suggestive of different fruits.

To:	Ralph Morgan <rmorgan@gemstonechocolates.com>
From:	Ariana Binocci <abinocci@gemstonechocolates.com>
Date:	March 12
Subject:	Updates

Dear Mr. Morgan,

You will be pleased to learn that food bloggers are raving about our chocolate's unique flavors and aromas. The public must like it too because our chocolates are completely sold out in Europe and Asia. There is even a waiting list for Midnight, our plain bar consisting of nothing but our darkest chocolate. So, implementing the alternative chemical method for preparing the cocoa beans put Gemstone Chocolates on the path to a major success.

And now, we must build on that success. We must double our output of all four Gemstone flavors immediately. That will require hiring and training new staff and establishing a second work shift. We also must increase the procurement of the ingredients used in the bars: nuts for the Vesper bar, caramel for the Twilight bar, and sea salt for the Eventide bar.

We should touch base tomorrow regarding specific targets. In the morning, I am scheduled to meet with the marketing department about the big advertising campaign they are putting together, but we could meet in the afternoon.

Sincerely,

Ariana Binocci
Executive Vice President, Gemstone Chocolates

A Gift for You

Dear Mr. Ewing,

Enclosed find the big package of Gemstone chocolate bars that I brought back from my trip to Korea. They seem like a lovely way to thank you for filling in for me while I was on vacation. My favorite is the one with sea salt, but I know how much you enjoy nuts. I hoped to get more of these as gifts for other staff members, but the shop I went to only allowed one jumbo variety pack per customer, and the other shops were sold out. Perhaps we can share some with them.

Your friend and colleague,

Paulette Kwon
Paulette Kwon

---

196. What is indicated in the report introduction about the traditional method of processing cocoa beans?

(A) It uses parts from banana plants.
(B) It requires less than a day to complete.
(C) It involves drying the cocoa beans.
(D) It adds bitter flavors to the cocoa beans.

197. With whom will Ms. Binocci meet on the morning of March 13 ?

(A) Agents who represent chocolate retailers
(B) Contractors who supply ingredients
(C) Specialists who understand product promotion
(D) Chefs who create new product recipes

198. What is most likely responsible for Gemstone Chocolate's recent success?

(A) Doubling productivity by hiring new staff
(B) Applying the moist incubation process
(C) Adopting imaginative packaging designs
(D) Revising the training of factory staff

199. What is indicated in the note about Mr. Ewing?

(A) He bought treats for his team members.
(B) He did Ms. Kwon's work while she was away.
(C) He just returned from a business trip.
(D) He is going on vacation soon.

200. What most likely is Ms. Kwon's favorite Gemstone chocolate bar?

(A) Midnight
(B) Vesper
(C) Twilight
(D) Eventide

Stop! This is the end of the test. If you finish before time is called, you may go back to Parts 5, 6, and 7 and check your work.

ETS
기출 모의고사

②회

🕐 시험 시간: 120분

	맞은 개수	환산 점수대
LISTENING TEST		
READING TEST		
총점		

*14쪽의 점수 환산표 및 산출법을 참조하세요.

LISTENING TEST

In the Listening test, you will be asked to demonstrate how well you understand spoken English. The entire Listening test will last approximately 45 minutes. There are four parts, and directions are given for each part. You must mark your answers on the separate answer sheet. Do not write your answers in your test book.

PART 1

Directions: For each question in this part, you will hear four statements about a picture in your test book. When you hear the statements, you must select the one statement that best describes what you see in the picture. Then find the number of the question on your answer sheet and mark your answer. The statements will not be printed in your test book and will be spoken only one time.

Statement (C), "They're sitting at a table," is the best description of the picture, so you should select answer (C) and mark it on your answer sheet.

1.

2.

GO ON TO THE NEXT PAGE ➜

ETS 기출

모의고사 2회

3.

4.

5.

6.

GO ON TO THE NEXT PAGE

PART 2

Directions: You will hear a question or statement and three responses spoken in English. They will not be printed in your test book and will be spoken only one time. Select the best response to the question or statement and mark the letter (A), (B), or (C) on your answer sheet.

7. Mark your answer on your answer sheet.

8. Mark your answer on your answer sheet.

9. Mark your answer on your answer sheet.

10. Mark your answer on your answer sheet.

11. Mark your answer on your answer sheet.

12. Mark your answer on your answer sheet.

13. Mark your answer on your answer sheet.

14. Mark your answer on your answer sheet.

15. Mark your answer on your answer sheet.

16. Mark your answer on your answer sheet.

17. Mark your answer on your answer sheet.

18. Mark your answer on your answer sheet.

19. Mark your answer on your answer sheet.

20. Mark your answer on your answer sheet.

21. Mark your answer on your answer sheet.

22. Mark your answer on your answer sheet.

23. Mark your answer on your answer sheet.

24. Mark your answer on your answer sheet.

25. Mark your answer on your answer sheet.

26. Mark your answer on your answer sheet.

27. Mark your answer on your answer sheet.

28. Mark your answer on your answer sheet.

29. Mark your answer on your answer sheet.

30. Mark your answer on your answer sheet.

31. Mark your answer on your answer sheet.

PART 3

Directions: You will hear some conversations between two or more people. You will be asked to answer three questions about what the speakers say in each conversation. Select the best response to each question and mark the letter (A), (B), (C), or (D) on your answer sheet. The conversations will not be printed in your test book and will be spoken only one time.

32. Why is the man calling the woman?

(A) To cancel an appointment
(B) To apologize for an error
(C) To announce a visitor
(D) To request a signature

33. What problem does the woman mention?

(A) There has been a scheduling misunderstanding.
(B) Some paperwork was not submitted.
(C) A device is malfunctioning.
(D) A meeting room is no longer available.

34. What will the man offer Mr. Bertrand?

(A) An apology
(B) A discounted rate
(C) A beverage
(D) Some reading material

35. Where is the conversation most likely taking place?

(A) At a property management office
(B) At a train station
(C) At a community center
(D) At a hardware store

36. What problem is being discussed?

(A) An electrical closet is locked.
(B) A kitchen pipe is leaking.
(C) A patio door is broken.
(D) A walkway needs to be repaired.

37. What does the woman agree to do?

(A) Record a video
(B) Reschedule a job
(C) Call a technician
(D) Sign for a delivery

38. What are the speakers mainly discussing?

(A) Redesigning a restaurant menu
(B) Providing landscaping services
(C) Purchasing some furniture
(D) Renovating a building

39. What does the woman warn against?

(A) Using a particular material
(B) Hiring unskilled staff
(C) Exceeding a budget
(D) Delaying an order

40. What will the woman send to the man?

(A) Photographs
(B) Product samples
(C) Cost estimates
(D) Vendor names

41. Where are the speakers?

(A) At an auto repair shop
(B) At a medical clinic
(C) At a computer store
(D) At a printing company

42. What are the speakers discussing?

(A) A delayed shipment
(B) A canceled appointment
(C) Missing information
(D) Mislabeled items

43. What will happen in the afternoon?

(A) A technician will arrive.
(B) A training will be held.
(C) A coworker will leave early.
(D) A contract will be finalized.

GO ON TO THE NEXT PAGE

44. What is the conversation mostly about?

(A) A location for a book fair
(B) A job applicant interview
(C) A speaker for a conference
(D) An idea for a new show

45. According to the man, what has made an item popular?

(A) Discounted prices
(B) Promotional events
(C) Celebrity endorsements
(D) Positive reviews

46. What does the woman ask the man to do?

(A) Send an e-mail
(B) Double-check some figures
(C) Schedule a seminar
(D) Develop a questionnaire

47. Where do the speakers most likely work?

(A) At an art studio
(B) At an advertising agency
(C) At a bank
(D) At an auto repair shop

48. What problem does the woman mention?

(A) A client is unhappy.
(B) A loan was not approved.
(C) Some information is outdated.
(D) Some staff members are unavailable.

49. What does the woman imply when she says, "This hasn't been sent to the client yet"?

(A) A deadline has been missed.
(B) A delivery service is experiencing delays.
(C) A project has been canceled.
(D) A correction can be made.

50. What is the purpose of the conversation?

(A) To finalize a Web site design
(B) To confirm an anniversary date
(C) To plan a shop's grand opening
(D) To discuss a new product line

51. What does the man suggest doing?

(A) Launching a campaign on social media
(B) Consulting with a marketing expert
(C) Negotiating for bulk pricing
(D) Hiring a well-known artist

52. Why is the woman concerned?

(A) A design requires approval.
(B) A deadline is approaching quickly.
(C) Some materials are expensive.
(D) Some competitors are gaining popularity.

53. What department do the speakers most likely work in?

(A) Public Relations
(B) Finance
(C) Human Resources
(D) Research and Development

54. What has Claudia Silvestri done?

(A) She has designed an airplane.
(B) She has written an article.
(C) She has developed some software.
(D) She has created a menu.

55. Why will the speakers meet this afternoon?

(A) To analyze some feedback
(B) To generate some ideas
(C) To lead a workshop
(D) To tour a facility

56. What are the speakers discussing?

(A) Boat maintenance
(B) Interior decorating
(C) Parade preparations
(D) Vehicle rentals

57. What specific problem does the man mention?

(A) An invoice is incorrect.
(B) Some material is torn.
(C) Some bad weather is predicted.
(D) A key is missing.

58. Why is Carmen unable to help the man this afternoon?

(A) She is waiting for information from a supervisor.
(B) She only works the morning shift.
(C) She has other work to do.
(D) She has a dentist's appointment.

59. Where do the speakers most likely work?

(A) At a factory
(B) At a university
(C) At a museum
(D) At a travel agency

60. What does the woman mean when she says, "I'm on my way to give a tour now"?

(A) She cannot help with a task.
(B) She cannot accept late arrivals.
(C) She has recently completed some training.
(D) She would like the man to join a tour.

61. What does the woman ask the man to do?

(A) Call a caterer
(B) Print some name tags
(C) Arrange guest transportation
(D) Review a brochure

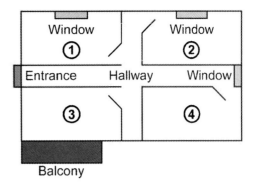

62. Who most likely is the man?

(A) An architect
(B) A mover
(C) A real estate agent
(D) A building manager

63. Look at the graphic. Which room does the woman refer to?

(A) Room 1
(B) Room 2
(C) Room 3
(D) Room 4

64. What does the woman offer?

(A) A bonus
(B) Some refreshments
(C) Some power tools
(D) A contract

GO ON TO THE NEXT PAGE

Pickup Location:	Location 1: Downtown Location 2: Walnut Street Location 3: Warehouse District Location 4: Mountain Avenue	v

Manor Hotel's Weekend Rates		
Room (per night)	Without gardens admission	With gardens admission
Single	$70	$90
Double	$80	$100

65. What type of business does the man work at?

(A) A bakery
(B) A furniture store
(C) An art supply store
(D) A hotel

66. Look at the graphic. At which location is the conversation taking place?

(A) Location 1
(B) Location 2
(C) Location 3
(D) Location 4

67. What does the man say he will do?

(A) Check an invoice
(B) Refund a purchase
(C) Provide a replacement item
(D) Schedule a delivery

68. What is Manor Hotel doing this weekend?

(A) Upgrading its grounds
(B) Offering free breakfast
(C) Partnering with a local business
(D) Hosting an annual festival

69. Why does the man say he can stay only one night?

(A) His business is open on Sundays.
(B) He has a limited budget.
(C) He has an early meeting.
(D) He is attending a party on Sunday.

70. Look at the graphic. How much will the man pay?

(A) $70
(B) $80
(C) $90
(D) $100

Directions: You will hear some talks given by a single speaker. You will be asked to answer three questions about what the speaker says in each talk. Select the best response to each question and mark the letter (A), (B), (C), or (D) on your answer sheet. The talks will not be printed in your test book and will be spoken only one time.

71. According to the speaker, what is Littleton known for?

(A) Porcelain pottery
(B) Baked goods
(C) Historic architecture
(D) Hiking trails

72. What does the speaker remind the listeners to do?

(A) Stay with the group
(B) Return to the bus on time
(C) Take photographs
(D) Bring warm clothing

73. How can the listeners receive a discount?

(A) By signing up for a mailing list
(B) By posting a review online
(C) By mentioning a tour company name
(D) By using a coupon

74. According to the speaker, what is located near the apartment building?

(A) A city park
(B) A university
(C) A train station
(D) A shopping center

75. What new feature of the building does the speaker emphasize?

(A) Enhanced security
(B) Energy efficiency
(C) Covered parking
(D) On-site storage space

76. What special offer is available until the end of April?

(A) Discounted rent
(B) Free Internet access
(C) Assistance with moving
(D) A gym membership

77. Who most likely is the speaker?

(A) A lawyer
(B) A courier
(C) An advertiser
(D) A computer technician

78. What does the speaker imply when he says, "the similarities are clear"?

(A) A logo is effective.
(B) A complaint is justified.
(C) Some instructions are easy to use.
(D) The quality of a product must be checked.

79. What information does the speaker request?

(A) A meeting date
(B) A list of contacts
(C) A conference location
(D) A travel itinerary

80. What does the speaker's farm produce?

(A) Cheese
(B) Herbs
(C) Coffee
(D) Fruit

81. What does a device assist with?

(A) Refilling a machine
(B) Monitoring visitors
(C) Controlling an indoor climate
(D) Tracking shipments

82. What are the listeners invited to do?

(A) Smell a fragrance
(B) Design some packaging
(C) Ask questions
(D) Take some samples

GO ON TO THE NEXT PAGE

83. What job position are the listeners training for?

(A) Bus driver
(B) Taxi operator
(C) Delivery truck driver
(D) Car rental agent

84. What information does the speaker request?

(A) Scheduling availability
(B) Clothing size
(C) Personal contact information
(D) Previous driving experience

85. According to the speaker, who can receive a discount?

(A) University students
(B) Medical professionals
(C) Retired individuals
(D) Loyalty-program members

86. Who are the listeners?

(A) Construction workers
(B) Business owners
(C) Government officials
(D) Television reporters

87. What does the speaker imply when she says, "Lauren is at a conference"?

(A) Some volunteers will be needed.
(B) A decision will be made at another time.
(C) The meeting should be recorded.
(D) The meeting will end early.

88. What will the listeners do next?

(A) Review a proposed budget
(B) Tour a construction site
(C) Look at some architectural renderings
(D) Address complaints from the public

89. What does the speaker ask the listeners to read?

(A) An inventory list
(B) A newspaper article
(C) A contract
(D) A safety guide

90. What is Narumi responsible for?

(A) Reimbursing meal expenses
(B) Tracking tool usage
(C) Distributing work assignments
(D) Speaking to reporters

91. What does the speaker imply when she says, "We have enough funding for six weeks"?

(A) The listeners should adjust their calendars.
(B) The listeners need to work quickly.
(C) More equipment should be ordered.
(D) Some assistants will be hired.

92. What did Ms. Iyanda do last month?

(A) She started a new job.
(B) She rented an apartment.
(C) She purchased some furniture.
(D) She moved across the country.

93. Why was Ms. Iyanda surprised?

(A) She won a contest.
(B) She reconnected with an old friend.
(C) She found some cash.
(D) She received an unusually high water bill.

94. What does the speaker encourage the listeners to do?

(A) Request songs
(B) Donate instruments
(C) Buy advertising space
(D) Attend a performance

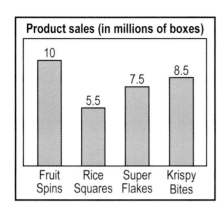

Product sales (in millions of boxes)

Fruit Spins	Rice Squares	Super Flakes	Krispy Bites
10	5.5	7.5	8.5

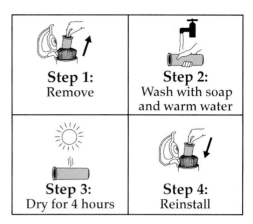

Step 1: Remove

Step 2: Wash with soap and warm water

Step 3: Dry for 4 hours

Step 4: Reinstall

95. What is the speaker mainly discussing?

(A) A price increase
(B) A new product line
(C) Ingredient modifications
(D) Packaging changes

96. Look at the graphic. Which cereal was used for a pilot project?

(A) Fruit Spins
(B) Rice Squares
(C) Super Flakes
(D) Krispy Bites

97. What will happen in two weeks?

(A) An advertising campaign will start.
(B) An executive will retire.
(C) A production facility will reopen.
(D) A product line will be discontinued.

98. Look at the graphic. Which step did not go as expected?

(A) Step 1
(B) Step 2
(C) Step 3
(D) Step 4

99. What did Murat suggest doing?

(A) Buying an extended warranty
(B) Using a scented product
(C) Cleaning a vehicle
(D) Mailing postcards to potential clients

100. What additional document will the speaker submit this week?

(A) An expense report
(B) A time sheet
(C) An inventory report
(D) A safety checklist

This is the end of the Listening test. Turn to Part 5 in your test book.

GO ON TO THE NEXT PAGE

READING TEST

In the Reading test, you will read a variety of texts and answer several different types of reading comprehension questions. The entire Reading test will last 75 minutes. There are three parts, and directions are given for each part. You are encouraged to answer as many questions as possible within the time allowed.

You must mark your answers on the separate answer sheet. Do not write your answers in your test book.

PART 5

Directions: A word or phrase is missing in each of the sentences below. Four answer choices are given below each sentence. Select the best answer to complete the sentence. Then mark the letter (A), (B), (C), or (D) on your answer sheet.

101. Ms. O'Dell said she would make her ------- about the new team leader tomorrow.

(A) decision
(B) decides
(C) decisive
(D) decisively

102. Use of the parking garage is limited to store employees ------- building residents.

(A) so
(B) for
(C) and
(D) until

103. Mr. Iwosu's team members appreciate ------- strong leadership skills.

(A) he
(B) his
(C) himself
(D) him

104. Please put the floor polisher ------- in the maintenance closet when you are finished with it.

(A) easy
(B) back
(C) very
(D) already

105. Many companies are updating their ------ regarding social media use by employees.

(A) supplies
(B) designs
(C) policies
(D) occasions

106. All silverware orders ------- before midnight tonight will be shipped free of charge.

(A) place
(B) places
(C) placed
(D) is placing

107. Residents are ------- asked to keep noise levels low when using the outdoor common areas.

(A) respect
(B) respectful
(C) respective
(D) respectfully

108. Reno is becoming a ------- place for technology companies to establish their headquarters.

(A) popular
(B) popularity
(C) popularly
(D) popularize

109. The Blixian Company's survey ------- that many of its employees have a long commute.

(A) looked
(B) found
(C) ordered
(D) chose

110. Read the application guidelines carefully ------- submitting your résumé and cover letter.

(A) over
(B) within
(C) before
(D) across

111. Because the budget is so -------, conference coordinators have planned a simple, low-cost welcoming event for attendees.

(A) fast
(B) sharp
(C) warm
(D) tight

112. Please let me know ------- I am eligible to receive a discount on my next purchase from your Web site.

(A) then
(B) often
(C) except
(D) whether

113. Montco Bank takes extraordinary steps to keep your personal information -------.

(A) safe
(B) safety
(C) saving
(D) saves

114. The director of product marketing is confident ------- brand awareness in the eastern region will continue to grow.

(A) that
(B) also
(C) about
(D) of

115. To meet heavy shipping demand, overtime will be ------- required across all production teams.

(A) hardly
(B) eagerly
(C) evenly
(D) deeply

116. The Wristly smartwatch ------- heart rate accurately but must be recharged every 48 hours.

(A) will be tracked
(B) tracks
(C) tracking
(D) to track

117. Faraj Antar hopes to pursue a ------- in broadcasting as a news reporter.

(A) trail
(B) view
(C) purpose
(D) career

118. Any ------- to the awards banquet menu must be approved by the head chef, Delmiro Rois.

(A) reactions
(B) modifications
(C) administrations
(D) portions

119. Aubern Financial does not charge fees for transferring money ------- accounts.

(A) onto
(B) upon
(C) beside
(D) between

120. Ana's Bread Company had been the only bakery in Springfield until a new ------- opened on Third Street last month.

(A) itself
(B) whose
(C) one
(D) another

GO ON TO THE NEXT PAGE

121. When books are packed too ------- in a box, the strong pressure can deform their bindings.

(A) keenly
(B) closely
(C) patiently
(D) greatly

122. The concert hall's acoustical design ------- to give audiences the best possible experience.

(A) adjustment
(B) were adjusting
(C) adjuster
(D) is being adjusted

123. To be competitive in the hospitality industry, many hotels offer guests a ------- breakfast.

(A) steady
(B) satisfied
(C) hearty
(D) positive

124. Input from management is ------- requested in order to finish tomorrow's workshop agenda.

(A) urged
(B) urgent
(C) urgency
(D) urgently

125. ------- the sensitive information they contain, completed forms should not be sent by e-mail.

(A) On account of
(B) Such as
(C) Rather than
(D) As though

126. Our consultants agree that a steep initial discount will provide enough ------- for customers to join the shopping club.

(A) motivate
(B) motivation
(C) motivates
(D) motivator

127. Although Ms. Choi's employment was only temporary, her contributions to our company have had a ------- effect.

(A) lasting
(B) presenting
(C) falling
(D) covering

128. The interns were given the option of stopping their work at 2:00 P.M. on Fridays, but ------- have chosen to do so.

(A) few
(B) nobody
(C) such
(D) anyone

129. Every quarter, Hanini Fashions ------- the employee who has made the most sales calls.

(A) reminds
(B) offers
(C) honors
(D) admits

130. ------- snowy weather, city bus services may be delayed or canceled.

(A) As much as
(B) In the event of
(C) In order that
(D) Even though

PART 6

Directions: Read the texts that follow. A word, phrase, or sentence is missing in parts of each text. Four answer choices for each question are given below the text. Select the best answer to complete the text. Then mark the letter (A), (B), (C), or (D) on your answer sheet.

Questions 131-134 refer to the following information.

Congratulations on your purchase of the Brantmerr B10 toaster oven. Please read the instructions carefully before operating the unit. Note that this ------- is intended for indoor use only.
131.
------- should never be operated in outdoor settings or without a user present. Every toaster made
132.
by Brantmerr undergoes rigorous inspection and testing processes before leaving the factory.
The B10 model is backed ------- a one-year warranty stating that Brantmerr will replace the unit
133.
free of charge if there are any manufacturing defects. ------- .
134.

131. (A) part
     (B) material
     (C) furniture
     (D) appliance

132. (A) It
     (B) Any
     (C) What
     (D) We

133. (A) by
     (B) from
     (C) into
     (D) down

134. (A) We now invite customers to tour our factory.
     (B) Minor alterations to the product's design are made yearly.
     (C) Evidence of improper usage will void this guarantee.
     (D) Brantmerr will support a recycling program for all electronics.

모의고사 2회

GO ON TO THE NEXT PAGE

Questions 135-138 refer to the following memo.

MEMO

To: All Staff
From: Service Innovation Team
Date: September 26
Subject: It's a go!

We have great news! Government officials have granted us permission to deliver components by drone from our Nombex Electronics warehouse beginning the first of the new year. Each drone has a round-trip range of 16 kilometers. This enables us to ------- as many as twenty local
135.
manufacturers and institutions. The drones are ------- automated. They use GPS, an onboard
136.
computer, and artificial intelligence to navigate to the destination and back on their own.

------- . Shipments that are too big or heavy will be delivered by our courier truck service.
137.

Employees who wish to see a drone in action may attend a ------- in the west parking lot at
138.
3:00 P.M. this Friday.

---

135. (A) invoice
(B) reach
(C) attract
(D) call

136. (A) full
(B) fullest
(C) fullness
(D) fully

137. (A) Our engineering department has also applied for several patents.
(B) Underwater drones are being used to explore the ocean floor.
(C) They can only carry loads that are below a certain weight and size.
(D) Our annual sale will occur during the same period.

138. (A) demonstration
(B) demonstrator
(C) demonstrated
(D) demonstrate

Questions 139-142 refer to the following e-mail.

To: karl.blankenship@myrtlemail.net
From: phyllis_casares@rochestercity.gov
Date: June 8
Subject: Re: Elm Avenue

Dear Mr. Blankenship:

Thank you for your message reporting the increased number of motorists using Elm Avenue to avoid the congestion on Interstate 38. ------- . Please be advised that this situation is ------- .
139. **140.**
The highway has been reduced to a single northbound lane while the construction crew completes some paving work. The project activity is scheduled to be completed within the next four days. ------- , we will have a police officer patrol the area. A radar speed detector will be
141.
installed ------- the traffic. Hopefully these measures will improve traffic movement and area
142.
safety.

Sincerely,

Phyllis Casares, Assistant Director
City Department of Transportation

ETS 기출

모의고사 2회

139. (A) You are welcome to join us at our next meeting.
(B) They regularly use our public transportation system.
(C) We are impressed by the rate at which it has grown.
(D) Several of your neighbors have submitted comments as well.

140. (A) identical
(B) temporary
(C) impossible
(D) doubtful

141. (A) If so
(B) After all
(C) On the contrary
(D) In the meantime

142. (A) to monitor
(B) monitored
(C) monitors
(D) be monitored

GO ON TO THE NEXT PAGE

Questions 143-146 refer to the following letter.

Theodore Newcombe
Edmonton Department Store
900 35th Avenue West
Edmonton, Alberta T5J 2R4

16 September

Dear Mr. Newcombe,

Last week, I visited your store to find a replacement for my old upright vacuum cleaner. Your employee Sarai Jebreen suggested I ------- a cordless model. I told Ms. Jebreen that I find
143.
cordless vacuums appealing, but I had two concerns. ------- . I was also skeptical that a cordless
144.
model would be strong enough for my needs. ------- assured me that you have powerful cordless
145.
vacuums in my price range. I did not think that such a vacuum existed. However, Ms. Jebreen demonstrated several models that worked surprisingly well. I purchased a Dirt Genie vacuum, and I am delighted with its performance. I am ------- pleased with the service I received from
146.
Ms. Jebreen!

Sincerely,

Leora Whang

---

143. (A) return
(B) design
(C) borrow
(D) consider

144. (A) I have purchased vacuum cleaner bags
        at Edmonton Department Store.
(B) It is easy to transport a cordless vacuum.
(C) I feared that a cordless vacuum would
        be too costly.
(D) The countertop was dirty when I
        dropped off my vacuum.

145. (A) You
(B) She
(C) Both
(D) These

146. (A) for example
(B) near
(C) likewise
(D) nevertheless

PART 7

Directions: In this part you will read a selection of texts, such as magazine and newspaper articles, e-mails, and instant messages. Each text or set of texts is followed by several questions. Select the best answer for each question and mark the letter (A), (B), (C), or (D) on your answer sheet.

Questions 147-148 refer to the following notice.

Tarterly Hotel

Date: 7 December
Time: 8:12 P.M.
Room Number: 394
Guest Name: Georgia Halperin

Dear Ms. Halperin,

Because we saw a "Do Not Disturb" sign on your door, we were unable to do the following.

☐ Provide daily cleaning service
☐ Address a reported maintenance issue
☒ Deliver your washed and ironed clothing
☐ Deliver additional toiletries or towels

When you are ready for us to help you with your request, please call our front desk by dialing 0 at any time of the day or night or visit the Guest Services desk in the main lobby between 8 A.M. and 7 P.M.

We hope you are enjoying your stay!

---

147. What did Ms. Halperin request from the hotel?

(A) Room cleaning
(B) Television repair
(C) Laundry service
(D) Extra soap

148. What is mentioned about the Guest Services desk?

(A) It is open 24 hours a day.
(B) It is located in the main lobby.
(C) It has Ms. Halperin's room key.
(D) It will call Ms. Halperin at 8 A.M.

GO ON TO THE NEXT PAGE

Simple Bank's Best Offer Yet

Sign up for a credit card with Simple Bank by December 31 and receive a $100 bonus! Simple Bank's credit card received the top ranking this year from Everyday-Consumers.com, and *Financial View* magazine has named it the best cash-back card for three years in a row. All cardholders enjoy the following benefits.

- 3% cash back on every in-store and online purchase

- Up to a 5% discount on hotels and restaurants

- Up to a 10% discount on bus, train, and light-rail fares

- No annual fee

Visit www.simplebank.com/creditcard now to sign up and collect your bonus! You do not need to have a checking or savings account at Simple Bank to become a cardholder.

149. What is indicated about the Simple Bank credit card?

(A) It is highly rated by financial professionals.
(B) It must be linked to a bank account.
(C) It charges cardholders an annual fee.
(D) It offers both cash-back and gift-card rewards.

150. What kind of purchases receive the largest discount?

(A) Restaurant meals
(B) Magazine subscriptions
(C) Hotel accommodations
(D) Transportation tickets

Questions 151-152 refer to the following museum exhibit notice.

> **Radhak Dhar** was a prolific illustrator who remains one of India's most revered graphic novelists. This exhibit displays examples of his work, including some of his earliest sketches and journals. While Dhar's graphic novels depict colourful, fantastical landscapes, many scholars believe his stories are loosely based on actual events from his life. Dhar's sketches and journals lend support to this theory. Dhar's journals also reveal his meticulous record keeping, with separate journals to track his progress on each project. Dhar's diligence and work ethic explain how he was able to produce such a tremendous volume of work.

151. What does the notice suggest about Mr. Dhar's graphic novels?

(A) They are not available in stores.
(B) They inspired a number of films.
(C) They are not completely fictional.
(D) They were created using computer graphics.

152. What does the notice mention about Mr. Dhar's journals?

(A) They were kept secret for years.
(B) They show how organized he was.
(C) They are too delicate to be handled.
(D) They were donated to a library in India.

GO ON TO THE NEXT PAGE

207

Ning Hsu [10:14 A.M.]
I'm at the construction site, and the workers are installing water pipes today. I need insulation to cover them. I phoned my regular contact at Tullyville Materials, but the call went directly to voice mail. Do you have the main number for Tullyville? Tullyville was able to deliver insulation very quickly the last time we needed it.

Daisy Guerra [10:15 A.M.]
Tullyville is the vendor we used for the Micklin project, right?

Ning Hsu [10:16 A.M.]
That's the one.

Daisy Guerra [10:17 A.M.]
I'm sure I have a purchase order with the main office number on it somewhere. I'll text the number to you as soon as I find it.

Ning Hsu [10:18 A.M.]
That would be a great help. In the meantime, I'll go ahead and remeasure the uncovered piping so I'll know exactly how much to request.

153. At 10:16 A.M., what does Mr. Hsu most likely mean when he writes, "That's the one"?

(A) Tullyville Materials helped with a previous construction project.
(B) Tullyville Materials is close to the current construction site.
(C) Ms. Guerra has identified the type of insulation that is needed.
(D) Ms. Guerra found a document that had been misplaced.

154. What will Mr. Hsu most likely do next?

(A) Order additional pipes
(B) Read a purchase order
(C) Visit the Micklin project site
(D) Take some measurements

New Electric Ferry Launches

OSLO (10 August)—Drammen Systems launched its third all-electric ferry on Monday. The Akselere 3 will travel twice daily between Harwich, England, and Rotterdam, the Netherlands.

The four-hour ferry route will be the longest route currently served by an electric-powered vessel. The launch of the Akselere 3 marks an important moment for electric-powered vessels. Previously, the longest route served by an all-electric vessel was the 30-minute route across the Aurlandsfjord.

Engineers at Oslo-based Drammen Systems said that the effort represents the work of ten years. They designed an innovative battery system to enable the ferry to run the long route. The ferry was constructed by Affidabile Shipyard in Genoa, Italy.

The battery will need to be charged on both sides of the journey. The ferry will be operated by Pomera Searider Services, which expects to transition to an all-electric fleet in the next decade.

"The transition to an electric ferry on this route is expected to reduce emissions significantly," said Agata C. Bakker, a spokesperson for Pomera Searider Services.

155. According to the article, what is important about the Akselere 3 ?

(A) It was developed in record time.
(B) It travels the longest route of any electric-powered ferry.
(C) It travels at an unusually high rate of speed.
(D) It is the first vessel designed by Drammen Systems.

156. Where was the Akselere 3 built?

(A) In Harwich
(B) In Rotterdam
(C) In Oslo
(D) In Genoa

157. The word "charged" in paragraph 4, line 1, is closest in meaning to

(A) commanded
(B) energized
(C) entrusted
(D) approached

GO ON TO THE NEXT PAGE

Two-Bedroom Apartment Available

3034 Jackson Avenue in Billings, Montana

This charming two-bedroom, one-bath unit with 110 square meters of living space is on the third floor of a twelve-unit apartment community. — [1] —. It features a remodeled kitchen with a brand-new dishwasher, oven, and refrigerator. Each bedroom has a large walk-in closet. — [2] —.

Located at the intersection of Jackson and Pullman Avenues in the heart of the city of Billings, the building is within walking distance of the Trident Nightlife District and Karsten College. — [3] —. Convenient public transit throughout the city is available via bus lines 8 and 15.

The monthly rent is $1,300. — [4] —. The lease term is twelve months, and payment of a security deposit equal to the first and last month's rent is required. To schedule an in-person showing, contact property manager Joan Wright at 406-555-0122.

158. What is indicated about the apartment?

(A) It is in the central part of the city.
(B) It was once used for student housing.
(C) It comes with free parking for residents.
(D) It is on the twelfth floor of a building.

159. What is a stated requirement for renters?

(A) Providing references
(B) Signing a 24-month lease
(C) Paying two months' rent as deposit
(D) Showing proof of current employment

160. In which of the positions marked [1], [2], [3], and [4] does the following sentence best belong?

"A grocery store and a weekend farmers market are also nearby."

(A) [1]
(B) [2]
(C) [3]
(D) [4]

Questions 161-163 refer to the following instructions.

Send Plutus is the world's top-rated service for transferring funds internationally. We will move your money securely, with no hidden fees, and at the best exchange rate available. For large or small transactions—for personal or business purposes—we have a solution for you. We operate entirely online, so you can start your transfer anytime, anywhere!

Follow these easy steps to move your money almost anywhere in the world.

1. Create a free account. Sign up online or use our phone app—at no cost.

2. Enter an amount to send. Indicate how much money you want to move.

3. Enter recipient information. Provide the details of your recipient's bank account.

4. Verify your identity. Enter a personal identification number that will be sent as a text message or in an e-mail.

5. Pay for your transfer. Send your money and pay the fee using a direct transfer from your bank account, a wire transfer, or a credit card.

6. You're done!

Go to www.sendplutus.com to sign up today.

161. What service does Send Plutus provide?

(A) Full-service online banking
(B) Advice on financial investments
(C) Bank security consultations
(D) International money transfers

162. What is suggested in the instructions about Send Plutus?

(A) It is a relatively new service.
(B) It has multiple international offices.
(C) It is intended solely for businesses.
(D) It requires the use of digital technology.

163. What is NOT mentioned as a way customers can pay for service from Send Plutus?

(A) Charging a credit card
(B) Making a wire transfer
(C) Mailing a check to Send Plutus
(D) Drawing money from a bank account

Legurian Responds to Lagging Sales

Longtime customers of Legurian may notice something different when they read through the company's autumn catalog next month. Instead of the big heavy-duty suitcases that the brand is known for, the catalog will feature smaller items, such as briefcases and shoulder bags. This change marks a dramatic shift for a company that once ran advertisements boasting that one Legurian suitcase can hold everything in a person's closet.

Legurian's change in strategy is due more to evolving travel patterns than to the latest fashion magazine trends.

"Simply put, people are taking fewer long trips, but more short trips," said Legurian CEO Gena Morelli. "People now have an easier time taking a couple of days off work, so they'll take advantage of the cheaper flights now being offered."

"Because of technology, they no longer have to travel to see family, so they're traveling more as tourists," she added. "The two-week trip is becoming rarer, so there's simply less need for large suitcases."

A few years ago, industry experts predicted that high airline luggage fees would depress sales of travel accessories. But that prediction turned out to be wrong. Instead, customers appear to be motivated more by convenience than by cost.

"Our new Peralta shoulder bag is a good example of what customers want," said Ms. Morelli. "It has a sleek, modern design and many small compartments. But what people really love is the fact that it's lightweight and has an ergonomic shoulder strap. They can walk around with it all day in complete comfort."

164. What is suggested in the article about Legurian?

(A) It no longer specializes in oversized luggage.
(B) It now produces closet storage systems.
(C) It provides time off for its employees to travel.
(D) It is not publishing an autumn catalog this year.

165. What trend is mentioned in the article?

(A) The cost of travel has increased significantly this year.
(B) Fashion magazines are promoting a wider variety of styles.
(C) Consumers are becoming more interested in trying different brands.
(D) Travelers are going on more trips for shorter periods of time.

166. The word "depress" in paragraph 5, line 3, is closest in meaning to

(A) reject
(B) sadden
(C) reduce
(D) force

167. According to Ms. Morelli, what do customers like most about the Peralta bag?

(A) It is affordable.
(B) It is easy to carry.
(C) It is visually attractive.
(D) It contains several pockets.

Questions 168-171 refer to the following e-mail.

```
┌─────────────────────────────────────────────────────────────┐
│                        *E-mail*                               │
├─────────────────────────────────────────────────────────────┤
│  To:        │ All employees                                   │
│  From:      │ Sunita Dahl                                     │
│  Date:      │ April 15                                        │
│  Subject:   │ Important information                           │
├─────────────────────────────────────────────────────────────┤
│  Dear Employees,                                              │
│                                                               │
│  Our company has grown significantly in the five years since  │
│  its founding, and our current office space no longer meets   │
│  our needs. — [1] —. Therefore, Urlane Technology will move   │
│  its headquarters in June to the Goldman-Poole Building       │
│  downtown. Our new office will be large enough for everyone   │
│  to have an individual work space, and there will still be    │
│  room for the company to expand. To facilitate this           │
│  undertaking, I will hold weekly move update meetings for     │
│  all department managers. — [2] —.                            │
│                                                               │
│  Professional movers will be handling the transport of        │
│  furniture and boxed materials, but employees will be         │
│  responsible for taking their laptops and confidential        │
│  materials with them to our new location. — [3] —. On May     │
│  15, our public relations department will issue a press       │
│  release to industry publications and send letters and        │
│  e-mails to our business partners and key customers           │
│  announcing our upcoming move. — [4] —. At that time,         │
│  please inform your customers and important contacts of our   │
│  new address. All other contact information, including your   │
│  telephone extension numbers, will remain the same.           │
│                                                               │
│  Sunita Dahl, Office Manager / Moving Coordinator             │
└─────────────────────────────────────────────────────────────┘
```

168. What is the purpose of the e-mail?

(A) To schedule a meeting
(B) To describe an upcoming change
(C) To welcome a new customer
(D) To announce a new product

169. What is indicated about Urlane Technology?

(A) It has been operating for five years.
(B) It has offices in more than one city.
(C) It employs fewer than 100 people.
(D) It recently purchased new laptops.

170. According to the e-mail, what will the public relations department do on May 15 ?

(A) Hold a meeting with department managers
(B) Transport boxed materials to another location
(C) Share information with company business partners
(D) Send an updated listing of telephone extension numbers to customers

171. In which of the positions marked [1], [2], [3], and [4] does the following sentence best belong?

"Right now, many employees are sharing office space meant for one person."

(A) [1]
(B) [2]
(C) [3]
(D) [4]

GO ON TO THE NEXT PAGE

Sakura Miyake [9:30 A.M.] Hi everyone. Sorry for the late notice, but I'm organizing a small surprise party for Jeff Koury tomorrow at 5:00 P.M.

Edouard Pellerin [9:31 A.M.] To celebrate his retirement in December?

Sakura Miyake [9:32 A.M.] No. He landed the Perch Foods account! It will be formally announced at the 2:00 P.M. staff meeting today.

Zoe Baez [9:33 A.M.] This is terrific news! We've been trying for years to persuade them to let us create their advertising.

Sakura Miyake [9:34 A.M.] I'll pick up a cake from Bergman's, and Stan promised to take care of the soft drinks.

Elijah Havelock [9:35 A.M.] What can I do?

Sakura Miyake [9:36 A.M.] If you're available around 4:00 tomorrow, I could use some help decorating the conference room.

Elijah Havelock [9:37 A.M.] You got it.

Edouard Pellerin [9:38 A.M.] There are some balloons and streamers left over from Latoya's anniversary party last month. They are in the storage closet. I'll grab them.

Sakura Miyake [9:39 A.M.] Thanks! Also check the cabinet in the break room. You will find paper plates, napkins, and plastic forks in there.

Zoe Baez [9:40 A.M.] I'm getting trained on the new graphic arts design software tomorrow from 4:00 to 5:30 P.M. Would it be too late if I come after that?

Sakura Miyake [9:41 A.M.] Not at all. Plus, I'm sure Jeff will want to give you his ideas for redesigning the Perch Foods logo.

172. Why is Ms. Miyake organizing a party for Mr. Koury?

(A) To celebrate his recruitment of a new client
(B) To congratulate him on his new position at Perch Foods
(C) To mark his upcoming retirement
(D) To observe his work anniversary

173. What does Mr. Pellerin say he will do?

(A) Lead the 2:00 P.M. staff meeting
(B) Gather some party supplies
(C) Order the cake
(D) Pick up the soft drinks

174. What is suggested about Ms. Baez?

(A) She oversees training for her company.
(B) She shares an office with Mr. Havelock.
(C) She lives near a bakery.
(D) She is a graphic artist.

175. At 9:41 A.M., what does Ms. Miyake imply when she writes, "Not at all"?

(A) She does not mind checking the budget.
(B) She will not tell Mr. Koury about the party.
(C) The party will still be going on after 5:30 P.M.
(D) The new software program is easy to learn.

GO ON TO THE NEXT PAGE

ETS 기출

모의고사 2회

Questions 176-180 refer to the following article and review.

Cucina Italiana Blends Local Art and Fine Flavors
By Alex Singh

MIAMI BEACH (June 12)—The much-anticipated opening of the new restaurant Cucina Italiana is set for July 1. When owner-chef Emilia Carafano began operating her regional Italian food truck in Brooklyn, New York, it was an instant sensation. As the business grew, she moved her operation into a more permanent space, creating a cozy eatery serving contemporary versions of many classic Italian dishes. The continued popularity of the original Cucina Italiana catapulted it to national prominence, with glowing reviews in food magazines and a profile of Carafano on a popular cooking show. Now Miami Beach will have its own branch of the acclaimed restaurant.

Beyond the excellent cuisine, the original Cucina Italiana also features the work of local artists. "At our New York restaurant, food and art go hand in hand," Ms. Carafano said. "I wanted to help artists who deserve a wider audience realize their dreams, just as I was able to do." To continue that worthy mission, the new restaurant will display the works of Florida-based artists.

---

https://www.customerreviewsite.com/restaurants

Cucina Italiana—Miami Beach (4 stars)

My sister and I were visiting for the weekend, and we were thrilled when we were able to get a reservation at Cucina Italiana just one week after it opened. What an experience! The beautiful artwork displayed created a lovely atmosphere, the service was prompt and professional, and the food was amazing. The smoked salmon ravioli was delicious, and the cannoli we ordered for dessert was the best we've ever had. Unfortunately, though, the restaurant was crowded and very loud. It was hard for us to hear each other talk, so that took away some of our enjoyment. Other than that, we had a wonderful evening.

—Barbara Oh, Orlando

176. What most likely is Mr. Singh's profession?

(A) Restaurant manager
(B) Artists' agent
(C) Newspaper writer
(D) Art critic

177. In the article, the word "opening" in paragraph 1, line 2, is closest in meaning to

(A) empty space
(B) vacancy
(C) launch
(D) first performance

178. According to the article, what is indicated about the original Cucina Italiana?

(A) It was founded by two sisters.
(B) It was unpopular at first.
(C) It was featured in a documentary.
(D) It was started as a food truck.

179. According to the review, what did Ms. Oh dislike about the new Cucina Italiana?

(A) The noise
(B) The location
(C) The prices
(D) The service

180. What can be concluded about the artwork Ms. Oh saw at the new Cucina Italiana?

(A) It was on display for a week only.
(B) It was painted by Ms. Garafano.
(C) It was a combination of classic and contemporary styles.
(D) It was created by artists from Florida.

GO ON TO THE NEXT PAGE

Professional Education Courses for November

Renbrook Corporation expects employees to register for a minimum of two professional education courses each year. Here are the courses that we will be offering during the month of November. If you are considering registration, speak with your supervisor first to confirm that a course is appropriate. All classes are 90 minutes long and meet on four mornings in November. Contact Ji-Tae Nan at jtnan@renbrookcorporation.com with any questions.

Course Number	Name and Description	Day and Time	Room
N22-01	Introduction to Business Analytics: How to apply fundamental data analysis to better understand and improve workplace processes	Mondays 8:30 AM	Main Building, Conference Room
N22-12	Business Analytics: Advance applications for data analysis (Please note that completion of the introductory-level course is a prerequisite.)	Wednesdays 8:30 AM	Main Building, Training Classroom
N22-03	Negotiating with Confidence: How to prepare for business negotiations and adopt strategies to maximize results	Tuesdays 11:00 AM	Parlin Building, Room 3
N22-44	Data Privacy: Maintaining client confidentiality and the security of company data	Fridays 11:00 AM	Parlin Building, Room 3

To:	Ji-Tae Nan
From:	Anders Wilson
Date:	October 7
Subject:	My course

Hello, Ji-Tae,

I have been scheduled to lead the N22-44 course in November. Unfortunately, I have just been asked to take charge of computer training during that time. Introducing employees to the new computer system is a corporate priority. I hope that another individual can be found to teach N22-44 and would like to suggest my assistant, Susan Logan. Another option might be to switch course assignments with the instructor assigned to teach N22-03, as I have experience teaching that course and it is scheduled for a time when I am available.

I apologize for any inconvenience.

Anders Wilson
Extension 3944

181. What is suggested in the schedule?

(A) Some courses are given twice a year.
(B) Some courses are being offered for the first time.
(C) Employees may take more than two courses each year.
(D) Employees who take courses may ask for a reduced workload.

182. What is mentioned about course N22-12 ?

(A) It is limited to department managers.
(B) It will meet in room 3.
(C) It follows an introductory course.
(D) It will be taught by Mr. Nan.

183. What is the purpose of the e-mail?

(A) To introduce a new employee
(B) To ask how to register for a course
(C) To recommend a new course
(D) To discuss a scheduling conflict

184. What topic is Ms. Logan most likely to be familiar with?

(A) Data security
(B) Workplace communication
(C) Client negotiations
(D) Business analytics

185. When is Mr. Wilson available to be an instructor in November?

(A) On Mondays
(B) On Tuesdays
(C) On Wednesdays
(D) On Fridays

GO ON TO THE NEXT PAGE

Architecture Review: Dream Peak

by Kirstin Blakely

MELBOURNE (2 August)—The city's new convention centre, Dream Peak, is scheduled to open in two weeks and is expected to be a boon to the city's hospitality industry. I was given a sneak peek last week while some finishing touches were being done. In a word, the facility is spectacular!

Located on Main Avenue between Maple and Oak Streets, Dream Peak is anchored by a sparkling 2,000-square-metre grand hall—an airy, sun-drenched space. It also has a 900-seat auditorium, a dedicated exhibition venue, and a variety of large and small meeting rooms spread over three levels. All meeting rooms feature state-of-the-art audiovisual technologies and high-speed Wi-Fi. Upcoming events this year include three trade shows, a puzzle convention, and a travel industry conference.

The grand opening, currently scheduled for 17 August, will feature live music, light refreshments, and a ribbon-cutting ceremony led by Deputy Mayor Jennifer Lane. The event is open to the public.

---

https://www.internationalwordpuzzlefans.org/events

| **Events** | Registration | About | Membership |

Don't Miss It!

This year's International Word Puzzle Convention will take place in Melbourne, Australia, from 3 to 5 November at the Dream Peak Convention Centre. Once again, Hari Chaudhari will serve as our master of ceremonies. The author of numerous puzzle books, Mr. Chaudhari edits the weekly puzzle section for the *London Announcer* newspaper. Advance registration is required to attend the convention. International Word Puzzle Fans members get a 10 percent discount on the registration fee. Visit the registration page to find a form to complete as well as information on special rates at nearby hotels.

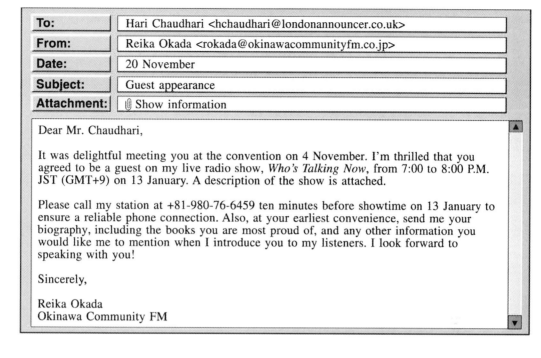

To:	Hari Chaudhari <hchaudhari@londonannouncer.co.uk>
From:	Reika Okada <rokada@okinawacommunityfm.co.jp>
Date:	20 November
Subject:	Guest appearance
Attachment:	🖉 Show information

Dear Mr. Chaudhari,

It was delightful meeting you at the convention on 4 November. I'm thrilled that you agreed to be a guest on my live radio show, *Who's Talking Now*, from 7:00 to 8:00 P.M. JST (GMT+9) on 13 January. A description of the show is attached.

Please call my station at +81-980-76-6459 ten minutes before showtime on 13 January to ensure a reliable phone connection. Also, at your earliest convenience, send me your biography, including the books you are most proud of, and any other information you would like me to mention when I introduce you to my listeners. I look forward to speaking with you!

Sincerely,

Reika Okada
Okinawa Community FM

186. What is the main topic of the article?

(A) How a convention center got its name
(B) The features of a convention center
(C) Popular tourist attractions in Melbourne
(D) A government official's recent activities

187. According to the article, what did Ms. Blakely do last week?

(A) She toured a building.
(B) She traveled to London.
(C) She booked a meeting space.
(D) She completed a long-term project.

188. What is indicated about the International Word Puzzle Convention?

(A) It is open to members only.
(B) It increased its registration fees.
(C) It has occurred annually for ten years.
(D) It is being held in a newly constructed venue.

189. What does the Web page mention about Mr. Chaudhari?

(A) He owns a respected newspaper.
(B) He is unable to attend an event.
(C) He has written multiple books.
(D) He lives in Okinawa.

190. What is suggested about Ms. Okada?

(A) She interviewed Deputy Mayor Lane.
(B) She once worked for Mr. Chaudhari.
(C) She is writing Mr. Chaudhari's biography.
(D) She was recently in Melbourne.

GO ON TO THE NEXT PAGE

Crestmont Walking Tour Itinerary
Sponsored by the Crestmont Visitor Center
Wednesday, June 5

8:15 A.M.   Meet at the front entrance of Sullivan Park, 214 Noank Avenue

8:30 A.M.   **Sullivan Park**
Enjoy a stroll through the flower gardens. The roses and zinnias are
spectacular at this time of year!

9:30 A.M.   **Edwards Hall**
The oldest surviving building in Crestmont, Edwards Hall is now the home
of the Crestmont Historical Society. The current exhibition is *A City
Grows: Portraits of Crestmont's Founding Families.*

10:30 A.M.   **The Old Train Station**
Trains no longer stop in Crestmont, but the former train station has been
converted into a lively venue for artists. We'll look in on several studios
and galleries before stopping at the Lunch Basket Café for a snack.

11:30 A.M.   **The Vanderwater Furniture Company**
Founded more than 100 years ago and still in business today, this company
introduced the iconic Vanderwater armchair, recognized worldwide as a
classic. Parts of the factory are open to visitors.

12:30 P.M.   **Nellie's Corner**
We will wrap up the tour at one of Crestmont's favorite souvenir shops,
where you can buy postcards, T-shirts, and other memorabilia.

E-mail

From:	Jhuli Sheth <jhuli.sheth@crestmontvisitorcenter.org>
To:	June 5 Tour Group
Date:	June 3
Subject:	Tour reminders and update

Dear All,

I hope you are excited about Wednesday's walking tour! There has been one change to
the itinerary you received earlier. Because Nellie's Corner is temporarily closed for
renovations, we will go instead to nearby Candlewick's (next to the movie theater), a
very similar place.

A couple of you have asked about adding other people to the tour. Unfortunately, we are
at our limit of 15, but there are still openings available for Friday's tour (June 7). To
purchase tickets, please call us at 555-0153. See you soon!

Jhuli Sheth
Crestmont Visitor Center

From: Hongxiu Kwon <hkwon@jaspermail.com>
To: Jhuli Sheth <jhuli.sheth@crestmontvisitorcenter.org>
Date: June 4
Subject: Re: Tour reminders and update

Dear Ms. Sheth,

I'm writing to let you know that I will be a little late for tomorrow's tour. I have an important business phone call in the morning, so I plan to meet up with the tour at the 9:30 a.m. stop.

Sincerely,

Hongxiu Kwon

191. What is indicated in the itinerary about the June 5 tour?

(A) It begins at a park entrance.
(B) It stops at Crestmont's city hall.
(C) It will be canceled in case of rain.
(D) It includes a free group photograph.

192. According to the itinerary, what has brought the city of Crestmont international fame?

(A) Its art galleries
(B) Its flower gardens
(C) Its portrait collection
(D) Its furniture production

193. What will tour participants most likely be able to do at Candlewick's?

(A) Shop for souvenirs
(B) Watch a movie about trains
(C) Take lessons from a local artist
(D) Learn about Crestmont's original residents

194. How can people purchase tickets for the June 7 tour?

(A) By going to a Web site
(B) By e-mailing Ms. Sheth
(C) By calling a phone number
(D) By speaking to the tour guide

195. Where will Ms. Kwon most likely meet up with her tour group?

(A) At Sullivan Park
(B) At Edwards Hall
(C) At The Old Train Station
(D) At The Vanderwater Furniture Company

GO ON TO THE NEXT PAGE

Questions 196-200 refer to the following e-mail, Web page, and memo.

To:	Residents of Barnhill
From:	Barnhill Waste Management Department
Date:	1 March
Subject:	Recycling service

Dear Resident:

As you may remember, on 5 January the Barnhill City Council voted to reduce the city budget for this year. Among the services affected by the reduction is the recycling pickup service for households in the community. Friday, 12 March, will be the last day of curbside recycling pickup. Starting on Monday, 15 March, you may deliver paper, cardboard, plastic items, aluminum cans, and glass bottles and jars to the city's waste management centre on Shelburne Road. Please be sure to sort your recyclables into the appropriate bins, which are clearly labelled.

If you wish, you may contract with one of the private waste management companies that offer fee-based curbside recycling service in our area. A list of these companies is available at www.barnhillcity.ie.

The Shelburne Road facility will continue to hold periodic collections of used engine and cooking oil, batteries, and latex paint.

Thank you for your cooperation.

Seamus Conner, Coordinator, Barnhill Waste Management Department

---

https://www.ecolandrecycling.ie/households

Ecoland Recycling's standard bin service for households is priced at €6 per month. Recyclables are picked up weekly. We collect aluminum cans, paper, cardboard, and glass bottles and jars. Objects made of plastic are not accepted.

The fee includes two large wheelie bins. You may order more bins at a cost of €2 each.

For new customers, we are offering a special deal: Pay in advance for the first year of service and receive a reduced price. Please call us at 020-912-0314 for more information.

MEMO

To: All recycling crews
From: Irwin Mitanni, Sales
Date: 10 April
Re: New Barnhill customers in Zone 3

Ecoland Recycling continues to add customers located in Barnhill. Please add the following four addresses to our regular Thursday route in Zone 3. All are fully paid up for the year.

Geoffrey Muellejans, 29 Main Street

Dianna Sperber, 661 Centre Road

Otis Rayano, 97 Fulton Street

Patricia Chen, 1300 Tarlow Lane

ETS 기출

모의고사 2회

196. What is the purpose of the e-mail?

(A) To introduce the city's new waste management coordinator
(B) To inform the public that a city service will be discontinued
(C) To ask city residents to reduce their use of disposable containers
(D) To request that city residents complete a survey about their recycling needs

197. What is indicated in the e-mail about the Barnhill City Council?

(A) It may resume recycling pickup in the future.
(B) It will raise the fee for trash pickup.
(C) It identified some ways to save money.
(D) It voted to expand the Shelburne Road facility.

198. What does the Web page indicate about Ecoland Recycling's standard service?

(A) It is less expensive than other services.
(B) It includes two pickups a week.
(C) It is intended for businesses.
(D) It costs €6 per month.

199. Why might Ecoland Recycling's Barnhill customers go to the Shelburne Road facility?

(A) To obtain extra bins
(B) To recycle plastic items
(C) To sign up for curbside pickup
(D) To learn about private recycling companies

200. What is suggested about the new customers in Ecoland Recycling's Zone 3 ?

(A) They are required to supply their own recycling bins.
(B) They previously had contracts with a different recycling company.
(C) They received a discount on their recycling contracts.
(D) They belong to a neighborhood homeowners association.

Stop! This is the end of the test. If you finish before time is called, you may go back to Parts 5, 6, and 7 and check your work.

ETS
기출 모의고사

3 회

⏱ 시험 시간: 120분

	맞은 개수	환산 점수대
LISTENING TEST		
READING TEST		
총점		

*14쪽의 점수 환산표 및 산출법을 참조하세요.

LISTENING TEST

In the Listening test, you will be asked to demonstrate how well you understand spoken English. The entire Listening test will last approximately 45 minutes. There are four parts, and directions are given for each part. You must mark your answers on the separate answer sheet. Do not write your answers in your test book.

PART 1

Directions: For each question in this part, you will hear four statements about a picture in your test book. When you hear the statements, you must select the one statement that best describes what you see in the picture. Then find the number of the question on your answer sheet and mark your answer. The statements will not be printed in your test book and will be spoken only one time.

Statement (C), "They're sitting at a table," is the best description of the picture, so you should select answer (C) and mark it on your answer sheet.

1.

2.

GO ON TO THE NEXT PAGE

3.

4.

5.

6.

GO ON TO THE NEXT PAGE

PART 2

7. Mark your answer on your answer sheet.

8. Mark your answer on your answer sheet.

9. Mark your answer on your answer sheet.

10. Mark your answer on your answer sheet.

11. Mark your answer on your answer sheet.

12. Mark your answer on your answer sheet.

13. Mark your answer on your answer sheet.

14. Mark your answer on your answer sheet.

15. Mark your answer on your answer sheet.

16. Mark your answer on your answer sheet.

17. Mark your answer on your answer sheet.

18. Mark your answer on your answer sheet.

19. Mark your answer on your answer sheet.

20. Mark your answer on your answer sheet.

21. Mark your answer on your answer sheet.

22. Mark your answer on your answer sheet.

23. Mark your answer on your answer sheet.

24. Mark your answer on your answer sheet.

25. Mark your answer on your answer sheet.

26. Mark your answer on your answer sheet.

27. Mark your answer on your answer sheet.

28. Mark your answer on your answer sheet.

29. Mark your answer on your answer sheet.

30. Mark your answer on your answer sheet.

31. Mark your answer on your answer sheet.

Directions: You will hear some conversations between two or more people. You will be asked to answer three questions about what the speakers say in each conversation. Select the best response to each question and mark the letter (A), (B), (C), or (D) on your answer sheet. The conversations will not be printed in your test book and will be spoken only one time.

32. Where does the woman most likely work?
(A) At a travel agency
(B) At an Internet service provider
(C) At a law firm
(D) At a real estate agency

33. What can the man do on a Web site?
(A) Purchase a ticket
(B) Apply for a job
(C) Cancel a service
(D) Open a customer account

34. Why does the woman apologize?
(A) A colleague is not available.
(B) A Web page is not working.
(C) An application was not processed.
(D) An expense will not be reimbursed.

35. What most likely is the woman's job?
(A) Architect
(B) Research scientist
(C) Marketing specialist
(D) Accountant

36. What does the woman ask for?
(A) Some receipts
(B) Some vendor addresses
(C) An electronic file location
(D) A delivery schedule

37. What will happen at 3:00 ?
(A) A product demonstration
(B) A press conference
(C) A client call
(D) A software upgrade

38. What does the man most likely sell?
(A) Picture frames
(B) Computers
(C) Outdoor lighting
(D) Eyeglasses

39. What does the woman ask about?
(A) The cost of an item
(B) The color of an item
(C) A delivery date
(D) A warranty

40. What does the man say will happen next week?
(A) A position will be filled.
(B) A repair will be completed.
(C) A product will be discounted.
(D) A shipment will arrive.

41. Who most likely are the speakers?
(A) Travel agents
(B) Event planners
(C) Restaurant chefs
(D) Magazine journalists

42. What specific event does the man highlight?
(A) A music performance
(B) A book fair
(C) A food festival
(D) An art exhibition

43. What does the woman say she will do next?
(A) Provide samples to clients
(B) Post a link to social media
(C) Review some résumés
(D) Print some handouts

GO ON TO THE NEXT PAGE

44. What job is the man interviewing for?

(A) Accountant
(B) Architect
(C) Graphic designer
(D) Software engineer

45. Where did the man see the job advertised?

(A) On social media
(B) On television
(C) On a billboard
(D) In the newspaper

46. What will the man most likely do next?

(A) Go to the security office
(B) Meet other colleagues
(C) Present a portfolio
(D) Ask about a company policy

47. Who most likely is the woman?

(A) A computer technician
(B) A hotel receptionist
(C) An event organizer
(D) A fitness trainer

48. Why does the man want to delay a program?

(A) He does not have the funding.
(B) He is leaving on a business trip.
(C) He feels unprepared.
(D) He is waiting for more participants.

49. What does the woman suggest?

(A) Using a mobile application
(B) Registering in advance
(C) Changing an appointment time
(D) Meeting regularly

50. Who most likely are the speakers?

(A) Baggage handlers
(B) Travel agents
(C) Airline pilots
(D) Airport security staff

51. What does the woman recommend that the man do?

(A) Arrive to work early
(B) Visit a restaurant
(C) Check a Web site for updates
(D) Take a city tour

52. What will the man most likely do next?

(A) Have his uniform cleaned
(B) Confirm his work schedule
(C) Purchase a meal
(D) Go through a security checkpoint

53. What recently happened at the speakers' company?

(A) A client ended a contract.
(B) A department hired a consultant.
(C) A headquarters was relocated.
(D) A business loan was rejected.

54. What does the woman say a company needs to focus on?

(A) Upgrading its technology
(B) Attending some industry conferences
(C) Organizing some team-building exercises
(D) Maintaining better communication

55. Why does Artem say he will schedule a meeting?

(A) To plan an event
(B) To welcome a new staff member
(C) To learn about some software
(D) To brainstorm some ideas

56. What are the speakers mainly discussing?

(A) A shopping trip
(B) An event for investors
(C) A construction project
(D) A staff survey

57. Why does the man say, "There's the York Shopping Center in Glenville"?

(A) To provide a recommendation
(B) To correct an assumption
(C) To express approval for a plan
(D) To extend an invitation

58. Why does the man want more time to review a document?

(A) Some information is missing.
(B) Another task is more urgent.
(C) A proposal is several pages long.
(D) A cost is higher than expected.

---

59. What most likely is the woman's job?

(A) Lawyer
(B) Financial analyst
(C) Scientist
(D) Real estate agent

60. What does the man say about Springfield?

(A) He was recently elected mayor there.
(B) He is interested in buying farmland there.
(C) It is the subject of an article he is writing.
(D) It is the city where he grew up.

61. Why does the woman say, "I'll be in that area tomorrow"?

(A) To complain about her heavy workload
(B) To explain why she turned down an invitation
(C) To indicate that a task can be completed on time
(D) To offer to give the man a ride

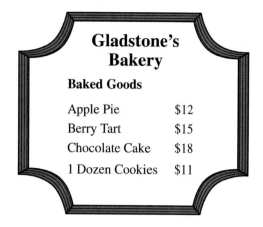

Gladstone's Bakery

Baked Goods

Apple Pie	$12
Berry Tart	$15
Chocolate Cake	$18
1 Dozen Cookies	$11

62. What type of event will the speakers attend?

(A) A theater performance
(B) A retirement party
(C) A corporate banquet
(D) An art exhibit opening

63. Look at the graphic. How much will the man pay for an item?

(A) $12
(B) $15
(C) $18
(D) $11

64. What does the woman offer to do?

(A) Take some photographs
(B) Prepare a conference room
(C) Pick up some supplies
(D) Contribute some money

GO ON TO THE NEXT PAGE

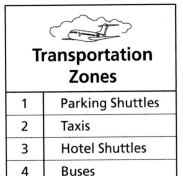

Transportation Zones

1	Parking Shuttles
2	Taxis
3	Hotel Shuttles
4	Buses

Lease Options

Term	Monthly Rent
Two years	$1,300
One year	$1,350
Six months	$1,450
Per month	$1,500

65. What does the man ask the woman to do?

(A) Enroll him in a rewards program
(B) Check his luggage
(C) Change a reservation
(D) Refund a ticket

66. Why is the man traveling?

(A) To purchase a home
(B) To attend a conference
(C) To conduct an interview
(D) To do some sightseeing

67. Look at the graphic. Where will the man most likely go next?

(A) To zone 1
(B) To zone 2
(C) To zone 3
(D) To zone 4

68. What feature of the apartment does the man like?

(A) The wood flooring
(B) The upgraded appliances
(C) The size of the kitchen
(D) The view from the living room

69. Look at the graphic. How much will the man pay?

(A) $1,300
(B) $1,350
(C) $1,450
(D) $1,500

70. What does the woman say she will do?

(A) Arrange for a professional cleaning
(B) Have a set of keys made
(C) Assign a parking space
(D) Provide a pass to a fitness center

PART 4

Directions: You will hear some talks given by a single speaker. You will be asked to answer three questions about what the speaker says in each talk. Select the best response to each question and mark the letter (A), (B), (C), or (D) on your answer sheet. The talks will not be printed in your test book and will be spoken only one time.

71. Where does the speaker work?
    (A) At a textile factory
    (B) At a picture frame shop
    (C) At a clothing store
    (D) At an interior design firm

72. What goal does the speaker mention?
    (A) Reducing expenses
    (B) Selling more than a competitor
    (C) Opening another location
    (D) Providing excellent customer service

73. What does the speaker say he will give to the listeners?
    (A) A work schedule
    (B) A uniform
    (C) A contact list
    (D) An alarm code

74. What are the listeners learning about?
    (A) How to use a computer program
    (B) How to complete a monthly inventory
    (C) How to order supplies
    (D) How to create a sales invoice

75. What will the listeners receive if they complete a webinar?
    (A) An extra vacation day
    (B) A gift card
    (C) A completion certificate
    (D) Tickets to a local festival

76. According to the speaker, what will the listeners do next?
    (A) Enter their employee identification numbers
    (B) Check an inventory list
    (C) Update some prices
    (D) Change column titles

77. What is the speaker scheduled to do on March 7 ?
    (A) Take an overseas trip
    (B) Give a flying lesson
    (C) Tour an airport
    (D) Purchase an aircraft

78. Why does the speaker prefer a particular aircraft?
    (A) It has a special navigation system.
    (B) It has an excellent reputation.
    (C) It has extra space for cargo.
    (D) It can reach very high speeds.

79. What does the speaker ask the listener to do?
    (A) Accompany him on a flight
    (B) Provide some documentation
    (C) Use a different airplane
    (D) Make a recommendation

80. What does the speaker remind the listeners about?
    (A) A change to a security code
    (B) A scheduled training session
    (C) A company policy
    (D) A visit by executives

81. What does the speaker say happened last month?
    (A) Sales increased.
    (B) Product defects declined.
    (C) More work shifts were added.
    (D) A new car model started production.

82. What goal is discussed?
    (A) Improving customer service
    (B) Merging with a competitor
    (C) Updating production technology
    (D) Expanding a business internationally

GO ON TO THE NEXT PAGE

83. Who is the speaker calling?

    (A) A travel agent
    (B) An architect
    (C) A building manager
    (D) A shuttle driver

84. What does the speaker mean when he says, "I'm leaving on a business trip tonight"?

    (A) He needs a ride to the airport.
    (B) He cannot complete some paperwork.
    (C) An itinerary was changed suddenly.
    (D) An appointment should be rescheduled.

85. What does the speaker say he will pay extra money for?

    (A) Overnight delivery
    (B) A parking space
    (C) A larger property
    (D) A scenic view

86. What type of artwork does the exhibit feature?

    (A) Oil paintings
    (B) Woven baskets
    (C) Clay pottery
    (D) Wooden carvings

87. What does the speaker imply when she says, "The other galleries in this museum are permanent"?

    (A) Maps are available.
    (B) Children are welcome.
    (C) Photography is allowed.
    (D) Admission is free.

88. What does the speaker offer to the listeners?

    (A) Art prints
    (B) Pamphlets
    (C) Headphones
    (D) Bottles of water

89. What does the company specialize in?

    (A) Creating digital art galleries
    (B) Printing photographs on canvases
    (C) Organizing commercial photography sessions
    (D) Compressing images for file attachments

90. What does the speaker say some software can assist with?

    (A) Importing files in batches
    (B) Labeling images by category
    (C) Overlaying text onto photographs
    (D) Selecting the appropriate size

91. According to the speaker, what advantage does the company have over its competitors?

    (A) It has low-cost subscription plans.
    (B) It is preferred by industry professionals.
    (C) It offers easy refunds.
    (D) It provides faster customer support.

92. Where is the talk taking place?

    (A) At a hair salon
    (B) At a jewelry store
    (C) At an automobile dealership
    (D) At a shoe store

93. Why does the speaker say, "the location's just down the street"?

    (A) To discourage the listeners from driving
    (B) To reassure the listeners about a change
    (C) To recommend taking a short break
    (D) To express disappointment about a decision

94. What will some new employees do?

    (A) Advertise products
    (B) Handle finances
    (C) Schedule appointments
    (D) Repair items

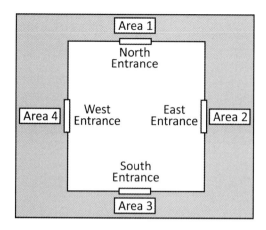

Radio Show	Broadcast Time	Host
Tech Chat	11:00	Sabine Klein
Local News	12:00	Jong-Gyu Cho
Food Bites	1:00	Shiori Azuma
Garden Blooms	2:00	Beatriz Flores

95. What is the talk mainly about?

(A) An annual company event
(B) A mobile-phone policy
(C) An employee survey
(D) A sustainability initiative

96. Look at the graphic. Where does the speaker say an amenity is available?

(A) In area 1
(B) In area 2
(C) In area 3
(D) In area 4

97. According to the speaker, how can the listeners submit recommendations?

(A) By using a link
(B) By sending an e-mail
(C) By speaking with a supervisor
(D) By scheduling a meeting

98. Look at the graphic. Who is the speaker substituting for?

(A) Sabine Klein
(B) Jong-Gyu Cho
(C) Shiori Azuma
(D) Beatriz Flores

99. According to the speaker, what will be the focus of an interview?

(A) Using environmentally friendly practices
(B) Writing a best-selling book
(C) Volunteering in the community
(D) Developing a successful business

100. Who does the speaker thank?

(A) The show's audience
(B) The production team
(C) The show's sponsor
(D) The station owner

This is the end of the Listening test. Turn to Part 5 in your test book.

GO ON TO THE NEXT PAGE

READING TEST

In the Reading test, you will read a variety of texts and answer several different types of reading comprehension questions. The entire Reading test will last 75 minutes. There are three parts, and directions are given for each part. You are encouraged to answer as many questions as possible within the time allowed.

You must mark your answers on the separate answer sheet. Do not write your answers in your test book.

PART 5

Directions: A word or phrase is missing in each of the sentences below. Four answer choices are given below each sentence. Select the best answer to complete the sentence. Then mark the letter (A), (B), (C), or (D) on your answer sheet.

101. Harbison and Company will be marking its 25-year anniversary ------- May 14.

(A) in
(B) at
(C) on
(D) to

102. Fashiontrack Athleticwear ------- thousands of workers at its retail locations worldwide.

(A) employs
(B) employer
(C) employable
(D) employing

103. Mr. Noe enjoys listening to audiobooks, ------- he does not mind his long commute to work.

(A) for
(B) but
(C) so
(D) or

104. Mr. Mansour ------- predicted the consumer demand for new coffee products.

(A) correct
(B) correcting
(C) corrects
(D) correctly

105. Connect Net provides Internet service to ------- 40 percent of Monroe County.

(A) here
(B) about
(C) fast
(D) today

106. The forms are ------- on our Web site and can be downloaded at your convenience.

(A) available
(B) availability
(C) availabilities
(D) availableness

107. When operating at ------- capacity, the refinery can process 30,000 liters of olive oil each day.

(A) full
(B) most
(C) rich
(D) tall

108. Employees are encouraged to update ------- in the shared calendar to avoid scheduling conflicts.

(A) appointing
(B) appointments
(C) appointed
(D) appoint

109. Senior management will conduct a ------- on how to lead effective meetings at 2:30 P.M. next Monday.
(A) search
(B) workshop
(C) manual
(D) decision

110. Connie's Adhesives is best known for manufacturing ------- multipurpose glues for automotive use.
(A) excel
(B) excellent
(C) excelled
(D) excels

111. After making your online purchase, please ------- the on-screen instructions to take a short survey.
(A) guide
(B) chase
(C) follow
(D) uphold

112. The IT technicians will give ------- two months to execute the software transition.
(A) themselves
(B) their
(C) they
(D) theirs

113. Employees must notify the human resources department of any address changes ------- ten days of moving.
(A) since
(B) under
(C) before
(D) within

114. Premium subscribers have lifetime ------- to courses on Eduton Academy's online learning platform.
(A) accessible
(B) access
(C) accessing
(D) accessed

115. The recipe recommends ------- the batter for at least three minutes to ensure the ingredients are well combined.
(A) measuring
(B) checking
(C) pouring
(D) mixing

116. Hickory Creek is not far from Fairview, so you can easily visit ------- in a single day.
(A) which
(B) both
(C) none
(D) fewer

117. Mr. Han left the ------- loan documents in an envelope on Mr. Oliver's desk.
(A) accomplished
(B) satisfied
(C) completed
(D) inhabited

118. Returns at Jebili's Treasure Trove ------- at the customer service desk near the entrance.
(A) to process
(B) have processed
(C) being processed
(D) are processed

119. Seasonal employees at Waterslide Park receive their ------- paycheck one week after the close of the season.
(A) final
(B) steady
(C) absolute
(D) fortunate

120. ------- time you make a purchase with your Pierce Card, a portion of the transaction will be donated to the charity of your choice.
(A) Yet
(B) Beside
(C) Each
(D) Until

GO ON TO THE NEXT PAGE

121. Griffley Architects is working ------- with Lim Construction to create a state-of-the-art office building on Bell Street.

   (A) previously
   (B) scarcely
   (C) cooperatively
   (D) immensely

122. Glate's laminate flooring looks just like ------- wood, but it is much easier to maintain.

   (A) authentication
   (B) authenticity
   (C) authenticate
   (D) authentic

123. It is possible to buy repurposed construction components, ------- it is not recommended.

   (A) then
   (B) similarly
   (C) because
   (D) though

124. A library card will be issued to any Mountain City resident ------- requests one.

   (A) who
   (B) what
   (C) whatever
   (D) whoever

125. ------- businesses switched to Birijon Web-Hosting Services after its closest competitor experienced server failures.

   (A) Despite
   (B) Over
   (C) Beyond
   (D) More

126. Having ------- the same salary for three years, Mr. Shadid will be relieved to learn he is getting a raise this month.

   (A) earned
   (B) offered
   (C) needed
   (D) required

127. Everyone should have received a copy of the staff directory that ------- last week.

   (A) distributed
   (B) distributing
   (C) was distributed
   (D) was distributing

128. Landscape artist Valerie Samson says the ------- for her paintings was a Mediterranean coastal village.

   (A) accessory
   (B) inspiration
   (C) hospitality
   (D) submission

129. After participating in many ------- structured debates, the political candidates appreciated a more relaxed group interview.

   (A) high
   (B) higher
   (C) highly
   (D) highest

130. Grandeur Tractors' quarterly profits were disappointing, and -------, the company had to sell off much of its inventory.

   (A) otherwise
   (B) comparatively
   (C) on the contrary
   (D) as a result

PART 6

Directions: Read the texts that follow. A word, phrase, or sentence is missing in parts of each text. Four answer choices for each question are given below the text. Select the best answer to complete the text. Then mark the letter (A), (B), (C), or (D) on your answer sheet.

Questions 131-134 refer to the following notice.

Department of Industry Temporarily Closed

Posted: January 5

The Department of Industry will be closed today, January 5, and tomorrow, January 6, for an important software update ------- a shutdown of the computer system. Be advised that ------- this
131.   132.
time period, license applications cannot be accepted online. However, to have an agent contact you, phone in and leave a voice message. Take note that you must include your full name and a ------- phone number. Both are required in order to receive a return call. ------- .
  133.   134.

131. (A) necessity
(B) necessitating
(C) necessary
(D) necessities

132. (A) by
(B) except
(C) as
(D) during

133. (A) valid
(B) validate
(C) validates
(D) validity

134. (A) You have successfully renewed your registration.
(B) We will have additional agents to assist with the calls.
(C) Users should regularly update their computers.
(D) Agents will assist with identification cards.

GO ON TO THE NEXT PAGE

Questions 135-138 refer to the following letter.

May 3

Celia Edgar
24 Crystal Beach Road
Middletown, OH 45055

Dear Ms. Edgar,

Thank you for letting us know about your move. Your ------- deliveries of milk and orange juice
135.
will come to your new address starting on May 10. Your delivery day will move from Tuesdays
to Thursdays, so please remember to put your empty bottles out every Wednesday night.

If you need to postpone a delivery, or if you wish to change the items in your order, you can do
so at www.mcgrathdairies.com/customerservice. We offer cottage cheese, yogurt, and eggs,
------- our fresh milk in glass bottles.
136.

We are pleased to count you among the growing number of people who ------- the convenience
137.
of home delivery. ------- .
138.

Sincerely,

Francis Bunuan
Manager, McGrath Dairies

135. (A) hourly
(B) daily
(C) weekly
(D) yearly

136. (A) as far as
(B) on account of
(C) in addition to
(D) with regard to

137. (A) enjoyment
(B) enjoyable
(C) enjoying
(D) enjoy

138. (A) We look forward to continuing to
serve you.
(B) We encourage you to recycle your
empty bottles.
(C) We are currently hiring new delivery
drivers.
(D) We regret that this service is no
longer available.

About Cerebellum

The Cerebellum app improves your mental acuity by challenging your mathematical and analytical thinking with a variety of ------- exercises. Track your progress in different skills via
            139.
your Cerebellum Proficiency Scores (CPS). These ------- are determined by evaluating users'
                                              140.
accuracy and response times. ------- . They range from 400 to 800 in each skill. Train at your
                            141.
own pace or compete with friends using the group-training function. Plan options include a $5

monthly or a $50 annual membership fee. Encourage ------- to sign up for a membership using
                                                142.
the promo code "CPSFRIEND" and get your first month free.

139. (A) engage
     (B) engages
     (C) engaged
     (D) engaging

140. (A) numbers
     (B) amounts
     (C) quantities
     (D) conclusions

141. (A) The referral bonus is limited to one per
         user.
     (B) Cerebellum is available wherever apps
         are sold.
     (C) CPS scores can be found in the My
         Performance section of the app.
     (D) People are looking for a way to test their
         knowledge.

142. (A) it
     (B) us
     (C) others
     (D) something

GO ON TO THE NEXT PAGE

Questions 143-146 refer to the following article.

VANCOUVER (6 April)—Lori's Sweet Treats Ice Cream announced today it is expanding internationally. ------- . In June it will open its first franchise south of the border in Seattle.
143.

"We have been looking to enter the market in the United States for years," said Lori Stout, the company's founder and CEO. "The ------- are now finally just right. The economy, the exchange
144.
rate—everything is favourable."

Lori's Sweet Treats Ice Cream ------- a menu that includes 40 flavours of ice cream. "We are
145.
known for our range of flavours," said Ms. Stout. "------- we serve the classics like chocolate and
146.
vanilla. But we also have some unusual ones that are very popular."

The Canadian company currently operates fourteen shops in the Vancouver area.

143. (A) Lori's Sweet Treats Ice Cream
employs more than 1,000 workers.
(B) Ice cream is enjoyed all over the
world.
(C) The popular ice cream chain has
been a Canadian staple for ten
years.
(D) The Vancouver-based company
recently hired a new general
manager.

144. (A) tools
(B) conditions
(C) portions
(D) temperatures

145. (A) boasts
(B) boaster
(C) boasting
(D) boastful

146. (A) There
(B) In fact
(C) Instead
(D) Of course

PART 7

Directions: In this part you will read a selection of texts, such as magazine and newspaper articles, e-mails, and instant messages. Each text or set of texts is followed by several questions. Select the best answer for each question and mark the letter (A), (B), (C), or (D) on your answer sheet.

Questions 147-149 refer to the following advertisement.

Airbest Airlines
Convenience, Comfort, Care

Named Best Customer Service by *International Business Travel Magazine*

- Daily flights operating out of St. Louis
- New European destinations: Frankfurt and Oslo
- Direct flights early in the morning and overnight (Get to meetings and back home within 24 hours!)
- Excellent amenities, including fully reclining seats, a wide selection of inflight entertainment options, and chef-prepared cuisine that passengers can select online before traveling

Book online at www.airbestairlines.com.

---

147. Who most likely is the advertisement for?

(A) Airline pilots
(B) Business travelers
(C) Airport employees
(D) Tour guides

148. What is indicated about Airbest Airlines?

(A) It was mentioned in a magazine.
(B) It is based in Oslo.
(C) It is hiring flight attendants.
(D) It recently acquired new airplanes.

149. What is included in the amenities on Airbest Airlines?

(A) Especially wide seats
(B) Entertainment choices unavailable elsewhere
(C) Wireless Internet service
(D) Food that can be ordered before a flight

GO ON TO THE NEXT PAGE

Questions 150-151 refer to the following e-mail.

To:	Mr. Jason Henare
From:	Ms. Sarah Rotessa
Re:	Access authorisation
Date:	8 August
Attachment:	📎 Signature verification form

Dear Mr. Henare,

The Bank of Pukekohe has received your request to grant another person access to your account. In order to proceed, we require both the current account holder and the person who needs access to complete a signature verification form.

As the account holder, you will need to print out the attached form and sign where indicated. You are also responsible for obtaining Ms. Mahoney's signature.

Once the form has been signed by you and Ms. Mahoney, either return the form by mail or scan it and send it back to me as an e-mail attachment.

If you have any questions, please contact me at 09 555 0109, ext. 513.

Thank you.

Sarah Rotessa, Personal Accounts Manager
Bank of Pukekohe
228 Wesley Street
Pukekohe, Auckland 2120

150. What is the purpose of the e-mail?

(A) To cancel a transaction
(B) To provide instructions
(C) To correct an error
(D) To announce policy changes

151. What is Ms. Mahoney expected to do?

(A) Pay a banking fee
(B) Forward an e-mail
(C) Sign a document
(D) Close a bank account

Questions 152-153 refer to the following notice.

Pinebrook Manors Policy Update: Good News for Grillers

The Pinebrook Manors Homeowners Association has recently made a policy change to Item 19.3 on page 28 of our *Community Standards Guide*. As of 9 June, homeowners will be permitted to use a charcoal, gas, or propane grill on their patios in the back of their houses without approval from the homeowners association. However, if you plan to connect a grill to the natural gas line, you will need written permission from the association before installation. The office has the appropriate forms for this request. In all cases, grills must be placed on the cement patio, no closer than four feet from the house.

Thank you. We hope you enjoy safe barbecuing!

---

152. Who is the notice written for?

(A) Workers at a construction company
(B) Business owners in a specific area
(C) Subscribers to a local newspaper
(D) Residents of a private community

153. What will be allowed as of June 9 ?

(A) The use of barbecue grills
(B) The installation of back patios
(C) Access to a public cooking area
(D) Paid access to a natural gas line

GO ON TO THE NEXT PAGE

Questions 154-155 refer to the following review.

Hoskuld Tours is the Best Tour Operator in Iceland!

If you're planning to visit Reykjavik, be sure to check out Hoskuld Tours. It offers the best group walking tours I've ever been on—and I have been on many, all over the globe. The guides are friendly and knowledgeable. Over the course of two and a half hours, you'll see just about every important landmark in central Reykjavik at a very reasonable cost. After the tour, you can enjoy a meal at one of the city's classy restaurants and spend the afternoon at the Icelandic History Museum.

Hoskuld Tours also offers boat excursions for whale watching. Unfortunately, I missed my chance. I would have gone on one of these excursions if my visit to Iceland had been longer, but I will definitely do it on my next visit.
—Elise Chae

---

154. What is suggested about Ms. Chae?

(A) She is an experienced traveler.
(B) She used to work in Reykjavik.
(C) She took a walking tour that lasted all day.
(D) She thinks that her restaurant meal cost too much.

155. What does Ms. Chae plan to do on her next visit to Iceland?

(A) Visit a museum
(B) See a city landmark
(C) Go whale watching
(D) Hire a private tour guide

Questions 156-157 refer to the following online chat discussion.

Miguel Canales [10:02 A.M.]
I ran the numbers again. The budget is still not balanced.

Joy Min [10:06 A.M.]
That's unfortunate. What do you suggest we do?

Miguel Canales [10:15 A.M.]
Because of the discrepancy, I would like to request an audit of last year's revenues and expenditures. I just wanted to let you know in advance.

Joy Min [10:17 A.M.]
I support that idea. Draw up the paperwork, and I will sign the approval. Let's start with an internal audit. We'll see what happens. If we need to, we can then hire an independent external auditing company.

Miguel Canales [10:18 A.M.]
Will do. Thanks.

156. What is the main topic of the discussion?

(A) Budget cuts
(B) A bookkeeping issue
(C) Unnecessary paperwork
(D) Employee feedback

157. At 10:17 A.M., what does Ms. Min most likely mean when she writes, "We'll see what happens"?

(A) She thinks Mr. Canales' clients will arrive soon.
(B) She will approve Mr. Canales' request.
(C) She will wait for some results before acting.
(D) She doubts that costs will increase.

GO ON TO THE NEXT PAGE

ETS 기출

모의고사 3회

Questions 158-160 refer to the following job posting.

Information Technology Infrastructure Manager

Erpop Video Services; Manchester, England

Description: Trains and supervises technology team to ensure the secure and stable operation of the company's IT systems. This includes maintaining and optimising network and server infrastructure, data communications, and the company's telephone system. The infrastructure manager also oversees end-user customer service to resolve hardware and software issues in a timely manner.

Assigns tasks to team members and evaluates their performance.

Reports to the director of Information Technology, who determines departmental policies and procedures and evaluates the manager's performance.

Qualifications: University degree in information technology and a minimum of five years of relevant experience.

To apply, send résumé to hr@erpopvideoservices.co.uk.

---

158. What is indicated about the posted job?

(A) It involves the security of campus buildings.
(B) It offers the possibility of job promotion.
(C) It requires the maintenance of a telephone system.
(D) It is a newly created position.

159. Who sets the IT infrastructure policies?

(A) The department manager
(B) The department director
(C) The infrastructure team members
(D) The company president

160. What is a stated requirement for the position?

(A) Experience in financial administration
(B) A high security clearance
(C) Ability to work flexible hours
(D) Previous work in a closely related role

To:	Kendra Klasnik <kendra.klasnik@mailhost.com>
From:	Marco Vargas <marco.vargas@buslono.com>
Subject:	Next week
Date:	September 13

Hello, Kendra,

Welcome to Buslono Industries! My name is Marco, and I will be your peer mentor. As was likely explained to you, all new hires are paired with a peer mentor for the first six weeks of their employment. I will be your point of contact to help answer questions about company policies and culture and to help you get settled into your new position. — [1] —.

I have been working for Buslono for nearly five years, first as a production assistant and now as a production leader. I have firsthand knowledge of the role you're about to take on. — [2] —.

On your first day, September 20, your first stop will be at the HR department, where Ms. Stacey will get you set up with paperwork and an employee ID. — [3] —. From there, I will give you a tour of the offices and introduce you to our colleagues. Then we can all get lunch together in the cafeteria. — [4] —.

I look forward to seeing you on Monday.

Marco Vargas
Production Leader, Buslono Industries

161. What is one reason Mr. Vargas wrote to Ms. Klasnik?

(A) To offer her a job
(B) To introduce himself
(C) To outline her responsibilities
(D) To answer a question about a policy

162. What is suggested about Ms. Klasnik?

(A) She will work in the production department.
(B) She knows the location of the cafeteria.
(C) She previously held a different position at Buslono Industries.
(D) She will be Ms. Stacey's supervisor.

163. In which of the positions marked [1], [2], [3], and [4] does the following sentence best belong?

"I will meet you in her office at 10:30 A.M."

(A) [1]
(B) [2]
(C) [3]
(D) [4]

Sandra Melendez [1:14 P.M.] I'm hoping one of you can help me with something.

Lester Tabayoyong [1:15 P.M.] I'll certainly try. What do you need?

Sandra Melendez [1:16 P.M.] I just called to schedule an appointment with Fountain of Clean, the company we've been using to wash the office windows.

Daria Krzyk [1:17 P.M.] The windows could sure use a cleaning! The construction project next door has kicked up a lot of dust.

Sandra Melendez [1:18 P.M.] Unfortunately, the Fountain of Clean telephone number has been disconnected, and their Web site is no longer available. It seems the company has gone out of business.

Lester Tabayoyong [1:19 P.M.] That's too bad. They always did a good job.

Sandra Melendez [1:20 P.M.] Do you know of any reliable window washers? Who did your last employer use?

Lester Tabayoyong [1:21 P.M.] I think they also used Fountain of Clean.

Daria Krzyk [1:22 P.M.] I'm afraid I can't help you.

Lester Tabayoyong [1:23 P.M.] Ask Mr. Gortimer. He was the head of maintenance at his old company and might have some ideas.

Sandra Melendez [1:24 P.M.] I'll get in touch with him right away.

164. What does Ms. Melendez need?

(A) A service provider recommendation
(B) A company handbook
(C) A client's telephone number
(D) A colleague's work history

165. Why does Ms. Krzyk mention a construction project?

(A) To justify a significant expense
(B) To note why the windows are particularly dirty
(C) To complain about excessive noise
(D) To express gratitude for additional office space

166. At 1:19 P.M., what does Mr. Tabayoyong most likely mean when he writes, "That's too bad"?

(A) He thought a task was performed poorly.
(B) He does not care about a problem.
(C) He cannot disclose a confidential source.
(D) He is disappointed to learn some information.

167. What will Ms. Melendez most likely do next?

(A) Contact a coworker
(B) Make a reservation
(C) Log on to a Web site
(D) Schedule a delivery

GO ON TO THE NEXT PAGE

ETS 기출

모의고사 3회

Lusaka Business Alliance
A Celebration of Accomplishments
Royal Nugget Hotel, Saturday, 12 June, 8:00–11:00 P.M.

On 12 June, the Lusaka Business Alliance (LBA) will be presenting several local business leaders with awards to acknowledge their accomplishments. The event will be held in the ballroom of the Royal Nugget Hotel. Tickets are K 500 per person.

On this occasion, we will also be presenting the Supremacy Award to Ms. Brenda Masebo for five decades of service to the Lusaka community. Her store, the Sketch Path, has for 40 years now been the place to go for the widest assortments of art and office supplies. Moreover, 15 years ago, she initiated the Lusaka Arts Jamboree, which brings numerous visual and performance artists to the city as well as tourists from across Central Africa. And last year, Ms. Masebo began an arts program for teens that has already drawn praise from the Ministry of Arts and Sciences.

We will end the evening with an art auction. Auction items can be viewed, and tickets for the event can be purchased on the LBA's Web site, www.lusakabusinessalliance.org.zm. All proceeds raised from the auction will benefit the XJK Foundation, whose mission is to support recreational opportunities for local youth.

168. What can be concluded about Ms. Masebo?

(A) She recently started a business.
(B) She has promoted the arts in various ways.
(C) She has traveled extensively in Central Africa.
(D) She used to be a government employee.

169. The word "drawn" in paragraph 2, line 7, is closest in meaning to

(A) tightened
(B) marked
(C) attracted
(D) illustrated

170. According to the announcement, what can visitors to the LBA Web site do?

(A) Buy admission tickets
(B) Sign up to receive e-mail updates
(C) View a list of current members
(D) Nominate a colleague for an award

171. What is one purpose of the event?

(A) To introduce the new director of an organization
(B) To announce the creation of a new award
(C) To celebrate a store's anniversary
(D) To raise money for a cause

Questions 172-175 refer to the following memo.

MEMO

To: Sales Team, KL International Home Goods
From: Alex Cardine, Director of Retail Sales
Date: October 29
Subject: Rice cookers

The central shipping warehouse has informed me that we have sold all our Jasmine 200 rice cookers. This is unfortunate because the Jasmine 200 is our most popular model and was expected to be a key item in our ongoing nationwide sale. We think many customers who see ads about the sale will inquire about it. — [1] —.

The discount for the Jasmine 200 was 15 percent off the regular price. To remedy the national sale situation, the corporate office will allow us to offer the Lotus 600 model with the same 15 percent discount. — [2] —. Since the Lotus 600 is the top-of-the-line rice cooker, we expect many customers will want to take advantage of this substantial discount and purchase it. — [3] —.

For those customers who are only interested in purchasing the Jasmine 200 during the sale, store managers may offer a rain check on the discount price. — [4] —. However, managers should inform those customers that there will be a six- to eight-week wait for that model.

---

172. What is one topic of the memo?

(A) A previously concluded sale
(B) A newly released product
(C) A recent pricing decision
(D) A quality control problem

173. What is suggested about the Lotus 600 ?

(A) It was not initially included in the nationwide sale.
(B) It is the company's most popular product.
(C) It is out of stock and needs to be reordered.
(D) It is not selling well because of its high cost.

174. According to the memo, what should store managers communicate to customers?

(A) Production of the Lotus 600 will be discontinued soon.
(B) Jasmine 200 rice cookers will not be available for six to eight weeks.
(C) KL International Home Goods products are already heavily discounted.
(D) Remodeling the store will take more than a month to complete.

175. In which of the positions marked [1], [2], [3], and [4] does the following sentence best belong?

"This problem needs to be addressed immediately."

(A) [1]
(B) [2]
(C) [3]
(D) [4]

GO ON TO THE NEXT PAGE

https://www.colettesbooks.co.uk/toppicks

Top Picks at Colette's Books

As spring comes to a close, readers turn to Colette's Books to find rewarding reads for the summer months. Every season, Colette's selects its top five new releases—and shoppers who purchase at least three of the five books receive 15% off their purchase.

Here are our picks for this summer.

• *Hidden by Clouds*, by Rachel Polk. In the not-too-distant future, explorers land on a planet in a nearby galaxy and discover it is already inhabited.

• *Ten Days at Sea*, by Ishan James. The author recounts the tale of a journey his grandparents made across the Atlantic in the late nineteenth century.

• *Taking to the Road*, by Paige Tse. A musician's life is changed when he responds to an advertisement to join a band for a multicity tour.

• *How I Got Here*, by Abel Umeh. Actor Abel Umeh takes a humorous look at his childhood and his eventual rise to celebrity.

• *Some Secrets Will Not Keep*, by Asami Ishida. Amateur detective Eriko Ogawa must use all her skills to solve a mystery in a small Japanese village.

Let us know what you think of this season's selections by sharing your comments using our online form at www.colettesbooks.co.uk/readercomments, and sign up for our newsletter at www.colettesbooks.co.uk/newsletter.

---

https://www.colettesbooks.co.uk/readercomments

Last month, a friend recommended that I check out Colette's Books top picks, and now I am hooked. For the summer, I purchased three books from the list, and I have just finished the first. I was pleasantly surprised by Ishan James's suspenseful and deeply personal story. Who would have guessed that a voyage could be so interesting? It would make an excellent film. I definitely look forward to reading more of Colette's summer selections over the next two months.

— Omar Pitafi

176. How often does Colette's Books create a list of top books?

(A) Every week
(B) Every month
(C) Every season
(D) Every year

177. How can customers of Colette's Books receive a discount?

(A) By joining a readers club
(B) By buying at least three recommended books
(C) By leaving a review on a Web site
(D) By subscribing to a weekly newsletter

178. What would a reader of *Hidden by Clouds* most likely be interested in?

(A) Contemporary music
(B) Detective stories
(C) Weather events
(D) Space travel

179. What book did Mr. Pitafi read?

(A) *Ten Days at Sea*
(B) *Taking to the Road*
(C) *How I Got Here*
(D) *Some Secrets Will Not Keep*

180. What will Mr. Pitafi most likely do in the near future?

(A) Watch a film based on a book he read
(B) Look for a book suggested by a friend
(C) Buy another book by an author he likes
(D) Read another book he recently purchased

GO ON TO THE NEXT PAGE

Questions 181-185 refer to the following policy and form.

Marjay Wireless Device Unlock Policy

Phones purchased from Marjay Wireless are programmed to lock to our wireless network, preventing them from operating with other wireless networks. Under certain conditions, Marjay Wireless will provide an unlock code to allow you to use your device on another carrier's network. However, because of differing technologies, an unlocked Marjay-issued phone may not work on another carrier's network, or the phone may have limited functionality. To have your phone unlocked by Marjay Wireless, you need to meet the following requirements:

1) The device has not been reported as lost or stolen.
2) The device is not associated with another account.
3) The device must be associated with an account with no past due or unpaid balances.
4) The device must be active for at least 60 days of paid service with Marjay Wireless.

To begin the unlock process, sign in to your Marjay account. First, select Settings, then Device, and fill out the form titled "Unlock Your Marjay Wireless Device." Additional customer support is available by calling 617-555-0122. You may also drop by your nearest Marjay Wireless store for assistance.

Unlock Your Marjay Wireless Device

Name of Account Holder	Ana Gaburo
Date of Request	October 1
Account #	5902515663
Account PIN	9318
Address of Account Holder	4069 Star View Way Chicago, IL 60601
Please let us know why you would like to unlock your Marjay device:	I have been a Marjay customer for one year and have been pleased with the service. I use the Marjay family plan and find the offer of five lines for only $100 a month to be very reasonable. I am almost finished paying for all the devices I purchased from Marjay. However, I will be relocating to Winnipeg, Canada, in November and after visiting there a few days ago, I realized that your coverage does not extend outside of the United States.

181. What does the policy mention about Marjay Wireless phones?

(A) They must be reported immediately to Marjay Wireless if they are stolen.
(B) They are offered at a discounted price.
(C) They may not work properly on other networks after they are unlocked.
(D) They can be unlocked 30 days after purchase from Marjay Wireless.

182. In the policy, the word "meet" in paragraph 1, line 6, is closest in meaning to

(A) join
(B) satisfy
(C) consider
(D) settle

183. What most likely must Ms. Gaburo do before her phone can be unlocked?

(A) Verify that her phone is compatible with other networks
(B) Report her phone as lost or stolen
(C) Finish paying for the phones on her account
(D) Close her existing account

184. Why does Ms. Gaburo want to unlock her Marjay Wireless phone?

(A) She is moving to an area not covered by Marjay Wireless.
(B) She is unhappy about the price of her plan.
(C) She is thinking about giving her phone to a family member.
(D) She is dissatisfied with Marjay Wireless' customer representatives.

185. What is indicated about Ms. Gaburo?

(A) She has been a Marjay Wireless customer for five years.
(B) She forgot her account PIN.
(C) She is the only user on her Marjay Wireless plan.
(D) She took a trip to Canada recently.

GO ON TO THE NEXT PAGE

Join us on June 23 to say goodbye to Tom's Food Palace, a landmark in the Knoxville community since it first opened over 40 years ago! Free commemorative T-shirts will be given away to the first 40 people who arrive between 4 and 6 P.M. at the restaurant's parking area.

You can also go online at www.tomsfoodpalace.com and purchase a brightly colored T- shirt. The front of the shirt reads "Tom's Food Palace" and the back reads "Happy Retirement, Tom!" Proceeds from the T-shirt sales will go to Tom's favorite charity, Cooking with Kids, an educational program supporting children in Knoxville schools.

East Tennessee Herald

Dear Editor:

I have been visiting Tom Hensley's restaurant for breakfast since I was a child. Last week, I brought my granddaughter with me. My favorite waitress, Ms. Rita, wore a T-shirt displaying a surprising message. She explained that Mr. Hensley had sold the business and that a barbeque restaurant will be taking its place. While I like barbeque, nothing will replace the warm atmosphere of Tom's Food Palace, especially at breakfast time! Ever the gracious host, Mr. Hensley customarily greets his morning guests at each table while making sure that their coffee cups are always full.

Your chance to visit this restaurant is quickly diminishing. Yesterday I was honored to be one of the first guests who attended Tom's retirement celebration outside of the restaurant. Readers of your newspaper should know they have limited time to enjoy one last meal there!

Tiffani Chester

```
┌─────────────────────────────────────────────┐
│  ┌───────────────────────────────────────┐  │
│  │                                       │  │
│  │          Brindel's Barbeque           │  │
│  │      (formerly Tom's Food Palace)     │  │
│  │                                       │  │
│  │      Specializing in chicken and ribs │  │
│  │                                       │  │
│  │    Grand opening of our newest location: │
│  │       1192 West River Road, Knoxville │  │
│  │                                       │  │
│  │            Opening July 17            │  │
│  │  Opening-day proceeds will be donated to Cooking with Kids. │
│  │                                       │  │
│  │   Mention this advertisement and get a free soft drink │
│  │     at any Brindel's Barbecue location, including: │
│  │                                       │  │
│  │        2300 Park Circle, Oak Ridge    │  │
│  │       4049 Swedesford Mall, Corryton  │  │
│  │         5 Lantern Lane, Maryville     │  │
│  │                                       │  │
│  └───────────────────────────────────────┘  │
└─────────────────────────────────────────────┘
```

186. What is the purpose of the flyer?

(A) To bring attention to a new charity
(B) To invite people to a retirement event
(C) To invite restaurant staff to an anniversary celebration
(D) To introduce a marketing campaign for a business

187. What is most likely true about Ms. Chester?

(A) She owns a catering business.
(B) She used to be employed at Tom's Food Palace.
(C) She received a free T-shirt on June 23.
(D) She has organized an event.

188. What does the letter suggest about Mr. Hensley?

(A) He has greeted Ms. Chester on multiple occasions.
(B) He is moving to another town.
(C) He is transferring his restaurant's ownership to a family member.
(D) He shared some breakfast recipes with Ms. Chester.

189. What do Tom's Food Palace and Brindel's Barbeque have in common?

(A) Both support an educational program.
(B) Both sell gifts online.
(C) Both were founded in Knoxville.
(D) Both have been in business for 40 years.

190. What does the advertisement promote?

(A) A festival on West River Road
(B) The opening of a new business location
(C) An offer for a discounted meal
(D) A hiring event for restaurant workers

Questions 191-195 refer to the following advertisement, e-mail, and profile.

Simpleze Business Solutions

Being a marketing manager means taking on the responsibilities of two jobs at once. You must develop a winning marketing strategy. At the same time, you must support team members' creativity and productivity. We offer a live online course for marketing managers that will help you understand how to balance these demands and sharpen your research and communication skills. Our one-day class highlights the most essential skills for your success. The course instructor is Mr. Ananth Roy, Chief Marketing Officer at Batesole Industries. Participation is capped at twelve registrants for each course date.

Online course dates (choose one): April 4; April 8; April 13; May 3

Cost:

• Early-bird Registration (by March 10): $299

• Regular Registration (by March 25): $349

From:	Marek Novotny <mnovotny@simplezebusinesssolutions.com>
To:	Pablo Espinoza <pespinoza@piscesmail.mx>
Date:	March 9
Subject:	Training course
Attachment:	📎 Profile

Dear Mr. Espinoza,

I am writing about the course you registered for earlier today. Unfortunately, the regular instructor, Mr. Roy, is unable to lead the course meeting on April 8 due to a scheduling conflict. The April 8 course will be taught by Elena Zamora instead. Ms. Zamora has extensive experience teaching marketing courses, and she has a weekly podcast about her work in the publishing industry. I have attached a profile of Ms. Zamora so that you can learn more about her.

If you prefer to take the course with Mr. Roy, I can change your registration to the class that meets on April 13. Please let us know if this option is acceptable to you.

Marek Novotny, Training Coordinator

Business Profile

Elena Zamora, Corporate Trainer

Ms. Zamora is a leading figure in the marketing field. After earning a degree in marketing from the University of Western Maine, she was hired as an analyst by Edgeware Products, a food manufacturer. In later years, she held positions as Chief Marketing Manager in several distinct industries. Five years ago, Ms. Zamora started her own business as a corporate trainer. When she is not facilitating business courses, she hosts her popular podcast *Paper Planes*.

191. According to the advertisement, why is a marketing manager job uniquely challenging?

(A) Marketing teams are hard to assemble.
(B) Marketing campaigns run for a long time.
(C) The job requires skills in multiple areas.
(D) The marketing industry is constantly changing.

192. What is suggested in the advertisement?

(A) Successful marketing cannot be taught online.
(B) Managers should be creative in their hiring decisions.
(C) Designing a good marketing plan takes several weeks.
(D) Developing effective communication strategies is important.

193. What is true about the course for which Mr. Espinoza registered?

(A) He paid $299 for it.
(B) It already had twelve registrants.
(C) His employer required him to take it.
(D) Its cost can be refunded.

194. What is indicated about Ms. Zamora?

(A) She teaches at the University of Western Maine.
(B) She founded Edgeware Products.
(C) She is a flight instructor.
(D) She is self-employed.

195. What is the topic of *Paper Planes* ?

(A) Publishing
(B) The food industry
(C) Corporate training
(D) Travel

GO ON TO THE NEXT PAGE

Questions 196-200 refer to the following articles and e-mail.

Hotel Chain Undergoing Changes

NEW YORK (July 6)—Greece-based Ceebeelux Properties continues to expand, redesign, and improve its hotels. Several Ceebeelux hotels are making changes intended to attract conferences and conventions, as well as private events, such as weddings.

Angelo Genelis, chief operating officer for Ceebeelux Properties, points to the company's hotel in Kingston, Jamaica, as a model for what the company is doing.

"We have just expanded the space for events," said Mr. Genelis. "In addition, areas can easily be reconfigured for different size groups. We can host a large convention, but we can also provide spaces for weddings or business meetings."

Ceebeelux hotels in cities around the world, including Sydney, Vancouver, and Miami, have also been recently renovated.

Upcoming Events

TORONTO (25 July)—The International Association of Small Business and Entrepreneurship (IASBE), based in Toronto, is holding its tenth annual conference from 17 to 24 November at the Ceebeelux Hotel in Kingston, Jamaica.

The IASBE conference attracts participants from all over the world. A keynote speaker will be featured each night, and hundreds of sessions and workshops will be held over the week.

Advanced registration is required to attend all convention events. To register, please visit www.iasbe.ca/conference. Discounted rates for conference attendees are available for all rooms booked by 25 September. For additional information about the convention programme and featured speakers, contact Daniel Olnisson at dolnisson@iasbe.ca.

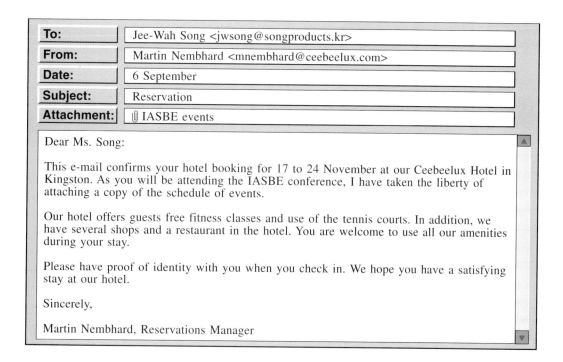

To:	Jee-Wah Song <jwsong@songproducts.kr>
From:	Martin Nembhard <mnembhard@ceebeelux.com>
Date:	6 September
Subject:	Reservation
Attachment:	📎 IASBE events

Dear Ms. Song:

This e-mail confirms your hotel booking for 17 to 24 November at our Ceebeelux Hotel in Kingston. As you will be attending the IASBE conference, I have taken the liberty of attaching a copy of the schedule of events.

Our hotel offers guests free fitness classes and use of the tennis courts. In addition, we have several shops and a restaurant in the hotel. You are welcome to use all our amenities during your stay.

Please have proof of identity with you when you check in. We hope you have a satisfying stay at our hotel.

Sincerely,

Martin Nembhard, Reservations Manager

196. What is suggested in the first article about Ceebeelux Properties?

(A) It is an international business.
(B) It hired a new chief operating officer.
(C) It recently moved its headquarters.
(D) It has merged with another hotel chain.

197. What is suggested about the tenth annual IASBE conference?

(A) It will cost more to attend than it did in previous years.
(B) It will be held at a newly remodeled hotel.
(C) It will feature Mr. Olnisson as a speaker.
(D) It will sell out by the end of November.

198. What can be concluded about Ms. Song?

(A) She plans to play tennis at the hotel.
(B) She plans to arrive early for the conference.
(C) She is eligible for a discounted hotel rate.
(D) She stayed at the Kingston Ceebeelux Hotel before.

199. What did Mr. Nembhard send with the e-mail?

(A) A schedule of fitness classes
(B) Menus from local restaurants
(C) Directions to the Ceebeelux Hotel
(D) Information about a conference

200. What does Mr. Nembhard ask Ms. Song to do?

(A) Complete a customer satisfaction survey
(B) Stop by the hotel desk for a store coupon
(C) Show identification at check-in
(D) Confirm her reservation dates

Stop! This is the end of the test. If you finish before time is called, you may go back to Parts 5, 6, and 7 and check your work.

ANSWER SHEET

ETS 기출 모의고사

수험번호

응시일자 : 20   년   월   일

성명	한글
	한자
	영자

LISTENING (Part I ~ IV)

READING (Part V ~ VII)

ANSWER SHEET

ETS 기출 모의고사

수험번호

응시일자 : 20   년   월   일

성명
- 한글
- 한자
- 영자

LISTENING (Part I ~ IV)

READING (Part V ~ VII)

ANSWER SHEET

ETS 기출 모의고사

수험번호

응시일자 : 20   년   월   일

성명 | 한글
성명 | 한자
성명 | 영자

LISTENING (Part I ~ IV)

1	ⓐ ⓑ ⓒ ⓓ
2	ⓐ ⓑ ⓒ ⓓ
3	ⓐ ⓑ ⓒ ⓓ
4	ⓐ ⓑ ⓒ ⓓ
5	ⓐ ⓑ ⓒ ⓓ
6	ⓐ ⓑ ⓒ ⓓ
7	ⓐ ⓑ ⓒ ⓓ
8	ⓐ ⓑ ⓒ ⓓ
9	ⓐ ⓑ ⓒ ⓓ
10	ⓐ ⓑ ⓒ ⓓ
11	ⓐ ⓑ ⓒ ⓓ
12	ⓐ ⓑ ⓒ ⓓ
13	ⓐ ⓑ ⓒ ⓓ
14	ⓐ ⓑ ⓒ ⓓ
15	ⓐ ⓑ ⓒ ⓓ
16	ⓐ ⓑ ⓒ ⓓ
17	ⓐ ⓑ ⓒ ⓓ
18	ⓐ ⓑ ⓒ ⓓ
19	ⓐ ⓑ ⓒ ⓓ
20	ⓐ ⓑ ⓒ ⓓ
21	ⓐ ⓑ ⓒ ⓓ
22	ⓐ ⓑ ⓒ ⓓ
23	ⓐ ⓑ ⓒ ⓓ
24	ⓐ ⓑ ⓒ ⓓ
25	ⓐ ⓑ ⓒ ⓓ
26	ⓐ ⓑ ⓒ ⓓ
27	ⓐ ⓑ ⓒ ⓓ
28	ⓐ ⓑ ⓒ ⓓ
29	ⓐ ⓑ ⓒ ⓓ
30	ⓐ ⓑ ⓒ ⓓ
31	ⓐ ⓑ ⓒ ⓓ
32	ⓐ ⓑ ⓒ ⓓ
33	ⓐ ⓑ ⓒ ⓓ
34	ⓐ ⓑ ⓒ ⓓ
35	ⓐ ⓑ ⓒ ⓓ
36	ⓐ ⓑ ⓒ ⓓ
37	ⓐ ⓑ ⓒ ⓓ
38	ⓐ ⓑ ⓒ ⓓ
39	ⓐ ⓑ ⓒ ⓓ
40	ⓐ ⓑ ⓒ ⓓ
41	ⓐ ⓑ ⓒ ⓓ
42	ⓐ ⓑ ⓒ ⓓ
43	ⓐ ⓑ ⓒ ⓓ
44	ⓐ ⓑ ⓒ ⓓ
45	ⓐ ⓑ ⓒ ⓓ
46	ⓐ ⓑ ⓒ ⓓ
47	ⓐ ⓑ ⓒ ⓓ
48	ⓐ ⓑ ⓒ ⓓ
49	ⓐ ⓑ ⓒ ⓓ
50	ⓐ ⓑ ⓒ ⓓ
51	ⓐ ⓑ ⓒ ⓓ
52	ⓐ ⓑ ⓒ ⓓ
53	ⓐ ⓑ ⓒ ⓓ
54	ⓐ ⓑ ⓒ ⓓ
55	ⓐ ⓑ ⓒ ⓓ
56	ⓐ ⓑ ⓒ ⓓ
57	ⓐ ⓑ ⓒ ⓓ
58	ⓐ ⓑ ⓒ ⓓ
59	ⓐ ⓑ ⓒ ⓓ
60	ⓐ ⓑ ⓒ ⓓ
61	ⓐ ⓑ ⓒ ⓓ
62	ⓐ ⓑ ⓒ ⓓ
63	ⓐ ⓑ ⓒ ⓓ
64	ⓐ ⓑ ⓒ ⓓ
65	ⓐ ⓑ ⓒ ⓓ
66	ⓐ ⓑ ⓒ ⓓ
67	ⓐ ⓑ ⓒ ⓓ
68	ⓐ ⓑ ⓒ ⓓ
69	ⓐ ⓑ ⓒ ⓓ
70	ⓐ ⓑ ⓒ ⓓ
71	ⓐ ⓑ ⓒ ⓓ
72	ⓐ ⓑ ⓒ ⓓ
73	ⓐ ⓑ ⓒ ⓓ
74	ⓐ ⓑ ⓒ ⓓ
75	ⓐ ⓑ ⓒ ⓓ
76	ⓐ ⓑ ⓒ ⓓ
77	ⓐ ⓑ ⓒ ⓓ
78	ⓐ ⓑ ⓒ ⓓ
79	ⓐ ⓑ ⓒ ⓓ
80	ⓐ ⓑ ⓒ ⓓ
81	ⓐ ⓑ ⓒ ⓓ
82	ⓐ ⓑ ⓒ ⓓ
83	ⓐ ⓑ ⓒ ⓓ
84	ⓐ ⓑ ⓒ ⓓ
85	ⓐ ⓑ ⓒ ⓓ
86	ⓐ ⓑ ⓒ ⓓ
87	ⓐ ⓑ ⓒ ⓓ
88	ⓐ ⓑ ⓒ ⓓ
89	ⓐ ⓑ ⓒ ⓓ
90	ⓐ ⓑ ⓒ ⓓ
91	ⓐ ⓑ ⓒ ⓓ
92	ⓐ ⓑ ⓒ ⓓ
93	ⓐ ⓑ ⓒ ⓓ
94	ⓐ ⓑ ⓒ ⓓ
95	ⓐ ⓑ ⓒ ⓓ
96	ⓐ ⓑ ⓒ ⓓ
97	ⓐ ⓑ ⓒ ⓓ
98	ⓐ ⓑ ⓒ ⓓ
99	ⓐ ⓑ ⓒ ⓓ
100	ⓐ ⓑ ⓒ ⓓ

READING (Part V ~ VII)

101	ⓐ ⓑ ⓒ ⓓ
102	ⓐ ⓑ ⓒ ⓓ
103	ⓐ ⓑ ⓒ ⓓ
104	ⓐ ⓑ ⓒ ⓓ
105	ⓐ ⓑ ⓒ ⓓ
106	ⓐ ⓑ ⓒ ⓓ
107	ⓐ ⓑ ⓒ ⓓ
108	ⓐ ⓑ ⓒ ⓓ
109	ⓐ ⓑ ⓒ ⓓ
110	ⓐ ⓑ ⓒ ⓓ
111	ⓐ ⓑ ⓒ ⓓ
112	ⓐ ⓑ ⓒ ⓓ
113	ⓐ ⓑ ⓒ ⓓ
114	ⓐ ⓑ ⓒ ⓓ
115	ⓐ ⓑ ⓒ ⓓ
116	ⓐ ⓑ ⓒ ⓓ
117	ⓐ ⓑ ⓒ ⓓ
118	ⓐ ⓑ ⓒ ⓓ
119	ⓐ ⓑ ⓒ ⓓ
120	ⓐ ⓑ ⓒ ⓓ
121	ⓐ ⓑ ⓒ ⓓ
122	ⓐ ⓑ ⓒ ⓓ
123	ⓐ ⓑ ⓒ ⓓ
124	ⓐ ⓑ ⓒ ⓓ
125	ⓐ ⓑ ⓒ ⓓ
126	ⓐ ⓑ ⓒ ⓓ
127	ⓐ ⓑ ⓒ ⓓ
128	ⓐ ⓑ ⓒ ⓓ
129	ⓐ ⓑ ⓒ ⓓ
130	ⓐ ⓑ ⓒ ⓓ
131	ⓐ ⓑ ⓒ ⓓ
132	ⓐ ⓑ ⓒ ⓓ
133	ⓐ ⓑ ⓒ ⓓ
134	ⓐ ⓑ ⓒ ⓓ
135	ⓐ ⓑ ⓒ ⓓ
136	ⓐ ⓑ ⓒ ⓓ
137	ⓐ ⓑ ⓒ ⓓ
138	ⓐ ⓑ ⓒ ⓓ
139	ⓐ ⓑ ⓒ ⓓ
140	ⓐ ⓑ ⓒ ⓓ
141	ⓐ ⓑ ⓒ ⓓ
142	ⓐ ⓑ ⓒ ⓓ
143	ⓐ ⓑ ⓒ ⓓ
144	ⓐ ⓑ ⓒ ⓓ
145	ⓐ ⓑ ⓒ ⓓ
146	ⓐ ⓑ ⓒ ⓓ
147	ⓐ ⓑ ⓒ ⓓ
148	ⓐ ⓑ ⓒ ⓓ
149	ⓐ ⓑ ⓒ ⓓ
150	ⓐ ⓑ ⓒ ⓓ
151	ⓐ ⓑ ⓒ ⓓ
152	ⓐ ⓑ ⓒ ⓓ
153	ⓐ ⓑ ⓒ ⓓ
154	ⓐ ⓑ ⓒ ⓓ
155	ⓐ ⓑ ⓒ ⓓ
156	ⓐ ⓑ ⓒ ⓓ
157	ⓐ ⓑ ⓒ ⓓ
158	ⓐ ⓑ ⓒ ⓓ
159	ⓐ ⓑ ⓒ ⓓ
160	ⓐ ⓑ ⓒ ⓓ
161	ⓐ ⓑ ⓒ ⓓ
162	ⓐ ⓑ ⓒ ⓓ
163	ⓐ ⓑ ⓒ ⓓ
164	ⓐ ⓑ ⓒ ⓓ
165	ⓐ ⓑ ⓒ ⓓ
166	ⓐ ⓑ ⓒ ⓓ
167	ⓐ ⓑ ⓒ ⓓ
168	ⓐ ⓑ ⓒ ⓓ
169	ⓐ ⓑ ⓒ ⓓ
170	ⓐ ⓑ ⓒ ⓓ
171	ⓐ ⓑ ⓒ ⓓ
172	ⓐ ⓑ ⓒ ⓓ
173	ⓐ ⓑ ⓒ ⓓ
174	ⓐ ⓑ ⓒ ⓓ
175	ⓐ ⓑ ⓒ ⓓ
176	ⓐ ⓑ ⓒ ⓓ
177	ⓐ ⓑ ⓒ ⓓ
178	ⓐ ⓑ ⓒ ⓓ
179	ⓐ ⓑ ⓒ ⓓ
180	ⓐ ⓑ ⓒ ⓓ
181	ⓐ ⓑ ⓒ ⓓ
182	ⓐ ⓑ ⓒ ⓓ
183	ⓐ ⓑ ⓒ ⓓ
184	ⓐ ⓑ ⓒ ⓓ
185	ⓐ ⓑ ⓒ ⓓ
186	ⓐ ⓑ ⓒ ⓓ
187	ⓐ ⓑ ⓒ ⓓ
188	ⓐ ⓑ ⓒ ⓓ
189	ⓐ ⓑ ⓒ ⓓ
190	ⓐ ⓑ ⓒ ⓓ
191	ⓐ ⓑ ⓒ ⓓ
192	ⓐ ⓑ ⓒ ⓓ
193	ⓐ ⓑ ⓒ ⓓ
194	ⓐ ⓑ ⓒ ⓓ
195	ⓐ ⓑ ⓒ ⓓ
196	ⓐ ⓑ ⓒ ⓓ
197	ⓐ ⓑ ⓒ ⓓ
198	ⓐ ⓑ ⓒ ⓓ
199	ⓐ ⓑ ⓒ ⓓ
200	ⓐ ⓑ ⓒ ⓓ

ETS 토익
단기공략
950+

LC

RC

기출
모의고사
3회

정답과 해설

PART 1
Listening Comprehension

UNIT 1 사진 묘사

01 인물 등장 사진

ETS 기출 유형연습   본책 p.19

1 (B)   **2** (A)

1   W-Br

(A) He's painting a cabin.
(B) He's sweeping a floor.
(C) He's adjusting his hat.
(D) He's putting wood inside a fireplace.

(A) 남자가 오두막을 페인트칠하고 있다.
(B) 남자가 바닥을 쓸고 있다.
(C) 남자가 모자를 고쳐 쓰고 있다.
(D) 남자가 벽난로 안에 장작을 넣고 있다.

해설   **인물 중심 사진**
(A) **동작 묘사 오답:** 남자가 오두막을 페인트칠하고 있는(is painting a cabin) 모습이 아니다.
(B) **정답:** 남자가 바닥을 쓸고 있는(is sweeping a floor) 모습이므로 정답이다.
(C) **동작 묘사 오답:** 남자가 모자를 고쳐 쓰고 있는(is adjusting his hat) 모습이 아니다.
(D) **동작 묘사 오답:** 남자가 벽난로 안에 장작을 넣고 있는(is putting wood inside a fireplace) 모습이 아니다.

어휘   cabin 오두막   sweep 쓸다   adjust (매무새를) 고치다, 바로잡다   fireplace 벽난로

2   W-Am

(A) Part of a window is being installed.
(B) Some wallpaper is being removed.
(C) He's taking off his gloves.
(D) He's closing the window blinds.

(A) 창문의 일부가 설치되고 있다.
(B) 벽지가 제거되고 있다.
(C) 남자가 장갑을 벗고 있다.
(D) 남자가 창문 블라인드를 닫고 있다.

해설   **인물/사물 혼합 사진**
(A) **정답:** 창문의 일부가 설치되고 있는(is being installed) 모습이므로 정답이다.
(B) **진행 상황 묘사 오답:** 벽지가 제거되고 있는(is being removed) 상황이 아니다.
(C) **동작 묘사 오답:** 남자가 장갑을 벗고 있는(is taking off his gloves) 모습이 아니다.
(D) **동작 묘사 오답:** 남자가 창문 블라인드를 닫고 있는(is closing the window blinds) 모습이 아니다.

어휘   install 설치하다   wallpaper 벽지   remove 제거하다   take off ~을 벗다

02 사물/풍경 사진

ETS 기출 유형연습   본책 p.21

1 (C)   **2** (C)

1   W-Am

(A) There is an open door between two pictures.
(B) A light fixture is suspended from the ceiling.
(C) A striped pillow has been placed on each bed.
(D) A night table drawer has been left open.

(A) 두 그림 사이에 열린 문이 있다.
(B) 조명 기구가 천장에 매달려 있다.
(C) 줄무늬 베개가 각 침대에 놓여 있다.
(D) 침실 협탁 서랍이 열려 있다.

해설   **사물 사진**
(A) **사진에 없는 명사를 이용한 오답:** 사진에 열린 문(an open door)이 보이지 않는다.
(B) **위치 묘사 오답:** 조명 기구가 천장에 매달려 있는(is suspended from the ceiling) 모습이 아니다.
(C) **정답:** 줄무늬 베개가 각 침대에 놓여 있는(has been placed on each bed) 모습이므로 정답이다.
(D) **상태 묘사 오답:** 침실 협탁 서랍이 열려 있는(has been left open) 상태가 아니다.

어휘   light fixture 조명 기구   suspend 매달다   ceiling 천장   pillow 베개   night table 침실 협탁   drawer 서랍

2   M-Au

(A) Umbrellas have been set up on a patio.
(B) A path winds through some sand dunes.

(C) Trees are growing on a hillside along the coast.

(D) Birds are flying through the sky over a beach.

(A) 파라솔들이 테라스에 설치되어 있다.

(B) 오솔길이 모래 언덕 사이로 구불구불 나 있다.

(C) 나무들이 해안을 따라 산비탈에 자라고 있다.

(D) 새들이 해변 위 하늘을 날고 있다.

해설 **사물/풍경 사진**

(A) **위치 묘사 오답:** 파라솔들이 테라스에 설치되어 있는 (have been set up on a patio) 모습이 아니다.

(B) **사진에 없는 명사를 이용한 오답:** 사진에 오솔길(A path) 과 모래 언덕(some sand dunes)이 보이지 않는다.

(C) **정답:** 나무들이 해안을 따라 산비탈에 자라고 있는(are growing on a hillside along the coast) 모습이므 로 정답이다.

(D) **사진에 없는 명사를 이용한 오답:** 사진에 새들(Birds)이 보이지 않는다.

어휘 patio 테라스   wind (도로나 강이) 구불구불하다
(sand) dune 모래 언덕   hillside 산비탈   coast 해안

ETS 기출 실전문제

본책 p.22

1 (C)	**2** (A)	**3** (D)	**4** (A)	**5** (A)	**6** (C)
7 (A)	**8** (D)				

1 W-Am

(A) The man is trimming some branches.

(B) The man is laying some bricks.

(C) The man is standing on some grass.

(D) The man is hanging up a water hose.

(A) 남자가 나뭇가지를 다듬고 있다.

(B) 남자가 벽돌을 쌓고 있다.

(C) 남자가 잔디 위에 서 있다.

(D) 남자가 호스를 걸고 있다.

해설 **인물 중심 사진**

(A) **동작 묘사 오답:** 남자가 나뭇가지를 다듬고 있는(is trimming some branches) 모습이 아니다.

(B) **동작 묘사 오답:** 남자가 벽돌을 쌓고 있는(is laying some bricks) 모습이 아니다.

(C) **정답:** 남자가 잔디 위에 서 있는(is standing on some grass) 모습이므로 정답이다.

(D) **동작 묘사 오답:** 남자가 호스를 걸고 있는(is hanging up a water hose) 모습이 아니다.

어휘 trim 다듬다   lay 쌓다

2 M-Au

(A) One of the women is waiting at a counter.

(B) One of the women is posting signs on a wall.

(C) One of the women is using a phone.

(D) One of the women is opening a drawer.

(A) 여자들 중 한 명이 카운터에서 기다리고 있다.

(B) 여자들 중 한 명이 표지판을 벽에 걸고 있다.

(C) 여자들 중 한 명이 전화기를 사용하고 있다.

(D) 여자들 중 한 명이 서랍을 열고 있다.

해설 **인물 중심 사진**

(A) **정답:** 여자들 중 한 명이 카운터에서 기다리고 있는(is waiting at a counter) 모습이므로 정답이다.

(B) **동작 묘사 오답:** 표지판을 벽에 걸고 있는(is posting signs on a wall) 여자의 모습이 보이지 않는다.

(C) **사진에 없는 명사를 이용한 오답:** 사진에 전화기(a phone)가 보이지 않는다.

(D) **동작 묘사 오답:** 서랍을 열고 있는(is opening a drawer) 여자의 모습이 보이지 않는다.

어휘 post 걸다, 게시하다

3 W-Br

(A) One of the people is lifting a coffee cup.

(B) One of the people is carrying a briefcase.

(C) Some people are watching a presentation.

(D) One of the people is facing a whiteboard.

(A) 사람들 중 한 명이 커피잔을 들어 올리고 있다.

(B) 사람들 중 한 명이 서류 가방을 들고 있다.

(C) 사람들이 발표를 보고 있다.

(D) 사람들 중 한 명이 화이트보드를 마주 보고 있다.

해설 **인물 중심 사진**

(A) **동작 묘사 오답:** 커피잔을 들어 올리고 있는(is lifting a coffee cup) 사람의 모습이 보이지 않는다.

(B) **동작 묘사 오답:** 서류 가방을 들고 있는(is carrying a briefcase) 사람의 모습이 보이지 않는다.

(C) **동작 묘사 오답:** 사람들이 발표를 보고 있는(are watching a presentation) 모습이 아니다.

(D) **정답:** 사람들 중 한 명이 화이트보드를 마주 보고 있는(is facing a whiteboard) 모습이므로 정답이다.

어휘 lift 들어올리다   briefcase 서류 가방   face 마주 보다

4 W-Am

(A) A house is undergoing some construction work.
(B) A worker is climbing up a ladder.
(C) A tent has been set up in front of a house.
(D) A worker is unloading furniture from a truck.

(A) 집이 공사 중이다.
(B) 작업자가 사다리를 오르고 있다.
(C) 천막이 집 앞에 설치되어 있다.
(D) 작업자가 트럭에서 가구를 내리고 있다.

해설 **인물/사물 혼합 사진**
(A) **정답:** 집이 공사 중인(is undergoing some construction work) 모습이므로 정답이다.
(B) **동작 묘사 오답:** 작업자가 사다리를 오르고 있는(is climbing up a ladder) 모습이 아니다.
(C) **사진에 없는 명사를 이용한 오답:** 사진에 천막(A tent)이 보이지 않는다.
(D) **사진에 없는 명사를 이용한 오답:** 사진에 가구(furniture)가 보이지 않는다.

어휘 undergo 겪다　ladder 사다리　unload (짐을) 내리다

5 W-Br

(A) Some people are seated on their motorcycles.
(B) Some people have parked their motorcycles in a garage.
(C) Some motorcycles have been locked to a lamppost.
(D) Some motorcycle riders are driving down the street.

(A) 사람들이 오토바이에 앉아 있다.
(B) 사람들이 차고에 오토바이를 주차해 놓았다.
(C) 오토바이들이 가로등에 묶여 있다.
(D) 오토바이 타는 사람들이 거리를 달리고 있다.

해설 **인물/사물 혼합 사진**
(A) **정답:** 사람들이 오토바이에 앉아 있는(are seated on their motorcycles) 모습이므로 정답이다.
(B) **위치 묘사 오답:** 사람들이 차고에 오토바이를 주차해 놓은(have parked their motorcycles in a garage) 모습이 아니다.
(C) **상태 묘사 오답:** 오토바이들이 가로등에 묶여 있는(have been locked to a lamppost) 상태가 아니다.
(D) **동작 묘사 오답:** 오토바이 타는 사람들이 거리를 달리고 있는(are driving down the street) 모습이 아니다.

어휘 motorcycle 오토바이　garage 차고, 주차장　lamppost 가로등

6 W-Am

(A) He's removing a wallet from his pocket.
(B) He's holding onto a railing for support.
(C) He's grasping the handle of a cart.
(D) He's stepping into a store.

(A) 남자가 주머니에서 지갑을 꺼내고 있다.
(B) 남자가 몸을 지탱하기 위해 난간을 잡고 있다.
(C) 남자가 카트 손잡이를 잡고 있다.
(D) 남자가 가게로 걸어 들어가고 있다.

해설 **인물 중심 사진**
(A) **사진에 없는 명사를 이용한 오답:** 사진에 지갑(a wallet)이 보이지 않는다.
(B) **동작 묘사 오답:** 남자가 몸을 지탱하기 위해 난간을 잡고 있는(is holding onto a railing for support) 모습이 아니다.
(C) **정답:** 남자가 카트 손잡이를 잡고 있는(is grasping the handle of a cart) 모습이므로 정답이다.
(D) **사진에 없는 명사를 이용한 오답:** 사진에 가게(a store)가 보이지 않는다.

어휘 railing 난간　grasp 잡다

7 M-Cn

(A) Luggage is being loaded onto an airplane.
(B) Some airplanes are lined up for takeoff.
(C) Some suitcases are being weighed on a scale.
(D) A technician is working on a propeller.

(A) 짐이 비행기에 실리고 있다.
(B) 비행기들이 이륙하려고 줄지어 있다.
(C) 저울로 여행 가방의 무게를 재고 있다.
(D) 기술자가 프로펠러에서 작업하고 있다.

해설 **인물/사물 혼합 사진**
(A) **정답:** 짐이 비행기에 실리고 있는(is being loaded onto an airplane) 모습이므로 정답이다.
(B) **사진에 없는 명사를 이용한 오답:** 사진에 비행기들(Some airplanes)이 보이지 않는다.
(C) **사진에 없는 명사를 이용한 오답:** 사진에 저울(a scale)이 보이지 않는다.
(D) **동작 묘사 오답:** 기술자가 프로펠러에서 작업하고 있는(is working on a propeller) 모습이 아니다.

어휘 luggage (여행용) 짐 load (짐을) 싣다 takeoff 이륙
suitcase 여행 가방 weigh 무게를 재다 scale 저울
technician 기술자

8 W-Br

(A) Some windows are covered by curtains.
(B) There are some potted plants in a kitchen.
(C) The doors of a cupboard have been left open.
(D) A dining area has been prepared for customers.

(A) 창문들이 커튼으로 가려져 있다.
(B) 화분에 심은 식물들이 부엌에 있다.
(C) 찬장 문들이 열려 있다.
(D) 식사 공간이 손님들을 위해 준비되어 있다.

해설 사물 사진
(A) **사진에 없는 명사를 이용한 오답:** 사진에 커튼(curtains)이 보이지 않는다.
(B) **위치 묘사 오답:** 화분에 심은 식물들이 부엌에(in a kitchen) 있는 모습이 아니다.
(C) **사진에 없는 명사를 이용한 오답:** 사진에 찬장(a cupboard)이 보이지 않는다.
(D) **정답:** 식사 공간이 손님들을 위해 준비되어 있는(has been prepared for customers) 모습이므로 정답이다.

어휘 potted plant 화분에 심은 식물 cupboard 찬장
prepare 준비하다

ETS 기출	고난도 실전문제	본책 p.24

1 (A)	2 (D)	3 (B)	4 (D)	5 (C)	6 (B)
7 (C)	8 (B)				

1 M-Au

(A) He's detaching a ceiling panel.
(B) He's looking through a box of supplies.
(C) He's replacing a glass door.
(D) He's carrying a ladder down a hallway.

(A) 남자가 천장 패널을 떼고 있다.
(B) 남자가 물품 상자를 뒤지고 있다.
(C) 남자가 유리문을 교체하고 있다.
(D) 남자가 복도를 따라 사다리를 운반하고 있다.

해설 인물 중심 사진
(A) **정답:** 남자가 천장 패널을 떼고 있는(is detaching a ceiling panel) 모습이므로 정답이다.
(B) **동작 묘사 오답:** 남자가 물품 상자를 뒤지고 있는(is looking through a box of supplies) 모습이 아니다.
(C) **동작 묘사 오답:** 남자가 유리문을 교체하고 있는(is replacing a glass door) 모습이 아니다.
(D) **동작 묘사 오답:** 남자가 복도를 따라 사다리를 운반하고 있는(is carrying a ladder down a hallway) 모습이 아니다.

어휘 detach 떼다 supplies 물품, 비품 replace 교체하다
hallway 복도

2 W-Am

(A) Maintenance work is being done on a staircase.
(B) People are examining a map on a wall.
(C) A pedestrian bridge crosses over a highway.
(D) An arched roof covers a building.

(A) 계단에서 보수 작업을 하고 있다.
(B) 사람들이 벽에 있는 지도를 살펴보고 있다.
(C) 보행자용 다리가 고속도로 위를 가로지른다.
(D) 아치 모양 지붕이 건물을 덮고 있다.

해설 인물/사물 혼합 사진
(A) **진행 상황 묘사 오답:** 계단에서 보수 작업을 하고 있는 (Maintenance work is being done) 상황이 아니다.
(B) **사진에 없는 명사를 이용한 오답:** 사진에 지도(a map)가 보이지 않는다.
(C) **위치 묘사 오답:** 보행자용 다리가 고속도로 위를 가로지르는(crosses over a highway) 모습이 아니다.
(D) **정답:** 아치 모양 지붕이 건물을 덮고 있는(covers a building) 모습이므로 정답이다.

어휘 maintenance (유지) 보수 staircase 계단
examine 살펴보다 pedestrian 보행자

3 M-Cn

(A) Some of the people are exiting a store.
(B) Some of the people are wearing backpacks.
(C) A seating area is being cleaned.
(D) Some television screens are being mounted on a wall.

(A) 사람들이 가게에서 나오고 있다.
(B) **사람들이 배낭을 메고 있다.**
(C) 좌석 구역이 청소되고 있다.
(D) 텔레비전 화면들이 벽에 설치되고 있다.

해설 **인물/사물 혼합 사진**
(A) **사진에 없는 명사를 이용한 오답:** 사진에 가게(a store)가 보이지 않는다.
(B) **정답:** 사람들이 배낭을 메고 있는(are wearing backpacks) 모습이므로 정답이다.
(C) **진행 상황 묘사 오답:** 좌석 구역이 청소되고 있는(is being cleaned) 상황이 아니다.
(D) **진행 상황 묘사 오답:** 텔레비전 화면들이 벽에 설치되고 있는(are being mounted on a wall) 상황이 아니다.

어휘 exit 나오다 mount 설치하다

4 M-Au

(A) Some merchandise is being restocked.
(B) A customer is pulling a cart.
(C) A worker is packing a shopping bag.
(D) A customer is purchasing some plants.

(A) 상품들이 다시 채워지고 있다.
(B) 손님이 카트를 끌고 있다.
(C) 직원이 쇼핑백에 물건을 담고 있다.
(D) **손님이 식물을 구입하고 있다.**

해설 **인물/사물 혼합 사진**
(A) **진행 상황 묘사 오답:** 상품들이 다시 채워지고 있는(is being restocked) 상황이 아니다.
(B) **동작 묘사 오답:** 손님이 카트를 끌고 있는(is pulling a cart) 모습이 아니다.
(C) **동작 묘사 오답:** 직원이 쇼핑백에 물건을 담고 있는(is packing a shopping bag) 모습이 아니다.
(D) **정답:** 손님이 식물을 구입하고 있는(is purchasing some plants) 모습이므로 정답이다.

어휘 merchandise 상품 restock (팔린 물건을) 다시 채우다
purchase 구입하다

5 M-Cn

(A) A server is filling a bottle with water.
(B) An employee is arranging some chairs.
(C) Some people are seated in an outdoor dining area.
(D) Some workers are putting plates away in a kitchen.

(A) 웨이터가 병에 물을 채우고 있다.
(B) 직원이 의자들을 정리하고 있다.
(C) **사람들이 야외 식사 공간에 앉아 있다.**
(D) 직원들이 부엌에서 접시를 치우고 있다.

해설 **인물 중심 사진**
(A) **동작 묘사 오답:** 웨이터가 병에 물을 채우고 있는(is filling a bottle with water) 모습이 아니다.
(B) **동작 묘사 오답:** 직원이 의자들을 정리하고 있는(is arranging some chairs) 모습이 아니다.
(C) **정답:** 사람들이 야외 식사 공간에 앉아 있는(are seated in an outdoor dining area) 모습이므로 정답이다.
(D) **사진에 없는 명사를 이용한 오답:** 사진에 직원들(Some workers)이 보이지 않는다.

어휘 arrange 정리하다 outdoor 야외의

6 W-Br

(A) Some boats are being taken out of the water.
(B) **A city skyline is visible in the distance.**
(C) Some people are walking on a beach.
(D) A man is picking up rocks along the shore.

(A) 보트들을 물 밖으로 끌어내고 있다.
(B) **멀리 도시의 스카이라인이 보인다.**
(C) 사람들이 해변을 걷고 있다.
(D) 남자가 해안에서 돌을 줍고 있다.

해설 **인물/사물 혼합 사진**
(A) **사진에 없는 명사를 이용한 오답:** 사진에 보트들(Some boats)이 보이지 않는다.
(B) **정답:** 멀리(in the distance) 도시의 스카이라인이 보이므로(A city skyline is visible) 정답이다.
(C) **동작 묘사 오답:** 사람들이 해변을 걷고 있는(are walking on a beach) 모습이 아니다.
(D) **동작 묘사 오답:** 남자가 해안에서 돌을 줍고 있는(is picking up rocks along the shore) 모습이 아니다.

어휘 visible 보이는 in the distance 멀리 shore 해안

7 M-Cn

(A) Some trees have fallen across a road.
(B) Some cars are backing out of a parking garage.
(C) Some work vehicles are parked on a road.
(D) Some workers are directing traffic.

(A) 나무들이 도로를 가로질러 쓰러져 있다.
(B) 차들이 후진으로 주차장을 빠져나오고 있다.

(C) 작업 차량들이 도로에 주차되어 있다.
(D) 작업자들이 교통 정리를 하고 있다.

해설 **사물/풍경 사진**
(A) **상태 묘사 오답:** 나무들이 도로를 가로질러 쓰러져 있는
(have fallen across a road) 상태가 아니다.
(B) **사진에 없는 명사를 이용한 오답:** 사진에 주차장(a
parking garage)이 보이지 않는다.
(C) **정답:** 작업 차량들이 도로에 주차되어 있는(are parked
on a road) 모습이므로 정답이다.
(D) **사진에 없는 명사를 이용한 오답:** 사진에 작업자들
(Some workers)이 보이지 않는다.

어휘 vehicle 차량

8 M-Au

(A) Some shelving units are being disassembled.
(B) Some bottles are lined up on a wire shelf.
(C) A laundry basket is being emptied on the
floor.
(D) A metal surface is being polished.

(A) 선반 유닛들이 분해되고 있다.
(B) 병들이 철제 선반 위에 나란히 놓여 있다.
(C) 바닥에서 빨래 바구니를 비우고 있다.
(D) 금속 표면이 닦이고 있다.

해설 **사물 사진**
(A) **진행 상황 묘사 오답:** 선반 유닛들이 분해되고 있는(are
being disassembled) 상황이 아니다.
(B) **정답:** 병들이 철제 선반 위에 나란히 놓여 있는(are lined
up on a wire shelf) 모습이므로 정답이다.
(C) **진행 상황 묘사 오답:** 바닥에서 빨래 바구니를 비우고 있
는(is being emptied) 상황이 아니다.
(D) **진행 상황 묘사 오답:** 금속 표면이 닦이고 있는(is being
polished) 상황이 아니다.

어휘 disassemble 분해하다 wire 철사 laundry 빨래
empty 비우다 surface 표면 polish 닦다

PART 2
Listening
Comprehension

UNIT 2 질의 응답

01 우회적인 답변

ETS 기출 유형연습   본책 p.28

1 (B)   **2** (B)   **3** (C)   **4** (A)   **5** (B)

1   M-Cn / W-Br
How do I sign up for the company baseball
team?
(A) It was an exciting championship.
(B) I didn't even know we had one!
(C) I'd like two tickets, please.

회사 야구팀에 가입하려면 어떻게 해야 하나요?
(A) 흥미진진한 선수권 대회였어요.
(B) 야구팀이 있는지도 몰랐어요!
(C) 표 두 장 주세요.

해설 **회사 야구팀 가입 방법을 묻는 How 의문문**
(A) **연상 어휘 오답:** 질문의 baseball team에서 연상 가능
한 championship을 이용한 오답이다.
(B) **정답:** 회사 야구팀 가입 방법을 묻는 질문에 야구팀이 있
는지도 몰랐다며 가입 방법을 알지 못함을 우회적으로 밝
히고 있으므로 정답이다.
(C) **연상 어휘 오답:** 질문의 baseball에서 연상 가능한
tickets를 이용한 오답이다.

어휘 sign up for ~에 가입하다

2   M-Au / W-Am
Shouldn't the reception desk be closer to the
door?
(A) I'll close the account.
(B) The owner hasn't decided yet.
(C) Yes, in the filing cabinet.

접수처가 문 쪽에 더 가까워야 하지 않을까요?
(A) 계좌를 해지하려고요.
(B) 사장님이 아직 결정하지 않았어요.
(C) 네, 문서 보관함에 있어요.

해설 **접수처의 위치를 제안하는 부정 의문문**
(A) **파생어 오답:** 질문의 closer와 파생어 관계인 close를
이용한 오답이다.
(B) **정답:** 접수처가 문 쪽에 더 가까워야 한다는 제안에 사장
님이 아직 결정하지 않았다며 당장 판단할 수 없음을 우회
적으로 밝히고 있으므로 정답이다.
(C) **연상 어휘 오답:** 질문의 desk에서 연상 가능한 filing
cabinet을 이용한 오답이다.

7

어휘 reception desk 접수처, 안내 데스크 account 계좌
filing cabinet 문서 보관함

3 W-Br / M-Au

Don't we need more parts for this machine?
(A) There are two main characters in the show.
(B) A new photocopier.
(C) Matthew takes care of all the ordering.

이 기계의 부품이 더 필요하지 않나요?
(A) 그 쇼에는 주인공이 두 명 있어요.
(B) 새 복사기예요.
(C) 주문은 전부 매튜가 맡아서 처리해요.

해설 **기계 부품이 더 필요한지 확인하는 부정 의문문**
(A) **연상 어휘 오답:** 질문의 parts에서 연상 가능한 main characters를 이용한 오답이다.
(B) **연상 어휘 오답:** 질문의 machine에서 연상 가능한 photocopier를 이용한 오답이다.
(C) **정답:** 기계 부품이 더 필요한지 묻는 질문에 주문은 전부 매튜가 맡아서 처리한다며 정보를 아는 사람을 알려 주고 있으므로 정답이다.

어휘 photocopier 복사기 take care of ~을 맡아서 처리하다

4 M-Au / M-Cn

I don't understand why today's shipment will be late.
(A) Have you seen the weather report?
(B) I'll take the train instead.
(C) 300 euros.

오늘 배송이 왜 늦는지 이해가 안 되네요.
(A) 일기예보 보셨어요?
(B) 저는 대신 기차를 탈게요.
(C) 300유로예요.

해설 **의견을 제시하는 평서문**
(A) **정답:** 오늘 배송이 왜 늦는지 이해가 안 된다는 말에 일기예보를 봤는지 물으면서 날씨 때문이라는 점을 우회적으로 밝히고 있으므로 정답이다.
(B) **연상 어휘 오답:** 평서문의 shipment에서 연상 가능한 train을 이용한 오답이다.
(C) **평서문과 상관없는 오답**

어휘 weather report 일기예보 instead 대신

5 M-Au / W-Br

Who's been appointed to direct this project?
(A) Oh no! The projector is broken.
(B) We voted on that at Wednesday's meeting.
(C) A three o'clock appointment.

누가 이 프로젝트를 총괄하도록 임명됐나요?
(A) 어떡해요! 프로젝터가 고장 났어요.
(B) 수요일 회의에서 투표했어요.
(C) 3시 약속이요.

해설 **프로젝트 관리자로 임명된 사람을 묻는 Who 의문문**
(A) **파생어 오답:** 질문의 project와 파생어 관계인 projector를 이용한 오답이다.
(B) **정답:** 프로젝트 관리자로 임명된 사람을 묻는 질문에 수요일 회의에서 투표했다며 임명이 아닌 투표로 결정되었음을 우회적으로 밝히고 있으므로 정답이다.
(C) **파생어 오답:** 질문의 appointed와 파생어 관계인 appointment를 이용한 오답이다.

어휘 appoint 임명하다 direct 총괄하다, 지휘하다
vote 투표하다 appointment 약속

02 의문사 의문문

ETS 기출 유형연습   본책 p.31

1 (A)   **2** (C)   **3** (C)   **4** (C)   **5** (C)

1 W-Am / M-Cn

Which fabric should we buy for the curtains?
(A) The one with the stripes.
(B) The light switch on the wall.
(C) A matching sofa.

커튼용으로 어떤 원단을 사야 할까요?
(A) 줄무늬 있는 거요.
(B) 벽에 있는 전등 스위치요.
(C) 어울리는 소파요.

해설 **사야 할 커튼용 원단을 묻는 Which 의문문**
(A) **정답:** 사야 할 커튼용 원단을 묻는 질문에 줄무늬가 있는 것이라고 구체적으로 대답하고 있으므로 정답이다.
(B) **질문과 상관없는 오답**
(C) **연상 어휘 오답:** 질문의 fabric에서 연상 가능한 sofa를 이용한 오답이다.

어휘 fabric 원단 matching 어울리는

2 M-Au / W-Br

Where should I get approval for this business trip?
(A) I enjoy traveling to France.
(B) The lawyer proved the case.
(C) Have you asked your manager?

이번 출장은 어디에서 승인을 받아야 하나요?
(A) 전 프랑스 여행을 좋아해요.
(B) 변호사가 사건을 입증했어요.
(C) 매니저에게 물어보셨나요?

해설 **출장 승인받을 곳을 묻는 Where 의문문**
(A) **연상 어휘 오답:** 질문의 trip에서 연상 가능한 traveling을 이용한 오답이다.
(B) **파생어 오답:** 질문의 approval과 파생어 관계인 proved를 이용한 오답이다.

(C) **정답:** 출장 승인받을 곳을 묻는 질문에 매니저에게 물어봤
는지 되물어 매니저가 알고 있음을 우회적으로 밝히고 있
으므로 정답이다.

어휘 approval 승인 business trip 출장 prove 입증하다

3 W-Br / M-Au

When will the company be restructured?
(A) The research and development division.
(B) This is my favorite sculpture.
(C) Sometime next quarter.

회사는 언제 구조 조정되나요?
(A) 연구 개발부예요.
(B) 이건 제가 가장 좋아하는 조각품이에요.
(C) 다음 분기 중으로요.

해설 **회사의 구조 조정 시기를 묻는 When 의문문**
(A) **연상 어휘 오답:** 질문의 company에서 연상 가능한
research and development division을 이용한 오
답이다.
(B) **유사 발음 오답:** 질문의 restructured와 부분적으로 발
음이 유사한 sculpture를 이용한 오답이다.
(C) **정답:** 회사의 구조 조정 시기를 묻는 질문에 다음 분기 중
이라고 대답하고 있으므로 정답이다.

어휘 restructure 구조 조정을 하다 division 부서
sculpture 조각품 quarter 분기

4 W-Br / M-Cn

Who's coming to the training session on Friday?
(A) No, I didn't.
(B) The conference room.
(C) Everyone from our department.

금요일 교육 세션에 누가 오나요?
(A) 아니요, 전 안 했어요.
(B) 회의실이에요.
(C) 우리 부서 전부예요.

해설 **금요일 교육 세션에 올 사람을 묻는 Who 의문문**
(A) **Yes/No 불가 오답:** Who 의문문에는 Yes/No 응답이
불가능하므로 오답이다.
(B) **연상 어휘 오답:** 질문의 training session에서 연상 가
능한 conference room을 이용한 오답이다.
(C) **정답:** 금요일 교육 세션에 올 사람을 묻는 질문에 우리 부
서 전부라고 구체적으로 밝히고 있으므로 정답이다.

어휘 department 부서

5 M-Au / W-Am

How are we going to get to Toronto?
(A) Is it a green suitcase?
(B) It's my favorite destination.
(C) Sky Airlines has reasonable prices.

토론토로 어떻게 가나요?
(A) 녹색 여행 가방인가요?
(B) 제가 가장 좋아하는 여행지예요.
(C) 스카이 항공이 가격이 저렴해요.

해설 **토론토로 가는 방법을 묻는 How 의문문**
(A) **연상 어휘 오답:** 질문의 get to Toronto에서 연상 가능
한 suitcase을 이용한 오답이다.
(B) **연상 어휘 오답:** 질문의 Toronto에서 연상 가능한
destination을 이용한 오답이다.
(C) **정답:** 토론토로 가는 방법을 묻는 질문에 스카이 항공이
가격이 저렴하다며 추천하고 있으므로 정답이다.

어휘 suitcase 여행 가방

03 일반/부정/부가 의문문

ETS 기출 유형연습 본책 p.33

1 (C) **2** (A) **3** (C) **4** (B) **5** (A)

1 W-Am / M-Cn

Has the new dining room set been placed in the
store showroom?
(A) The menu changed recently.
(B) There's only limited seating available.
(C) A customer bought it this morning.

새 식탁 세트가 매장 전시실에 배치됐나요?
(A) 최근에 메뉴가 바뀌었어요.
(B) 이용할 수 있는 좌석이 한정되어 있어요.
(C) 오늘 아침에 고객이 구매했어요.

해설 **새 식탁 세트가 매장 전시실에 배치되었는지 묻는 일반 의문문**
(A) **연상 어휘 오답:** 질문의 dining에서 연상 가능한 menu
를 이용한 오답이다.
(B) **연상 어휘 오답:** 질문의 dining room에서 연상 가능한
seating을 이용한 오답이다.
(C) **정답:** 새 식탁 세트가 매장 전시실에 배치되었는지 묻는
질문에 오늘 아침에 고객이 구매했다며 이미 팔렸음을 밝
히고 있으므로 정답이다.

어휘 showroom 전시실 limited 한정된 available 이용할
수 있는

2 M-Au / W-Am

Do you know where the stairway is?
(A) This building has only one level.
(B) Yes, I know him too.
(C) In about ten minutes.

계단이 어디 있는지 아세요?
(A) 이 건물은 한 층뿐이에요.
(B) 네, 저도 그를 알아요.
(C) 약 10분 뒤예요.

해설 **계단 위치를 묻는 간접 의문문**
   (A) **정답:** 계단 위치를 묻는 질문에 이 건물은 한 층뿐이라며 계단이 없음을 우회적으로 밝히고 있으므로 정답이다.
   (B) **어휘 반복 오답:** 질문의 know를 반복 이용한 오답이다.
   (C) **질문과 상관없는 오답**

어휘 stairway 계단

3 M-Cn / W-Br

Aren't we going to look over the budget numbers?
(A) Twenty-three copies.
(B) A slight increase.
(C) Our accountant's on his way.

예산 수치를 검토해야 하지 않나요?
(A) 23부예요.
(B) 조금 올랐어요.
(C) 회계사가 오고 있어요.

해설 **예산 수치 검토 여부를 확인하는 부정 의문문**
   (A) **연상 어휘 오답:** 질문의 numbers에서 연상 가능한 Twenty-three를 이용한 오답이다.
   (B) **연상 어휘 오답:** 질문의 budget과 numbers에서 연상 가능한 increase를 이용한 오답이다.
   (C) **정답:** 예산 수치를 검토할 것인지 묻는 질문에 회계사가 오고 있다며 도착하면 진행할 것임을 우회적으로 밝히고 있으므로 정답이다.

어휘 budget 예산   slight 조금의   increase 인상
   accountant 회계사

4 W-Br / M-Au

You still have last year's invoices, don't you?
(A) I like your new office.
(B) Mr. Hamada's in charge of Accounting now.
(C) Tickets are half-price today.

작년 송장 아직 가지고 있죠, 그렇지 않나요?
(A) 당신의 새 사무실이 마음에 들어요.
(B) 지금은 하마다 씨가 회계를 담당하고 있어요.
(C) 오늘은 표가 반값이군요.

해설 **작년 송장을 아직 가지고 있는지 확인하는 부가 의문문**
   (A) **질문과 상관없는 오답**
   (B) **정답:** 작년 송장을 아직 가지고 있는지 묻는 질문에 지금은 하마다 씨가 회계를 담당한다며 대답할 수 있는 사람을 알려 주고 있으므로 정답이다.
   (C) **연상 어휘 오답:** 질문의 invoices에서 연상 가능한 half-price를 이용한 오답이다.

어휘 invoice 송장   in charge of ~을 담당하는

5 M-Au / W-Am

Isn't the shipment ready yet?
(A) No, there's been a delay.
(B) The door on your right.
(C) On a monthly basis.

배송 준비가 아직도 안 됐나요?
(A) 안 됐어요, 지연이 있었어요.
(B) 오른쪽에 있는 문이에요.
(C) 월 단위예요.

해설 **배송 준비 여부를 확인하는 부정 의문문**
   (A) **정답:** 배송 준비가 되었는지 묻는 질문에 안 됐어요(No)라고 대답한 후 지연이 있었다며 일관된 내용을 덧붙이고 있으므로 정답이다.
   (B) **질문과 상관없는 오답**
   (C) **질문과 상관없는 오답**

어휘 on a ~ basis ~ 단위로

04 기타 의문문/평서문

ETS 기출 유형연습   본책 p.35

1 (B)   **2** (C)   **3** (A)   **4** (B)   **5** (C)

1 M-Au / W-Am

We'd like you to come work in our laboratory.
(A) Isn't that your lab coat?
(B) I just accepted another offer.
(C) A fifteen percent pay increase.

우리 실험실에 오셔서 일해 주셨으면 합니다.
(A) 당신 실험실 가운 아니에요?
(B) 방금 다른 제안을 수락했어요.
(C) 15퍼센트 임금 인상이요.

해설 **요청하는 평서문**
   (A) **연상 어휘 오답:** 평서문의 laboratory에서 연상 가능한 lab coat를 이용한 오답이다.
   (B) **정답:** 실험실에서 일해달라는 요청에 방금 다른 제안을 수락했다며 우회적으로 거절하고 있으므로 정답이다.
   (C) **연상 어휘 오답:** 평서문의 work에서 연상 가능한 pay increase를 이용한 오답이다.

어휘 laboratory 실험실   accept 수락하다

2 W-Br / M-Cn

Why don't we all go and see a play together?
(A) I've never played basketball.
(B) I left it in the cafeteria.
(C) The new musical got great reviews.

우리 다 같이 연극 보러 가는 거 어때요?
(A) 저는 농구를 해본 적이 없어요.
(B) 제가 구내식당에 두고 왔어요.
(C) 신작 뮤지컬 평이 아주 좋던데요.

해설 **제안하는 의문문**
   (A) **파생어 오답:** 질문의 play와 파생어 관계인 played를 이용한 오답이다.
   (B) **질문과 상관없는 오답**

(C) **정답:** 연극을 보러 가자는 제안에 신작 뮤지컬 평이 아주 좋다며 연극이 아닌 뮤지컬을 보러 가고 싶다는 의견을 우회적으로 표현하고 있으므로 정답이다.

어휘 review 논평, 후기

3 M-Cn / W-Am

With production levels increasing, we'll need additional staff.
(A) I'll post an advertisement.
(B) Attendance is mandatory.
(C) Put it on a higher shelf.

생산량이 증가함에 따라, 추가 인력이 필요할 것입니다.
(A) 제가 공고를 게시할게요.
(B) 출석은 의무입니다.
(C) 더 높은 선반에 올려놓으세요.

해설 **의견을 제시하는 평서문**
(A) **정답:** 생산량 증가에 따라 추가 인력이 필요하다는 말에 공고를 게시하겠다며 의견에 우회적으로 동의하고 있으므로 정답이다.
(B) **평서문과 상관없는 오답**
(C) **연상 어휘 오답:** 평서문의 increasing에서 연상 가능한 higher를 이용한 오답이다.

어휘 additional 추가의 post 게시하다 attendance 출석. 참석 mandatory 의무의

4 M-Cn / W-Br

Do you want a paper copy of your receipt, or should I e-mail it to you?
(A) Just a cup of coffee, please.
(B) I only keep electronic records.
(C) It cost fifteen euros.

영수증 종이 사본을 드릴까요, 아니면 이메일로 보내 드릴까요?
(A) 커피 한 잔만 주세요.
(B) 저는 전자 기록만 보관해요.
(C) 15유로로 들었어요.

해설 **선호하는 영수증의 형태를 묻는 선택 의문문**
(A) **유사 발음 오답:** 질문의 copy와 부분적으로 발음이 유사한 coffee를 이용한 오답이다.
(B) **정답:** 선호하는 영수증의 형태를 묻는 질문에 전자 기록만 보관한다며 이메일을 선호한다는 것을 우회적으로 밝히고 있으므로 정답이다.
(C) **연상 어휘 오답:** 질문의 receipt에서 연상 가능한 It cost fifteen euros를 이용한 오답이다.

어휘 receipt 영수증 electronic 전자의 cost (비용이) 들다

5 W-Am / M-Au

Our company logo is really outdated.
(A) September third is fine.
(B) A good location to open a business.
(C) The marketing team has several good ideas.

우리 회사 로고는 정말 구식이에요.
(A) 9월 3일이 괜찮아요.
(B) 사업을 시작하기 좋은 위치죠.
(C) 마케팅 팀에 여러 가지 좋은 아이디어가 있어요.

해설 **의견을 제시하는 평서문**
(A) **연상 어휘 오답:** 평서문에 나온 outdated의 date에서 연상 가능한 September third를 이용한 오답이다.
(B) **연상 어휘 오답:** 평서문의 company에서 연상 가능한 business를 이용한 오답이다.
(C) **정답:** 회사 로고가 구식이라는 말에 마케팅 팀에 좋은 아이디어가 있다며 해결책을 우회적으로 제시하고 있으므로 정답이다.

어휘 outdated 구식의

ETS 기출 실전문제
본책 p.36

1 (C)	2 (C)	3 (A)	4 (B)	5 (C)	6 (A)
7 (C)	8 (B)	9 (A)	10 (A)	11 (A)	12 (B)
13 (A)	14 (B)	15 (A)	16 (C)	17 (A)	18 (B)
19 (A)	20 (C)				

1 W-Br / M-Au

Why did the shipment arrive so late?
(A) Sure, I can unload the boxes.
(B) No, I took a different route.
(C) Because there was a lot of road construction.

배송품이 왜 이렇게 늦게 도착했죠?
(A) 물론이죠. 제가 상자를 내릴 수 있어요.
(B) 아니요, 저는 다른 길로 갔어요.
(C) 도로 공사가 많았기 때문이에요.

해설 **배송품이 늦게 도착한 이유를 묻는 Why 의문문**
(A) **Yes/No 불가 오답:** Why 의문문에는 Yes/No 응답이 불가능한데, Sure도 일종의 Yes 응답이라고 볼 수 있으므로 오답이다.
(B) **Yes/No 불가 오답:** Why 의문문에는 Yes/No 응답이 불가능하므로 오답이다.
(C) **정답:** 배송품이 늦게 도착한 이유를 묻는 질문에 도로 공사가 많았기 때문이라며 구체적인 이유를 제시하고 있으므로 정답이다.

어휘 unload (짐을) 내리다

2 M-Cn / W-Br

How did the conference call with the clients go?
(A) I'll go with you.
(B) At least two chairs, please.
(C) They're going to renew their contract.

고객과의 전화 회의는 어떻게 됐나요?
(A) 제가 같이 갈게요.
(B) 의자는 2개 이상 주세요.
(C) 그들은 계약을 갱신할 거예요.

해설 **전화 회의의 결과를 묻는 How 의문문**

(A) **어휘 반복 오답:** 질문의 go를 반복 이용한 오답이다.

(B) **연상 어휘 오답:** 질문의 conference에서 연상 가능한 chairs를 이용한 오답이다.

(C) **정답:** 전화 회의의 결과를 묻는 질문에 고객들이 계약을 갱신할 예정이라며 회의가 잘 진행되었다는 점을 우회적으로 밝히고 있으므로 정답이다.

어휘 conference call 전화 회의   renew 갱신하다
contract 계약

3   W-Br / M-Cn

Who's contacting the catering service?

(A) It's already been taken care of.

(B) No, on the left.

(C) I'll have some more, thanks.

누가 출장 요리 업체에 연락할 건가요?

(A) 이미 처리됐어요.

(B) 아니요, 왼쪽이에요.

(C) 더 먹을게요, 감사합니다.

해설 **출장 요리 업체에 연락할 사람을 묻는 Who 의문문**

(A) **정답:** 출장 요리 업체에 연락할 사람을 묻는 질문에 이미 처리되었다고 응답하고 있으므로 정답이다.

(B) **Yes/No 불가 오답:** Who 의문문에는 Yes/No 응답이 불가능하므로 오답이다.

(C) **연상 어휘 오답:** 질문의 catering에서 연상 가능한 have some more를 이용한 오답이다.

어휘 catering 출장 요리(업)

4   M-Cn / W-Br

Where are the storage lockers located in this airport?

(A) Yes, the walkway needs some repairs.

(B) It's my first day working here.

(C) From Montreal to Vancouver.

이 공항에는 보관함이 어디에 있나요?

(A) 네, 통로는 수리가 필요해요.

(B) 전 오늘이 근무 첫날이에요.

(C) 몬트리올에서 밴쿠버까지요.

해설 **보관함의 위치를 묻는 Where 의문문**

(A) **Yes/No 불가 오답:** Where 의문문에는 Yes/No 응답이 불가능하므로 오답이다.

(B) **정답:** 보관함의 위치를 묻는 질문에 오늘이 근무 첫날이라 위치를 모른다고 우회적으로 밝히고 있으므로 정답이다.

(C) **연상 어휘 오답:** 질문의 airport에서 연상 가능한 From Montreal to Vancouver를 이용한 오답이다.

어휘 storage 보관   repair 수리

5   W-Am / M-Au

When will you finish editing the manuscript?

(A) With some updated software.

(B) The author's signature is unique.

(C) I just returned from vacation yesterday.

원고 편집은 언제 완료되나요?

(A) 업데이트된 소프트웨어로요.

(B) 저자의 서명이 독특하네요.

(C) 전 휴가 끝내고 어제 막 돌아왔어요.

해설 **원고 편집 완료 시기를 묻는 When 의문문**

(A) **연상 어휘 오답:** 질문의 editing에서 연상 가능한 updated software를 이용한 오답이다.

(B) **연상 어휘 오답:** 질문의 manuscript에서 연상 가능한 author를 이용한 오답이다.

(C) **정답:** 원고 편집 완료 시기를 묻는 질문에 휴가를 끝내고 어제 막 돌아왔다면서 종료 시점을 모른다고 우회적으로 밝히고 있으므로 정답이다.

어휘 edit 편집하다   manuscript 원고   author 저자
signature 서명   unique 독특한

6   W-Am / M-Cn

Have you stocked the shelves at the front of the store?

(A) Yes, everything's on display.

(B) He's an architect.

(C) I watered them yesterday.

매장 앞쪽 선반에 물품을 채우셨나요?

(A) 네, 모두 진열되어 있어요.

(B) 그는 건축가예요.

(C) 제가 어제 물을 줬어요.

해설 **물품을 채웠는지 묻는 일반 의문문**

(A) **정답:** 물품을 채웠는지 묻는 질문에 네(Yes)라고 긍정한 뒤, 모두 진열되어 있다며 긍정 답변과 일관된 내용을 덧붙이고 있으므로 정답이다.

(B) **질문과 상관없는 오답**

(C) **질문과 상관없는 오답**

어휘 stock 채우다   architect 건축가   water 물을 주다

7   W-Br / M-Cn

Isn't the video game competition going to be in Beijing again?

(A) Gregor often wins first prize.

(B) This computer is brand new.

(C) Each year a different country hosts the event.

비디오 게임 대회가 또 베이징에서 열리는 거 아닌가요?

(A) 그레고르가 종종 1등을 해요.

(B) 이 컴퓨터는 새것이에요.

(C) 해마다 다른 나라가 행사를 주최해요.

해설 대회가 베이징에서 개최되는지 확인하는 부정 의문문

    (A) **연상 어휘 오답:** 질문의 competition에서 연상 가능한 first prize를 이용한 오답이다.

    (B) **연상 어휘 오답:** 질문의 video game에서 연상 가능한 computer를 이용한 오답이다.

    (C) **정답:** 대회가 베이징에서 개최되는지 묻는 질문에 해마다 다른 나라가 행사를 주최한다면서 베이징에서 개최되지 않는다는 것을 우회적으로 밝히고 있으므로 정답이다.

어휘 host 개최하다

---

8   W-Am / M-Cn

Why are all employees gathering for a picnic on Friday?

(A) No, use a metal frame for the picture.

(B) Haven't you heard of our company's tradition?

(C) The grocery store on Elm Road.

금요일에 왜 전 직원이 모여 소풍을 가는 거죠?

(A) 아니요, 그 사진은 금속 액자를 쓰세요.

(B) 우리 회사 전통에 대해 못 들어 보셨나요?

(C) 엘름 로에 있는 식료품점이에요.

해설 금요일에 전 직원이 소풍 가는 이유를 묻는 **Why 의문문**

    (A) **Yes/No 불가 오답:** Why 의문문에는 Yes/No 응답이 불가능하므로 오답이다.

    (B) **정답:** 금요일에 전 직원이 소풍 가는 이유를 묻는 질문에 회사 전통에 대해 들어보지 못했는지 되물어 회사 전통을 이유로 제시하고 있으므로 정답이다.

    (C) **질문과 상관없는 오답**

어휘 tradition 전통   grocery store 식료품점

---

9   M-Cn / W-Br

These chairs are very expensive.

(A) They're high quality.

(B) Yes, I'd like that.

(C) The store didn't close.

이 의자들은 아주 비싸네요.

(A) 품질이 좋아요.

(B) 네, 그렇게 해 주세요.

(C) 가게가 문을 닫지 않았어요.

해설 의견을 제시하는 **평서문**

    (A) **정답:** 의자가 비싸다는 말에 품질이 좋다며 비싼 이유를 설명하고 있으므로 정답이다.

    (B) **평서문과 상관없는 오답**

    (C) **평서문과 상관없는 오답**

---

10   W-Br / M-Au

How many copies of the presentation should we prepare?

(A) I'll need to check with my supervisor.

(B) In the cabinet by the mailboxes.

(C) The speaker was well prepared.

발표 자료는 몇 부를 준비해야 하나요?

(A) 상사에게 확인해 볼게요.

(B) 우편함 옆 캐비닛에 있어요.

(C) 발표자가 준비를 잘 했어요.

해설 준비해야 하는 발표 자료의 부수를 묻는 **How many 의문문**

    (A) **정답:** 발표 자료를 몇 부 준비해야 하는지 묻는 질문에 상사에게 확인해 보겠다며 자신은 모른다는 것을 우회적으로 밝히고 있으므로 정답이다.

    (B) **연상 어휘 오답:** 질문의 copies of the presentation에서 연상 가능한 cabinet을 이용한 오답이다.

    (C) **연상 어휘 및 파생어 오답:** 질문의 presentation에서 연상 가능한 speaker와 질문의 prepare와 파생어 관계인 prepared를 이용한 오답이다.

어휘 supervisor 상사, 관리자   mailbox 우편함

---

11   W-Am / M-Cn

Who needs my help downloading the software?

(A) The instructions seem easy to follow.

(B) I received a discount.

(C) Please print your name carefully.

소프트웨어를 다운로드하는 데 도움이 필요한 분 계신가요?

(A) 설명서가 따라 하기 쉬운 것 같아요.

(B) 저는 할인받았어요.

(C) 이름을 정자로 쓰세요.

해설 도움이 필요한 사람을 묻는 **Who 의문문**

    (A) **정답:** 도움이 필요한 사람을 묻는 질문에 설명서가 따라 하기 쉽다며 도움이 필요하지 않다고 우회적으로 밝히고 있으므로 정답이다.

    (B) **연상 어휘 오답:** 질문의 downloading에서 연상 가능한 received를 이용한 오답이다.

    (C) **질문과 상관없는 오답**

어휘 instructions 설명서

---

12   M-Cn / W-Am

Could you start counting the money in the envelope?

(A) The stamps are in that drawer.

(B) Of course—just a moment.

(C) No, I took that course already.

봉투에 든 돈을 세기 시작해 주시겠어요?

(A) 우표는 저 서랍 안에 있어요.

(B) 그러죠. 잠시만요.

(C) 아니요, 전 이미 그 강좌를 들었어요.

해설 요청하는 **의문문**

    (A) **연상 어휘 오답:** 질문의 envelope에서 연상 가능한 stamps를 이용한 오답이다.

    (B) **정답:** 봉투에 든 돈을 세기 시작해 달라는 요청에 그러죠(Of course)라고 긍정한 뒤 긍정 답변과 일관된 내용을 덧붙이고 있으므로 정답이다.

    (C) **질문과 상관없는 오답**

어휘 envelope 봉투   drawer 서랍

13 W-Am / W-Br

What's that desk made out of?
(A) Here's the paperwork from the manufacturer.
(B) I've got some news.
(C) Yes, in the lobby.

저 책상은 무엇으로 만들었나요?
(A) 여기 제조사 서류예요.
(B) 소식이 있어요.
(C) 네, 로비에서요.

해설 **책상의 원자재를 묻는 What 의문문**
(A) **정답:** 책상의 원자재를 묻는 질문에 정보를 알 수 있는 제조사 서류를 주고 있으므로 정답이다.
(B) **연상 어휘 오답:** 질문의 desk에서 연상 가능한 news를 이용한 오답이다.
(C) **Yes/No 불가 오답:** What 의문문에는 Yes/No 응답이 불가능하므로 오답이다.

어휘 manufacturer 제조사

14 M-Cn / W-Am

I'm headed to the lunchtime yoga class in the break room.
(A) No, I haven't been there.
(B) Our conference call starts in ten minutes.
(C) Down the street to the left.

저는 휴게실에서 열리는 점심시간 요가 수업에 가요.
(A) 아니요, 저는 거기 가본 적 없어요.
(B) 10분 후에 전화 회의가 시작돼요.
(C) 길을 따라 왼쪽이에요.

해설 **상황을 설명하는 평서문**
(A) **평서문과 상관없는 오답**
(B) **정답:** 휴게실에서 열리는 점심시간 요가 수업에 간다는 말에 10분 후에 전화 회의가 시작된다며 업무 일정을 알려 주고 있으므로 정답이다.
(C) **연상 어휘 오답:** 평서문의 headed to에서 연상 가능한 Down the street to the left를 이용한 오답이다.

어휘 be headed to ~으로 향하다, 가다

15 W-Am / W-Br

Do you think the budget will be finalized this month or next month?
(A) The deadline hasn't been changed.
(B) No, thanks. I'm not hungry.
(C) I enjoyed the final chapter.

예산이 이번 달에 확정될까요, 다음 달에 확정될까요?
(A) 마감일은 바뀌지 않았어요.
(B) 괜찮아요. 배고프지 않아요.
(C) 전 마지막 장이 재미있었어요.

해설 **예산 확정 시기를 묻는 선택 의문문**
(A) **정답:** 예산 확정이 이번 달인지 다음 달인지 묻는 질문에 마감일은 바뀌지 않았다며 예산 확정 시기에 변화가 없음을 우회적으로 밝히고 있으므로 정답이다.

(B) **유사 발음 오답:** 질문의 think와 부분적으로 발음이 유사한 thanks를 이용한 오답이다.
(C) **파생어 오답:** 질문의 finalized와 파생어 관계인 final을 이용한 오답이다.

어휘 finalize 확정하다

16 W-Br / M-Au

Won't you be coming to lunch with us?
(A) No, I'd prefer a red one.
(B) Because it's his favorite sandwich.
(C) I have an all-day meeting.

와서 우리랑 같이 점심 먹지 않을래요?
(A) 아니요, 저는 빨간 것이 더 좋아요.
(B) 그가 제일 좋아하는 샌드위치니까요.
(C) 저는 하루 종일 회의가 있어요.

해설 **점심을 같이 먹자고 제안하는 부정 의문문**
(A) **질문과 상관없는 오답**
(B) **연상 어휘 오답:** 질문의 lunch에서 연상 가능한 sandwich를 이용한 오답이다.
(C) **정답:** 같이 점심을 먹자고 제안하는 질문에 하루 종일 회의가 있다며 제안을 우회적으로 거절하고 있으므로 정답이다.

어휘 prefer 선호하다

17 M-Au / W-Am

The office is too warm today, isn't it?
(A) It'll be nice to go outside.
(B) I think the office furniture looks great.
(C) Sure, I'll close the account.

오늘은 사무실이 너무 덥네요, 그렇지 않나요?
(A) 밖에 나가면 좋겠어요.
(B) 사무용 가구가 멋지네요.
(C) 물론이죠, 계좌를 해지하겠습니다.

해설 **사무실이 더운지 확인하는 부가 의문문**
(A) **정답:** 사무실이 너무 덥다는 말에 밖에 나가면 좋겠다며 동조하고 있으므로 정답이다.
(B) **어휘 반복 오답:** 질문의 office를 반복 이용한 오답이다.
(C) **질문과 상관없는 오답**

18 W-Am / M-Au

Would you like to register to win one of our door prizes?
(A) I can hold that open for you.
(B) OK, I'm feeling lucky today.
(C) His opinion surprised me.

경품 추첨에 응모하시겠어요?
(A) 제가 문을 잡아드릴게요.
(B) 네, 오늘 예감이 좋아요.
(C) 그의 의견에 놀랐어요.

해설 **제안하는 의문문**
(A) **연상 어휘 오답:** 질문의 door에서 연상 가능한 hold

that open을 이용한 오답이다.
(B) **정답**: 경품에 응모하라는 제안에 네(OK)라고 제안을 받아들인 뒤, 오늘 예감이 좋다며 긍정 답변과 일관된 내용을 덧붙이고 있으므로 정답이다.
(C) **유사 발음 오답**: 질문의 prizes와 부분적으로 발음이 유사한 surprised를 이용한 오답이다.

어휘 door prize 경품

19 M-Au / W-Am
Isn't the market going to be crowded?
(A) It's a weekday morning.
(B) The local farmers market.
(C) A marketing consultant.
시장이 붐비지 않을까요?
(A) 평일 오전이잖아요.
(B) 지역 농산물 직판장이에요.
(C) 마케팅 컨설턴트예요.

해설 **시장이 붐빌지 확인하는 부정 의문문**
(A) **정답**: 시장이 붐빌지 묻는 질문에 평일 오전이라며 붐비지 않을 것이라고 우회적으로 밝히고 있으므로 정답이다.
(B) **어휘 반복 오답**: 질문의 market을 반복 이용한 오답이다.
(C) **파생어 오답**: 질문의 market과 파생어 관계인 marketing을 이용한 오답이다.

어휘 crowded 붐비는   farmers market 농산물 직판장

20 W-Am / M-Cn
I rewrote our business proposal.
(A) That's all the way across town.
(B) Every once in a while.
(C) Could you send it to me?
제가 사업 제안서를 다시 썼어요.
(A) 마을 반대편에 있어요.
(B) 가끔요.
(C) 저한테 보내 주실래요?

해설 **상황을 설명하는 평서문**
(A) **평서문과 상관없는 오답**
(B) **평서문과 상관없는 오답**
(C) **정답**: 사업 제안서를 다시 썼다는 말에 보내 달라고 요청하고 있으므로 정답이다.

어휘 proposal 제안(서)   every once in a while 가끔

ETS 기출 고난도 실전문제   본책 p.38

1 (C)	2 (C)	3 (C)	4 (B)	5 (C)	6 (C)
7 (B)	8 (B)	9 (C)	10 (A)	11 (B)	12 (B)
13 (B)	14 (B)	15 (C)	16 (A)	17 (A)	18 (A)
19 (B)	20 (C)				

1 W-Br / M-Au
When will the maintenance crew replace the outdoor fence?
(A) Those boxes are heavy.
(B) Close the door at the top of the stairs, please.
(C) It's going to start snowing soon.
정비팀은 언제 야외 울타리를 교체하나요?
(A) 저 상자들은 무거워요.
(B) 계단 꼭대기에 있는 문을 닫아 주세요.
(C) 곧 눈이 올 텐데요.

해설 **야외 울타리 교체 시기를 묻는 When 의문문**
(A) 질문과 상관없는 오답
(B) **파생어 오답**: 질문의 outdoor와 파생어 관계인 door를 이용한 오답이다.
(C) **정답**: 야외 울타리 교체 시기를 묻는 질문에 곧 눈이 온다면서 교체 시기가 늦어진다고 우회적으로 밝히고 있으므로 정답이다.

어휘 maintenance 정비   replace 교체하다

2 M-Cn / W-Br
Why haven't the results been e-mailed to the clients?
(A) No, send them to Alvaro.
(B) About 2,000 dollars.
(C) Isn't that scheduled for next week?
왜 결과가 고객들에게 이메일로 전송되지 않았나요?
(A) 아니요, 알바로에게 보내세요.
(B) 2,000달러 정도예요.
(C) 다음 주에 예정되어 있지 않나요?

해설 **결과가 이메일로 전송되지 않은 이유를 묻는 Why 의문문**
(A) **Yes/No 불가 오답**: Why 의문문에는 Yes/No 응답이 불가능하므로 오답이다.
(B) **질문과 상관없는 오답**
(C) **정답**: 결과가 이메일로 전송되지 않은 이유를 묻는 질문에 다음 주에 예정된 것이 아닌지 되물어 아직 시기가 아님을 우회적으로 표현하고 있으므로 정답이다.

어휘 result 결과

3 W-Br / W-Am
How does this red shirt look on me?
(A) Have you started reading it?
(B) A shortened timeline.
(C) It's a great color on you.
이 빨간 셔츠 저한테 어때요?
(A) 읽기 시작했어요?
(B) 단축된 시간표예요.
(C) 색이 정말 잘 어울려요.

해설 **빨간 셔츠가 어울리는지 묻는 How 의문문**
(A) **유사 발음 오답**: 질문의 red와 부분적으로 발음이 유사한

reading을 이용한 오답이다.

(B) **유사 발음 오답**: 질문의 shirt와 부분적으로 발음이 유사한 shortened를 이용한 오답이다.

(C) **정답**: 셔츠가 어울리는지 묻는 질문에 색이 정말 잘 어울린다고 밝히고 있으므로 정답이다.

어휘   shortened 단축된

---

4   M-Cn / W-Br

Are you moving into this neighborhood?
(A) A famous director.
(B) My new job's only a few streets away.
(C) I hope you enjoyed it.

이 동네로 이사 오시나요?
(A) 유명한 감독이에요.
(B) 새 직장이 거리 몇 개만 지나면 있어요.
(C) 즐거우셨길 바라요.

해설   **이 동네로 이사 오는지 묻는 일반 의문문**

(A) **연상 어휘 오답**: 질문의 moving을 movie로 잘못 들었을 때 연상 가능한 director를 이용한 오답이다.

(B) **정답**: 이 동네로 이사 오는지 묻는 질문에 새 직장이 거리 몇 개만 지나면 있다며 이사 오는 것을 우회적으로 밝히고 있으므로 정답이다.

(C) **연상 어휘 오답**: 질문의 moving을 movie로 잘못 들었을 때 연상 가능한 enjoyed를 이용한 오답이다.

어휘   neighborhood 동네

---

5   W-Am / M-Au

Where's the art festival going to be held?
(A) Mostly building materials.
(B) Please show me where the exit is.
(C) Let's take a look at the Web site.

예술제는 어디에서 열리나요?
(A) 대부분 건축 자재예요.
(B) 출구가 어디인지 알려 주세요.
(C) 웹사이트를 살펴봅시다.

해설   **예술제가 열리는 장소를 묻는 Where 의문문**

(A) **질문과 상관없는 오답**

(B) **어휘 반복 오답**: 질문의 Where를 반복 이용한 오답이다.

(C) **정답**: 예술제가 열리는 장소를 묻는 질문에 웹사이트를 살펴보자며 정보를 알 수 있는 방법을 제시하고 있으므로 정답이다.

어휘   material 자재

---

6   W-Br / M-Cn

Could we start closing the store early on Saturdays?
(A) Oh, it's really close by.
(B) That's in the cosmetics department.
(C) Yes, business has been slow.

이제부터 토요일에는 가게를 일찍 닫을 수 있을까요?
(A) 아, 정말 가깝네요.

(B) 그건 화장품 부서에 있어요.
(C) 네, 매출이 부진하네요.

해설   **제안하는 의문문**

(A) **파생어 오답**: 질문의 closing과 파생어 관계인 close를 이용한 오답이다.

(B) **연상 어휘 오답**: 질문의 store에서 연상 가능한 cosmetics를 이용한 오답이다.

(C) **정답**: 토요일에는 가게를 일찍 닫을 수 있을지 제안하는 질문에 네(Yes)라고 긍정한 뒤 매출이 부진하다며 긍정 답변과 일관된 내용을 덧붙이고 있으므로 정답이다.

어휘   cosmetics 화장품   slow 매출이 부진한

---

7   W-Am / W-Br

What do you think about the new security camera?
(A) The electronics store on Wilton Avenue.
(B) We just installed it yesterday.
(C) Several photographs.

새 보안 카메라 어떠세요?
(A) 윌튼 가에 있는 전자 제품 매장이에요.
(B) 어제 막 설치했어요.
(C) 사진 몇 장이요.

해설   **새 보안 카메라에 대한 의견을 묻는 What 의문문**

(A) **연상 어휘 오답**: 질문의 camera에서 연상 가능한 electronics를 이용한 오답이다.

(B) **정답**: 새 보안 카메라에 대한 의견을 묻는 질문에 어제 막 설치했다며 아직 두고 봐야 한다는 취지로 응답하고 있으므로 정답이다.

(C) **연상 어휘 오답**: 질문의 camera에서 연상 가능한 photographs를 이용한 오답이다.

어휘   security 보안   electronics 전자 제품   install 설치하다

---

8   W-Br / M-Au

The product testers reported that our new model of shoe is uncomfortable.
(A) A variety of colors.
(B) The leather is very stiff.
(C) He's the morning news reporter.

제품 검수자들이 우리 신발 신모델이 불편하다고 보고했어요.
(A) 다양한 색상이요.
(B) 가죽이 너무 뻣뻣해요.
(C) 그는 아침 뉴스 기자예요.

해설   **정보를 전달하는 평서문**

(A) **연상 어휘 오답**: 평서문의 product와 shoe에서 연상 가능한 A variety of colors를 이용한 오답이다.

(B) **정답**: 제품 검수자들이 신발 신모델이 불편하다고 보고했다는 말에 가죽이 너무 뻣뻣하다며 동조하고 있으므로 정답이다.

(C) **파생어 오답**: 평서문의 reported와 파생어 관계인 reporter를 이용한 오답이다.

어휘   uncomfortable 불편한   a variety of 다양한
leather 가죽   stiff 뻣뻣한

9 M-Cn / W-Br

Is the financial report ready?
(A) It's a new filing cabinet.
(B) That might not be enough money.
(C) I'm still waiting for the numbers.

재무 보고서가 준비됐나요?
(A) 새 문서 보관함이에요.
(B) 그 돈으로 부족할 수도 있어요.
(C) 아직 수치를 기다리고 있어요.

해설　**재무 보고서가 준비되었는지 묻는 일반 의문문**
(A) **연상 어휘 오답:** 질문의 report에서 연상 가능한 filing cabinet을 이용한 오답이다.
(B) **연상 어휘 오답:** 질문의 financial에서 연상 가능한 money를 이용한 오답이다.
(C) **정답:** 재무 보고서가 준비되었는지 묻는 질문에 아직 수치를 기다리고 있다며 준비가 덜 되었다고 우회적으로 밝히고 있으므로 정답이다.

어휘　financial 재무의

10 M-Au / M-Cn

Would you like me to send out these customer surveys today?
(A) They're being revised.
(B) A customer complaint.
(C) Last month on the fifth.

이 고객 설문지를 오늘 보낼까요?
(A) 그건 수정 중이에요.
(B) 고객 불만이에요.
(C) 지난달 5일이요.

해설　**제안하는 의문문**
(A) **정답:** 고객 설문지를 오늘 보내겠다는 제안에 수정 중이라며 아직 보낼 수 없다고 우회적으로 밝히고 있으므로 정답이다.
(B) **어휘 반복 오답:** 질문의 customer를 반복 이용한 오답이다.
(C) **연상 어휘 오답:** 질문의 today에서 연상 가능한 Last month on the fifth를 이용한 오답이다.

어휘　revise 수정하다　complaint 불만, 항의

11 M-Cn / M-Au

Are you looking for an office with a view?
(A) I previewed the documents.
(B) I'll take whatever's available.
(C) Because this chair is uncomfortable.

전망이 좋은 사무실을 찾으시나요?
(A) 제가 서류를 사전에 검토했어요.
(B) 이용 가능한 곳이면 어디든 괜찮아요.
(C) 이 의자가 불편해서요.

해설　**전망 좋은 사무실을 찾는지 묻는 일반 의문문**
(A) **파생어 오답:** 질문의 view와 파생어 관계인 previewed를 이용한 오답이다.
(B) **정답:** 전망 좋은 사무실을 찾는지 묻는 질문에 이용 가능한 곳이면 어디든 괜찮다며 전망은 크게 중요하지 않다는 것을 우회적으로 표현하고 있으므로 정답이다.
(C) **연상 어휘 오답:** 질문의 office에서 연상 가능한 chair를 이용한 오답이다.

어휘　preview 사전에 검토하다　uncomfortable 불편한

12 M-Cn / W-Br

Isn't the keynote speech taking place at the hotel?
(A) No, I don't speak Spanish.
(B) I have the schedule here.
(C) My presentation went well.

기조연설은 호텔에서 하는 거 아닌가요?
(A) 아니요, 저는 스페인어를 못해요.
(B) 저한테 일정표가 있어요.
(C) 발표는 잘 진행됐어요.

해설　**기조연설을 호텔에서 하는지 확인하는 부정 의문문**
(A) **파생어 오답:** 질문의 speech와 파생어 관계인 speak를 이용한 오답이다.
(B) **정답:** 기조연설을 호텔에서 하는지 묻는 질문에 자신에게 일정표가 있다며 정보를 알 수 있는 수단을 제공하고 있으므로 정답이다.
(C) **연상 어휘 오답:** 질문의 keynote speech에서 연상 가능한 presentation을 이용한 오답이다.

어휘　keynote speech 기조연설

13 M-Cn / W-Am

Do you think I should buy an electric bicycle?
(A) I'll change the lightbulb.
(B) They are more affordable these days.
(C) I thought it was by the sink.

제가 전기 자전거를 사야 할까요?
(A) 제가 전구를 바꿀게요.
(B) 요즘은 가격이 더 저렴해요.
(C) 싱크대 옆에 있는 줄 알았어요.

해설　**전기 자전거를 사야 할지 묻는 일반 의문문**
(A) **연상 어휘 오답:** 질문의 electric에서 연상 가능한 lightbulb를 이용한 오답이다.
(B) **정답:** 전기 자전거를 사야 할지 묻는 질문에 요즘은 가격이 더 저렴하다며 우회적으로 구매를 권유하고 있으므로 정답이다.
(C) **파생어 및 유사 발음 오답:** 질문의 think와 파생어 관계인 thought를 이용했고, think와 부분적으로 발음이 유사한 sink를 이용한 오답이다. 질문의 buy와 발음이 유사한 by를 이용한 오답이기도 하다.

어휘　lightbulb 전구　affordable 저렴한

14 W-Br / M-Au

Where can I file a missing-luggage report?
(A) Twenty-three kilograms maximum.
(B) Let me see your claim ticket.
(C) It's supposed to be sunny all day.

분실 수하물 신고는 어디에서 하면 되나요?
(A) 최대 23kg입니다.
(B) 보관증을 보여 주세요.
(C) 하루 종일 맑다고 하네요.

해설 **분실 수하물 신고 장소를 묻는 Where 의문문**
(A) **연상 어휘 오답:** 질문의 luggage에서 연상 가능한 Twenty-three kilograms를 이용한 오답이다.
(B) **정답:** 분실 수하물 신고 장소를 묻는 질문에 수하물 보관증을 요구하며 이곳이 신고 장소임을 우회적으로 표현하고 있으므로 정답이다.
(C) **질문과 상관없는 오답**

어휘 luggage 수하물, (여행용) 짐　claim ticket (수하물) 보관증

15 M-Cn / M-Au

How long do the fountains in the park stay on?
(A) A lovely fishpond.
(B) Sure, let's meet in the park.
(C) Ivan is the head groundskeeper.

공원에 있는 분수는 얼마나 오래 틀어 놓나요?
(A) 예쁜 연못이네요.
(B) 그래요. 공원에서 만나요.
(C) 이반이 수석 관리인이에요.

해설 **공원에 있는 분수를 틀어 놓은 시간을 묻는 How long 의문문**
(A) **연상 어휘 오답:** 질문의 fountains에서 연상 가능한 fishpond를 이용한 오답이다.
(B) **Yes/No 불가 오답:** How long 의문문에는 Yes/No 응답이 불가능한데, Sure도 일종의 Yes 응답이라고 볼 수 있으므로 오답이다.
(C) **정답:** 공원 분수를 얼마나 오래 틀어 놓는지 묻는 질문에 이반이 수석 관리인이라며 정보를 아는 사람을 알려 주고 있으므로 정답이다.

어휘 fountain 분수　fishpond (물고기가 사는) 연못
groundskeeper (공원) 관리인

16 M-Cn / W-Am

Would you be willing to take a survey about the service you received today?
(A) How long is it?
(B) No, that seat's not taken.
(C) I found a pair of them yesterday.

오늘 받은 서비스에 대한 설문 조사에 참여하시겠어요?
(A) 얼마나 걸리죠?
(B) 아니요, 그 자리는 비었어요.
(C) 제가 어제 한 쌍 찾았어요.

해설 **요청하는 의문문**
(A) **정답:** 오늘 받은 서비스에 대한 설문 조사를 해달라는 요청에 얼마나 걸리는지 되물으며 시간에 따라 결정할 의사를 표현하고 있으므로 정답이다.
(B) **파생어 오답:** 질문의 take와 파생어 관계인 taken을 이용한 오답이다.
(C) **연상 어휘 오답:** 질문의 today에서 연상 가능한 yesterday를 이용한 오답이다.

어휘 be willing to 기꺼이 ~하다　take a survey 설문 조사에 참여하다

17 M-Au / W-Am

You managed to get tickets for the show, didn't you?
(A) Yes, balcony seats.
(B) The manager of a basketball team.
(C) Sure, I'll show you the apartment later.

공연 표를 간신히 구하셨죠, 그렇지 않나요?
(A) 네, 발코니 좌석이에요.
(B) 농구팀 감독이에요.
(C) 물론이죠. 나중에 아파트를 보여 드릴게요.

해설 **공연 표를 구했는지 확인하는 부가 의문문**
(A) **정답:** 공연 표를 구했는지 묻는 질문에 네(Yes)라고 긍정한 뒤 발코니 좌석이라며 긍정 답변과 일관된 내용을 덧붙이고 있으므로 정답이다.
(B) **파생어 오답:** 질문의 managed와 파생어 관계인 manager를 이용한 오답이다.
(C) **어휘 반복 오답:** 질문의 show를 반복 이용한 오답이다.

어휘 manage to 간신히 ~하다

18 M-Cn / W-Br

Excuse me, the strawberry jam isn't in aisle five anymore.
(A) This market was just reorganized.
(B) Yes, I'll take some more.
(C) I do shop online.

실례합니다. 딸기잼이 이제는 5번 통로에 없네요.
(A) 이 마트가 얼마 전에 재정비됐어요.
(B) 네, 조금 더 살게요.
(C) 저는 온라인으로 쇼핑해요.

해설 **상황을 설명하는 평서문**
(A) **정답:** 딸기잼이 이제는 5번 통로에 없다는 말에 마트가 얼마 전에 재정비되었다며 이유를 밝히고 있으므로 정답이다.
(B) **연상 어휘 오답:** 평서문의 anymore에서 연상 가능한 some more를 이용한 오답이다.
(C) **연상 어휘 오답:** 평서문의 strawberry jam과 aisle five에서 연상 가능한 shop을 이용한 오답이다.

어휘 aisle 통로　reorganize 재정비하다

19 W-Br / M-Au

Should we open our restaurant in the historic district or the financial district?
(A) Yes, I like that building.
(B) The historic district has more tourists.
(C) A map of the city.

식당을 역사 지구에 열어야 할까요, 금융가에 열어야 할까요?
(A) 네, 저 건물이 마음에 들어요.
(B) 역사 지구에 관광객이 더 많아요.
(C) 도시 지도예요.

해설 **식당 개업 장소를 묻는 선택 의문문**
(A) **연상 어휘 오답:** 질문의 historic district과 financial district에서 연상 가능한 building을 이용한 오답이다.
(B) **정답:** 식당 개업 장소를 묻는 질문에 역사 지구에 관광객이 더 많다며 역사 지구를 우회적으로 선택하고 있으므로 정답이다.
(C) **연상 어휘 오답:** 질문의 district에서 연상 가능한 map과 city를 이용한 오답이다.

어휘 historic 역사적인 district 지구, 구역 financial 금융의 tourist 관광객

20 M-Cn / W-Br

We should buy more computer monitors.
(A) I've made a lunch reservation for five people.
(B) Two hundred dollars.
(C) We've been instructed to cut back on costs.

컴퓨터 모니터를 더 사야 해요.
(A) 5명으로 점심 예약했어요.
(B) 200달러예요.
(C) 비용을 줄이라는 지시를 받았어요.

해설 **의견을 제시하는 평서문**
(A) **평서문과 상관없는 오답**
(B) **연상 어휘 오답:** 평서문의 buy에서 연상 가능한 Two hundred dollars를 이용한 오답이다.
(C) **정답:** 컴퓨터 모니터를 더 사야 한다는 말에 비용을 줄이라는 지시를 받았다며 살 수 없음을 우회적으로 밝히고 있으므로 정답이다.

어휘 make a reservation 예약하다 instruct 지시하다 cut back on ~을 줄이다

PART 3&4
Listening Comprehension

UNIT 3 대화/담화 빈출 유형

01 주제/목적, 직업/장소

❶ 주제/목적 문제
본책 p.42

정답 단서 패턴 ①

> 남1 내일 신문 1면에 실릴 기사를 골라야 합니다. 히로시, 어떻게 생각하세요?
> 남2 동물원 확장에 대해 다뤄야 할 것 같아요. 곧 완공될 예정이고 동물원은 마을에서 가장 많은 사람들이 찾는 곳 중 하나거든요.
>
> 어휘 expansion 확장 site 장소

문제 화자들은 주로 무엇을 논의하고 있는가?
정답 신문 기사 선택하기

정답 단서 패턴 ②

> 여 안녕하세요, 여러분. 아시다시피, 우리는 이 공장에 대한 연례 안전 점검을 실시하기 위해 회사의 품질 보증 부서에서 왔습니다.
>
> 어휘 assurance 보증 safety inspection 안전 점검

문제 화자가 방문한 목적은 무엇인가?
정답 점검을 실시하려고

❷ 직업/장소 문제

정답 단서 패턴 ①

> 여 지금까지 훈련 잘했어요, 안드레이. 이제 곧 혼자서 차를 고칠 수 있을 거예요.
> 남 고마워요, 실비아. 다음 단계가 기대되네요. 오늘은 스포츠카 수리에 대해 배울 예정이죠, 그렇죠?

문제 화자들은 누구인 것 같은가?
정답 자동차 정비사

정답 단서 패턴 ②

> 여 안녕하십니까, 승객 여러분. 런던발 마드리드행 그린웨이 항공 59편 탑승 전 안내 방송입니다.
>
> 어휘 passenger 승객

문제 청자들은 어디에 있는 것 같은가?
정답 공항

[1-3] M-Au / W-Am

M Hi, Marta. This is Klaus from Casella Press. **1 We're delighted with your book proposal about starting a different career later in life, and we'd like to offer you a contract.**

W That's wonderful news! It's difficult to find resources about this topic. **2 Since there's nothing else like it on the market right now, I think the book will be a success.**

M **2 Exactly — that was my thinking too.** Now, we'll need to consider a suitable timeline for getting the chapters done.

W Sure. **3 I think we should build in extra time, though.** As you know, I'd like to include guest entries from professionals in different fields who can provide industry-specific input. Collecting those could take a while.

남 안녕하세요, 마르타. 카셀라 프레스의 클라우스예요. **1** 인생 후반에 다른 일을 시작하는 것에 관한 책을 제안해 주셔서 기뻐요. 계약을 제안하고 싶습니다.

여 좋은 소식이네요! 이 주제에 관한 자료를 찾기가 어려워요. **2** 지금 시중에 비슷한 게 없어서 책이 성공할 것 같아요.

남 **2** 맞아요. 제 생각도 그래요. 이제 챕터들을 마무리하는 데 적당한 일정을 고려해야 합니다.

여 그렇죠. **3** 그런데 시간을 더 확보해야 할 것 같아요. 아시다시피 업계별 특화된 정보를 제공할 수 있는 다양한 분야의 전문가들의 특별 기고문을 포함하고 싶어요. 모으려면 시간이 좀 걸릴 수도 있어요.

어휘 proposal 제안 contract 계약 resource 자료, 자원 suitable 적당한 specific 특정한, 구체적인

1 남자는 왜 전화하고 있는가?
(A) 계약을 논의하려고
(B) 추천서를 요청하려고
(C) 회의 일정을 확정하려고
(D) 마케팅 캠페인을 준비하려고

해설 전화의 목적
남자가 첫 대사에서 인생 후반에 다른 일을 시작하는 것에 관한 책을 제안해 줘서 기쁘다(We're delighted with your book proposal ~)며 계약을 제안하고 싶다(we'd like to offer you a contract)고 했으므로 정답은 (A)이다.

어휘 letter of reference 추천서

2 화자들은 왜 제품이 성공할 것이라고 생각하는가?
(A) 발상이 독창적이다.
(B) 비슷한 제품들이 인기가 많다.
(C) 시장 실험이 긍정적이었다.
(D) 사전 주문이 예상보다 많다.

해설 제품이 성공할 것이라고 생각하는 이유
여자가 첫 대사에서 지금 시중에 비슷한 게 없어서 책이 성공할 것 같다(Since there's nothing else like it on the market right now, I think the book will be a success)고 했고 남자가 맞다면서 자신의 생각도 그렇다고 호응했으므로 정답은 (A)이다.

어휘 original 독창적인 advance 사전의 anticipate 기대하다

(Paraphrasing) 대화의 there's nothing else like it on the market → 정답의 An idea is original.

3 여자는 어떤 일에 시간이 더 걸린다고 말하는가?
(A) 초안 오류 수정   (B) 그래픽 디자이너 선택
(C) 전문가 의견 수렴   (D) 장소 방문

해설 여자가 시간이 더 걸린다고 말하는 일
여자가 마지막 대사에서 시간을 더 확보해야 할 것 같다면서 업계별 특화된 정보를 제공할 수 있는 다양한 분야의 전문가들의 특별 기고문을 포함하고 싶은데(As you know, I'd like to include guest entries from professionals in different fields who can provide industry-specific input), 모으려면 시간이 좀 걸릴 수도 있다(Collecting those could take a while)고 했으므로 정답은 (C)이다.

어휘 correct 수정하다 draft 초안

(Paraphrasing) 대화의 guest entries from professionals ~ input → 정답의 input from professionals

[4-6] 방송

W-Br Welcome to another episode of my podcast, *Technology World*, the show where we discuss innovative technology. **4 Our guest today is Joshua Lee. He works at an offshore hydroelectric station that transforms energy from ocean waves into electricity. 5 Mr. Lee is a mechanical engineer, and he designed the generator that produces the power for the station.** For his design, he received an Innovation in Engineering Award. **6 Mr. Lee, let me ask you some questions about your typical day working at the station.**

혁신적인 기술에 대해 이야기하는 제 팟캐스트 〈테크놀로지 월드〉의 새로운 에피소드에 오신 것을 환영합니다. **4** 오늘 게스트는 조슈아 리인데요. 파도에서 나오는 에너지를 전기로 바꾸는 연안 수력 전기 발전소에서 일하고 있습니다. **5** 리 씨는 기계 공학자로, 발전소 전력을 생산하는 발전기를 설계했어요. 이 설계로 기술 혁신상을 받았죠. **6** 리 선생님, 발전소에서 일하는 평범한 하루에 대해 몇 가지 여쭤 볼게요.

어휘 innovative 혁신적인 offshore 연안의 hydroelectric 수력 전기의 transform 바꾸다 generator 발전기 typical 평범한, 전형적인

4 조슈아 리는 어디에서 일하는가?

(A) 자동차 제조업체 　　　(B) 대학 실험실

(C) 자연 보호 구역 　　　**(D) 발전소**

해설　**조슈아 리의 근무 장소**

초반부에 오늘 게스트는 조슈아 리(Our guest today is Joshua Lee)라고 한 뒤 파도에서 나오는 에너지를 전기로 바꾸는 연안 수력 전기 발전소에서 일하고 있다(He works at an offshore hydroelectric station ~)고 했으므로 정답은 (D)이다.

어휘　manufacturer 제조업체

nature preserve 자연 보호 구역

(Paraphrasing) 담화의 an offshore hydroelectric station → 정답의 a power station

5 조슈아 리는 무엇으로 상을 받았는가?

(A) 학술 논문 　　　**(B) 기계 설계**

(C) 경영 계획 　　　(D) 자원봉사 프로젝트

해설　**조슈아 리가 상을 받은 이유**

중반부에 리 씨는 기계 공학자로, 발전소 전력을 생산하는 발전기를 설계했고(Mr. Lee is a mechanical engineer, and he designed the generator that produces the power for the station). 이 설계로 기술 혁신상을 받았다(For his design, he received an Innovation in Engineering Award)고 했으므로 정답은 (B)이다.

(Paraphrasing) 담화의 the generator that produces the power for the station → 정답의 A machine

6 조슈아 리는 다음으로 무엇에 대해 이야기하겠는가?

(A) 장래 계획 　　　(B) 연구 경력

(C) 매일 하는 직무 　　　(D) 학력

해설　**조슈아 리가 다음에 이야기할 내용**

후반부에 화자가 조슈아 리에게 발전소에서 일하는 평범한 하루에 대해 몇 가지 물어보겠다(Mr. Lee, let me ask you some questions about your typical day working at the station)고 했으므로 정답은 (C)이다.

어휘　responsibility 직무, 책임

(Paraphrasing) 담화의 typical day working at the station → 정답의 daily responsibilities

02　문제점/걱정거리, 세부 사항

❶ 문제점/걱정거리 문제

본책 p.44

정답 단서 패턴 ①

> 여　매표소가 일찍 열어서 오늘 공연 티켓을 구할 수 있어 다행이에요. 오늘 오전에 웹사이트에 문제가 많았어요.
>
> 남　죄송합니다. 웹사이트에 문제가 있습니다.

문제　화자들은 어떤 문제를 논의하는가?

정답　웹사이트가 작동하지 않는다.

정답 단서 패턴 ②

> 여　안녕하세요, 두재 씨. 이번 분기에 생산할 베개에 필요한 충전재를 충분히 확보하고 싶은데요.
>
> 남　깃털과 폴리에스테르 충전재는 납품받았지만 폼 충전재 배송이 지연되고 있습니다.

어휘　filling 충전재

문제　남자는 어떤 문제를 언급하는가?

정답　배송이 늦는다.

❷ 세부 사항 문제

정답 단서 패턴 ①

> 여　안녕하세요, 여러분. 와 주셔서 감사합니다. 제가 지난 주말에 테니스를 치다가 손목을 삐었어요. 심각한 정도는 아니지만 적어도 앞으로 2주 동안은 환자를 수술할 수 없을 것 같습니다.

어휘　sprain 삐다　wrist 손목　operate 수술하다

문제　지난 주말에 화자에게 무슨 일이 있었는가?

정답　손목을 다쳤다.

정답 단서 패턴 ②

> 여　이번 달에 맞춤 제작 드레스 주문이 정말 많이 늘었어요.
>
> 남　알아요. 정말 대단하죠. 하지만 모든 의류 품목이 수작업으로 제작되기 때문에 양이 너무 많아서 감당하기 어려운 지경이에요.

어휘　custom-designed 맞춤 제작된

문제　남자는 제품에 관해 무엇이라고 말하는가?

정답　수제품이다.

> **ETS 기출 유형연습**　　　본책 p.45
>
> **1** (A)　**2** (D)　**3** (B)　**4** (B)　**5** (C)　**6** (A)

[1-3] M-Cn / W-Br / W-Am　　　3인 대화

> M　Hi. You must be Farida and Carmen. **1 I understand you're looking for a commercial retail space for your tea shop.**
>
> W1　Yes. Until now, we've operated exclusively online. But we'd like to offer in-store service.
>
> W2　**2 We'd also like to host events that involve the community, such as discussion groups and book signings.**
>
> W1　**2 Right—our priority is to engage with the local community.**
>
> M　OK. A retail space just opened up in Greenson, which is a nice mix of commercial and residential properties. **3 The only problem is that the space will need a lot of work.** Do you have a budget for renovations?

남 안녕하세요. 파리다 씨와 카르멘 씨죠? **1 찻집을 차릴 상업용 소매 공간을 찾고 계신다고요.**

여1 네. 지금까지는 온라인으로만 운영해 왔어요. 하지만 매장 내 서비스를 제공하고 싶어요.

여2 **2 아울러 토론 단체, 저자 사인회 같은 지역 사회와 관련된 행사도 주최하고 싶어요.**

여1 **2 맞아요. 우리의 우선순위는 지역 사회와 소통하는 거예요.**

남 알겠습니다. 그린슨에 소매 공간이 방금 나왔는데, 상가와 주택이 잘 섞여 있어요. **3 문제가 딱 하나 있는데 이 공간은 손을 많이 봐야 해요.** 개조에 필요한 예산이 있나요?

어휘 commercial 상업의 retail 소매의 operate 운영하다 involve 관련되다 priority 우선순위 engage with ~와 소통하다 property 건물, 부동산 renovation 개조

---

1 대화는 주로 무엇에 관한 것인가?
(A) 소매 공간 선택
(B) 입사 지원서 검토
(C) 인테리어 디자이너 선정
(D) 신제품군 테스트

해설 **대화의 주제**
남자가 첫 대사에서 찻집을 차릴 상업용 소매 공간을 찾고 있다고 알고 있다(I understand you're looking for a commercial retail space for your tea shop)고 한 뒤 소매 공간에 관한 대화가 이어지므로 정답은 (A)이다.

어휘 application 지원(서)

---

2 여자들은 우선순위가 무엇이라고 말하는가?
(A) 혁신적인 아이디어 내기
(B) 지속 가능한 방식 채택하기
(C) 효율적인 사업 모델 따르기
(D) 지역 사회와 상호작용하기

해설 **여자들이 우선순위라고 말하는 것**
두 번째 여자가 첫 대사에서 토론 단체, 저자 사인회 같은 지역 사회와 관련된 행사도 주최하고 싶다(We'd also like to host events that involve the community, ~)고 하자 첫 번째 여자가 맞다고 호응하며 우선순위는 지역 사회와 소통하는 것(our priority is to engage with the local community)이라고 했으므로 정답은 (D)이다.

어휘 sustainable 지속 가능한 practice 방식, 관행 efficient 효율적인 interact with ~와 상호작용하다

Paraphrasing 대화의 to engage with the local community → 정답의 To interact with the community

---

3 남자는 어떤 문제를 언급하는가?
(A) 요금이 예상보다 비쌀 것이다.
(B) 개조가 필요할 것이다.
(C) 시장은 경쟁이 무척 치열하다.
(D) 일부 자료는 이용할 수 없다.

해설 **남자가 언급하는 문제**
남자가 마지막 대사에서 문제가 하나 있는데 이 공간은 손을 많이 봐야 한다(The only problem is that the space will need a lot of work)고 했으므로 정답은 (B)이다.

어휘 competitive 경쟁하는 unavailable 이용할 수 없는

Paraphrasing 대화의 the space will need a lot of work → 정답의 Some renovations will be needed.

[4-6] 견학 정보

W-Am OK, folks. To your left, you'll see our press shop. **4 Here, heavy machines press massive rolls of reinforced steel into shapes that make up the parts of a vehicle—the door frames, the roofs, and so on. 5 These machines are very efficient—able to stamp out up to 800 parts each day.** Now let's walk into the main assembly area where these molds are welded together and then painted. **6 Kavi is going to tell you about the process the company goes through every year when we choose the colors that will be available for each model.**

네, 여러분. 왼쪽에 프레스 공장이 있습니다. **4 이곳에서는 중장비들이 거대한 철근 롤을 문틀, 지붕 등 차량의 부품을 구성하는 모양으로 압착합니다. 5 이 기계들은 하루에 최대 800개의 부품을 찍어낼 수 있을 정도로 매우 효율적이에요.** 이제 이 금형을 용접하고 도장하는 주요 조립 구역으로 들어가 보겠습니다. **6 각 모델에 사용할 색상을 선택할 때 회사가 매년 어떤 과정을 거치는지 카비가 알려 줄 거예요.**

어휘 folks 여러분 massive 거대한 reinforced steel (강화) 철근 assembly 조립 weld 용접하다

---

4 견학은 어디에서 진행되고 있는 것 같은가?
(A) 자동차 박물관
(B) 자동차 공장
(C) 우체국
(D) 건설 현장

해설 **견학의 장소**
초반부에 이곳에서는 중장비들이 거대한 철근 롤을 문틀, 지붕 등 차량의 부품을 구성하는 모양으로 압착한다(Here, heavy machines press ~ make up the parts of a vehicle—the door frames, the roofs, and so on)고 했으므로 자동차를 만드는 공장임을 알 수 있다. 따라서 정답은 (B)이다.

---

5 화자는 기계의 어떤 장점을 언급하는가?
(A) 유지 보수가 쉽다.
(B) 가볍다.
(C) 효율적이다.
(D) 원격으로 작동할 수 있다.

해설 **화자가 언급하는 기계의 장점**
중반부에 이 기계들은 하루에 최대 800개의 부품을 찍어낼 수 있을 정도로 매우 효율적이다(These machines are very efficient—able to stamp out up to 800 parts each day)라고 했으므로 정답은 (C)이다.

어휘 lightweight 가벼운 remotely 원격으로, 멀리서

6 화자에 따르면, 카비는 무엇에 대해 이야기할 것인가?

(A) 페인트 색상　　　　(B) 유지 보수 일정
(C) 운영 허가증　　　　(D) 보험 옵션

해설 카비가 이야기할 내용

후반부에 각 모델에 사용할 색상을 선택할 때 회사가 매년 어떤 과정을 거치는지 카비가 알려 줄 것이다(Kavi is going to tell you about the process ~ when we choose the colors that will be available for each model)라고 했으므로 정답은 (A)이다.

어휘 insurance 보험

03 제안/요청, 다음에 할 일

❶ 제안/요청 문제
본책 p.46

정답 단서 패턴 ①

> 남 이 코트를 큰 사이즈밖에 못 찾았는데 저는 미디엄 사이즈를 입어요. 뒤에 다른 사이즈가 있나요?
> 여 없습니다. 하지만 코트 안에 여러 겹을 입고 싶을 수도 있으니 큰 코트를 구입하는 걸 추천드려요.
>
> **어휘** layer 겹, 층　underneath 안에, 속에

문제 여자는 남자에게 무엇을 하라고 권하는가?
정답 큰 사이즈 구매

정답 단서 패턴 ②

> 여 탑승객 검사를 시작할 수 있도록 확인을 위해 탑승권을 제시해 주시기 바랍니다. 기다려 주셔서 감사합니다. 저희 항공사를 이용해 주셔서 감사드립니다.
>
> **어휘** boarding pass 탑승권　verification 확인

문제 화자는 청자들에게 무엇을 하라고 요청하는가?
정답 탑승권 제시

❷ 다음에 할 일 문제

정답 단서 패턴 ①

> 여 음, 문에 점심시간에 대한 정보가 게시되어 있지 않았어요.
> 남 알려 주셔서 감사합니다. 어제 창문을 청소했어요. 누군가 영업 시간 표지판을 옮겼을 수 있어요. 다시 걸어 놓을게요.

문제 남자는 무엇을 할 것이라고 말하는가?
정답 표지판 제자리에 두기

정답 단서 패턴 ②

> 여 지난달에 귀하에게 딱 맞는 받침대들을 판매했습니다. 제 컴퓨터에 재고가 있는지 확인해 볼게요.
>
> **어휘** pedestal 받침대　in stock 재고가 있는

문제 여자는 다음에 무엇을 할 것인가?
정답 재고 확인

ETS 기출 유형연습　　　　본책 p.47

1 (D)　**2** (A)　**3** (C)　**4** (B)　**5** (C)　**6** (A)

[1-3] M-Cn / W-Br

> M Kelly. **1 Since the mayor wants to increase community involvement, let's talk about what our city can do to make it happen.**
> W **2 I know many of our city's residents have been wanting to build a community garden. Why don't we move forward with that idea?**
> M **3 Well, I'm supposed to meet with some members of the city council tomorrow.** Why don't I mention the garden idea to them? That way we'll know whether to proceed with it.
>
> 남 켈리. **1 시장님께서 지역 사회 참여를 늘리고 싶어 하시니,** 이를 위해 우리 시에서 할 수 있는 일이 무엇인지 이야기해 봅시다.
> 여 **2 제가 알기로 우리 시의 많은 주민이 마을 정원을 만들고 싶어 합니다. 이 아이디어를 추진하는 게 어떨까요?**
> 남 **3 음, 내일 시의회 의원들과 만나기로 했어요.** 제가 그들에게 정원 아이디어를 얘기해 볼까요? 그러면 진행 여부를 알 수 있을 겁니다.

어휘 increase 늘리다　involvement 참여　council 의회　proceed 진행하다

1 화자들은 어디에서 일하는 것 같은가?

(A) 도서관　　　　(B) 박물관
(C) 농산물 직판장　　(D) 시청

해설 화자들의 근무 장소

남자가 첫 대사에서 시장이 지역 사회 참여를 늘리고 싶어 한다(Since the mayor wants to increase community ~)면서 이를 위해 우리 시에서 할 수 있는 일이 무엇인지 이야기해 보자(let's talk about what our city can do to make it happen)고 했으므로 정답은 (D)이다.

2 여자는 무엇을 제안하는가?

(A) 마을 정원 조성　　(B) 자선 걷기 대회 준비
(C) 주차 구역 확장　　(D) 주말 강좌 제공

해설 여자의 제안 사항

여자가 첫 대사에서 우리 시의 많은 주민이 마을 정원을 만들고 싶어 한다(I know many of our city's residents have been wanting to build a community garden)면서 이 아이디어를 추진하는 게 어떨지(Why don't we move forward with that idea?) 제안하고 있으므로 정답은 (A)이다.

어휘 charity 자선　expand 확장하다

3 남자는 내일 무엇을 할 것인가?

(A) 후기 작성하기　　(B) 면접 실시하기
(C) 회의 참석하기　　(D) 광고 내기

해설 **남자가 내일 할 일**
남자가 마지막 대사에서 내일 시의회 의원들과 만나기로 했다(Well, I'm supposed to meet with some members of the city council tomorrow)고 했으므로 정답은 (C)이다.

[4-6] 회의 발췌

> W-Br   As you know, the Espinoza exhibit is going to be opening in the winter. **⁴We have some wonderful plans for merchandise to sell here in our museum gift shop during the exhibit. ⁵I'm particularly excited about the T-shirts we'll have with Espinoza's paintings on them. Shirts with art printed on them are specialty items that are often big sellers**—I'm sure this will go over well with the patrons. Now, I want to make sure that you are all familiar with our new merchandise so you can promote it to the customers. **⁶If you'll turn your attention to the screen, you'll see a mock-up of what the shirts will look like.**
>
> 아시다시피 겨울에 에스피노자 전시회가 열립니다. ⁴전시 기간 동안 이곳 미술관 기념품점에서 상품을 판매할 멋진 계획이 있어요. ⁵특히 에스피노자의 그림이 그려진 티셔츠를 판매할 예정이라 기대돼요. 예술 작품이 인쇄된 셔츠는 종종 아주 잘 팔리는 특별 상품이죠. 분명 고객들 반응이 좋을 겁니다. 자, 고객에게 홍보할 수 있도록 여러분 모두 새로운 상품에 대해 꼭 숙지하시기 바랍니다. ⁶화면에 주목하시면 셔츠가 어떤 모습일지 시안이 보일 겁니다.
>
> 어휘 exhibit 전시(회) merchandise 상품 go over with ~에게 받아들여지다 patron 고객, 후원자 familiar with ~에 대해 잘 아는 promote 홍보하다 mock-up 시안, 모형

4 화자는 어디에서 일하는 것 같은가?
(A) 의류 제조업체
(B) 미술관 기념품점
(C) 미술용품점
(D) 소프트웨어 회사

해설 **화자의 근무 장소**
초반부에 전시 기간 동안 이곳 미술관 기념품점에서 상품을 판매할 멋진 계획이 있다(We have some wonderful plans ~ in our museum gift shop during the exhibit)고 했으므로 정답은 (B)이다.

5 화자는 무엇을 기대하고 있는가?
(A) 직원 추가 채용
(B) 온라인 광고
(C) 특별 상품 판매
(D) 축하 행사 참석

해설 **화자가 기대하는 것**
초반부에 전시회 기간 동안 상품을 판매할 계획이 있다고 한 뒤 특히 에스피노자의 그림이 그려진 티셔츠를 판매할 예정이라 기대된다(I'm particularly excited about the T-shirts we'll have with Espinoza's paintings on them)고 했고 예술 작품이 인쇄된 셔츠는 종종 아주 잘 팔리는 특별 상품이다(Shirts with art printed on them are specialty items that are often big sellers)라고 했으므로 정답은 (C)이다.

6 화자는 다음에 무엇을 할 것인가?
(A) 이미지 제시하기
(B) 통계 제시하기
(C) 다과 나눠주기
(D) 의견 수렴하기

해설 **화자가 다음에 할 일**
후반부에 화면에 주목하면 셔츠가 어떤 모습일지 시안이 보일 것이다(If you'll turn your attention to the screen, you'll see a mock-up of what the shirts will look like)고 했으므로 정답은 (A)이다.

어휘 statistics 통계 distribute 나눠주다, 배포하다 refreshments 다과

(Paraphrasing) 담화의 a mock-up of what the shirts will look like → 정답의 some images

---

ETS 기출 실전문제
본책 p.48

1 (B)	2 (D)	3 (B)	4 (B)	5 (A)	6 (C)
7 (C)	8 (B)	9 (D)	10 (C)	11 (C)	12 (A)
13 (A)	14 (B)	15 (C)	16 (B)	17 (A)	18 (D)

[1-3] M-Au / W-Am

> M   **¹Ms. Sullivan, I enjoyed the presentation you just gave. It's been my favorite session of the day so far. ²The packaging system your company is developing to extend the shelf life of fresh fruits and vegetables is fascinating.**
>
> W   Thank you! There's a lot of room for innovation in the field of packaging. And once we access more funding, we can expand our trials beyond grapes and tomatoes.
>
> M   That's what I wanted to approach you about. **³I've been looking to expand my investment portfolio, and your project seems like a promising opportunity.** Here's my card. **³I'd love to meet later to talk more about your company.**
>
> 남   ¹설리번 씨, 방금 하신 발표 잘 들었습니다. 오늘 하루 중 지금까지 가장 마음에 드는 세션이었어요. ²신선 과일과 채소의 유통기한을 연장하기 위해 귀사가 개발하고 있는 포장 시스템이 흥미롭네요.
>
> 여   감사합니다! 포장 분야에는 혁신의 여지가 많습니다. 그리고 자금을 더 확보하면 포도와 토마토 이외에도 실험을 확대할 수 있습니다.
>
> 남   바로 그 건 때문에 만나고 싶었습니다. ³투자 포트폴리오를 확대하려고 모색하고 있었는데, 당신의 프로젝트가 유망한 기회인 것 같아요. 제 명함입니다. ³나중에 만나서 귀사에 대해 더 이야기하고 싶습니다.
>
> 어휘 extend 연장하다 shelf life 유통기한 room 여지, 가능성 innovation 혁신 funding 자금 expand 확대하다 trial 실험 promising 유망한 opportunity 기회

1 화자들은 어디에 있는 것 같은가?
(A) 식료품점   (B) 회의장
(C) 실험실   (D) 창고

해설 **대화의 장소**
남자가 첫 대사에서 여자에게 방금 한 발표 잘 들었다(Ms. Sullivan, I enjoyed the presentation you just gave)면서 오늘 하루 중 지금까지 가장 마음에 드는 세션이었다(It's been my favorite session ~)고 했으므로 화자들이 여러 발표가 진행된 회의장에 있다는 것을 알 수 있다. 따라서 정답은 (B)이다.

2 여자는 어떤 업계에 종사하는가?
(A) 건설   (B) 교육
(C) 의학 연구   (D) 식품 포장

해설 **여자가 종사하는 업계**
남자가 첫 대사에서 여자에게 신선 과일과 채소의 유통기한을 연장하기 위해 귀사가 개발하고 있는 포장 시스템이 흥미롭다(The packaging system your company is developing ~ of fresh fruits and vegetables is fascinating)고 했으므로 정답은 (D)이다.

(Paraphrasing) 대화의 fresh fruits and vegetables
→ 정답의 Food

3 남자는 왜 여자와 회의를 잡고 싶어 하는가?
(A) 여자에게 업계 인맥을 소개하려고
(B) 여자의 회사에 대한 투자를 논의하려고
(C) 기사를 위해 여자를 인터뷰하려고
(D) 사업 관련 조언을 주려고

해설 **남자가 회의를 잡으려는 이유**
남자가 마지막 대사에서 투자 포트폴리오를 확대하려고 모색하고 있었다(I've been looking to expand my investment portfolio)면서 여자의 프로젝트가 유망한 기회인 것 같다(your project seems like a promising opportunity)고 한 뒤 나중에 만나서 여자의 회사에 대해 더 이야기하고 싶다(I'd love to meet later to talk more about your company)고 했으므로 정답은 (B)이다.

[4-6] M-Cn / W-Br

M Hi, Sung-Hee. **4,5 QJ Industries called me in for a face-to-face sales meeting at noon tomorrow.** I think they're finally ready to sign a contract.
W Wow, that's great. You've been working on that account for a long time.
M Right. **5 And I'm actually wondering if you can come with me.** That way you can answer any questions on the technical side.
W Well, I'm supposed to do some software training for our staff in the morning, but I should be finished before noon.

M OK, that works. **6 I'll have my car with me tomorrow, so I can drive us both there.**

남 안녕하세요, 성희 씨. **4,5** QJ 산업에서 내일 정오에 열리는 대면 영업회의에 오라고 하네요. 드디어 계약할 준비가 된 모양이예요.
여 와, 잘됐네요. 그 거래처를 오랫동안 공들이셨잖아요.
남 맞아요. **5** 실은 성희 씨가 저와 함께 가실 수 있는지 궁금해요. 그렇게 되면 성희 씨가 기술 측면은 어떤 질문에도 대답할 수 있을 텐데요.
여 음, 오전에 직원들을 위한 소프트웨어 교육을 해야 해요. 하지만 정오 전에는 끝날 거예요.
남 좋아요, 그럼 됐어요. **6** 제가 내일 차를 가지고 가니까 둘 다 거기까지 같이 타고 가면 돼요.

어휘 call ~ in ~에게 요청하다 account 고객; 계좌
technical 기술적인 be supposed to ~해야 한다

4 남자의 직업은 무엇인 것 같은가?
(A) 변호사   (B) 영업사원
(C) 수리기사   (D) 재정 고문

해설 **남자의 직업**
남자가 첫 대사에서 QJ 산업에서 내일 정오에 열리는 대면 영업회의에 오라고 한다(QJ Industries called me in for a face-to-face sales meeting at noon tomorrow)고 했으므로 정답은 (B)이다.

5 남자는 여자에게 무엇을 해 달라고 요청하는가?
(A) 회의 참석   (B) 소프트웨어 업데이트
(C) 약속 연기   (D) 교육 자료 제작

해설 **남자의 요청 사항**
남자가 첫 대사에서 내일 정오에 QJ 산업과 대면 영업회의가 있다고 했고, 두 번째 대사에서 여자에게 실은 함께 갈 수 있는지 궁금하다(And I'm actually wondering if you can come with me)고 했으므로 정답은 (A)이다.

어휘 postpone 연기하다

6 남자는 무엇을 하겠다고 제안하는가?
(A) 안건 이메일 송부   (B) 발표 준비
(C) 교통편 제공   (D) 문서 복사

해설 **남자의 제안 사항**
남자가 마지막 대사에서 내가 내일 차를 가지고 가니까 둘 다 거기까지 같이 타고 가면 된다(I'll have my car with me tomorrow, so I can drive us both there)고 했으므로 정답은 (C)이다.

어휘 agenda 안건 transportation 교통(편)

W **7 Thank you for inviting me to come on your research boat, Professor Volkov.**

M1 Certainly, Ms. Rotimi. **8 I'm glad reporters like you are interested in our research on marine ecosystems. This is my colleague, Oleg Klein.** He studies the impact of rising water temperatures on the biology of crustacean species, so he can answer any questions about that.

M2 Pleased to meet you, Ms. Rotimi. So, what exactly is your assignment?

W **9 I'm going to write a magazine article about crab populations.** It's part of a broader series about wildlife in the Chesapeake Bay region.

여 7 연구선에 초대해 주셔서 감사합니다, 볼코프 교수님.

남1 별말씀을요. 8 선생님 같은 기자들이 해양 생태계에 대한 우리 연구에 관심이 있다니 기쁘네요. 이 사람은 제 동료 올레그 클라인입니다. 수온 상승이 갑각류의 생태에 미치는 영향을 연구하고 있으니 관련된 질문은 무엇이든 대답할 수 있죠.

남2 만나서 반가워요, 로티미 씨. 정확히 어떤 일을 맡으셨나요?

여 9 게 개체군에 관한 잡지 기사를 쓰려고 해요. 체서피크만 지역의 야생동물에 관한 광범위한 연속 기사의 일부예요.

어휘 marine 해양의 ecosystem 생태계 biology 생태, 생물학 crustacean 갑각류 assignment 임무 population 개체군 wildlife 야생동물

---

7 대화는 어디에서 이루어지는가?

(A) 여행사   (B) 지역 시장

(C) 배   (D) 비행기

해설 **대화의 장소**

여자가 첫 대사에서 연구선에 초대해 줘서 고맙다(Thank you for inviting me to come on your research boat, Professor Volkov)고 했으므로 정답은 (C)이다.

8 남자들은 누구인가?

(A) 식당 요리사   **(B) 해양 생물학자**

(C) 여행 가이드   (D) 안전 감독관

해설 **남자들의 직업**

첫 번째 남자가 첫 대사에서 당신 같은 기자들이 해양 생태계에 대한 우리 연구에 관심이 있다니 기쁘다(I'm glad reporters like you are interested in our research on marine ecosystems)고 했고 이 사람은 동료 올레그 클라인이다(This is my colleague, Oleg Klein)라고 두 번째 남자를 소개했으므로 정답은 (B)이다.

어휘 inspector 감독관

9 여자는 무엇을 할 것이라고 말하는가?

(A) 장비 구매하기   (B) 도서관 가기

(C) 휴가 가기   **(D) 기사 작성하기**

해설 **여자가 할 것이라고 말하는 일**

여자가 마지막 대사에서 게 개체군에 관한 잡지 기사를 쓰려고 한다(I'm going to write a magazine article about crab populations)고 했으므로 정답은 (D)이다.

[10-12] 안내 방송

W-Br Your attention, please. **10 We are sorry to announce one more delay due to track maintenance:** the seven forty-five Fastrail service to Bridgetown will be delayed by about 45 minutes. We apologize for any inconvenience. The comfort of all riders as they await their transport is important to us. **11 To ensure everyone has a place to sit in the waiting area, please do not block or take up seats with your luggage.** Personal belongings can be stored under your seat or in your lap. **12 Riders with tickets for a delayed service can receive a discounted item at the snack bar. Have your ticket ready to show the cashier.**

안내 말씀드립니다. 10 선로 정비로 인해 한 번 더 지연을 알리게 되어 죄송합니다. 브리지타운행 745 패스트레일 운행이 45분 정도 지연될 예정입니다. 불편을 드려 죄송합니다. 저희로서는 교통편을 기다리는 동안 모든 승객이 편안하게 계시는 것이 중요합니다. 11 모두 대합실에 앉을 수 있도록 짐으로 좌석을 막거나 차지하지 마세요. 개인 소지품은 좌석 아래나 무릎에 보관하면 됩니다. 12 지연된 열차의 표를 소지한 승객은 매점에서 할인 상품을 받을 수 있습니다. 계산원에게 보여줄 수 있도록 표를 준비하세요.

어휘 maintenance 정비 inconvenience 불편 comfort 편안함 take up ~을 차지하다 belongings 소지품

---

10 안내 방송은 어디에서 나오고 있는가?

(A) 공항   (B) 버스 터미널

(C) 기차역   (D) 여객선 터미널

해설 **안내 방송의 장소**

초반부에 선로 정비로 인해 한 번 더 지연을 알리게 되어 죄송하다(We are sorry to announce one more delay due to track maintenance)고 했으므로 정답은 (C)이다.

11 화자는 승객 소지품에 대해 무엇이라고 말하는가?

(A) 방치되면 안 된다.

(B) 인식표가 있어야 한다.

(C) 좌석에 두면 안 된다.

(D) 사물함에 보관해야 한다.

해설 **화자가 승객 소지품에 대해 말하는 것**

중반부에 모두 대합실에 앉을 수 있도록 짐으로 좌석을 막거

나 차지하지 말라(To ensure everyone has a place to sit ~, please do not block or take up seats with your luggage)고 했으므로 정답은 (C)이다.

어휘 unattended 방치된 identification tag 인식표

12 일부 청자들은 물품 구매 시 어떻게 절약할 수 있는가?
(A) 표를 보여줘서
(B) 모바일 애플리케이션을 다운로드해서
(C) 후기를 게시해서
(D) 할인 카드를 신청해서

해설 **청자들이 물품 구매 시 절약할 수 있는 방법**
후반부에 지연된 열차의 표를 소지한 승객은 매점에서 할인 상품을 받을 수 있다(Riders with tickets for a delayed service can receive a discounted item at the snack bar)고 한 뒤 계산원에게 보여줄 수 있도록 표를 준비하라(Have your ticket ready to show the cashier)고 했으므로 정답은 (A)이다.

[13-15] 방송

M-Au Thanks for tuning in to our radio show, *Innovate*. **13 Each week, we test different cameras to tell you which one's worth buying.** Many of you asked about a model that takes great pictures at night. Well, for taking low-light photos, we've found that the best camera is the Revue 10x. **14 However, this camera's very heavy.** So if you're a casual photographer going on your next vacation, it's probably not for you. **15 When I travel, I prefer the Lightmaster 200.** It has many of the same features as the Revue 10x, but it's much lighter. **15 But don't take my word alone: it's a very popular model.**

라디오 쇼 〈이노베이트〉를 청취해 주셔서 감사합니다. **13매주 다양한 카메라를 테스트해서 어떤 제품이 구매할 가치가 있는지 알려 드립니다.** 많은 분들이 밤에 사진이 잘 찍히는 모델에 대해 물어보셨습니다. 음, 저조도 사진을 찍을 때 가장 좋은 카메라는 레뷰 10x입니다. **14하지만 이 카메라는 아주 무겁습니다.** 따라서 다음 휴가 때 편하게 취미 삼아 사진을 찍을 분이라면 이 제품은 아마 맞지 않을 겁니다. **15저는 여행 갈 때 라이트마스터 200을 선호합니다.** 레뷰 10x와 동일한 기능이 많지만 훨씬 더 가볍죠. **15하지만 저 혼자만의 생각은 아닙니다. 아주 인기 있는 모델이에요.**

어휘 tune in to (채널을) ~에 맞추다 casual 편한

13 화자는 무엇에 대해 이야기하고 있는가?
(A) 카메라
(B) 노트북 컴퓨터
(C) 실외 조명
(D) 여행 가방

해설 **담화의 주제**
초반부에 매주 다양한 카메라를 테스트해서 어떤 제품이 구매할 가치가 있는지 알려 준다(Each week, we test different cameras to tell you which one's worth

buying)고 한 뒤 다양한 카메라에 대한 내용이 이어지므로 정답은 (A)이다.

14 화자는 제품에 대해 어떤 문제를 언급하는가?
(A) 비싸다.
(B) 무겁다.
(C) 사용하기가 복잡하다.
(D) 볼품없다.

해설 **화자가 언급하는 제품의 문제점**
중반부에 하지만 이 카메라는 아주 무겁다(However, this camera's very heavy)고 했으므로 정답은 (B)이다.

어휘 complicated 복잡한

15 화자가 "아주 인기 있는 모델이에요"라고 말할 때 무엇을 의미하는가?
(A) 교체 부품이 두루 쓰일 수 있다.
(B) 제품 신뢰성이 떨어질 수 있다.
(C) 많은 사람들이 의견에 동의한다.
(D) 제품이 빨리 매진될 수 있다.

해설 **아주 인기 있는 모델이라는 말의 의도**
후반부에 본인은 여행 갈 때 라이트마스터 200을 선호한다(When I travel, I prefer the Lightmaster 200)고 한 뒤, 하지만 나 혼자 생각은 아니다(But don't take my word alone)라고 한 뒤 인용문을 언급했으므로 화자뿐만 아니라 다른 사람들에게도 인기 있는 모델이라는 것을 표현하려는 의도로 볼 수 있다. 따라서 정답은 (C)이다.

어휘 replacement 교체 reliable 신뢰할 수 있는

[16-18] 회의 발췌

M-Cn Thanks for attending this product research and development meeting. I'd like to provide an update on our new all-season car tires. If you'll recall, **16 we had to postpone the testing of the tires due to a shipping delay on the manufacturer's end.** But now the results are in, and overall, the tires performed well on both wet and dry road surfaces. **17 Next week the product testers will begin comparing our tires to some competing models.** We're optimistic that our product will compare favorably. **18 Also, Magali from our graphic design team has prepared some drafts of the logo for the tires. Magali, can you share those with us now?**

제품 연구 개발 회의에 참석해 주셔서 감사합니다. 사계절용 자동차 타이어 신제품에 대한 최근 소식을 알려 드리려고 합니다. 기억하실지 모르겠지만, **16제조사 측의 배송 지연으로 타이어 테스트를 연기해야 했죠.** 하지만 이제 결과를 입수했는데, 대체로 타이어는 젖은 노면과 마른 노면 모두에서 우수한 성능을 보였습니다. **17다음 주에 제품 테스트 담당자들이 우리 타이어를 경쟁 모델들과 비교할 겁니다.** 우리 제품이 더 좋은 평가를 받으리라 낙관합니다. **18그리고 그래픽 디자인 팀의 마갈리가 타이어 로고 초안을 준비했어요. 마갈리, 지금 보여 주실래요?**

16 화자에 따르면, 제품 테스트가 왜 예정보다 늦어졌는가?
(A) 테스트 구역이 폐쇄됐다.
(B) 배송이 지연됐다.
(C) 소프트웨어가 업데이트됐다.
(D) 장비가 고장 났다.

해설 **제품 테스트가 늦어진 이유**
초반부에 제조사 측의 배송 지연으로 타이어 테스트를 연기해야 했다(we had to postpone the testing of the tires due to a shipping delay on the manufacturer's end)고 했으므로 정답은 (B)이다.

어휘 behind schedule 예정보다 늦은

(Paraphrasing) 담화의 postpone the testing
→ 질문의 product testing behind schedule
담화의 a shipping delay → 정답의 A delivery was delayed.

17 화자는 다음 주에 어떤 일이 일어날 것이라고 말하는가?
(A) 제품들이 비교된다.
(B) 일부 직원이 휴가를 간다.
(C) 보도 자료 초안이 작성된다.
(D) 제조업체에 연락한다.

해설 **화자가 다음 주에 일어날 것이라고 말하는 일**
중반부에 다음 주에 제품 테스트 담당자들이 타이어를 경쟁 모델들과 비교할 것(Next week the product testers will begin comparing our tires to some competing models)이라고 했으므로 정답은 (A)이다.

어휘 press release 보도 자료

18 청자들은 다음에 무엇을 할 것 같은가?
(A) 안전 동영상 시청하기 (B) 보고서 검토하기
(C) 휴식하기 (D) 로고 보기

해설 **청자들이 다음에 할 일**
후반부에 그래픽 디자인 팀의 마갈리가 타이어 로고 초안을 준비했다(Also, Magali ~ has prepared some drafts of the logo for the tires)면서 마갈리에게 지금 보여 달라(Magali, can you share those with us now?)고 했으므로 정답은 (D)이다.

ETS 기출 | **고난도 실전문제** | 본책 p.50

1 (B)	**2** (C)	**3** (A)	**4** (D)	**5** (C)	**6** (D)
7 (D)	**8** (A)	**9** (C)	**10** (C)	**11** (A)	**12** (D)
13 (C)	**14** (B)	**15** (D)	**16** (C)	**17** (D)	**18** (C)

[1-3] W-Br / M-Au

W Oliver, you've been working as an apprentice here for a month. How are things going?
M Great. **1It's been helpful learning how to remove dents and scratches from cars in a hands-on setting.**
W Very good. **2Well, today you're going to learn something new. You'll work with one of our expert paint technicians and learn how to mix paint for a custom auto paint job.**
M OK.
W **3And don't forget what I told you when you started this apprenticeship—if you'd like to make this a long-term career, work hard. We're always hiring!**

여 올리버, 여기 수습생으로 일한 지 한 달이죠. 어때요?
남 좋아요. 1자동차의 찌그러진 부분과 긁힌 부분 없애는 법을 실습을 통해 배우니 도움이 됐어요.
여 잘됐네요. 2자, 오늘은 새로운 걸 배울 텐데요. 도색 전문 기술자 한 명과 함께 작업하면서 맞춤형 자동차 도색 작업을 위해 페인트 섞는 방법을 배울 거예요.
남 알겠습니다.
여 3그리고 이 수습직을 시작할 때 제가 한 말 잊지 마세요. 이 일을 장기적으로 하고 싶다면 열심히 일하세요. 상시 채용하고 있으니까요!

1 화자들은 어디에 있는가?
(A) 가전제품 매장 **(B) 자동차 외장 수리점**
(C) 미술학교 (D) 페인트 가게

해설 **대화의 장소**
남자가 첫 대사에서 자동차의 찌그러진 부분과 긁힌 부분 없애는 법을 실습을 통해 배우니 도움이 됐다(It's been helpful learning how to remove dents and scratches from cars in a hands-on setting)고 한 것으로 보아 대화의 장소가 차량의 외부를 수리하는 정비소임을 알 수 있다. 따라서 정답은 (B)이다.

어휘 appliance 가전제품

2 남자는 오늘 무엇을 할 것인가?
(A) 보관 구역 정리 (B) 작업 공간 청소
(C) 새로운 기술 습득 (D) 수정된 정책 검토

해설 **남자가 오늘 할 일**
여자가 두 번째 대사에서 오늘은 새로운 걸 배운다(Well, today you're going to learn something new)고 한 뒤 도색 전문 기술자 한 명과 함께 작업하면서 맞춤형 자동차 도색 작업을 위해 페인트 섞는 방법을 배울 것(You'll work with one of our expert paint technicians and learn how to mix paint for a custom auto paint job)이라고 했으므로 정답은 (C)이다.

3 여자는 남자에게 무엇에 대해 상기시키는가?

(A) 취업 기회   (B) 안전 지침

(C) 비품 배달   (D) 작업 일정표

해설 **여자가 남자에게 상기시키는 것**

여자가 마지막 대사에서 수습직을 시작할 때 자신이 한 말을 잊지 말라(And don't forget what I told you ~)고 한 뒤 이 일을 장기적으로 하고 싶다면 열심히 일하라(if you'd like to make this a long-term career, work hard)며 상시 채용하고 있다(We're always hiring!)고 했으므로 정답은 (A)이다.

[4-6] W-Br / W-Am / M-Cn   **3인 대화**

> **W1** Amany, there you are. **⁴I'd like to introduce you to Oleg, the sustainability consultant—who will help us formulate our line of household detergents.**
>
> **W2** Nice to meet you, Oleg. We're grateful that you're here—and looking forward to the talk that you're giving to our staff.
>
> **M** **⁵I'm looking forward to helping you develop eco-friendly cleaning products.** I've provided consulting services for many businesses like yours. There's so much interest in moving toward sustainability these days.
>
> **W1** Sorry to interrupt, **⁶but speaking of the talk—we need to get the projector running with the slideshow.**
>
> 여1 아마니, 여기 있었네요. **⁴가정용 세제 제품군을 만들 때 우리를 도와 줄 지속 가능성 컨설턴트 올레그를 소개할게요.**
>
> 여2 반가워요. 올레그 씨. 와 주셔서 감사합니다. 우리 직원들에게 해 주실 발표에 기대가 많습니다.
>
> 남 **⁵친환경 청소용품 개발을 돕게 되어 기대가 큽니다.** 저는 귀사와 같은 많은 기업에 컨설팅 서비스를 제공했어요. 요즘 지속 가능성을 향한 움직임에 대한 관심이 매우 높아요.
>
> 여1 방해해서 죄송하지만, **⁶발표 얘기가 나와서 말인데 프로젝터를 켜서 슬라이드쇼를 틀어야 해요.**

어휘 sustainability 지속 가능성   formulate 만들다 detergent 세제   eco-friendly 친환경의   interrupt 방해하다

---

4 화자들은 어떤 종류의 제품을 논의하고 있는가?

(A) 무늬 섬유   (B) 기계 부품

(C) 주방용품   **(D) 청소용품**

해설 **화자들이 논의하고 있는 제품**

첫 번째 여자가 첫 대사에서 가정용 세제 제품군을 만들 때 도움을 줄 지속 가능성 컨설턴트 올레그를 소개하겠다(I'd like to introduce you to Oleg, ~ who will help us formulate our line of household detergents)고 했으므로 정답은 (D)이다.

Paraphrasing 대화의 household detergents

→ 정답의 Cleaning supplies

5 남자는 여자들의 회사를 위해 무엇을 할 것인가?

(A) 데이터베이스 보안

(B) 해외 시장 점유율 확대

(C) 지속 가능한 제품 개발 지원

(D) 직원 사기 고취

해설 **남자가 여자들의 회사를 위해 할 일**

남자가 첫 대사에서 친환경 청소용품 개발을 돕게 되어 기대가 크다(I'm looking forward to helping you develop eco-friendly cleaning products)고 했으므로 정답은 (C)이다.

어휘 market share 시장 점유율   morale 사기, 의욕

Paraphrasing 대화의 eco-friendly cleaning products → 정답의 sustainable products

6 여자들은 다음에 무엇을 할 것 같은가?

(A) 음식 납품 일정 잡기   (B) 데이터 수집하기

(C) 비품 주문하기   **(D) 발표 준비하기**

해설 **여자들이 다음에 할 일**

첫 번째 여자가 마지막 대사에서 발표 얘기가 나와서 말인데 프로젝터를 켜서 슬라이드쇼를 틀어야 한다(but speaking of the talk—we need to get the projector running with the slideshow)고 했으므로 정답은 (D)이다.

어휘 catering 음식 납품(업)

Paraphrasing 대화의 the talk

→ 정답의 a presentation

[7-9] W-Br / M-Au

> **W** **⁷The city road repairs director just informed me that there's going to be urgent maintenance work along Maple Avenue to repave a large part of the road this week. It'll affect the number 33 bus schedule.**
>
> **M** **⁸OK, let me look at the city map and find a temporary route for the bus to detour around the construction zone.**
>
> **W** Great, thank you! The sooner you can do that, the better. **⁹Since we didn't have a lot of notice about the work, I want to get signs posted and update the Web site so riders know as soon as possible.**
>
> 여 **⁷시** 도로 보수 책임자가 이번 주에 메이플 가를 따라 도로 상당 부분을 재포장하는 긴급 정비 작업이 있을 예정이라고 방금 알려 줬어요. 33번 버스 시간표에 영향을 미칠 겁니다.
>
> 남 **⁸알겠어요.** 도시 지도를 보고 버스가 공사 구역을 우회할 수 있는 임시 노선을 찾아볼게요.

여 좋아요, 감사합니다! 빨리 할수록 좋아요. ⁹작업에 대해 충분한 공지가 없었으니 승객들이 가능한 한 빨리 알 수 있도록 표지판을 게시하고 웹사이트를 수정하고 싶어요.

> **어휘** urgent 긴급한 repave (도로 등을) 재포장하다 affect 영향을 미치다 temporary 임시의 detour 우회하다

7 대화의 목적은 무엇인가?
(A) 인력 부족 해소 (B) 프로젝트 예산 협의
(C) 보도 자료 승인 **(D) 서비스 차질 논의**

해설 **대화의 목적**
여자가 첫 대사에서 시 도로 보수 책임자가 알려 주기를 이번 주에 메이플 가를 따라 도로 상당 부분을 재포장하는 긴급 정비 작업이 있다(there's going to be urgent maintenance work ~ to repave a large part of the road this week)고 하면서 33번 버스 시간표에 영향을 미칠 것(It'll affect the number 33 bus schedule)이라고 했으므로 정답은 (D)이다.

어휘 address 해소하다 shortage 부족 negotiate 협의하다 approve 승인하다 disruption 차질, 중단

> **Paraphrasing** 대화의 affect the number 33 bus schedule → 정답의 a service disruption

8 남자는 무엇을 할 것이라고 말하는가?
(A) 새 노선 알아내기 (B) 도급업자 고용하기
(C) 비품 주문 변경하기 (D) 프로젝트 마감일 변경하기

해설 **남자가 할 것이라고 말하는 일**
남자가 첫 대사에서 도시 지도를 보고 버스가 공사 구역을 우회할 수 있는 임시 노선을 찾아보겠다(OK, let me look at the city map and find a temporary route for the bus to detour ~)고 했으므로 정답은 (A)이다.

어휘 determine 알아내다 contractor 도급업자

> **Paraphrasing** 대화의 find a temporary route for the bus to detour → 정답의 Determine a new route

9 여자는 무엇을 할 계획인가?
(A) 직원들에게 작업 할당하기
(B) 기자 회견 준비하기
(C) 정보 공개하기
(D) 버스 운전기사들에게 정책 변경 통지하기

해설 **여자의 계획**
여자가 마지막 대사에서 작업에 대해 충분한 공지가 없었으니 승객들이 가능한 한 빨리 알 수 있도록 표지판을 게시하고 웹사이트를 수정하고 싶다(Since we didn't have a lot of notice about the work, I want to get signs posted and update the Web site so riders know as soon as possible)고 했으므로 정답은 (C)이다.

어휘 assign 할당하다 press conference 기자 회견 make ~ public ~을 공개하다

> **Paraphrasing** 대화의 get signs posted and update the Web site → 정답의 Make some information public

[10-12] 설명

> **W-Br** Hello, everyone. ¹⁰**I've just gotten word that the food critic from the *Daily Times* will be dining at our restaurant this evening.** As you know, the *Daily Times* has a huge circulation, so a good review is important. It's a big night for us, and I want to be sure that things go smoothly. ¹¹**We'll have a couple of extra waitstaff working, so I apologize because you may get fewer tables than usual.** ¹²**The specials menu has been prepared, and of course, you'll all be expected to memorize it, as you typically do.** If we all do our part, I'm sure the evening will be a great success.
>
> 안녕하세요, 여러분. ¹⁰오늘 저녁 〈데일리 타임즈〉의 음식 평론가가 우리 식당에서 식사한다는 소식을 방금 들었어요. 아시다시피 〈데일리 타임즈〉는 발행 부수가 엄청 나서 좋은 후기가 중요해요. 우리로선 아주 중요한 밤이니 순조롭게 진행되도록 제대로 준비하고 싶어요. ¹¹추가로 종업원 두어 명이 더 근무할 예정이라 평소보다 담당 테이블이 적을 수 있다는 점 양해해 주세요. ¹²특별 메뉴가 준비됐으니 당연히 다들 평소 하시던 대로 외우셔야 합니다. 우리 모두 각자의 역할을 다한다면 저녁은 분명 대성공일 겁니다.

> **어휘** critic 평론가 circulation 발행 부수 waitstaff 종업원들 memorize 외우다

10 화자는 어떤 소식을 공유하는가?
(A) 영업시간이 연장됐다.
(B) 신규 지점이 개업할 것이다.
(C) 업체가 평가를 받을 것이다.
(D) 직원이 승진했다.

해설 **화자가 공유하는 소식**
초반부에 오늘 저녁 〈데일리 타임즈〉의 음식 평론가가 우리 식당에서 식사한다는 소식을 방금 들었다(I've just gotten word that the food critic from the *Daily Times* will be dining at our restaurant this evening)고 했으므로 정답은 (C)이다.

어휘 extend 연장하다 promote 승진시키다

11 화자는 왜 사과하는가?
(A) 테이블 할당이 줄었다.
(B) 주차장이 수리 중이다.
(C) 행사가 연기됐다.
(D) 급여 지급이 약간 지연됐다.

해설 **화자가 사과하는 이유**
중반부에 추가로 종업원 두어 명이 더 근무할 예정이라 평소보다 담당 테이블이 적을 수 있다는 점 양해해 달라(We'll

have a couple of extra waitstaff working, so I apologize because you may get fewer tables than usual)고 했으므로 정답은 (A)이다.

(Paraphrasing) 담화의 get fewer tables than usual
→ 정답의 Table assignments have been reduced.

12 청자들은 무엇을 외우라고 요청받는가?
(A) 비밀번호　　　　　(B) 인사말
(C) 고객 명단　　　　　(D) 메뉴

해설　**청자들이 외우라고 요청받은 것**
후반부에 특별 메뉴가 준비됐으니 당연히 다들 평소 하던 대로 외워야 한다(The specials menu has been prepared. ~ you'll all be expected to memorize it, as you typically do)고 했으므로 정답은 (D)이다.

[13-15] 광고

M-Au 　**13 This Saturday and Sunday from nine A.M. to five P.M. the annual Kinneyville Market will be held.** That's right! **13 Over 300 vendors will be selling their goods inside the convention center.** Shop for everything from handmade jewelry to homemade cooking sauces, all in one convenient location! **14 The first 100 attendees each day will receive a bag of samples from selected vendors.** Interested in selling your own wares? **15 Visit kmarket.com to find out how to reserve a booth.** See you this weekend!

13 이번 주 토요일과 일요일 오전 9시부터 오후 5시까지 해마다 있는 키니빌 마켓이 열립니다. 맞습니다! 13 300명이 넘는 판매자들이 컨벤션 센터 안에서 상품을 판매합니다. 수제 쥬얼리부터 집에서 만든 요리 소스까지 모든 것을 한 장소에서 편리하게 쇼핑하세요! 14 매일 참석자 중 선착순 100명은 선정된 판매자들의 견본 한 봉지를 받습니다. 상품 판매에 관심 있으신가요? 15 kmarket.com을 방문해 부스 예약 방법을 알아보세요. 이번 주말에 만나요!

어휘　annual 연례의　vendor 판매자　convenient 편리한
attendee 참석자　wares 상품　reserve 예약하다

13 무엇이 광고되고 있는가?
(A) 스포츠 경기　　　　(B) 지역 퍼레이드
(C) 실내 시장　　　　　(D) 요리 시연회

해설　**광고되고 있는 것**
초반부에 이번 주 토요일과 일요일 오전 9시부터 오후 5시까지 해마다 있는 키니빌 마켓이 열린다(This Saturday and Sunday from nine A.M. to five P.M. the annual Kinneyville Market will be held)고 한 뒤 300명이 넘는 판매자들이 컨벤션 센터 안에서 상품을 판매한다(Over 300 vendors will be selling their goods inside the convention center)고 했으므로 정답은 (C)이다.

어휘　demonstration 시연회

14 일부 참석자는 무엇을 받을 것인가?
(A) 할인 쿠폰　　　　　(B) 제품 견본
(C) 무료 주차　　　　　(D) 티셔츠

해설　**참석자가 받을 것**
후반부에 매일 참석자 중 선착순 100명은 선정된 판매자들의 견본 한 봉지를 받는다(The first 100 attendees each day will receive a bag of samples from selected vendors)고 했으므로 정답은 (B)이다.

(Paraphrasing) 담화의 a bag of samples from selected vendors → 정답의 Product samples

15 청자들은 웹사이트에서 무엇을 할 수 있는가?
(A) 대회 참가 신청하기　　(B) 운전 경로 찾기
(C) 일정 다운로드하기　　(D) 부스 예약하기

해설　**청자들이 웹사이트에서 할 수 있는 일**
후반부에 kmarket.com을 방문해 부스 예약 방법을 알아보라(Visit kmarket.com to find out how to reserve a booth)고 했으므로 정답은 (D)이다.

[16-18] 회의 발췌

M-Cn 　**16 As an update, I'm happy to report that the new holographic nail polish we launched last quarter has been selling even better than expected.** As you may know, Adeola was in charge of researching that product. **17 But now it's time for us to start generating ideas for our next nail polish collection—which is why I called this meeting.** To build on the success of our holographic collection, I think we should consider releasing another specialty line—maybe with metallic glitter. **18 We'd need more details about how that would affect our costs,** though, since it's important to keep the products at a reasonable price point.

16 지난 분기에 출시한 새로운 홀로그램 매니큐어가 예상보다 훨씬 잘 팔리고 있다는 최신 소식을 전하게 되어 기쁘네요. 아시다시피, 아데올라가 해당 제품의 연구를 담당했죠. 17 하지만 이제 다음 매니큐어 컬렉션에 대한 아이디어를 짤 때가 됐어요. 그래서 이 회의를 소집했고요. 홀로그램 컬렉션의 성공을 발판으로 삼아서 또 다른 특별 제품군 출시를 고려해야 한다고 생각해요. 금속 반짝이가 있는 그런 제품일 수도 있겠죠. 하지만 제품을 합리적인 가격대로 유지하는 게 중요하기 때문에 18 비용에 어떤 영향을 미칠지 더 자세한 내용이 필요해요.

어휘　nail polish 매니큐어　launch 출시하다
in charge of ~을 담당하는　generate 내다, 생성하다
glitter 반짝이　affect 영향을 미치다　reasonable 합리적인

16 화자는 왜 "아데올라가 해당 제품의 연구를 담당했죠"라고
말하는가?
(A) 결정을 정당화하려고　　　(B) 오해를 바로잡으려고
(C) 동료를 칭찬하려고　　　　(D) 제조 지연을 설명하려고

해설 **아데올라가 해당 제품의 연구를 담당했다는 말의 의도**
초반부에 지난 분기에 출시한 새로운 홀로그램 매니큐어가 예
상보다 훨씬 잘 팔리고 있다는 최신 소식을 전하게 되어 기
쁘다(As an update, ~ the new holographic nail
polish we launched last quarter has been selling
even better than expected)고 한 뒤 인용문을 언급했
으므로 제품 연구를 담당했던 아데올라를 칭찬하기 위한 의도
임을 알 수 있다. 따라서 정답은 (C)이다.

17 화자에 따르면, 회의의 주제는 무엇인가?
(A) 예산 수립하기　　　　　(B) 고객 응대하기
(C) 판매 방법 논의하기　　　(D) 아이디어 내기

해설 **회의의 주제**
중반부에 이제 다음 매니큐어 컬렉션에 대한 아이디어를 짤
때가 됐고 그래서 이 회의를 소집했다(But now it's time
for us to start generating ideas for our next nail
polish collection—which is why I called this
meeting)고 했으므로 정답은 (D)이다.

어휘 approach 방법

18 화자는 무엇에 대해 더 자세한 내용을 원하는가?
(A) 일정표　　　　　　　　(B) 판매자
(C) 비용　　　　　　　　　(D) 인력 배치

해설 **화자가 자세한 내용을 원하는 것**
후반부에 비용에 어떤 영향을 미칠지 더 자세한 내용이 필
요하다(We'd need more details about how that
would affect our costs)고 했으므로 정답은 (C)이다.

PART 3 & 4

Listening
Comprehension

UNIT 4 대화 / 담화 고난도 유형

01 의도 파악

정답 단서 패턴 ①　　　　　　　　　　　　본책 p.54

남　안녕하세요. 방금 신문에서 다음 주에 도서관에서 무료 사진 강좌를 개최한다는 기사를 읽었습니다. 등록하고 싶어요. 여　제가 한번 볼게요. 음 컴퓨터 시스템이 또 다운됐네요. 한 시간 정도 후에 다시 전화해 주시겠어요?

어휘 sign up ~에 등록[신청]하다

문제 여자가 "컴퓨터 시스템이 또 다운됐네요"라고 말할 때 무엇을
의미하는가?
정답 남자의 요청을 들어줄 수 없다.

여　안타깝게도 이 열차의 도입은 약 6개월 정도 지연될 예정 입니다. 현재 많은 주민들이 저희 부서에 연락해 더 빠른 일정을 요청하고 있습니다. 하지만 콜벤스키 제조에서 생산을 담당하고 있습니다.

어휘 introduction 도입, 소개　approximately 약, 대략
timeline 일정

문제 화자는 왜 "콜벤스키 제조에서 생산을 담당하고 있습니다"라고
말하는가?
정답 오해를 바로잡으려고

정답 단서 패턴 ②

남　제시카, 방금 한국에 있는 제작사에서 전화가 왔어요. 여　누가 저에게 한국에서 영화를 만들어 달라고 요청하나요? 남　사실 〈블루 샌드〉의 판권을 사서 한국 출연진으로 리메이크 하고 싶다고 하더라고요. 여　와우! 그렇다면 그들이 선택한 감독과 출연진에 대한 최종 결정을 제가 내렸으면 해요. 계약서에 그런 내용이 모두 포함될 수 있나요? 이런 협상을 해본 적이 없어서요. 남　에이전트로서 제가 모든 것을 처리해 드릴게요. 관련된 모든 사람의 프로필을 보기 전에는 아무것도 서명하지 않을 거예요. 여　알았어요. 이번 달은 제가 좀 바빠서요. 남　아, 그들은 아직 우리에게 명단을 보내지 않았어요.

어휘 right 판권, 권리　negotiate 협상하다

문제 남자는 왜 "그들은 아직 우리에게 명단을 보내지 않았어요"
라고 말하는가?
정답 여자에게 일이 급하지 않다는 것을 확신시켜 주려고

여　안녕하세요, 여러분. 기억하시겠지만, 현재 진행 중인 프로젝트 중 하나는 다음 달에 출시될 새로운 러닝화 라인에 대한 광고를 회사 웹사이트에 삽입하는 것입니다. 드디어

제품 사진을 받았으니 웹페이지를 완성하는 데 필요한 모든 것이 갖춰졌을 거예요. 하지만 사진이 예상보다 늦게 도착해서 예정보다 늦어졌어요. 이 페이지 작업 외에도 모두가 진행 중인 다른 프로젝트가 있다는 것을 알고 있지만 이것은 금요일에 출시될 예정입니다.

어휘 insert 삽입하다 release 출시하다 behind schedule 예정보다 늦은 launch 출시하다

문제 여자가 "이것은 금요일에 출시될 예정입니다"라고 말할 때 무엇을 의미하는가?
정답 프로젝트가 빨리 완료되어야 한다.

ETS 기출 유형연습

1 (A) **2** (B) **3** (A) **4** (B) **5** (B) **6** (A)

[1-3] W-Am / M-Au

W **1,2 Koji, what kind of gardening workshop do you think our store should offer this spring?**

M **2 The workshop on flowers, shrubs, and soil for landscaping purposes has been well attended in the past.** Our customers like to make informed choices for their homes.

W That workshop was very popular. Maybe we can get some feedback from past participants to see what updates we could make to the materials.

M Good idea. **3 I'll compile an e-mail distribution list from our records.**

여 1,2코지, 이번 봄에 우리 가게에서 어떤 원예 강습을 제공해야 할까요?
남 2예전에 조경용 꽃과 관목, 토양에 관한 강습이 참석자가 많았어요. 고객들은 집을 위해 충분한 정보를 바탕으로 한 선택을 하고 싶어 하죠.
여 그 강습은 인기가 아주 많았어요. 어쩌면 과거 참가자들에게 의견을 받아서 자료에 어떤 부분을 개정할 수 있는지 확인해도 되겠어요.
남 좋은 생각이네요. 3기록을 보고 이메일 배포 목록을 작성할게요.

어휘 shrub 관목 landscaping 조경 well attended 참가자가 많은 informed 정보에 근거한 participant 참가자 distribution 배포

1 대화는 어디에서 이루어지는 것 같은가?
(A) 원예점 (B) 가구 할인점
(C) 건설 현장 (D) 부동산 중개소

해설 대화의 장소
여자가 첫 대사에서 이번 봄에 우리 가게에서 어떤 원예 강습을 제공해야 할지(Koji, what kind of gardening workshop do you think our store should offer this spring?) 물었으므로 정답은 (A)이다.

2 여자가 "그 강습은 인기가 아주 많았어요"라고 말할 때 무엇을 의미하는가?
(A) 지금은 강습 참가자 수가 줄었다.
(B) 강습이 다시 제공되어야 한다.
(C) 강사는 축하를 받아야 한다.
(D) 일부 자료는 재인쇄할 필요가 없을 것이다.

해설 강습이 인기가 아주 많았다는 말의 의도
여자가 어떤 원예 강습을 제공해야 할지 묻자 남자가 예전에 조경용 꽃과 관목, 토양에 관한 강습이 참석자가 많았다 (The workshop on flowers, shrubs, and soil for landscaping purposes has been well attended in the past)고 대답한 뒤 인용문을 언급했으므로 강습이 인기가 많았음을 상기시키며 강습을 다시 제공하자는 의도임을 알 수 있다. 따라서 정답은 (B)이다.

3 남자는 무엇을 만들겠다고 제안하는가?
(A) 목록 (B) 지도
(C) 발표 자료 (D) 일정표

해설 남자가 만들겠다고 제안하는 것
남자가 마지막 대사에서 기록을 보고 이메일 배포 목록을 작성하겠다(I'll compile an e-mail distribution list from our records)고 했으므로 정답은 (A)이다.

[4-6] 방송

W-Br Welcome back to the *Channel 4 Nightly News*. Today we're on location at the electronics store Charged Up. **4,5 It's nine P.M. now and the store is closed, but Charged Up will be opening its doors at midnight for the product launch of a new video game called *Mars Race*.** I'm standing outside the store, where people have been lined up for over two hours! They've brought chairs, blankets, and even picnic dinners! **6 If you'd like to know more about *Mars Race*, we've got the link to a promotional video on our Web site.**

다시 〈채널 4 저녁 뉴스〉입니다. 오늘 저희는 전자제품 매장 차지드 업에서 현장 중계로 진행합니다. 4,5지금은 오후 9시고 매장은 문을 닫았지만, 차지드 업은 〈마스 레이스〉라고 불리는 새로운 비디오 게임의 제품 출시로 인해 자정에 문을 엽니다. 저는 매장 밖에 서 있는데요, 사람들이 두 시간 넘게 줄을 서고 있습니다! 의자, 담요, 심지어 저녁 도시락까지 가지고 왔네요! 6〈마스 레이스〉에 대해 더 자세히 알고 싶으시면, 저희 웹사이트에 홍보 동영상 링크가 있습니다.

어휘 on location 현장 중계의 electronics 전자제품 promotional 홍보의

4 화자는 무엇을 논의하고 있는가?
(A) 연예인 출연 (B) 비디오 게임 출시
(C) 음악회 (D) 저자 사인회

PART 3&4

UNIT 4

33

해설 **담화의 주제**
　초반부에 지금은 오후 9시고 매장은 문을 닫았지만, 차지드 업은 〈마스 레이스〉라고 불리는 새로운 비디오 게임의 제품 출시로 인해 자정에 문을 연다(It's nine P.M. now and the store is closed, but Charged Up will be opening its doors at midnight for the product launch of a new video game called *Mars Race*)고 했으므로 정답은 (B)이다.

어휘 celebrity 연예인, 유명인사

(Paraphrasing) 담화의 the product launch of a new video game → 정답의 A video game release

5 여자가 "사람들이 두 시간 넘게 줄을 서고 있습니다"라고 말할 때 무엇을 의미하는가?
　(A) 직원이 더 필요하다.　　(B) 제품이 인기가 많다.
　(C) 주차장이 꽉 찼다.　　(D) 이벤트가 지연되었다.

해설 **사람들이 두 시간 넘게 줄을 서고 있다는 말의 의도**
　초반부에 지금은 오후 9시고 매장은 문을 닫았지만, 차지드 업은 〈마스 레이스〉라고 불리는 새로운 비디오 게임의 제품 출시로 인해 자정에 문을 연다(It's nine P.M. now and the store is closed, but Charged Up will be opening its doors at midnight for the product launch of a new video game called *Mars Race*)고 한 뒤 인용문을 언급했으므로 사람들이 새로 출시되는 게임에 관심이 많다는 의미임을 알 수 있다. 따라서 정답은 (B)이다.

6 화자에 따르면, 청자들은 어떻게 더 많은 정보를 얻을 수 있는가?
　(A) 링크를 클릭해서　　(B) 매장에 가서
　(C) 매표소에 연락해서　　(D) 소책자를 읽어서

해설 **청자들이 더 많은 정보를 얻을 수 있는 방법**
　후반부에 〈마스 레이스〉에 대해 더 자세히 알고 싶다면, 우리 웹사이트에 홍보 동영상 링크가 있다(If you'd like to know more about *Mars Race*, we've got the link to a promotional video on our Web site)고 했으므로 정답은 (A)이다.

02 시각 정보 연계

❶ 목록(List) / 표(Table)
본책 p.56

여 첫 번째 그룹은 처음 두 장면에 있는 여러분 모두입니다. 메인 룸에서 리허설을 하면 돼요. 세 번째 장면인 과거로의 여행에 있는 두 번째 그룹은 극작가에게 가서 이야기를 나눠야 해요. 그녀가 방금 그 장면을 크게 수정했기 때문에 다시 한 번 검토해야 합니다.

어휘 playwright 극작가　substantial 상당한　revision 수정　go over ~을 검토하다

페이지	장면
1-10	오프닝 장면
11-15	정원에서
16-20	**과거로의 여행**
21-28	고난
29-32	결말

어휘 ordeal 고난, 시련

문제 시각 정보에 따르면, 대본의 어떤 페이지가 수정되었는가?
정답 16-20

❷ 지도(Map) / 평면도(Floor plan)

남 다음 주에 있을 사진 촬영에 대한 정보를 알려 드리기 위해 전화했어요. 전문적인 사진을 찍을 수 있는 좋은 장소를 찾았어요. 공공 도서관과 법원 사이에 있는 작은 정원이에요. 사진을 찍기에 완벽한 장소가 될 거예요. 웹사이트와 명함에도 잘 어울릴 거라고 확신해요.

어휘 shoot 촬영　courthouse 법원

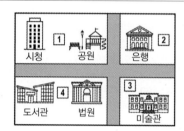

문제 시각 정보에 따르면, 화자는 어느 장소를 언급하는가?
정답 장소 4

ETS 기출 유형연습 1
본책 p.57

1 (D)　**2** (B)　**3** (B)　**4** (A)　**5** (C)　**6** (B)

[1-3] W-Am / M-Cn　　아파트 목록

W Hi. My name is Sabine Hoffman. **1 I came yesterday morning to view some of your apartments for rent.**

M **1 Yes, I remember you.** You were interested in a one-bedroom apartment. We have several available.

W Actually, I've changed my mind. **2 I'd like to rent a two-bedroom apartment instead. And I won't need garage parking. With this mild climate, I'm OK parking outdoors.**

M OK. **3 Here's a map of the complex that shows where the available apartments are. Let me know which location you'd like.**

여 안녕하세요. 제 이름은 사빈 호프만입니다. **1** 어제 아침에 임대 아파트를 보러 왔어요.

남 **1** 네, 기억합니다. 방 하나짜리 아파트에 관심 있으셨죠. 빈 아파트가 몇 군데 있어요.

여 실은 생각이 바뀌었어요. **2** 대신 방 두 개짜리 아파트를 임대하고 싶어요. 그리고 차고 주차는 필요 없고요. 기후가 온화해서 야외 주차도 괜찮아요.

남 알겠습니다. **3** 여기 비어 있는 아파트의 위치를 보여주는 단지 지도예요. 원하는 위치를 알려 주세요.

어휘 available 비어 있는, 이용 가능한 complex (건물) 단지

방 개수	주차	월세
1개	야외	850달러
2 2개	야외	950달러
3개	차고	1,200달러
4개	차고	1,450달러

1 여자는 어제 무엇을 했는가?
(A) 임대 계약을 했다.
(B) 가구를 옮겼다.
(C) 남자에게 차량을 구입했다.
(D) 남자의 사업장을 방문했다.

해설 **여자가 어제 한 일**
여자가 첫 대사에서 어제 아침에 임대 아파트를 보러 왔다(I came yesterday morning to view some of your apartments for rent)고 하자 남자가 기억한다(Yes, I remember you)면서 여자가 방문했다는 사실을 언급하고 있으므로 정답은 (D)이다.

2 시각 정보에 따르면, 여자는 얼마를 지불할 것인가?
(A) 850달러   **(B) 950달러**
(C) 1,200달러   (D) 1,450달러

해설 **시각 정보 연계**
여자가 두 번째 대사에서 방 두 개짜리 아파트를 임대하고 싶고 차고 주차는 필요 없다(I'd like to rent a two-bedroom apartment instead. And I won't need garage parking)고 하며 기후가 온화해서 야외 주차도 괜찮다(With this mild climate, I'm OK parking outdoors)고 했다. 아파트 목록을 보면 방 두 개에 야외 주차인 아파트는 월세 950달러이므로 정답은 (B)이다.

3 남자는 여자에게 무엇을 해 달라고 요청하는가?
(A) 측정   **(B) 위치 선택**
(C) 지불 정보 제공   (D) 참고 자료 송부

해설 **남자의 요청 사항**
남자가 마지막 대사에서 비어 있는 아파트의 위치를 보여주는 단지 지도를 주면서(Here's a map of the complex that shows where the available apartments are) 원하는 위치를 알려 달라(Let me know which location you'd like)고 했으므로 정답은 (B)이다.

어휘 take measurements 측정하다 reference 참고 자료

[4-6] 회의 발췌 + 지도

W-Am Welcome to our board of directors meeting. **4** I'm thrilled to share the good news that last month's auction to raise money for the museum was a huge success. Thanks to the generous donations we received, we'll be able to start the renovation work we've been planning. **5** We'll begin with the gallery next to the garden—it'll be closed for the next three months. **6** I know you might be concerned about the level of noise with all the construction going on, but don't worry—we're planning to do most of the work in the evenings, so our visitors won't be bothered.

이사회에 참석해 주셔서 감사합니다. **4** 지난달 박물관 기금 마련을 위한 경매를 성황리에 마쳤다는 희소식을 전하게 되어 기쁘네요. 아낌없이 기부 받은 덕택에 우리가 계획하고 있던 보수 공사를 시작할 수 있게 됐어요. **5** 정원 옆에 있는 갤러리부터 시작할 겁니다. 갤러리는 앞으로 석 달 동안 문을 닫을 예정인데요. **6** 공사가 진행되는 동안 소음에 대해 걱정하실 수도 있겠지만, 걱정하지 마세요. 작업은 대부분 저녁에 할 계획이니 방문객들에게 방해가 되지는 않을 겁니다.

어휘 auction 경매 raise money 모금하다 donation 기부(금) renovation 보수 be concerned about ~을 걱정하다 bother 방해하다

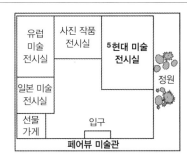

4 화자는 어떤 좋은 소식을 전하는가?
(A) 모금 행사가 성공적이었다.
(B) 계약이 마무리되었다.
(C) 새로운 전시회가 열렸다.
(D) 표 판매가 늘었다.

해설 **화자가 전하는 좋은 소식**
초반부에 지난달 박물관 기금 마련을 위한 경매를 성황리에 마쳤다는 희소식을 전하게 되어 기쁘다(I'm thrilled to share the good news that last month's auction to raise money for the museum was a huge success)고 했으므로 정답은 (A)이다.

어휘 fund-raiser 모금 행사

(Paraphrasing) 담화의 auction to raise money for the museum was a huge success → 정답의 A fund-raiser was successful.

5 시각 정보에 따르면, 프로젝트는 어디에서 시작할 것인가?

(A) 유럽 미술 전시실 　(B) 사진 작품 전시실

(C) 현대 미술 전시실 　(D) 일본 미술 전시실

해설 **시각 정보 연계**

중반부에 정원 옆에 있는 갤러리부터 시작한다(We'll begin with the gallery next to the garden)고 했다. 지도를 보면 정원 옆에 있는 갤러리는 현대 미술 전시실이므로 정답은 (C)이다.

6 화자는 무엇에 관해 청자들을 안심시키는가?

(A) 프로젝트가 지연되지 않을 것이다.

(B) 소음은 문제가 되지 않을 것이다.

(C) 꽃은 선물 가게에서 판매될 것이다.

(D) 갤러리는 저녁에 문을 열 것이다.

해설 **화자가 안심시키는 것**

후반부에 공사가 진행되는 동안 소음에 대해 걱정할 수도 있겠지만 걱정하지 말라(I know you might be concerned about the level of noise ~, but don't worry)고 하면서 작업은 대부분 저녁에 할 계획이니 방문객들에게 방해가 되지는 않을 것(we're planning to do ~, so our visitors won't be bothered)이라고 했으므로 정답은 (B)이다.

❸ 그래프(Graph)

본책 p.58

> 남　교육에는 이 로봇이 기존 로봇과 어떻게 다른지에 대한 시연이 포함됩니다. 이번 업그레이드를 통해 생산량이 증가할 것으로 예상하고 있어요. 실제로 다음 분기에는 처음으로 1,000대를 넘을 것으로 예상하고 있습니다.
>
> **어휘** project 예상하다　surpass 넘어서다

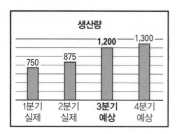

문제 시각 정보에 따르면, 화자는 몇 분기를 언급하는가?

정답 3분기

❹ 기타

> 여　프레시 리넨과 라벤더 필드 모두 마음에 들지만 프레시 리넨이 가장 마음에 들어요.
>
> 남　저도 프레시 리넨을 선호해요. 저렴하지는 않지만 호텔 체인 전체에 통일성을 주기 위해 독특한 객실 향을 원해요.
>
> 여　맞아요. 향기는 고객이 호텔에 들어올 때 가장 먼저 경험하는 것 중 하나이니 좋은 향기를 만들어 봅시다.
>
> **어휘** distinctive 독특한　fragrance 향기　uniformity 통일성

문제 시각 정보에 따르면, 화자들이 선호하는 제품의 금액은 얼마인가?

정답 17달러

ETS 기출 유형연습 2

본책 p.59

1 (A)　**2** (C)　**3** (A)　**4** (B)　**5** (B)　**6** (C)

[1-3] W-Br / M-Au

그래프

> W　Hey, Yoon-Ho. Thanks for presenting at the company's Digital Marketing conference. **¹ According to the survey results, your session was the most helpful.**
>
> M　Glad to hear it! Overall, was the conference a success?
>
> W　Yes, but **² the air conditioning broke in the morning and wasn't fixed until after lunch.** So most of the complaints were about how hot it was during the morning sessions.
>
> M　That's a shame.
>
> W　Well, at least the air conditioning started working again by lunchtime. **³ But we still had to refund half of everyone's registration fee because of the inconvenience.**
>
> 여　윤호 씨. 회사 디지털 마케팅 콘퍼런스에서 발표하느라 고생했어요. **¹ 설문 조사 결과에 따르면, 윤호 씨 세션이 가장 유익했어요.**
>
> 남　다행이네요! 전반적으로 콘퍼런스가 성공적이었나요?
>
> 여　네. **² 그런데 아침에 에어컨이 고장 나서 점심시간이 지나서야 수리가 됐어요.** 그래서 불만 대부분이 오전 세션에 너무 더웠다는 거였어요.
>
> 남　아쉽네요.
>
> 여　음. 그래도 점심시간 무렵에는 에어컨이 다시 작동하기 시작했어요. **³ 하지만 불편을 드린 점 때문에 모두에게 등록비 절반을 환불해 드려야 했어요.**
>
> **어휘** refund 환불하다　registration fee 등록비　inconvenience 불편

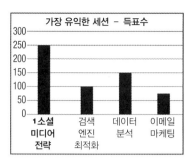

가장 유익한 세션 - 득표수

소셜 미디어 전략	검색 엔진 최적화	데이터 분석	이메일 마케팅

어휘 strategy 전략 optimization 최적화 analytics 분석(론)

1 시각 정보에 따르면, 남자는 어떤 발표를 했는가?

(A) 소셜 미디어 전략 (B) 검색 엔진 최적화
(C) 데이터 분석 (D) 이메일 마케팅

해설 시각 정보 연계
여자가 첫 대사에서 설문 조사 결과에 따르면, 윤호 씨 세션이 가장 유익했다(According to the survey results, your session was the most helpful)고 했다. 그래프를 보면 가장 유익한 세션은 득표수가 가장 많았던 소셜 미디어 전략이므로 정답은 (A)이다.

2 여자는 어떤 문제를 언급하는가?

(A) 초청 연사가 늦었다.
(B) 음식이 부족했다.
(C) 에어컨이 작동하지 않았다.
(D) 인터넷 연결이 불안정했다.

해설 여자가 언급하는 문제
여자가 두 번째 대사에서 아침에 에어컨이 고장 나서 점심시간이 지나서야 수리가 됐다(the air conditioning broke in the morning and wasn't fixed until after lunch)고 했으므로 정답은 (C)이다.

어휘 unreliable 불안정한

(Paraphrasing) 대화의 the air conditioning broke
→ 정답의 The air conditioning was not working.

3 여자는 회의 참석자들이 무엇을 받았다고 말하는가?

(A) 일부 환불 (B) 무료 주차
(C) 식권 (D) 판촉물

해설 회의 참석자들이 받은 것
여자가 마지막 대사에서 하지만 불편을 드린 점 때문에 모두에게 등록비 절반을 환불해 줘야 했다(But we still had to refund half of everyone's registration fee because of the inconvenience)고 했으므로 정답은 (A)이다.

어휘 partial 일부의 promotional 판촉의, 홍보의

(Paraphrasing) 대화의 refund half of everyone's
registration fee → 정답의 A partial refund

[4-6] 연설 + 수상 후보자

W-Am This is an incredible night. There were other talented musicians I had to compete with for this honor. **4 I'm humbled and thrilled to be accepting this award for my song "The Promise,"** but I was simply amazed by my fellow nominee's vocals for "Here and There" and also by the musical vision for "Beyond the City." Wow. **5 As for me, my life truly changed when I received a guitar for my tenth birthday.** I started playing all the tunes I heard on the radio. **6 Now—decades later—as an adult, my songs are based on my personal experiences, so my lyrics give voice to everything I am.** Thank you for this recognition.

믿을 수 없는 밤이네요. 이 영광을 두고 경쟁해야 했던 다른 재능 있는 음악가들도 있었어요. **4 제 노래 〈약속〉으로 이 상을 받게 되어 겸허하고 기쁘지만**, 〈이곳저곳〉을 부른 동료 후보자의 보컬과 〈도시 너머〉의 음악적 통찰에 그저 놀랐습니다. 우와. **5 제 경우 10번째 생일에 기타를 받으면서 인생이 확 바뀌었죠.** 라디오에서 들은 곡조는 죄다 연주하기 시작했죠. **6 수십 년이 지나 성인이 된 지금, 제 노래들은 제가 몸소 겪은 경험을 바탕으로 하고 있어서 가사는 제 전부를 표현하고 있습니다.** 이렇게 인정해 주셔서 감사합니다.

어휘 honor 영광 humbled 겸허한 accept 받다 nominee 후보자 decade 10년 lyrics 가사 recognition 인정

올해의 노래 후보

폴리나 에반스	4 라켈 클레멘트
〈이곳저곳〉	〈약속〉
아사코 시미즈	에밀리 몰리나
〈변하는 시절〉	〈도시 너머〉

4 시각 정보에 따르면, 누가 연설을 하고 있는가?

(A) 폴리나 에반스 (B) 라켈 클레멘트
(C) 아사코 시미즈 (D) 에밀리 몰리나

해설 시각 정보 연계
초반부에 자신의 노래 〈약속〉으로 이 상을 받게 되어 겸허하고 기쁘다(I'm humbled and thrilled to be accepting this award for my song "The Promise")고 했다. 수상 후보자를 보면 〈약속〉을 부른 가수는 라켈 클레멘트이므로 정답은 (B)이다.

5 화자는 무엇이 진로에 영향을 주었다고 말하는가?

(A) 음악 수업 듣기 (B) 기타 받기
(C) 콘서트 참석하기 (D) 특정 뮤직비디오 보기

해설 화자가 진로에 영향을 주었다고 말하는 것
중반부에 자신의 경우 10번째 생일에 기타를 받으면서 인생이 확 바뀌었다(As for me, my life truly changed

when I received a guitar for my tenth birthday)고 했으므로 정답은 (B)이다.

어휘 particular 특정한

(Paraphrasing) 담화의 received a guitar
→ 정답의 Being given a guitar

6 화자는 자신의 노래에 대해 무엇이라고 설명하는가?
(A) 작곡하는 데 오래 걸린다.
(B) 영화에 사용되었다.
(C) 자신에 대해 많은 것을 드러낸다.
(D) 대개 지역 스튜디오에서 녹음한다.

해설 **화자가 자신의 노래에 대해 설명하는 것**
후반부에 수십 년이 지나 성인이 된 지금, 자신의 노래들은 몸소 겪은 경험을 바탕으로 하고 있어서 가사는 자기를 전부 표현하고 있다(Now—decades later—as an adult, my songs are based on my personal experiences, so my lyrics give voice to everything I am)고 했으므로 정답은 (C)이다.

어휘 reveal 드러내다

(Paraphrasing) 담화의 give voice to everything I am
→ 정답의 reveal a lot about her

ETS 기출 실전문제

본책 p.60

1 (A)	**2** (D)	**3** (B)	**4** (D)	**5** (A)	**6** (B)
7 (B)	**8** (D)	**9** (C)	**10** (B)	**11** (C)	**12** (A)
13 (B)	**14** (D)	**15** (C)	**16** (D)	**17** (C)	**18** (B)

[1-3] W-Br / M-Cn

W Mr. Silvestri. **1 With your health condition, you would benefit from a daily routine of low-impact aerobic exercise. 1, 2 I refer many of my patients to a personal trainer. 2 How would you feel about that?**

M Well, it's true I don't know much about fitness routines.

W Good. **3 A trainer has the expertise and knowledge to come up with a good exercise regimen for you. We have trainers here at the medical clinic. Would you like to meet one now?**

M **3 Sure.** I have some time.

여 실베스트리 씨. 1 선생님 건강 상태로 보아, 저강도 유산소 운동을 매일 하면 도움이 될 겁니다. 1, 2 제가 많은 환자를 개인 트레이너에게 보내고 있는데, 2 어떻게 생각하세요?
남 음. 사실 운동 루틴이라면 제가 잘 모르긴 해요.
여 괜찮아요. 3 트레이너는 선생님에게 좋은 운동 요법을 제안할 수 있는 전문 기술과 지식이 있어요. 여기 병원에 트레이너들이 있는데, 지금 바로 만나 보실래요?
남 3 그러죠. 시간 있어요.

어휘 benefit from ~에서 도움을 받다 low-impact 저강도의, 부담이 적은 aerobic exercise 유산소 운동 refer A to B A를 B에게 보내다[소개하다] expertise 전문 기술[지식] regimen 운동[식이] 요법

1 여자는 누구인 것 같은가?
(A) 의사　　　　　　(B) 변호사
(C) 프로 선수　　　　(D) 약사

해설 **여자의 직업**
여자가 첫 대사에서 남자의 건강 상태로 보아, 저강도 유산소 운동을 매일 하면 도움이 된다(With your health condition, you would benefit from a daily routine of ~ aerobic exercise)면서 많은 환자를 개인 트레이너에게 보내고 있다(I refer many of my patients to a personal trainer)고 했으므로 정답은 (A)이다.

2 남자는 왜 "사실 운동 루틴이라면 제가 잘 모르긴 해요"라고 말하는가?
(A) 오해를 풀려고
(B) 결정에 불만을 표현하려고
(C) 더 적합한 후보자를 추천하려고
(D) 제안에 동의하려고

해설 **운동 루틴에 대해 잘 모른다는 말의 의도**
여자가 첫 대사에서 많은 환자를 개인 트레이너에게 보내고 있다(I refer many of my patients to a personal trainer)면서 어떻게 생각하는지(How would you feel about that?) 묻자 남자가 인용문을 언급했으므로 운동 루틴에 대해 잘 알지 못한다는 점을 인정하면서 여자의 제안에 동의하고 있음을 나타낸다. 따라서 정답은 (D)이다.

어휘 qualified 적임인 candidate 후보

3 남자는 다음에 무엇을 할 것인가?
(A) 양식 작성하기　　**(B) 전문가와 면담하기**
(C) 전화 걸기　　　　(D) 결제하기

해설 **남자가 다음에 할 일**
여자가 마지막 대사에서 트레이너는 남자에게 좋은 운동 요법을 제안할 수 있는 전문 기술과 지식이 있다(A trainer has the expertise and knowledge to come up with a good exercise regimen for you)면서 여기 병원에 트레이너들이 있는데(We have trainers here at the medical clinic), 지금 바로 만나 볼지(Would you like to meet one now?) 묻자 남자가 그렇게 하겠다(Sure)고 했으므로 정답은 (B)이다.

[4-6] M-Au / W-Am

M Gabriela, we should talk about adding more restaurants to our amusement park. But **4 we would need to consider what new dining options our customers would like.**

W **5, 6 Right, we could find out by asking customers to complete a short survey when** they purchase tickets.** They could tell us the types of food they'd like to have in the park.

M ⁶**That's a good idea.**

W It wouldn't take long to create a draft.

M Oh, great. Thanks!

남 가브리엘라, 놀이공원에 식당을 더 추가하는 방안에 대해 의논해야 해요. ⁴그런데 고객들이 새로운 먹거리로 어떤 걸 원하는지 고려해야 합니다.

여 ⁵,⁶맞아요, 고객들이 표를 살 때 간단한 설문 조사를 해 달라고 하면 알 수 있어요. 공원에서 먹고 싶은 음식 종류를 알려 주겠죠.

남 ⁶좋은 생각이네요.

여 초안을 만드는 데 오래 걸리지 않을 거예요.

남 오, 좋아요. 고마워요!

어휘 amusement park 놀이공원   draft 초안

---

4 남자는 무엇을 의논하고 싶어하는가?

(A) 고객 불만   (B) 급여 인상

(C) 영업시간   **(D) 먹거리**

해설 **남자가 의논하고 싶어하는 것**

남자가 첫 대사에서 고객들이 새로운 먹거리로 어떤 걸 원하는지 고려해야 한다(we would need to consider what new dining options our customers would like)고 했으므로 정답은 (D)이다.

5 여자는 무엇을 제안하는가?

(A) 고객 의견 받기   (B) 표 가격 변경하기

(C) 지역 연예인 섭외하기   (D) 지역 사회 행사 후원하기

해설 **여자의 제안 사항**

여자가 첫 번째 대사에서 고객들이 표를 살 때 간단한 설문 조사를 해 달라고 하면 알 수 있다(Right, we could find out by asking customers to complete a short survey when they purchase tickets)고 했으므로 정답은 (A)이다.

어휘 entertainer 연예인

(Paraphrasing) 대화의 asking customers to complete a short survey → 정답의 Getting customer feedback

6 여자가 "초안을 만드는 데 오래 걸리지 않을 거예요"라고 말할 때 무엇을 의미하는가?

(A) 곧 남자를 만날 수 있다.

(B) 기꺼이 일을 완수하려고 한다.

(C) 자원봉사자 몇 사람이 필요하다.

(D) 문서가 거의 완성되었다.

해설 **초안을 만드는 데 오래 걸리지 않는다는 말의 의도**

여자가 첫 번째 대사에서 고객들이 표를 살 때 간단한 설문 조사를 해 달라고 하면 알 수 있다(we could find out by asking customers to complete a short survey when they purchase tickets)고 했고, 이 제안에 남자가 좋은 생각(That's a good idea)이라고 호응한 뒤 여자

가 인용문을 언급했으므로 시간이 얼마 걸리지 않으니 본인이 하겠다는 의지를 나타낸다. 따라서 정답은 (B)이다.

[7-9] 녹음 메시지

M-Au Hello. ⁷**You've reached the law offices of Smith and Jones, specializing in real estate law for over twenty years.** If you are a current client, you may enter the extension of your attorney now. ⁸**Are you new to our practice? If you would like to schedule a consultation, please leave your name and phone number, and we will connect you to an expert on our team as soon as possible.** Please be advised, our office building is undergoing renovations. ⁹**When you visit, just follow the signs to our office.**

안녕하세요. ⁷20년 이상 부동산 법률을 전문으로 하고 있는 스미스 앤 존스 법률사무소입니다. 현재 고객이시면 지금 담당 변호사의 내선번호를 입력해 주세요. ⁸저희 사무소가 처음이신가요? 상담 예약을 원하시면 성함과 전화번호를 남겨 주세요. 그러면 저희 팀 전문가와 최대한 빨리 연결해 드리겠습니다. 참고로 사무소 건물이 보수 공사 중입니다. ⁹방문하실 때 표지판을 따라 사무실로 오세요.

어휘 specialize in ~을 전문으로 하다   real estate 부동산   extension 내선번호   attorney 변호사   practice (전문직) 사무소   consultation 상담   expert 전문가   undergo 받다, 겪다   renovation 보수, 개조

---

7 화자는 어디에서 일하는가?

(A) 부동산 중개소   **(B) 법률사무소**

(C) 건축회사   (D) 진료소

해설 **화자의 근무 장소**

초반부에 20년 이상 부동산 법률을 전문으로 하고 있는 스미스 앤 존스 법률사무소이다(You've reached the law offices of ~, specializing in real estate law for over twenty years)라고 했으므로 정답은 (B)이다.

어휘 architecture 건축(술)

8 화자는 신규 고객에게 어떤 정보를 요청하는가?

(A) 추천한 사람   (B) 원하는 지불 방식

(C) 만날 수 있는 시간   **(D) 연락할 수 있는 방법**

해설 **신규 고객에게 요청하는 정보**

중반부에 사무소가 처음인지(Are you new to our practice?) 물은 다음, 상담 예약을 원하면 이름과 전화번호를 남겨달라(If you would like to schedule a consultation, please leave your name and phone number)면서 팀 전문가와 최대한 빨리 연결해 주겠다(we will connect you to an expert on our team as soon as possible)고 했으므로 정답은 (D)이다.

어휘 refer 추천하다

9 남자가 "사무소 건물이 보수 공사 중입니다"라고 말할 때 무엇을 의미하는가?

(A) 더 이상 서비스가 제공되지 않는다.
(B) 운영 시간이 연장되었다.
(C) 사무실을 찾기 어려울 수도 있다.
(D) 업체가 신규 지점을 열었다.

해설 **사무소 건물이 보수공사 중이라는 말의 의도**
후반부에 인용문을 언급한 뒤 방문할 때 표지판을 따라 사무실로 오라(When you visit, just follow the signs to our office)고 했으므로 사무실이 보수 공사 중이라서 찾기 어려울 수도 있다는 것을 나타내고 있으므로 정답은 (C)이다.

어휘 operation 운영 extend 연장하다

[10-12] 팟캐스트

W-Br **10** You're listening to today's episode of *For Profit*, a weekly podcast about managing your finances. Today we'll be speaking with author Claudia Aslan. Her new book, *Helpful Money Habits*, is a must read for anyone on a budget, especially those who are looking to build their savings. **11** Now, I've heard from many listeners that they think books about personal finances are dense and hard to understand. But, they haven't read Ms. Aslan's book. **12** If you don't already own the book, there's a link to purchase it on our Web site.

10 여러분은 재정 관리를 주제로 진행하는 주간 팟캐스트인 〈포 프로핏〉의 오늘의 에피소드를 듣고 계십니다. 오늘은 저자 클라우디아 아슬란과 함께 이야기를 나누겠습니다. 그녀의 신간 〈유용한 돈 습관〉은 예산을 세우는 분이라면 누구나, 특히 저축을 늘리고자 하는 분들이 꼭 읽어 봐야 할 책입니다. **11** 자, 많은 청취자들이 개인 재정에 관한 책들은 난해하고 이해하기 어렵다고 이야기하는데요. 하지만 그런 분들은 아슬란 씨의 책을 읽어 보지 않은 겁니다. **12** 만약 아직 책이 없으시면 저희 웹사이트에 책을 구매할 수 있는 링크가 있습니다.

어휘 profit 이익 budget 예산 dense 난해한

10 팟캐스트는 주로 무엇에 관한 것인가?

(A) 회사 창업　　　(B) 재무 관리
(C) 운동 습관　　　(D) 출판 정보

해설 **팟캐스트의 주제**
초반부에 여러분은 재정 관리를 주제로 진행하는 주간 팟캐스트인 〈포 프로핏〉의 오늘의 에피소드를 듣고 있다(You're listening to today's episode of *For Profit*, a weekly podcast about managing your finances)고 했으므로 정답은 (B)이다.

(Paraphrasing) 담화의 managing your finances
→ 정답의 Financial management

11 화자는 왜 "그런 분들은 아슬란 씨의 책을 읽어 보지 않은 겁니다"라고 말하는가?

(A) 지연에 대해 사과하려고
(B) 실망감을 표현하려고
(C) 의견에 이의를 제기하려고
(D) 결정에 대해 설명하려고

해설 **그런 분들은 아슬란 씨의 책을 읽어 보지 않았다는 말의 의도**
중반부에 많은 청취자들이 개인 재정에 관한 책들은 난해하고 이해하기 어렵다고 이야기한다(Now, I've heard from many listeners that they think books about personal finances are dense and hard to understand)고 한 뒤 인용문을 언급했으므로 아슬란의 책은 그렇지 않다면서 의견에 반박하기 위한 의도임을 알 수 있다. 따라서 정답은 (C)이다.

12 화자는 웹사이트에서 무엇을 이용할 수 있다고 말하는가?

(A) 제품 링크　　　(B) 할인 코드
(C) 설문 조사 결과　　(D) 고객 후기

해설 **화자가 웹사이트에서 이용할 수 있다고 말하는 것**
후반부에 만약 아직 책이 없으면 웹사이트에 책을 구매할 수 있는 링크가 있다(If you don't already own the book, there's a link to purchase it on our Web site)고 했으므로 정답은 (A)이다.

(Paraphrasing) 담화의 a link to purchase it
→ 정답의 A product link

[13-15] W-Br / M-Au　　　　　　　　그래프

W　Hello, Mr. Patel. My name is Hah-Nul Kwon, and **13** I write a column about international trade for *Weekly International*. I'm calling to ask you a few questions about the report you recently published on the modes of transport used for imports.

M　Sure. What would you like to know?

W　**14** Well, I can't find records to support what you say about imports by sea. Could you tell me how you arrived at that percentage?

M　Yes, but you've caught me at a bad time. **15** I'm on a train, and it's a bit noisy. Can I call you back when there are fewer distractions?

여　안녕하세요, 파텔 씨. 제 이름은 권하늘입니다. **13** 〈위클리 인터내셔널〉에 국제 무역에 관한 칼럼을 쓰고 있어요. 최근 수입에 사용되는 운송 수단에 대해 발표하신 보고서와 관련해 몇 가지 여쭤보고 싶어서 전화드렸어요.

남　네. 어떤 게 궁금하신가요?

여　**14** 해운을 통한 수입에 대해 말씀하신 내용을 뒷받침할 만한 기록을 찾을 수가 없네요. 해당 비율이 어떻게 도출된 건지 설명해 주시겠어요?

남　네, 그런데 곤란한 시간에 연락하셨네요. **15** 기차 안이라서 좀 시끄러워요. 방해가 덜한 시간에 다시 전화드려도 될까요?

어휘 transport 운송 import 수입 support 뒷받침하다
distraction 집중을 방해하는 것

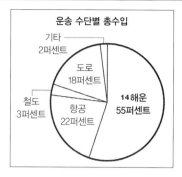

운송 수단별 총수입

기타 2퍼센트
도로 18퍼센트
철도 3퍼센트
항공 22퍼센트
14해운 55퍼센트

13 여자는 누구인 것 같은가?

(A) 조종사   **(B) 기자**
(C) 공무원   (D) 여행사 직원

해설 여자의 직업

여자가 첫 대사에서 〈위클리 인터내셔널〉에 국제 무역에 관한 칼럼을 쓰고 있다(I write a column about international trade for *Weekly International*)고 했으므로 정답은 (B)이다.

14 시각 정보에 따르면, 여자는 어떤 비율을 확인하려고 하는가?

(A) 2퍼센트   (B) 18퍼센트
(C) 22퍼센트   **(D) 55퍼센트**

해설 시각 정보 연계

여자가 두 번째 대사에서 해운을 통한 수입에 대해 말한 내용을 뒷받침할 만한 기록을 찾을 수가 없다(Well, I can't find records to support what you say about imports by sea)면서 해당 비율이 어떻게 도출된 건지 설명해 달라(Could you tell me how you arrived at that percentage?)고 했다. 그래프를 보면 해운을 통한 수입 비율은 55퍼센트이므로 정답은 (D)이다.

15 남자는 왜 여자에게 다시 전화해야 하는가?

(A) 회사 규정을 확인해야 한다.
(B) 서류를 찾을 수 없다.
(C) 주변이 무척 시끄럽다.
(D) 남자와 이야기하려고 기다리는 사람들이 있다.

해설 남자가 여자에게 다시 전화해야 하는 이유

남자가 마지막 대사에서 기차 안이라서 좀 시끄럽다(I'm on a train, and it's a bit noisy)면서 방해가 덜한 시간에 다시 전화해도 될지(Can I call you back when there are fewer distractions?) 물었으므로 정답은 (C)이다.

[16-18] 방송 + 영상 목록

W-Br   I hope you enjoyed this video on growing ginger at home. You learned what type of soil to use, how deep to place the ginger in the soil, and when to water the plant. **16In fact, if you're interested in watering your garden plants**

in general, my video on avoiding mistakes is perfect for you. Highly recommended! **17I'd also like to thank Kevin Graham, owner of Kevin's Garden Supplies, for donating the materials I used in this video.** Finally, regular viewers know I post new videos weekly. **18However, I'm taking a break from gardening this summer to learn about traditional dances in Spain,** so my next video probably won't be posted until September.

집에서 생강 기르기에 관한 이 동영상이 재미있으셨기를 바랍니다. 어떤 흙을 써야 하는지, 생강을 흙 속에 얼마나 깊이 심어야 하는지, 언제 물을 줘야 하는지 배우셨습니다. **16사실, 텃밭 식물에 물을 주는 것에 전반적으로 관심이 있으시면 피해야 할 실수에 관한 제 동영상이 안성맞춤이죠. 강력 추천합니다! 17또한 제가 이 동영상에 사용했던 재료를 기증해 주신 케빈 원예용품점의 케빈 그레이엄 사장님께도 감사드립니다.** 마지막으로, 방송을 꾸준히 보시는 시청자라면 제가 매주 새로운 동영상을 올린다는 점 아실 텐데요. **18그런데 스페인 전통 춤을 배우느라 이번 여름에는 텃밭 가꾸기를 잠시 쉬려고 합니다.** 그래서 다음 동영상은 아마도 9월에나 올라갈 것 같습니다.

어휘 ginger 생강 avoid 피하다 donate 기증하다
traditional 전통적인

동영상	길이
적절한 토마토 작물 관리	13분 55초
바질 가지치기 방법	5분 30초
돋음 텃밭 준비	17분 45초
16물 주기 실수 방지	**11분 20초**

어휘 prune 가지치기하다

16 시각 정보에 따르면, 화자가 추천하는 영상의 길이는?

(A) 13분 55초   (B) 5분 30초
(C) 17분 45초   **(D) 11분 20초**

해설 시각 정보 연계

초반부에 텃밭 식물에 물을 주는 것에 전반적으로 관심이 있으면 피해야 할 실수에 관한 자신의 동영상이 안성맞춤(In fact, if you're interested in watering your garden plants in general, my video on avoiding mistakes is perfect for you)이라면서 강력 추천한다(Highly recommended!)고 했다. 영상 목록을 보면 물 주기 실수 방지 동영상의 길이는 11분 20초이므로 정답은 (D)이다.

17 화자는 왜 케빈 그레이엄에게 감사를 표하는가?

(A) 그래픽을 만들어서   (B) 작업 공간을 제공해서
(C) 재료를 공급해서   (D) 동영상 대본을 작성해서

해설 화자가 케빈 그레이엄에게 감사하는 이유

중반부에 이 동영상에 사용했던 재료를 기증해 준 케빈 원예용품점의 케빈 그레이엄 사장에게도 감사하다(I'd also like to thank Kevin Graham, ~, for donating the materials I used in this video)고 했으므로 정답은 (C)이다.

PART 3&4   UNIT 4

Paraphrasing 담화의 donating the materials
→ 정답의 supplying materials

18 화자는 올여름에 무엇을 배울 것인가?
    (A) 제물낚시   (B) 전통 춤
    (C) 초상화 그리기   (D) 등산

해설 **화자가 올 여름에 배울 것**
후반부에 스페인 전통 춤을 배우느라 이번 여름에는 텃밭 가꾸기를 잠시 쉬려고 한다(However, I'm taking a break from gardening this summer to learn about traditional dances in Spain)고 했으므로 정답은 (B)이다.

ETS 기출   **고난도 실전문제**   본책 p.62

1 (D)	**2** (B)	**3** (C)	**4** (A)	**5** (B)	**6** (D)
7 (B)	**8** (A)	**9** (D)	**10** (B)	**11** (A)	**12** (C)
13 (D)	**14** (D)	**15** (B)	**16** (B)	**17** (C)	**18** (B)

[1-3] M-Cn / W-Am

> **M** Usha, I've been incredibly happy with your work over the past year. **1 I've been especially impressed with your problem-solving skills.**
> **W** Thank you. I enjoy my position on the factory floor.
> **M** Now, we like to encourage our employees to grow professionally. **2 Do you have any career goals?**
> **W** **3 I have been thinking about going to night school to earn a degree in assembly-line mechanics. But I know the factory already has enough mechanics.**
> **M** Well, Alberto's about to retire.
> **W** Really? In that case, does the company offer a tuition assistance program?
>
> **남** 우샤, 지난 한 해 동안 하신 일에 더 없이 만족하고 있습니다. **1특히 문제 해결 능력이 대단하시던데요.**
> **여** 감사합니다. 작업 현장에서 일하는 게 즐거워요.
> **남** 자, 저희 회사는 직원들이 전문적으로 성장하도록 장려하고 있어요. **2커리어 목표가 있나요?**
> **여** **3야간 학교에 다니면서 조립 라인 기계학 학위를 딸까 생각해 봤어요. 하지만 공장에는 이미 기계공이 충분한 걸로 알아요.**
> **남** 음, 알베르토가 곧 은퇴할 예정이에요.
> **여** 정말요? 그렇다면 회사에서 학비 지원 프로그램을 제공하나요?
>
> 어휘 assembly-line 조립 라인   mechanics 기계학
> mechanic 기계공   retire 은퇴하다   tuition 학비

1 남자는 여자의 어떤 점이 특별히 인상 깊었는가?
    (A) 학력이 높다.
    (B) 기꺼이 위험을 감수한다.

    (C) 긍정적인 태도를 가지고 있다.
    (D) 문제 해결 능력이 좋다.

해설 **남자가 깊은 인상을 받은 여자의 역량**
남자가 첫 대사에서 특히 문제 해결 능력이 대단하다(I've been especially impressed with your problem-solving skills)고 했으므로 정답은 (D)이다.

어휘 educational background 학력

2 남자는 여자에게 무엇에 관해 묻는가?
    (A) 추천서   (B) 직업 목표
    (C) 휴가 계획   (D) 선호하는 직장 위치

해설 **남자의 질문 사항**
남자가 두 번째 대사에서 커리어 목표가 있는지(Do you have any career goals?) 물었으므로 정답은 (B)이다.

Paraphrasing 대화의 career → 정답의 professional

3 남자가 "알베르토가 곧 은퇴할 예정이에요"라고 말할 때 무엇을 의미하는가?
    (A) 남자가 파티를 계획하고 있다.
    (B) 팀은 프로젝트를 빨리 끝내야 한다.
    (C) 일자리가 날 것이다.
    (D) 사무실 용도가 변경될 것이다.

해설 **알베르토가 곧 은퇴할 예정이라는 말의 의도**
여자가 야간 학교에 다니면서 조립 라인 기계학 학위를 딸까 생각해 봤다(I have been thinking about going to night school to earn a degree in assembly-line mechanics)면서 하지만 공장에는 이미 기계공이 충분한 걸로 안다(But I know the factory already has enough mechanics)고 하자 남자가 인용문을 언급했으므로 알베르토가 곧 은퇴함에 따라 기계공 자리가 공석이 될 것임을 암시한다. 따라서 정답은 (C)이다.

어휘 opportunity 기회   repurpose 용도를 바꾸다

[4-6] M-Au / W-Br

> **M** Hi, Mona. How's it going?
> **W** Hi, Andrew. **4 I was just working out some of the engineering issues on one of our robot prototypes**—the robot that mops floors.
> **M** Oh! **5 That's actually what I'm calling about. The investors we spoke with last week just got back to me.**
> **W** Oh, great. What do they think?
> **M** They're really interested. Nothing is in writing yet, but they may be willing to invest 250,000 euros.
> **W** That is so exciting. **6 Let's get back together with them and finalize the deal.**
> **M** Well, we're meeting with another group on Friday.

남	안녕, 모나. 어떻게 지내요?
여	안녕, 앤드류. ⁴로봇 시제품 중 하나의 기술적 문제 몇 가지를 해결하고 있었어요. 바닥 닦는 로봇 말이에요.
남	오! ⁵사실 그것 때문에 전화했어요. 지난주에 이야기를 나눴던 투자자들이 다시 연락했거든요.
여	오, 잘됐네요. 그들은 어떻게 생각해요?
남	관심이 많아요. 아직 서면으로 된 건 없지만, 25만 유로를 선뜻 투자할지도 몰라요.
여	신나네요. ⁶그 사람들을 다시 만나서 계약을 마무리하죠.
남	음, 금요일에 다른 그룹과 만나기로 했어요.

어휘 **prototype** 시제품 **mop** 닦다 **finalize** 마무리하다

---

4 여자는 누구인 것 같은가?

(A) 엔지니어   (B) 대학 교수
(C) 재무 상담가   (D) 소매점 직원

해설 **여자의 직업**
여자가 첫 대사에서 로봇 시제품 중 하나의 기술적 문제 몇 가지를 해결하고 있었다(I was just working out some of the engineering issues on one of our robot prototypes)고 했으므로 정답은 (A)이다.

어휘 **associate** 직원

5 남자는 왜 여자에게 전화하고 있는가?

(A) 의견을 물으려고   **(B) 소식을 전하려고**
(C) 프로젝트에 협력하려고   (D) 회의를 취소하려고

해설 **남자가 전화하는 이유**
남자가 두 번째 대사에서 사실 그것 때문에 전화했다(That's actually what I'm calling about)면서 지난주에 이야기를 나눴던 투자자들이 다시 연락했다(The investors we spoke with last week just got back to me)고 알리고 있으므로 정답은 (B)이다.

6 남자는 왜 "금요일에 다른 그룹과 만나기로 했어요"라고 말하는가?

(A) 고마움을 표하려고   (B) 일정에 대해 불평하려고
(C) 규정에 반대하려고   **(D) 대기를 권하려고**

해설 **금요일에 다른 그룹과 만나기로 했다는 말의 의도**
여자가 마지막 대사에서 그 사람들을 다시 만나서 계약을 마무리하자(Let's get back together with them and finalize the deal)고 하자 남자가 인용문을 언급했으므로 다른 그룹과 만난 이후에 최종 결정을 내리자고 제안하는 의도임을 알 수 있다. 따라서 정답은 (D)이다.

[7-9] 회의 발췌

M-Au I just want to give everyone in the department a quick update on my team's work. ⁷ **We're nearly done developing the software for optimizing delivery routes.** Basically, the software will ensure that our drivers use the safest, most cost-effective routes. I'd especially

---

like to highlight the work of our new team member, So-Jin Cho. ⁸ **She's helped us tremendously,** and this is her first month on the job. ⁸ **So a big thanks to her!** ⁹ **We'll be publishing our project details in the company's internal newsletter later this week, so look out for that.**

부서 직원 모두에게 팀 업무 진행 상황을 간단히 알려 드리려고 합니다. ⁷배송 경로를 최적화하는 소프트웨어 개발이 거의 끝났습니다. 기본적으로 소프트웨어는 운전자가 가장 안전하고 경제적인 경로를 이용할 수 있도록 보장하죠. 특히 새로운 팀원인 조소진 씨의 노고를 강조하고 싶은데요. ⁸소진 씨는 엄청나게 도움이 됐어요. 게다가 이번이 근무 첫 달입니다. ⁸정말 감사합니다! ⁹이번 주 후반에 사내 소식지에 프로젝트 세부 정보를 게시할 예정이니 꼭 챙겨 보세요.

어휘 **nearly** 거의 **optimize** 최적화하다 **cost-effective** 경제적인 **tremendously** 엄청나게

7 화자는 누구인 것 같은가?

(A) 회계사   **(B) 소프트웨어 엔지니어**
(C) 공사장 인부   (D) 배송 기사

해설 **화자의 직업**
초반부에 배송 경로를 최적화하는 소프트웨어 개발이 거의 끝났다(We're nearly done developing the software ~ delivery routes)고 했으므로 정답은 (B)이다.

8 남자가 "이번이 근무 첫 달입니다"라고 말할 때 무엇을 의미하는가?

(A) 직원이 한 일에 감명을 받았다.
(B) 아직 직원을 만나지 못했다.
(C) 직원은 추가 교육이 필요하다.
(D) 직원의 업무량이 줄었다.

해설 **이번이 근무 첫 달이라는 말의 의도**
중반부에 소진 씨가 엄청나게 도움이 됐다(She's helped us tremendously)고 한 뒤 인용문을 언급했고 뒤이어 정말 고맙다(So a big thanks to her!)고 했으므로 정답은 (A)이다.

9 화자에 따르면, 소식지에는 무엇이 실릴 것인가?
(A) 회사 행사 사진
(B) 위치 안내
(C) 신입 사원 명단
(D) 팀 프로젝트에 대한 세부 정보

해설 **소식지에 실릴 내용**
후반부에 이번 주 후반에 사내 소식지에 프로젝트 세부 정보를 게시할 예정(We'll be publishing our project details in the company's internal newsletter later this week)이라고 했으므로 정답은 (D)이다.

(Paraphrasing) 담화의 project details
→ 정답의 Details about a team's project

PART 3&4   UNIT 4

[10-12] 전화 메시지

W-Am Hello, Ms. Salazar. My name's Amina, and I'm calling from Jebreen Septic Services. **10 You requested a price quote on our Web site to install a new septic system for your house.** I've sent you a preliminary quote, but **11 the final price will depend on an assessment of the soil on your property. To do that, you'll need to schedule a time for us to come out and perform the assessment. 12 This will determine the optimal place for excavation.** Just keep in mind, our team can't dig once the weather gets cold.

안녕하세요, 살라자르 씨. 저는 제브린 정화 서비스의 아미나라고 합니다. 10 집에 새로운 정화조를 설치하기 위해 저희 웹사이트에 가격 견적을 요청하셨네요. 예비 견적을 보내 드렸습니다만, 11 최종 가격은 주택 부지의 토양 평가에 따라 달라집니다. 그러려면 저희가 가서 평가를 수행할 시간을 정해 주셔야 합니다. 12 이렇게 해서 최적의 굴착 위치를 판단합니다. 유념하세요. 날씨가 추워지면 저희 팀은 땅을 팔 수 없습니다.

어휘 quote 견적(서) septic system 정화조, 하수 처리 설비 preliminary 예비의 depend on ~에 따라 달라지다 assessment 평가 property 부지, 부동산 optimal 최적의 excavation 땅 파기 dig (땅을) 파다

---

10 화자에 따르면, 청자는 무엇을 요청했는가?
(A) 고객 목록
(B) 비용 견적서
(C) 디지털 이미지
(D) 등기부 등본

해설 청자의 요청 사항
초반부에 집에 새로운 정화조를 설치하기 위해 웹사이트에 가격 견적을 요청했다(You requested a price quote ~ for your house)고 했으므로 정답은 (B)이다.

어휘 estimate 견적(서) property deed (부동산) 등기부 등본

11 화자에 따르면, 청자는 다음에 무엇을 해야 하는가?
(A) 토양 평가 준비
(B) 정화용 펌프 주문
(C) 허가 신청
(D) 신용카드 번호 제공

해설 청자가 다음에 해야 할 일
중반부에 최종 가격은 주택 부지 토양 평가에 따라 달라진다(the final price will depend on an assessment of the soil on your property)면서 그러려면 우리가 가서 평가를 수행할 시간을 정해 주어야 한다(To do that, you'll need to schedule a time for us to come out and perform the assessment)고 했으므로 정답은 (A)이다.

어휘 permit 허가

12 화자는 왜 "날씨가 추워지면 저희 팀은 땅을 팔 수 없습니다" 라고 말하는가?
(A) 다른 회사를 추천하기 위해
(B) 비용 인상을 설명하기 위해
(C) 긴급함을 알리기 위해
(D) 계획을 변경하기 위해

해설 날씨가 추워지면 땅을 팔 수 없다는 말의 의도
후반부에 이렇게 해서 최적의 굴착 위치를 판단한다(This will determine the optimal place for excavation)고 한 뒤 인용문을 언급했으므로 날씨가 추워지기 전에 작업을 서둘러야 한다는 의도임을 알 수 있다. 따라서 정답은 (C)이다.

어휘 urgency 긴급함

[13-15] M-Au / W-Am 휴대폰 화면

M Thanks for shopping at Baja's Grocers. **14 That'll be $98.**

W That's more than I expected!

M **13 Have you heard that we just launched our new app last week?** We now offer great discounts for our app users.

W Actually, I did download the app recently. Let me open it up and scan it. **14 Wow, that's a significant savings for $98.** Thanks for reminding me about this.

M You're welcome. **15 We also have an in-store special in the bakery department—buy one, get one free. I can put your purchase on hold while you check it out.**

W **15 Thanks, I'll be right back!**

남 바하 식료품점에서 구매해 주셔서 감사합니다. 14 98달러입니다.
여 예상보다 많이 나왔네요!
남 13 지난주에 새로운 앱을 출시했다는 소식 들으셨나요? 지금 앱 사용자에게 대폭 할인을 제공하고 있어요.
여 실은 최근에 앱을 다운받았거든요. 열어서 살펴볼게요. 14 와, 98달러면 꽤 절약되네요. 알려 줘서 고마워요.
남 별말씀을요. 15 베이커리 매장에서 매장 내 특별 행사가 있는데 하나를 사면 하나를 공짜로 드려요. 살펴보시는 동안 구매품은 보관해 놓을게요.
여 15 고마워요, 금방 올게요!

어휘 launch 출시하다 significant 상당한

바하 식료품점
주간 특별 행사

25달러 이상 구매 시 3달러 할인!
40달러 이상 구매 시 5달러 할인!
60달러 이상 구매 시 7달러 할인!
14 75달러 이상 구매 시 9달러 할인!

---

13 가게는 지난주에 무엇을 했는가?
(A) 웹사이트를 업데이트했다.
(B) 온라인 서비스를 확대했다.
(C) 배송 서비스를 시작했다.
(D) 모바일 애플리케이션을 출시했다.

해설 **가게가 지난주에 한 일**
남자가 두 번째 대사에서 지난주에 새로운 앱을 출시했다는 소식을 들었는지(Have you heard that we just launched our new app last week?) 물었으므로 정답은 (D)이다.

14 시각 정보에 따르면, 여자는 얼마나 아끼겠는가?
(A) 3달러   (B) 5달러
(C) 7달러   **(D) 9달러**

해설 **시각 정보 연계**
남자가 첫 대사에서 여자가 구매한 금액을 98달러(That'll be $98)라고 했고 여자가 두 번째 대사에서 98달러면 꽤 절약된다(Wow, that's a significant savings for $98)고 했다. 휴대폰 화면을 보면 75달러 이상 구매 시 9달러 할인이므로 정답은 (D)이다.

15 여자는 다음에 무엇을 할 것 같은가?
(A) 물품 반납하기   **(B) 베이커리 매장으로 가기**
(C) 설문 조사 질문에 답하기   (D) 가게에서 나가기

해설 **여자가 다음에 할 일**
남자가 베이커리 매장에서 매장 내 특별 행사가 있는데 하나를 사면 하나를 공짜로 준다(We also have an in-store special in the bakery department ~ free)면서 살펴보는 동안 구매품은 보관해 놓겠다(I can put ~ while you check it out)고 하자 여자가 고맙다며 금방 오겠다(Thanks, I'll be right back!)고 했으므로 정답은 (B)이다.

[16-18] 연설 + 경주 코스 지도

M-Au Welcome, everyone, to the tenth annual Summerville ten-kilometer race! **16 This year, we have more participants than we've ever had!** The run will begin shortly, but **17 I just wanted to remind you that about halfway through the course, you'll cross a pair of bridges.** Make sure to run carefully when you get there, as the ground may be a little slippery. OK. **18 Now head over to our refreshments area to fill up your water bottles and grab an energy bar for the race.**

제10회 연례 서머빌 10km 경주대회에 오신 여러분, 환영합니다! **16올해는 참가자가 역대 최고로 많습니다!** 곧 달리기가 시작되겠지만, **17코스 중간쯤에 다리 두 개를 건넌다는 점, 기억하세요.** 그곳에 도착하면 땅이 조금 미끄러울 수도 있으니까 조심해서 달리세요. 자, 그럼 **18경주를 위해 식음료 구역으로 이동해 물병을 채우고 에너지 바를 챙기세요.**

어휘 annual 연례의, 해마다 열리는   participant 참가자   shortly 곧   slippery 미끄러운   head over to ~으로 향하다   refreshments 식음료, 다과

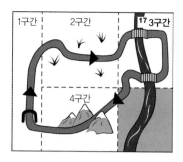

16 화자에 따르면, 올해 경주대회의 특별한 점은 무엇인가?
(A) 평소보다 길다.   **(B) 경주자가 더 많다.**
(C) 상품을 준다.   (D) 아이들이 참가할 수 있다.

해설 **올해 경주대회의 특별한 점**
초반부에 올해는 참가자가 역대 최고로 많다(This year, we have more participants than we've ever had!)고 했으므로 정답은 (B)이다.

어휘 than usual 평소보다

17 시각 정보에 따르면, 화자는 경주의 어느 구간을 언급하는가?
(A) 1구간   (B) 2구간
(C) 3구간   (D) 4구간

해설 **시각 정보 연계**
중반부에 코스 중간쯤에 다리 두 개를 건넌다는 점을 기억하라(I just wanted to remind you ~, you'll cross a pair of bridges)고 했다. 경주 코스 지도를 보면 다리가 두 개 있는 구간은 3구간이므로 정답은 (C)이다.

18 청자들은 다음에 무엇을 할 것인가?
(A) 면책 동의서에 서명하기   **(B) 물품 챙기기**
(C) 사진 찍기   (D) 줄서기

해설 **청자들이 다음에 할 일**
후반부에 경주를 위해 식음료 구역으로 이동해 물병을 채우고 에너지 바를 챙기라(Now head over to ~ to fill up your water bottles and grab an energy bar for the race)고 했으므로 정답은 (B)이다.

어휘 waiver 면책 동의서

Paraphrasing 담화의 fill up your water bottles and grab an energy bar → 정답의 Gather supplies

PART 5&6

Reading Comprehension

UNIT 5 문법 빈출 유형

01 명사/대명사/형용사/부사

ETS 기출 유형연습　　　　본책 p.70

1 (C)　　**2** (A)　　**3** (B)　　**4** (D)

1　(C) 명사 자리_복합명사

번역 햄프턴의 도로 보수는 이번 주 주요 창고에서 컴퓨터 출하를 약간 지연시켰다.

해설 빈칸 앞에 가산명사 Road가 단수의 형태로 있지만 한정사를 동반하지 않고 있으므로, 동사 caused의 주어 역할을 할 수 없다. 따라서 빈칸은 주어 역할을 하는 명사 자리이며, Road와 함께 '도로 보수'라는 의미의 복합명사를 이루는 '수리, 보수'라는 뜻의 (C) repairs가 정답이다. 명사인 (B) repairer(수리공)는 road와 함께 복합명사를 만들 수는 있으나 가산 단수명사이므로 앞에 한정사가 필요하다.

어휘 delay 지연　warehouse 창고

2　(A) 지시대명사_those

번역 노바 피스트 케이터링은 시선을 끄는 소셜 미디어 게시물을 매주 제작하는 데 전념할 의향이 있는 사람들을 찾고 있다.

해설 빈칸에는 관계사절(who are willing to ~ on a weekly basis)의 수식을 받고 전치사 for의 목적어 역할을 하는 대명사가 필요하다. 관계사절의 동사가 복수동사 are이므로 관계대명사 who와 함께 '~ 하는 사람들'이라는 뜻으로 쓰이는 복수 지시대명사 (A) those가 정답이다. (C) someone과 (D) anyone은 뒤에 단수동사가 와야 하고, 인칭대명사 (B) them은 지문에 them을 나타내는 복수명사가 없을 뿐 아니라, 일반적으로 뒤에 수식구가 오지 않는다.

어휘 feast 진수성찬　commit 전념하다　catchy 시선을 끄는　post 게시물　on a weekly basis 주 단위로

3　(B) 부사 어휘_시제 부사

번역 최근 채용된 포트폴리오 매니저들은 내일 A 회의실에서 열릴 상급 교육 세션에 참석해야 함을 다시 한번 알려 드립니다.

해설 빈칸 앞의 동사구 were hired를 수식하여 '최근에 채용된'이라는 의미가 되어 적절하므로 '최근에'라는 뜻으로 과거 시제와 어울리는 부사 (B) recently가 정답이다. (A) soon(곧)은 미래 시제, (C) often(자주)은 현재 시제, (D) yet(아직)은 주로 의문문이나 부정문과 어울린다.

어휘 advanced 상[고]급의　session (특정 활동을 위한) 시간

4　(D) 형용사 자리

번역 일부 철물점에서는 제설기와 고압 세척기 같은 크고 값비싼 장비를 시간 단위로 대여해 준다.

해설 빈칸은 명사 items의 수식어 자리로, 분사 (B) costing과 형용사 (D) costly가 가능하다. costing은 '~의 비용이 들고 있는'이라는 의미로 해석이 어색할 뿐 아니라, 상태동사이므로 진행형의 현재분사로는 거의 쓰이지 않는다. 따라서 '비용이 많이 드는, 비싼'이라는 의미의 형용사 (D) costly가 정답이다.

어휘 hardware store 철물점　snowblower 제설기　power washer 고압 세척기　by the hour 시간 단위로

02 동사

ETS 기출 유형연습　　　　본책 p.73

1 (C)　　**2** (B)　　**3** (B)

1　(C) 동사 어형_수 일치+태

번역 브래드포드는 제품을 위한 공간이 제한적인 매장에 이상적으로, 자사 제품 중 가장 폭이 좁은 진열장입니다.

해설 빈칸은 선행사 stores를 수식하는 관계사절(that ~ products)의 동사 자리로 선행사와 수가 일치하는 복수동사가 들어가야 한다. 또한 '제한된 공간을 가진 매장'이라는 의미가 되어야 하므로 '가지다'라는 의미의 (C) have가 정답이다. (D) have been은 '제한된 공간이었던 매장'이라는 의미를 만들므로 문맥상 부적절하다.

어휘 narrow (폭이) 좁은　ideal 이상적인　limited 제한된

2　(B) 동사 어휘_5형식 동사

번역 보고서 작성은 짧게 해 주시고 관련 없는 자료는 포함하지 말아 주십시오.

해설 빈칸 뒤에 목적어 the written report와 목적격 보어인 형용사 short가 있고, 문맥상 '보고서는 짧게 해 달라'는 의미가 되어야 하므로 5형식 동사가 필요하다. 따라서, '유지하다, (특정 상태로) 있게 하다'를 뜻하는 (B) keep이 정답이다. (A) maintain과 (D) retain도 '유지하다'라는 의미이지만 3형식 동사로 목적격 보어를 취하지 않으며, (C) allow(허락하다)는 목적격 보어로 to부정사가 쓰인다.

어휘 irrelevant 상관없는

3　(B) 동사 어형_태+시제

번역 다음 달 자오 키친 서플라이의 할인 판매 기간 동안 판매되는 모든 가전제품에는 환불 보증이 포함될 것입니다.

해설 빈칸은 주어 All appliances의 동사 자리로 복수동사가 들어가야 하므로, 단수동사 (A) includes와 동명사/현재분사인 (C) including은 제외된다. 또한 빈칸 앞 next month라는 미래 시간 표현과 뒤에 목적어 a money-back guarantee가 있으므로 미래 시제이면서 능동태 동사인 (B) will include가 정답이다.

어휘 appliances 가전제품   guarantee 보증

03 전치사와 부사절 접속사

ETS 기출 유형연습
본책 p.75

1 (A)   **2** (A)   **3** (C)

1 **(A) 접속사 자리_부사절 접속사+분사**

번역 고객에게 서신을 보낼 때는 반드시 협회의 수정된 레터헤드를 사용하세요.

해설 콤마 뒤 명령문 형태의 주절이 있으므로, 빈칸 뒤 sending ~ customers는 분사구문 또는 동명사구로 볼 수 있다. 문맥상 '서신을 보낼 때'라는 의미가 되어야 자연스러우므로 분사구문을 이끄는 부사절 접속사 (A) When이 정답이다. 전치사 (B) During은 명동사를 목적어로 취하지 않고, 부사인 (C) Meanwhile(그동안에)과 (D) Yet(아직)은 문법적으로는 분사를 수식할 수 있지만 문맥상 적절하지 않다.

어휘 correspondence 서신   association 협회
letterhead 편지 윗부분에 인쇄하는 이름 및 주소

2 **(A) 전치사 어휘**

번역 회의 참석자들은 첫 번째 세션에 참여하려면 오전 8시 30분까지 참가 수속을 마쳐야 한다.

해설 빈칸은 완전한 절에 시점을 나타내는 8:30 A.M.을 연결하는 자리이므로 전치사가 들어가야 한다. 문맥상 '오전 8시 30분까지 참가 수속을 마쳐야 한다'는 내용이 되어야 하므로 '(어느 시점)까지' 행위의 완료를 나타내는 전치사 (A) by가 정답이다. (B) until(~까지)은 특정 시점까지 어떤 상태가 지속되는 경우에 쓰이고, (C) since는 '(과거 시점) 이후'라는 뜻으로 현재완료 시제와 쓰이므로 부적절하며, (D) within(~이내)은 기간의 표현과 쓰여야 하므로 오답이다.

어휘 check in 수속을 밟다, 등록하다

3 **(C) 접속사 자리_부사절 접속사**

번역 우리 아티스트가 쿡 광고주의 로고를 수정했으나 고객은 여전히 만족하지 않는다.

해설 빈칸 뒤에 주어와 동사를 갖춘 완전한 절이 왔으므로 부사절 접속사가 들어가야 한다. 문맥상 '우리 아티스트가 로고를 수정했지만'이라는 의미가 되어야 자연스러우므로 '(비록) ~하지만'을 뜻하는 (C) Although가 정답이다. (A) As long as도 부사절 접속사이지만 '~하는 한'이라는 뜻으로 문맥상 어울리지 않는다.

어휘 account 광고주, 고객   satisfied 만족하는   even so 그렇기는 하지만   nonetheless 그럼에도 불구하고

ETS 기출 실전문제
본책 p.76

1 (A)	**2** (A)	**3** (B)	**4** (B)	**5** (A)	**6** (D)
7 (B)	**8** (A)	**9** (A)	**10** (C)	**11** (B)	**12** (C)
13 (D)	**14** (D)	**15** (C)	**16** (B)	**17** (A)	**18** (D)

1 **(A) 명사 자리_동사의 주어**

번역 케이블 TV 공급업체 간의 경쟁으로 가정용 가입자에 대한 가격이 낮아졌다.

해설 빈칸은 동사 has led의 주어 역할을 하는 명사 자리이다. 따라서 (A) Competition과 (C) Competitor 중 하나를 선택해야 하는데, 빈칸 앞에 한정사가 없으므로 가산 단수명사인 Competitor(경쟁자)는 들어갈 수 없다. 따라서 '경쟁'을 뜻하는 불가산명사 (A) Competition이 정답이다.

어휘 residential 주거의   competitive 경쟁력 있는; 경쟁이 치열한

2 **(A) 형용사 자리_주격 보어**

번역 최근 시행된 마케팅 설문 조사는 시나바이트의 액션 어드벤처 게임의 가격이 너무 높다는 것을 보여 준다.

해설 빈칸은 명사절인 that절 안의 동사 is의 보어 자리로, 형용사와 부사의 원급을 강조하는 부사 too(너무)의 수식을 받고 있다. 따라서 형용사 (A) high가 정답이다. 비교급인 (B) higher는 too와 어울리지 않으므로 오답이다.

어휘 indicate 보여 주다, 암시하다

3 **(B) 접속사 자리_부사절 접속사**

번역 지난 분기 매출액이 22퍼센트 증가했기 때문에 직원 교육에 사용 가능한 자금이 더 많이 있다.

해설 빈칸 뒤에 주어와 동사를 갖춘 완전한 절이 왔으므로 부사절 접속사가 들어가야 한다. 따라서 '~ 때문에'라는 뜻의 부사절 접속사 (B) Since가 정답이다. (A) Due to(~ 때문에)와 (C) Like(~처럼)는 전치사이고, (D) Thus(그러므로)는 접속부사이므로 품사상 답이 될 수 없다.

어휘 revenue 수익   quarter 분기

4 **(B) 동사 어형_수 일치**

번역 승인 받은 직원만이 환자 기록에 대한 접근 권한을 받는다.

해설 빈칸은 주어 Only authorized employees의 동사 자리로, 복수주어인 employees와 수가 일치하는 (B) are granted가 정답이다. 참고로 4형식 동사인 grant는 '~에게 …을 부여하다, 승인하다'라는 뜻으로, 수동태 뒤에 목적어가 올 때 '~을 받다'라는 의미로 해석된다.

어휘 authorized 승인된   access 접근, 이용   patient 환자

5 **(A) 명사 자리_동사의 주어**

번역 인테리어 디자인 컨퍼런스의 주요 연사는 조명 시스템의 혁신에 대해 논의할 것입니다.

해설 빈칸은 동사구 will discuss의 주어 역할을 하는 명사 자리이다. '가장 중요한, 으뜸가는'을 의미하는 형용사 lead의 수식을 받아 '주요 연사'라는 의미가 되어야 자연스러우므로 '연사'라는 뜻의 명사 (A) speaker가 정답이다. 참고로 '주연 배우, 선임; 납'이라는 의미의 명사이기도 한 lead는 문맥상 명사가 아니므로 형용사 (D) spoken의 수식을 받을 수 없다.

어휘 innovations 혁신   spoken 구두의, 구어체의

6   (D) 전치사 자리

번역 15매 이상의 티켓을 구입하시기 전에 단체 할인 및 좌석 배치와 관련하여 극장 매표소에 문의하십시오.

해설 동명사 purchasing과 함께 쓰여 '구입하기 전에'라는 의미를 나타내는 전치사 (D) Before가 정답이다. 부사절 접속사인 (C) Although(~이긴 하지만)는 분사구문을 이끌 수 있지만 문맥상 어울리지 않고, (A) Otherwise(그렇지 않으면)는 접속부사, (B) Whatever(~하는 것은 무엇이든지)는 복합관계대명사이다.

어휘 regarding ~에 관하여   arrangement 배치

7   (B) 전치사 어휘

번역 전액 환불을 받으시려면 모발 관리 제품이 개봉되지 않은 상태로 구매 후 30일 이내에 반품되어야 합니다.

해설 빈칸 뒤의 숫자 기간 명사구 30 days를 목적어로 취해 '30일 이내에'라는 내용이 되어야 하므로 '~이내에'를 뜻하는 (B) within이 정답이다. (C) during은 뒤에 숫자 기간이 아닌 기간을 뜻하는 명사나 명사구를 취하므로 오답이다.

어휘 full refund 전액 환불

8   (A) 동사 어휘

번역 플래티넘 트리니다드의 웹사이트는 저렴한 연회비로 다양한 일반 비즈니스 업무를 위한 견본을 제공합니다.

해설 빈칸 뒤의 templates를 목적어로 취해 '견본을 제공한다'는 의미가 되어야 적절하므로 '제공하다'라는 뜻의 타동사 (A) provides가 정답이다. (B) belongs(속하다)는 자동사로 목적어를 취하지 않고, (D) notifies(~에게 알리다)는 사람 목적어만 취하므로 templates가 목적어가 될 수 없다.

어휘 annual fee 연회비   template 견본

9   (A) 동사 어형_시제

번역 월요일까지 충분한 인원의 팀원들이 전화 회의에 관심을 표할 경우 메이어 씨가 회의를 준비할 것이다.

해설 If절에 동사가 보이지 않으므로 빈칸은 동사 자리이다. 주절의 동사가 미래 시제(will set)이고 월요일까지 일어날 일에 대한 내용인 것으로 보아 미래 시제가 와야 하지만, 조건절인 If절에는 미래 시제 대신 현재 시제가 쓰이므로 (A) express가 정답이다.

어휘 set up ~을 준비[마련]하다

10   (C) 형용사 어휘

번역 릭스비 출판은 여러 다른 주제를 다루는 교과서를 제공한다.

해설 현재분사 covering의 목적어 역할을 하는 명사구 different topics 앞에 빈칸이 있으므로, 한정사인 (A) any나 (C) several이 들어갈 수 있다. 복수명사 topics와 수 일치하고 '여러 다른 주제를 다루는 교과서'라는 내용이 되어야 적절하므로, '여러 가지의'라는 뜻의 수량 형용사 (C) several이 정답이다. (A) any는 '어떤, 어느'라는 의미로 문맥상 어색하다.

어휘 cover 다루다

11   (B) 형용사 자리_목적격 보어

번역 새로운 회계 시스템은 사무용품 구매를 더 편리하게 해 줄 것이다.

해설 동사 make는 목적격 보어로 형용사나 명사를 취하여 5형식 문장을 만들 수 있다. 빈칸은 목적어인 동명사구 buying office supplies를 보충 설명함과 동시에 부사 more의 수식을 받아 '사무용품 구매를 더 편리하게 만든다'는 의미가 되어야 하므로 '편리한'을 뜻하는 형용사 (B) convenient가 정답이다. (A) convenience와 (D) conveniences는 명사로 보어 역할을 할 수는 있지만 buying office supplies와 동격이 아니므로 답이 될 수 없다.

어휘 office supplies 사무용품   convenience 편의

12   (C) 부사 자리_동사 수식

번역 원격 근무자는 적절한 교육과 온라인 도구로 대부분의 광고 캠페인 작업에서 생산적으로 협업할 수 있다.

해설 빈칸 앞에는 자동사 collaborate, 뒤에는 전치사 on이 있으므로 빈칸에는 동사 collaborate를 수식하는 부사가 들어가야 한다. 따라서 '생산적으로'라는 의미의 부사 (C) productively가 정답이다.

어휘 proper 적절한   remote 원격의   collaborate 협업하다   productive 생산적인   productivity 생산성

13   (D) 인칭대명사의 격_목적격

번역 카본 씨와 리 씨의 직속 직원들은 그들이 제공하는 뛰어난 진로 지도에 감사한다.

해설 빈칸은 관계사절(who report to -------)에서 전치사 to의 목적어 역할을 하는 자리이다. 문맥상 'Ms. Carbone과 Mr. Lee의 직속인 직원들'이라는 내용이 되어야 하므로 Ms. Carbone과 Mr. Lee를 대신하는 인칭대명사의 목적격인 (D) them이 정답이다.

어휘 report to ~의 직속이다. 지시를 받다   exceptional 뛰어난   guidance 지도

14   (D) 명사 자리_동사의 주어

번역 참석자들은 내일 있을 포커스 그룹 회의에서 열 가지 광고의 효과에 대한 순위를 매겨달라는 요청을 받을 것이다.

해설 빈칸은 동사 will be asked의 주어 자리이므로 명사가 들어가야 하고, 문맥상 '참석자들은 요청을 받을 것이다'라는 내

용이 되어야 자연스러우므로 '참석자들'을 뜻하는 명사 (D) Attendees가 정답이다. (C) Attendant(안내원)는 가산 단수명사이므로 앞에 한정사가 있거나 복수명사이어야 주어 역할을 할 수 있다.

어휘 rank (순위를) 매기다   effectiveness 효과 attendance 참석(률)

[15-18] 제품 안내서

혁신적인 물 여과에 있어 세계적인 선두업체인 플럭소퓨어가 설치하는 물 ¹⁵정화 시스템을 구입해 주셔서 감사합니다. 구입하신 제품인 피셰 II는 플럭소퓨어가 새롭게 설계한 전매특허 필터를 사용합니다. ¹⁶피셰 II의 2리터 물병은 식용 등급의 재활용 플라스틱으로 만들어졌습니다. 물병을 채우시려면 필터를 뚜껑에 돌려서 끼우시고 편리한 깔때기 모양의 주입구에 수돗물을 부은 후 물이 필터¹⁷를 통해 통과할 때까지 기다리세요. 그런 다음 ¹⁸맛을 해치는 일반 오염 물질이 없는 물을 마시거나 요리할 수 있습니다. 피셰 II를 처음 사용하시기 전에 삽화가 포함된 동봉된 안내 책자를 읽어 보세요.

어휘 innovative 혁신적인   filtration 여과   employ 이용하다   proprietary 전매특허의   jug 물병, 단지 screw 돌려서 조이다   lid 뚜껑   tap water 수돗물 funnel-shaped 깔때기 모양의   entry port 입구 contaminant 오염 물질   spoil 망치다   booklet 소책자

15 (C) 명사 자리_복합명사

해설 동명사 purchasing의 목적어 역할을 하는 명사 자리로, 빈칸 앞의 명사 water, 빈칸 뒤의 명사 system과 함께 쓰여 '물 정화 시스템'이라는 의미의 복합명사를 만들 수 있는 '정화'라는 뜻의 (C) purification이 정답이다.

어휘 purify 정화하다

16 (B) 문맥에 맞는 문장 고르기

번역 (A) 또한 피셰 II는 모든 홈 밸류 매장에서 찾을 수 있습니다.
(B) 피셰 II의 2리터 물병은 식용 등급의 재활용 플라스틱으로 만들어졌습니다.
(C) 피셰 II에 재활용 플라스틱을 사용하는 것은 환경에 도움이 됩니다.
(D) 피셰 II의 낮은 가격에 필적할 수 있는 회사는 없습니다.

해설 빈칸 앞에서 피셰 II는 새롭게 설계한 전매특허 필터(proprietary, redesigned filter)를 사용한다며 필터에 대해 홍보하고 있고, 빈칸 뒤에서 물병(the jug)과 필터(the filter)의 사용법을 안내하고 있으므로, 빈칸에는 물병에 대해 홍보하는 내용이 들어가면 자연스럽다. 따라서 식용등급의 재활용 플라스틱으로 만들었다며 물병에 쓰인 재료에 대해 언급하고 있는 (B)가 정답이다.

어휘 furthermore 또한, 게다가   food-grade 식용 등급의

17 (A) 전치사 어휘

해설 빈칸 뒤의 명사 the filter를 목적어로 취해 '물이 필터를 통해 통과한다'는 의미가 되어야 하므로 '~을 통해'를 뜻하는 (A) through가 정답이다. (B) toward는 '~을 향하여', (C) plus는 '~도 또한', (D) along은 '~을 따라'라는 의미이다.

18 (D) 명사 자리_동사의 목적어

해설 빈칸은 선행사 contaminants를 수식하는 관계사절(that 이하)의 동사 spoil의 목적어 자리이고, 빈칸 앞에 소유격 its가 있으므로 명사가 들어가야 한다. 따라서 '맛'을 뜻하는 명사 (D) flavor가 정답이다.

어휘 flavorful 맛있는   flavorless 맛이 없는

ETS 기출   고난도 실전문제   본책 p.78

1 (A)	2 (D)	3 (D)	4 (D)	5 (C)	6 (B)
7 (B)	8 (A)	9 (D)	10 (C)	11 (D)	12 (D)
13 (B)	14 (A)	5 (D)	16 (C)	17 (D)	18 (C)

1 (A) 동사 어형_태

번역 고객은 온라인 뱅킹 서비스를 통해 계좌를 관리하도록 권장된다.

해설 빈칸은 주어 Clients의 동사 자리이다. 동사 encourage(권장하다)는 일반적으로 「encourage+목적어+to부정사」의 5형식 구조로 쓰이는데, 빈칸 뒤에 목적어 없이 to부정사구가 바로 왔으므로 「be encouraged+to부정사」의 수동태 구조임을 알 수 있다. 따라서 (A) are encouraged가 정답이다.

2 (D) 명사 자리_복합명사

번역 가입자 계약을 늘리는 것이 내년 영업 팀의 최우선 과제이다.

해설 동사 is의 주어로 쓰인 동명사 Increasing의 목적어 역할을 하는 명사 자리로, 빈칸 앞의 명사 subscriber와 함께 쓰여 '구독자 계약'이라는 의미의 복합명사를 만드는 '계약, 약속'이라는 뜻의 (D) engagement가 정답이다.

어휘 subscriber 가입자, 구독자   priority 우선 사항 engage 관여하다   engaged 바쁜, 작업 중인

3 (D) 부사 어휘

번역 제품 개발 팀은 자사의 식물성 물병이 플라스틱 폐기물을 크게 줄일 수 있기를 희망한다.

해설 동사구 will reduce를 수식하여 '폐기물을 크게 줄인다'는 내용이 되어야 자연스러우므로, '크게, 상당히'라는 뜻으로 증감 동사와 어울리는 부사 (D) significantly가 정답이다. (B) fairly는 '꽤, 상당히'라는 뜻이지만 형용사나 부사를 강조하는 부사이므로 동사를 수식하지 않는다.

어휘 plant-based 식물성의   waste 폐기물   seldom 거의 ~하지 않는

4　(D) 인칭대명사의 격_주격

번역 그 승합차는 기술자가 필요한 도구를 더 쉽게 찾을 수 있도록 개조되었다.

해설 빈칸과 동사 need는 선행사인 the tools를 부연 설명하는 관계사절로, 빈칸 앞에는 목적격 관계대명사 which 또는 that이 생략되어 있다. 따라서 빈칸은 동사 need의 주어 자리이며, the technicians를 대신하여 '그들(기술자들)이 필요로 하는 도구'라는 의미가 되어야 하므로 (D) they가 정답이다.

어휘 van 승합차, 밴　retrofit 장치를 개조하다 enable 가능하게 하다

5　(C) 접속사 자리_부사절 접속사

번역 윈저 아파트 단지 주민은 손님과 함께 있는 한 손님을 단지 내 수영장으로 데려올 수 있다.

해설 빈칸 앞뒤로 완전한 절이 있으므로 빈칸은 부사절 접속사 자리이다. 따라서 '~하는 한'이라는 의미의 부사절 접속사 (C) as long as가 정답이다. 명사절/부사절 접속사인 (D) whether는 부사절을 이끌 때 등위접속사 or와 함께 'whether A or B(A이든 B이든)'의 형태로 쓰이므로 빈칸에 적절하지 않다.

어휘 complex 단지　on-site 현장의　host (손님을 초대한) 주인　in view of ~을 고려하여

6　(B) 재귀대명사

번역 안젤로 씨는 자신이 휘플리 제조의 다음 분기 매출을 예측할 수 없다는 것을 알게 되었다.

해설 5형식 동사 found의 목적어 자리에 들어갈 대명사를 찾는 문제이다. 목적격 보어에 unable to predict ~ sales가 나왔으므로, 주어인 Ms. Angelo를 대신하여 '안젤로 씨는 자신이 다음 분기 매출을 예측할 수 없다는 것을 알게 되었다'는 내용이 되어야 한다. 따라서 재귀대명사 (B) herself가 정답이다.

어휘 predict 예측하다　manufacturing 제조업 quarter 분기

7　(B) 명사 자리_동사의 목적어

번역 티켓 소지자는 오후 5시에 시더 레인 경기장으로의 입장이 허용된다.

해설 4형식 동사 allow(~에게 …을 허용하다)는 간접목적어가 주어가 되는 수동태가 되면 뒤에 직접목적어가 남아 '~을 허용받다'라는 의미가 된다. 따라서 빈칸은 be allowed의 목적어 역할을 하는 명사 자리이며, '티켓 소지자는 입장을 허용받는다'는 의미가 되어야 자연스러우므로, '입장'이라는 뜻의 명사 (B) entry가 정답이다.

어휘 holder 소지자, 보유자

8　(A) 동사 어휘

번역 래드보드 테크놀로지스는 오랫동안 여러 분야의 엔지니어들에게 최고의 고용주였다.

해설 현재완료 시제 has 뒤에 과거분사 형태의 동사 어휘를 고르는 문제이다. 빈칸 뒤 명사구 a premier employer를 보어로 취해 '오랫동안 최고의 고용주였다'는 내용이 되어야 자연스러우므로 '~이다'를 뜻하는 be동사의 과거분사 (A) been이 정답이다.

어휘 premier 최고의　multiple 다수의　field 분야

9　(D) 부사 어휘

번역 새 백화점은 공사 지연으로 2월 15일 개장일을 연기해야 할 수도 있지만, 그 날짜에 문을 열 가능성이 높다.

해설 동사구 will open을 수식하여 '새 백화점은 2월 15일에 문을 열 가능성이 높다'는 의미가 되어야 적절하므로 '가능성이 있게, 잠재적으로'라는 뜻으로 미래 시제와 어울리는 부사 (D) potentially가 정답이다.

어휘 delay 지연　extend 연장하다

10　(C) 형용사 어휘

번역 이번 주 브라운스 커피하우스에서 대용량 커피를 구입하시고 어느 식품 품목이든 반값 할인을 받으세요.

해설 복합명사 food item을 수식하기에 적절한 형용사나 한정사를 고르는 문제이다. food item은 가산 단수명사로 앞에 관사나 소유격과 같은 한정사가 반드시 필요하므로, '어느, 어떤'을 뜻하는 한정사 (C) any가 정답이다. 참고로, (D) whole(전체의)은 앞에 the나 소유격을 동반해야 한다.

11　(D) 동사 어휘

번역 회의 참석자들은 체크인 구역에서 도시락이 배포될 예정이라고 알림을 받았다.

해설 빈칸에는 be동사와 함께 수동태를 이뤄 빈칸 뒤 that절과 연결되는 동사가 들어가야 한다. '도시락이 배포될 것이라는 알림을 받았다'는 내용이 되어야 하므로, '상기시키다, 알려 주다'라는 뜻으로 능동태는 「remind+목적어+that절」, 수동태는 「be reminded+that절」의 구조로 쓰이는 (D) reminded가 정답이다.

어휘 engage 고용하다; 관여하다　elect 선출하다

12　(D) 형용사 자리_명사 수식

번역 9월 30일까지 모든 로든 자동차 서비스 센터에서 무료 브레이크 점검을 제공합니다.

해설 빈칸은 brake inspections(브레이크 점검)를 수식하는 형용사 자리이다. '무료 점검'이라는 내용이 되어야 자연스러우므로 '무료의'라는 뜻의 형용사 (D) complimentary가 정답이다. 참고로 과거분사인 (B) complimented(칭찬받는)와 현재분사인 (C) complimenting(~을 칭찬하는)도 명사를 수식할 수는 있지만 문맥상 적절하지 않다.

어휘 inspection 점검　compliment 칭찬; 칭찬하다

13　(B) 전치사 자리

번역 레이크우드 몰 지점은 페니 풋웨어의 가장 분주한 매장임에도 불구하고 이번 분기에 매출 감소를 보고했다.

해설 빈칸 뒤의 동명사 being을 목적어로 취해 '페니 풋웨어의 가장 분주한 매장임에도 불구하고'라는 의미가 되어야 하므로 '~에도 불구하고'라는 뜻의 전치사 (B) Despite가 정답이다. 부사절 접속사인 (A) Unless(~이 아닌 한)는 분사구문을 이끌 수 있으나 문맥상 적합하지 않고, (C) Otherwise(그렇지 않으면)은 접속부사, (D) Yet은 부사(아직)/등위접속사(그렇지만)이다.

14 (A) 동사_시제 일치의 예외

번역 영업시간 이후에 도움이 필요하신 고객께서는 비상 번호로 메시지를 남기시기를 권고 드립니다.

해설 가주어 It으로 시작하는 문장의 진주어 역할을 하는 that절에 동사가 필요하므로 빈칸은 동사 자리이다. 요청 및 권고(be advised) 동사 뒤에 오는 that절에는 「(should)+동사원형」을 써야 하므로 동사원형 (A) leave가 정답이다.

어휘 advise 권고하다   emergency 비상

[15-18] 이메일

수신: GT 잉크 고객 서비스
발신: 조제트 심슨
날짜: 5월 14일
제목: OS-1147 계정

좋은 아침입니다.

6월 1일부로 저의 잉크 배송 요금제를 업그레이드하고자 합니다. 저의 월별 잉크 주문을 검토하고 나서 **15전에** 생각했던 것보다 더 많은 잉크를 사용하는 것을 알게 되었습니다. 표준 요금제에서 매월 350쪽까지 인쇄하기에 충분한 잉크가 포함된 **16프리미엄** 요금제로 제 계정을 변경해 주세요. 각 배송마다 대용량 검은색 잉크와 표준 컬러 잉크 카트리지가 필요합니다. **17제가 이해하기로는, 월 비용이 20달러 증가할 것입니다. 18이를** 그에 맞춰 제 계정에 청구하는 데에 대한 저의 승인이라고 여기시면 됩니다.

감사합니다.

조제트 심슨

어휘 plan 요금제   as of ~부로   high-capacity 대용량의
authorization 승인   accordingly 그에 맞춰

15 (D) 부사 어휘

해설 빈칸은 동사 thought을 수식하는 부사 자리로, 문맥상 검토 결과 '전에 생각했던 것보다' 더 많은 잉크를 사용하고 있었다는 내용이 되어야 자연스럽다. 따라서 '이전에'라는 뜻으로 과거 시제와 어울리는 부사 (D) previously가 정답이다. (A) eventually는 '결국', (B) separately는 '별도로', (C) suddenly는 '갑자기'라는 의미이다.

16 (C) 형용사 어휘

해설 표준 요금제(the standard plan)보다 더 높은 사양의 요금제를 나타낼 수 있는 형용사가 들어가야 한다. 따라서 '고급의'라는 뜻의 (C) premium이 정답이다.

어휘 limited 제한된   functional 실용적인. 기능 위주인

17 (D) 문맥에 맞는 문장 고르기

번역 (A) 잉크젯 프린터는 이월 주문 중이며 곧 도착할 것입니다.
(B) 적시에 제 전화에 답신해 주셔서 감사합니다.
(C) 또한, 즉시 귀하의 서비스에 대한 저의 구독을 중단해 주세요.
(D) 제가 이해하기로는, 월 비용이 20달러 증가할 것입니다.

해설 빈칸 앞에서 표준 요금제에서 프리미엄 요금제로 변경해 달라(change my account from the standard plan to the premium one)고 했고, 빈칸 뒤 문장에서는 이를 그에 맞춰 자신의 계정에 청구하는 데에 대한 승인으로 간주하라(You may consider ~ my account accordingly)고 했다. 따라서 빈칸에는 월간 비용이 20달러 오를 것으로 이해한다며 고급 요금제로 변경함에 따라 청구될 금액의 인상분에 대해 확인하고 있는 (D)가 정답이다.

어휘 back order (재고가 없어) 처리 못하는 주문. 이월 주문
in a timely manner 적시에   discontinue 중단하다
effective 시행되는   immediately 즉시

18 (C) 지시대명사_this

해설 빈칸은 5형식 동사 consider의 목적어 자리이므로, 빈칸 뒤에 오는 목적격 보어 my authorization to bill my account accordingly와 동격을 이뤄야 한다. 앞에서 프리미엄 요금제로 변경해 달라고 했고, 월 비용이 20달러 더 증가할 것으로 알고 있다고 했으므로 이 내용 전체를 '이를'로 대신 받아 '이를 제 계정에 청구하는 데에 대한 저의 승인으로 간주하면 된다'는 내용이 되어야 적절하므로 이미 언급한 내용을 가리키는 지시대명사 (C) this(이것)가 정답이다.

PART 5&6   Reading Comprehension

UNIT 6 문법 고난도 유형

01 to부정사/동명사, 분사와 분사구문

ETS 기출 유형연습   본책 p.83

1 (B)   2 (B)   3 (C)

1 (B) to부정사_부사적 용법

번역 매직 클리어 스프레이는 유리 표면의 줄무늬 자국을 방지하기 위해 특별히 만들어졌다.

해설 빈칸 앞에 완전한 절(Magic ~ formulated)이 있고 빈칸 뒤에 명사가 있으므로, 빈칸에는 뒤에 나온 명사 streaks를 목적어로 취하면서 앞에 나온 완전한 절을 수식할 수 있는 준동사가 들어가야 한다. 문맥상 '줄무늬 자국을 방지하기 위해'

라는 내용이 적절하므로 '~하기 위해서'라는 목적의 의미를 지니는 to부정사구 (B) to prevent가 정답이다.

어휘 formulate 만들어 내다   streak 줄무늬 자국

2 **(B) 분사형 형용사_명사 수식**

번역 새로운 회계 소프트웨어는 맞춤형 재무 보고서를 더 쉽게 작성할 수 있도록 해 준다.

해설 빈칸은 to generate의 목적어 역할을 하는 명사구 financial reports를 수식하는 자리이고, '맞춤형의 재무 보고서'라는 의미가 되어야 하므로 '맞춤형의'를 뜻하는 분사형 형용사 (B) customized가 정답이다.

어휘 generate 생성하다   customs 세관
customize 주문 제작하다

3 **(C) 분사구문_현재분사**

번역 철거 팀원들은 노후한 건물에 들어갈 때 주의해야 한다.

해설 부사절 접속사 when 뒤에는 주어와 동사를 갖춘 완전한 절이 뒤따라야 하는데, 빈칸과 명사구 the deteriorated building만 나와 있다. 따라서 빈칸은 when 부사절이 축약된 분사구문의 분사 자리이며, 빈칸 뒤 목적어 the deteriorated building이 있으므로 능동의 형태인 현재분사 (C) entering이 정답이다.

어휘 demolition 철거   cautious 주의하는   deteriorated 노후한   entrance 입구

02 명사절과 관계사절

1 (B)   **2** (B)   **3** (A)

1 **(B) 명사절 접속사_의문형용사**

번역 홍 씨는 한산한 시간에 어느 버스 노선이 운행되는지 알아야 한다.

해설 빈칸은 to know의 목적어 역할을 하는 명사절을 이끄는 접속사 자리이다. 또한 뒤에 온 복합명사 bus routes를 수식하여 '어느 버스 노선'이라는 의미가 되어야 하므로 '어느, 어떤'이라는 뜻으로 명사와 결합하여 명사절을 이끄는 의문형용사 (B) which가 정답이다. (D) until은 부사절 접속사로 목적어 역할을 하는 명사절을 이끌 수 없다.

어휘 run 운행하다   off-peak 한산한, 비수기의

2 **(B) 복합관계대명사**

번역 장 박사를 대신하는 사람은 누구든 일주일에 한번은 저녁에 환자 진료를 볼 수 있어야 한다.

해설 문장의 동사가 replaces와 must be 두 개 있으므로, 빈칸은 접속사 자리이다. 빈칸 뒤 replaces Dr. Chang을 이끌어 must be의 주어 역할을 하는 명사절의 접속사가 필요한데, '장 박사를 대신하는 사람은 누구든'이라는 의미가 되어

야 하므로 복합관계대명사 (B) Whoever가 정답이다. (A) Whose(누구의) 또한 명사절을 이끌 수 있지만 뒤에 명사를 동반하는 의문형용사이므로 빈칸에는 적절하지 않다.

어휘 replace 대신하다   available 시간이 있는

3 **(A) 관계대명사_주격**

번역 고객에게 공개하기 전에 오해의 소지가 있는 용어가 있는지 계약서를 꼼꼼히 읽어야 한다.

해설 빈칸 이하(might be misleading)는 선행사 language를 수식하는 관계절로, 빈칸 뒤에 동사 might be가 있으므로 주격 관계대명사인 (A) that이 정답이다. (B) in that은 '~이라는 점에서'라는 뜻의 부사절 접속사, (C) what은 명사절 접속사로 선행사를 수식하지 않으며, 소유격 관계대명사인 (D) whose는 주격 자리에 올 수 없다.

어휘 release 공개하다   language 용어, 표현   misleading 오해의 소지가 있는

03 비교/도치 구문, 병렬 구조

1 (C)   **2** (B)   **3** (D)

1 **(C) 형용사의 비교급**

번역 그로 씨의 동료들은 그보다 더 이상을 받을 만한 사람은 없다고 말했다.

해설 빈칸 앞뒤에 be동사 is와 전치사 of가 있으므로 빈칸은 보어 역할을 하는 명사나 형용사 자리이다. 뒤에 비교급과 함께 쓰는 than(~보다)이 나왔으므로 형용사의 비교급인 (C) worthier가 정답이다

어휘 colleague 동료   be worthy of ~을 받을 만하다

2 **(B) 병렬 구조**

번역 저명한 문학잡지인 〈라구나 리뷰〉는 기성 작가와 신진 작가를 모두 자랑스럽게 다룬다.

해설 상관접속사 both A and B로 연결된 형용사 established와 함께 병렬 구조를 이루어 명사 writers를 수식하는 형용사를 고르는 문제이다. '기성 작가와 신진 작가 둘 다'라는 의미가 되어야 하므로 '떠오르는, 신생의'를 뜻하는 분사형 형용사 (B) emerging이 정답이다.

어휘 respected 높이 평가되는   literary 문학의
established 기성의, 저명한   emerge 부상하다, 알려지다

3 **(D) 부정어 도치**

번역 기기 사용 설명서 어디에도 깜박이는 주황색 불빛에 대한 정보가 없다.

해설 문장 중간에 '~이 있다'라는 의미의 「there be동사 + 명사」 구문이 is there information으로 도치되어 있고, '어디에도 정보가 없다'는 내용이 되어야 자연스러우므로, 문장 맨 앞

에 오면 주어와 동사가 도치되는 부정부사 (D) Nowhere(어디에도 없다)가 정답이다.

어휘 appliance 가전제품 blinking 깜박거리는

ETS 기출 실전문제

본책 p.88

1 (C)	**2** (B)	**3** (A)	**4** (C)	**5** (C)	**6** (D)
7 (B)	**8** (A)	**9** (D)	**10** (D)	**11** (A)	**12** (B)
13 (D)	**14** (B)	**15** (B)	**16** (C)	**17** (A)	**18** (A)

1 **(C) 동명사 자리**

번역 한국 작가 배경진은 선명한 색감의 유화를 통해 색과 빛을 감상하는 새로운 방법을 제시한다.

해설 앞에 전치사 of, 뒤에 명사구 color and light가 있으므로 빈칸에는 명사구를 수식하는 형용사나 전치사의 목적어 역할을 하면서 명사구를 목적어로 취하는 동명사가 들어갈 수 있다. 문맥상 '색과 빛을 감상하는 새로운 방법'이 되어야 자연스러우므로 '감상하다'를 뜻하는 동사 appreciate의 동명사 (C) appreciating이 정답이다.

어휘 vivid 색이 선명한 oil painting 유화 appreciative 감사하는 appreciation 감상, 감사

2 **(B) to부정사_명사적 용법**

번역 시의회는 최근 태양 전지판을 설치하고자 하는 업체들이 따라야 할 일련의 지침을 승인했다.

해설 관계사 that절의 주어 businesses를 수식하는 현재분사 wishing의 목적어 자리이다. wish는 to부정사를 목적어로 취해 '~하기를 바라다'라는 의미를 나타내므로 to부정사 (B) to install이 정답이다.

어휘 city council 시의회 guidelines 지침 solar panel 태양 전지판

3 **(A) 명령문의 동사원형_병렬 구조**

번역 패치빌 수영 클럽의 연간 회원권을 구매하고 일 년 내내 실내 수영장을 즐기세요.

해설 빈칸 앞 등위접속사 and가 앞에 있는 명령문(Purchase ~ Club)과 뒤에 오는 다른 명령문을 병렬로 연결하는 구조로, 빈칸에는 앞의 명령문의 동사원형 Purchase에 맞춰 동사원형이 들어가야 하므로 (A) enjoy가 정답이다.

어휘 year-round 일 년 내내

4 **(C) 부사 자리_비교급 강조**

번역 출판사에 따르면, 업데이트된 대수학 교재를 통해 해당 과목을 훨씬 더 쉽게 이해할 수 있다.

해설 빈칸은 makes의 목적격 보어 역할을 하는 비교급 형용사 easier를 강조하는 부사 자리이다. 따라서 '훨씬 더'라는 의미로 비교급을 강조하는 부사 (C) much가 정답이다. (A) any는 부정문이나 의문문에서 비교급 강조를 할 수 있지만 긍정문에서는 쓰이질 않고, (B) further는 far의 비교급이다.

어휘 algebra 대수(학) subject 과목, 주제

5 **(C) 분사구문**

번역 관리자는 업무를 배정할 때 회사의 요구 사항과 직원의 이익 사이에서 균형을 잡아야 한다.

해설 부사절 접속사 When 뒤에 주어가 보이지 않으므로 부사절이 축약된 구조인 분사구문이 와야 한다. 빈칸 뒤의 명사구 work tasks를 목적어로 취해 '업무를 할당할 때'라는 의미가 되어야 하므로 현재분사 (C) assigning이 정답이다.

어휘 interest 이익, 관심 assign 배정[할당]하다

6 **(D) 접속사 자리_부사절 접속사**

번역 클리어 숏 디지털 카메라는 기본 설정으로 자동 초점이 켜지는 반면, 대부분의 다른 브랜드는 사용자가 메뉴를 열도록 합니다.

해설 빈칸 앞뒤 모두 주어와 동사를 갖춘 완전한 절이 있으므로, 빈칸은 부사절 접속사 자리이다. 따라서 '반면'이라는 뜻의 부사절 접속사 (D) whereas가 정답이다. (B) whatever는 복합관계대명사로 부사절을 이끌 수는 있지만 뒤에 불완전한 절이 온다.

어휘 autofocus 자동 초점 default 기본 설정값

7 **(B) to부정사_형용사적 용법**

번역 린더 컴퍼니는 마케팅 팀에 합류할 그래픽 디자이너를 찾고 있습니다.

해설 빈칸은 앞에 나온 a graphic designer를 수식하는 동시에 뒤의 its marketing team을 목적어로 취하는 형용사 용법의 준동사 자리이다. 문맥상 '마케팅 팀에 합류할 그래픽 디자이너'라는 내용이 되어야 하므로 미래의 의미를 지닌 to부정사 (B) to join이 정답이다. 참고로 (A) joining은 현재분사로 명사를 수식할 수는 있으나, 진행의 의미를 지니고 있어 앞으로 일할 직원을 찾는다는 구인 광고에는 적합하지 않다.

8 **(A) 형용사의 비교급**

번역 웨슬리 세탁기는 다른 브랜드보다 적은 물을 사용하여 옷을 세탁한다.

해설 명사 water를 수식하기에 적절한 형용사 어휘를 고르는 문제이다. 뒤에 than이 온 것으로 보아 비교급 형용사가 들어가야 하며, '다른 브랜드보다 적은 물을 사용하여'라는 의미가 되어야 적절하므로 '더 적은'을 뜻하는 (A) less가 정답이다.

9 **(D) 관계대명사_주격**

번역 지난달에 합류한 펄로프 씨를 제외한 시범 사업 팀원들은 모두 6월에 영입되었다.

해설 빈칸 이하(joined us last month)는 선행사 Ms. Perloff를 수식하는 관계사절로, 빈칸 뒤에 동사 joined가 나오므로 주격 관계대명사인 (D) who가 정답이다. (A) personally는 부사, (B) herself는 재귀대명사, (C) alone은 형용사/부사이므로 품사상 답이 될 수 없다.

어휘 besides ~외에 pilot project 시범 사업

10 (D) 과거분사_명사 수식

번역 겟짓 프린팅 사는 회사의 글로벌 사업 전반에 걸쳐 재활용된 자재를 활용한다.

해설 빈칸은 동사 utilizes의 목적어 역할을 하는 명사 materials를 수식하는 형용사 자리이다. 따라서 '재활용된'이라는 뜻의 과거분사 (D) recycled가 정답이다.

어휘 utilize 활용하다 operation 사업, 운영

11 (A) 명사절 접속사_복합관계대명사

번역 리더십 팀은 장기근속 보너스 제공을 포함하여 직원 유지에 필요한 것은 무엇이든 할 것이다.

해설 빈칸 뒤 동사 is needed의 주어 역할을 하면서 동시에 빈칸 이하의 절(is needed to retain employees)을 본동사 will do의 목적어가 될 수 있도록 명사절로 만들어 주는 접속사가 필요하다. '직원 유지에 필요한 것은 무엇이든'이라는 의미가 되어야 하므로 '~한 것은 무엇이든'을 뜻하는 복합관계대명사 (A) whatever가 정답이다.

어휘 retain 유지[보유]하다 long-term 장기적인

12 (B) to부정사_부사적 용법

번역 스피디 배송 서비스에서 운전기사로 등록하고 직불카드 계좌로 매일 수입을 입금 받으세요.

해설 빈칸은 명령문의 동사 Sign up을 수식하는 부사적 용법의 준동사 자리이다. 문맥상 '운전하기 위해 등록하라', 즉 '운전기사로 등록하고 수입을 입금 받아라'는 내용이 되어야 적절하므로 to부정사인 (B) to drive가 정답이다. (D) to be driven은 to부정사이지만 문맥상 수동의 의미가 적절하지 않아 답이 될 수 없다. 참고로 drive(운전하다)는 자동사, 타동사 둘 다 가능하다.

어휘 sign up 등록하다 earnings 수입 deposit 입금 debit card 직불 카드

13 (D) 명사절 접속사_whether

번역 지노 씨의 은퇴 파티 계획을 도울 수 있는지 인사부의 카미다 씨에게 알려 주세요.

해설 빈칸에는 know의 목적어 역할을 하는 명사절을 이끄는 접속사가 필요하다. 빈칸 뒤에 완전한 절이 있고 '파티 계획을 도울 수 있는지'라는 내용이 되어야 자연스러우므로 '~인지 (아닌지)'를 뜻하는 명사절 접속사 (D) whether가 정답이다. 명사절 접속사인 (B) what은 불완전한 문장이 뒤따르고, (C) whose는 뒤에 명사가 와야 한다.

14 (B) 분사구문_현재분사

번역 시바리 홈 퍼니싱즈는 최근 지점 두 곳을 새로 열었는데, 이는 도시의 위축된 소매 부문에서 이례적인 일이 되었다.

해설 앞에 완전한 절과 콤마가 있고 빈칸 뒤의 구문을 연결해 앞 절을 수식하는 자리이므로, 빈칸은 분사구문을 이끄는 분사 자리이다. 또한 빈칸 뒤에 목적어가 있고, 문맥상 '이(it)를 이례적인 일로 만들었다'는 내용이 되어야 하므로 능동을 나타내는 현재분사 (B) making이 정답이다.

어휘 furnishings 가재도구 exception 예외 shrinking 줄어드는 retail 소매 sector 부문

[15-18] 블로그 게시물

> 간식으로 만들 수 있는 것은 감자뿐만이 아니다. 많은 채소와 콩류가 쉽게 바삭바삭한 **15** 간식으로 바뀐다. 예를 들어, 병아리콩은 양념한 뒤 베이킹 시트에 한 층으로 올려 바삭해질 때까지 구워서 건조할 수 있다. **16** 그렇게 구워진 공 모양의 바삭한 병아리콩들은 단백질과 섬유질로 가득하다. 가지 또한 좋은 선택이다. **17** 얇게 썰어 살짝 육포 같은 맛이 나는 것으로 구울 수 있다. 케일 잎은 기름과 양념을 넣고 **18** 섞어 20분간 구우면 감자칩과 비슷한 질감이 만들어진다.

어휘 treat 간식 legume 콩과 식물 transform 변형시키다 crispy 바삭한 chickpea 병아리콩 season 양념하다 roast 굽다 layer 층 eggplant 가지 beef jerky 육포 seasoning 양념 texture 질감 akin to ~와 유사한

15 (B) 명사 어휘

해설 앞 문장에서 간식으로 만들 수 있는 것은 감자뿐이 아니(It's not just potatoes ~ into treats)라고 했으므로, 뒤 문장에서는 '많은 채소와 콩류도 쉽게 간식으로 바뀐다'는 의미가 되어야 자연스럽다. 따라서 '간식'을 의미하는 (B) snacks가 정답이다. (A)의 meal은 '식사', (C)의 bar는 '초콜렛 바', (D)의 dip은 '소스'를 뜻한다.

16 (C) 문맥에 맞는 문장 고르기

번역 (A) 메인 코스를 위한 수많은 조리법을 온라인에서 찾을 수 있다.
(B) 집에서 요리할 때 칼로리 섭취량을 조절하기가 더 쉽다.
(C) 그렇게 구워진 공 모양의 바삭한 병아리콩들은 단백질과 섬유질로 가득하다.
(D) 최신 오븐 모델에는 베이킹, 컨벡션 오븐 및 에어프라이 설정이 포함되어 있다.

해설 앞에서 간식으로 만들 수 있는 재료에 대해 언급하며 병아리콩을 간식으로 만드는 조리법을 예로 들고 있고, 빈칸 뒤에는 가지라는 새로운 재료에 대해 언급하고 있다. 따라서 빈칸에는 병아리콩으로 만든 간식에 대한 부연 설명이 들어가야 적절하므로, 병아리콩을 간식으로 조리한 결과물은 단백질과 섬유질로 가득하다고 언급하고 있는 (C)가 정답이다.

어휘 countless 무수한 intake 섭취(량) resulting 결과로 초래된 batch (빵, 콩) 한 번 굽는 분량 crunchy 바삭한 packed with ~이 가득 찬

17 (A) 부사 자리_동사 수식

해설 빈칸은 수동태 동사구 be와 sliced 사이에서 동사를 수식하는 부사 자리이므로, '얇게'라는 의미의 부사 (A) thinly가 정답이다.

18 (A) 분사구문_과거분사

해설 부사절 접속사 When 뒤에 주어와 동사가 보이지 않으므로 부사절이 축약된 구조인 분사구문이 와야 한다. 빈칸 뒤에 목

적어가 보이지 않고, 등위접속사 and 뒤에 과거분사 baked
가 연결되어 있어 빈칸에도 동일하게 과거분사가 들어가 '기름
과 양념을 넣고 섞어 구우면'이라는 의미가 되어야 자연스럽
다. 따라서 (A) mixed가 정답이다.

ETS 기출 고난도 실전문제
본책 p.90

1 (C)	2 (B)	3 (C)	4 (C)	5 (A)	6 (A)
7 (A)	8 (C)	9 (B)	10 (D)	11 (B)	12 (C)
13 (B)	14 (C)	15 (A)	16 (D)	17 (B)	18 (C)

1 (C) to부정사_부사적 용법

번역 옆 사무실 회의에 방해되지 않도록 탁자를 가능한 한 조용히 옮겨주세요.

해설 빈칸 앞 so as는 to부정사와 함께 '~하기 위해'라는 의미로 쓰이는데 not이 있으므로 '~하지 않기 위해'라는 부정의 뜻이 된다. 빈칸 뒤 명사구 the meeting을 목적어로 취해 '회의를 방해하지 않기 위해'라는 의미가 되어야 자연스러우므로 to부정사인 (C) to disrupt가 정답이다.

2 (B) 부사 어휘_원급 비교 강조

번역 한 씨는 구형 냉장고 수리가 거의 신형 냉장고 구입 비용만큼 든다는 것을 알고 놀랐다.

해설 빈칸은 be동사 is의 보어 역할을 하는 형용사의 원급 비교 as expensive as를 강조하는 부사 자리로, '거의 새 냉장고 구입 비용만큼 비싸다'라는 의미가 되어야 자연스러우므로, 원급 비교 구문을 강조하는 '거의'라는 의미의 부사 (B) nearly가 정답이다. (A) mutually(서로), (C) closely(면밀히)는 문맥과 맞지 않고, (D) substantially(상당히)는 비교급을 수식하므로 빈칸에 들어갈 수 없다.

3 (C) 현재분사_명사 수식

번역 매장의 전화는 연례 세일에 대한 정보를 요청하는 고객들로 하루 종일 울리고 있다.

해설 빈칸은 명사 customers를 뒤에서 수식하면서 동시에 information을 목적어로 취하는 준동사 자리이다. 문맥상 '정보를 요청하는 고객들'이라는 내용이 되어야 자연스러우므로, '~한, ~하고 있는'이라는 의미로 명사를 수식하는 현재분사 (C) requesting이 정답이다. to부정사인 (A) to request도 명사를 수식할 수 있지만, '~할, ~하기 위한'이라는 미래의 의미를 나타내므로 문맥상 적합하지 않다.

4 (C) 관계대명사_소유격

번역 스털링 뮤직은 작년 수익이 3천만 파운드를 넘어선 여섯 개의 음반사 중의 하나가 된 것을 영광으로 생각합니다.

해설 빈칸 이하는 선행사 the half-dozen record labels를 수식하는 관계사절로, 선행사와 빈칸 뒤에 오는 명사 revenues(수익)가 '여섯 개 음반사의 수익'이라는 소유격 의미로 연결되어야 자연스러우므로 소유격 관계대명사 (C)

whose가 정답이다. (A) which는 주격/목적격 관계대명사로 뒤에 불완전한 절이 와야 하고, (B) in which는 뒤에 완전한 절이 올 수는 있지만 '여섯 개 음반사에서'라는 의미가 되므로 문맥상 적합하지 않다.

어휘 half-dozen 여섯 개(의) surpass 뛰어넘다

5 (A) 동명사_동사의 목적어

번역 이 회사의 금융 위원회는 올해 잠재적으로 위험한 투자를 하는 것에 강력히 반대한다.

해설 빈칸은 동사 opposes(반대하다)의 목적어 자리로, 뒤에 오는 any potential risky investments를 목적어로 취하는 준동사가 필요하다. 동사 oppose는 동명사를 목적어로 취하는 동사이므로 (A) making이 정답이다.

어휘 committee 위원회 potential 잠재적인 risky 위험한

6 (A) 동사 어휘_5형식 동사

번역 공장의 새로운 자동화 시스템으로 회사는 더 짧은 시간에 더 많은 의류를 생산할 수 있게 된다.

해설 목적어(the company) 뒤의 목적격 보어 자리에 to부정사 (to produce more ~ less time)가 왔고, '자동화 시스템은 회사가 더 많은 의류를 생산할 수 있게 해 준다'는 의미가 되어야 하므로 「동사+목적어+to부정사」라는 5형식 구조로 쓰여 '~을 가능하게 하다'를 뜻하는 (A) enables가 정답이다. 참고로, (D) ensures(보장하다)는 주로 that절을 목적어로 취하므로 5형식 구문에는 적절하지 않다.

어휘 automated 자동화된 garment 의류

7 (A) 원형부정사

번역 주택 담보 대출 금리가 5년 만에 최저치에 도달했으며, 이는 주택 매매의 급격한 상승을 설명하는 데 도움이 된다.

해설 빈칸은 관계사절의 동사 helps의 목적어 자리로, 뒤에 오는 the sharp rise를 목적어로 취하는 준동사가 필요하다. help는 to부정사나 원형부정사를 목적어로 취하므로 원형부정사 (A) explain이 정답이다.

어휘 mortgage 주택 담보 대출 hit a low 최저치에 도달하다 sharp 급격한 rise 상승

8 (C) 관계대명사_수량 표현 of+목적격 관계대명사

번역 요리사 아미나 디알로의 요리책에는 세네갈 요리를 위한 조리법이 있는데, 그 요리 대부분은 조리가 간단하다.

해설 빈칸을 포함한 콤마 이후의 절은 주절에 있는 선행사 Senegalese dishes를 수식하는 관계사절로, 사물 선행사 Senegalese dishes를 받는 관계대명사 which가 필요하다. 또한 빈칸 앞 수량 대명사 most를 단서로 선행사의 부분 수량을 나타내는 「수량대명사+of which/whom」의 구조를 떠올려 볼 수 있는데, most of which가 쓰이면 '요리책에는 세네갈 요리를 위한 조리법이 있는데, 그 세네갈 요리의 대부분이 조리가 쉽다'는 내용이 되어 문맥이 자연스럽다. 따라서 (C) of which가 정답이다.

9 (B) 현재분사_명사 수식

번역 몬세라트 역사학회 관리 이사회가 새 예산을 승인했다.

해설 정관사 The와 명사 board 사이에 빈칸이 있으므로 형용사 자리이다. '관리 이사회'라는 의미가 되어야 하므로 '관리[운영]하는'을 뜻하는 현재분사형 형용사 (B) governing이 정답이다. (A) governed는 수동 의미를 지닌 과거분사로 board(이사회)는 관리의 대상이 아니므로 답이 될 수 없다.

10 (D) 형용사 자리_분사구문

번역 새로운 디자인의 FZ-550 오토바이는 이전 모델과 다르게, 더욱 강력하지만 무게는 더 가볍다.

해설 빈칸은 전치사구 from previous models와 함께 콤마 뒤 절을 수식하는 분사구문을 이끄는 자리로, 「부사절 접속사 + 주어 + be동사」가 생략된 형태이다. 따라서 빈칸에는 보어가 되는 명사 (C) Difference(차이점)나 형용사 (D) Different(다른)가 들어갈 수 있는데, 문맥상 '새 오토바이는 이전 모델과 다르다'는 내용이 되어야 자연스러우므로 형용사 (D) Different가 정답이다.

11 (B) 동사 자리_가정법 도치

번역 구매에 만족하지 못하실 경우 원래 포장에 제품을 넣어 14일 이내에 저희에게 반품해 주세요.

해설 Should로 문장이 시작된 것으로 보아 가정법 미래의 도치 구문임을 알 수 있다. 따라서 「Should + 주어 + 동사원형」의 형태가 되어야 하고, 빈칸 뒤 '만족되지 않은'을 뜻하는 형용사 unsatisfied가 있으므로 (B) be가 정답이다.

12 (C) 명사절 접속사_that

번역 시공업체는 로비의 깨진 타일을 교체하는 데 3시간이 걸릴 것으로 추정했다.

해설 빈칸에는 동사 estimated의 목적어 역할을 하는 명사절을 이끄는 접속사가 필요한데, 빈칸 뒤에 완전한 절이 있고 문맥상 '타일 교체에 3시간이 걸릴 것'이라는 내용이 되어야 자연스러우므로 명사절 접속사 (C) that이 정답이다. (B) in which는 앞에 선행사가 필요한 관계사이며, (D) what은 명사절 접속사이지만 뒤에 불완전한 절이 온다.

어휘 contractor 시공업체 estimate 추정하다

13 (B) 접속사 자리/어휘_분사구문

번역 세입자의 문에 열쇠 없는 도어 록을 설치한 이후 집주인은 잠금장치 수리 및 교체 비용을 최소 500달러 절약했다.

해설 빈칸 이하 콤마 전(installing ~ doors)까지는 콤마 뒤 완전한 절을 수식하는 구문으로, 빈칸에는 동명사를 목적어로 취하는 전치사나 분사구문을 이끄는 부사절 접속사가 들어갈 수 있다. 문장의 동사가 현재완료 시제인 has saved이므로, '~한 이후로'라는 뜻으로 현재완료와 어울려 분사구문을 이끄는 부사절 접속사 (B) Since가 정답이다. (A) Once는 부사절 접속사(일단 ~하면)/부사(한 번)로 부사절이 축약된 구조에서 쓰일 수는 있지만 현재완료 시제와 어울리지 않는다.

어휘 keyless 열쇠가 없는 entry pad 도어 록 tenant 세입자 landlord 집주인 lock 잠금장치

14 (C) 명사절 접속사_복합관계대명사

번역 두 번째로 높은 득표수를 획득한 사람이 누구든 우표 클럽의 부회장으로 임명될 것이다.

해설 will be named의 주어 역할을 하는 동시에 빈칸 이하의 receives ~ votes를 문장의 주어가 될 수 있도록 만들어 주는 명사절 접속사가 필요하다. 문맥상 '두 번째로 높은 득표수를 받은 사람이 누구든'이라는 내용이 되어야 하므로 '~한 사람은 누구든지'를 의미하는 복합관계대명사 (C) Whoever가 정답이다.

어휘 vote 표 name 임명하다 vice president 부회장

[15-18] 기사

고베 (5월 18일)—테이스티 스무디는 이곳 고베의 선별된 몇몇 지점에서 자동화된 스무디 키오스크를 테스트 중이다. 키오스크는 여섯 개의 스무디를 추가 맞춤 선택 사항과 함께 **15제공한다**. 음료가 터치스크린을 통해 선택되고 나면 기계에서 주문을 준비한다. 직원이 상주할 필요가 없다. 하지만 직원 한 팀이 각 키오스크의 재료 사용을 **16원격으로** 확인하고 필요에 따라 기계를 다시 채우도록 재고 관리자가 파견된다.

17지금까지 회사에서는 긍정적인 고객 피드백만을 보고해 왔다. 만약 테스트 기계의 인기가 지속될 경우, 테이스티 스무디는 전국에 더 많은 키오스크를 설치할 예정이다. 이로 인해 회사에서는 전통적인 스무디 가게를 열 공간이 없는 **18장소에서** 제품을 판매할 수 있게 될 것이다.

어휘 automated 자동화된 select 선별된 customized 맞춤형의 via ~을 통해 present (자리에) 있는 ingredient 재료 stocker 재고 관리자 dispatch 파견하다 nationwide 전국적으로

15 (A) 동사 어형_시제

해설 첫 문장에서 테이스티 스무디라는 업체가 자동화된 스무디 키오스크를 테스트 중(Tasty Smoothie is testing automated smoothie kiosks)이라며 첫 문단 전반에 걸쳐 이 키오스크에 대해 현재 시제를 사용하여 설명하고 있다. 빈칸이 있는 문장 역시 키오스크에서 제공하는 스무디 메뉴 옵션에 대해 설명하는 문장이므로 현재 시제가 쓰여야 자연스럽다. 따라서 (A) provide가 정답이다.

16 (D) 부사 어휘

해설 앞 문장에서 직원이 상주해 있을 필요가 없다(No workers need to be present)고 했으므로, 직원이 키오스크의 재료 사용을 현장이 아닌 곳에서 확인한다는 의미가 되어야 한다. 따라서 '멀리서, 원격으로'라는 뜻의 (D) remotely가 정답이다. (A) conditionally는 '조건부로', (B) abruptly는 '갑자기', (C) distinctly는 '분명히'라는 의미이다.

17 (B) 문맥에 맞는 문장 고르기

번역 (A) 테이스티 스무디는 키오스크를 유지 관리하기 위해 더 많은 직원을 고용할 것으로 예상한다.
(B) 지금까지 회사에서는 긍정적인 고객 피드백만을 보고해 왔다.
(C) 재료가 있는 한 고객의 선택은 영향을 받지 않을 것이다.
(D) 다행히 키오스크는 대학 캠퍼스에 위치해 있다.

해설 앞에서 테이스티 스무디가 일부 선별 지점에서 자동화 스무디 키오스크를 테스트 중(Tasty Smoothie is testing ~ in Kobe)이라고 했고, 뒤 문장에는 이 테스트 기계의 인기가 지속될 경우 취하게 될 조치에 대해 언급하고 있다. 따라서 뒤 문장의 '인기가 지속된다(continue to be popular)'라는 내용과 자연스럽게 연결되려면 테스트 중인 키오스크가 고객들 사이에서 긍정적인 평가를 받았다는 내용이 들어가야 적절하므로, 지금까지 긍정적인 고객 피드백만을 보고했다고 언급하고 있는 (B)가 정답이다.

어휘 maintain 유지 관리하다 to date 지금까지
affect 영향을 주다

18 (C) 관계부사

해설 빈칸은 완전한 절(there is no space for a traditional smoothie shop)을 이끌어 장소 명사인 places를 수식하는 역할을 한다. 따라서 관계부사 (C) where이 정답이다. (A) as와 (D) though는 부사절 접속사로 완전한 두 절을 연결할 수는 있으나 문맥상 적합하지 않고, (B) that은 주격/목적격 관계사로 뒤에 불완전한 절이 온다.

PART 5&6
Reading Comprehension

UNIT 7 어휘 Collocation

01 동사+명사, 동사+전치사

> **ETS 기출 유형연습** 본책 p.95
>
> **1** (A)   **2** (C)

1 (A)

번역 핀 건축 협회는 밴쿠버 광역 지역에 새 사무실을 위한 장소를 물색해 왔다.

해설 locations를 목적어로 취하는 타동사 자리로, '새 사무실을 위한 장소를 물색해 왔다'는 내용이 되어야 자연스러우므로 동사 scout(조사하다, 찾아다니다)의 현재분사형 (A) scouting이 정답이다. (B)의 look(보다)은 자동사로 목적어를 취할 수 없고, (C)의 watch(시청하다, 감시하다)는 움직이는 대상을 목적어로 취하므로 locations와 어울리지 않으며, (D)의 transmit은 '전송하다'라는 의미이다.

어휘 architectural 건축학의

2 (C)

번역 어제의 인터넷 문제는 구식 소프트웨어의 사용에서 기인했다.

해설 빈칸 뒤에 전치사 from이 있으므로 자동사가 필요하다. 문맥상 '문제가 구식 소프트웨어의 사용에서 기인했다'는 내용이 되어야 적절하므로 from과 함께 '~에서 기인하다'라는 의미를 나타내는 (C) originated가 정답이다.

어휘 outdated 구식의, 구 버전의   interpret 해석하다

02 명사+명사, 명사+전치사/전치사+명사

> **ETS 기출 유형연습** 본책 p.97
>
> **1** (D)   **2** (D)

1 (D)

번역 모든 서류 가방과 소포는 도착 즉시 프런트 데스크에서 스캔됩니다.

해설 빈칸은 완전한 절에 명사 arrival을 연결하는 전치사 자리이다. 문맥상 '가방과 소포는 도착 즉시 스캔된다'라는 의미가 되어야 하므로 '~ 즉시, ~할 때'를 뜻하는 시간 전치사 (D) upon이 정답이다.

2 (D)

번역 하리치 출판사의 인사 위원회는 다음 주부터 선임 편집자 직에 대한 지원자 면접을 시작할 예정이다.

해설 동사구 will begin의 주어 역할을 하는 명사 자리로, 앞의 명사 search와 함께 '인사 위원회'라는 복합명사를 만드는 '위원회'라는 의미의 (D) committee가 정답이다.

어휘 publishing 출판사 senior 선임의 editor 편집자
society 사회, 단체 process 과정, 절차

03 형용사+명사, 형용사+전치사

> **ETS 기출 유형연습** 본책 p.99
>
> **1** (B)   **2** (A)

1 (B)

번역 탑 트레이닝 앱은 다양한 피트니스 수업을 가르칠 수 있는 검증된 강사와 체육관을 연결해 준다.

해설 빈칸은 명사 instructors(강사)를 수식하는 형용사 자리이다. 문맥상 '다양한 수업을 가르칠 수 있는 검증된 강사'라는 의미가 되어야 자연스러우므로 '검증[공인]된, 자격증을 갖춘'이라는 뜻의 (B) certified가 정답이다.

어휘 identical 동일한 defensive 수비의 academic 학업의

2 (A)

번역 하튼 극장은 가족들을 대상으로 하는 일련의 프리쇼 워크숍을 시작했다.

해설 명사구 a series of preshow workshops를 뒤에서 수식하는 형용사 어휘를 고르는 문제이다. '가족을 대상으로 하는 워크숍'이라는 의미가 되어야 적절하므로 전치사 at과 함께 '~을 대상으로 하는'을 의미하는 (A) aimed가 정답이다. 참고로, (B) designed(설계된)는 전치사 at 보다는 for와 어울리므로 빈칸에 적절하지 않다.

어휘 a series of 일련의 preshow 프리쇼

04 부사+동사, 부사+형용사

ETS 기출 유형연습
본책 p.101

1 (B) **2** (D)

1 (B)

번역 무용 애호가들은 안무가 진 월의 신작 발레 〈미드나잇 문〉의 초연을 열렬히 기다리고 있다.

해설 동사구 are awaiting과 어울리는 부사를 고르는 문제이다. 공연을 기다리는 팬들에 관한 내용이므로 '열렬히 기다리고 있다'는 의미가 되어야 자연스러우므로 '열렬히'라는 뜻의 (B) enthusiastically가 정답이다.

어휘 patron 고객, 후원자 choreographer 안무가 deliberately 고의로 sympathetically 동정하여 courageously 용감하게

2 (D)

번역 〈마이너스 위클리〉에 실린 백 씨의 에세이는 독자들로부터 매우 비판적인 피드백을 받고 있다.

해설 형용사 critical과 어울리는 부사를 고르는 문제로, 문맥상 '매우 비판적인 피드백'이라는 의미가 되어야 적절하므로 '매우'라는 뜻의 (D) highly가 정답이다.

어휘 generate 발생시키다 critical 비판적인 neatly 깔끔하게

ETS 기출 실전문제
본책 p.102

1 (C)	**2** (D)	**3** (B)	**4** (A)	**5** (B)	**6** (C)
7 (D)	**8** (A)	**9** (C)	**10** (B)	**11** (A)	**12** (A)
13 (A)	**14** (B)	**15** (A)	**16** (B)	**17** (D)	**18** (D)

1 (C) 명사 어휘

번역 졸업 후 올루지미 씨는 고향인 잉가와에 있는 회사에 일자리 기회를 찾아보기로 했다.

해설 빈칸은 동사 seek의 목적어 자리로, 명사 job과 '일자리 기회'라는 복합명사를 이루는 (C) opportunity(기회)가 정답이다.

어휘 following ~ 후에 seek 찾다. 모색하다 firm 회사

2 (D) 형용사 어휘

번역 그렌만 카페의 모든 직원은 1년에 새 유니폼 한 벌을 무상으로 받을 자격이 됩니다.

해설 과거분사 형태의 형용사 어휘를 고르는 문제로, '직원은 유니폼을 무상으로 받을 자격이 된다'는 의미가 되어야 자연스럽다. 따라서 뒤에 오는 전치사 to와 함께 '~에 자격이 되는'을 나타내는 형용사 (D) entitled가 정답이다. (A)의 deserve는 '~을 누릴 자격이 있다'는 뜻의 타동사로 능동태로 쓰이고, (B) permitted와 (C) allowed는 to부정사와 어울려 '~하도록 허용되는'이라는 뜻으로 쓰인다.

어휘 at no charge 무상으로, 무료로

3 (B) 명사 어휘

번역 기계 공학자 협회는 최근 서울에서 개최한 콘퍼런스에 관한 의견을 구하고 있다.

해설 빈칸은 동사구 is looking for의 목적어 역할을 하는 동시에 뒤에 오는 전치사 on(~에 관한)과 어울리는 명사 자리이다. '협회에서 최근 콘퍼런스에 관한 의견을 구하고 있다'라는 의미가 되어야 자연스러우므로 '(개선) 의견'이라는 뜻의 (B) feedback이 정답이다.

어휘 mechanical 기계의 association 협회 statement 성명 conduct 행동. 수행

4 (A) 부사 어휘

번역 슈라이버 씨의 프레젠테이션 직후 로비에서 환영회가 열릴 예정이다.

해설 전치사구 following the presentation을 수식하기에 알맞은 부사를 골라야 한다. 행사 식순에 관련된 내용이므로 '프레젠테이션 후 즉시 환영회가 열린다'는 내용이 되어야 적절하다. 따라서 '즉시'를 뜻하는 (A) immediately가 정답이다.

어휘 reception 환영회 foyer 로비 mutually 상호간에

5 (B) 동사 어휘

번역 스피드스트롬 테크놀로지스는 금전 등록기를 거래 처리가 두 배 더 빠른 것으로 교체할 예정이다.

해설 빈칸 뒤에 목적어 역할을 하는 명사구 the cash register와 전치사 with가 있고, 문맥상 '금전 등록기를 더 빠른 것으로 교체할 것'이라는 의미가 되어야 적절하므로 전치사 with와 함께 쓰여 '~을 …으로 교체하다'를 뜻하는 (B) replace가 정답이다.

어휘 cash register 금전 등록기 transaction (상)거래

6 (C) 전치사구 어휘

번역 일정 문제로 인해 이번 주 금요일 세미나는 대면보다는 컴퓨터상으로 진행될 예정입니다.

해설 빈칸은 '컴퓨터상으로, 가상으로'라는 의미의 부사 virtually 를 상관접속사 rather than이 대등하게 연결하고 있으므로, 부사 역할을 하며 virtually와 의미상 대조를 이루는 전치사 구 (C) in person(대면으로, 직접)이 정답이다.

어휘 scheduling issue 일정상의 문제   rather than ~보다는

7   (D) 명사 어휘

번역 정 조선소는 노스 베이 해안가에 새 조선소를 건설 중이다.

해설 동사구 is constructing의 목적어 역할을 하는 명사 자리 로, 빈칸 앞의 명사 boatbuilding(조선)과 함께 '조선 시설' 이라는 복합명사를 만들어 '새로운 조선소를 건설 중이다'라는 내용이 되어야 적절하다. 따라서 '시설'을 뜻하는 (D) facility 가 정답이다.

어휘 shipyard 조선소   waterfront 해안가

8   (A) 동사 어휘

번역 알린스 세라믹스 스튜디오는 보수 공사가 진행 중이며 10월 1일에 다시 문을 열 예정입니다.

해설 renovations를 목적어로 취하는 타동사 자리로, '스튜디오 는 보수 공사가 진행 중이다'라는 내용이 되어야 자연스러우므 로 '(변화, 공사 등)을 겪다'라는 뜻의 동사 undergo의 현재 분사 (A) undergoing이 정답이다.

어휘 renovation 보수 공사   establish 설립하다

9   (C) 부사 어휘

번역 모든 예약 변경 사항은 고객 서비스 팀장인 이시다 씨에게 바 로 보내져야 한다.

해설 동사구 should be sent를 수식하여 '이시다 씨에게 바로 보내져야 한다'는 의미가 되어야 자연스러우므로 '바로, 곧장' 을 뜻하는 (C) directly가 정답이다.

어휘 distinctly 뚜렷하게   curiously 신기하게도

10   (B) 전치사 어휘

번역 주주들의 대리 투표용지는 9월 6일 정오까지가 기한이다.

해설 '기한인, 예정인'을 뜻하는 형용사 due와 어울려 '9월 6일 정 오까지가 기한인'이라는 의미를 이루는 전치사 (B) by(~까 지)가 정답이다.

어휘 proxy 대리   ballot 투표용지   shareholder 주주

11   (A) 동사 어휘

번역 화가 조슈아 루벤의 풍경화가 그라니도스 미술관의 새 전시회 에서 선보인다.

해설 앞에 있는 be동사와 함께 수동태를 이루는 과거분사 형태 의 동사 어휘를 고르는 문제이다. 문맥상 '풍경화가 전시회 에서 선보인다'는 내용이 되어야 적절하므로 '특별히 선보이 다, 특징으로 삼다'를 뜻하는 동사 feature의 과거분사 (A) featured가 정답이다.

어휘 landscape painting 풍경화   exhibit 전시회 broadcast 방송하다   demonstrate 시연하다

12   (A) 형용사 어휘

번역 고속도로가 완공되면 운전자들은 주변 도시 지역으로 빠르게 이동할 수 있게 된다.

해설 전치사 to의 목적어인 urban areas를 수식하는 형용 사 자리로, 문맥상 '주변 지역으로 빠르게 이동한다'는 의 미가 되어야 자연스럽다. 따라서 '주변의'라는 의미의 (A) surrounding이 정답이다.

어휘 urban 도시의   perfunctory 형식적인

13   (A) 부사 어휘

번역 캄로 인더스트리스의 근로 복지 혜택은 회사 웹사이트에 명확 히 기재되어 있다.

해설 동사구 are listed를 수식하는 부사를 고르는 문제이다. '근 로 복지 혜택이 명확히 기재되어 있다'는 내용이 되어야 적절 하므로 '명확하게'라는 의미의 (A) clearly가 정답이다.

어휘 benefits 근로 복지, 복리 후생   eagerly 간절히

14   (B) 형용사 어휘

번역 미션 제약사는 직원에게 매우 다양한 교육 기회를 제공한다.

해설 '다양한'을 뜻하는 a variety of에서 명사 variety(종류, 다양성)을 수식하기에 적절한 형용사를 고르는 문제이다. a variety of의 의미를 강조하기 위해 '광범위한'을 뜻하는 형 용사 wide가 덧붙어 a wide variety of(매우 다양한)라는 관용어구로 쓰이므로 (B) wide가 정답이다.

어휘 pharmaceuticals 제약사   educational 교육의

[15-18] 기사

> **시, 새로운 시립 센터 별관 설계 업체 선정**
>
> 로크헤이븐 (6월 9일)—로크헤이븐 시의회는 기존 시립 센터의 새로운 별관 설계를 위한 르플랫 건축 협회의 고용을 승인했다. **15 이 결정은 시의회의 가장 최근 월례 회의에서 내려졌다.** 새로운 별관에는 시장 집무실, 재무 담당관 사무실, 공원 및 공익사업 부서 가 **16 들어설 것이다.** 다른 **17 용도로는** 로크헤이븐 역사 협회를 위 한 사무실 공간과 작은 카페가 포함될 수 있다.
>
> "새 별관의 최종 구성은 비용과 제안된 설계의 매력 모두에 달려 있습니다."라고 이반 헨즈데일 로크헤이븐 시의회 의장은 말했다. "우리는 르플랫이 **18 초기** 설계에서 무엇을 제시하는지 보기를 기 대하고 있습니다."
>
> **어휘** name 지명하다   municipal 시의   wing 별관 architectural 건축학의   associate 동료, 회원   existing 기존의   controller 재무 담당관   utilities (전기, 가스 등) 공익사업   configuration 구성, 배치   attractiveness 매력 proposed 제안된   come up with ~을 제시하다

15 (A) 문맥에 맞는 문장 고르기

번역 (A) 이 결정은 시의회의 가장 최근 월례 회의에서 내려졌다.
(B) 의회는 2년 임기로 선출된 7명의 의원으로 구성된다.
(C) 다음 의회 회의는 7월 23일에 열릴 예정이다.
(D) 많은 건축가들이 이 일에 지원하도록 권유받았다.

해설 앞에서 시의회에서 시립 센터의 새 별관 설계를 위한 르플랫 건축 협회 고용을 승인했다(The Loch Haven City Council has approved ~ center)고 했다. 따라서 시의회의 승인을 나타내는 이 결정(The decision)이 언제 이루어졌는지를 언급하고 있는 (A)가 정답이다.

어휘 elect 선출하다 term 임기 architect 건축가

16 (B) 동사 어형_시제

해설 빈칸은 주어 The new wing의 동사 자리로, 앞에서 시의회에서 새로운 별관 설계를 위한 업체 고용을 승인했다고 했으므로 새로운 별관은 미래에 건설될 건물임을 알 수 있다. 빈칸이 있는 문장은 앞으로 새 별관이 수용하게 될 시설을 열거한 내용이므로 동사 house(장소를 제공하다, 수용하다)의 미래 시제인 (B) will house가 정답이다.

17 (D) 명사 어휘

해설 앞 문장에서 새 별관에 들어설 시설을 나열했고, 빈칸이 있는 문장 역시 별관에 포함될 수 있는 시설을 추가적으로 보여주고 있다. 따라서 빈칸에 들어갈 명사는 별관에 입주할 시설물을 통해 파악할 수 있는 건물의 용도나 쓰임새를 나타내는 단어가 들어가 '다른 용도로는 역사 협회 사무실과 카페가 포함될 수 있다'는 내용이 되어야 적절하므로 '용도'를 뜻하는 (D) uses가 정답이다.

18 (D) 형용사 어휘

해설 앞에서 시의회에서 시립 센터의 새로운 별관 설계를 위해 르플랫을 고용하기로 했다고 발표했고 새로운 별관의 구성은 비용과 제안된 설계의 매력에 달려 있다고 설명한 것으로 보아 르플랫이 설계를 시작하기 전 단계임을 알 수 있다. 따라서 '르플랫이 초기 설계에 제시하는 것'이라는 내용이 되어야 적절하므로 '처음의, 초기의'라는 의미의 (D) initial이 정답이다.

어휘 alternate 대안의 competitive 경쟁력 있는
balanced 균형 잡힌

ETS 기출 고난도 실전문제 본책 p.104

1 (D)	2 (A)	3 (B)	4 (A)	5 (A)	6 (A)
7 (C)	8 (D)	9 (A)	10 (C)	11 (D)	12 (D)
13 (D)	14 (B)	15 (B)	16 (A)	17 (C)	18 (C)

1 (D) 부사 어휘

번역 더 시한 미술관은 쌍방향 전시를 더 많이 기획하기 위해 소프트웨어 프로그램에 많은 투자를 해왔다.

해설 동사구 has invested를 수식하여 적절한 문맥을 이루는 부사를 고르는 문제이다. 동사 invest는 heavily와 어울려 '많은 투자를 하다'라는 의미로 자주 쓰이는데, 지문에서도 '소프트웨어 프로그램에 많은 투자를 했다'라는 내용이 자연스러우므로 '아주 많이'를 뜻하는 (D) heavily가 정답이다.

어휘 invest in ~에 투자하다 interactive 상호적인, 쌍방향의
randomly 무작위로 instantly 즉시 roughly 대략

2 (A) 동사 어휘

번역 협상이 예상보다 오래 걸렸기 때문에 루카스 씨는 출발을 하루 미뤄야 했다.

해설 had to의 to부정사에 들어갈 동사 어휘를 고르는 문제이다. her departure를 목적어로 취하고 by one day의 수식을 받아 '출발을 하루 미뤄야 했다'는 내용이 되어야 적절하므로 '미루다, 연기하다'를 뜻하는 (A) postpone이 정답이다. (C) cancel(취소하다)은 by one day와 문맥이 연결되지 않아 오답이다.

어휘 negotiation 협상 longer than expected 예상보다 더 오래 compromise 타협하다

3 (B) 명사 어휘

번역 제안된 개발은 지역 주민들의 상당한 반대에 직면했다.

해설 동사 faced의 목적어 역할을 하며 전치사구 from local residents의 수식을 받아 '주민들의 반대에 직면했다'는 내용이 되어야 자연스러우므로 '반대'를 뜻하는 (B) opposition이 정답이다.

어휘 face 직면하다 substantial 상당한 resident 주민
prediction 예측 deduction 공제

4 (A) 동사 어휘

번역 로스코 드라이 클리너스는 직원을 위한 파티를 주최하고 고객에게 할인을 제공함으로써 창립 5주년을 기념할 예정이다.

해설 빈칸 뒤의 명사구 its five-year anniversary를 목적어로 취해 '5주년을 기념할 것'이라는 내용이 되어야 자연스러우므로 '기념[축하]하다'를 뜻하는 (A) observe가 정답이다.

어휘 dry cleaner 세탁소 anniversary 기념일

5 (A) 명사 어휘

번역 트램모비단 모터스 사가 지은 최신 공장은 하루 900대의 차량을 생산할 수 있는 능력을 갖추고 있다.

해설 빈칸은 뒤의 to부정사인 to produce의 수식을 받아 '900대의 차량을 생산할 수 있는 능력을 갖추고 있다'라는 내용이 되어야 하므로 '(생산) 능력, 수용력'을 의미하는 (A) capacity가 정답이다.

어휘 judgment 판단 association 제휴 contraction 축소

6 (A) 형용사 어휘

번역 비전문가의 눈에는 모조 원석이 광산에서 나온 천연 원석과 동일해 보인다.

해설 동사 appears 뒤 보어 자리에서 주어 a simulated gemstone을 보충 설명하는 형용사를 고르는 문제이다. 빈칸 뒤 전치사 to가 핵심 단서로, '모조 원석이 천연 원석과 동일해 보인다'는 내용이 되어야 하므로 전치사 to와 함께 '~와 동일한'을 뜻하는 (A) identical이 정답이다.

어휘 untrained 비전문가의, 훈련받지 않은   simulated 모조의   gemstone 원석   mine 광산   suitable 적합한

7 (C) 명사 어휘

번역 로자 씨는 매출을 올린 검증된 실적을 보유하고 있기 때문에 입사 지원자 중 가장 강력한 후보이다.

해설 동사 has의 목적어 역할을 하는 명사 자리로, 빈칸 앞의 명사 track(기록, 행적)과 함께 '실적'이라는 의미의 복합명사를 만들어 '검증된 실적을 보유하고 있다'는 내용이 되어야 적절하므로 '기록'을 뜻하는 (C) record가 정답이다.

어휘 generate 만들어 내다, 창출하다   retort 반박

8 (D) 부사 어휘

번역 니시카와 씨의 연구소 부소장직 전환은 예상보다 더 신속하게 이루어졌다.

해설 동사 happened를 수식하여 '전환이 예상보다 신속하게 이루어졌다'는 내용이 되어야 자연스러우므로 '신속하게'를 뜻하는 (D) swiftly가 정답이다.

어휘 transition 전환   anticipate 예상하다   partially 부분적으로   ultimately 궁극적으로   adequately 충분히

9 (A) 동사 어휘

번역 샤봇 병원 회계부에서 고객님의 청구 관련 문의 사항을 해결해 드릴 수 있습니다.

해설 빈칸은 명사구 your billing-related questions를 목적어로 취하는 타동사 자리이다. 문맥상 '회계부에서 문의 사항을 해결할 수 있다'는 의미가 되어야 적절하므로 '해결하다, 다루다'라는 뜻의 (A) address가 정답이다. 참고로 (C) attend가 '처리하다'라는 의미로 쓰일 때는 자동사로 전치사 to를 동반해야 하고, (B) respond(응답하다)와 (D) appeal(호소하다) 또한 전치사 to와 함께 쓰이는 자동사이다.

어휘 billing-related 청구와 관련된

10 (C) 명사 어휘

번역 설문 조사에 따르면, 많은 사람들이 자신의 창의력을 표현하기 위한 발산 수단으로 베이킹을 시작한다.

해설 전치사 as(~으로서)의 목적어 역할을 하는 명사 자리로, 문맥상 '창의력 표현을 위한 발산 수단으로'라는 의미가 되어야 적절하므로 전치사 for와 함께 '(표현 등의) 발산 수단'을 뜻하는 (C) outlet이 정답이다.

어휘 take up ~을 시작하다   creativity 창의력   entry 참가   outcome 결과   obstacle 장애물

11 (D) 동사 어휘

번역 오늘 싱가포르 바이어와의 전화 회의는 목요일 오전으로 일정

이 변경될 예정이다.

해설 회의 일정에 관한 내용으로 '오늘 회의가 목요일 오전으로 일정이 변경된다'는 의미가 되어야 적절하므로 '일정을 변경하다'라는 뜻의 동사 reschedule의 과거분사 (D) rescheduled가 정답이다. 참고로 (A)의 plan(계획하다)은 일정을 처음 준비할 때 쓰이는데, 문맥상 이미 계획된 Today's conference call이라는 대상과 어울리지 않아 오답이다.

12 (D) 전치사 어휘

번역 직원들은 적절한 안전 장비 없이는 창고 출입이 불가합니다.

해설 장소를 나타내는 명사 the warehouse를 목적어로 취해 '창고에 출입이 허용되지 않는다'는 내용이 되어야 자연스러우므로 '~ 안에(서)'를 뜻하는 위치/장소 전치사 (D) in이 정답이다. 참고로 방향을 나타내는 전치사 (B) to 또한 '~에'라는 의미를 나타내지만 permitted와 함께 쓰이지 않는다.

어휘 proper 적절한   safety gear 안전 장비

13 (D) 명사 어휘

번역 경기 침체에도 불구하고, 전자 산업은 올해 24퍼센트의 수익 성장을 달성했다.

해설 빈칸은 전치사 Despite의 목적어 역할을 하는 명사 자리로, 문맥상 '경기 침체에도 불구하고'라는 내용이 되어야 자연스럽다. 따라서 in the economy와 함께 '경기 침체'라는 의미를 이루는 '침체'라는 뜻의 (D) downturn이 정답이다.

어휘 realize 달성[실현]하다   protocol (조약의) 원안   longevity 수명   drawback 결점

14 (B) 부사 어휘

번역 하우스 연구소는 학제 간 훈련을 받은 과학자 직원들로부터 대단히 큰 이득을 본다.

해설 동사 benefits를 수식하여 '대단히 크게 이득을 본다'는 내용이 되어야 적절하므로 '대단히, 엄청나게'라는 뜻의 (B) immensely가 정답이다.

어휘 laboratory 연구소   interdisciplinary 학제 간의, 여러 학문 분야가 관련된   jointly 공동으로   evenly 고르게   impulsively 충동적으로

[15-18] 발표

소중한 고객 여러분께:

웨스트 그로브 가에서 10년의 멋진 시간을 뒤로하고, 테리스 식료품점이 베일 쇼핑센터로 이전하게 되었음을 알려 드리게 되어 기쁩니다. 우리는 **15** 한때 베넷츠 백화점이 있던 자리를 인수할 예정입니다. **16** 더 넓은 건물은 고객 여러분께 더 나은 서비스를 제공하는 데 도움이 될 것입니다. 우리의 새로운 식료품점은 특별한 상품을 진열할 수 있는 더 넓은 공간과 함께 덜 혼잡한 경험을 제공할 것입니다. 고객들은 쇼핑센터 옆에 있는 넉넉한 주차 공간과 버스 정류장을 이용하게 됩니다. 게다가 햇살 가득한 카페가 매장 전면에 자리 잡을 예정입니다. 개점식은 9월 10일로 **17** 계획되어 있습니다. **18** 그동안 서비스 중단으로 불편을 드려 죄송합니다.

어휘 valued 소중한 take over ~을 인수하다 ample
충분한 what's more 게다가 feature 특별히 포함하다
disruption 중단

15 (B) 부사 어휘

해설 빈칸은 명사 the space를 뒤에서 수식하는 과거분사구
(occupied by Bennett's Department Store)를 수식
하는 부사 자리이다. 식료품점 이전 소식을 전하며 새롭게 옮
겨가게 될 장소에 관해 소개하고 있으므로 '한때 백화점이 있
던 자리'라는 내용이 되어야 적절하다. 따라서 '한때'라는 뜻의
(B) once가 정답이다.

어휘 barely 간신히 further 더; 더 멀리

16 (A) 문맥에 맞는 문장 고르기

번역 (A) 더 넓은 건물은 고객 여러분께 더 나은 서비스를 제공하는
     데 도움이 될 것입니다.
   (B) 새로운 장소를 찾는 작업이 진행 중입니다.
   (C) 매장은 현재 새로운 경영진 관리하에 운영되고 있습니다.
   (D) 회사 임원들은 합병이 좋은 아이디어였다는 데
       동의합니다.

해설 앞에서 테리스 식료품점이 한때 백화점이 있었던 자리로 이전
한다고 했고, 빈칸 뒤에서 새 식료품점은 더 넓은 공간과 함께
덜 혼잡할 것(Our new grocery store will offer a less
crowded experience, with a lot more space)이라
고 했다. 따라서 빈칸에는 새로 이전할 장소는 더 넓고 더 나
은 서비스를 제공할 것이라는 내용이 들어가야 연결이 자연스
러우므로 (A)가 정답이다.

어휘 ongoing 진행 중인 merger 합병

17 (C) 동사 어형_태+시제

해설 주어 The grand opening의 동사 자리로, 빈칸 뒤에 목적
어가 없으므로 수동태가 들어가야 한다. 또한 앞 내용 전반에
걸쳐 새롭게 이전할 식료품점에 대해 미래 시제로 설명하고
있고, 빈칸이 있는 문장에서는 재개점 일자에 대한 현재의 계
획을 언급하고 있으므로 현재 시제인 (C) is planned가 정
답이다.

18 (C) 접속부사

해설 앞 문장에서는 개점식이 9월 10일로 계획되어 있다고 했고,
빈칸 뒤에서는 그때까지 서비스가 중단되는 데 대해 양해를
구하고 있다. 따라서 개점식까지의 기간을 나타내는 '그동안'
이라는 뜻의 (C) In the meantime이 정답이다.

어휘 nearby 근처에 on the contrary 그와는 반대로

PART 7
Reading Comprehension

UNIT 8 독해

1 주제/목적, 세부 사항

❶ 주제/목적
본책 p.110

기출 대표 예제 | 이메일

> 안녕하세요, 김 씨.
>
> 제가 내일 아침 고위 인사들을 사우스 캐니언에 모시고 가게 되었
> 다는 연락을 방금 받았습니다. 원래 저에게 배정된 오전 8시 일정
> 을 맥널 씨가 진행하도록 처리해 주십시오. 감사합니다.
>
> 그건 그렇고, 호수로 가는 길에 나뭇가지들이 떨어져 있어 길이 일
> 부 막혀 있다는 것을 알고 계시나요? 이로 인해 넘어질 위험이 있
> 습니다.

어휘 dignitary 고위 인사 arrange (~하도록) 조처하다
assign 배정하다 incidentally 그건 그렇고 partially
부분적으로 pose (문제를) 야기하다 tripping 걸려 넘어지는
hazard 위험

이메일의 한 가지 목적은 무엇인가?
(A) 사우스 캐니언 투어 시간을 옮기려고
(B) 김 씨에게 안전 문제에 대해 알리려고

❷ 세부 사항

기출 대표 예제 | 광고

> **개봉 박두!**
>
> 〈우리의 다음 비행〉은 전형적인 사랑 이야기가 아닙니다. 배우 줄
> 리아나 번스와 데이비드 오월라비가 하노이의 한 공항에서 우연히
> 만나는 여행자로 출연합니다.
>
> 텐캐스트 앱에서의 스트리밍은 4월 10일 금요일에 시작합니다. 가
> 입자들은 www.tencastnow.com/ournextflight에서 영화의 하
> 이라이트를 보면서 미리 보기를 할 수 있습니다.

어휘 typical 전형적인 star 주연을 맡다 by accident
우연히 subscriber 가입자 sneak peek 미리 보기, 예고편

광고에 따르면, 웹사이트에서 무엇을 찾을 수 있는가?
(A) 구독 정보
(B) 영화의 일부 미리 보기

ETS 기출 유형연습
본책 p.111

1 (C) 2 (D) 3 (B) 4 (B) 5 (C) 6 (C)
7 (D)

[1-3] 공지

https://www.sanburyfarmersmarket.net/announcements

소개	공지	제품	판매자 설문 조사

지난 5년 동안 샌버리 파머스 마켓의 판매자들은 다양한 고품질의 과일, 채소, 조리 식품 및 디저트를 제공해 왔습니다. **1새로운 시즌이 활기차게 시작됨에 따라 우리는 추가 판매자를 찾고 있습니다.** 귀하의 식품이 적합하다고 생각하신다면 이 웹사이트의 '판매자 설문 조사' 페이지를 방문하셔서 예비 판매자 설문지를 작성하시길 권장드립니다. 귀하의 정보를 검토하는 즉시 귀하의 제품 및 시장 참여 가능성에 대해 논의하기 위해 연락을 드릴 수 있습니다. 해당되는 경우 설문 조사의 끝부분에 '모든 토양은 유기농입니다'와 같은 경작 방식에 관한 설명을 포함시켜 주십시오.

2샌버리 파머스 마켓은 7번 도로 바로 남쪽에 있는 헨리 가의 타운 플라자 빌딩 1층에 있습니다. 이 편리한 위치는 샌버리의 건축 유산 지구 중심부에 있어 유동 인구가 많습니다. 우리 시즌은 5월 초부터 10월 말까지 진행됩니다. **3마켓은 금요일과 토요일 오전 11시부터 오후 8시까지 열립니다.** 이번 시즌에는 높은 수요에 따라 우리의 가장 큰 판매처인 캐리스 그로서리가 목요일에도 오전 9시부터 오후 3시까지 문을 열도록 특별히 조정했습니다.

어휘 a wide selection of 다양한 off to a start 시작하는 fit 적합한 것 complete 작성하다 questionnaire 설문지 prospective 장래의 applicable 해당되는 description 설명 soil 토양 architectural 건축학의 heritage 유산 district 구역[지구] foot traffic 유동 인구 by demand 수요에 따라

1 공지의 한 가지 목적은 무엇인가?
(A) 일부 보수 공사에 대한 업데이트를 제공하려고
(B) 지역 사회의 축하 행사를 홍보하려고
(C) 새로운 식품 판매자를 모집하려고
(D) 회사 기념일을 축하하려고

해설 주제/목적
첫 번째 단락의 두 번째 문장에서 새로운 시즌이 활기차게 시작됨에 따라 추가 판매자를 찾고 있다(With our new season ~ seeking additional vendors)면서, 귀하의 식품이 적합하다고 생각한다면 이 웹사이트의 '판매자 설문 조사' 페이지를 방문하여 예비 판매자 설문지를 작성할 것을 권한다(If you think your food products would be a good fit, ~ Web site)고 했으므로 (C)가 정답이다.

어휘 renovation 보수 publicize 홍보하다 recruit 모집하다 mark 기념[축하]하다 anniversary 기념일

(Paraphrasing) 지문의 vendors → 정답의 sellers

2 샌버리 파머스 마켓에 대해 명시된 것은?
(A) 건물의 2개 층을 차지하고 있다.
(B) 10년 넘게 운영되고 있다.
(C) 유기농으로 재배한 식품만 판매한다.
(D) 역사적인 지구에 위치하고 있다.

해설 Not/True
두 번째 단락의 첫 문장에서 샌버리 파머스 마켓은 7번 도로 바로 남쪽에 있는 헨리 가의 타운 플라자 빌딩 1층에 있다(Sanbury Farmers Market is ~ on Henry Street,

just south of Route 7)고 했고, 이 위치는 샌버리의 건축 유산 지구 중심부에 있어 유동 인구가 많다(This ~ architectural heritage district, has heavy foot traffic)고 했다. 따라서 샌버리 파머스 마켓이 역사 지구에 위치해 있다는 것을 알 수 있으므로 (D)가 정답이다.

어휘 occupy 차지하다 decade 10년 grow 재배하다

(Paraphrasing) 지문의 heritage → 정답의 historic

3 샌버리 파머스 마켓은 최근에 무엇을 변경했는가?
(A) 쇼핑객을 위한 주차 공간을 확장했다.
(B) 매장 중 한 곳의 운영 시간을 늘렸다.
(C) 시즌 일정을 연장했다.
(D) 이전 고객 설문 조사의 데이터를 발표했다.

해설 세부 사항
두 번째 단락의 네 번째 문장에서 마켓은 금요일과 토요일 오전 11시부터 오후 8시까지 열린다(The market is open ~ on Fridays and Saturdays)고 했고, 이번 시즌에는 높은 수요에 따라 가장 큰 판매처인 캐리스 그로서리가 목요일에도 오전 9시부터 오후 3시까지 문을 열도록 특별히 조정했다(And this season, ~ Carrie's Grocery, to be open on Thursdays as well—from 9:00 A.M. to 3:00 P.M.)고 했다. 따라서 입점 매장 중 한 곳인 캐리스 그로서리의 영업일을 하루 더 늘렸으므로 (B)가 정답이다.

어휘 lengthen 연장하다

[4-7] 웹페이지

https://www.bartrumcity.gov/BCHC/home

4,530년 전에 설립된 바트럼시 역사 위원회(BCHC)는 바트럼시 역사 지구의 고유한 특성을 보존하는 것을 사명으로 하는 시 운영 기관입니다. 4위원회의 책임에는 구역 내에서 시행되는 재개발 프로젝트가 이 특성에 부합하는지 확인하는 일이 포함됩니다. 구역 내에 위치한 150년 된 주택들을 포함하여 BCHC가 감독하는 건축물에 대한 어떠한 변경이라도 허가가 필요합니다.

건물 변경 제안서는 검토를 위해 BCHC의 건축 유산 위원회에 제출되어야 합니다. 검토 과정은 60일까지 소요될 수 있습니다. 리모델링 사업이 승인되면 400달러의 수수료로 건축 허가증이 발급됩니다. 역사 건축물 정비를 전문으로 하는 지역 시공사들의 목록 또한 요청할 수 있습니다.

6건물 변경 요청서 제출을 고려 중인 사람은 역사 보존 건축가인 베스 파타키 씨에게 문의하도록 적극 권장됩니다. 그녀는 프로젝트 시행 전과 진행 중에 프로젝트 팀에게 안내 및 지침 사항을 제공할 수 있습니다. patakib@bartrumcity.gov로 이메일 연락이 가능합니다.

프로젝트가 완료되는 즉시 현장 점검이 실시됩니다. **7점검 결과가 만족스러울 경우, 변경 프로젝트가 BCHC의 지침을 완전히 준수하여 수행되었음을 명시하는 확인 인증서가 발급됩니다.**

어휘 commission 위원회 city-run 시가 운영하는 body 단체 mission 사명 preserve 보존하다 in keeping with ~와 일치하여 modification 변경, 수정 structure 건축물 oversee 감독하다 residence 주택 architectural 건축학의 heritage 유산 building permit

4 웹페이지의 한 가지 목적은 무엇인가?
(A) 바트럼시 역사 지구의 의의를 설명하려고
(B) 한 단체의 직무에 관해 자세히 설명하려고
(C) 신청 절차의 변경 사항을 설명하려고
(D) 프로젝트에 대한 업데이트를 제공하려고

해설 **주제/목적**
첫 문장에서 30년 전에 설립된 바트럼시 역사 위원회(BCHC)는 바트럼시 역사 지구의 고유한 특성을 보존하는 것을 사명으로 하는 시에서 운영하는 기관(Established 30 years ago, the Bartrum City Historical Commission (BCHC) is a city-run body whose mission is to preserve ~ historical district)이라고 했고, 위원회의 책임에는 구역 내에서 진행되는 재개발 프로젝트가 이 특성에 부합하는지를 확인하는 것이 포함된다(The commission's responsibilities include ~ in keeping with this special character)며 조직이 맡고 있는 임무에 대해 설명하고 있으므로 (B)가 정답이다.

어휘 significance 의의, 중요성 give details 자세히 설명하다

5 바트럼시 역사 위원회에 대해 언급된 것은?
(A) 150개의 역사적 건물을 감독한다.
(B) 건축가로만 구성되어 있다.
(C) 정부에서 운영한다.
(D) 30명의 자원봉사자를 구하고 있다.

해설 **Not/True**
첫 문장에서 30년 전에 설립된 바트럼시 역사 위원회(BCHC)는 바트럼시 역사 지구의 고유한 특성을 보존하는 것을 사명으로 하는 시에서 운영하는 기관(Established 30 years ago, the Bartrum City Historical Commission (BCHC) is a city-run body)이라고 했으므로 (C)가 정답이다.

어휘 be made up of ~으로 구성되다 solely 오로지

(Paraphrasing) 지문의 city-run → 정답의 operated by the government

6 바트럼시 역사 지구의 건물주들은 왜 파타키 씨에게 연락해야 하는가?
(A) 구역 지도를 구하려고
(B) 시공사들의 입찰을 비교하려고
(C) 리모델링 변경에 대한 조언을 구하려고
(D) 바트럼시의 역사에 대해 알아보려고

해설 **세부 사항**
세 번째 단락의 첫 문장에서 건물 변경 요청서 제출을 고려 중인 사람은 역사 보존 건축가인 베스 파타키 씨에게 문의하도록 적극 권장된다(Individuals considering submitting a building modification request ~ Ms. Beth

Pataki)고 했고, 그녀는 프로젝트 팀에게 안내 및 지침 사항을 제공할 수 있다(She can offer guidance ~ project)고 했으므로 (C)가 정답이다.

어휘 obtain 입수하다 bid 입찰

(Paraphrasing) 지문의 building modification → 정답의 remodeling changes
지문의 guidance and directives → 정답의 recommendations

7 확인 인증서에 대해 명시된 것은?
(A) 추가 수수료가 필요하다.
(B) 확보하는 데 최장 60일이 걸린다.
(C) 파타키 씨가 서명을 한다.
(D) 프로젝트가 점검을 통과할 경우 주어진다.

해설 **Not/True**
마지막 문장에서 점검 결과가 만족스러울 경우 변경 프로젝트가 BCHC의 지침을 완전히 준수하여 수행되었음을 명시하는 확인 인증서가 발급된다(If the inspection result is satisfactory, a Certificate of Validation will be issued, ~ guidelines)고 했다. 따라서 (D)가 정답이다.

(Paraphrasing) 지문의 the inspection result is satisfactory → 정답의 passes inspection

02 Not/True, 추론/암시

❶ Not/True
본책 p.114

기출 대표 예제 | 웹페이지

https://www.hotelverra.co.kr
투숙객이 호텔 베라에서의 경험을 공유하는 것을 환영합니다. 투숙객이 게시하는 모든 피드백은 호텔 경영진에 의해 확인됩니다. **필요에 따라 경영진이 이곳에서 직접 답변합니다.**

어휘 address 다루다

웹페이지에 대해 사실인 것은?
(A) 후기 작성자는 계정을 만들어야 한다.
(B) 관리자는 웹페이지에 올라온 의견에 답변할 수 있다.

❷ 추론/암시

기출 대표 예제 | 공지

등록된 세시토 기타 소유자로서 귀하는 악기 관리, 수리 및 부속품에 관하여 필요한 **모든 정보를 손쉽게 바로 얻을 수 있습니다.**

미국과 캐나다의 모든 등록된 세시토 기타 소유자는 앨범 리뷰, 음악가 인터뷰, 그리고 신제품에 대한 모든 최신 소식이 수록된 잡지 〈기타 유니버스〉의 무료 구독을 제공받습니다.

어휘 registered 등록된 instrument 악기 accessories 부속품 at your fingertips 즉시 이용할 수 있는 complimentary 무료의

공지는 누구를 대상으로 하는 것 같은가?
(A) 악기 판매업자
(B) 세시토 기타 고객

ETS 기출 유형연습
본책 p.115

1 (C) **2** (B) **3** (D) **4** (A) **5** (C) **6** (B)
7 (D)

[1-3] 기사

자유롭게 자랄 수 있는 녹지

엘크 (7월 12일)—**1 랜돌프 카운티 관계자들이 도로변 녹지가 관리되는 방식을 근본적으로 바꾸기 위한 계획을 발표했다.**

2 새로운 계획에 따르면, 대부분 지역의 잔디는 매년 한 번만 깎게 된다. 일부 지역에는 나무와 야생화를 심을 예정이다. 이러한 공간에는 고속도로변 그리고 도심 지역의 도로와 인도 사이 부지가 포함된다. 이 공간들은 전통적으로 한 달에 두세 번씩 깎아야 하는 잔디가 심어져 왔다.

랜돌프 카운티의 대변인인 던 리우에 따르면, **3(A), 3(B) 이번 변화에는 호우 기간 동안 배수를 개선하는 부가적인 이점이 있기는 하지만 주로 야생 동물의 서식지를 개선하기 위해 이루어지는 것이라고 한다. 3(C) 또한 이로 인해 랜돌프 카운티가 도로 유지관리 예산의 일부를 다른 필요한 곳에 사용할 수 있게 된다.** 통근자들은 나무 및 야생화를 심는 동안 일부 도로를 따라 교통 흐름이 영향을 받을 수 있다는 점을 알고 있어야 한다.

어휘 fundamentally 근본적으로 freeway 고속도로
sidewalk 보행로 urban 도시의 district 지역, 지구
spokesperson 대변인 primarily 주로 habitat 서식지
drainage 배수 divert 전용하다 portion 부분
commuter 통근자 traffic flow 교통 흐름

1 기사의 목적은 무엇인가?
(A) 유원지 공간 개장을 알리려고
(B) 카운티 예산 삭감에 반대 주장을 하려고
(C) 곧 시행될 정책을 설명하려고
(D) 랜돌프 카운티 관광을 홍보하려고

해설 주제/목적
첫 문장에서 랜돌프 카운티 관계자들이 도로변 녹지가 관리되는 방식을 근본적으로 바꾸기 위한 계획을 발표했다(Randolph County officials have announced plans to fundamentally change ~ spaces are managed)는 소식을 전한 뒤 정책 변경 사항에 대해 설명하는 글이 뒤따르고 있으므로 (C)가 정답이다.

2 기사에 따르면, 일어날 변화 한 가지는 무엇인가?
(A) 더 많은 주차 공간이 조성될 것이다.
(B) 도로변 잔디가 덜 깎일 것이다.
(C) 여러 카운티 도로가 확장될 것이다.
(D) 지역 채소 농원을 위해 토지가 따로 확보될 것이다.

해설 세부 사항
두 번째 단락의 첫 문장에서 새로운 계획에 따르면 대부분 지역의 잔디는 매년 한 번만 깎게 된다(Under the new

---

plan, the grass in most areas will be cut only once per year)고 했으므로 (B)가 정답이다.

어휘 widen 넓히다 set aside ~을 확보하다, 떼어놓다

(Paraphrasing) 지문의 only once per year
→ 정답의 less often

3 변화로 인해 예상되는 결과로 언급된 것이 아닌 것은?
(A) 야생 동물 서식지 개선
(B) 침수 위험 감소
(C) 기타 프로젝트에 대한 재정 지원 증가
(D) 주택 소유자의 부동산 가치 상승

해설 Not / True
세 번째 단락의 첫 문장에서 이번 변화에는 호우 기간 동안 배수를 개선하는 부가적인 이점이 있기는 하지만 주로 야생 동물의 서식지를 개선하기 위해 이루어지는 것(the change is being made primarily to improve habitats for wildlife. ~ improving drainage during rainstorms)이라고 했으므로 (A)와 (B), 두 번째 문장에서 또한 이로 인해 랜돌프 카운티가 도로 유지관리 예산의 일부를 다른 필요한 곳에 사용할 수 있게 된다(It ~ divert portions of the road-maintenance budget to other needs)고 했으므로 (C) 또한 언급되었지만, 부동한 가치 상승에 대한 언급은 없으므로 (D)가 정답이다.

어휘 flooding 침수 funding 재정 지원 property 부동산

(Paraphrasing) 지문의 divert ~ budget to other needs → (C)의 funding for other projects

[4-7] 기사

팟캐스트에서 미래를 보는 기업들

시드니 (5월 9일)—**4 팟캐스트 수의 증가는 소기업들이 새로운 고객들을 끌어들일 수 있는 더 많은 기회를 제시하고 있다.** 광고 시간 및 홍보의 대가로 팟캐스트 제작자에게 후원금을 지불하는 것이 하나의 방법으로 활용되고 있다.

"확실히, TV나 라디오 광고에서 할 수 있는 만큼 많은 사람들에게 다가가지는 못합니다."라고 **5 울버비에서 문을 연지 1년이 채 안 된 레갈라도 플라워스의 주인인 비토 레갈라도**는 말했다. "하지만 팟캐스트 청취자들은 특히 주의 깊게 듣는 청중입니다."

베인스 테크니컬 아카데미에서 광고 과정을 가르치는 레오라 트럼퍼는 이에 동의한다. "청취자들은 그들이 애청하는 팟캐스트를 후원하는 업체들에 대한 세부 정보를 기억하는 것 같습니다."라고 그녀는 말한다.

후원의 이점은 요리사 티나 롱고가 진행하는 시드니 기반 팟캐스트인 〈콘티넨탈 테이블〉에 의해 잘 설명된다. **6 매주 롱고 씨는 호주의 각기 다른 지역에서 요리를 어떻게 준비하는지 설명한다. 7 팟캐스트의 후원사 중 한 곳인 스파이스 라이프는 단 2회 만에 온라인 판매 25퍼센트 성장이라는 경험을 했다.**

"대부분의 당사 주문과는 달리, 이 주문들은 시드니 외부 사람들로부터 온 것입니다."라고 **5, 7 스파이스 라이프의 소유주인 유코우 이와세 씨**는 말했다. "롱고 씨는 저희 향신료 라인을 좋아하고 그녀의 쇼에서 이를 홍보하는데, 그녀의 팬들은 우리와 같은 새로운 업체를 시도해 볼 만한 충분한 자신감을 얻습니다."

어휘 reel in ~을 끌어들이다　approach 접근법
employ 이용하다　in exchange for ~에 대한 대가로
endorsement 홍보　particularly 특히　attentive 주의를
기울이는　illustrate 예증하다　episode 1회 방송분
take a chance on (운에 맡기고) ~을 해보다

4　기사의 목적은 무엇인가?
(A) 광고의 새로운 트렌드를 설명하려고
(B) 몇몇 새로운 팟캐스트의 내용을 집중 조명하려고
(C) 소기업의 판촉비를 분석하려고
(D) 다양한 형태의 방송 미디어를 비교하려고

해설　**주제 / 목적**
첫 문장에서 팟캐스트 수의 증가는 소기업들이 새로운 고객들을 끌어들일 수 있는 더 많은 기회를 제시한다(The rising number of podcasts ~ to reel in new customers)며, 광고 시간 및 홍보의 대가로 팟캐스트 제작자에게 후원금을 지불하는 것이 하나의 방법으로 활용되고 있다(One approach being employed is to pay ~ endorsements)고 새로운 광고 방식에 대해 설명하고 있으므로 (A)가 정답이다.

어휘　emerging 최근 생겨나는　expenditure 비용

5　레갈라도 씨와 이와세 씨 둘 다에 대해 사실인 것은?
(A) 베인스 테크니컬 아카데미에 다녔다.
(B) 같은 텔레비전 쇼에서 광고한다.
(C) 비교적 신생 업체를 운영한다.
(D) 〈콘티넨털 테이블〉의 게스트였다.

해설　**Not / True**
두 번째 단락의 첫 문장에서 레갈라도 씨는 울롬비에서 문을 연지 1년이 채 안 된 레갈라도 플라워의 주인(Vito Regalado, owner of Regalado Flowers in Wollombi, which opened less than a year ago)이라고 했고, 마지막 단락의 첫 문장에서 스파이스 라이프의 소유주인 유코우 이와세 씨(Yuukou Iwase, owner of Spice Life)를 소개하며, 롱고 씨는 자신의 향신료를 좋아하고 홍보하는데, 그녀의 팬들에게 자신과 같은 새로운 업체를 시도해 보게 한다(Ms. Longo likes our line of spices ~ a chance on a new business like ours)라며 그 또한 신생 업체를 운영한다고 언급했다. 따라서 레갈라도 씨와 이와세 씨 모두 새로 생긴 업체를 운영하고 있음을 알 수 있으므로 (C)가 정답이다.

어휘　relatively 비교적

6　롱고 씨의 팟캐스트 주제는 무엇인가?
(A) 여행　　　　　　(B) 요리
(C) 실내 디자인　　　(D) 호주의 역사

해설　**세부 사항**
네 번째 단락의 두 번째 문장에서 매주 롱고 씨는 호주의 각기 다른 지역에서 요리를 어떻게 준비하는지 설명한다(Each week, Ms. Longo describes how to prepare a dish ~ Australia)고 했으므로 (B)가 정답이다.

7　롱고 씨의 팟캐스트 청취자들에 대해 암시된 것은?
(A) 자신의 팟캐스트를 시작했다.
(B) 일주일에 한 번 신선한 꽃을 구매한다.
(C) 롱고 씨에게 주제를 추천한다.
(D) 이와세 씨의 회사에서 제품을 주문했다.

해설　**추론 / 암시**
네 번째 단락의 마지막 문장에서 롱고 씨의 팟캐스트 후원사 중 한 곳인 스파이스 라이프는 단 2회 만에 매출 성장을 경험했다(One of the podcast's sponsors, Spice Life, experienced ~ sales after just two episodes)고 했고, 마지막 단락의 첫 문장에서 스파이스 라이프의 소유주인 유코우 이와세 씨(Yuukou Iwase, owner of Spice Life)를 소개하며, "롱고 씨는 저희 향신료 라인을 좋아하고 그녀의 쇼에서 이를 홍보하는데 그녀의 팬들은 우리와 같은 새로운 업체를 시도해 볼 만한 자신감을 얻습니다."("Ms. Longo ~ a chance on a new business like ours.")라는 이와세 씨의 말을 인용하고 있다. 따라서 롱고 씨의 팟캐스트 청취자들이 이와세 씨의 회사인 스파이스 라이프의 향신료 제품을 주문했다는 것을 알 수 있으므로 (D)가 정답이다.

03　**의도 파악, 동의어, 문장 삽입**

❶ 의도 파악　　　　　　　　　　本책 p.118

기출 대표 예제 | 온라인 채팅

> 마리사 코아리 (오전 10시 45분)
> 여러분. 좋은 아침입니다. **직원 감사 오찬을 어디에서 할지에 대해 생각해 보셨나요?**
>
> 수지 볼랜드 (오전 10시 47분)
> 그걸 벌써 계획하고 계신지 몰랐어요.
>
> 타일러 렘쿨 (오전 10시 49분)
> 우리가 항상 이용하는 곳에 문제가 있나요?
>
> 마리사 코아리 (오전 10시 51분)
> **칸디치스 키친은 지금 보수 공사 중이에요.** 7월까지는 문을 열지 않을 예정인데, 우리 행사는 항상 6월에 있어요.

오전 10시 49분에 렘쿨 씨가 "우리가 항상 이용하는 곳에 문제가 있나요?"라고 쓴 의도는 무엇인가?
(A) 행사가 취소된 것을 알지 못했다.
(B) 칸디치스 키친을 이용해야 한다고 생각한다.

❷ 동의어

기출 대표 예제 | 기사

> 록스비 지역에 주거 부문 외에도 저장 공간이 필요한 업체들의 비율이 평균 이상이라는 점이 눈에 띈다. 아넬 스토리지라는 한 시설은 인근 산업 단지에 있는 상업 기업들로부터 거의 모든 **고객층을 끌어들인다.**

세 번째 단락 4행의 "draws"와 의미가 가장 가까운 단어는?
(A) 선화를 그리다
(B) 끌어들이다

❸ 문장 삽입

기출 대표 예제 | 웹페이지

https://landmersupply.com			
구입	주문 제작	**소개**	연락처

브리티시컬럼비아주 밴쿠버에 본사를 둔 랜드머 서플라이는 포켓 사이즈의 종이 노트, 메모장, 여행 일지를 제조하는 회사입니다.

오늘날 많은 사람들이 휴대폰을 사용해 삶을 기록하여 점점 더 종이를 쓰지 않는 세상에서, **종이 제품**은 여전히 그 어느 때만큼 의미가 있을 수 있습니다. 이 제품들은 배터리가 방전되거나 인터넷 연결이 잘 되지 않아 낙담할 일이 없습니다. 이 점이 사진작가들과 해외 여행객들이 여행 중 메모를 위해 저희 메모장에 의존한다고 말하는 이유입니다. 저희 제품을 애용해 주시는 고객들은 이 디지털 시대에 사업이 계속 성장할 수 있도록 도움을 주셨습니다. 작년에 당사의 판매량은 역대 최고였습니다!

어휘 pocket-size 포켓 크기의, 소형의 journal 일지
increasingly 점점 더 paperless 종이를 쓰지 않는
document 기록하다 relevant (삶 등에) 의의가 있는
jot down ~을 (급히) 적다 era 시대 volume 총량

[1], [2]로 표시된 곳 중에서 다음 문장이 들어가기에 가장 적합한 위치는?
"이 제품들은 배터리가 방전되거나 인터넷 연결이 잘 되지 않아 낙담할 일이 없습니다."
(A) [1]
(B) [2]

ETS 기출 유형연습
본책 p.120

1 (D) **2** (A) **3** (D) **4** (A) **5** (C) **6** (A)
7 (D) **8** (A)

[1-2] 문자 메시지

후안 로사스 (오후 7시 38분)
안녕하세요. 아직 근무하고 계시나요? 부탁이 있어요.

라니쉬 더글러스 (오후 7시 44분)
네. 어떻게 도와드릴까요?

후안 로사스 (오후 7시 46분)
제 사무실로 가 주세요. 가서 문자 주세요.

라니쉬 더글러스 (오후 7시 54분)
알았어요. 저 여기 왔어요.

후안 로사스 (오후 7시 55분)
제 실험실 책상에 있는 파란색 타이머 보이시나요? 몇 시로 맞춰져 있나요?

라니쉬 더글러스 (오후 7시 56분)
오전 3시 45분이요.

후안 로사스 (오후 7시 58분)
1,2타이머를 재설정해 주시겠어요? 1집에 와서 자료를 검토했는데, 기계가 오전 5시 45분에 시작되면 더 좋은 결과가 나올 것 같아요.

라니쉬 더글러스 (오후 8시)
2했어요.

후안 로사스 (오후 8시 1분)
신세를 졌네요, 라니쉬. 내일 봬요!

어휘 owe 신세를 지다

1 오전 5시 45분에 일어날 일은?
(A) 로사스 씨가 타이머를 다시 설정할 것이다.
(B) 사무실 문이 열릴 것이다.
(C) 더글러스 씨가 알람 시계 때문에 깰 것이다.
(D) 일부 장비가 자동으로 켜질 것이다.

해설 세부 사항
7시 58분에 로사스 씨가 타이머를 재설정해 주겠냐(Could you reset the timer?)고 부탁하면서, 집에 와서 자료를 검토했는데 기계가 오전 5시 45분에 시작되면 더 좋은 결과가 나올 것 같다(I reviewed ~ better results if the machine starts at 5:45 in the morning)고 했다. 따라서 오전 5시 45분에 기계가 타이머에 맞춰 자동으로 작동될 것임을 알 수 있으므로 (D)가 정답이다.

(**Paraphrasing**) 지문의 the machine starts
→ 정답의 equipment will turn on

2 오후 8시 1분에 로사스 씨가 "신세를 졌네요, 라니쉬"라고 쓴 의도는?
(A) 더글러스 씨의 도움에 감사한다.
(B) 실수한 것에 대해 유감스럽게 생각한다.
(C) 대출을 즉시 상환할 생각이다.
(D) 실험 결과를 분석할 것이다.

해설 의도 파악
7시 58분에 로사스 씨가 더글러스 씨에게 타이머를 재설정해 달래(Could you reset the timer?)고 요청한 것에 대해 8시에 더글러스 씨가 했다(Done)고 응답하자, 8시 1분에 로사스 씨가 신세를 졌다(I owe you, Ranish)고 말했다. 따라서 로사스 씨는 부탁을 들어준 더글러스 씨에게 감사를 표현하고자 한 말임을 알 수 있으므로 (A)가 정답이다.

어휘 grateful 감사하는 regret 유감스럽게 생각하다
promptly 즉시

[3-5] 정보

머니 리버 추천 프로그램

³ 머니 리버 앱 사용자라면, 안전하고 확실하게 일상적인 금융 거래를 하는 것이 얼마나 쉬운지 이미 알고 계십니다. 그런데 친구나 가족에게 똑같은 편리함을 ⁴ 제공하는 동시에 본인도 보너스 지급을 받을 수 있다는 사실을 알고 계셨나요? 여러분이 추천하신 분이 첫 구매를 할 때마다 5달러를 받게 됩니다! 여기 약관을 간단히 살펴보세요.

• 머니 리버 모바일 앱을 사용하시거나 www.moneyriver.com/referral로 웹사이트를 방문하셔서 직접 누군가를 추천하세요.

• ⁵ 1년에 최대 10명까지 추천하세요.

• 혜택은 미국과 캐나다 사용자로 제한됩니다.

• 보너스 보상은 보통 영업일 기준 10일 이내에 사용자의 머니 리버 계정에 표시됩니다.

지금 첫 추천을 하시고 머니 리버 프로그램을 최대한 활용하세요!

어휘 referral 추천, 소개 transaction 거래 securely 확실히, 안전하게 extend 주다, 베풀다 refer 소개하다 terms 약관, 조항 offer 혜택, 특가 reward 보상 take advantage of ~을 활용하다

3 머니 리버 앱은 사용자가 무엇을 하는 데 도움이 되도록 설계되었는가?
(A) 친구들과의 채팅 (B) 여행 준비
(C) 창업 (D) 간단한 구매

해설 세부 사항
첫 문장에서 머니 리버 앱 사용자라면 일상적인 금융 거래를 안전하고 확실하게 하는 것이 얼마나 쉬운지 알고 있다(As a Money River app user, ~ make everyday financial transactions safely and securely)고 한 것으로 보아 머니 리버 앱이 쉽고 안전한 거래를 위한 것임을 알 수 있으므로 (D)가 정답이다.

(Paraphrasing) 지문의 transactions
→ 정답의 purchases

4 첫 번째 단락 2행의 "extend"와 의미가 가장 가까운 단어는?
(A) 제공하다 (B) 복원하다
(C) 연장하다 (D) 가속화하다

해설 동의어 찾기
의미상 친구나 가족에게 똑같은 편리함을 '제공하다'라는 뜻으로 쓰였으므로 '제공하다, 권하다'라는 의미의 (A) offer가 정답이다.

5 머니 리버 추천 프로그램에 대해 명시된 것은?
(A) 전 세계 어디에서나 사용할 수 있다.
(B) 24시간 이내에 사용자 계정에 보너스가 지급된다.
(C) 연간 최대 10회의 추천이 가능하다.
(D) 앱을 통해서만 시작할 수 있다.

해설 Not/True
세 번째 단락에서 1년에 최대 10명까지 추천하라(Refer up to ten individuals within one year)고 명시했으므로 (C)가 정답이다.

어휘 credit 입금하다 initiate 개시하다

(Paraphrasing) 지문의 up to → 정답의 a maximum of

[6-8] 보도 자료

즉각 발표용

연락처: 이본 스테파니안, ystepanian@skarnov.ca

토론토 (8월 21일)—건강 증진 에너지 음료의 선두 제조업체인 스카노프 사에서 곧 인기 있는 비고레이트 브랜드 에너지 음료를 500밀리리터 알루미늄 병으로 선보일 것이다. 이 더 커진 병은 몇 주 내로 일반적인 250밀리리터 병과 함께 매장 진열대에 등장할 예정이다. ⁸ 작은 병과 마찬가지로 500밀리리터 병도 재사용 및 완전한 재활용이 가능하다. 이는 비고레이트 브랜드가 친환경적이라는 것을 보장한다.

스카노프는 좀 더 건강한 음료를 향한 소비자 요구를 충족시키기 위해 10년 전 비고레이트 에너지 음료를 출시했다. 비고레이트는 딸기, 복숭아, 레몬이라는 세 가지 맛있는 100퍼센트 천연 맛으로 제공된다. 업체 측은 내년에 이 제품군에 두 가지 맛을 더 추가할 것으로 예정하고 있다.

⁶ 비고레이트 제품은 현재 대부분의 슈퍼마켓에서 판매되고 있으며, 더 큰 병 옵션이 브랜드의 가시성을 높여 주기를 업체 측은 기대하고 있다. ⁶ 에너지 음료는 또한 다양한 음식점, 피트니스 센터, 그리고 호텔에서도 구입 가능하다.

⁷ 스카노프는 최근 다양한 소셜 미디어 플랫폼과 헬스 및 피트니스 팟캐스트를 통해 마케팅 강화를 시작했다. 더 많은 정보는 www.skarnov.ca/vigorate에서 확인할 수 있다.

어휘 immediate 즉각적인 release 발표 leading 선두의 alongside ~와 함께 standard 일반적인, 표준의 reusable 재사용 가능한 recyclable 재활용 가능한 visibility 가시성 launch 시작하다 push 분발, 노력

6 비고레이트의 250밀리리터 병에 대해 암시된 것은?
(A) 다양한 장소에서 구입할 수 있다.
(B) 이전에는 유리로 만들어졌다.
(C) 곧 500밀리리터 병을 대체할 것이다.
(D) 노란색 용기에 판매될 것이다.

해설 추론/암시
세 번째 단락의 첫 문장에서 비고레이트 제품은 현재 대부분의 슈퍼마켓에서 판매되고 있다(Vigorate products are currently sold in most supermarkets)고 했고, 다양한 음식점, 피트니스 센터, 그리고 호텔에서도 구입할 수 있다(The energy drinks ~ at many restaurants, fitness centres, and hotels)고 했다. 따라서 비고레이트 음료가 다양한 곳에서 판매되고 있음을 알 수 있으므로 (A)가 정답이다.

지문의 supermarkets/restaurants, fitness centres, and hotels → 정답의 a variety of places

7 보도 자료에 따르면, 스카노프 사가 최근에 한 일은?
(A) 음료의 재료를 바꿨다.
(B) 새로운 생산 시설을 열었다.
(C) 슈퍼마켓에서 판매를 중단했다.
(D) 광고 활동을 늘렸다.

해설 세부 사항
마지막 단락의 첫 번째 문장에서 스카노프는 최근 다양한 소셜 미디어 플랫폼과 헬스 및 피트니스 팟캐스트를 통해 마케팅 강화를 시작했다(Skarnov has recently launched a marketing push ~ podcasts)고 했으므로 (D)가 정답이다.

어휘 ingredient 재료 facility 시설 effort 노력, 활동
(Paraphrasing) 지문의 a marketing push → 정답의 advertising efforts

8 [1], [2], [3], [4]로 표시된 곳 중에서 다음 문장이 들어가기에 가장 적합한 위치는?
"이는 비고레이트 브랜드가 친환경적이라는 것을 보장한다."
(A) [1]　　　　　　(B) [2]
(C) [3]　　　　　　(D) [4]

해설 문장 삽입
주어진 문장에서 이(This)는 비고레이트 브랜드가 친환경적이라는 것을 보장한다고 했으므로, 주어진 문장 앞에는 브랜드가 친환경적이라는 특성을 보여줄 수 있는 내용이 있어야 한다. 따라서 음료 병이 재사용 및 완전 재활용이 가능하다(reusable and fully recyclable)고 언급한 문장 뒤 [1]에 들어가는 것이 자연스러우므로 (A)가 정답이다.

04 연계 문제

연계 문제
본책 p.123

기출 대표 예제 | 구인 광고 + 일정표

앱 개발자 구함

방갈로르에 기반을 두고 최근에 설립된 소프트웨어 스타트업인 **게임세이크**에서 팀을 구성하는 데 도움을 줄 풀타임 앱 개발자를 찾습니다. 지원자들은 최신 앱 개발 도구에 대한 경험이 있어야 하고, 온라인 소비자의 요구를 이해해야 하며, 현장에서 풀타임으로 근무할 수 있어야 합니다. 일주일에 2~3일 원격으로 근무하는 것은 고용 후 첫 6개월 뒤에 협의 가능합니다.

자세한 정보를 원하시면, 무료 라이브 웨비나 중 하나에 참석하세요. 날짜 및 등록할 링크를 원하시면, vmisra@gamesake.co.in으로 **빈 미스라 부사장**에게 이력서를 보내 주세요. 제목란에 '프로젝트 8900'이라고 적으세요.

어휘 on-site 현장에서 remotely 원격으로 negotiable 협의 가능한 initial 초기의 vice president 부사장

프로젝트 8900 웨비나		
진행자	**날짜, 시간**	**세션**
리안 산얄 씨	11월 11일 오전 10시	202
시타 티파니 씨	11월 12일 오후 2시	203
빈 미스라 씨	**11월 13일 오후 12시 30분**	**204**
리안 산얄 씨	11월 14일 오후 8시	205

게임세이크의 부사장에 대해 결론지을 수 있는 것은?
(A) 11월 13일에 웨비나를 진행할 것이다.
(B) 가상 현실 앱을 개발하기 위한 도구를 만들었다.

ETS 기출 유형연습
본책 p.124

1 (A)	2 (C)	3 (A)	4 (D)	5 (A)	6 (B)
7 (D)	8 (C)	9 (C)	10 (B)		

[1-5] 광고 + 기사

뮤지컬 공연 해외 투어

〈오르페우스의 재방문〉은 오르페우스와 에우리디케의 신화를 바탕으로 한 짜릿한 새 뮤지컬입니다. 이 공연은 눈과 귀를 위한 향연입니다! 수상 경력의 작곡가 아드리엔 안사리가 쓴 〈오르페우스의 재방문〉은 분명 모든 관람객에게 즐거움을 줄 것입니다. **1투어 일정**에는 유럽의 수도 네 곳에서 열리는 공연이 포함됩니다.

4시사회:
4월 9일–28일: 워드라이트 극장 (영국 이스트본)

투어 일정:
5월 4–15일: 피나클 극장 (영국 런던)
5월 18–29일: 센터 뮤지크 (프랑스 파리)
6월 1–12일: 라벤슈타인 홀 (벨기에 브뤼셀)
6월 15–26일: 더 디아망 (네덜란드 암스테르담)

어휘 electrifying 짜릿한, 열광시키는 myth 신화 feast 향연, 성찬 composer 작곡가 delight 즐겁게 하다 capital 수도 preview 시사회

극장 개보수 완료

리즈 카네코 작성

이스트본 **3**(3월 10일)—**4**호평 받는 워드라이트 극장이 대대적인 보수 공사 끝에 4월 9일 다시 문을 연다. **2**이 1950년대 건물은 수도관 파손으로 인한 구조적 손상으로 4년 전 문을 닫았다. 극장 이사회가 높은 수리 비용 때문에 곤란을 겪음에 따라 이용객들은 극장이 다시 문을 열지 못할 것을 우려했다.

320년간 이 극장의 이사회 구성원이었던 크리스텔라 마모르가 지난 3월 새로운 회장으로 임명되었다. "지난 12개월 동안 보수 공사가 완료되는 것을 보는 것은 제가 마주했던 가장 큰 도전 과제 중 하나였지만, 이 중요한 건물을 지역 사회의 이익을 위해 되살릴 수 있다는 것은 큰 선물입니다."라고 마모르 씨는 말했다.

건물에 대한 작업에는 기반 보수, 세부적인 석고 장식 복원, 새로운 냉난방 시스템 설치, 극장의 좌석 및 무대 기술 업그레이드가 포함되었다.

지역 관객들은 아드리안 안사리가 쓴 고대 신화의 새 뮤지컬 버전의 첫 공연을 볼 수 있다는 기대감에 설레고 있다. 감독인 시마 쿠

마르는 이스트본 출신으로 워드라이트의 재건을 위한 자금 조성을 도왔다. 그녀의 노력은 쇼를 이곳으로 가져오는 데 **5필수적이었다.**

어휘 acclaimed 호평받는 era 시대 structural 구조상의 water main 수도관 patron 고객 fear 염려하다 struggle 고투하다 costly 많은 비용이 드는 appoint 임명하다 chairperson 의장 challenge 난제, 도전 face 직면하다 foundation 기반 restoration 복원 plaster 석고 decoration 장식 installation 설치 prospect 기대감 ancient 고대의 vital 필수적인

1 광고에서 〈오르페우스의 재방문〉의 해외 투어에 대해 명시하는 것은?
(A) 4개국이 포함될 것이다.
(B) 투자자로부터 자금을 지원받을 것이다.
(C) 5월에 시사회를 열 예정이다.
(D) 안사리 씨의 강연이 포함될 것이다.

해설 **Not / True**
광고의 첫 단락 마지막 문장에서 투어 일정에는 유럽의 수도 네 곳에서 열리는 공연이 포함된다(The touring schedule includes performances in four European capital cities)고 했으므로 (A)가 정답이다.

(Paraphrasing) 지문의 European capital cities → 정답의 different countries

2 워드라이트 극장은 왜 보수 공사를 했는가?
(A) 이용객들이 더 편안한 좌석을 요구했다.
(B) 현대 제작물을 올리기에 무대가 너무 작았다.
(C) 건물이 침수 피해를 입었다.
(D) 쿠마르 씨가 개보수를 위한 비용을 댄다고 제안했다.

해설 **세부 사항**
기사의 첫 단락 두 번째 문장에서 이 1950년대 건물은 수도관 파손으로 인한 구조적 손상으로 4년 전 문을 닫았다(The 1950s-era building ~ owing to structural damage caused by a broken water main)고 했으므로 (C)가 정답이다.

어휘 undergo (변화 등을) 겪다 suffer 고통을 겪다

(Paraphrasing) 지문의 damage caused by a broken water main → 정답의 water damage

3 마모르 씨가 극장 이사회 회장을 맡은 기간은?
(A) 1년 　　　　　　(B) 2년
(C) 12년 　　　　　(D) 20년

해설 **세부 사항**
기사의 첫 단락 도입부에 작성일이 3월 10일(10 March)이라고 나와 있고, 두 번째 단락의 첫 문장에서 20년간 이 극장의 이사회 구성원이었던 크리스텔라 마모르가 지난 3월 새로운 회장으로 임명되었다(Cristela Marmor ~ was appointed as the new chairperson last March)고 했으므로 마모르 씨가 극장 이사회 회장을 맡은 지 1년이 되었다는 것을 알 수 있다. 따라서 (A)가 정답이다.

4 〈오르페우스의 재방문〉에 대해 암시된 것은?
(A) 1950년대에 쓰여졌다.
(B) 전문 기술을 활용한다.
(C) 이스트본 출신이 썼다.
(D) 재개관한 극장의 첫 작품이 될 것이다.

해설 **연계**
광고의 중반부에 〈오르페우스의 재방문〉의 시사회(Previews)가 4월 9일-28일에 워드라이트 극장(9-28 April: Wordwright Theatre)에서 열린다고 나와 있고, 기사의 첫 문장에서 호평 받는 워드라이트 극장이 대대적인 보수 공사 끝에 4월 9일 다시 문을 연다(On 9 April, the acclaimed Wordwright Theatre will reopen its doors after a major renovation project)고 했다. 따라서 〈오르페우스의 재방문〉은 워드라이트 극장이 재개관일에 올리는 첫 작품임을 알 수 있으므로 (D)가 정답이다.

어휘 specialized 전문적인

5 기사에서 네 번째 단락 7행의 "vital"과 의미가 가장 가까운 단어는?
(A) 필수적인 　　　　(B) 기운을 돋우는
(C) 원기 왕성한 　　　(D) 생산적인

해설 **동의어 찾기**
의미상 감독인 시마 쿠마르의 노력이 쇼를 극장으로 가져오는 데 '필수적'이었다는 뜻으로 쓰였으므로 '필수적인'을 뜻하는 (A) essential이 정답이다.

[6-10] 공지 + 이메일 + 온라인 댓글

모두를 위한 캘런 여름 축제에 오세요!

6매년 열리는 캘런 여름 축제가 올해 7월 11일부터 7월 14일까지 (우천 시 연기 날짜: 7월 25일부터 7월 28일까지) 도시 남부 박람 회장에서 열립니다. 축제는 매일 오전 9시부터 오후 9시까지 열릴 예정입니다. **6여름 축제는 100년이 넘는 전통 행사입니다!** www. callansummerfair.ie를 방문하셔서 역사에 대해 더 읽어 보시고 올해 축제에 대한 티켓 정보와 일정을 확인하세요.

늘 그랬듯이 축제는 수많은 노점상, 먹거리 가판대, 공연 등으로 구성됩니다. 판매자나 공연자로 참여하고 싶은 경우 다미엔 도허티에 게 ddougherty@callansummerfair.ie로 이메일을 보내세요. 또한 **7올해의 행사에 도움을 줄 자원봉사자도 여전히 필요합니다.** 아이슬린 말로니에게 amaloney@callansummerfair.ie로 연락해 주세요.

어휘 fair 축제 마당 fairground 박람회장 dozens of 많은, 수십의 vendor 노점상 stall 가판대

수신: 조나스 스컬라 〈jskerla@callancitycouncil.ie〉
발신: 아이슬린 말로니 〈amaloney@callansummerfair.ie〉
날짜: 7월 19일
제목: 준비 사항

스컬라 씨께:

8원래 날짜에 비가 와서 행사가 연기됨에 따라 다음 주 축제를 위해 모든 것이 준비되었는지 확인하고자 합니다. 박람회장 작업 팀

과 정비 직원들은 공지를 받았나요? 박람회장은 7월 25일 전에 새로 잔디를 깎아야 하고, 청소 작업 팀은 축제 기간과 마지막 날 이후에 쓰레기를 치워야 할 겁니다. 다음 주에는 어떠한 스포츠 행사도 없을 예정이라서 애초에 예상했던 것보다 더 많은 사람들을 보게 될 것 같습니다. **10우리는 언제나 더 많은 자원봉사자들이 정비 직원들과 함께 일하도록 할 수 있습니다. 물론 그들은 무료 축제 입장권을 받게 될 것입니다.** 운이 좋으면 이번에는 날씨가 더 쾌적할 겁니다!

7아이슬린 말로니
캘런 여름 축제 기획 책임자

어휘 rain out 우천으로 연기하다   mow (잔디를) 깎다
rubbish 쓰레기   initially 처음에   anticipate 예상하다
maintenance 정비   complimentary 무료의
admission 입장

---

https://www.callansummerfair.ie/comments

지난해 제 연구의 일환으로 캘런 시의회 사무소에서 근무했습니다. **10스컬라 씨의 제안으로 저는 정비 팀이 여름 축제를 준비하는 것을 돕는 일에 자원했습니다.** 그리고 **97월 26일에 축제에 참석했는데 축제는 무척 재미있었습니다!** 음식, 음악, 전시는 훌륭했고, 모든 것이 잘 짜여 있었습니다. 만약 향후 아일랜드에 다시 갈 일이 있다면 축제에 다시 참석하고 싶습니다.

–오순희 (대한민국 서울)

어휘 demonstration 시연   organise 준비[조직]하다

---

6 공지에서 축제에 대해 명시하는 것은?
(A) 시 주민들에게만 개방한다.
(B) 1세기 이상 매년 열렸다.
(C) 그 역사가 곧 연구자들에 의해 편찬될 것이다.
(D) 매년 다른 장소에서 개최된다.

해설 **Not / True**
공지의 첫 문장에서 매년 열리는 캘런 여름 축제(The annual Callan Summer Fair)라고 했고, 세 번째 문장에서 여름 축제는 100년이 넘는 전통 행사(The summer fair has been a tradition for over a hundred years!)라고 했으므로, 축제는 100년이 넘는 기간 동안 매년 열렸다는 것을 알 수 있다. 따라서 (B)가 정답이다.

어휘 occur 일어나다   compile 편찬[편집]하다

(Paraphrasing) 지문의 over a hundred years
→ 정답의 more than a century

7 공지를 읽은 사람은 왜 기획 책임자에게 연락해야 하는가?
(A) 먹거리 가판대를 임대하려고
(B) 공연을 위해 등록하려고
(C 업데이트된 행사 일정표를 받으려고
(D) 축제에서 도움을 주는 자원봉사를 하려고

해설 **연계**
공지의 두 번째 단락 세 번째 문장에서 올해의 행사에 도움을 줄 자원봉사자도 여전히 필요하다(we still need volunteers to assist us with this year's event)며 아이슬린 말로니에게 그녀의 이메일로 연락해 달라(If you

---

are interested, please contact Aislinn Maloney at amaloney@callansummerfair.ie)고 했고, 이메일 하단에 아이슬린 말로니(Aislinn Maloney)는 캘런 여름 축제 기획 책임자(Planning Director, Callan Summer Fair)라고 나와 있다. 따라서 공지를 접한 사람이 자원봉사자로 지원하려면 행사 기획 책임자인 아이슬린 말로니에게 문의해야 하므로 (D)가 정답이다.

8 말로니 씨가 스컬라 씨에게 보낸 이메일에 언급하는 것은?
(A) 박람회장의 잔디를 깎기 위해 사람들을 고용했다.
(B) 축제에 스포츠 행사가 포함될 것이다.
(C) 우천으로 인해 축제 일정이 변경되었다.
(D) 판매자가 먹거리 가판대를 임대하는 비용이 인상되었다.

해설 **Not / True**
이메일의 첫 문장에서 말로니 씨가 스컬라 씨에게 원래 날짜에 비가 와서 행사가 연기됨에 따라 다음 주 축제를 위해 모든 것이 준비되었는지 확인하고자 한다(I wanted to check ~ for the fair next week, as we were rained out on our original dates)고 했으므로 (C)가 정답이다.

어휘 mow 잔디를 깎다

(Paraphrasing) 지문의 rained out
→ 정답의 rescheduled because of rainy weather

9 오 씨는 왜 축제 웹사이트에 댓글을 남겼는가?
(A) 축제 티켓 가격을 문의하려고
(B) 축제 개최 시기를 알아보려고
(C) 축제에서의 경험을 설명하려고
(D) 향후 축제에 대해 제안을 하려고

해설 **주제 / 목적**
온라인 댓글의 세 번째 문장에서 오 씨가 7월 26일에 축제에 참석했는데 축제는 무척 재미있었다(I attended the fair on 26 July, and it was so much fun!)며 축제에 참석하고 난 감상평을 남겼으므로 (C)가 정답이다.

10 오 씨에 대해 사실일 것 같은 것은?
(A) 현재 스컬라 씨를 위해 일하고 있다.
(B) 축제에 무료로 참석했다.
(C) 내년에 아일랜드에서 공부할 예정이다.
(D) 축제를 위해 음식과 음악을 계획하는 일을 도왔다.

해설 **연계**
이메일의 다섯 번째 문장에서 언제나 더 많은 자원봉사자들이 정비 직원들과 함께 일하도록 할 수 있다(We ~ use more volunteers to work with the maintenance staff)며 물론 그들은 무료 축제 입장권을 받게 될 것(They will, of course, receive complimentary admission to the fair)이라고 했고, 온라인 댓글의 두 번째 문장에서 오 씨는 스컬라 씨의 제안으로 정비 팀이 여름 축제를 준비하는 것을 돕는 일에 자원했다(At Mr. Skerla's suggestion, I volunteered to help ~ prepare for the summer fair)고 했다. 따라서 오 씨는 자원봉사자로서 축제에 무료로 입장했음을 알 수 있으므로 (B)가 정답이다.

Paraphrasing 지문의 complimentary admission
→ 정답의 attend ~ for free

ETS 기출 실전문제
본책 p.128

1 (B)	**2** (C)	**3** (A)	**4** (C)	**5** (B)	**6** (C)
7 (B)	**8** (C)	**9** (D)	**10** (C)	**11** (B)	**12** (A)
13 (A)	**14** (D)	**15** (C)			

[1-3] 설명

> **세이프스프레이 커버 보호제—사용 설명**
>
> 세이프스프레이 커버 보호제는 차나 주스와 같은 액체로 인한 얼룩을 방지하는 데 도움을 주는 친환경 섬유 처리제입니다. **1유해한 화학 물질이 함유되지 않은 세이프스프레이는** 직물 표면에 수분을 튕겨내는 미세막을 생성합니다. 직물 커버로 된 의자 및 기타 푹신한 가구가 수분으로 인해 손상되는 것을 방지하며 가볍고 상쾌한 향이 나는 사용하기 쉬운 제품입니다.
>
> **2세이프스프레이를 사용하시려면 병을 잘 흔든 다음 약품을 사용할 직물로부터 6인치 떨어진 곳에서 들어 주세요.** 그런 다음 쓸어내리는 동작으로 표면에 분사하세요. 직물이 **3흠뻑 젖어서는** 안 되니 너무 많이 사용하지 마세요. 소재가 완전히 마르도록 두세요. 최대한 보호하기 위해서는 몇 달마다 다시 도포해 주세요.

어휘 upholstery (소파 등의) 커버 protector 보호제 fabric 섬유 prevent 방지하다 stain 얼룩 chemical 화학 물질 repel (물 등을) 튕기다 microlayer 미세층 scent 향기 saturated 흠뻑 젖은 reapply 다시 도포하다

1 세이프스프레이 커버 보호제에 대해 명시된 것은?
(A) 알아 챌 수 있는 향이 없다.
(B) 무독성 성분으로 만들어졌다.
(C) 단단한 표면을 손상시킬 수 있다.
(D) 1년에 한 번만 사용해야 한다.

해설 **Not / True**
첫 번째 단락 두 번째 문장에서 유해한 화학 물질이 함유되지 않은 세이프스프레이(Free from harmful chemicals, Safespray)라고 했으므로 (B)가 정답이다.

어휘 detectable 알아 챌[감지할] 수 있는 fragrance 향 nontoxic 무독성의

Paraphrasing 지문의 Free from harmful chemicals
→ 정답의 nontoxic

2 설명에 따르면, 제품을 사용하기 전에 해야 할 일은?
(A) 환기를 위해 창문 열기
(B) 병에 물 넣기
(C) 병을 잘 흔들어 주기
(D) 처치 부위 깨끗이 닦기

해설 **세부 사항**
두 번째 단락의 첫 문장에서 세이프스프레이를 사용하려면 병을 잘 흔들라(To use Safespray, shake the bottle well)고 했으므로 (C)가 정답이다.

어휘 thoroughly 완전히, 철저히

Paraphrasing 지문의 well → 정답의 thoroughly

3 두 번째 단락 3행의 "saturated"와 의미가 가장 가까운 단어는?
(A) 흠뻑 젖은 (B) 만족하는
(C) 강렬한 (D) 순수한

해설 **동의어 찾기**
의미상 직물이 '흠뻑 젖으면' 안 된다는 뜻으로 쓰였으므로 '흠뻑 젖은'을 뜻하는 (A) soaked가 정답이다.

[4-6] 광고

> **현대 사진 박물관—교육 워크숍**
>
> 시의 시각 예술가 협회에 의해 설립된 현대 사진 박물관은 예술 형태로서의 사진에 대한 관심을 높이는 것을 목표로 합니다. 대중에게 무료로 개방되는 박물관은 메인 갤러리에서 다양한 현대 사진을 전시합니다. **4또한 빈티지 카메라, 부속품, 필름 롤, 그리고 역사적으로 흥미로운 기타 관련 물건들의 전시도 선보입니다.**
>
> 박물관 직원들의 사진에 대한 열정을 공유하고자, 창의적 표현 수단으로서 사진에 초점을 둔 무료 교육 워크숍을 제공합니다. 사진 촬영 사전 경험이 필수 사항이 아니며 모든 기술 수준의 참가자를 환영합니다.
>
> '건축을 담다'라는 제목의 이번 달 워크숍은 4월 13일 토요일 오후 3시 30분에서 6시까지 센트럴 시티 광장에서 열립니다. **6이 강좌는 유명 도시 사진작가인 강사 브라이언 캠포스의 유익한 강의로 시작됩니다.** 참가자들은 건물 사진 촬영 기법에 대한 그의 전문적인 조언을 받게 될 것입니다. 그런 다음 광장 구역을 답사하고 사진을 찍을 충분한 시간이 제공됩니다. **5모든 종류의 카메라가 이 강좌에 적합합니다.**
>
> 이 세션은 참가자 10명으로 제한되며 박물관 웹사이트를 통한 온라인 등록이 필수입니다. 참가자들은 센트럴 시티 비즈니스 호텔 옆 광장과 접해 있는 피크닉 구역에서 모일 예정입니다. 날씨가 안 좋을 경우, 강좌 일정은 다른 시간대로 변경됩니다.

어휘 found 설립하다 showcase 전시하다 an array of 다수의 contemporary 현대의 accessories 부속품 enthusiasm 열정 means 수단 plaza 광장 informative 유익한 noted 유명한 urban 도시의 ample 충분한 explore 답사하다 suitable 적합한 assemble 모이다 alongside ~ 옆에

4 광고에서 박물관에 대해 명시된 것은?
(A) 소정의 입장료가 부과된다.
(B) 현대적인 외관으로 유명하다.
(C) 오래된 사진 장비를 전시한다.
(D) 교육자 단체에 의해 설립되었다.

해설 **Not / True**
첫 번째 단락 마지막 문장에서 박물관은 빈티지 카메라, 부속품, 필름 롤, 그리고 역사적으로 흥미로운 기타 관련 물건들의 전시도 선보인다(It also features exhibits of vintage cameras, ~ other related objects of historical interest)고 했으므로 (C)가 정답이다.

어휘 charge 부과하다   exterior 외관

(Paraphrasing) 지문의 vintage cameras ~ objects of historical interest → 정답의 old photographic equipment

5 '건축을 담다' 워크숍에 대해 명시된 것은?
(A) 한 달에 두 번 제공될 예정이다.
(B) 특정한 유형의 카메라가 필요하지 않다.
(C) 날씨가 안 좋을 경우 실내에서 진행된다.
(D) 피크닉 구역에서의 무료 간식이 포함되어 있다.

해설 **Not / True**
세 번째 단락의 마지막 문장에서 모든 종류의 카메라가 이 강좌에 적합하다(All types of cameras are suitable for this class)고 안내했으므로 (B)가 정답이다.

6 [1], [2], [3], [4]로 표시된 곳 중에서 다음 문장이 들어가기에 가장 적합한 위치는?
"참가자들은 건물 사진 촬영 기법에 대한 그의 전문적인 조언을 받게 될 것입니다."
(A) [1]   (B) [2]
(C) [3]   (D) [4]

해설 **문장 삽입**
주어진 문장에서 참가자들이 사진 촬영에 대한 그의(his) 조언을 받는다고 했으므로, 주어진 문장 앞에는 사진 촬영에 대해 조언해 줄 수 있는 남자가 등장해야 한다. 따라서 유명 도시 사진작가인 강사 브라이언 캠포스(instructor Brian Campos, a noted urban photographer)가 수업을 진행한다고 언급한 문장 뒤 [3]에 들어가는 것이 글의 흐름상 자연스러우므로 (C)가 정답이다.

[7-10] 문자 메시지

리처드 코헨 (오후 3시 42분) 안녕하세요, 여러분. **7**우리 월례 모임에 대해 점검하고, 배정받은 독서도 확인하며, 새로운 클럽 회원인 카리마 알라위도 환영하려고 합니다!

카리마 알라위 (오후 3시 45분) 감사합니다, 리처드. 샌프란시스코 베이 지역에서 마음이 맞는 분들을 만나게 되어 정말 좋아요. 여러분이 제가 여기 이사 온 이후 처음으로 만난 분들입니다.

엔조 토마소 (오후 3시 47분) 이 그룹에 오신 것을 환영해요, 카리마! **8**리처드는 제가 살리나스에서 이사 왔을 때 이곳에서 처음 맺은 인연이기도 해요. 열혈 독서가들을 연결해 주는 것이 그의 평생 사명 같아요.

리처드 코헨 (오후 3시 49분) 제가 좋아서 하는 일이에요. 이번 달에는 윌리엄 실즈의 〈멕시코만행〉을 읽을 예정이에요. 미시시피 강을 따라 가는 증기선 여행을 시간순으로 기록한 회고록이죠. 모두 책을 구하실 수 있었나요?

카리마 알라위 (오후 3시 52분) 네. 저는 샌브루노의 저희 아파트 근처에 있는 브래들리 앤 뉴웰에서 샀어요. 중고 페이퍼백은 10달러가 안 되었어요.

사라 모리타 (오후 3시 56분) 그 서점을 한번 가 봐야겠어요. 작은 업체에 도움이 되는 걸 좋아하지만, **9**원하는 것보다 아타카마에

서 더 자주 구매한다는 사실을 인정해야겠어요. 거기는 선택의 폭이 넓고 온라인으로 구매할 책을 검색하기도 쉽거든요.

리처드 코헨 (오후 3시 59분) 좋아요. 그럼 모두 준비가 된 것 같네요. **10**5월 28일 오전 11시에 미션베이에 있는 베를린 카페에서 모두 만납시다.

카리마 알라위 (오후 4시) 모임 전에 조언이 좀 필요해요. 저는 차가 없고, 시내에서 길을 찾는 것도 좀 자신이 없어요.

사라 모리타 (오후 4시 2분) 샌브루노에서 L열차를 타면 금방 갈 수 있어요. 제가 밀브레이에 사는데 사시는 곳과 그리 멀지 않아요. 대중교통이 시내를 돌아다니기에 정말 편리한 것 같아요.

어휘 verify 확인하다   assigned 할당된   like-minded 생각이 비슷한   avid 열렬한   bound for ~ 행의   memoir 회고록   chronicle 연대순으로 기록하다   steamboat 증기선   journey 여행   browse 검색하다   public transit 대중교통

7 메시지 작성자들은 누구일 것 같은가?
(A) 출판사 직원   (B) 독서회 회원
(C) 역사 소설 작가   (D) 서점 주인

해설 **추론 / 암시**
3시 42분에 코헨 씨가 우리 월례 모임 점검과 배정받은 독서 확인, 신규 클럽 회원 환영을 하려고 한다(I wanted ~ our newest club member, Karima Alaoui!)고 한 것으로 보아 메시지 작성자들은 도서회의 회원들이라는 것을 알 수 있다. 따라서 (B)가 정답이다.

8 오후 3시 49분에 코헨 씨가 "제가 좋아서 하는 일이에요"라고 쓴 의도는?
(A) 샌프란시스코에 사는 것이 좋다.
(B) 주제에 관한 자신의 의견을 공유하게 되어 기쁘다.
(C) 그룹을 조직하는 것이 즐겁다.
(D) 독자들의 피드백을 감사하게 여긴다.

해설 **의도 파악**
3시 47분에 토마소 씨가 살리나스에서 이사 왔을 때 리처드는 이곳에서 처음 맺은 인연(Richard was also my first connection ~ Salinas)이라면서 열혈 독서가들을 연결해 주는 것이 그의 평생 사명 같다(His life mission ~ connecting avid readers)고 칭찬하자, 3시 49분에 코헨 씨가 좋아서 하는 일이다(it's my pleasure)라고 했다. 따라서 코헨 씨가 독서회에 사람들을 연결시켜 주는 일이 즐겁다는 의도로 한 말임을 알 수 있으므로 (C)가 정답이다.

9 아타카마는 어떤 종류의 업체일 것 같은가?
(A) 사무용품점   (B) 사립 도서관
(C) 출판사   **(D) 온라인 매장**

해설 **추론 / 암시**
3시 56분에 모리타 씨가 원하는 것보다 아타카마에서 더 자주 구매한다는 걸 인정해야겠다(I must admit that I buy from Atacama ~ like)면서, 거기는 선택의 폭이 넓고 온라인으로 구매할 책을 검색하기도 쉽다(They ~ easy to browse for books to buy online)고 했으므로 아타카마가 온라인 서점임을 알 수 있다. 따라서 (D)가 정답이다.

10 메시지 작성자들이 직접 만날 장소는?

(A) 살리나스   (B) 샌브루노

(C) 미션베이   (D) 밀브레이

해설 **세부 사항**

3시 59분에 코헨 씨가 5월 28일 오전 11시에 미션베이에 있는 베를린 카페에서 모두 만나자(See everyone ~ in Mission Bay)고 했으므로 (C)가 정답이다.

[11-15] 이메일 + 영수증

> 수신: 마케팅 팀
>
> 발신: 셰인 홀리데이
>
> **13** 날짜: 5월 6일
>
> **13** 제목: 내일 회의
>
> 좋은 아침입니다, 팀원 여러분.
>
> 내일 우리 회의는 곧 있을 마케팅 활동에 초점을 둘 것입니다. **11** 작년에 북미로 진출한 덕분에 우리의 가장 인기 있는 제품 일부를 재디자인하고 새로운 제품을 출시하게 되었습니다.
>
> **13** 회의는 현재 오후 2시 30분부터 5시까지 오크 회의실에서 열릴 예정입니다. 회의가 오래 진행될 경우, 식사가 제공될 것입니다. 필수적인 정보가 논의되고 팀 의견이 필요한 결정이 내려질 것이므로 참석에 만전을 기해 주십시오. **12** 특히 유럽에서 판매 둔화세를 보이고 있는 여성 운동화 **14** 라인의 브랜드 이미지를 쇄신하기 위한 계획을 다룰 것입니다. 제품 개발 팀의 아서 그린이 참석하여 신상 디자인 및 색상의 실물 모형을 보여줄 것입니다. 우리는 반드시 이 신발들이 시장에서 다시 제자리를 되찾을 수 있게 해야 합니다.
>
> 셰인 홀리데이
>
> 소프트 스프린트 슈즈 마케팅 부사장

어휘 effort 활동, 노력   launch 출시하다   input 의견   rebrand 브랜드 이미지를 쇄신하다   slowdown 둔화   mock-up (실물 크기의) 모형   regain 되찾다

> **엘로이지스 식당**
>
> **11 킬링 로**
>
> **페리베일**
>
> **UB6 7JB**
>
> **www.eloiseseatery.co.uk**
>
> **13** 날짜: 5월 7일   **13** 주문 접수: 오후 4시
>
> 고객: 셰인 홀리데이   sholliday@softsprintshoes.co.uk
>
> 배송 주소: 소프트 스프린트 슈즈
>
> 워즈워스 비즈니스 센터
>
> 본햄 로
>
> 페리베일
>
> HA0 1BW

주문: 피시앤칩스 대형 트레이 1개	125파운드
이탈리안 토마토 소스 파스타 대형 트레이 1개	80파운드
15(B) 혼합 그린 샐러드 1개	40파운드
(10인분, 이탈리안 드레싱)	
15(D) 1리터 탄산수 5병	9파운드
나이프, 포크, 스푼 아니요 **15(A)** 냅킨 네	
총	254파운드

어휘 eatery 식당   cutlery 날붙이(나이프, 포크 등)

11 이메일에서 소프트 스프린트 슈즈에 대해 암시된 것은?

(A) 제품 디자이너 채용이 진행 중이다.

(B) 최근 새로운 시장에서 신발을 판매하기 시작했다.

(C) 북미 지역에 새로운 생산 센터를 열 계획이다.

(D) 지난 1년 동안 매출이 크게 증가했다.

해설 **추론/암시**

이메일의 첫 단락 두 번째 문장에서 작년에 북미로 진출한 덕분에 당사의 인기 있는 제품 일부를 재디자인하고 새로운 제품을 출시하게 되었다(Expanding into North America last year ~ launch some new ones)고 한 것으로 보아 최근 새로운 시장인 북미 지역에서 제품을 판매하기 시작했음을 알 수 있다. 따라서 (B)가 정답이다.

어휘 in the process of ~을 진행 중인   revenue 수익, 매출액

12 이메일에서 홀리데이 씨가 언급한 문제는?

(A) 어느 한 제품이 더 이상 잘 팔리지 않는다.

(B) 새로운 제품의 생산이 지연되었다.

(C) 일부 직원이 퇴사했다.

(D) 제품 후기가 부정적이었다.

해설 **세부 사항**

이메일의 두 번째 단락 네 번째 문장에서 홀리데이 씨가 특히 유럽에서 판매 둔화세를 보이고 있는 여성 운동화 라인의 브랜드 이미지 쇄신을 위한 계획을 다룰 것(We will address ~ a slowdown in sales, especially in Europe)이라며 여성 운동화 라인의 매출이 전보다 줄었다고 언급했으므로 (A)가 정답이다.

(Paraphrasing) 지문의 a slowdown in sales

→ 정답의 no longer selling well

13 마케팅 회의에 대해 결론지을 수 있는 것은?

(A) 오후 5시 이후에 끝났다.

(B) 참석이 저조했다.

(C) 식당에서 열렸다.

(D) 회사 사장의 연설이 포함되었다

해설 **연계**

이메일의 날짜가 5월 6일(6 May), 제목은 내일 회의(Tomorrow's meeting)이다. 두 번째 단락 첫 문장에서 회의는 오후 2시 30분부터 5시까지 열릴 예정(The meeting ~ from 2:30 P.M. to 5:00 P.M.)이고, 회의가 오래 진행될 경우 식사가 제공된다(In the event that the meeting runs long, a meal will be provided)고 했으며, 엘로이지스 식당 영수증의 상단에 날짜가 5월 7일(Date: 7 May), 주문 접수가 오후 4시(Order received: 4:00 P.M.)로 표기되어 있다. 따라서 5월 7일 회의가 길어져 오후 4시에 식사를 주문한 것으로 보아 회의가 5시 이후에 끝났다는 것을 짐작할 수 있으므로 (A)가 정답이다.

14 이메일의 두 번째 단락 5행의 "line"과 의미가 가장 가까운 단어는?

(A) 열   (B) 노선

(C) 경계   (D) 컬렉션

의미상 여성 운동화 '라인', 즉 '제품군'이라는 뜻으로 쓰였으므로 '(의류 등의) 컬렉션'이라는 의미의 (D) collection이 정답이다.

15 영수증에 따르면, 홀리데이 씨의 주문에 포함되지 않은 것은?
(A) 냅킨 (B) 샐러드
(C) 디저트 (D) 음료

해설 **Not/True**
영수증의 하단에 혼합 그린 샐러드 1개(1 mixed greens salad)가 있으므로 (B), 1리터 탄산수 5병(5 ~ sparkling water)이 있으므로 (D), 냅킨에 네(Napkins Yes)라고 표기되어 있으므로 (A)는 포함된 것을 알 수 있다. 디저트는 영수증에 보이지 않으므로 (C)가 정답이다.

ETS기출 고난도 실전문제
본책 p.134

1 (A)	**2** (D)	**3** (A)	**4** (C)	**5** (A)	**6** (C)
7 (B)	**8** (D)	**9** (C)	**10** (A)	**11** (C)	**12** (D)
13 (B)	**14** (A)	**15** (C)	**16** (B)	**17** (A)	**18** (A)
19 (B)	**20** (D)				

[1-4] 편지

유럽 티타늄 회의

6월 28일

리제트 오졸스
벨리어드 가 1365
브뤼셀, BE 1000

오졸스 씨께,

¹**티타늄 금속 산업의 국제 교역 단체인 유럽 티타늄 회의(ETC)에 가입해 주셔서 감사합니다.** ETC는 티타늄의 독특한 특성과 현대 제조업에서 중대한 역할에 관해 엔지니어 및 비즈니스 전문가를 교육하는 데 전념하고 있습니다.

²**ETC 회원으로서 귀하는 당 회의의 기술 문헌 및 전문가 팀의 지원을 이용할 수 있습니다.** 귀하는 연례 유럽 티타늄 박람회와 티타늄 산업 관련 주제를 다루는 정기 워크숍에 참석할 수 있습니다.

⁴**제조업에서 티타늄의 유용성은 매년 증가하고 있습니다.** 항공 우주 및 의료 산업에서의 높은 수요가 이 성장을 주도하고 있습니다. ³**티타늄의 낮은 무게, 우수한 강도, 유연성뿐만 아니라 녹과 기타 형태의 부식에 대한 저항력 때문에 티타늄은 여러 용도에서 철과 강철의 훌륭한 대안이 됩니다.** 향후 행사에서 뵙기를 기대합니다.

시구르드 빈제
사무국장
유럽 티타늄 회의

어휘 congress 회의, 협회 properties 특성 crucial 중대한 manufacturing 제조업 literature 문헌 exposition 박람회 periodic 정기적인 pertinent to ~와 관련 있는 flexibility 유연성 resistance 저항력 rust 녹 corrosion 부식 alternative 대안 application 특정 용도, 적용

---

1 빈제 씨는 왜 오졸스 씨에게 편지를 썼는가?
(A) 전문 단체에 가입한 것을 환영하려고
(B) 티타늄 산업에서 일자리를 제공하려고
(C) 그녀의 회사가 제조한 티타늄 구매를 협상하려고
(D) 교역 콘퍼런스에서 연설하도록 권하려고

해설 **주제/목적**
첫 문장에서 빈제 씨가 오졸스 씨에게 티타늄 금속 산업의 국제 교역 단체인 유럽 티타늄 회의(ETC)에 가입해 주어 감사하다(Thank you for joining the European Titanium Congress ~ industry)고 했으므로 전문 단체 가입을 환영하는 편지임을 알 수 있다. 따라서 (A)가 정답이다.

2 ETC에 대해 언급된 것은?
(A) 티타늄을 제조 및 판매한다.
(B) 학술 연구에 자금을 지원한다.
(C) 정부가 티타늄 교역 문제를 해결하는 데 도움을 준다.
(D) 기술 전문가에게 문의할 기회를 제공한다.

해설 **세부 사항**
두 번째 단락의 첫 문장에서 ETC 회원으로서 당사의 기술 문헌 및 전문가 팀의 지원을 이용할 수 있다(As an ETC member, you have access to our technical literature ~ experts)며 전문가 팀의 도움을 받을 수 있다고 언급했으므로 (D)가 정답이다.

어휘 fund 자금을 대다 resolve 해결하다 access 대면 기회

(Paraphrasing) 지문의 experts → 정답의 specialists

3 티타늄이 철과 강철의 훌륭한 대체제인 이유로 언급된 것이 아닌 것은?
(A) 가격이 저렴하다. (B) 가볍다.
(C) 유연하다. (D) 튼튼하다.

해설 **Not/True**
세 번째 단락의 세 번째 문장에서 티타늄의 낮은 무게, 우수한 강도, 유연성뿐만 아니라 녹과 기타 형태의 부식에 대한 저항력 때문에 여러 용도에서 티타늄은 철과 강철의 훌륭한 대안(Titanium's low weight, superior strength, and flexibility, ~ applications)이라고 했으므로 (B), (C), (D)는 모두 언급되었다. 따라서 (A)가 정답이다.

(Paraphrasing) 지문의 low weight → (B)의 lightweight

4 [1], [2], [3], [4]로 표시된 곳 중에서 다음 문장이 들어가기에 가장 적합한 위치는?
"항공 우주 및 의료 산업에서의 높은 수요가 이 성장을 주도하고 있습니다."
(A) [1] (B) [2]
(C) [3] (D) [4]

해설 **문장 삽입**
주어진 문장에서 항공 우주와 의료 산업에서 높은 수요가 이 성장(This growth)을 주도하고 있다고 했으므로, 주어진 문장 앞에는 산업과 관련된 성장에 대한 내용이 있어야 한다. 따라서 제조업에서 티타늄의 유용성이 매년 증가(increases)하고 있다며 티타늄의 성장세에 대해 언급한 문장 뒤 [3]에 들

어가는 것이 자연스러우므로 (C)가 정답이다.

어휘 drive 주도하다　aerospace 항공 우주 산업

[5-6] 문자 메시지

> **레나 헨더슨 (오전 9시 29분)**
> 아마라 베이크숍의 레나입니다. **5뒷문에 주차했고 배송품을 내려 놓을 준비가 되었어요.**
>
> **조 나카무라 (오전 9시 30분)**
> 안녕하세요, 레나. 저희 주방 직원은 45분 전에 도착하실 줄 알고 있었어요!
>
> **레나 헨더슨 (오전 9시 31분)**
> 맞아요. 저희가 일손이 부족해서 빵과 디너 롤 굽는 데 평소보다 오래 걸렸어요.
>
> **조 나카무라 (오전 9시 32분)**
> 좀 더 일찍 알려 주셨으면 좋았을 텐데요. 저희 음식 납품 팀이 이미 나머지 음식을 트럭에 실었어요. 연회장에 오전 10시 30분에 도착해야 하니까 가지고 오신 제품을 즉시 우리 트럭에 실어야 해요.
>
> **레나 헨더슨 (오전 9시 33분)**
> 죄송합니다. **6이런 일이 또 생기면 반드시 미리 알려 드리겠습니다.**
>
> **조 나카무라 (오전 9시 34분)**
> 적어도 한 시간 전에는요. 지금 우리 팀원 한 명이 하역장 입구에서 만나 뵐 거예요.
>
> **어휘** short-staffed 직원이 부족한　loading dock 하역장

5 헨더슨 씨는 어디에 있을 것 같은가?
(A) 차량　　　　　　(B) 주방
(C) 제과점　　　　　(D) 연회장

해설 **추론/암시**
오전 9시 29분에 헨더슨 씨가 뒷문에 주차했고 배송품을 내릴 준비가 되었다(I'm parked ~ ready to unload your delivery)고 한 것으로 보아 헨더슨 씨는 현재 주차한 차량에서 대기 중인 것임을 짐작할 수 있다. 따라서 (A)가 정답이다.

6 오전 9시 34분에 나카무라 씨가 "적어도 한 시간 전에는요" 라고 쓴 의도는?
(A) 적재 작업이 한 시간 걸릴 것으로 예상한다.
(B) 자동차로 한 시간 이상 걸릴 것이라고 믿는다.
(C) 더 일찍 알림을 받기를 원한다.
(D) 헨더슨 씨가 곧 팀원 몇 명을 만나기를 희망한다

해설 **의도 파악**
9시 33분에 헨더슨 씨가 이런 일이 또 생기면 미리 알리겠다(I'll be sure to give you some notice ~ again)고 하자 9시 34분에 나카무라 씨가 적어도 한 시간 전에는요(At least one hour in advance)라고 응답했으므로, 나카무라 씨는 지연이 있을 경우 일찍 알려 주기를 당부하려는 의도로 한 말임을 알 수 있다. 따라서 (C)가 정답이다.

어휘 alert (문제 등을) 알리다

[7-10] 편지

> **황거레이 공익 기업　·　166 노던 크레센트　·　황거레이 0112**
>
> 4월 2일
>
> 소중한 고객님께:
>
> **7저희가 고객님의 정확한 전화번호를 기록 보관하고 있나요?** 요즘 거의 모든 사람들이 휴대폰을 가지고 있습니다. 사실, 고객님은 휴대폰 사용만 선호하여 유선 전화를 포기한 수백만 뉴질랜드인 중 한 분일 수 있습니다. 고객님의 현재 전화번호가 등록되어 있지 않으면, 황거레이 공익 기업은 고객님이 전화를 주실 때 인식할 수 없습니다. 이는 고객님이 저희 서비스를 필요로 하실 때 저희가 얼마나 신속하게 대응하는지에 영향을 미칠 수 있습니다.
>
> 저희는 여러 방법으로 고객님의 전화번호를 사용합니다. **8문제 보고를 위해 전화나 문자를 주실 때 자사의 자동화 시스템은 즉시 고객님의 번호를 자택 주소에 연계시킵니다.** 이를 통해 고객님의 문제에 보다 빠르게 대응할 수 있습니다. 그리고 계정과 관련하여 고객 관리 센터로 전화를 하실 경우 등록되어 있는 고객인지를 확인하기 위해 고객님의 전화번호를 이용합니다.
>
> 회선 및 장비를 업그레이드하기 위한 서비스 일시 중단 일정을 잡을 때 등록되어 있는 전화번호로 전화를 걸어 미리 알려 드립니다. 사전 알림은 서비스 **9중단**의 불편을 줄이고 미리 대비할 수 있도록 해 줍니다.
>
> **10(B), (D)전화번호를 확인하시거나 업데이트하시려면, 황거레이 공익 기업 웹사이트 또는 휴대폰 앱을 통해 계정에 로그인하시거나** (09) 429 9755로 전화하십시오. 10(C)우편으로 납부하시는 경우 고지서 뒷면에 전화번호를 기재하십시오.
>
> 더 나은 서비스를 제공할 수 있도록 도와주셔서 감사합니다.
>
> 황거레이 공익 기업 고객 관리 팀
>
> **어휘** utility (수도·가스 등의) 공익사업　on file 기록 보관되어　landline 유선 전화　in favour of ~에 찬성하여　exclusively 오로지 ~만　associate 연관 짓다　verify 확인하다　temporary 일시적인　outage (서비스) 중단　advance 사전의　lessen 줄이다

7 편지의 목적은 무엇인가?
(A) 휴대폰 앱의 업데이트를 공지하려고
(B) 고객에게 한 가지의 정보를 계속 업데이트하도록 장려하려고
(C) 고객에게 곧 있을 정비 사업에 관해 알리려고
(D) 공과금의 최근 변동 사항을 설명하려고

해설 **주제/목적**
첫 문장에서 해당 업체가 고객의 정확한 전화번호를 기록 보관하고 있는지(Do we have your correct telephone number on file?) 묻는 것으로 보아 연락 정보를 최근 것으로 업데이트해 줄 것을 고객에게 당부하기 위한 편지임을 알 수 있다. 따라서 (B)가 정답이다.

어휘 maintenance 정비　utility rate 공과금

8 황거레이 공익 기업에서 고객의 전화번호를 사용하는 한 가지 방식은 무엇인가?
(A) 결제 알림 전송
(B) 지역 사회 봉사 활동 활성화

(C) 가장 많은 전력을 사용하는 고객 식별

(D) 발신자와 서비스 지점 연결

해설 세부 사항

두 번째 단락의 두 번째 문장에서 문제 보고를 위해 고객이 전화나 문자를 주면 자동화 시스템은 즉시 고객의 번호를 자택 주소에 연계시킨다(When you call ~ associates your number with your home address)고 했으므로 전화번호를 통해 발신자인 고객이 서비스 받는 위치를 파악한다는 것을 알 수 있다. 따라서 (D)가 정답이다.

어휘 reminder 알림 메시지 outreach 봉사 활동

(Paraphrasing) 지문의 associates → 정답의 link

9 세 번째 단락 3행의 "break"와 의미가 가장 가까운 단어는?

(A) 탈출   (B) 개점

(C) 중단   (D) 기회

해설 동의어 찾기

의미상 서비스 '중단'이라는 뜻으로 쓰였으므로 '중단'을 뜻하는 (C) interruption이 정답이다.

10 편지에 언급된 의사소통 방법이 아닌 것은?

(A) 이메일   (B) 전화 통화

(C) 우편 서비스   (D) 스마트폰 앱

해설 세부 사항

마지막 단락의 첫 문장에서 전화번호를 확인하거나 업데이트하려면 황거레이 공익 기업 웹사이트 또는 휴대폰 앱을 통해 로그인하거나 (09) 429 9755로 전화하라(To check ~ Web site or mobile app or call (09) 429 9755)고 했으므로 (B)와 (D). 우편으로 납부하는 경우 고지서 뒷면에 전화번호를 기재하라(If you pay your bills by mail, ~ bill)고 했으므로 (C)는 연락 방법으로 언급되었다. 하지만 이메일에 대한 언급은 없으므로 (A)가 정답이다.

(Paraphrasing) 지문의 by mail → (C)의 Postal service

[11-15] 기사 + 이메일

락-E 그리고 그의 암석

캐롤리 스팽글러 작성

리버풀 (3월 4일)—어떤 연예인들은 스포츠 기념품이나 예술 작품과 같은 물건을 수집하기를 좋아하지만, 다른 어떤 연예인들은 덜 평범한 물건을 모은다. 본래 자메이카 킹스턴 출신인 레게 음악 슈퍼스타 락-E는 특이한 수집품 한 가지를 보관하고 있다.

11(A) 어린 시절 락-E(본명은 오언 터프튼)는 지질학자인 아버지로부터 지구 광물, 특히 암석에 대한 많은 것을 배웠다. 초등학교 때는 그것이 그가 이야기하고 싶어 하는 전부였다. 곧, **11(B)** 그의 학교 친구들은 그에게 락-E라는 별명을 지어 주었다. 그는 나중에 그것을 자신의 예명으로 택하게 된다.

락-E는 자라서도 지질학에 대한 흥미를 결코 잃지 않았다. **12** 20년의 경력 동안, 그는 공연했던 모든 도시에서 돌을 주웠다. 각각의 돌에는 도시의 이름과 공연 날짜가 새겨져 있다. **11(D), 14** 이 돌들은 그의 맨체스터 자택의 특별한 정원에 배치되어 있다.

락-E가 방문객들에게 그의 암석 수집품을 보여줄 때면, 방문객

들은 종종 각 암석의 광물 구성물과 지질학적 기원에 대한 그의 전문 지식에 놀라움을 금치 못한다. 그의 새 매니저인 프리티 마라즈는 "락-E가 갖고 있는 이 암석들에 대한 풍부한 정보는 정말 놀랍습니다. 게다가 그것들은 락-E 브랜드에 큰 가치를 더해 줍니다."라고 말했다.

어휘 memorabilia 기념품 ordinary 평범한 mineral 광물 particularly 특히 geologist 지질학자 adopt 택하다 outgrow 자라면서 ~에 흥미를 잃다 geological 지질학적인 fascination 매료됨 engrave 새기다 composition 구성 요소 origin 기원 remark 언급하다 astounding 놀라운

수신: 락-E ⟨rock_e@dandeliondance.co.uk⟩

발신: 프리티 마라즈 ⟨preeti.maraj@nightglitz.co.uk⟩

날짜: 3월 9일

제목: 의견 요청드립니다.

록-E께,

14 지난주 당신의 집에서 있었던 친목 모임에 초대해 주셔서 감사합니다. **15** 거기서 그린패스트 밴드의 멤버들을 보게 되어 더욱 특별했습니다. 모르시겠지만 그들과 저의 인연은 그들이 저를 에이전트로 고용했던 15년 전으로 거슬러 올라갑니다. 저는 이곳 리버풀에서 막 일을 시작했고, 그들은 저의 첫 고객이었습니다.

말할 필요도 없이, 당신의 암석 수집품을 직접 보는 것도 즐거웠습니다. 솔직히 말하자면 처음에는 돌 수집이라는 발상이 놀라웠지만 곰곰이 생각해 보니 더 이해가 갔습니다. 그 돌들은 마치 사진처럼 당신의 이력에 대해 이야기해 줍니다.

13 곧 있을 호주 투어를 위해 투어 로고, 도시, 콘서트 날짜가 새겨진 돌을 판매 상품으로 넣어도 되겠다는 생각이 들었습니다. 이 기념 돌을 티셔츠 및 기타 제품과 온라인에서 판매할 수 있습니다.

그런 작업을 하는 업체 몇 군데를 이미 찾아봤습니다. 하지만 더 알아보기 전에 **13** 이 아이디어에 관심이 있는지 궁금합니다. 어떻게 생각하는지 알려 주세요.

프리티 마라즈

나이트글리츠 탤런트 에이전시 대표

어휘 input 의견 gathering 모임 treat 특별한 것[선물] launch 시작하다 needless to say 말할 필요도 없이 initially 처음에 reflect on ~을 곰곰이 생각하다 make sense 타당하다 occur to ~에게 생각이 떠오르다 merchandising 판매, 판촉 imprint 새기다 commemorative 기념하는 explore 알아보다

11 기사에서 락-E에 대해 언급된 것이 아닌 것은?

(A) 아버지로부터 지질학에 대해 배웠다.

(B) 어린 시절의 별명을 직업적 이름으로 썼다.

(C) 공연자가 되기 전에 자메이카에 있는 대학을 다녔다.

(D) 손님들이 볼 수 있도록 자신의 암석 수집품을 전시한다.

해설 Not/True

기사의 두 번째 단락 첫 문장에서 어린 시절 락-E는 지질학자인 아버지로부터 암석에 대한 많은 것을 배웠다(As a child, Rock-E ~ rocks, from his father, a geologist)고 했으므로 (A). 같은 단락의 세 번째 문장에서 그의 학교 친구들은 그에게 락-E라는 별명을 지어주었고(his schoolmates nicknamed him Rock-E). 그는 나중에 그것을 예명으로 택하게 된다(He ~ adopt that as his stage name)고 했으므로 (B). 세 번째 단락의 마지막 문장에서 이 돌들은 그의 맨체스터 자택 정원에 배치되어 있다(The stones are arranged ~ home)고 했으므로 (D)는 언급되어 있다. 따라서 (C)가 정답이다.

12 락-E의 수집품 암석에 대해 명시된 것은?
(A) 그의 팬들이 그에게 주었다.
(B) 그가 자란 고향을 떠올리게 한다.
(C) 그에 관한 다큐멘터리에 등장할 것이다.
(D) 그가 공연했던 도시의 이름이 있다.

해설 **Not/True**
기사의 세 번째 단락 두 번째 문장에서 20년 동안 그는 공연했던 모든 도시에서 돌을 주웠다(Over ~, a rock in every city where he has played)고 했고, 각각의 돌에는 도시의 이름과 공연 날짜가 새겨져 있다(Each one ~ engraved with the name of the city and the performance date)고 했으므로 (D)가 정답이다.

어휘 feature 특집으로 다루다 bear (눈에 보이게) 있다[지니다]

(Paraphrasing) 지문의 engraved with → 정답의 bear

13 마라즈 씨가 락-E에게 이메일을 보낸 한 가지 이유는 무엇인가?
(A) 그의 배경에 대해 문의하려고
(B) 마케팅 아이디어를 추진하려고
(C) 자신의 다른 고객들에게 그를 소개하려고
(D) 리버풀에서 열리는 축하 행사에 초대하려고

해설 **주제/목적**
이메일의 세 번째 단락 첫 문장에서 마라즈 씨가 락-E에게 곧 있을 호주 투어를 위해 투어 로고, 도시, 콘서트 날짜가 새겨진 돌을 판매 상품으로 넣어도 되겠다는 생각이 들었다(For your upcoming tour ~ concert date imprinted on it)고 했고, 마지막 단락의 두 번째 문장에서 이 아이디어에 관심이 있는지 궁금하다(I'd like ~ the idea appeals to you)면서 어떻게 생각하는지 알려 달라(Please ~ what you think)고 했으므로 마케팅 아이디어를 제안하려고 이메일을 썼다는 것을 알 수 있다. 따라서 (B)가 정답이다.

14 마라즈 씨에 대해 사실일 것 같은 것은?
(A) 최근 맨체스터에 갔었다.
(B) 전문 음악가였다.
(C) 락-E의 유일한 홍보 대리인이었다.
(D) 락-E의 수집품 암석 중 한 개를 선물받았다.

해설 **연계**
기사의 세 번째 단락 마지막 문장에서 이 돌들은 그(락-E)의 맨체스터 자택의 특별 정원에 배치되어 있다(The stones ~ Manchester home)고 했고, 이메일의 첫 문장에서 마라즈 씨가 락-E에게 지난주 집에서 열린 친목 모임에 초대해 주어 감사하다(Thanks for inviting me ~ at your house last week)고 했다. 따라서 마라즈 씨는 최근 락-E의 맨체스터 자택에 다녀왔다는 것을 알 수 있으므로 (A)가 정답이다.

어휘 publicity agent 홍보 대리인

15 그린패스트 밴드의 멤버들에 대해 암시된 것은?
(A) 현재 호주에서 투어 중이다.
(B) 특이하다고 생각되는 품목을 수집한다.
(C) 최소한 15년 동안 함께했다.
(D) 그룹에 새로운 멤버를 추가했다.

해설 **추론/암시**
이메일의 첫 단락 두 번째 문장에서 마라즈 씨가 그린패스트 밴드의 멤버들을 보게 되어 더욱 특별했다(It ~ the band Greenfast there)면서, 그들과의 인연은 그들이 자신을 에이전트로 고용했던 15년 전으로 거슬러 올라간다(You ~ goes back fifteen years when they hired me as their agent)고 했다. 따라서 그린패스트 밴드는 결성된 지 최소 15년이 지났다는 것을 알 수 있으므로 (C)가 정답이다.

[16-20] 광고 + 이메일 + 후기

라센비 매트는 믿을 수 있습니다.

라센비 매트는 40년 이상 호주에서 가장 큰 재생고무 바닥 매트 제조업체입니다. 우리는 매년 수백만 개의 자동차 타이어를 소각로와 쓰레기 매립지에 보내지 않고, 다양한 용도의 내구성 좋은 맞춤형 매트로 탈바꿈시킵니다.

19우리는 주로 농업, 해양 및 임업 분야 고객에게 서비스를 제공하지만 전국 각지의 학교에도 매트를 공급하고 있습니다. **16**(03) 5550 0821로 연락하셔서, 제품군에 관한 질문에 답하거나 직접 주문을 지원 또는 당사의 유통 협력사 및 소매업체에 대한 정보를 제공할 수 있는 영업 담당자와 상담하십시오. 제품 및 구매처의 전체 목록이 필요하시면 www.lassenbymats.com.au로 당사 웹사이트를 방문하십시오.

어휘 rely on ~을 신뢰하다 recycled 재생된 incinerator 소각로 landfill 쓰레기 매립지 transform 탈바꿈하다 durable 내구성이 좋은 customisable 맞춤형의 application 용도 primarily 주로 marine 해양의 forestry 임업, 삼림 관리 distribution 유통 retailer 소매업체

수신: 가렛 샌본 〈gsanborne@opalmail.com.au〉
발신: 로버트 펜들리 〈rfendley@lassenbymats.com.au〉
날짜: 6월 14일 화요일
제목: 귀하의 주문

샌본 씨께,

귀하의 라센비 매트가 발송되어 6월 17일 금요일에 도착할 예정입니다. 다음은 도움이 될 만한 몇 가지 제안 사항입니다.

1. 배송 당일 부재중이실 경우, 이 메시지에 답장을 주시고 배송 상자를 건물 어디에 두길 바라는지 알려 주십시오.

2. **17**매트를 설치할 장소가 건조하고 먼지가 없는지 확인해 주십시오. 그러면 매트가 제대로 밀착되어 자리에 고정되는 데 도움이 됩니다. 초기 설치 후에는 대부분의 여건을 견딜 수 있습니다.

3. 매트는 포장에서 꺼낼 때 강한 냄새가 나겠지만, 환기가 잘 되는 곳에 몇 시간 포장을 벗겨 두면 냄새는 빠르게 사라집니다.

4. **²⁰매트의 한쪽 면은 밀착도를 높이기 위해 돌기가 있는 질감으로 되어 있습니다. 매트는 필요에 따라 매끄러운 면 또는 질감 처리된 면이 위로 향하도록 설치할 수 있습니다.**

거래에 감사드리며, 문의 사항이 있으시면 알려 주십시오!

로버트 펜들리
라센비 매트 선임 영업 담당

어휘 ship 출하하다 present (자리에) 있는 property 건물
adhere 부착되다 properly 제대로 initial 초기의
withstand 견뎌내다 odour 냄새 well-ventilated 환기가
잘 되는 spot 장소 dissipate 소멸되다 raised 돋아진,
양각의 texture 질감 traction 밀착력 face 향하다

---

https://www.lassenbymats.com.au/productreviews/25391

뛰어난 제품!

¹⁹저는 상업용 어선을 운용하고 있으며 미끄럼 방지 매트를 찾아보던 중 라센비 매트를 발견했습니다. ¹⁸영업 사원인 로버트 펜들리와 상담했을 때 그의 전문 지식과 저의 특정 요구 사항을 빠르게 파악하는 점에 감탄했습니다. ²⁰제 보트에서는 울퉁불퉁한 면이 위를 향하도록 매트를 설치했는데, 선원들이 보트의 갑판이 위험해질 수 있는 습한 상황에서 작업하기 때문에 저희에겐 안성맞춤이었습니다. 이 회사와 제품을 적극 추천합니다.

—가렛 샌본

어휘 operate 운용하다 slip-resistant 미끄럼 방지의
impressed 감명받은 expertise 전문 지식 grasp 파악,
이해 bumpy 울퉁불퉁한 deck 갑판

---

16 광고에서 라센비 매트에 대해 암시하는 것은?
(A) 최근에 제조법을 변경했다.
(B) 자사 제품의 일부를 다른 업체를 통해 판매한다.
(C) 특정 고객에게 무료 설치를 제공한다.
(D) 수익의 일정 비율을 교육 기관에 기부한다.

해설 추론/암시
광고의 두 번째 단락 두 번째 문장에서 주어진 전화번호로 연락하여 당사의 유통 협력사 및 소매업체에 대한 정보를 제공할 영업 담당자와 상담하라(Contact us ~ about our distribution partners and retailers)고 한 것으로 보아, 라센비 매트는 유통 협력사나 소매업체를 활용한 다양한 판매 경로가 있다는 것을 알 수 있으므로 (B)가 정답이다.

어휘 formula 제조법 portion 일부 institution 기관

(Paraphrasing) 지문의 distribution partners and retailers → 정답의 other companies

17 이메일에서 매트에 대해 명시하는 것은?
(A) 깨끗한 표면에 놓으면 더 나은 성능을 발휘한다.
(B) 손상된 경우 반품해야 한다.
(C) 설치를 위한 특별한 장비가 필요하다.
(D) 다양한 색상으로 구입할 수 있다.

해설 Not/True
이메일의 제안 사항 중 2번 항목에서 매트를 설치할 장소가 건조하고 먼지가 없게 하라(Make sure ~ dry and free

of dirt)면서 그렇게 하면 매트가 제대로 밀착되어 자리에 고정되는 데 도움이 된다(This will help the mats ~ stay in place)고 했다. 따라서 (A)가 정답이다.

(Paraphrasing) 지문의 free of dirt → 정답의 clean

18 후기에 따르면, 샌본 씨는 무엇이 인상 깊었나?
(A) 직원의 지식   (B) 제품 시연
(C) 고객의 추천 후기   (D) 마케팅 영상

해설 세부 사항
후기의 두 번째 문장에서 샌본 씨가 영업 사원인 로버트 펜들리와 상담했을 때 그 직원의 전문 지식과 샌본 씨의 요구 사항을 빠르게 파악하는 점에 감탄했다(When ~ impressed with his expertise and quick grasp of my particular needs)고 했으므로 (A)가 정답이다.

어휘 demonstration 시연 testimonial 추천 후기

(Paraphrasing) 지문의 expertise → 정답의 knowledge

19 샌본 씨에 대해 결론지을 수 있는 것은?
(A) 선원 중 한 명으로부터 라센비 매트를 추천받았다.
(B) 라센비 매트가 서비스를 제공하는 주요 산업 분야 중 하나에서 일한다.
(C) 라센비 매트의 일자리에 지원할 예정이다.
(D) 과거에 라센비 매트에서 주문한 적이 있다.

해설 연계
광고의 두 번째 단락 첫 문장에서 해당 업체는 주로 농업, 해양 및 임업 분야 고객에게 서비스를 제공한다(We primarily serve ~ marine, and forestry clients)고 했고, 후기의 첫 문장에서 샌본 씨가 자신은 상업용 어선을 운용하고 있으며 미끄럼 방지 매트를 찾아보던 중 라센비 매트를 발견했다(I operate a commercial fishing boat, ~ slip-resistant mats)고 했다. 따라서 샌본 씨는 라센비 매트가 주로 서비스를 제공하는 해양 산업에 종사하고 있다는 것을 알 수 있으므로 (B)가 정답이다.

20 펜들리 씨의 제안 사항 중 샌본 씨가 적용했을 것 같은 것은?
(A) 제안 1   (B) 제안 2
(C) 제안 3   **(D) 제안 4**

해설 연계
이메일의 제안 사항 중 4번 항목에서 매트의 한쪽 면은 밀착도를 높이기 위해 돌기가 있는 질감으로 되어 있다(One side ~ a raised texture for added traction)고 했고, 매트는 필요에 따라 매끄러운 면 또는 질감 처리된 면이 위로 향하도록 설치할 수 있다(The mats can be installed ~ on your needs)고 했다. 후기의 세 번째 문장에서 샌본 씨는 자신의 보트에서는 울퉁불퉁한 면이 위를 향하도록 매트를 설치했다(For my boat, we installed the mats with the bumpy side up)고 했으므로, 샌본 씨는 4번 제안 사항에 있듯이 자신의 필요에 따라 매트의 돌기 있는 면이 위를 향하도록 설치했다는 것을 알 수 있다. 따라서 (D)가 정답이다.

LISTENING TEST

1 (A)	**2** (B)	**3** (C)	**4** (A)	**5** (C)
6 (D)	**7** (C)	**8** (A)	**9** (A)	**10** (B)
11 (C)	**12** (B)	**13** (A)	**14** (B)	**15** (B)
16 (B)	**17** (A)	**18** (B)	**19** (C)	**20** (A)
21 (B)	**22** (C)	**23** (A)	**24** (C)	**25** (A)
26 (C)	**27** (C)	**28** (A)	**29** (A)	**30** (B)
31 (B)	**32** (C)	**33** (D)	**34** (A)	**35** (D)
36 (D)	**37** (C)	**38** (A)	**39** (B)	**40** (C)
41 (B)	**42** (A)	**43** (D)	**44** (D)	**45** (B)
46 (C)	**47** (D)	**48** (C)	**49** (B)	**50** (C)
51 (B)	**52** (C)	**53** (C)	**54** (A)	**55** (C)
56 (B)	**57** (D)	**58** (C)	**59** (C)	**60** (B)
61 (A)	**62** (B)	**63** (C)	**64** (D)	**65** (C)
66 (A)	**67** (D)	**68** (D)	**69** (C)	**70** (C)
71 (C)	**72** (D)	**73** (B)	**74** (C)	**75** (D)
76 (B)	**77** (C)	**78** (B)	**79** (B)	**80** (B)
81 (D)	**82** (A)	**83** (D)	**84** (A)	**85** (C)
86 (B)	**87** (A)	**88** (D)	**89** (B)	**90** (A)
91 (D)	**92** (A)	**93** (C)	**94** (B)	**95** (A)
96 (D)	**97** (C)	**98** (C)	**99** (D)	**100** (B)

READING TEST

101 (A)	**102** (A)	**103** (D)	**104** (A)	**105** (B)
106 (D)	**107** (B)	**108** (B)	**109** (A)	**110** (D)
111 (B)	**112** (D)	**113** (A)	**114** (C)	**115** (B)
116 (B)	**117** (C)	**118** (B)	**119** (C)	**120** (C)
121 (C)	**122** (D)	**123** (C)	**124** (D)	**125** (A)
126 (A)	**127** (D)	**128** (A)	**129** (D)	**130** (D)
131 (B)	**132** (A)	**133** (B)	**134** (B)	**135** (D)
136 (D)	**137** (B)	**138** (C)	**139** (D)	**140** (C)
141 (D)	**142** (D)	**143** (C)	**144** (B)	**145** (D)
146 (D)	**147** (B)	**148** (A)	**149** (C)	**150** (A)
151 (C)	**152** (A)	**153** (C)	**154** (C)	**155** (C)
156 (D)	**157** (A)	**158** (D)	**159** (B)	**160** (C)
161 (C)	**162** (C)	**163** (D)	**164** (B)	**165** (C)
166 (A)	**167** (D)	**168** (A)	**169** (D)	**170** (C)
171 (B)	**172** (C)	**173** (A)	**174** (A)	**175** (B)
176 (A)	**177** (C)	**178** (D)	**179** (A)	**180** (B)
181 (D)	**182** (A)	**183** (C)	**184** (A)	**185** (B)
186 (B)	**187** (B)	**188** (D)	**189** (C)	**190** (C)
191 (A)	**192** (B)	**193** (C)	**194** (D)	**195** (D)
196 (A)	**197** (C)	**198** (B)	**199** (B)	**200** (D)

PART 1

1 M-Cn

(A) The man is serving food.
(B) The man is taking off his hat.
(C) The man is lifting a pitcher of water.
(D) The man is washing some fruit.

(A) 남자가 음식을 제공하고 있다.
(B) 남자가 모자를 벗고 있다.
(C) 남자가 물주전자를 들어올리고 있다.
(D) 남자가 과일을 씻고 있다.

해설 **인물 중심 사진**
(A) **정답:** 남자가 음식을 제공하고 있는(is serving) 모습이므로 정답이다.
(B) **동작 묘사 오답:** 남자가 모자를 벗고 있는(is taking off) 모습이 아니다.
(C) **동작 묘사 오답:** 남자가 물주전자를 들어올리고 있는(is lifting) 모습이 아니다.
(D) **동작 묘사 오답:** 남자가 과일을 씻고 있는(is washing) 모습이 아니다.

어휘 lift 들어올리다 pitcher 주전자

2 M-Au

(A) They're assembling a wooden box.
(B) They're bending over a work project.
(C) One of the men is carrying some tools.
(D) One of the men is pointing at a car.

(A) 사람들이 나무 상자를 조립하고 있다.
(B) 사람들이 작업물 위로 몸을 굽히고 있다.
(C) 남자들 중 한 명이 도구를 나르고 있다.
(D) 남자들 중 한 명이 차를 가리키고 있다.

해설 **인물 중심 사진**
(A) **동작 묘사 오답:** 사람들이 나무 상자를 조립하고 있는(are assembling) 모습이 아니다.
(B) **정답:** 사람들이 작업물 위로 몸을 굽히고 있는(are bending over) 모습이므로 정답이다.
(C) **동작 묘사 오답:** 남자들 중 한 명이 도구를 나르고 있는(is carrying) 모습이 아니다.
(D) **동작 묘사 오답:** 남자들 중 한 명이 차를 가리키고 있는(is pointing) 모습이 아니다.

어휘 assemble 조립하다 bend 굽히다, 숙이다 tool 도구 point at ~을 가리키다

3 W-Br

(A) A cup has been placed next to a printer.
(B) She's checking her mobile phone.
(C) Documents are stacked on a desk.
(D) She's wiping off a computer keyboard.

(A) 컵이 프린터 옆에 놓여 있다.
(B) 여자가 휴대폰을 확인하고 있다.
(C) 서류들이 책상 위에 쌓여 있다.
(D) 여자가 컴퓨터 키보드를 닦고 있다.

해설 **인물/사물 혼합 사진**
(A) **위치 묘사 오답:** 컵이 프린터 옆에(next to a printer) 놓여 있는 모습이 아니다.
(B) **동작 묘사 오답:** 여자가 휴대폰을 확인하고 있는(is checking) 모습이 아니다.
(C) **정답:** 서류들이 책상 위에 쌓여 있는(are stacked on a desk) 모습이므로 정답이다.
(D) **동작 묘사 오답:** 여자가 컴퓨터 키보드를 닦고 있는(is wiping off) 모습이 아니다.

어휘 stack 쌓다 wipe off ~을 닦다

4 M-Cn

(A) A potted plant has been set on the floor.
(B) Some posters have been hung on the walls.
(C) An entrance is blocked by a ladder.
(D) Some elevator doors are open.

(A) 화분이 바닥에 놓여 있다.
(B) 포스터들이 벽에 걸려 있다.
(C) 입구가 사다리로 막혀 있다.
(D) 엘리베이터 문들이 열려 있다.

해설 **사물 사진**
(A) **정답:** 화분이 바닥에 놓여 있는(has been set on the floor) 모습이므로 정답이다.
(B) **사진에 없는 명사를 이용한 오답:** 사진에 포스터(Some posters)가 보이지 않는다.
(C) **사진에 없는 명사를 이용한 오답:** 사진에 사다리(a ladder)가 보이지 않는다.
(D) **상태 묘사 오답:** 엘리베이터 문들이 열려 있는(are open) 상태가 아니다.

어휘 potted 화분에 심은 ladder 사다리

5 W-Am

(A) The woman is standing in line at the register.
(B) The woman is pushing a cart down an aisle.
(C) The woman is examining clothes on a rack.
(D) The woman is taking items out of a cart.

(A) 여자가 계산대에 줄을 서 있다.
(B) 여자가 통로를 따라 카트를 밀고 있다.
(C) 여자가 옷걸이에 있는 옷을 살펴보고 있다.
(D) 여자가 카트에서 물건을 꺼내고 있다.

해설 **인물 중심 사진**
(A) **동작 묘사 오답:** 여자가 계산대에 줄을 서 있는(is standing) 모습이 아니다.
(B) **동작 묘사 오답:** 여자가 통로를 따라 카트를 밀고 있는(is pushing) 모습이 아니다.
(C) **정답:** 여자가 옷걸이에 있는 옷을 살펴보고 있는(is examining) 모습이므로 정답이다.
(D) **동작 묘사 오답:** 여자가 카트에서 물건을 꺼내고 있는(is taking items out) 모습이 아니다.

어휘 register 계산대 aisle 통로 examine 살펴보다
rack 걸이

6 M-Au

(A) One of the people is picking up a notebook.
(B) Some chairs have been stored in a closet.
(C) Some people are putting together a bookshelf.
(D) One of the people is erasing a whiteboard.

(A) 사람들 중 한 명이 공책을 집어 들고 있다.
(B) 의자들이 벽장에 보관되어 있다.
(C) 사람들이 책장을 조립하고 있다.
(D) 사람들 중 한 명이 화이트보드를 지우고 있다.

해설 **인물/사물 혼합 사진**
(A) **동작 묘사 오답:** 사람들 중 한 명이 공책을 집어 들고 있는(is picking up) 모습이 아니다.
(B) **사진에 없는 명사를 이용한 오답:** 사진에 벽장(a closet)이 보이지 않는다.
(C) **사진에 없는 명사를 이용한 오답:** 사진에 책장(a bookshelf)이 보이지 않는다.
(D) **정답:** 사람들 중 한 명이 화이트보드를 지우고 있는(is erasing) 모습이므로 정답이다.

어휘 store 보관하다 put together ~을 조립하다, 합치다

PART 2

7 M-Cn / W-Br

When is the final proposal due?
(A) An interesting e-mail.
(B) Just my initials.
(C) By Thursday afternoon.

최종 제안서는 기한이 언제까지인가요?
(A) 흥미로운 이메일이네요.
(B) 제 이니셜만요.
(C) 목요일 오후까지예요.

해설 **최종 제안서의 기한을 묻는 When 의문문**
(A) **연상 어휘 오답:** 질문의 proposal에서 연상 가능한 e-mail을 이용한 오답이다.
(B) **질문과 상관없는 오답**
(C) **정답:** 최종 제안서의 기한을 묻는 질문에 목요일 오후까지라고 구체적인 시점으로 응답하고 있으므로 정답이다.

어휘 proposal 제안서 due 예정된, ~하기로 되어 있는

8 M-Au / W-Am

Who can fix my computer?
(A) I'm available now to help you.
(B) It's at the car repair shop.
(C) I don't need another one.

제 컴퓨터를 고쳐 줄 수 있는 분 있나요?
(A) 지금 시간이 되니 제가 도와 드릴게요.
(B) 자동차 정비소에 있어요.
(C) 다른 건 필요 없어요.

해설 **컴퓨터 수리가 가능한 사람을 묻는 Who 의문문**
(A) **정답:** 컴퓨터를 고칠 수 있는 사람을 묻는 질문에 자신이 도와주겠다고 응답하고 있으므로 정답이다.
(B) **연상 어휘 오답:** 질문의 fix에서 연상 가능한 car repair shop을 이용한 오답이다.
(C) **질문과 상관없는 오답**

어휘 available 시간이 되는

9 M-Cn / W-Br

Why are you at work early this morning?
(A) Because I have a project deadline.
(B) Any time after eight thirty A.M.
(C) I'm sorry, but I can't.

오늘 아침에 왜 일찍 출근했죠?
(A) 프로젝트 마감일이라서요.
(B) 오전 8시 30분 이후라면 언제든지요.
(C) 죄송하지만 그럴 수 없어요.

해설 **오늘 아침에 일찍 출근한 이유를 묻는 Why 의문문**
(A) **정답:** 오늘 아침에 일찍 출근한 이유를 묻는 질문에 프로젝트 마감일이라며 구체적인 이유를 제시하고 있으므로 정답이다.
(B) **연상 어휘 오답:** 질문의 this morning에서 연상 가능한 eight thirty A.M.을 이용한 오답이다.
(C) **질문과 상관없는 오답**

10 M-Au / W-Am

Which magazine did you advertise in?
(A) No, the reception is outdoors.
(B) It's called *World Travels*.
(C) Thanks, I had a lot of fun.

어떤 잡지에 광고했나요?
(A) 아니요, 접수처는 실외에 있습니다.
(B) 〈월드 트래블즈〉라고 해요.
(C) 감사합니다. 정말 즐거웠어요.

해설 **광고한 잡지를 묻는 Which 의문문**
(A) **Yes/No 불가 오답:** Which 의문문에는 Yes/No로 응답할 수 없다.
(B) **정답:** 광고한 잡지를 묻는 질문에 〈월드 트래블즈〉라는 구체적인 잡지명으로 응답하고 있으므로 정답이다.
(C) **질문과 상관없는 오답**

어휘 advertise 광고하다 reception 접수처

11 M-Cn / W-Am

You're coming to the office today, aren't you?
(A) Yes, he watched the news.
(B) I prefer the other sample.
(C) No, I'm visiting a client.

오늘 사무실에 오시죠, 그렇지 않나요?
(A) 네, 그는 뉴스를 봤어요.
(B) 저는 다른 샘플이 더 좋아요.
(C) 아니요, 고객을 만나러 가요.

해설 **사무실 방문 여부를 확인하는 부가 의문문**
(A) **질문과 상관없는 오답**
(B) **질문과 상관없는 오답**
(C) **정답:** 사무실 방문 여부를 확인하는 질문에 No라고 답한 뒤, 고객을 만나러 간다며 부정 답변과 일관된 내용을 덧붙이고 있으므로 정답이다.

12 M-Cn / W-Br

Could I schedule an appointment with Dr. Taylor for Thursday?
(A) They sell vitamins.
(B) Sorry—she's busy that day.
(C) I agree with him.

목요일에 테일러 박사님 예약을 잡을 수 있을까요?
(A) 그들은 비타민을 판매해요.
(B) 죄송합니다. 박사님은 그날 바쁘세요.
(C) 그의 말에 동의합니다.

해설 **요청하는 의문문**
(A) **연상 어휘 오답:** 질문의 Dr. Taylor에서 연상 가능한 vitamins를 이용한 오답이다.
(B) **정답:** 목요일에 예약을 잡아 달라는 요청에 죄송하다(Sorry)고 거절한 뒤, 그날은 박사님이 바쁘다며 부정 답변과 일관된 내용을 덧붙이고 있으므로 정답이다.
(C) **연상 어휘 오답:** 질문의 Dr. Taylor에서 연상 가능한 대명사 him을 이용한 오답이다.

13 W-Am / M-Cn

Where do you plan to go on vacation?
(A) To a lake just north of here.
(B) He worked for a company overseas.
(C) Yes, I'll be checking luggage.

휴가는 어디로 갈 계획인가요?
(A) 여기서 바로 북쪽에 있는 호수로요.
(B) 그는 해외에 있는 회사에서 일했어요.
(C) 네, 짐을 확인하겠습니다.

해설 **휴가 장소를 묻는 Where 의문문**
(A) **정답:** 휴가 장소를 묻는 질문에 여기서 바로 북쪽에 있는 호수라고 구체적인 장소로 응답하고 있으므로 정답이다.
(B) **연상 어휘 오답:** 질문의 go on vacation에서 연상 가능한 overseas를 이용한 오답이다.
(C) **연상 어휘 오답:** 질문의 go on vacation에서 연상 가능한 luggage를 이용한 오답이다.

어휘 overseas 해외 luggage 짐

14 M-Au / W-Am

How soon can you start your new position?
(A) The building on the corner.
(B) As soon as you want me to.
(C) That'll be 25 dollars.

얼마나 빨리 새 직책을 맡을 수 있나요?
(A) 모퉁이에 있는 건물이요.
(B) 당신이 원하는 즉시요.
(C) 25달러예요.

해설 **새 직책을 맡을 수 있는 시점을 묻는 How soon 의문문**
(A) **연상 어휘 오답:** 질문의 position을 '위치'로 잘못 이해했을 때 연상 가능한 on the corner를 이용한 오답이다.
(B) **정답:** 새 직책을 맡을 수 있는 시점을 묻는 질문에 당신이 원하는 즉시라며 언제든 가능함을 제시하고 있으므로 정답이다.
(C) **질문과 상관없는 오답**

어휘 position 직책

15 W-Br / W-Am

Why did she win an employee award?
(A) Oh, congratulations!
(B) Because the client liked her prototype.
(C) Yes, I would.

그녀가 왜 직원상을 수상했나요?
(A) 어머나, 축하해요!
(B) 고객이 그녀의 시제품을 좋아했기 때문이에요.
(C) 네, 그럴게요.

해설 **그녀가 직원상을 수상한 이유를 묻는 Why 의문문**
(A) **연상 어휘 오답:** 질문의 win an employee award에서 연상 가능한 congratulations를 이용한 오답이다.
(B) **정답:** 직원상을 받은 이유를 묻는 질문에 고객이 그녀의 시제품을 좋아했기 때문이라며 구체적인 이유로 응답하고 있으므로 정답이다.

(C) **Yes/No 불가 오답:** Why 의문문에는 Yes/No로 응답할 수 없다.

어휘 prototype 시제품

16 W-Br / M-Au

Should we go for lunch now or finish taking inventory first?
(A) No, it's not broken.
(B) Let's eat now.
(C) The new receptionist.

지금 점심을 먹으러 갈까요, 아니면 재고 조사부터 먼저 끝낼까요?
(A) 아니요, 고장 나지 않았어요.
(B) 지금 먹어요.
(C) 새로 온 접수 담당자예요.

해설 **먼저 할 일을 묻는 선택 의문문**
(A) **Yes/No 불가 오답:** 문장과 문장을 연결하는 경우를 제외하고는 선택 의문문에 Yes/No로 응답할 수 없다.
(B) **정답:** 먼저 할 일을 묻는 선택 의문문에 지금 점심을 먹자고 전자를 선택해 응답하고 있으므로 정답이다.
(C) **질문과 상관없는 오답**

어휘 take inventory 재고 조사를 하다 receptionist 안내 직원, 접수 담당자

17 M-Au / W-Am

Are you going to the gallery?
(A) I need a ride.
(B) The light switch.
(C) In the file cabinet.

미술관에 가시나요?
(A) 태워 주세요.
(B) 조명 스위치요.
(C) 파일 캐비닛에 있어요.

해설 **미술관에 가는지 묻는 일반 의문문**
(A) **정답:** 미술관에 가는지 묻는 질문에 태워 달라고 하면서 미술관에 가는 것을 우회적으로 표현하고 있으므로 정답이다.
(B) **질문과 상관없는 오답**
(C) **질문과 상관없는 오답**

18 M-Cn / W-Br

When will the updated payroll policy go into effect?
(A) An online calendar.
(B) At the end of the quarter, I think.
(C) No, the first shift.

변경된 급여 정책은 언제부터 시행되나요?
(A) 온라인 달력이요.
(B) 분기 말일 거예요.
(C) 아니요, 첫 번째 교대 근무예요.

변경된 정책의 시행 시점을 묻는 When 의문문
- (A) 연상 어휘 오답: 질문의 When에서 연상 가능한 calendar를 이용한 오답이다.
- (B) 정답: 변경된 급여 정책 시행 시점을 묻는 질문에 분기 말이라고 구체적인 시점으로 응답하고 있으므로 정답이다.
- (C) Yes/No 불가 오답: When 의문문에는 Yes/No로 응답할 수 없다.

어휘 payroll 급여   policy 정책   go into effect 시행되다
quarter 분기   shift 교대 [근무]

---

19 W-Am / W-Br

Can I help you carry those boxes?
(A) That pamphlet was helpful.
(B) I already ate, thanks.
(C) They're not very heavy.

상자 옮기는 거 도와드릴까요?
(A) 그 팸플릿이 유용했어요.
(B) 벌써 먹었어요. 고마워요.
(C) 별로 무겁지 않아요.

해설 제안하는 의문문
- (A) 파생어 오답: 질문의 help와 파생어 관계인 helpful을 이용한 오답이다.
- (B) 연상 어휘 오답: 질문의 Can I help you에서 연상 가능한 I already와 thanks를 이용한 오답이다.
- (C) 정답: 상자 옮기는 일을 도와주겠다는 제안에 별로 무겁지 않다며 거절 의사를 간접적으로 표현하고 있으므로 정답이다.

---

20 M-Au / W-Am

Would you like to leave at five or six?
(A) Five o'clock would be better.
(B) The auditorium is on the third floor.
(C) He's the committee chair.

5시에 출발하시겠어요, 아니면 6시에 출발하시겠어요?
(A) 5시가 낫겠어요.
(B) 강당은 3층에 있어요.
(C) 그는 위원장이에요.

해설 출발 시점을 묻는 선택 의문문
- (A) 정답: 5시와 6시 중에 언제 출발할지 묻는 질문에 5시가 낫겠다며 전자를 선택해 응답하고 있으므로 정답이다.
- (B) 연상 어휘 오답: 질문의 five, six에서 연상 가능한 third를 이용한 오답이다.
- (C) 질문과 상관없는 오답

어휘 auditorium 강당   committee 위원회   chair 의장

---

21 W-Br / M-Au

Should I test the projector in the meeting room now?
(A) It came equipped with a navigation system.
(B) The cleaning staff is still in there.
(C) He mailed the invoices.

지금 회의실에서 프로젝터를 테스트할까요?
(A) 내비게이션이 장착돼 나와요.
(B) 아직 청소 직원이 안에 있어요.
(C) 그가 청구서를 부쳤어요.

해설 프로젝터 테스트 여부를 묻는 일반 의문문
- (A) 연상 어휘 오답: 질문의 projector에서 연상 가능한 equipped를 이용한 오답이다.
- (B) 정답: 프로젝터를 지금 테스트해야 할지 묻는 질문에 청소 직원이 아직 있다면서 지금은 테스트할 수 없음을 간접적으로 밝히고 있으므로 정답이다.
- (C) 질문과 상관없는 오답

어휘 equipped 장비를 갖춘   invoice 청구서

---

22 M-Au / W-Am

When was the last time the budget meeting was postponed?
(A) A spreadsheet.
(B) That's not my wallet.
(C) This is the first that I know of.

예산 회의가 마지막으로 연기되었을 때가 언제인가요?
(A) 스프레드시트예요.
(B) 그건 제 지갑이 아니에요.
(C) 제가 알기로는 이번이 처음이에요.

해설 예산 회의가 마지막으로 연기된 시점을 묻는 When 의문문
- (A) 질문과 상관없는 오답
- (B) 연상 어휘 오답: 질문의 budget에서 연상 가능한 wallet을 이용한 오답이다.
- (C) 정답: 예산 회의가 마지막으로 연기된 시점을 묻는 질문에 자신이 알기로는 이번이 처음이라고 응답하고 있으므로 정답이다.

어휘 postpone 연기하다

---

23 M-Cn / W-Br

I can help you process the order for shipment.
(A) No, thanks—I already handled it.
(B) Fifty kilograms of cement.
(C) Some errors in the process document.

배송 주문 처리를 도와드릴 수 있어요.
(A) 괜찮아요. 이미 처리했어요.
(B) 시멘트 50킬로그램이에요.
(C) 절차 문서에 몇 가지 오류가 있어요.

해설 제안하는 평서문
- (A) 정답: 배송 주문 처리를 도와줄 수 있다고 제안하는 평서문에 괜찮다며 거절한 후, 이미 처리했다고 일관된 내용을 덧붙이고 있으므로 정답이다.
- (B) 연상 어휘 오답: 평서문의 shipment에서 연상 가능한 Fifty kilograms를 이용한 오답이다.
- (C) 어휘 반복 오답: 평서문의 process를 반복 이용한 오답이다.

어휘 process 처리하다;절차   shipment 배송   handle 처리하다

24 W-Am / M-Cn

Mr. Ruiz replaced the ink cartridge in the copier.
(A) Print your name here.
(B) About 300 dollars.
(C) Oh, that was the last one.

루이즈 씨가 복사기 잉크 카트리지를 교체했어요.
(A) 여기에 이름을 인쇄체로 적으세요.
(B) 300달러 정도예요.
(C) 아, 그게 마지막이었군요.

해설 정보를 전달하는 평서문
(A) **연상 어휘 오답:** 평서문의 ink cartridge와 copier에서 연상 가능한 Print를 이용한 오답이다.
(B) **평서문과 상관없는 오답**
(C) **정답:** 루이즈 씨가 복사기 잉크 카트리지를 교체했다는 평서문에 그것이 마지막이었다며 관련된 내용으로 호응하고 있으므로 정답이다.

어휘 replace 교체하다 **print** (글자를) 인쇄체로 쓰다

25 W-Br / M-Au

Doesn't this meal usually come with a salad?
(A) The restaurant menu has changed.
(B) Yes, the manager does.
(C) I'll have a tea with milk, please.

이 식사는 보통 샐러드가 같이 나오지 않나요?
(A) 식당 메뉴가 바뀌었어요.
(B) 네, 매니저님이 해요.
(C) 밀크티 주세요.

해설 식사 구성을 확인하는 부정 의문문
(A) **정답:** 식사 구성을 확인하는 질문에 식당 메뉴가 바뀌었다고 설명하고 있으므로 정답이다.
(B) **연상 어휘 오답:** 식당에서 식사 구성을 확인하는 질문에서 연상 가능한 manager를 이용한 오답이다.
(C) **연상 어휘 오답:** 질문의 meal에서 연상 가능한 tea with milk를 이용한 오답이다.

26 W-Br / W-Am

I haven't heard anything about the new office space.
(A) The stapler on the desk.
(B) It was a difficult bicycle race.
(C) It won't be announced until Wednesday.

새 사무실 공간에 대해 들은 바가 없어요.
(A) 책상 위에 있는 스테이플러요.
(B) 어려운 자전거 경주였어요.
(C) 수요일은 돼야 발표돼요.

해설 상황을 설명하는 평서문
(A) **연상 어휘 오답:** 평서문의 office space에서 연상 가능한 stapler와 desk를 이용한 오답이다.
(B) **유사 발음 오답:** 평서문의 space와 부분적으로 발음이 유사한 race를 이용한 오답이다.
(C) **정답:** 새 사무실 공간에 대해 들은 바가 없다는 평서문에 수요일은 돼야 발표된다며 정보를 확인할 수 있는 시점을 알려 주고 있으므로 정답이다.

27 W-Am / M-Cn

Do you want more cheese on your pizza?
(A) Next to the window, please.
(B) You might want to call in the morning.
(C) I don't want to pay any extra.

피자에 치즈를 더 넣을까요?
(A) 창가로 부탁해요.
(B) 아침에 전화하시는 게 좋겠어요.
(C) 추가 요금을 내고 싶지 않아요.

해설 재료 추가 여부를 묻는 일반 의문문
(A) **연상 어휘 오답:** 질문의 Do you want more에서 연상 가능한 please를 이용한 오답이다.
(B) **어휘 반복 오답:** 질문의 want를 반복 이용한 오답이다.
(C) **정답:** 피자에 치즈를 더 원하는지 묻는 질문에 추가 요금을 내고 싶지 않다며 우회적으로 부정하고 있으므로 정답이다.

28 M-Cn / W-Br

Who's going to be in the parade?
(A) It was rescheduled for next month.
(B) The post office downtown.
(C) Along Main Street.

누가 퍼레이드에 참석하나요?
(A) 다음 달로 일정이 변경됐어요.
(B) 시내 우체국이에요.
(C) 메인 가를 따라서요.

해설 퍼레이드 참석자를 묻는 Who 의문문
(A) **정답:** 퍼레이드 참석자를 묻는 질문에 다음 달로 일정이 변경됐다며 아직 모른다는 것을 우회적으로 밝히고 있으므로 정답이다.
(B) **연상 어휘 오답:** 질문의 parade에서 연상 가능한 downtown을 이용한 오답이다.
(C) **연상 어휘 오답:** 질문의 parade에서 연상 가능한 Along Main Street를 이용한 오답이다.

29 W-Am / M-Cn

We have to set up the conference tables for the seminar.
(A) Which room is it going to be in?
(B) Several folding metal chairs.
(C) The name tag goes around your neck.

세미나를 위해 회의 탁자를 준비해야 합니다.
(A) 어느 방에서 세미나가 진행되나요?
(B) 접이식 금속 의자 몇 개요.
(C) 이름표를 목에 걸어야 해요.

해설 의견을 제시하는 평서문
(A) **정답:** 세미나를 위해 회의 탁자를 준비해야 한다는 평서문에 어느 방에서 세미나가 진행되는지 관련 내용을 묻고 있으므로 정답이다.
(B) **연상 어휘 오답:** 평서문의 tables에서 연상 가능한 chairs를 이용한 오답이다.
(C) **연상 어휘 오답:** 평서문의 conference와 seminar에서 연상 가능한 name tag를 이용한 오답이다.

어휘 set up ~을 준비하다, 설치하다

30 W-Br / M-Au

Should we register for the certification course today or tomorrow?
(A) Have you ever shopped there?
(B) The deadline has already passed.
(C) No, it wasn't damaged.

자격증 취득 과정에 오늘 등록해야 하나요, 아니면 내일 등록해야 하나요?
(A) 거기서 쇼핑해 본 적이 있나요?
(B) 이미 기한이 지났어요.
(C) 아니요, 파손되지 않았어요.

해설 **자격증 취득 과정의 등록 시점을 묻는 선택 의문문**
(A) **연상 어휘 오답:** 질문의 register를 '계산대'로 잘못 이해 했을 때 연상 가능한 shopped를 이용한 오답이다.
(B) **정답:** 자격증 취득 과정의 등록 시점을 묻는 질문에 이미 기한이 지났다며 등록할 수 없음을 우회적으로 밝히고 있으므로 정답이다.
(C) **Yes/No 불가 오답:** 문장과 문장을 연결하는 경우를 제외하고는 선택 의문문에는 Yes/No로 응답할 수 없다.

어휘 register 등록하다 certification 인증, 자격(증)

31 M-Au / W-Am

The construction project we visited last month should be completed.
(A) A brand-new office building.
(B) The walls are still being painted.
(C) From the Internet.

저희가 지난달에 방문한 건축 프로젝트는 완료되어야 합니다.
(A) 새 사무실 건물이에요.
(B) 아직 벽에 페인트칠을 하고 있어요.
(C) 인터넷에서요.

해설 **의견을 제시하는 평서문**
(A) **연상 어휘 오답:** 평서문의 construction project에서 연상 가능한 office building을 이용한 오답이다.
(B) **정답:** 지난달 방문했던 건축 프로젝트가 완료되어야 한다는 평서문에 아직 벽을 칠하고 있다며 완료되기까지 시간이 걸림을 우회적으로 나타내고 있으므로 정답이다.
(C) **평서문과 상관없는 오답**

어휘 construction 건축

PART 3

[32-34] W-Br / M-Au

W Hi, Doo-Jae. **32 The sales team meets at nine. Are you ready?**
M Yes. I compiled the data on the team's quarterly sales figures and put together the slide deck last night. **33 I just sent you an e-mail with all the information a moment ago.**

W Perfect! Oh, and are you planning to go to the company bowling night next week?
M Probably not. I don't bowl very much.
W It's not competitive! **34 And honestly, it's a really good way to interact with coworkers outside of work.** I think you'd enjoy it.

여 안녕하세요, 두재 씨. **32 영업팀이 9시에 모여요. 준비되셨나요?**
남 네. 어제저녁에 팀의 분기별 매출액 자료를 모아서 슬라이드 문서로 정리했어요. **33 방금 모든 정보를 포함한 이메일을 보내 드렸어요.**
여 훌륭해요! 아, 그리고 다음 주에 회사 볼링 저녁 모임에 가시나요?
남 아마 안 갈 것 같아요. 제가 볼링을 잘 안 쳐서요.
여 이건 경쟁이 아니에요! **34 솔직히 회사 밖에서 동료들과 어울리기에 정말 좋은 방법이죠.** 재미있을 거에요.

어휘 quarterly 분기의 competitive 경쟁의 interact with ~와 어울리다

32 화자들은 무엇을 준비하고 있는가?
(A) 회사 야유회 (B) 스포츠 대회
(C) 팀 회의 (D) 무역 박람회

해설 **화자들이 준비하는 것**
여자가 첫 대사에서 영업팀이 9시에 모인다(The sales team meets at nine)고 하면서 준비됐는지(Are you ready?) 묻고 있으므로 (C)가 정답이다.

어휘 retreat 야유회 competition 대회, 시합

33 남자는 방금 무엇을 했는가?
(A) 예약을 했다. (B) 제품 설명서를 출력했다.
(C) 비품을 주문했다. **(D) 정보를 이메일로 보냈다.**

해설 **남자가 방금 한 일**
남자가 첫 대사에서 방금 모든 정보를 포함한 이메일을 보냈다(I just sent you an e-mail with all the information a moment ago)고 말하고 있으므로 (D)가 정답이다.

어휘 description 설명(서) supplies 비품, 용품

34 여자에 따르면, 남자는 왜 행사에 참여해야 하는가?
(A) 동료들과 어울리려고
(B) 컴퓨터 실력을 향상시키려고
(C) 잠재 고객을 만나려고
(D) 자선기금을 모으려고

해설 **남자가 행사에 참여해야 하는 이유**
여자가 마지막 대사에서 회사 밖에서 동료들과 어울리기에 정말 좋은 방법(it's a really good way to interact with coworkers outside of work)이라며 행사 참여를 권하고 있으므로 (A)가 정답이다.

어휘 socialize with ~와 어울리다 potential 잠재적인 raise (돈을) 모으다 charity 자선

(Paraphrasing) 대화의 interact with
→ 정답의 socialize with

[35-37] M-Cn / W-Br

M Hello. I'm calling about a car I rented on Monday. I'm supposed to return it to the Springfield airport on Sunday but my travel plans changed, and **35 I was wondering if I could drop the car off in Oakland instead.**

W Sure. I can notify our Oakland branch that you'll return the car there.

M Great—thank you.

W **36 Please be aware that the Oakland office closes early on Sundays, so you'll need to drop it off that afternoon by two.**

M OK. **37 I'll make sure to note that on my phone calendar.** I don't want to pay any late fees.

남 안녕하세요. 월요일에 빌린 차 때문에 전화 드렸습니다. 일요일에 스프링필드 공항에 반납하기로 했는데 여행 계획이 바뀌었어요. **35 대신 오클랜드에 차를 반납할 수 있는지 궁금합니다.**

여 물론이죠. 고객님이 그곳에 차를 반납할 거라고 제가 오클랜드 지사에 통보하면 됩니다.

남 잘됐네요. 감사합니다.

여 **36 오클랜드 사무실은 일요일에 일찍 문을 닫으니 그날 오후 2시까지 차를 반납하셔야 하는 점 유념해 주세요.**

남 알겠습니다. **37 휴대폰 달력에 꼭 메모해 두어야겠어요.** 연체료는 내기 싫거든요.

어휘 drop off (물건을) 가져다 주다, 놓고 가다
notify 통보하다 branch 지점 late fee 연체료

35 남자는 왜 전화를 하고 있는가?
(A) 자동차 대여 기간을 연장하려고
(B) 렌터카가 고장난 것을 알리려고
(C) 렌터카 요금을 문의하려고
(D) 다른 도시에서 렌터카를 반납해도 되는지 문의하려고

해설 **전화의 목적**
남자가 첫 대사에서 일요일에 스프링필드 공항에 반납하기로 했는데 여행 계획이 바뀌었다며 대신 오클랜드에 차를 반납해도 될지(I was wondering if I could drop the car off in Oakland instead) 묻고 있으므로 (D)가 정답이다.

어휘 extend 연장하다 charge 요금

(Paraphrasing) 대화의 drop the car off in Oakland instead → 정답의 returning a rental car in a different city

36 여자는 남자에게 무엇에 대해 주의를 주는가?
(A) 도로 폐쇄   (B) 일기예보
(C) 정책 변경   (D) 영업 종료 시간

해설 **여자가 남자에게 주의를 주는 것**
여자가 마지막 대사에서 오클랜드 사무실은 일요일에 일찍 문을 닫으므로 그날 오후 2시까지 차를 반납해야 하는 점을 유

념해 달라(Please be aware that the Oakland office closes early on Sundays, so you'll need to drop it off that afternoon by two)고 했으므로 (D)가 정답이다.

어휘 closure 폐쇄 forecast 예보

37 남자는 다음에 무엇을 할 것 같은가?
(A) 항공 일정 확인하기
(B) 결제하기
(C) 달력 업데이트하기
(D) 다른 대여 사무실에 전화하기

해설 **남자가 다음에 할 일**
여자가 사무실이 문을 닫는 시간을 알려 주자 남자가 마지막 대사에서 휴대폰 달력에 꼭 메모해 두겠다(I'll make sure to note that on my phone calendar)고 말하고 있으므로 (C)가 정답이다.

(Paraphrasing) 대화의 note that on my phone calendar → 정답의 Update a calendar

[38-40] M-Au / W-Br

M Hey, Marion. **38 With the game room and lounge being closed for renovations, I was really counting on our hotel's outdoor swimming pool and tennis courts to keep guests entertained.** But it looks like rain for the whole week.

W Yeah, we definitely need to plan for bad weather. **39 There are two art museums and a bowling alley in the city center.** We could use the shuttle to take guests there and pay their way for whatever activity they're interested in.

M I didn't even think of something like that—but it's a great idea! **40 We might even be able to get group discounts. I'll call and ask.**

남 안녕하세요, 마리온. **38 게임장과 라운지가 보수 공사로 문을 닫아서 저는 투숙객 접대에 호텔 야외 수영장과 테니스 코트만 믿고 있었거든요.** 하지만 이번 주 내내 비가 올 모양이에요.

여 네, 날씨가 안 좋은 경우를 대비한 계획이 꼭 필요해요. **39 도심에 미술관 두 곳과 볼링장이 있어요.** 셔틀을 이용해 투숙객을 모시고 가서 그들이 관심 있는 활동에 비용을 지불할 수 있어요.

남 그런 건 생각지도 못했는데 정말 기막힌 아이디어예요! **40 어쩌면 단체 할인도 받을 수 있을 거예요. 전화해서 물어볼게요.**

어휘 renovation 보수, 수리 count on ~에 의지하다
definitely 반드시 bowling alley 볼링장
pay one's way ~의 돈을 지불하다

38 화자들은 어디에 있는 것 같은가?
(A) 호텔   (B) 피트니스 센터
(C) 박물관   (D) 버스 터미널

해설 **대화의 장소**
남자가 첫 대사에서 게임장과 라운지가 보수 공사로 문을 닫았다(With the game room and lounge being closed for renovations)면서 투숙객 접대에 호텔 야외 수영장과 테니스 코트만 믿고 있었다(I was really counting on our hotel's outdoor swimming pool and tennis courts to keep guests entertained)고 한 것으로 보아 (A)가 정답이다.

39 여자에 따르면, 도심에서 무엇을 찾을 수 있는가?
(A) 식사 옵션   (B) 실내 활동
(C) 주차장   (D) 산책로

해설 **도심에서 찾을 수 있는 것**
여자가 첫 대사에서 도심에 미술관 두 곳과 볼링장이 있다(There are two art museums and a bowling alley in the city center)고 말하고 있으므로 (B)가 정답이다.

(Paraphrasing) 대화의 two art museums and a bowling alley → 정답의 Indoor activities

40 남자는 무엇을 조사할 것이라고 말하는가?
(A) 연령 요건   (B) 운전 경로
(C) 이용 가능한 할인   (D) 운영 시간

해설 **남자가 조사할 것**
여자가 마지막 대사에서 도심에 있는 미술관과 볼링장으로 투숙객을 모시고 갈 것을 제안하자 남자가 마지막 대사에서 단체 할인도 가능할지 모른다(We might even be able to get group discounts)면서 전화해서 물어보겠다(I'll call and ask)고 했으므로 (C)가 정답이다.

어휘 requirement 요건

[41-43] M-Cn / W-Am

M Hi. This is Rawad from the Tile Warehouse. I'm calling about the order you placed for floor tile. We've just been notified that the tile is on back order. **41 We won't be able to ship your tile for at least two months.**
W Oh dear. Construction starts in a week.
M **42 We carry a very similar tile from another manufacturer. It's a bit more expensive, but I can give it to you for the same price to make up for the inconvenience.**
W **43 I think I'll still have to see the tile in person before I decide. I could stop by tomorrow evening.**

남 여보세요. 타일 웨어하우스의 라와드입니다. 바닥 타일 주문 건으로 전화드렸습니다. 방금 타일이 입고 대기 중이라는 통보를 받았습니다. **41 최소 두 달 동안은 타일을 배송해 드릴 수 없습니다.**
여 이런, 일주일 후에 공사가 시작돼요.
남 **42 저희가 다른 제조사에서 나온 아주 비슷한 타일을 취급하고 있어요. 가격이 살짝 더 비싸지만, 불편을 보상해 드리기 위해 같은 가격에 드릴 수 있습니다.**

여 **43 그래도 결정하기 전에 타일을 직접 봐야 할 것 같아요. 내일 저녁에 들를게요.**

어휘 back order (재고가 없어) 처리 못한 주문
manufacturer 제조사 inconvenience 불편
in person 직접

41 무엇에 관한 대화인가?
(A) 청구서 오류   **(B) 배송 지연**
(C) 분실 청구서   (D) 파손 제품

해설 **대화의 주제**
남자가 첫 대사에서 주문한 타일이 입고 대기 중이어서 최소 두 달 동안 타일을 배송할 수 없다(We won't be able to ship your tile for at least two months)고 말한 뒤 해결 방안에 관한 대화가 이어지고 있으므로 (B)가 정답이다.

어휘 billing 청구서 작성 misplaced 분실된

(Paraphrasing) 대화의 We won't be able to ship your tile for at least two months. → 정답의 A delayed shipment

42 남자는 무엇을 제안하는가?
(A) 대체 품목   (B) 전액 환불
(C) 설치 할인   (D) 익일 배송

해설 **남자의 제안 사항**
남자가 마지막 대사에서 다른 제조사에서 나온 아주 비슷한 타일을 취급하고 있다(We carry a very similar tile from another manufacturer)면서 가격이 더 비싸지만, 불편을 보상하기 위해 같은 가격에 주겠다(It's a bit more expensive, but I can give it to you for the same price to make up for the inconvenience)고 제안하고 있으므로 (A)가 정답이다.

어휘 substitute 대체품 installation 설치

(Paraphrasing) 대화의 a very similar tile from another manufacturer → 정답의 A substitute item

43 여자는 왜 매장에 방문할 것인가?
(A) 불만을 제기하려고   (B) 기기를 반품하려고
(C) 주문품을 찾아가려고   **(D) 제품을 보려고**

해설 **여자가 매장을 방문하는 이유**
여자가 마지막 대사에서 결정하기 전에 타일을 직접 보겠다(I think I'll still have to see the tile in person before I decide)면서 내일 저녁에 들르겠다(I could stop by tomorrow evening)고 했으므로 (D)가 정답이다.

어휘 complaint 불만 appliance 기기, 전자제품

(Paraphrasing) 대화의 see the tile
→ 정답의 view a product

[44-46] M-Cn / W-Br

M **44 Don't you think our plans for the summer internships are coming along nicely, Yuping?**

W **44 They really are!** Actually, that reminds me— I had an idea. Why don't we pair each intern with a mentor—you know, someone from our staff?

M I like that idea. That way, interns will have someone they can go to with questions.

W **45 I'd be happy to assign a mentor to each intern.**

M Well, **46 before you make those assignments, let's see what our colleagues' schedules look like. I'll send out an e-mail to see who's available to be a mentor.**

남 **44** 여름 인턴십 계획이 순조롭게 진행되고 있는 것 같지 않나요, 유핑?

여 **44** 그러게요! 실은 그러고 보니, 저한테 아이디어가 있어요. 인턴마다 우리 직원 한 명씩 멘토로 짝지어 주는 건 어때요?

남 그거 좋은 생각인데요. 그렇게 하면 인턴들이 질문이 있을 때 찾아갈 수 있는 사람이 생기겠죠.

여 **45** 인턴마다 멘토를 배정하는 일은 제가 기꺼이 하겠습니다.

남 그럼 **46** 배정하기 전에 동료들의 일정이 어떤지 살펴봅시다. 누가 멘토 역할을 할 시간이 있는지 이메일을 보낼게요.

어휘 come along 순조롭게 진행되다 assign 배정하다 assignment 배정 colleague (직장) 동료

---

44 화자들은 무엇을 준비하고 있는가?
(A) 회사 기념 행사   (B) 제품 출시
(C) 비즈니스 강의   **(D) 인턴십 프로그램**

해설 화자들이 준비하는 것
남자가 첫 대사에서 여름 인턴십 계획이 순조롭게 진행되는 것 같지 않은지(Don't you think our plans for the summer internships are coming along nicely) 여자에게 묻고 있고 여자가 그렇다(They really are!)고 호응하며 관련 아이디어를 제안하고 있으므로 (D)가 정답이다.

45 여자는 무엇을 하겠다고 제안하는가?
(A) 워크숍 운영   **(B) 배정 작업**
(C) 초대장 발송   (D) 관리자에게 연락

해설 여자의 제안 사항
여자가 마지막 대사에서 인턴마다 멘토를 배정하는 일을 기꺼이 하겠다(I'd be happy to assign a mentor to each intern)고 제안하고 있으므로 (B)가 정답이다.

어휘 supervisor 관리자

46 남자는 어떤 정보를 수집할 것인가?
(A) 비용 견적   (B) 최신 정책
(C) 직원 확보 가능성   (D) 좌석 선호도

해설 남자가 수집할 정보
남자가 마지막 대사에서 배정하기 전에 동료들의 일정이 어떤지 살펴보자(before you make those assignments,

let's see what our colleagues' schedules look like)고 하면서 누가 멘토 역할을 할 시간이 있는지 이메일을 보내겠다(I'll send out an e-mail to see who's available to be a mentor)고 했으므로 (C)가 정답이다.

어휘 estimate 견적(서) availability 이용 가능성

[47-49] M-Au / W-Br

M **47 Now that we've prepared the vegetables for tomorrow's lunch service and stored them in the refrigerator**, there's just one more thing I need you to do before we close for the evening.

W Sure—what's that?

M **48 Clean the flattop grill. First, scrape off any remaining food. Then spray it down with vinegar and wipe it off.** Everything you need is on that shelf.

W OK. Oh, and **49 didn't you mention that we need to wear protective gloves when we clean?**

M **49 Right. Here's a pair for you to use.**

남 **47** 내일 점심 서비스에 쓸 채소를 준비해서 냉장고에 보관했으니 저녁에 문 닫기 전에 한 가지만 더 해 주시면 됩니다.

여 그러죠. 뭐가요?

남 **48** 플랫톱 그릴을 청소하는 것이요. 먼저 남은 음식물을 긁어내 주세요. 그런 다음 식초를 뿌리고 닦아내세요. 필요한 것은 전부 저 선반에 있습니다.

여 알겠습니다. 그런데 **49** 청소할 때 보호 장갑을 착용해야 한다고 말씀하지 않으셨나요?

남 **49** 맞습니다. 여기 한 켤레가 있으니 쓰세요.

어휘 vinegar 식초 protective 보호하는

---

47 화자들은 어디에서 일하는 것 같은가?
(A) 원예용품점   (B) 식품 가공 공장
(C) 가전제품 매장   **(D) 식당**

해설 화자들의 근무 장소
남자가 첫 대사에서 내일 점심 서비스에 쓸 채소를 준비해서 냉장고에 보관했다(Now that we've prepared the vegetables for tomorrow's lunch service and stored them in the refrigerator)고 했고 이후 그릴 청소 등 영업 종료 전에 해야 할 일에 관해 대화가 이어지고 있으므로 (D)가 정답이다.

48 남자는 무엇을 하는 방법을 설명하고 있는가?
(A) 기계 부품 교체   (B) 영수증 정리
(C) 기기 청소   (D) 진열

해설 남자가 설명하는 것
남자가 두 번째 대사에서 플랫톱 그릴을 청소하라(Clean the flattop grill)고 하면서 먼저 남은 음식물을 긁어내라(First, scrape off any remaining food)고 한 뒤, 식초를 뿌리고 닦아내라(Then spray it down with vinegar

and wipe it off)고 청소 방법을 설명하고 있으므로 (C)가 정답이다.

어휘 set up a display 진열하다

(Paraphrasing) 대화의 the flattop grill
→ 정답의 an appliance

49 남자는 여자에게 무엇을 건네는가?
(A) 점검 목록 (B) 안전 장갑
(C) 작업 스케줄 (D) 주문서

해설 **남자가 여자에게 건네는 것**
여자가 마지막 대사에서 청소할 때 보호 장갑을 착용해야 한다고 하지 않았는지(didn't you mention that we need to wear protective gloves when we clean?) 묻자 남자가 그렇다(Right)고 대답하면서 여자에게 사용할 장갑 한 켤레를 주고(Here's a pair for you to use) 있으므로 (B)가 정답이다.

(Paraphrasing) 대화의 protective gloves
→ 정답의 Safety gloves

[50-52] W-Am / M-Cn / M-Au **3인 대화**

W **50 As the official spokesperson for Sanquel Transport**, I'd like to welcome you both aboard the largest container ship in our fleet.

M1 Thank you for allowing us to interview you for our newspaper. I'll be recording our conversation today.

M2 And I'll be taking photographs as we tour the ship. **51 I just need you to sign this photo release form so we can publish the pictures.**

W **51 No problem. 52 When you scheduled the interview, you said you wanted me to focus on our environmental initiatives, correct?**

M1 **52 Right**—the measures you've taken to reduce your environmental impact.

W Great. Let's start in the engine room. We use a low-sulfur fuel, which reduces air pollution.

여 **50 산쿠엘 트랜스포트의 공식 대변인으로서** 우리 선단에서 가장 큰 컨테이너선에 탑승하신 두 분을 환영합니다.

남1 신문 인터뷰를 허락해 주셔서 감사합니다. 오늘 대화를 녹음하겠습니다.

남2 그리고 저는 배를 둘러보면서 사진을 찍겠습니다. **51 저희가 사진을 게재할 수 있도록 이 사진 공개 동의서에 서명해 주시면 됩니다.**

여 **51 문제없습니다. 52 인터뷰 일정을 잡을 때 우리의 환경 관련 방침에 초점을 맞추고 싶다고 하셨죠?**

남1 **52 그렇습니다.** 귀사가 환경에 미치는 영향을 줄이기 위해 취한 조치들이요.

여 좋습니다. 엔진실부터 시작하죠. 우리는 저유황유를 사용해 대기 오염을 줄입니다.

어휘 spokesperson 대변인 aboard (배 등에) 탄, 승선한 fleet 선단 release 공개 environmental 환경의 initiative (목표를 달성하기 위한) 계획 measure 조치 impact 영향 low-sulfur 저유황의 fuel 연료

50 여자는 어떤 업계에서 일하는 것 같은가?
(A) 제조업 (B) 기술업
(C) 운송업 (D) 방송업

해설 **여자의 근무 업계**
여자가 첫 대사에서 산쿠엘 트랜스포트의 공식 대변인(As the official spokesperson for Sanquel Transport)이라고 자신의 신분을 밝히고 있으므로 (C)가 정답이다.

(Paraphrasing) 대화의 Transport → 정답의 Shipping

51 여자는 어떤 서류에 서명하도록 요청받는가?
(A) 임대 계약서 (B) 사진 공개 동의서
(C) 항목별 영수증 (D) 직원 계약서

해설 **여자가 서명하도록 요청받은 서류**
두 번째 남자가 배를 둘러보며 사진을 찍겠다고 하면서 사진을 게재할 수 있도록 사진 공개 동의서에 서명해 달라(I just need you to sign this photo release form so we can publish the pictures)고 요청하자 여자가 문제없다(No problem)고 허락했으므로 (B)가 정답이다.

52 인터뷰의 초점은 무엇이 될 것인가?
(A) 지역 사회 봉사 활동 (B) 사업장 안전
(C) 환경 친화 정책 (D) 고용 유지 전략

해설 **인터뷰의 초점**
여자가 두 번째 대사에서 인터뷰 일정을 잡을 때 환경 관련 방침에 초점을 맞추고 싶다고 했는지(When you scheduled the interview, you said you wanted me to focus on our environmental initiatives, correct?) 물었고 첫 번째 남자가 그렇다(Right)고 응답했으므로 (C)가 정답이다.

어휘 outreach 봉사 활동 retention 유지

(Paraphrasing) 대화의 environmental initiatives
→ 정답의 Environmentally friendly policies

[53-55] M-Au / W-Br

M Tatyana, I'm looking forward to helping you improve your company's image. Why don't we start by discussing the outcomes you'd like from this project?

W Well, our shoe outlet has a loyal customer base, but it hasn't grown much. **53, 54 We'd like to expand our customer base by appealing to younger consumers. 54 I just don't know where to begin with that.**

M I've done a lot of research in this area.

W That's good to hear.

M We'll look at the market, but **55 reaching this audience segment these days means relying heavily on social media.** That's how we'll attract younger customers.

남 타티아나, 귀사의 이미지 개선에 도움이 되기를 고대하고 있습니다. 이 프로젝트에서 원하시는 결과에 대해 논의하는 것부터 시작할까요?

여 음, 우리 신발 할인점은 충성도 높은 고객층을 보유하고 있지만, 크게 성장하지는 못했어요. 53, 54 젊은 소비자들에게 어필해 고객층을 확대하고 싶어요. 54 단지 어디서부터 시작해야 할지 모르겠습니다.

남 제가 이 분야에서 연구를 많이 했습니다.

여 다행이네요.

남 시장을 살펴보겠지만, 55 요즘 이 대상 고객층에 도달하려면 소셜 미디어에 크게 의존해야 합니다. 그래야 젊은 고객을 끌어들일 수 있어요.

어휘 outcome 결과 loyal 충성도 높은 expand 확장하다 audience (광고) 대상 segment 부분

---

53 여자는 무엇을 하고 싶다고 말하는가?
(A) 비즈니스 컨벤션 개최   (B) 신제품군 디자인
(C) 고객층 확대   (D) 멤버십 프로그램 시작

해설 **여자가 하고 싶은 일**
여자가 첫 대사에서 젊은 소비자들에게 어필해 고객층을 확대하고 싶다(We'd like to expand our customer base by appealing to younger consumers)고 했으므로 (C)가 정답이다.

54 남자는 왜 "제가 이 분야에서 연구를 많이 했습니다"라고 말하는가?
(A) 안심시키려고   (B) 정정하려고
(C) 제안에 반대하려고   (D) 결정을 설명하려고

해설 **화자의 의도**
여자가 첫 대사에서 젊은 소비자들에게 어필해 고객층을 넓히고 싶다(We'd like to expand our customer base by appealing to younger consumers)고 말한 뒤 어디서부터 시작해야 할지 모르겠다(I just don't know where to begin with that)고 하자 남자가 인용문을 언급한 것으로 보아 여자를 안심시키려고 한 말임을 알 수 있다. 따라서 (A)가 정답이다.

어휘 reassurance 안심

55 남자에 따르면, 계획의 초점은 무엇이 되어야 하는가?
(A) 공정 효율   (B) 고객 보상
(C) 제품 품질   (D) 소셜 미디어

해설 **계획의 초점이 되어야 하는 것**
남자가 마지막 대사에서 요즘 이 대상 고객층에 도달하려면 소셜 미디어에 크게 의존해야 한다(reaching this audience segment these days means relying heavily on social media)고 했으므로 (D)가 정답이다.

어휘 efficiency 효율 reward 보상

[56-58] M-Cn / M-Au / W-Am   3인 대화

M1 So, Joshua, **56 you've had the cast off your leg for a whole week. That must be a relief.**

M2 **56 It sure is!** I hope Dr. Bora gives me the OK today to resume normal activities.

M1 Well, the doctor will be right in to go over the results of your X-rays with you.

W Good morning, Joshua! **57 Let me pull up your X-rays on this computer.** As you can see, your leg is healing nicely.

M2 That's great. Will I be able to return to work soon?

W Well, that depends. **58 I'll need to evaluate you.** Let's start with your range of motion.

남1 조슈아, 56 일주일 내내 다리 깁스를 풀고 있었네요. 한시름 덜었네요.

남2 그러게요! 56 오늘 보라 박사님께서 일상 활동을 재개해도 괜찮다고 허락해 주시면 좋겠어요.

남1 자, 의사 선생님이 엑스레이 결과를 확인하러 바로 들어오실 거예요.

여 안녕하세요, 조슈아! 57 이 컴퓨터에 엑스레이를 띄울게요. 보다시피, 다리가 잘 아물고 있어요.

남2 잘됐네요! 곧 업무에 복귀할 수 있을까요?

여 음, 그건 상황에 따라 다르죠. 58 진단해 봐야겠어요. 운동 범위부터 시작해 보죠.

어휘 cast 깁스 relief 안심 resume 다시 시작하다 evaluate 진단하다 range 범위

---

56 화자들은 어디에 있는 것 같은가?
(A) 사진관   (B) 진료소
(C) 스포츠 경기장   (D) 피트니스 센터

해설 **대화의 장소**
첫 번째 남자가 첫 대사에서 일주일 내내 다리 깁스를 풀고 있었으니(you've had the cast off your leg for a whole week) 한시름 덜었겠다(That must be a relief)고 이야기하자 두 번째 남자가 그러게요(It sure is!)라고 답하면서 오늘 보라 박사님이 일상 활동을 재개해도 괜찮다고 허락해 주면 좋겠다(I hope Dr. Bora gives me the OK today to resume normal activities)고 한 것으로 보아 병원에서 이루어지는 대화임을 알 수 있다. 이후 보라 박사와 두 번째 남자의 대화가 이어지고 있으므로 (B)가 정답이다.

57 여자는 컴퓨터 화면에 무엇을 보여주는가?
(A) 일정표   (B) 계약서
(C) 가격   (D) 결과

해설 **여자가 컴퓨터 화면에 보여주는 것**
여자가 첫 대사에서 이 컴퓨터에 엑스레이를 띄우겠다(Let me pull up your X-rays on this computer)고 했으므로 (D)가 정답이다.

어휘 contract 계약(서)

58 여자는 다음에 무엇을 하고 싶어 하는가?

(A) 포트폴리오 논의　　　(B) 정책 확인

(C) 진단　　　(D) 일정 변경

해설　여자가 다음에 하고 싶은 일

여자가 마지막 대사에서 진단해 봐야겠다(I'll need to evaluate you)고 했으므로 (C)가 정답이다.

어휘　perform 수행하다　**revise** 변경[수정]하다

[59-61] W-Am / M-Au

W	Thanks for calling Focus Advertisers.
M	Hi. **59 My company sells a variety of kitchenware,** and we'd like to hire you to create a new ad to give our products a more modern image.
W	Sure. **60 We could start by identifying the dish sets and cookware you'd like to showcase.** We'd put together a cost estimate, after which we'd create a rough draft of a new ad campaign.
M	**60 I'll text you the link to our online catalog right now.**
W	Great. **61 I can also give you the names of some modeling agencies we've worked with before.**
M	We'd like to supply our own models.

여　포커스 애드버타이저스에 전화 주셔서 감사합니다.

남　안녕하세요. **59 저희 회사는 다양한 주방용품을 판매하고 있어요.** 귀사에 의뢰해 자사 제품에 더 현대적인 이미지를 부여할 새로운 광고를 만들고 싶어요.

여　그렇군요. **60 먼저 소개하고 싶은 접시 세트와 조리 기구를 확인하는 일부터 하죠.** 견적서를 작성한 후, 새 광고 캠페인의 대략적인 초안을 제작하려고요.

남　**60 지금 바로 저희 온라인 카탈로그 링크를 문자로 보내 드릴게요.**

여　좋습니다. **61 이전에 함께 일했던 몇몇 모델 에이전시의 이름도 알려 드릴 수 있습니다.**

남　우리는 자체 모델을 제공하고 싶습니다.

어휘　kitchenware 주방용품　**identify** 확인하다
cost estimate 비용 견적(서)　**rough** 대략적인　**draft** 초안

59 남자의 회사는 어떤 유형의 제품을 판매하는가?

(A) 아동복　　　(B) 배송 상자

(C) 주방용품　　　(D) 냉동식품

해설　남자의 회사에서 판매하는 제품의 종류

남자가 첫 대사에서 우리 회사는 다양한 주방용품을 판매하고 있다(My company sells a variety of kitchenware)고 했으므로 (C)가 정답이다.

(Paraphrasing)　대화의 a variety of kitchenware
→ 정답의 Kitchen supplies

60 여자는 문자 메시지로 무엇을 받을 것인가?

(A) 비밀번호　　　(B) 하이퍼링크

(C) 가상 티켓　　　(D) 사진

해설　여자가 문자 메시지로 받을 것

여자가 두 번째 대사에서 먼저 소개하고 싶은 접시 세트와 조리 기구를 확인하는 일부터 하자(We could start by identifying the dish sets and cookware you'd like to showcase)고 제안하자 남자가 지금 바로 온라인 카탈로그 링크를 문자로 보내 주겠다(I'll text you the link to our online catalog right now)고 했으므로 (B)가 정답이다.

어휘　virtual 가상의

(Paraphrasing)　대화의 the link to our online catalog
→ 정답의 A hyperlink

61 남자는 왜 "우리는 자체 모델을 제공하고 싶습니다"라고 말하는가?

(A) 제안을 거절하려고　　　(B) 놀라움을 나타내려고

(C) 주소를 요청하려고　　　(D) 제품 품질을 지키려고

해설　화자의 의도

여자가 마지막 대사에서 이전에 함께 일했던 모델 에이전시의 이름도 알려 줄 수 있다(I can also give you the names of some modeling agencies we've worked with before)고 하자 남자가 인용문을 언급했으므로 (A)가 정답이다.

어휘　decline 거절하다　**defend** 지키다

[62-64] W-Am / M-Cn　　　표

W	Hello?
M	Hi—Christina? This is Suresh Bajaj. **62 We met at the conference in Mumbai.**
W	Oh—hi, Suresh! **62 Nice hearing from you.** You gave a great presentation on emerging markets in Southeast Asia. I learned a lot!
M	Thank you. **63 You had asked me to follow up a week after the conference regarding the investment apps my company provides. I was calling to find out if you've checked out any of them.**
W	**64 I downloaded one last week, actually. It seems like a great way to invest in small-scale stocks.** I've got to thank you for your recommendation.
M	Glad it worked out for you.

여　여보세요?

남　여보세요, 크리스티나? 수레쉬 바자즈예요. **62 우리 뭄바이에서 열린 회의에서 만났죠.**

여　아, 안녕하세요, 수레쉬! **62 반가워요.** 동남아시아 신흥 시장에 대해 멋진 발표를 하셨죠. 많이 배웠어요!

남 감사합니다. ⁶³회의 일주일 후에 저희 회사가 제공하는 투자 앱에 대해 알려 달라고 요청하셨죠. 확인해 보신 앱이 있는지 알아보려고 전화드렸습니다.

여 ⁶⁴실은 지난주에 하나 내려받았어요. 소형주 투자에 괜찮은 방법인 것 같아요. 추천해 주셔서 고마워요.

남 잘 되셨다니 다행입니다.

어휘 emerging market 신흥 시장 regarding ~에 관하여 investment 투자 stock 주식 recommendation 추천

투자 옵션	유용한 앱
국채	릴리아드
부동산	파운데이션즈
대형주	문샷
⁶⁴소형주	페이즈

62 화자들은 어디에서 만났는가?
(A) 대학교
(B) 회의
(C) 공항
(D) 취업 면접

해설 **화자들이 만난 장소**
남자가 첫 대사에서 우리는 뭄바이에서 열린 회의에서 만났다 (We met at the conference in Mumbai)고 말하자 여자가 반갑다(Nice hearing from you)며 호응하고 있으므로 (B)가 정답이다.

63 남자는 왜 전화를 하고 있는가?
(A) 여자에게 마감일을 상기시키려고
(B) 여자에게 취업 기회를 제공하려고
(C) 요청에 대한 후속 조치를 하려고
(D) 안건을 마무리하는 데 도움이 되려고

해설 **전화의 목적**
남자가 두 번째 대사에서 여자가 회의 일주일 후에 우리 회사가 제공하는 투자 앱에 대해 알려 달라고 요청했다(You had asked me to follow up a week after the conference regarding the investment apps my company provides)고 하면서 확인한 앱이 있는지 알아보려고 전화했다(I was calling to find out if you've checked out any of them)고 했으므로 (C)가 정답이다.

64 시각 정보에 따르면, 여자는 어떤 애플리케이션을 내려받았는가?
(A) 릴리아드
(B) 파운데이션즈
(C) 문샷
(D) 페이즈

해설 **시각 정보 연계**
여자가 마지막 대사에서 지난주에 앱을 하나 내려받았다(I downloaded one last week, actually)고 말하면서 소형주 투자에 괜찮은 방법인 것 같다(It seems like a great way to invest in small-scale stocks)고 했다. 표에 따르면 소형주 투자 앱은 페이즈이므로 (D)가 정답이다.

W ⁶⁵**I'm just about to post the pool schedule online. Could you take a look at it first?**

M Sure. Oh, I forgot to tell you—⁶⁶**the high school team wants to practice every Saturday morning for the next few months. So there's a conflict with this morning class.**

W OK. ⁶⁶**Should I cancel it?**

M ⁶⁶**Yeah, let's do that.** The high school team will need that time. Oh, and ⁶⁷**we'll have to make up some entry badges so they can get into the locker room. Do you have time to help me with them now?**

여 ⁶⁵곧 수영장 일정을 인터넷에 올리려고 해요. 먼저 봐 주시겠어요?

남 그러죠. 아, 제가 깜빡하고 얘기를 안 했네요. ⁶⁶고등학교 팀이 앞으로 몇 달 동안 매주 토요일 오전에 연습하고 싶다고 하네요. 이번 오전 수업과 겹쳐요.

여 알겠습니다. ⁶⁶취소할까요?

남 ⁶⁶네, 그렇게 하죠. 고등학교 팀에서 그 시간이 필요할 거예요. 아, 그리고 ⁶⁷그들이 탈의실에 들어갈 수 있도록 출입 배지를 만들어야겠네요. 지금 도와줄 시간이 있나요?

어휘 conflict (일정) 겹침

수영장 주말 일정표		
수업	요일	시간
⁶⁶수중 에어로빅	토요일	오전 9시
초급 수영	토요일	오후 1시
스쿠버 다이빙	일요일	오전 8시
인명 구조 훈련	일요일	오후 2시

65 여자는 남자에게 무엇을 해 달라고 요청하는가?
(A) 수영장 청소하기
(B) 운동 구역 열기
(C) 정보 검토하기
(D) 회원 목록 확인하기

해설 **여자의 요청 사항**
여자가 첫 대사에서 곧 수영장 일정을 인터넷에 올리려고 한다(I'm just about to post the pool schedule online)며 먼저 봐 달라(Could you take a look at it first?)고 했으므로 (C)가 정답이다.

(Paraphrasing) 대화의 take a look at it
→ 정답의 Review some information

66 시각 정보에 따르면, 어떤 수업이 취소될 것인가?
(A) 수중 에어로빅
(B) 초급 수영
(C) 스쿠버 다이빙
(D) 인명 구조 훈련

해설 **시각 정보 연계**
남자가 고등학교 팀이 앞으로 몇 달 동안 매주 토요일 오전에 연습하고 싶어 한다(the high school team wants to practice every Saturday morning for the next

few months)며 이번 오전 수업과 겹친다(So there's a conflict with this morning class)고 했다. 그러자 여자가 취소할지(Should I cancel it?) 물었고 남자가 그렇게 하자(Yeah, let's do that)며 동의했다. 일정표에 따르면 토요일 오전 수업은 수중 에어로빅(Water aerobics)이므로 (A)가 정답이다.

67 화자들은 다음에 무엇을 할 것 같은가?
(A) 팀 코치에게 연락　　(B) 수영장 규칙 게시
(C) 수업 지도　　**(D) 배지 준비**

해설　**화자들이 다음에 할 일**
남자가 마지막 대사에서 고등학교 팀이 탈의실에 들어갈 수 있도록 출입 배지를 만들어야 한다(we'll have to make up some entry badges so they can get into the locker room)며 지금 도와줄 시간이 있는지(Do you have time to help me with them now?) 묻고 있으므로 (D)가 정답이다.

(Paraphrasing) 대화의 make up some entry badges
→ 정답의 Prepare some badges

[68-70] M-Cn / W-Br　　　　　　　　　**웹페이지**

M　**68 Now that we've finalized the movie script, it's time to select locations for filming.** Our representative in Barcelona found some promising places.

W　**68 Let's rent a car and drive out to the locations to see if they meet our needs.**

M　Good idea. Does Tuesday work for you?

W　Sure. I'm just checking the rental car company's Web site to see what they have available.

M　Hmm. **69 I think we should go with the SUV since we'll be hauling cameras and equipment to check the lighting conditions.**

W　OK. While I'm reserving the vehicle, **70 you should probably call our contact in Barcelona to let him know we're coming.**

남　68 이제 영화 대본이 완성됐으니 촬영 장소를 정할 때요. 바르셀로나에 있는 담당자가 몇 군데 유망한 장소를 찾았습니다.

여　68 차를 빌려 그 장소들로 몰고 나가서 우리 조건에 맞는지 확인해 보죠.

남　좋아요. 화요일 괜찮으신가요?

여　그럼요. 렌터카 회사 웹사이트에서 이용 가능한 차가 무엇인지 볼게요.

남　흠. 69 조명 상태를 확인하기 위해 카메라와 장비를 운반해야 하니까 SUV로 골라야 할 것 같네요.

여　알겠습니다. 제가 차량을 예약하는 동안 70 바르셀로나에 있는 연락처로 전화해서 우리가 간다고 알려 주세요.

어휘　script 대본　representative 담당자　promising 유망한　haul 운반하다　equipment 장비

소형차　일 45유로
중형차　일 60유로
69 SUV　일 80유로
트럭　일 85유로

68 화자들은 어떤 업계에서 일하는 것 같은가?
(A) 부동산　　(B) 음식 조달
(C) 관광　　**(D) 영화**

해설　**화자들의 근무 업계**
남자가 첫 대사에서 영화 대본이 완성되었으니 촬영 장소를 정할 때(Now that we've finalized the movie script, it's time to select locations for filming)라고 말하자 여자가 차를 빌려 몰고 나가서 조건에 맞는지 알아보자(Let's rent a car and drive out to the locations to see if they meet our needs)고 했으므로 (D)가 정답이다.

69 시각 정보에 따르면, 화자들은 차량 대여에 얼마를 지불하겠는가?
(A) 일 45유로　　(B) 일 60유로
(C) 일 80유로　　(D) 일 85유로

해설　**시각 정보 연계**
남자가 마지막 대사에서 조명 상태를 확인하기 위해 카메라와 장비를 운반해야 하므로 SUV로 골라야 한다(I think we should go with the SUV since we'll be hauling cameras and equipment to check the lighting conditions)고 했다. 웹페이지를 보면 SUV 대여료는 일 80유로이므로 (C)가 정답이다.

70 남자는 다음에 무엇을 할 것 같은가?
(A) 사진 발송
(B) 모바일 애플리케이션 설치
(C) 동료에게 연락
(D) 지도 인쇄

해설　**남자가 다음에 할 일**
여자가 마지막 대사에서 바르셀로나에 있는 연락처로 전화해서 우리가 간다고 알려 주라(you should probably call our contact in Barcelona to let him know we're coming)고 했으므로 (C)가 정답이다.

(Paraphrasing) 대화의 call our contact
→ 정답의 Contact a colleague

PART 4

[71-73] 회의 발췌

W-Br **71 As the leader of the product development team**, I can report to the board of directors that the new 23Xi smartphone is nearly ready to go to market. My team has been working on the technological upgrades for over a year, and I'm very pleased with everything we have accomplished! **72 This model is packed with features, including a powerful satellite messaging capability. 73 I anticipate sales will exceed all our expectations** because no other smartphone on the market has this advantage.

71 제품 개발팀 팀장으로서 신형 23Xi 스마트폰이 출시될 준비가 거의 다 되었다고 이사회에 보고할 수 있습니다. 저희 팀은 1년 넘게 기술 개선 작업을 해왔고, 저는 저희 팀이 이룬 모든 것에 매우 만족합니다! **72** 이 모델은 강력한 위성 메시지 송수신 기능을 포함하여 다양한 기능들이 탑재되어 있습니다. 시중에 있는 어떤 스마트폰도 이런 장점이 없기 때문에 **73** 판매량이 우리 모두의 기대를 뛰어넘을 것으로 예상합니다.

어휘 board of directors 이사회 accomplish 성취하다, 이루다 satellite 위성 capability 능력 anticipate 예상하다 exceed 넘어서다 expectation 예상

71 화자는 누구인가?
(A) 영업 사원 (B) 이사진
(C) 제품 개발자 (D) 데이터 분석가

해설 **화자의 직업**
화자가 도입부에 제품 개발팀 팀장(As the leader of the product development team)이라고 했으므로 (C)가 정답이다.

어휘 analyst 분석가

(Paraphrasing) 담화의 the leader of the product development team → 정답의 A product developer

72 화자는 어떤 기능을 언급하는가?
(A) 강화 유리 스크린 (B) 고급 카메라
(C) 연장된 배터리 수명 **(D) 위성 메시지 송수신**

해설 **화자가 언급한 기능**
화자가 중반부에 이 모델은 강력한 위성 메시지 송수신 기능을 포함하여 다양한 기능들이 탑재되어 있다(This model is packed with features, including a powerful satellite messaging capability)고 했으므로 (D)가 정답이다.

어휘 shatterproof 강화 처리를 한, 산산이 부서지지 않는

73 화자는 무슨 일이 일어날 것으로 예상한다고 말하는가?
(A) 입사 지원이 늘어날 것이다.
(B) 수요가 높을 것이다.

(C) 생산이 지연될 것이다.
(D) 제품 후기가 긍정적일 것이다.

해설 **화자가 예상한다고 말하는 것**
후반부에 판매량이 기대를 뛰어넘을 것으로 예상한다(I anticipate sales will exceed all our expectations)고 했으므로 (B)가 정답이다.

어휘 demand 수요 favorable 긍정적인, 호의적인

(Paraphrasing) 담화의 sales will exceed all our expectations → 정답의 Demand will be high.

[74-76] 방송

M-Au Good evening. **74 I'm reporting live from Middleboro International, 75 where travel delays are mounting this evening after a computer glitch caused the cancellation of many flights.** This technical problem is affecting multiple airlines, and passengers are not happy. With delays and cancellations rippling throughout the air travel system, pressure is mounting on airport authorities to fix the issue. **76 I've been trying to contact the public relations officer here at the airport for a comment, but without success.** We'll update you as we get more information.

안녕하세요. **74** 미들버러 인터내셔널에서 생중계로 전합니다. **75** 컴퓨터 결함으로 많은 항공편이 취소된 후 오늘 저녁 여행 지연 사태가 증가하고 있는데요. 이 기술 문제가 여러 항공사에 영향을 미치고 있어 승객들이 불평하고 있습니다. 항공 여행 시스템 전반에 걸쳐 지연과 취소 사태가 번지면서 공항 당국에 문제 해결에 대한 압박이 가중되고 있습니다. **76** 의견을 듣기 위해 이곳 공항의 홍보 담당자에게 연락을 시도했지만, 연결이 되지 않았습니다. 보다 자세한 정보는 입수하는 대로 알려 드리겠습니다.

어휘 mount 증가하다 glitch (기술의) 결함 cancellation 취소 affect 영향을 미치다 ripple 퍼지다 pressure 압력 authorities 당국, 관계자 public relations 홍보

74 화자는 어디에 있는가?
(A) 녹음실 (B) 컨벤션 센터
(C) 공항 (D) 기차역

해설 **화자가 있는 장소**
도입부에 미들버러 인터내셔널에서 생중계로 전한다(I'm reporting live from Middleboro International)면서 컴퓨터 결함으로 많은 항공편이 취소되어 오늘 저녁 여행 지연 사태가 증가하고 있다(where travel delays are mounting this evening after a computer glitch caused the cancellation of many flights)고 했으므로 (C)가 정답이다.

75 무엇이 문제를 일으켰는가?
(A) 악천후 (B) 직원 부족
(C) 초과 예약 **(D) 컴퓨터 오작동**

해설 **문제의 원인**

도입부에 컴퓨터 결함으로 많은 항공편이 취소되어 오늘 저녁 여행 지연 사태가 증가하고 있다(where travel delays are mounting this evening after a computer glitch caused the cancellation of many flights)고 했으므로 (D)가 정답이다.

어휘 shortage 부족   malfunction 오작동

(Paraphrasing) 담화의 a computer glitch
→ 정답의 A computer malfunction

76 화자는 무엇을 하려고 시도했다고 말하는가?
(A) 장비 교체   **(B) 관계자에게 연락**
(C) 임무 완수   (D) 예약 변경

해설 **화자가 시도한 일**

후반부에 의견을 듣기 위해 여기 공항의 홍보 담당자에게 연락을 시도했지만 연락이 닿지 않았다(I've been trying to contact the public relations officer here at the airport for a comment, but without success)고 했으므로 (B)가 정답이다.

어휘 official 관계자   assignment 과제, 임무

(Paraphrasing) 담화의 the public relations officer
→ 정답의 an official

[77-79] 연설

W-Br Thank you so much, everyone, for this celebration. I can't believe my time with the company is coming to an end. **77 After nearly 30 years of working here, I'm ready to retire. 78 During my time at this company, I've been dedicated to making sure that all staff members have a safe environment to work in.** I'm proud that the safety policies we've implemented have proven to be effective. And I couldn't have asked for a better group of people to work with. **79 Do you know that I still have a welcome note that Gregor Hoffman, our previous CEO, sent to me during my first month of work? It's framed and hanging on my wall.**

여러분, 축하해 주셔서 정말 감사합니다. 회사와 함께한 시간이 끝나간다니 믿기지 않아요. 77 이곳에서 30년 가까이 근무했고 이제 은퇴하려 합니다. 78 이 회사에 있는 동안 저는 모든 직원이 안전하게 일할 수 있는 환경을 만드는 데 전념했습니다. 우리가 시행한 안전 정책이 효과적이라는 사실이 입증되어 뿌듯합니다. 그리고 이보다 더 좋은 팀원들과 함께 일할 수는 없었을 겁니다. 79 이거 아세요? 근무 첫 달에 전 CEO인 그레고르 호프만이 제게 보낸 환영 편지를 아직도 간직하고 있답니다. 액자에 담겨 벽에 걸려 있어요.

어휘 retire 은퇴하다   be dedicated to ~에 전념하다 implement 시행하다   effective 효과적인   previous 이전의

77 어떤 종류의 행사가 열리고 있는가?
(A) 기념일 축하 행사   (B) 제품 출시
(C) 은퇴 축하 파티   (D) 개업식

해설 **열리고 있는 행사**

도입부에서 축하에 감사의 인사를 전한 뒤, 이 회사에서 30년 가까이 근무했고 이제 은퇴하려 한다(After nearly 30 years of working here, I'm ready to retire)고 밝히고 있으므로 (C)가 정답이다.

78 화자는 회사에 어떤 도움을 주었는가?
(A) 임원 교육   **(B) 안전 보장**
(C) 매출 증대   (D) 전시 디자인

해설 **화자가 회사에 도움을 준 것**

초반부에 회사에 있는 동안 모든 직원이 안전하게 일할 수 있는 환경을 만드는 데 전념했다(During my time at this company, I've been dedicated to making sure that all staff members have a safe environment to work in)고 했으므로 (B)가 정답이다.

어휘 executive 임원

(Paraphrasing) 담화의 making sure ~ a safe environment to work in → 정답의 Ensuring safety

79 화자의 벽에는 무엇이 있는가?
(A) 서명한 사진   (B) 업계 상
(C) 수제 시계   **(D) 환영 편지**

해설 **화자의 벽에 있는 것**

근무 첫 달에 전 CEO인 그레고르 호프만이 보낸 환영 편지를 아직도 간직하고 있다(Do you know that I still have a welcome note that Gregor Hoffman, our previous CEO, sent to me during my first month of work?)고 말한 뒤, 액자에 담겨 벽에 걸려 있다(It's framed and hanging on my wall)고 했으므로 (D)가 정답이다.

[80-82] 전화 메시지

M-Cn Hello, Ms. Ogawa. I'm returning your call regarding the funding request that I submitted yesterday. As you saw in the request, **80 I'd like to hold a picnic in Grant Park next Saturday for the members of the marketing team. Everyone worked so hard on the Davidson campaign, and I want to thank them for their efforts.** Now, in your message, **81 you questioned the necessity of some of the items I'm requesting funding for**—in particular, the rental fee for the tent. Well, I just checked, and the forecast is calling for rain. If you have any other concerns, please let me know. **82 I'm hoping to send out invitations by the end of the week.**

안녕하세요, 오가와 씨. 제가 어제 제출한 자금 지원 요청 건으로 전화하셔서 회신드립니다. 요청서에서 보셨듯이 80 마케팅 팀원들을 위해 다음 주 토요일 그랜트 파크에서 야유회를 열고자 합니다. 모두 데이비드슨 캠페인으로 고생이 많았으니 노고에 고마움을 표하고 싶거든요. 보내신 메시지에서 81 제가 자금 지원을 요청한 항목 중 일부, 특히 텐트 임대료가 필요한지 질문하셨습니다. 음, 방금 확인했는데, 예보에서 비가 온다고 합니다. 다른 우려 사항이 있으면 말씀해 주세요. 82 이번 주말까지 초대장을 보내고 싶습니다.

어휘 regarding ~에 관하여 funding 자금 지원 in particular 특히 forecast 예보 concern 우려, 걱정

80 화자는 왜 행사를 열기 원하는가?
(A) 자선 단체를 지원하려고
(B) 직원들에게 감사하려고
(C) 신임 회사 임원을 환영하려고
(D) 사내 수상을 발표하려고

해설 **화자가 행사 개최를 원하는 이유**
초반부에 마케팅 팀원들을 위해 다음 주 토요일 그랜트 파크에서 야유회를 열고 싶다(I'd like to hold a picnic in Grant Park next Saturday for the members of the marketing team)고 한 뒤, 모두 데이비드슨 캠페인으로 고생이 많았으니 노고에 고마움을 표하고 싶다(Everyone worked so hard on the Davidson campaign, and I want to thank them for their efforts)고 행사의 목적을 밝히고 있으므로 (B)가 정답이다.

어휘 charity 자선 (단체) executive 경영[운영]진
(Paraphrasing) 담화의 a picnic → 문제의 an event

81 화자는 왜 "예보에서 비가 온다고 합니다"라고 말하는가?
(A) 실수를 인정하려고
(B) 장소에 대해 불만을 제기하려고
(C) 행사 연기를 제안하려고
(D) 요청의 타당성을 설명하려고

해설 **화자의 의도**
중반부에서 메시지 수신자에게 자금 지원을 요청한 항목 중 일부, 특히 텐트 임대가 필요한지 질문했다(you questioned the necessity of some of the items I'm requesting funding for—in particular, the rental fee for the tent)고 한 뒤 인용문을 언급했으므로, 날씨 때문에 텐트 임대가 필요하다는 점을 설명하기 위해 한 말임을 알 수 있다. 따라서 (D)가 정답이다.

어휘 acknowledge 인정하다 venue 장소 postpone 연기하다 justify 당위성을 설명하다

82 화자는 이번 주말까지 무엇을 하고 싶다고 말하는가?
(A) 초대장 발송
(B) 음식 주문 확정
(C) 장식품 구매
(D) 자격증 인쇄

해설 **화자가 주말까지 하고 싶은 일**
후반부에 이번 주말까지 초대장을 보내고 싶다(I'm hoping to send out invitations by the end of the week)고 했으므로 (A)가 정답이다.

어휘 confirm 확정하다 certificate 증명서, 자격증

[83-85] 방송

W-Am 84 **On tomorrow's *Science Still Matters* show, I'll be interviewing physicist Dr. Claudia Tong.** 83,84 **Dr. Tong heads a team of scientists researching alternative energy sources.** 84 **She'll explain the science behind fusion energy research.** Many people believe that fusion energy will eventually be the main source of energy around the globe. But when? Dr. Tong will discuss the obstacles scientists need to overcome before fusion power can be produced commercially. 85 **Our guest will also answer some questions from our listeners. So post your questions on my social media page**, and be sure to tune in to tomorrow's show.

84 내일 〈사이언스 스틸 매터즈〉 쇼에서 저는 물리학자 클라우디아 통 박사를 인터뷰할 예정입니다. 83,84 통 박사는 대체 에너지원을 연구하는 과학자 팀을 이끌고 있습니다. 84 박사는 핵융합 에너지 연구의 이면에 있는 과학에 대해 설명할 겁니다. 많은 사람들이 핵융합 에너지가 결국 전 세계에서 주요 에너지원이 될 것이라고 믿고 있죠. 하지만 언제쯤일까요? 통 박사는 핵융합 전력을 상업적으로 생산하기 전에 과학자들이 극복해야 하는 장애물에 대해 논의할 예정입니다. 85 게스트는 청취자들의 질문에도 답할 예정입니다. 그러니 여러분의 질문을 제 소셜 미디어 페이지에 올리고, 내일 쇼를 꼭 청취해 주세요.

어휘 physicist 물리학자 alternative energy 대체 에너지 fusion energy 핵융합 에너지 globe 지구 obstacle 장애물 overcome 극복하다 commercially 상업적으로 tune in to ~에 채널을 맞추다. 청취[시청]하다

83 클라우디아 통은 누구인가?
(A) 기자 (B) 환경 운동가
(C) 사장 (D) 연구원

해설 **클라우디아 통의 직업**
도입부에서 통 박사는 대체 에너지원을 연구하는 과학자 팀을 이끌고 있다(Dr. Tong heads a team of scientists researching alternative energy sources)고 했으므로 (D)가 정답이다.

84 내일 방송은 어떤 주제에 초점을 맞출 것인가?
(A) 대체 에너지원 개발 (B) 과학 교육 개선
(C) 신기술 규제 (D) 더 안전한 과학 발전

해설 **내일 방송의 주제**
도입부에서 내일 〈사이언스 스틸 매터즈〉 쇼에서 물리학자 클라우디아 통 박사를 인터뷰할 예정(On tomorrow's ~ show, I'll be interviewing Dr. Claudia Tong)이라고 한 뒤, 통 박사는 대체 에너지원을 연구하는 과학자 팀을 이끌고 있다(Dr. Tong heads a team of scientists researching alternative energy sources)고 소개하고, 박사는 핵융합 에너지 연구의 이면에 있는 과학에 대해 설

명할 예정(She'll explain the science behind fusion energy research)이라고 했으므로 (A)가 정답이다.

어휘 regulate 규제하다 advance 발전

85 화자는 청자들에게 소셜 미디어에서 무엇을 하라고 요청하는가?
(A) 향후 방송 주제 제안   (B) 이전 방송 청취
(C) 게스트에게 할 질문 게시   (D) 주제 관련 추가 정보 이용

해설 **화자가 요청하는 것**
후반부에 게스트는 청취자들의 질문에도 답할 예정(Our guest will also answer some questions from our listeners)이라고 한 뒤, 질문을 소셜 미디어 페이지에 올려 달라(So post your questions on my social media page)고 했으므로 (C)가 정답이다.

어휘 additional 추가의

[86-88] 전화 메시지

M-Au Hi, Susana. It's Jacob. **86 I wanted to let you know that things are going smoothly so far at the Hamburg branch office. My flight arrived on time last night, so I was able to start training the new employees this morning as scheduled. 87 I think they're going to be a great addition to our sales team**—they were all very engaged and asked a lot of questions about our target client base. Looking forward to your arrival next week. It's a beautiful place, but it's been a bit cold here, and **88 I didn't pack the right clothes. Remember that we're planning to go hiking on the weekend.** See you next week.

안녕하세요. 수잔나. 제이콥입니다. **86 지금까지 함부르크 지사는 순조롭게 진행되고 있다는 것을 알려 드리고 싶었어요. 어젯밤 비행기가 제시간에 도착해서 예정대로 오늘 아침부터 신입 사원 교육을 시작할 수 있었어요. 87 그들은 우리 영업팀에 큰 도움이 될 것 같아요.** 모두들 아주 열심이었고 우리의 목표 고객층에 대한 질문을 많이 했어요. 다음 주에 오시기를 고대하고 있습니다. 아름다운 곳이지만 여기 날씨가 좀 추워요. 그런데 **88 저는 적당한 옷을 챙기지 못했어요. 주말에 하이킹 갈 계획이니 잊지 마세요.** 다음 주에 뵙겠습니다.

어휘 so far 지금까지 branch 지점 engaged 열심인

86 화자는 왜 함부르크에 있는가?
(A) 고객을 만나려고   (B) 직원을 교육하려고
(C) 친척을 방문하려고   (D) 지점장을 선임하려고

해설 **화자가 함부르크에 있는 이유**
도입부에서 지금까지 함부르크 지사는 순조롭게 진행되고 있다(I wanted to let you know that things are going smoothly so far at the Hamburg branch office)고 하면서 어젯밤 비행기가 제시간에 도착해 예정대로 오늘 아침부터 신입 사원 교육을 시작할 수 있었다(My flight arrived on time last night, so I was able to start training

---

the new employees this morning as scheduled)고 했으므로 (B)가 정답이다.

어휘 relative 친척 appoint 선임하다

87 화자는 어떤 부서에서 일하는가?
(A) 영업   (B) 정보 기술
(C) 인사   (D) 지역 사회 공헌

해설 **화자의 근무 부서**
중반부에 그들은 우리 영업팀에 큰 도움이 될 것 같다(I think they're going to be a great addition to our sales team)고 했으므로, 화자가 영업팀 소속임을 알 수 있다. 따라서 (A)가 정답이다.

88 화자는 왜 "여기 날씨가 좀 추워요"라고 말하는가?
(A) 보고서에 반대 의견을 내려고
(B) 정보를 바로잡으려고
(C) 지연에 대해 설명하려고
(D) 조언하려고

해설 **화자의 의도**
후반부에 인용문을 언급한 뒤 나는 적당한 옷을 챙기지 못했다(I didn't pack the right clothes)며 주말에 하이킹 갈 계획이니 잊지 말라(Remember that we're planning to go hiking on the weekend)고 했다. 따라서 추운 날씨에 하이킹을 해야 하므로 두꺼운 옷을 챙겨 오라고 조언하기 위해 한 말이므로 (D)가 정답이다.

[89-91] 방송

M-Cn Thanks for tuning in to WQWR for your morning news! **89 The Littleton City Council met last night and approved the budget for renovations to the airport.** A spokesperson for the airport announced that the project will begin next month. **90 Changes include the opening of a new shuttle station at the airport,** among other large construction projects. Renovations will provide hundreds of jobs and are expected to be completed in a year. **91 Up next, the traffic report from our man on the spot, Johnny Tremblay.**

WQWR 아침 뉴스를 시청해 주셔서 감사합니다! **89 어젯밤 리틀턴 시의회가 모여 공항 보수 공사 예산을 승인했습니다.** 공항 대변인은 공사가 다음 달에 시작된다고 발표했습니다. **90 변화에는 공항에 새 셔틀 역 개설을 포함해** 다른 대규모 건설 공사들이 있습니다. 보수 공사로 수백 개의 일자리가 공급될 것이며 1년 후에 완공될 것으로 예상합니다. **91 다음은 현장에 있는 조니 트렘블레이가 교통 상황을 전하겠습니다.**

어휘 approve 승인하다 budget 예산 renovation 보수 공사 spokesperson 대변인 on the spot 현장에서

89 화자는 어젯밤에 어떤 일이 있었다고 말하는가?
(A) 스포츠 경기   (B) 시의회 회의
(C) 비즈니스 컨벤션   (D) 쇼핑몰 개장

해설 **지난밤 일어난 일**

도입부에서 어젯밤 리틀턴 시의회가 모여 공항 보수 공사 예산을 승인했다(The Littleton City Council met last night and approved the budget for renovations to the airport)고 했으므로 (B)가 정답이다.

90 화자에 따르면, 공항에 무엇이 추가되고 있는가?

(A) 셔틀 역 　　　　　 (B) 호텔

(C) 푸드코트 　　　　 (D) 실내 정원

해설 **공항에 추가되고 있는 것**

중반부에서 변화에는 공항에 새 셔틀 역 개설이 포함되어 있다(Changes include the opening of a new shuttle station at the airport)고 했으므로 (A)가 정답이다.

91 청자들은 다음에 무엇을 들을 것인가?

(A) 주식 시장 최신 정보 　 (B) 광고

(C) 일기 예보 　　　　　 (D) 교통 정보

해설 **청자들이 다음에 들을 것**

후반부에 다음은 현장에 있는 조니 트렘블레이가 교통 상황을 전하겠다(Up next, the traffic report from our man on the spot, Johnny Tremblay)고 했으므로 (D)가 정답이다.

[92-94] 회의 발췌

> **W-Am** Good morning, **92 maintenance team. As you know, we'll be closing the parking area of this apartment complex next week.** I've hired contractors to repaint the lines for the parking spaces, and we'll need all apartment residents to use alternate parking. The owner of the shopping center just opposite us has agreed to let residents park their cars in his parking area temporarily. But it's across the highway, **93 so we'll try to get this work over with as quickly as possible. 94 I made some signs with this information. Silvia, could you please post them in the entryways and elevators of each building?**
>
> 좋은 아침입니다. **92 관리팀 여러분.** 아시다시피, 우리는 다음 주에 이 아파트 단지의 주차장을 폐쇄할 예정입니다. 주차 구역의 선을 다시 그리기 위해 도급업체를 고용했고 모든 아파트 거주민은 대체 주차장을 이용해야 합니다. 바로 맞은편에 있는 쇼핑센터 소유주가 거주자들이 임시로 그의 주차장에 차를 주차하는 데 동의했습니다. 그렇지만 간선도로 건너편에 있어요. **93 그러니 최대한 빨리 이 작업을 끝내도록 노력해 보겠습니다. 94 제가 이 정보를 담은 안내문을 몇 개 만들었습니다. 실비아, 각 동 입구 통로와 엘리베이터에 안내문을 게시해 주겠어요?**
>
> **어휘** maintenance 관리 　contractor 도급업자[체]　resident 거주민　alternate 대체하는　opposite 맞은편에　temporarily 임시로　entryway 입구 통로

92 화자는 누구인 것 같은가?

(A) 아파트 단지 관리자 　 (B) 주차장 안내원

(C) 상업 도색 작업자 　　 (D) 부동산 중개업자

해설 **화자의 직업**

도입부에 관리팀(maintenance team)을 상대로 우리가 다음 주에 이 아파트 단지의 주차장을 폐쇄할 예정(As you know, we'll be closing the parking area of this apartment complex next week)이라고 했으므로 (A)가 정답이다.

어휘 attendant 안내원　commercial 상업의

93 화자가 "간선도로 건너편에 있어요"라고 말할 때, 무엇을 의미하는가?

(A) 쇼핑센터가 찾기 쉽다. 　 (B) 식당이 가볼 만하다.

(C) 위치가 불편하다. 　　　　 (D) 제안을 고려하고 있다.

해설 **화자의 의도**

중반부에 인용문을 언급한 뒤 최대한 빨리 작업을 끝내도록 노력해 보겠다(so we'll try to get this work over with as quickly as possible)고 한 것으로 보아 대체 주차장의 위치가 불편함을 전하려는 의도이다. 따라서 (C)가 정답이다.

94 화자는 실비아에게 무엇을 하라고 요청하는가?

(A) 도급업체에 전화하기 　 (B) 안내문 달기

(C) 차량 이동하기 　　　　 (D) 페인트 구입하기

해설 **화자의 요청 사항**

후반부에 정보를 담은 안내문을 만들었다(I made some signs with this information)면서 실비아에게 각 동 입구 통로와 엘리베이터에 게시해 달라(Silvia, could you please post them in the entryways and elevators of each building?)고 요청했으므로 (B)가 정답이다.

[95-97] 회의 발췌 + 그래프

> **M-Au** OK, everyone. **95 Let's take a look at last year's sales for our shampoos, conditioners, and other hair care products.** As you can see from this graph, sales in department stores were especially strong. But I want to focus on one of the other categories. **96 Although it made up only fifteen percent of our sales, it's actually a promising market. 97 But clients in that market prefer to have a large selection of scents to choose from, so I propose that we develop new fragrances for our products.**
>
> 자, 여러분. **95 샴푸, 컨디셔너, 그리고 기타 모발 관리 제품의 지난해 판매량을 살펴봅시다.** 이 그래프에서 볼 수 있듯이, 백화점 매출이 특히 강세였습니다. 하지만 저는 다른 카테고리 중 하나에 집중하고 싶은데요. **96 비록 우리 매출에서 15퍼센트만 차지했지만, 실은 유망한 시장입니다. 97 그런데 그 시장의 고객들은 선택할 수 있는 향이 많은 것을 선호하므로, 우리 제품에 새로운 향을 개발할 것을 제안합니다.**

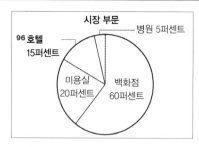

시장 부문

병원 5퍼센트
96 호텔
15퍼센트
미용실
20퍼센트
백화점
60퍼센트

95 화자의 회사는 어떤 유형의 제품을 판매하는가?
(A) 모발 관리 제품   (B) 가향차
(C) 장식용 양초   (D) 세탁 세제

해설 **화자의 회사에서 판매하는 제품의 종류**
도입부에서 샴푸, 컨디셔너, 그리고 기타 모발 관리 제품의
지난해 판매량을 살펴보자(Let's take a look at last
year's sales for our shampoos, conditioners, and
other hair care products)고 했으므로 (A)가 정답이다.

어휘 flavored 향이 첨가된 decorative 장식용의
detergent 세제

96 시각 정보에 따르면, 화자는 어떤 시장 부문에 집중하고 싶어
하는가?
(A) 병원   (B) 백화점
(C) 미용실   **(D) 호텔**

해설 **시각 정보 연계**
중반부에 카테고리 중 하나에 집중하고 싶다고 한 뒤, 비록 우
리 매출에서 15퍼센트만 차지했지만 유망한 시장(Although
it made up only fifteen percent of our sales, it's
actually a promising market)이라고 했다. 그래프에 따
르면 매출에서 15퍼센트를 차지하는 시장은 호텔이므로 (D)
가 정답이다.

97 화자는 어떤 새로운 마케팅 특성을 제공하기를 원하는가?
(A) 대량 주문 할인   (B) 다양한 제품 크기
(C) 다양한 향   (D) 전자 소식지

해설 **화자가 제공하고 싶어 하는 것**
후반부에 호텔 시장의 고객들은 선택할 수 있는 향이 많
은 것을 선호한다(But clients in that market prefer
to have a large selection of scents to choose
from)며 우리 제품에 새로운 향을 개발할 것을 제안(I
propose that we develop new fragrances for our
products)하고 있으므로 (C)가 정답이다.

(Paraphrasing) 담화의 a large selection of scents
→ 정답의 Different scents

[98-100] 전화 메시지 + 가격표

M-Cn Hi. This is Arzu Toprak. **98 I received
a vegetable delivery from your company on
Tuesday, and the spinach is already brown and
going bad. 99 And you've recently increased
the unit price of spinach too!** Frankly, I'm
disappointed. It seems like the quality of your
products has gone down over the past few
months. **100 I've owned many restaurants over
the years.** If the quality of our deliveries doesn't
improve soon, I'm going to look somewhere else.

여보세요. 아르주 토프락입니다. **98** 화요일에 귀사에서 채소를 배달
받았는데 시금치가 이미 갈색이 되어 썩고 있어요. **99** 게다가 최근
에 시금치 단가도 인상했잖아요! 솔직히 실망스럽습니다. 지난 몇
달 동안 상품 품질이 하락한 것 같습니다. **100** 저는 수년째 여러 식
당을 소유하고 있는데요. 배달 품질이 곧 개선되지 않으면 다른 곳
을 알아보려고 합니다.

어휘 spinach 시금치 unit 단위 frankly 솔직히

채소 유형	단가
양배추	15달러
양파	20달러
토마토	23달러
99 시금치	25달러

98 전화의 목적은 무엇인가?
(A) 환불을 요청하려고
(B) 배송 일정을 업데이트하려고
(C) 불만을 제기하려고
(D) 주소를 변경하려고

해설 **전화의 목적**
도입부에서 화요일에 채소를 배달받았는데 시금치가 이미 갈
색이 되어 썩고 있다(I received a vegetable delivery
from your company on Tuesday, and the
spinach is already brown and going bad)고 한 뒤,
이어서 단가는 인상된 데 반해 품질은 하락했다며 실망감을
표시하고 있으므로 (C)가 정답이다.

99 시각 정보에 따르면, 최근에 어떤 단가가 올랐는가?
(A) 15달러   (B) 20달러
(C) 23달러   **(D) 25달러**

해설 **시각 정보 연계**
초반부에 최근에 시금치 단가도 인상했다(And you've
recently increased the unit price of spinach too!)
고 말했다. 가격표에 따르면 시금치 단가는 25달러이므로 (D)
가 정답이다.

100 화자는 누구인 것 같은가?
(A) 슈퍼마켓 관리자   **(B) 식당 주인**
(C) 배달 기사   (D) 농부

해설 화자의 직업

후반부에 나는 수년째 여러 식당을 소유하고 있다(I've owned many restaurants over the years)고 했으므로 (B)가 정답이다.

PART 5

101 인칭대명사의 격_소유격

번역 야외 조각으로 유명한 이리나 레예스는 종이에도 예술 작품을 창작한다.

해설 전치사 for의 목적어 역할을 하는 명사구 outdoor sculptures를 한정 수식하는 자리이다. 따라서 소유격 인칭대명사 (A) her가 정답이다.

어휘 sculpture 조각(품)   artwork 예술 작품

102 접속사 자리_등위접속사

번역 고 박사와 그의 동료들은 재활 의학에 특별한 관심이 있다.

해설 주어 역할을 하는 명사구 Dr. Ko와 his partners를 연결해 줄 등위접속사가 필요하다. '고 박사와 그의 동료들은 재활 의학에 관심이 있다'는 내용의 문장이므로 '~와, 그리고'를 뜻하는 등위접속사 (A) and가 정답이다. 등위접속사 (C) so는 단어 및 구는 연결하지 않고 절과 절을 연결하며, (D) both는 대명사/형용사/부사로 접속사 기능을 할 수 없다.

어휘 rehabilitative 재활의

103 전치사 자리

번역 갓 만든 샌드위치는 주차장 뒤쪽의 푸드 트럭에서 구입할 수 있다.

해설 빈칸은 완전한 절에 명사구 the rear of the parking lot을 연결하는 자리이므로 전치사가 들어가야 한다. 따라서 보기 중 유일한 전치사로 장소와 함께 '~에서'라는 의미로 쓰이는 전치사 (D) at이 정답이다.

어휘 rear 뒤쪽

104 명사 자리_to부정사의 목적어 / 수 일치

번역 그로버 가든 센터로 제품을 반품하려는 고객은 영수증을 제시해야 합니다.

해설 빈칸은 동사 wish의 목적어 역할을 하는 to부정사 to return의 목적어 역할을 하는 명사 자리이고, 앞에 부정관사 an이 있으므로 단수명사가 들어가야 한다. 따라서 (A) item(제품)이 정답이다. (B) items는 복수명사, (C) itemize는 동사, (D) itemized는 동사의 과거형/과거분사이므로 품사상 빈칸에 들어갈 수 없다.

어휘 present 제시[제출]하다

105 전치사 어휘

번역 넬슨 시에 있는 밀돈 가공 공장은 더 빠른 생산을 위해 장비를 업그레이드했다.

해설 빈칸 뒤 명사구 Nelson City와 함께 The Mildorn Processing Plant를 수식하기에 적절한 전치사를 골라야 한다. 뒤에 나온 Nelson City가 중요한 단서가 되어 '~에 있는'이라는 의미로 도시와 함께 쓰이는 장소 전치사 (B) in이 정답이다.

106 부사 자리_동사 수식

번역 시 공무원들은 공공 도서관 보수 공사가 꾸준히 진행되었다고 보고했다.

해설 빈칸 앞에 자동사 progress(진행되다)의 현재완료 시제 have progressed가 있으므로 빈칸은 동사구를 수식하는 부사 자리이다. 따라서 '꾸준히'라는 의미의 부사 (D) steadily가 정답이다.

어휘 city officials 시 공무원

107 전치사 어휘

번역 델핀 해군 박물관은 월요일부터 금요일 오전 10시부터 오후 5시 30분까지 연다.

해설 '오전 10시부터 오후 5시 30분까지'라는 내용이 되어야 적절하므로, '~까지'를 뜻하는 시간 전치사 (B) until이 정답이다. (A) since는 '~부터[이후]'라는 뜻으로 주로 완료 시제 동사와 함께 쓰이며, (C) during은 '~동안'이라는 뜻으로 기간 명사와 어울리며, (D) except는 '~을 제외하고'라는 의미로 문맥상 부적절하다.

어휘 naval 해군의

108 동사 자리_수 일치

번역 앰버 주방용품은 모든 제품에 1년 보증을 제공합니다.

해설 빈칸은 주어 Amber Kitchen Supply의 동사 자리이고, 주어가 3인칭 단수이므로 단수동사가 들어가야 한다. 따라서 (B) provides가 정답이다. (A) provider는 명사, (D) providing은 동명사/현재분사이므로 품사상 답이 될 수 없고, (C) provide는 복수동사이므로 오답이다.

어휘 warranty 보증

109 형용사 어휘

번역 블레인스빌 다운타운 원형 극장은 도시 주민들에게 인기 있는 많은 행사들을 주최한다.

해설 선행사 many events를 수식하는 관계사절 내의 be동사 뒤 주격 보어 자리이므로 many events를 보충 설명하기에 적절한 형용사가 필요하다. 빈칸 뒤의 전치사구 with the city's residents와 어울려 '도시 주민들에게 인기 있는 많은 행사'라는 문맥이 되어야 적절하므로 '인기 있는'을 뜻하는 형용사 (A) popular가 정답이다. (B) careful은 '조심하는', (C) happy는 '행복한', (D) helpful은 '도움이 되는'이라는 의미로 문맥상 어울리지 않는다.

어휘 amphitheater 원형 극장

ETS 기출

모의고사 1회

110 명사 자리_복합명사 / 수 일치

번역 베스트폼 문구점은 이제 우편, 온라인 및 소매점을 통해 양질의 종이 제품을 판매한다.

해설 전치사 in의 목적어 역할을 하는 명사 자리로, 빈칸 앞의 명사 retail과 함께 '소매점'이라는 의미의 복합명사를 만들 수 있어야 한다. 또한 전치사 in과 retail 사이에 한정사가 보이지 않는 것으로 보아 빈칸에는 가산명사 store(상점)의 복수형이 들어가야 한다. 따라서 (D) stores가 정답이다. (A) store는 단수명사, (B) stored는 동사/과거분사, (C) storing은 동명사/현재분사이므로 빈칸에 들어갈 수 없다.

어휘 stationery 문구류   quality 양질[고급]의

111 상관접속사

번역 신규 주민은 계정 활성화를 위해 이메일 또는 전화로 유잉 수자원부에 연락해야 한다.

해설 빈칸 뒤에 or가 보이고 '이메일 또는 전화로 연락해야 한다'라는 의미가 되어야 하므로, or와 함께 상관접속사를 이루어 'A 또는 B (둘 중 하나)'라는 뜻을 완성하는 (B) either가 정답이다. (A) than은 '~보다'라는 뜻으로 형용사나 부사의 비교급과 쓰이며, (C) besides는 전치사/부사, (D) as if는 접속사로 뒤에 절이 와야 한다.

어휘 activate 활성화시키다

112 동사 어형_태

번역 소프트웨어 엔지니어 직책을 위한 지원서는 vntsystems.net에서 온라인으로 제출되어야 한다.

해설 빈칸은 주어 Applications의 동사 자리이다. Applications(지원서)는 제출되는 대상이고, 빈칸 뒤에 목적어가 보이지 않으므로 submit(제출하다)은 수동태로 쓰여야 한다. 따라서 (D) must be submitted가 정답이다. (A) submitted, (B) are submitting, (C) must submit은 모두 능동태 동사 형태이므로 빈칸에 들어갈 수 없다.

113 부사 어휘

번역 이사회는 새로운 구성원, 특히 기술 분야에서 경력이 있는 사람을 찾고 있다.

해설 부사는 일반적으로 명사를 수식하지 않지만 명사구 앞에서 의미를 강조하는 역할을 할 수 있다. 문맥상 '특히 기술 분야에 경력이 있는 사람'이라는 의미가 되어야 적절하므로 '특히'라는 뜻의 (A) especially가 정답이다. (B) sincerely는 '진심으로', (C) positively는 '긍정적으로', (D) seriously는 '진지하게'라는 의미이다.

어휘 board of directors 이사회   sector 분야

114 전치사 자리 / 어휘

번역 아케미스 카페는 두 달간의 보수 공사를 끝내고 다시 고객을 맞이하기를 고대하고 있다.

해설 빈칸 앞에 완전한 절(Akemi's Café is looking forward to welcoming back customers)이 있고 뒤에 명사구 a two-month renovation project가 있으므로 빈칸은 전치사 자리이다. 문맥상 '두 달간의 보수 공사를 끝낸 뒤'가 되어야 적절하므로 '뒤에, 후에'를 뜻하는 전치사 (C) after가 정답이다. (A) because of는 '~때문에'라는 뜻으로 의미상 어울리지 않고, (B) now that과 (D) when은 접속사로 뒤에 절이 와야 하므로 답이 될 수 없다.

115 형용사 자리_명사 수식

번역 10년의 긴 휴식 후, 더 미스 라이더스 밴드는 라이브 쇼를 재개할 것이다.

해설 빈칸 앞에 부정관사, 뒤에 명사 break가 있으므로 명사를 수식하는 형용사 자리이다. '10년의 긴 휴식'이라는 의미가 되어야 적합하므로 '긴, 늘어난'을 뜻하는 형용사 (B) extended가 정답이다. (A) extend는 동사, (C) extension은 명사이므로 품사상 답이 될 수 없고, 타동사 extend의 현재분사인 (D) extending은 목적어를 동반하여 명사를 후치 수식하므로 명사를 앞에서 수식하는 자리에는 어울리지 않는다.

어휘 resume 재개하다

116 동사 어휘

번역 여행자는 집을 떠나기 전에 필요한 서류를 모두 챙겼는지 확인해야 한다.

해설 전치사 before의 목적어 역할을 하는 동명사 자리에 들어갈 동사 어휘를 고르는 문제이다. '집을 떠나기 전에'라는 의미가 되어야 자연스러우므로 '떠나다'라는 뜻의 동사 leave의 동명사형 (B) leaving이 정답이다. (A)의 expand는 '확대하다', (C)의 allow는 '허락하다', (D)의 manage는 '관리하다'라는 의미이다.

117 형용사 자리_명사 수식

번역 퀘일룩스 창고는 저렴한 요금으로 모든 주거용 보관 요구 사항에 적합한 시설을 갖추고 있다.

해설 빈칸 앞에 소유격 대명사 your, 뒤에 명사구 storage needs가 있으므로 명사구를 수식하는 형용사 자리이다. '주거용 보관 요구'라는 의미가 되어야 자연스러우므로 '주거의, 주거용의'라는 뜻의 형용사 (C) residential이 정답이다. (A) residing은 '거주하는'이라는 뜻으로 의미상 부적절하고, (B) to reside는 to부정사, (D) resides는 동사이므로 품사상 답이 될 수 없다.

어휘 depot 창고   facility 시설   storage 보관   rate 요금

118 부사 어휘

번역 가장 출중한 이력서들을 검토한 결과, 에이지 아라카키 씨가 확실히 그 직책에 가장 적합한 사람이었다.

해설 문맥상 '확실히 그 직책에 가장 적합한 사람'이라는 의미가 되어야 적절하므로 '확실히, 분명히'라는 뜻의 (B) clearly가 정답이다. (A) neutrally는 '중립적으로', (C) usually는 '보통'이라는 뜻으로 문맥상 어울리지 않고, (D) very는 최상급을 강조할 때 정관사 the와 최상급 사이에 들어간다.

어휘 qualified 자격이 있는   position 지위

119 부정대명사

번역 기존 대리점이 있던 곳에서 몇 블록 떨어진 곳에 오토바이 대리점이 개점한다.

해설 전치사 from의 목적어 역할을 하는 명사절의 주어 역할을 하는 동시에, 주절에 언급된 단수명사 A motorcycle dealership을 받아 '예전 대리점'을 의미하는 부정대명사가 필요하므로 (C) one이 정답이다. '(둘 중) 다른 하나'를 뜻하는 대명사 the other는 형용사의 수식을 받지 않으므로 (D) other는 빈칸에 들어갈 수 없다.

어휘 motorcycle 오토바이   dealership 대리점

120 부사 어휘

번역 로봇 공학 전문가 바자즈 씨는 산업 자동화에 관심 있는 기업들에 수시로 자문 서비스를 제공한다.

해설 현재 시제 동사 provides를 수식하여 '자문 서비스를 수시로 제공한다'라는 의미가 되어야 자연스러우므로 '수시로'라는 뜻으로 현재 시제와 어울리는 빈도 부사 (C) frequently가 정답이다. (A) highly는 '매우', (B) comparably는 '비슷하게', (D) deeply는 '깊이'라는 의미이다.

어휘 robotics 로봇 공학   industrial 산업의
automation 자동화

121 형용사 자리_명사 수식

번역 마케팅팀은 고객 설문조사를 계속 수행하기로 공동 결정을 내렸다.

해설 빈칸 앞에 부정관사 a, 뒤에 명사 decision이 있으므로 명사를 수식하는 형용사 자리이다. 따라서 '집단의, 공동의'라는 의미의 형용사 (C) collective가 정답이다. (A) collect와 (B) collects는 동사, (D) collectively는 부사이므로 품사상 적합하지 않다.

어휘 conduct (특정 활동을) 하다   collectively 일괄적으로

122 동사 어휘

번역 각 셰프웨어 팬에는 12년간 고객 만족 보장이 제공된다.

해설 빈칸 뒤에 목적어가 보이지 않으므로 자동사가 들어가야 한다. 전치사 with와 함께 '딸려 있다, 함께 제공되다'라는 뜻의 자동사 (D) comes가 정답이다. (A)의 include는 타동사로 '포함시키다', (B)의 serve는 자동사로 '근무하다', 타동사로 '(음식 등) 제공하다'라는 의미이며, (C)의 adjust는 자동사로 '적응하다', 타동사로 '조정하다'라는 의미이다.

어휘 satisfaction 만족   guarantee 보장

123 부사 자리_동사 수식

번역 배송 업체는 뉴캐슬에 있는 공장에서 제품을 운반할 때 가끔 지연을 겪었다.

해설 빈칸은 has와 experienced 사이에서 동사구를 수식하는 부사 자리이므로, '가끔'이라는 의미의 부사 (C) occasionally가 정답이다. (A) occasioned는 동사/과거분사, (B) occasional은 형용사, (D) occasioning은 동명사/현재분사이므로 품사상 빈칸에 들어갈 수 없다.

어휘 delay 지연   occasion 야기하다; 경우   occasional 가끔의

124 접속사 자리_부사절 접속사

번역 일단 모든 필수 서류가 접수되면 계약이 체결됩니다.

해설 빈칸은 두 개의 완전한 절을 이어주는 접속사 자리이다. 문맥상 '일단 서류가 접수되면'이라는 의미가 되어야 하므로 '일단 ~하면'이라는 뜻의 부사절 접속사 (D) once가 정답이다. (A) yet은 '하지만'이라는 뜻의 등위접속사로 의미상 어울리지 않고, (B) instead는 '대신에'라는 뜻의 부사, (C) similarly는 '유사하게'라는 뜻의 부사로 품사상 적합하지 않다.

어휘 award a contract 계약해 주다

125 명사 어휘

번역 작업 설명서에는 교대 근무를 시작할 때 어떤 장비 부품에 윤활유를 발라야 하는지 명시되어 있다.

해설 전치사구 of the shift의 수식을 받아 '교대 근무를 시작할 때'라는 의미가 되어야 자연스러우므로 '시작'을 뜻하는 (A) start가 정답이다. (B) day는 '날', (C) place는 '장소', (D) side는 '쪽[측]'이라는 의미이다.

어휘 operations manual 작업 설명서   state 명시하다
lubricate 윤활유를 바르다

126 지시대명사

번역 럭키 브릿지 레스토랑의 관리자는 초과 근무를 희망하는 사람들에게 신청서에 이름을 써 달라고 요청했다.

해설 빈칸은 동사 asked의 목적어 자리이고, 현재분사구(willing to work overtime)의 수식을 받아 '초과 근무를 희망하는 사람들'이라는 의미가 되어야 하므로 분사구의 후치 수식을 받아 '~하는 사람들'이라는 뜻으로 쓸 수 있는 지시대명사 (A) those가 정답이다. (B) which와 (C) who는 뒤에 동사를 포함한 절이 와야 하고, (D) yours는 인칭대명사로 후치 수식을 받지 않는다.

어휘 overtime 초과 근무   sign-up sheet 참가 신청서

127 동사 자리

번역 예상했던 대로 내부 감사 결과 회사에서 소액의 출장비를 초과 지급했다는 것이 드러났다.

해설 주어 the internal audit의 동사 자리로 that절을 목적어로 취한다. 따라서 '드러내다'라는 뜻의 동사 (D) revealed가 정답이다. (A) having revealed와 (B) revealing은 동명사/현재분사, (C) to reveal은 to부정사로 품사상 빈칸에 들어갈 수 없다.

어휘 internal 내부의   audit 감사   overpay 초과 지급하다
expense 경비

128 명사 어휘

번역 장식품 재고 물량의 최신 목록은 페스탈 시즌스 사가 연휴 성수기를 위해 대비를 잘 하고 있음을 보여 준다.

해설 형용사 latest와 전치사구 of decorations in stock의

수식을 받아 '장식품 재고 물량의 최신 목록'이라는 의미가 되어야 적합하므로 '물품 목록'이라는 뜻의 (B) inventory가 정답이다. (A) proposal은 '제안(서)', (C) consideration은 '고려 (사항)', (D) commitment는 '약속'이라는 의미이다.

어휘 in stock 재고가 있는   indicate 보여 주다

129 명사 어휘

번역 프린슨 테크놀로지스의 온라인 카탈로그에는 소프트웨어 제품에 대한 상세한 설명이 들어 있다.

해설 형용사 detailed와 전치사구 of its software products의 수식을 받아 '소프트웨어 제품에 대한 상세한 설명이 들어 있다'는 내용이 되어야 자연스럽다. 따라서 '설명'을 뜻하는 (D) descriptions가 정답이다. (C) predictions는 '예측'이라는 의미로 문맥상 적절하지 않다.

어휘 contain ∼이 들어 있다   detailed 상세한

130 형용사 어휘

번역 모든 은행 이체 내역은 검토 대상이며 문제가 확인될 경우 지연될 수 있다.

해설 빈칸 뒤 to review의 review는 뒤에 목적어가 없으므로 명사이며 to는 전치사임을 알 수 있다. 문맥상 '모든 은행 이체는 검토의 대상이다'라는 내용이 되어야 적절하므로, 전치사 to와 함께 'be subject to'의 형태로 '∼의 대상이다'라는 의미를 나타내는 형용사 (D) subject가 정답이다. (A) required는 'be required to부정사'의 형태로 쓰이며, (B) imaginary는 '상상의', (C) conscious는 '의식하는'이라는 뜻으로 문맥에 어울리지 않는다.

어휘 transfer 송금   delay 지연시키다   identify 확인하다

PART 6

[131-134] 기사

> **노리치 농업 브랜즈, 신규 냉동 채소 공장 개장**
>
> 노리치 농업 브랜즈가 이믈리에 새로운 채소 가공 공장을 완공했다. 이 공장은 근처에 위치한 노후 **131시설**을 대체한다. 새 공장에서는 연간 천만 킬로그램의 옥수수, 완두콩, 그리고 콩을 가공할 수 있다. **132이 수치는 기존 공장 대비 20퍼센트 증가한 수치에 해당한다.** 새로운 공장은 **133또한** 제품 1킬로그램당 25퍼센트 적은 양의 물을 사용하게 된다.
>
> 새로운 부지에서 가공되는 채소는 지역 재배자들에게서 공급받을 예정이다. 노리치는 채소가 가장 잘 익었을 때 수확되어 가공되도록 **134하기 위해** 현지 공급자 네트워크와 긴밀히 협력한다.

> **어휘** agricultural 농업의 frozen 냉동된 processing 가공 outdated 구식인 process 가공하다 pea 완두콩 annually 매년 site 부지, 장소 ripe 익은, 숙성한

131 명사 어휘

해설 앞 문장에서 새 공장을 완공했다(has completed construction of its new vegetable-processing plant)고 했으므로 빈칸이 있는 문장의 주어 It이 가리키는

것은 '새로운 공장'이고, 빈칸에 들어갈 명사는 새 공장이 대체하는 대상임을 알 수 있다. 따라서 '새 공장은 낡은 시설을 대체한다'는 의미가 되어야 적절하므로 '시설'을 뜻하는 (B) facility가 정답이다. (A) shop은 '가게', (C) machine은 '기계', (D) monument는 '기념물'이라는 의미이다.

132 문맥에 맞는 문장 고르기

번역 (A) 이 수치는 기존 공장 대비 20퍼센트 증가한 수치에 해당한다.
(B) 노리치는 50년 이상 지역 경제의 일부였다.
(C) 지역의 몇몇 가족들은 노리치에서 대대로 근무했다.
(D) 채식 위주의 식단은 건강한 대안이 될 수 있다.

해설 빈칸 앞에서 새 공장은 매년 천만 킬로그램(10 million kilos)의 곡물을 가공할 수 있다고 안내하고 있으므로, 빈칸에는 10 million kilos를 '이 수치(this figure)'로 받아 수치가 나타내는 의미를 설명하는 내용이 들어가야 자연스럽다. 따라서 해당 수치가 기존 공장과 비교했을 때 얼마나 증가한 것인지에 대해 언급하고 있는 (A)가 정답이다.

어휘 figure 수치   represent ∼에 상당하다
for generations 대대로   alternative 대안

133 부사 어휘

해설 앞 문장에서 새 공장에서는 연간 천만 킬로그램의 곡물을 가공할 수 있고 이는 기존 공장 대비 20퍼센트 증가한 수치에 해당한다며 새로운 공장의 이점인 증대된 가공 용량에 대해 언급하고 있다. 빈칸이 있는 문장은 가공 공정에 더 적은 물을 사용하게 된다며 새로운 공장의 또 다른 이점을 덧붙여 언급하고 있으므로 '또한'이라는 뜻으로 추가의 의미를 나타내는 (D) also가 정답이다. (A) therefore는 '그러므로', (B) instead는 '대신에', (C) quite는 '꽤'라는 의미이다.

134 to부정사_부사적 용법

해설 빈칸 앞에 완전한 절이 있고 뒤에 that절이 있으므로, that절을 목적어로 취하면서 앞 절의 내용을 수식할 수 있는 준동사가 들어가야 한다. 따라서 '채소가 가장 잘 익었을 때 수확되고 가공되도록 하기 위해'라는 목적을 나타내면서 부사적 역할을 하는 to부정사 (B) to ensure가 정답이다. (A) ensured 동사/과거분사, (C) ensures와 (D) will ensure는 동사로 구조상 빈칸에 들어갈 수 없다.

[135-138] 이메일

> 수신: 그레이터 메트로 은행
> 발신: 조 마이클슨
> 날짜: 12월 2일
> 제목: 대출 요청
> 첨부: 사업 계획서
>
> 담당자 분께,
>
> 저는 지역 제과점인 조스 브레즈 앤 트리츠를 소유 및 운영하고 있습니다. 제과점은 지난 5년 동안 점점 더 **135성공적**이었습니다. **136사실**, 제과점이 아주 잘 되고 있어서 커피숍을 열 계획이고, 그곳에서 제 제과 제품도 판매할 것입니다. 새로운 고객에게 서비스를 제공할 수 있도록 이 신규 점포는 도시 북쪽에 위치할 계획입니

다. 다만 저의 계획을 현실화하기 위해 대출을 신청해야 합니다. **137 귀 은행에서 저에게 이 대출을 제공해 줄 수 있기를 바랍니다.**

제가 대출금을 정확히 **138 어떻게** 사용할 것인지 확인하실 수 있도록 이 이메일에 제 사업 계획서를 첨부했습니다. 검토하신 후, 다음 단계와 관련하여 연락 주시기를 바랍니다.

감사합니다. 조 마이클슨

어휘 loan 대출(금) make ~ a reality 실현하다
precisely 정확히 regarding ~에 관하여

135 형용사 어휘

해설 빈칸 뒤 문장에서 제과점이 아주 잘 돼서(my bakery is doing so well) 빵 제품을 판매할 커피숍을 열 계획이라고 한 것으로 보아 해당 문장은 '제과점은 지난 5년간 점점 더 성공적이었다'는 내용이 되어야 적절하다. 따라서 '성공한'을 뜻하는 (D) successful이 정답이다. (A) important는 '중요한', (B) necessary는 '필수적인', (C) affordable은 '저렴한'이라는 의미이다.

136 접속부사

해설 앞 문장에서 제과점이 5년 동안 성공적이었다고 했고, 빈칸 뒤에서 제과점이 아주 잘 돼서 커피숍을 열어 제과도 판매할 계획이라고 했다. 따라서 '사실'이라는 뜻으로 앞의 정보를 강화하거나 확인하는 진술을 이어나갈 때 사용하는 (A) In fact가 정답이다. (B) Of course는 '물론', (D) On the contrary는 '그와는 반대로'라는 의미이다. 참고로, '또한'이라는 의미의 (C) In addition은 앞 문장과 별도로 추가 정보를 나열하므로 빈칸에는 적절하지 않다.

137 문맥에 맞는 문장 고르기

번역 (A) 충분한 돈이 모이는 대로 제과점을 개조할 것입니다.
(B) 저의 첫 사업을 시작하기 위해서 대출도 필요했습니다.
(C) 고객들은 저의 제품을 적극 추천합니다.
(D) 귀 은행에서 저에게 이 대출을 제공해 줄 수 있기를 바랍니다.

해설 빈칸 앞에서 제과점이 잘 되고 있어 커피숍을 열어 제과 제품을 판매할 계획이고 이를 실현하기 위해 대출이 필요하다며 대출 신청 사유에 대해 설명하고 있고, 빈칸 뒤에서 대출금 사용 계획이 포함된 사업 계획서를 첨부했다며 대출 승인에 필요한 서류를 제출하고 있음을 언급했다. 따라서 빈칸에는 은행에서 대출을 지급해 주기를 희망하는 내용이 들어가야 적절하므로 (D)가 정답이다.

138 명사절 접속사

해설 빈칸은 완전한 절(I plan to use the loan)을 이끌어 동사 see의 목적어로 만드는 명사절 접속사 자리이다. 빈칸 앞의 부사 precisely의 수식을 받아 '제가 대출금을 정확히 어떻게 사용할 것인지'라는 내용이 되어야 자연스러우므로 '어떻게'라는 뜻으로 완전한 절을 이끄는 명사절 접속사 (C) how가 정답이다. (A) for는 전치사, (D) much는 한정사/대명사/부사로 구조상 빈칸에 들어갈 수 없고, (B) that은 '~이라는 것'이라는 뜻의 명사절 접속사로 문맥상 오답이다.

[139-142] 편지

> 10월 10일
>
> 줄리아 수자 고메스
> 벌라마 팜스 주식회사
> 버크 로 548
> 멜버른
> 빅토리아 3126
>
> 고메스 씨께:
>
> 벌라마 팜스에서 기계 공학자로 **139 일할** 기회를 주셔서 감사합니다. 지난달 **140 면접** 때 귀하와 다른 기술자분들을 만나 뵀던 일은 정말 즐거웠습니다. 하지만 저는 이미 수고 농업에서 비슷한 직책을 맡게 되었습니다. 이 회사는 제 집과 더 가까워서, 여기서 근무하면 가족과 더 많은 시간을 가질 수 있을 것입니다. **141 귀사의 제품에 대한 저의 관심을 고려했을 때 이 결정은 매우 힘들었습니다.** 향후 콘퍼런스나 다른 농업 관련 행사에서 **142 다시** 뵙기를 바랍니다.
>
> 레너드 헤일

어휘 mechanical 기계의 thoroughly 완전히
agroindustrial 농공업의 agricultural 농업의

139 to부정사_형용사적 용법

해설 빈칸은 전치사구 as a mechanical engineer를 이끌며 앞에 있는 명사 opportunity를 수식하는 역할을 한다. opportunity는 to부정사와 함께 쓰여 '~할 기회'라는 뜻을 나타내므로 (A) to work가 정답이다. (B) works는 동사/명사로 품사상 들어갈 수 없고, (C) that worked는 관계사절, (D) working은 현재분사구를 이루어 앞에 오는 명사를 수식할 수는 있지만 여기서 opportunity는 work의 주체가 아니므로 정답이 될 수 없다.

140 명사 어휘

해설 앞에서 벌라마 팜스에서 일할 기회를 주어 감사하다고 언급한 뒤 빈칸이 있는 문장에서 지난달 만났던 일이 즐거웠다고 했으므로, 지난달 이들은 구직을 위한 면접에서 만났음을 알 수 있다. 따라서 '면접'을 뜻하는 (C) interview가 정답이다.

141 문맥에 맞는 문장 고르기

번역 (A) 수고 농공업은 확실히 인상적인 기업입니다.
(B) 기꺼이 더 많은 추천서를 제공해 드리겠습니다.
(C) 그 일자리에 맞는 훌륭한 친구를 추천할 수 있습니다.
(D) 귀사의 제품에 대한 저의 관심을 고려했을 때 이 결정은 매우 힘들었습니다.

해설 앞 내용에서 벌라마 팜스에서 일할 기회를 주어 감사하지만 수고 농공업이라는 다른 회사에서 직책을 맡게 되었다(I have already taken ~ at Sugo Agroindustrial)는 소식과 함께 이러한 결정을 내리게 된 이유에 대해 설명하고 있다. 따라서 빈칸에는 벌라마 팜스의 제품에 대한 자신의 관심을 고려했을 때 쉽지 않은 결정이었다며 고용 제안을 정중하게 거절하는 내용이 들어가야 자연스러우므로 (D)가 정답이다.

어휘 reference 추천서 given ~을 고려하면

142 부사 어휘

해설 앞 내용에서 면접 때 만나서 즐거웠지만 이미 다른 회사에서 근무하게 되었다고 했으므로 빈칸이 있는 문장은 '향후 다른 기회에 다시 뵙기를 바란다'는 내용이 되어야 자연스럽다. 따라서 '다시'를 뜻하는 부사 (D) again이 정답이다.

[143-146] 공지

> ### 공청회 공고
>
> 설베리 시의회는 10월 3일 화요일 저녁 7시 30분에 공청회를 개최할 예정입니다. 회의 목적은 클리프턴 로 **143 확장** 계획에 대해 논의하는 것입니다. 주된 목표는 보행자 및 자전거 이용자를 위해 이 도로를 더 안전하게 만드는 것입니다. 이 **144 프로젝트**의 이차적인 목표는 교통 체증을 완화하는 것입니다. 변경**145 되면** 상점, 사무실, 집 및 사업장에 쉽게 접근할 수 있어야 합니다. 이러한 이유로 기존의 인도가 확장되고 필요한 곳에 새로운 신호등이 설치될 것으로 예상됩니다. **146 제안된 계획의 세부 사항은 설베리 시 웹사이트에서 확인하실 수 있습니다.** 시민들은 회의 참석 전에 계획에 대한 모든 참고 가능한 정보를 검토해 보시기를 권장 드립니다.
>
> **어휘** public meeting 공청회 council 의회 primary 주된 pedestrian 보행자 secondary 이차적인 modification 수정, 변경 existing 기존의 sidewalk 인도

143 동사 어휘

해설 빈칸 뒤에서 '클리프턴 로를 ~하려는 계획'의 주된 목표는 도로를 더 안전하게 만드는 것이고 이차적 목표는 교통 체증을 완화하는 것이라고 했고, 뒤이어 기존의 인도를 확장한다는 내용도 언급하고 있다. 따라서 '클리프턴 로를 확장하려는 계획'이라는 의미가 되어야 적절하므로 '확장하다'라는 뜻을 나타내는 (C) widening이 정답이다.

144 명사 어휘

해설 앞 문장에서 회의가 클리프턴 로 확장 계획(the plan for widening Clifton Road)에 대해 논의하기 위한 것이라고 했으므로 해당 문장은 앞 문장에서 언급된 '도로 확장 계획'의 이차적인 목표에 대한 것임을 알 수 있다. 따라서 도로 확장 계획을 대신할 수 있는 '계획, 프로젝트'라는 뜻의 (B) project가 정답이다. (A) crew는 '작업팀', (C) signage는 '신호 체계', (D) gathering은 '모임'이라는 의미이다.

145 과거분사

해설 빈칸은 주어 Any modifications와 동사 must allow 사이에서 주어를 수식하는 자리이다. 빈칸 뒤에 목적어가 없고 '만들어진 변경은'이라는 의미가 되어야 하므로 과거분사 (D) made가 정답이다. 전치사 (A) prior to(~ 전에)와 (B) as of(~ 부로), 동명사/현재분사 (C) having set은 뒤에 목적어가 필요하므로 빈칸에 들어갈 수 없다.

146 문맥에 맞는 문장 고르기

번역 (A) 점주들은 인도에 장애물이 없도록 주의해 주셔야 합니다.
(B) 저희는 현재 도시 계획 회사로부터 제안서를 받고 있습니다.

(C) 몇몇 주민들은 교통 연구를 의뢰했는지에 대해 문의하셨습니다.
(D) 제안된 계획의 세부 사항은 설베리 시 웹사이트에서 확인하실 수 있습니다.

해설 앞에서 설베리 시의회가 도로 확장 계획에 대한 공청회를 개최한다고 공지하며 공사 계획의 목표 및 내용에 대해 간략히 요약하고 있고, 빈칸 뒤에서는 공청회 참석 전에 계획에 대한 모든 가능한 정보를 검토해 볼 것(review all available information)을 권하고 있다. 따라서 빈칸에는 공사 계획에 대한 세부 정보를 확인할 수 있는 방법에 대해 알려 주는 내용이 들어가야 자연스러우므로 (D)가 정답이다.

어휘 obstruction 장애물 urban-planning 도시 계획 firm 회사 commission 의뢰하다 municipal 시의

PART 7

[147-148] 이메일

> 수신: 티켓 소지자
> 발신: 마젠타 극장
> 날짜: 11월 12일
> 제목: 클로이 창 콘서트
>
> 티켓 소지자분들께:
>
> **147 유감스럽게도 내일 저녁 8시 클로이 창 공연은 가수의 건강 문제로 연기되었음을 알려 드립니다.** 이러한 상황으로 인해 실망 또는 불편을 드려 죄송합니다. **148 공연 일정을 조율하는 동안 티켓을 보관해 주실 것을 요청드립니다.** 현재 여러분께서는 다른 조치를 취하실 필요가 없습니다. 변경된 공연 일자에 대한 자세한 내용은 확보되는 대로 이메일로 보내 드리겠습니다.
>
> 문의 사항이 있으시면 마젠타 극장 매표소로 555-0112번으로 연락하십시오. 다시 한번 불편을 드려 진심으로 사죄드립니다.
>
> 마젠타 극장 직원 일동
>
> **어휘** regret to 유감스럽게도 ~하다 postpone 연기하다 disappointment 실망 retain 보관[보유]하다

147 이메일의 목적은 무엇인가?
(A) 티켓 구매를 위한 새로운 절차 설명
(B) 공연의 변경 사항 고지
(C) 고객에게 공연 할인 티켓 제공
(D) 다가오는 콘서트 투어 홍보

해설 **주제/목적**
첫 문장에서 유감스럽게도 내일 저녁 8시 클로이 창 공연은 가수의 건강 문제로 연기되었음을 알려 드린다(We regret to inform you that tomorrow's 8:00 P.M. performance ~ has been postponed because the singer is ill)고 했으므로 공연 일정이 변경되었다는 소식을 전하기 위해 이메일을 썼다는 것을 알 수 있다. 따라서 (B)가 정답이다.

어휘 procedure 절차 patron 고객 promote 홍보하다

148 티켓 소지자는 무엇을 해야 하는가?

(A) 티켓 보관하기

(B) 창 씨에게 이메일 보내기

(C) 즉시 매표소로 전화하기

(D) 저녁 8시까지 극장에 도착하기

해설 **세부 사항**

세 번째 문장에서 공연 일정을 조율하는 동안 티켓을 보관해 주실 것을 요청드린다(We ask that you please retain your tickets while we work to reschedule the performance)고 했으므로 (A)가 정답이다.

(Paraphrasing) 지문의 retain → 정답의 save

[149-150] 공지

다가오는 볼라노 런치

우리가 가장 좋아하는 연중행사 시기가 왔습니다! **149 가장 인기 있는 우리의 제휴 식당 중 하나인 볼라노에서 우리의 지속적인 사업 협력을 기념하여 6월 2일 키요티 이벤트 기획의 전 직원에게 다시 한번 무료 점심을 제공합니다.** 볼라노와 함께 이벤트를 진행한 모두가 알고 있듯이 그들의 음식은 맛있습니다. 점심 식사 등록을 위해 5월 31일까지 접수 담당자와 이야기하세요. 충분한 음식이 모두에게 제공될 수 있도록 하겠습니다.

점심 식사는 정오부터 구내식당에서 뷔페식으로 제공될 예정입니다. 음료도 제공될 예정이므로 이벤트를 위해 어떠한 것도 준비할 필요가 없습니다. **150 볼라노 직원들을 위한 감사 카드를 돌릴 예정이니 6월 1일까지 카드에 꼭 서명해 주세요.** 모두 거기서 만나기를 기대합니다.

어휘 in honour of ~을 기념하여 collaboration 협력 register for ~에 등록하다 circulate 돌리다, 회람하다

149 볼라노는 왜 키요티 이벤트 기획 직원들에게 점심을 제공하는가?

(A) 키요티 이벤트 기획의 기념일을 축하하려고

(B) 새로운 메뉴의 샘플을 공유하려고

(C) 사업 제휴에 대한 감사를 표현하려고

(D) 새로운 음식 공급 과정을 시연하려고

해설 **세부 사항**

두 번째 문장에서 가장 인기 있는 제휴 식당 중 하나인 볼라노에서 지속적인 사업 협력을 기념하여 6월 2일 키요티 이벤트 기획의 전 직원에게 다시 한번 무료 점심을 제공한다 (Bolano, one of our most popular restaurant partners, is once again providing a free lunch ~ in honour of our continued business collaboration)고 했다. 따라서 볼라노는 키요티 이벤트와 협력 관계를 유지하는 것에 대한 감사의 뜻으로 무료 점심을 제공한다는 것을 알 수 있으므로 (C)가 정답이다.

어휘 appreciation 감사 demonstrate 시연하다

(Paraphrasing) 지문의 our continued business collaboration → 정답의 a business partnership

---

150 행사 전에 직원들은 무엇을 요청받았는가?

(A) 카드에 서명 (B) 결제

(C) 식당 방문 (D) 장식품 준비

해설 **세부 사항**

두 번째 단락의 세 번째 문장에서 볼라노 직원들을 위한 감사 카드를 돌릴 예정이니 6월 1일까지 카드에 꼭 서명해 달라 (We will be circulating a thank-you card ~ make sure to add your signature by 1 June)고 요청하고 있는 것으로 보아 (A)가 정답이다.

(Paraphrasing) 지문의 add your signature → 정답의 Sign

[151-152] 광고

151 파멜라스 아동복 – 지금 바로 쇼핑하세요!

아이들의 놀이복은 지루하거나 진부해서는 안 됩니다! 파멜라스 아동복에서는 아동복이 편하고 저렴하며 세련되어야 한다고 믿습니다. 이러한 이유로 저희는 아동복 전 라인에 걸쳐 고급 소재와 세심한 디자인만을 사용합니다.

게다가, **152 부모님들은 아이들이 입고 노는 옷은 튼튼하고 세탁하기 쉬워야 한다고 요구하십니다. 저희 청바지, 멜빵바지, 티셔츠, 신발, 수영복, 치노 팬츠, 반바지, 스웨터는 모두 세탁기로 세탁할 수 있고 얼룩에 강하며 빨리 마릅니다.**

오늘 15개의 저희 매장 중 한 곳에서 여러분의 아이들을 위한 옷 놀이 약속을 잡으세요! 아니면 온라인으로 https://pamelasclothesforkids.com에서 저희를 찾아보세요.

어휘 trite 진부한 affordable 저렴한 quality 고급의 thoughtful 사려 깊은 demand 요구하다 sturdy 튼튼한 launder 세탁하다 overalls 멜빵바지 chino 치노 팬츠 stain resistant 얼룩이 지지 않는 youngster 아이

151 광고되고 있는 것은 무엇인가?

(A) 새로운 브랜드 (B) 패션쇼

(C) 옷 가게 (D) 어린이 모임

해설 **주제/목적**

광고 상단의 제목이 파멜라스 아동복에서 지금 바로 쇼핑하세요(Pamela's Clothes for Kids — shop now!)인 것으로 보아 아동복 가게가 광고되고 있음을 알 수 있다. 따라서 (C)가 정답이다.

어휘 gathering 모임

152 아동복 라인에 대해 명시된 것은?

(A) 쉽게 세탁할 수 있는 옷이 포함되어 있다.

(B) 학교 관계자의 승인을 받았다.

(C) 유명한 패션 디자이너가 제작했다.

(D) 곧 소매점에서 구매 가능하다.

해설 **Not/True**

두 번째 단락의 첫 문장에서 부모들은 아이들이 입고 노는 옷은 튼튼하고 세탁하기 쉬워야 한다고 요구한다(moms and dads demand that the clothes ~ easy to launder)고 한 뒤 자사의 옷들은 모두 세탁기로 세탁할 수 있고 얼룩에 강하며 빨리 마른다 (all machine washable, stain resistant, and quick drying)고 했다. 따라서 해당 아동복 라인은 세탁이 쉬운 옷들로 구성되어 있음을 언급하고 있으므로 (A)가 정답이다.

어휘 approve 승인하다 school official 학교 관계자

(Paraphrasing) 지문의 easy to launder
→ 정답의 easily cleaned

[153-154] 문자 메시지

루이스 올리베라 (오전 8시 10분)
할랜드시 송수관 프로젝트에 채용할 엔지니어를 논의하기 위한 오늘 오후 2시 회의를 확인 중입니다. **154**우리는 엔지니어 다섯 명의 면접을 봤고 두 자리를 채워야 합니다.

수잔 아놀드 (오전 8시 12분)
네, 가겠습니다. **153**오후 2시까지 다른 회의가 예정되어 있어서 몇 분 늦을 수도 있습니다. 가는 길에 제가 문자를 드리면 어떨까요?

루이스 올리베라 (오전 8시 15분)
그러면 되겠네요. 설계 계획도 보여드리고 싶어요. 인사과의 사만다 마르티네즈도 회의에 참석하나요?

수잔 아놀드 (오전 8시 17분)
154그녀는 이번 주에 콘퍼런스에 가 있지만 이메일로 제게 채용 지침을 보냈습니다. 그녀는 월요일까지 우리가 최종 결정을 내리기를 원합니다.

루이스 올리베라 (오전 8시 20분)
알겠습니다. 오늘 오후에 뵙겠습니다.

어휘 water pipeline 송수관 fill (공석을) 채우다
on one's way 가는 길에 determination 결정

153 오전 8시 15분에 올리베라 씨가 "그러면 되겠네요"라고 쓴 의도는 무엇인가?
(A) 수송관 설계 계획에 찬성한다.
(B) 알림 메시지를 보내겠다는 아놀드 씨의 제안에 동의한다.
(C) 다른 날에 아놀드 씨와 만나고 싶어 한다.
(D) 아마 더 많은 엔지니어가 필요할 것이라는 점을 알고 있다.

해설 의도 파악
8시 12분에 아놀드 씨가 오후 2시까지 다른 회의가 잡혀 있어서 몇 분 늦을 수도 있다(I have another meeting scheduled until 2:00 P.M., so I might be a few minutes late)며 가는 길에 문자로 알려 주면 어떨지(Why don't I text you when I am on my way?)를 제안하자, 8시 15분에 올리베라 씨가 그러면 되겠다(That makes sense)고 답했다. 따라서 올리베라 씨는 문자를 보내겠다는 아놀드 씨의 제안을 받아들인다는 의도로 한 말임을 알 수 있으므로 (B)가 정답이다.

어휘 in favor of ~에 찬성하여 notification 알림

154 아놀드 씨와 올리베라 씨는 월요일까지 무엇을 해야 하는가?
(A) 입사 지원자 면접
(B) 콘퍼런스 발표 준비
(C) 채용 대상자 결정
(D) 마르티네즈 씨가 보낸 지침 편집

해설 세부 사항
8시 10분에 올리베라 씨가 엔지니어 다섯 명의 면접을 봤고 두 자리를 채워야 한다(We interviewed five engineers, and we have two positions to fill)고 했고, 8시 17분에 아놀드 씨가 그녀(사만다 마르티네즈)는 이번 주에 콘퍼런스에 가 있지만 이메일로 채용 지침을 보냈다(She's away ~ but she e-mailed the hiring guidelines to me)며 월요일까지 우리가 최종 결정을 내리기를 원한다(She wants our final determination by Monday)고 했다. 따라서 아놀드 씨와 올리베라 씨는 월요일까지 채용 지침에 따라 면접 참가자 중 최종 합격자 두 명을 결정해야 한다는 것을 알 수 있으므로 (C)가 정답이다.

어휘 candidate 지원자 edit 편집하다

[155-157] 웹페이지

https://www.taoblar.com/features

연혁	특징	구매	문의

디자인이 잘된 탁상용 램프는 집이든 사무실이든 모든 작업 공간에 필수적입니다. 하지만 사람들은 별생각 없이 램프를 구입하는 경향이 있고, 일부는 분명히 이상적이지 않은 조명 해결책을 선택할 것입니다. 하지만 우리는 약간의 계획을 세우는 것만으로도 소비자들이 돈을 낭비하거나 형편없는 제품에 실망하는 일을 피할 수 있다고 생각합니다.

155타오블라 주식회사에서 생산한 모든 제품은 필요한 곳에 빛을 비출 수 있도록 완전한 조절이 가능합니다. 예를 들어 **156**TT-1 모델은 당사의 가장 작고 효율적인 램프로, 작거나 좁은 컴퓨터 책상을 위해 특별히 설계되었습니다. TT-1은 매우 집중적인 조명인 반면 TT-2와 TT-3 모델은 더 큰 작업 공간을 위해 설계되어 더 넓게 빛을 비춥니다. **155**또한 타오블라 주식회사의 모든 램프는 조도를 조절할 수 있으며 사용자가 원하는 정도로 램프의 밝기를 조절할 수 있는 간단한 스위치가 달려 있습니다. 이것은 눈의 피로와 피로감을 방지하는 데 도움이 됩니다.

저희 램프는 모든 유형의 작업장에서 주요 제품이 되었습니다. **155,157**최근 최고의 디자인 전문가 패널이 자사 제품군의 특징을 조사하고 타오블라 주식회사가 우수 디자인 상을 수상할 만한 자격이 있었다고 결론지었습니다. 저희의 모든 제품을 보시려면 구매 페이지를 방문하세요.

어휘 feature 특징 vital 필수적인 tend to ~하는 경향이 있다 undoubtedly 의심 없이, 분명히 settle on ~을 결정하다 less-than-ideal 이상적이지 못한 manufacture 제조[생산]하다 adjustable 조절 가능한 direct 향하게 하다 compact 작고 효율적인 narrow 좁은 cast (빛을) 발하다 dimmable 조도 조절이 가능한 knob 노브, (돌리는) 스위치 eyestrain 눈의 피로 fatigue 피로 mainstay 주요 지지물, 주축 specialist 전문가 examine 조사하다 worthy of ~을 받을 만한 offering 판매품

155 웹페이지에서 설명하는 것은 무엇인가?
(A) 컴퓨터 워크스테이션을 위한 조립 지침
(B) 산업 디자인 시상 축하 행사
(C) 타오블라 주식회사 제품의 바람직한 면
(D) 타오블라 주식회사가 제품 생산에 사용하는 공정

해설 **주제/목적**

두 번째 단락의 첫 문장에서 타오블라 주식회사에서 생산한 모든 제품은 필요한 곳에 빛을 비출 수 있도록 완전한 조절이 가능하다(Every product ~ is fully adjustable to direct light where needed)고 했고, 같은 단락의 네 번째 문장에서 또한 모든 타오블라 주식회사의 램프는 조도를 조절할 수 있으며 사용자가 원하는 정도로 램프의 밝기를 조절할 수 있는 간단한 스위치가 달려 있다(Furthermore, all Taoblar, Inc., lamps are dimmable and have a simple knob ~ whatever degree the user wishes)고 했으며, 마지막 단락의 두 번째 문장에서 최근 최고의 디자인 전문가 패널이 자사 제품군의 특징을 조사하고 타오블라 주식회사가 우수 디자인 상을 수상할 만 했다고 결론지었다(Recently, a panel of top design specialists ~ concluded that Taoblar, Inc., was worthy of their Excellence in Design award)고 했다. 웹페이지 전반에 걸쳐 타오블라 주식회사 램프의 장점에 대해 설명하고 있으므로 (C)가 정답이다.

어휘 assembly 조립 desirable 바람직한 aspect 측면

156 TT-1 모델에 대해 암시된 것은?

(A) 유명한 예술 작품을 기반으로 한다.

(B) 현재 품절됐다.

(C) 회사의 베스트셀러 제품이다.

(D) 회사가 만드는 가장 작은 모델이다.

해설 **추론/암시**

두 번째 단락의 두 번째 문장에서 TT-1 모델은 당사의 가장 작고 효율적인 램프(The Model TT-1 ~ is our most compact lamp)라고 했으므로 TT-1은 타오블라 주식회사에서 생산하는 가장 작은 모델임을 알 수 있다. 따라서 (D)가 정답이다.

어휘 out of stock 재고가 없는

(Paraphrasing) 지문의 most compact
→ 정답의 smallest

157 타오블라 주식회사에 대해 명시된 것은?

(A) 제품이 업계의 인정을 받았다.

(B) 제품이 내구성으로 유명하다.

(C) 최근 중요한 조명 부품을 새로 디자인했다.

(D) 다른 지역에 더 많은 매장을 열 계획이다.

해설 **Not/True**

세 번째 단락의 두 번째 문장에서 최근 최고의 디자인 전문가 패널이 자사 제품군의 특징을 조사하고 타오블라 주식회사가 우수 디자인 상을 수상할 만한 자격이 있었다고 결론지었다(Recently, a panel of top design specialists ~ concluded that Taoblar, Inc., was worthy of their Excellence in Design award)고 했다. 따라서 타오블라 주식회사의 제품이 업계의 인정을 받고 있음을 알 수 있으므로 (A)가 정답이다.

어휘 recognition 인정 durability 내구성 component 부품, 구성 요소

[158-160] 이메일

수신: 수 고 〈sue_koh@swipemail.com〉
발신: 고객 지원 〈customer_relations@harborhopferries.ca〉
날짜: 7월 24일
제목: 고객님의 최근 여행

고 씨께,

158 7월 7일 갈리아노 섬으로 가셨다가 7월 12일 돌아오시는 데 하버홉 페리즈를 이용해 주셔서 감사드립니다. 저희 서비스에 만족하셨기를 바랍니다.

159 50년 동안 하버홉 페리즈는 근사한 해변, 경치 좋은 자전거 및 하이킹 코스, 상점 그리고 레스토랑을 즐기려는 방문객들을 섬으로 실어 나르며, 갈리아노 섬의 경제를 지원하고 강화하는 것을 도왔습니다. 섬의 경제를 활성화하는 데 있어 저희의 역할은 작을지 모르지만, 그럼에도 불구하고 저희는 이것을 매우 진지하게 생각합니다. 따라서 **160** 저희가 대중을 위한 서비스를 지속적으로 개선할 수 있도록 저희와의 경험에 대한 몇 가지 질문에 잠시 시간을 내어 답변해 주실 것을 요청드립니다. 저희 웹사이트 www.harborhopferries.ca/survey에서 설문 조사를 작성하시면 됩니다.

감사의 선물로 다음 여행 비용에 적용하실 수 있는 20퍼센트 할인권을 보내 드립니다. 발급일로부터 최대 6개월까지 사용하실 수 있습니다.

시간 내주셔서 감사드리며 다시 뵙기를 기대합니다.

고객 지원, 하버홉 페리즈

어휘 strengthen 강화하다 spectacular 장관인, 멋진
scenic 경치 좋은 trail 코스, 등산로 boost 신장시키다
nevertheless 그럼에도 불구하고 voucher 상품권
good 유효한 issue 발급

158 고 씨에 대해 암시된 것은?

(A) 자전거를 배에 가지고 탔다.

(B) 하버홉 페리즈를 자주 이용한다.

(C) 보통 7월에 갈리아노 섬을 방문한다.

(D) 갈리아노 섬에서 며칠 밤을 보냈다.

해설 **추론/암시**

첫 문장에서 고 씨에게 7월 7일 갈리아노 섬으로 가셨다가 7월 12일 돌아오시는 데 하버홉 페리즈를 이용해 주어 감사하다(Thank you for using Harborhop Ferries on 7 July to go to Galiano Island and on 12 July to return from it)고 한 것으로 보아 고 씨가 갈리아노 섬에서 며칠 묵었음을 짐작할 수 있다. 따라서 (D)가 정답이다.

159 하버홉 페리즈에 대해 명시된 것은?

(A) 배에 선상 레스토랑이 있다.

(B) 50년 동안 사업을 해 왔다.

(C) 하루에 여러 차례 갈리아노 섬으로 운행 서비스를 제공한다.

(D) 6개월 뒤 갈리아노 섬으로의 운행을 중단할 예정이다.

해설 **Not/True**

두 번째 단락의 첫 문장에서 50년 동안 하버홉 페리즈는 방문객들을 섬으로 실어 나르며 갈리아노 섬의 경제를 지원하고 강화하는 것을 도왔다(For 50 years now, Harborhop

Ferries has helped ~ Galiano Island, bringing visitors to the area)고 했으므로, 하버홉 페리즈가 50년 간 페리 운영 사업을 지속해 왔음을 알 수 있다. 따라서 (B)가 정답이다.

어휘 onboard 선상[기내]의

160 이메일의 목적은 무엇인가?
(A) 페리 예약 확인
(B) 페리 운행의 변경 사항 고지
(C) 제공된 서비스에 대한 피드백 요청
(D) 섬의 경제 성장에 대한 보고

해설 **주제/목적**
두 번째 단락의 세 번째 문장에서 하버홉 페리즈가 대중을 위 한 서비스를 지속적으로 개선할 수 있도록 이용 경험에 대한 몇 가지 질문에 잠시 시간을 내어 답변해 줄 것을 요청(so as to keep improving our service to the public, we invite you to take a few minutes to answer some questions about your experience with us)하고 있 다. 따라서 고객들에게 설문조사에 참여해 줄 것을 요청하기 위해 이메일을 썼다는 것을 알 수 있으므로 정답은 (C)이다.

[161-163] 이메일

수신: 안젤리나 노보아
발신: 올리버 로빈슨
제목: 정보
날짜: 10월 1일
첨부: 로빈슨 1권

안젤리나에게,

161직원 건강 위원회의 일원으로서 우리가 최근 이곳 월본 제조 에서 걷기 동호회를 시작했다는 것을 알고 계실 거예요. 벌써 직원 32명이 등록했다는 걸 알면 기쁠 거예요! **162**그룹 걷기는 10월 16 일로 계획되어 있는데 그 전에 더 많은 회원이 가입할 수도 있어요. 그룹은 걷기 출발점인 구내식당에서 만날 계획이에요.

161지난 회의에 참석을 못하셔서, 위원회에서 직원들이 제출한 건 강한 조리법을 담은 요리책을 만들기로 결정했다는 것도 알려 드리 고 싶었어요. 조리법은 사내 웹사이트에서 수집할 수 있어요. 아니 면, **163**조리법을 인쇄해서 책으로 제본할 수도 있는데, 그러면 기 금 모금용으로 판매할 수도 있고요. 책은 항상 친구와 가족을 위한 훌륭한 선물이잖아요. 승인을 위해 관리자들에게 보낼 제안서를 첨 부했어요. 어떻게 생각하시는지 알려 주세요!

올리버

어휘 wellness 건강 committee 위원회 contain ~이 들어 있다 alternatively 그렇지 않으면 bound 제본된 fund-raiser 기금 모금자, 기금 모금 행사

161 로빈슨 씨가 노보아 씨에게 왜 이메일을 보냈는가?
(A) 동호회에 가입을 권하려고
(B) 기금 모금 행사에 초대하려고
(C) 위원회 활동에 대해 업데이트해 주려고
(D) 그녀가 대회에서 우승했다는 것을 알려 주려고

해설 **주제/목적**
첫 문장에서 직원 건강 위원회의 일원으로서 최근 이곳 월본 제조에서 걷기 동호회를 시작했다는 것을 알고 있을 것(As a member of the Employee Wellness Committee, you know that we recently started a walking club here at Walbourne Manufacturing)이라고 한 뒤 회원 등록 현황과 일정을 알려 주고 있고, 두 번째 단락의 첫 문장에서 지난 회의에 참석을 못해서 위원회에서 직원들 이 제출한 건강한 조리법을 담은 요리책을 만들기로 결정했다는 것을 알려 주고자 했다(Since you were unable to attend the last meeting, I also wanted to let you know that the committee has decided to create a cookbook ~)고 했다. 로빈슨 씨가 노보아 씨에게 이메일 전반에 걸쳐 직원 건강 위원회와 관련된 새로운 소식을 알려 주고 있으므로 (C)가 정답이다.

162 10월 16일에 무엇이 열릴 예정인가?
(A) 독서회   (B) 온라인 파티
(C) 운동 행사   (D) 기획 회의

해설 **세부 사항**
세 번째 문장에서 그룹 걷기는 10월 16일로 계획되어 있다 (A group walk is planned for 16 October)고 했으므 로 운동 행사가 열린다는 것을 알 수 있다. 따라서 (C)가 정답 이다.

163 [1], [2], [3], [4]로 표시된 곳 중에서 다음 문장이 들어가기에 가장 적합한 위치는?
"책은 항상 친구와 가족을 위한 훌륭한 선물이잖아요."
(A) [1]   (B) [2]
(C) [3]   (D) [4]

해설 **문장 삽입**
주어진 문장에서 책(Books)은 훌륭한 선물이 된다고 했으므 로, 책과 관련된 내용을 언급한 문장과 연결되어야 한다. [4] 앞에서 조리법을 책으로 제본할 수 있다(we could have the recipes ~ bound as a book)며 책을 처음 언급했 다. 또한 선물용으로 책을 언급한 주어진 문장이 [4]에 들어 가면, 책을 기금 모금용으로 판매할 수도 있다(which we could then sell as a fund-raiser)는 앞 문장을 자연스 럽게 뒷받침해 준다. 따라서 (D)가 정답이다.

[164-167] 이메일

수신: 영화 채팅 배포 목록
발신: 〈newsletter@filmchat.ca〉
날짜: 10월 17일
제목: 일일 영화 채팅

영화 채팅 친구 여러분께,

오늘 집중 조명할 것은 초기 피터 쿠차르스키의 영화입니다. **164**지난 10년 동안 쿠차르스키는 〈10억 달러 구조〉와 〈먼 우주 모 험〉과 같은 강렬한 액션 영화를 감독했습니다. 이러한 성공들은 쿠 차르스키의 명성을 굳혀 주었습니다. 하지만 블록버스터를 감독하 기 전 쿠차르스키는 다른 영화 장르들을 탐구했습니다.

15년 전 그의 첫 영화 〈눈의 노래〉는 가족 드라마입니다. **166이 영화는 배우이자 뮤지션인 브라탄 말리노프스키가 연기한 밝고 창의적인 손자와 함께 살며 안나 베드나르스카가 연기한 나이 든 가게 주인의 이야기입니다.** **165어느 날, 책을 읽던 중 손자는 자신에게 깊은 영향을 준 시를 한 편 만나게 됩니다. 사실, 이것은 그와 할머니의 삶을 모두 바꿔 놓습니다.**

이 주제는 쿠차르스키의 후기 영화들의 주제와 완전히 다릅니다. 그럼에도 불구하고, 감동을 불러일으키는 영화를 만드는 쿠차르스키의 재능을 이미 확인할 수 있습니다. 할머니와 손자 사이에는 가끔 오해도 있지만, 이는 명백한 사랑과 헌신의 순간들로 상쇄됩니다. 모든 상황에 유머를 가미하는 감독의 능력 또한 주목할 만합니다.

쿠차르스키의 이런 **167부드러운** 면을 보시려면 이번 주 토요일 낮 12시에 열리는 비쥬 영화제에서 〈눈의 노래〉 특별 주간 상영회를 확인하세요.

어휘 distribution 배포 decade 10년 intense 강렬한 rescue 구조 establish 확립시키다 reputation 명성 portray 연기하다, 묘사하다 poem 시 profound 심오한 subject matter 주제, 소재 and yet 그럼에도 불구하고 evoke (감정 등을) 일으키다 occasional 가끔의 misunderstanding 오해 offset 상쇄하는 것 obvious 명백한 devotion 헌신 noticeable 주목할 만한 matinee (영화 등의) 주간 상영

164 이메일에 따르면, 피터 쿠차르스키는 무엇으로 유명한가?

(A) 연극 연기 (B) 영화 감독
(C) 음악 작곡 (D) 언론 출판

해설 **세부 사항**

두 번째 문장에서 지난 10년 동안 쿠차르스키는 강렬한 액션 영화를 감독했다(In the past decade, Kucharsky has directed intense action films)고 했고, 이러한 성공들은 쿠차르스키의 명성을 굳혀 주었다(These successes have established Kucharsky's reputation)고 했다. 따라서 피터 쿠차르스키는 영화 감독으로 유명하다는 것을 알 수 있으므로 (B)가 정답이다.

어휘 compose 작곡하다 journalism 언론, 저널리즘

(Paraphrasing) 지문의 films → 정답의 movies

165 영화 〈눈의 노래〉에서 무엇이 주인공들의 삶에 변화를 일으키는가?

(A) 사업 실패 (B) 가족 행사
(C) 문학 작품 (D) 오해

해설 **세부 사항**

두 번째 단락의 세 번째 문장에서 영화 〈눈의 노래〉에 대해 설명하면서 어느 날 책을 읽던 중 손자는 자신에게 깊은 영향을 준 시를 한 편 만나게 된다(One day, while reading a book, the grandson comes across a poem that has a profound effect on him)고 했고, 이것이 그와 할머니의 삶을 모두 바꿔 놓는다(In fact, it transforms both his and his grandmother's lives)고 했으므로 이 영화의 주인공들은 시, 즉 문학 작품을 통해 삶이 바뀌었음을 알 수 있다. 따라서 (C)가 정답이다.

어휘 literature 문학

(Paraphrasing) 지문의 a poem → 정답의 A work of literature

166 브라탄 말리노프스키는 누구인가?

(A) 연기자 (B) 소식지 구독자
(C) 소년의 할아버지 (D) 가게 주인

해설 **세부 사항**

두 번째 단락의 두 번째 문장에서 이 영화는 배우이자 뮤지션인 브라탄 말리노프스키가 연기한 밝고 창의적인 손자와 함께 살며, 안나 베드나르스카가 연기한 나이 든 가게 주인의 이야기(It tells the story of an older shop owner ~ who lives with her bright and creative grandson, portrayed by actor and musician Bratan Malinowski)라고 했다. 따라서 브라탄 말리노프스키는 영화에서 손자 역을 맡은 연기자임을 알 수 있으므로 (A)가 정답이다.

어휘 performer 연기자 newsletter 소식지

167 네 번째 단락 1행의 "softer"와 의미가 가장 가까운 단어는?

(A) 더 새로운 (B) 더 매끄러운
(C) 더 조용한 (D) 더 온화한

해설 **동의어 찾기**

의미상 감독이 가진 '부드러운' 면이라는 뜻으로 쓰였으므로 (D) gentler가 정답이다.

[168-171] 회람

> **회람**
>
> 수신: 난베로 전 직원
> 발신: 클라이브 바타야, 회장
> 날짜: 4월 18일
> 제목: 새로운 안식 휴가 혜택
>
> 난베로는 새로운 안식 휴가 프로그램을 도입하게 되어 기쁘게 생각합니다. **170직원들은 10년 근속 이후 자격이 주어지며 최대 6주 동안 휴가를 신청할 수 있습니다.** **168난베로는 안식 기간 동안 직원에게 평상시 급여의 50퍼센트를 제공할 것입니다.**
>
> 안식 휴가는 직원들이 평소에는 추구할 수 없었던 활동을 자유롭게 참여할 수 있도록 해 줍니다. **169여기에는 여행, 특히 해외여행, 자원봉사, 특히 장기 프로젝트나 해외 자원봉사, 관심 분야나 경력과 관련된 주제 연구, 진로 개발이나 변경을 위한 공부나 교육, 또는 글쓰기나 그림과 같은 예술 관련 활동 등이 포함될 수 있습니다.**
>
> 안식 휴가는 원하는 시작일보다 최소 3개월 전에 신청해야 합니다. **171사전 요청은 관리자가 여러분이 부재중인 동안 업무를 대신할 방안을 마련할 수 있도록 해 줍니다.** 사용 가능한 유급 휴가(PTO) 일수를 사용해 안식 휴가를 연장할 수 있습니다.
>
> **170이 새로운 혜택으로 우리 베테랑 직원들에게 감사의 뜻이 전달되기를 진정으로 바랍니다.** 전체 규정을 확인하고 안식 휴가 신청서를 이용하려면 난베로 직원 인트라넷의 인사부 탭을 방문하십시오. 신청서는 온라인으로 작성되어 전자상으로 제출되어야 합니다.

168 안식 휴가를 요청하는 직원에게 무엇이 요구되는가?

(A) 이 기간 동안 감봉받을 의향이 있어야 한다.

(B) 휴가 중에 다른 회사에서 근무하지 않기로 동의해야 한다.

(C) 안식 휴가에서 돌아올 때 보고서를 제출해야 한다.

(D) 휴가 중에 가끔 경영진과 연락해야 한다.

해설 **세부 사항**

첫 단락의 세 번째 문장에서 난베로는 안식 휴가 기간 동안 직원에게 평상시 급여의 50퍼센트를 제공할 것(Nanvero is offering staff members 50 percent of their usual salary while taking sabbatical)이라고 했으므로 안식 휴가를 신청하는 직원은 급여가 줄어드는 것을 감안해야 한다는 것을 알 수 있다. 따라서 (A)가 정답이다.

어휘 be willing to 기꺼이 ~하다 occasionally 가끔 check in with ~와 연락하다

(Paraphrasing) 지문의 50 percent of their usual salary → 정답의 reduced pay

169 안식 휴가 요청 사유로 언급된 것이 아닌 것은?

(A) 연구하기   (B) 해외여행하기

(C) 직업 기술 개발하기   (D) 가족과 시간 보내기

해설 **Not / True**

두 번째 단락의 두 번째 문장에서 안식 휴가 동안 할 수 있는 활동에 대해 언급하며 여기에는 여행, 특히 해외여행, 자원봉사, 특히 장기 프로젝트나 해외 자원봉사, 관심 분야나 경력과 관련된 주제 연구, 진로 개발이나 변경을 위한 공부나 교육, 또는 글쓰기나 그림과 같은 예술 관련 활동 등이 포함될 수 있다(These may include traveling, especially overseas; ~ researching topics of interest or relevance to their careers; studying or training to advance or change careers; or pursuing arts-related activities, such as writing or painting)고 했다. 가족과 시간을 보내는 것은 언급되지 않았으므로 정답은 (D)이다.

어휘 conduct (특정 활동을) 하다 professional 전문의

(Paraphrasing)
지문의 researching → 보기 (A)의 Conducting research
지문의 travelling ~ overseas → 보기 (B)의 Travelling internationally
지문의 studying or training to ~ change careers → 보기 (C)의 Advancing professional skills

170 회람에 따르면, 난베로는 왜 새로운 정책을 시행하는가?

(A) 직원 이직률을 낮추려고

(B) 잠재적 직원을 유치하려고

(C) 장기근속 직원에게 포상하려고

(D) 직원 급여를 절약하려고

해설 **세부 사항**

첫 단락의 두 번째 문장에서 직원들은 10년 근속 이후 자격이 주어진다(Employees become eligible after ten years of service)고 했고, 마지막 단락의 첫 문장에서 이 새로운 혜택으로 우리 베테랑 직원들에게 감사의 뜻이 전달되기를 진정으로 바란다(We sincerely hope this new benefit will show our appreciation for our veteran employees)고 했다. 따라서 10년 이상 근무한 장기근속 직원들을 위해 새로운 혜택을 마련한 것임을 알 수 있으므로 (C)가 정답이다.

어휘 implement 시행하다 turnover 이직률 potential 잠재적인 reward 보상하다 long-term 장기의

(Paraphrasing) 지문의 veteran employees → 정답의 long-term employees

171 [1], [2], [3], [4]로 표시된 곳 중에서 다음 문장이 들어가기에 가장 적합한 위치는?

"안식 휴가는 원하는 시작일보다 최소 3개월 전에 신청해야 합니다."

(A) [1]   (B) [2]

(C) [3]   (D) [4]

해설 **문장 삽입**

주어진 문장에서 안식 휴가는 시작일보다 최소 3개월 전(at least three months prior to the desired start date)에 신청해야 한다고 했으므로, 휴가 사전 신청과 관련된 내용과 연결되어야 자연스럽다. 세 번째 단락의 [2] 뒤에서 사전 요청으로 휴가 기간 동안 업무를 대체할 방안을 마련할 수 있게 된다(arrange coverage for your job)며 휴가를 미리 신청해야 하는 이유에 대해 설명하고 있다. 따라서 주어진 문장은 [2]에 들어가는 것이 글의 흐름상 적절하므로 (B)가 정답이다.

[172-175] 온라인 채팅

앤 와이머 (오전 11시 21분)
여러분, 좋은 아침입니다. **173** 다음 주에 있을 산업 박람회를 위해 모든 것이 준비되었는지 확인하고 싶습니다. 우리에게 아주 중요한 행사인데, 저는 사촌 결혼식에 갈 예정입니다.

래리 보닛 (오전 11시 22분)
행사 진행자가 우리 부스가 준비되었다고 확인해 주었습니다. 그녀는 또 우리가 전기 콘센트, 무선 인터넷, 시연 공간을 이용할 수 있다고 확실히 말해 주었습니다.

성해진 (오전 11시 25분)
저한테 포스터랑 안내 책자가 있습니다. 사진이 굉장히 멋집니다! 부스에서 재생할 동영상도 있습니다. **172** 어떤 것은 우리가 카운터, 바닥, 가전제품을 설치하는 것을 보여주고, 다른 것은 전후 비교 구성 방식으로 우리 프로젝트를 보여주며, 하나는 말튼 하우스의 조리 공간을 완전히 재설계한 것을 강조해 보여줍니다. **174** 우리 인턴 제이콥이 소셜 미디어를 담당하고 있습니다. 그가 우리 웹사이트에 행사 시연을 실시간으로 방송해 줄 것입니다.

래리 보닛 (오전 11시 26분)
174 제이콥을 발견한 것은 우리에게 행운이에요!

성해진 (오전 11시 27분)
의문의 여지가 없습니다! 그러니까, 네, 자료와 미디어 모두 준비되었습니다.

마사 바렐라 (오전 11시 28분)
저는 여기서 가정 방문 견적과 판매를 처리하고 있겠습니다. ¹⁷⁵이번 분기가 시작되었을 때처럼 유지된다면 우리의 매출액이 그 어느 때보다 더 높을 것임을 알려 드리고 싶습니다.

앤 와이머 (오전 11시 30분)
훌륭하네요! 알겠습니다. 목요일 오전에 짧게 회의를 하겠지만, 문제가 생길 경우 그 전에 저에게 알려 주세요.

어휘 assure 확언[장담]하다 outlet 콘센트 demonstration 시연 brochure 안내 책자 stunning 굉장히 멋진 put in ~을 설치하다 appliances 가전제품 format 구성 방식 handle 처리하다 luck out 운이 좋다 in-home (서비스, 활동 등이) 가정 내에서 제공되는 estimate 견적 quarter 분기 sales figures 매출액 arise 발생하다

172 메시지 작성자들은 어디에서 일할 것 같은가?
(A) 사진관
(B) 전기용품 상점
(C) 행사 기획 회사
(D) 주방 리모델링 업체

해설 **추론/암시**
11시 25분에 성 씨가 박람회에서 재생할 동영상을 언급하면서 어떤 것은 우리가 카운터, 바닥, 가전제품을 설치하는 것을 보여주고, 다른 것은 전후 비교 구성 방식으로 우리 프로젝트를 보여주며, 하나는 말튼 하우스의 조리 공간을 완전히 재설계한 것을 강조해 보여준다(Some show us putting in counters, floors, and appliances, ~ and one highlights our total redesign of the cooking area at the Marlton house)라고 한 것으로 보아 메시지 작성자들은 조리 공간을 리모델링하는 업체에서 근무하고 있음을 알 수 있다. 따라서 (D)가 정답이다.

(Paraphrasing) 지문의 redesign of the cooking area → 정답의 kitchen-remodeling

173 와이머 씨는 왜 사촌의 결혼식을 언급하는가?
(A) 산업 박람회에 불참하는 이유를 설명하려고
(B) 동료들에게 산업 박람회 일정 변동 사항을 알리려고
(C) 산업 박람회에 늦게 도착할 수 있음을 알리려고
(D) 산업 박람회를 다른 종류의 행사와 비교하려고

해설 **세부 사항**
11시 21분에 와이머 씨가 다음 주에 있을 산업 박람회를 위해 모든 것이 준비되었는지 확인하고 싶다(I want to make certain everything is set for the trade show next week)면서 아주 중요한 행사인데 자신은 사촌의 결혼식에 가서 없을 예정(I'll be away at my cousin's wedding)이라고 했다. 따라서 와이머 씨는 사촌의 결혼식에 가야 해서 산업 박람회에 참석할 수 없음을 알리려는 것이므로 (A)가 정답이다.

174 오전 11시 27분에 성 씨가 "의문의 여지가 없습니다"라고 쓴 의도는 무엇인가?
(A) 인턴이 일을 잘했다는 것에 동의한다.
(B) 실시간으로 방송된 행사가 성공적이었다고 생각한다.

(C) 일부 제품이 배송되었음을 확인할 수 있다.
(D) 소셜 미디어 이용이 중요하다고 믿는다.

해설 **의도 파악**
11시 25분에 성 씨가 인턴 제이콥이 소셜 미디어를 담당하고 있다(Our intern Jacob has been handling the social media)며 그가 웹사이트에 행사 시연을 실시간 송출할 것(He'll be live streaming our event demonstrations on our Web site)이라고 했고, 11시 26분에 보닛 씨가 제이콥을 발견한 것은 우리에게 행운이다(We really lucked out when we found Jacob!)라고 하자 11시 27분에 성 씨가 의문의 여지가 없다(There's no question about it!)고 호응했다. 따라서 성 씨는 인턴 제이콥이 담당 업무를 잘했다는 것에 동조하려는 의도로 한 말임을 알 수 있으므로 정답은 (A)이다.

175 바렐라 씨가 명시하는 것은?
(A) 약속 일정이 조정되어야 한다는 것
(B) 판매가 순조로운 속도로 증가하고 있다는 것
(C) 분기가 예상보다 부진하게 시작되었다는 것
(D) 영업 회의에 늦을 수도 있다는 것

해설 **Not/True**
11시 28분에 바렐라 씨가 이번 분기가 시작되었을 때처럼 유지된다면 매출액이 그 어느 때보다 더 높을 것임을 알려 드리고 싶다(I want to point out that if this quarter continues the way it's begun, our sales figures will be higher than they've ever been)며 매출 증가 소식을 전하고 있으므로 (B)가 정답이다.

어휘 favorable 순조로운

(Paraphrasing) 지문의 be higher → 정답의 increasing

[176-180] 점검 목록 + 보고서

브로만 제조		
작업장 안전 점검 목록		**완료일: 4월 11일**
점검자: 타마르 누리야, 운영부		

구역	작업	완료 시간
작업장	• 출입구에 보안경이 비치되어 있는지 확인합니다. • 연장의 상태가 양호한지 확인합니다. • 모든 전기 코드의 손상 및 마모 여부를 확인합니다. • 작업 공간에 파편이나 위험 요소가 있는지 점검합니다. • ¹⁷⁶구급상자의 재고를 조사하고 사용되거나 유통 기한이 지난 물품은 교체합니다.	¹⁷⁶오전 9시
¹⁷⁸창고	• ¹⁷⁸통로에 위험한 장애물이 없는지 확인합니다. • 선반 및 상자 더미가 안정적인지 확인합니다.	오전 10시 15분
사무실	• 전기 히터 또는 기타 발열 장치가 없는지 확인하기 위해 각 사무실 및 칸막이 공간을 점검합니다.	오전 11시

구분	내용	시간
	• 각 코드에 한 개의 장치만 연결되어 있는지 확인하기 위해 연장 코드를 점검합니다.	
구내식당	• 냉장고 온도가 섭씨 3~5도 사이인지 확인합니다.	오전 11시 45분

어휘 safety inspection 안전 점검 inspector 점검자 operation 운영 workshop 작업장 verify 확인하다 fraying 마모 debris 파편, 잔해 hazard 위험 요소 inventory 재고(품) first aid kit 구급상자 expired 기한이 지난 supplies 물품 aisle 통로 hazardous 위험한 obstruction 장애물 shelving 선반 stack 더미 stable 안정적인 cubicle 칸막이 공간 present 있는 extension cord 연장 코드, 멀티 탭 lunchroom 구내식당

작업장 안전 준수 보고서

제출자: 타마르 누리야

보고일: 4월 11일

177 이번 달 안전 점검을 수행하는 동안 다음과 같은 규정 미준수 사례를 목도하였습니다.

작업장에서, 7번 작업 공간의 테이블 톱은 날이 무디고 녹슬어 톱이 부드럽게 움직이는 데 방해가 될 수 있습니다. 수리될 때까지 사용하지 못하도록 톱에 꼬리표를 붙였습니다.

178 창고에서, 통로에 쌓여 있는 상자들을 발견했는데 이는 걸려 넘어질 위험이 있습니다. 관리자에게 상자들을 선반 위에 **179** 올려 놓도록 이야기했습니다.

180 114호 사무실에서, 사용 중인 전기 커피포트를 발견했습니다. 사용자에게 플러그를 뽑고 물건을 치우라고 권고했으며 불시에 후속 점검을 진행하겠다고 말했습니다.

어휘 compliance (규정) 준수 file (서류 등을) 제출하다 observe 목격하다 instance 사례 saw 톱 dull 무딘 rusty 녹슨 blade 날 tag 꼬리표를 붙이다 tripping 발이 걸려 넘어지는 occupant 사용자 state 말하다 unannounced 미리 알리지 않은 follow-up 후속의

176 점검 목록에 따르면, 구급상자는 언제 다시 채워졌는가?

(A) 오전 9시
(B) 오전 10시 15분
(C) 오전 11시
(D) 오전 11시 45분

해설 세부 사항

점검 목록의 작업장(Workshop) 작업(Tasks)란의 마지막 항목으로 구급상자의 재고를 확인하고 사용되거나 유통 기한이 지난 물품은 교체한다(Take inventory of the first aid kit and replace any used and expired supplies)고 나와 있고, 완료 시간(Time Completed)이 오전 9시(9:00 a.m.)로 되어 있으므로 (A)가 정답이다.

177 점검 목록은 얼마나 자주 사용되는가?

(A) 매일
(B) 매주
(C) 매달
(D) 매년

해설 세부 사항

보고서의 첫 문장에서 이번 달 안전 점검을 수행하는 동안 다음과 같은 규정 미준수 사례를 목도하였다(While performing the safety inspection for this month, I observed

~ noncompliance)고 한 것으로 보아 매달 안전 점검을 수행한다는 것을 알 수 있다. 따라서 (C)가 정답이다.

178 누리야 씨는 어디에서 장애물을 발견했는가?

(A) 사무실
(B) 작업장
(C) 구내식당
(D) 창고

해설 연계

점검 목록의 창고(Storeroom)란의 첫 번째 항목에서 통로에 위험한 장애물이 없는지 확인한다(Make sure aisles are clear of hazardous obstructions)고 했고, 보고서의 세 번째 단락 첫 문장에서 누리야 씨가 창고에서 통로에 쌓여 있는 상자들을 발견했는데 걸려 넘어질 수 있다(In the storeroom, I found boxes stacked in an aisle where they were a tripping hazard)고 했다. 따라서 누리야 씨는 창고 통로에 장애물이 있는지 점검하던 중 상자들이 쌓여 있는 것을 발견한 것이므로 (D)가 정답이다.

(**Paraphrasing**) 지문의 boxes stacked in an aisle → 질문의 obstruction

179 보고서의 세 번째 단락 2행의 "placed"와 의미가 가장 가까운 단어는?

(A) 놓인
(B) 주어진
(C) 정렬된
(D) 확인된

해설 동의어 찾기

의미상 상자가 선반 위에 '놓이다'라는 뜻으로 쓰였으므로 (A) put이 정답이다.

180 누리야 씨가 하겠다고 명시하는 것은?

(A) 연장 수리
(B) 사무실 재방문
(C) 상자에 라벨 부착
(D) 추가 보고서 제출

해설 세부 사항

보고서의 마지막 단락 첫 문장에서 누리야 씨는 114호 사무실에서 사용 중인 전기 커피포트를 발견했다(In office 114, I found an electric coffeepot in use)고 한 뒤, 사용자에게 플러그를 뽑고 물건을 치우라고 권고했으며 불시에 후속 점검을 진행하겠다고 말했다(I advised the occupant ~ and stated that I would make an unannounced follow-up inspection)고 했다. 따라서 누리야 씨는 후속 점검을 위해 114호 사무실을 다시 방문할 계획임을 예고한 것이므로 (B)가 정답이다.

[181-185] 제작 일정표 + 기사

롱 로드 프로덕션스

영화 제목: 〈앵커드 어센트〉
감독: 리 지앙
목표 관객: 18세~30세, 모험 이야기 애호가

제작 일정 개요 (잠정)

사전 제작 준비: 1월

• **181** 1월 25일 – 투자자 대상 재무 전망 보고
• 출연자 계약 완료 – 버논 스카피디, 젠 안
• 촬영 장소 허가 및 계약 확보

184 제작: 2~5월
- 본 촬영
- **181** 2월 28일과 5월 25일 – 투자자 대상 중간 재무 보고

후반 작업: 6~8월
- 영화 편집 완료

홍보 캠페인 및 개봉: 9~10월
- 9월 15일: 파인랜즈 영화제 시사회
- 10월 1일: 영화관 일반 배급
- **181** 투자자 대상 주간 수익 보고

어휘 ascent 오름, 오르막 enthusiast 애호가 tentative 잠정적인 projection 전망 investor 투자자 finalise 완결하다 secure 확보하다 permit 허가(증) principal 주된 interim 중간의 premiere 시사회 general 일반적인 distribution 배급 revenue 수익

리 지앙 감독이 말하는
〈앵커드 어센트〉

골웨이 (10월 15일)—한 달의 지연 끝에 〈앵커드 어센트〉가 이번 주 파인랜즈 영화제에서 첫 상영되었다. 이 영화는 칭송 받는 산악인 퀸 디콘의 실화를 다룬다.

182 리 지앙 감독에 따르면, 영화 제작진은 투자자들 사이에 우려를 불러일으킨 제작 차질을 여러 번 겪었다. 첫째, 배우 버논 스카피디와의 긴 협상이 그의 출연료 요구를 맞출 수 없게 되자 결국 무산되었다. "다행히, **184** 마크 토벨이 그 역할을 맡을 수 있었고 2월 초에 바로 우리 출연진에 합류했습니다."라고 지앙 씨는 설명했다. "그래서 그때까지는 제작 마감일을 지킬 수 있었습니다. 하지만 **183** 이례적인 폭설 기간과 통행이 불가능한 도로로 인해 야외 장면 촬영이 6주간 연기되었습니다."

야외 촬영의 지연은 롱 로드 프로덕션스가 촬영 허가 연장을 위해 비용을 지불해야 한다는 것을 의미했다. "그렇지만 결국 한 달 늦게 시작한 덕분에 낮 시간이 길어져서 잃어버린 시간을 일부 만회하는 데 도움이 되었습니다." **185** 만약 파인랜즈 영화제에서의 관객 반응이 시사하는 바가 있다면, 이 영화의 재정적 후원자들은 투자 수익에 상당히 만족할 것이다.

〈앵커드 어센트〉는 11월 1일에 영화관에서 일반 상영될 예정이다.

어휘 acclaimed 칭송 받는 endure 견디다 setback 차질 lengthy 너무 긴 negotiation 협상 ultimately 결국 fall through 실현되지 못하다 postpone 연기하다 impassable 통행할 수 없는 extension 연장 in the end 결국 make up ~을 벌충하다 indication 암시, 조짐 backer 후원자

---

181 제작 일정표에 따르면, 투자자에 대해 사실인 것은?
(A) 연령이 18세에서 30세 사이이다.
(B) 촬영 장소를 선정했다.
(C) 파인랜즈 영화제에 참석했다.
(D) 수차례의 재정 관련 업데이트를 받았다.

해설 **Not/True**

제작 일정표의 중반부에 1월 25일에 투자자 대상 재무 전망 보고(25 January — Financial projection report to investors), 2월 28일과 5월 25일에 투자자 대상 중간 재무 보고(28 February and 25 May — Interim finance reports to investors), 후반에 투자자 대상 주간 수익 보고(Weekly revenue report to investors) 일

정이 나와 있는 것으로 보아 투자자들은 여러 차례에 걸쳐 재정 관련 보고를 받았음을 알 수 있다. 따라서 (D)가 정답이다.

Paraphrasing 지문의 report(s) → 정답의 updates

182 기사의 목적은 무엇인가?
(A) 영화를 제작하는 동안 직면한 어려움을 설명하려고
(B) 영화에 영감을 준 실화에 관해 이야기하려고
(C) 지앙 씨의 경력에 대한 세부 정보를 전달하려고
(D) 촬영 허가를 받는 방법을 설명하려고

해설 **주제/목적**

기사의 두 번째 단락 첫 문장에서 리 지앙 감독에 따르면 영화 제작진은 투자자들 사이에 우려를 불러일으킨 제작 차질을 여러 번 겪었다(According to the director, Lee Jiang, the film crew endured several production setbacks that caused concern among investors)고 언급하며 뒤이어 수차례의 제작 차질에 관해 설명하고 있다. 따라서 영화를 제작하는 동안 경험한 어려움에 대해 이야기하기 위해 기사를 쓴 것이므로 (A)가 정답이다.

어휘 encounter 직면하다 obtain 얻다

Paraphrasing 지문의 setbacks → 정답의 difficulties

183 〈앵커드 어센트〉 촬영이 중단된 원인은 무엇인가?
(A) 국경일 준수
(B) 영화감독 변경
(C) 기상 악화
(D) 새로운 장소에 대한 비용 지불 필요성

해설 **세부 사항**

기사의 두 번째 단락 마지막 문장에서 이례적인 폭설 기간과 통행이 불가능한 도로로 인해 야외 장면 촬영이 6주간 연기되었다(filming of outdoor scenes was postponed for six weeks due to an unusually heavy snow season and impassable roads)고 했으므로 (C)가 정답이다.

어휘 observance 준수

Paraphrasing 지문의 an unusually heavy snow season → 정답의 Poor weather conditions

184 토벨 씨는 제작 일정 어느 단계에서 영화에 참여했는가?
(A) 제작　　　　　　(B) 사전 제작 준비
(C) 후반 작업　　　　(D) 홍보 캠페인 및 개봉

해설 **연계**

기사의 두 번째 단락 세 번째 문장에서 마크 토벨이 그 역할을 맡을 수 있었고 2월 초에 출연진에 합류했다(Mark Tobel ~ joined our cast right at the beginning of February)고 했는데, 제작 일정표를 보면 2월은 제작(Production) 단계이다. 따라서 (A)가 정답이다.

185 기사에 따르면, 파인랜즈 영화제의 관객에 대해 언급된 것은?
(A) 스카피디 씨가 영화에 출연하기를 기대했다.
(B) 영화를 좋아했다.
(C) 9월에 영화를 관람했다.
(D) 티켓에 추가 비용을 냈다.

해설 **Not/True**

기사의 세 번째 단락 마지막 문장에서 만약 파인랜즈 영화제에서의 관객 반응이 시사하는 바가 있다면 이 영화의 재정적 후원자들은 투자 수익에 상당히 만족할 것(If the audience response at the Pinelands Film Festival is any indication, the movie's financial backers will be quite pleased with their return on investment)이라고 했으므로 관객들이 영화에 좋은 반응을 보였다는 것을 알 수 있다. 따라서 정답은 (B)이다.

[186-190] 이메일 + 일정표 + 지도

> **186 수신: 해리스 노프림**
>
> 발신: 살 폴레스트로
>
> 날짜: 9월 10일
>
> 제목: 새퍼턴 박물관 청소 서비스
>
> 안녕하세요, 해리스.
>
> 아시다시피 **186,187 박물관이 일주일에 한 번 시민들에게 문을 닫는 날 청소 서비스가 방문합니다.** 9월 15일 오전 8시에 청소부들이 도착하면 그들을 들여보내 주세요. 그리고 **189 도자기 갤러리의 큰 창문을 청소하도록 해 주세요.** 종종 창문을 가리고 있는 무거운 커튼 때문에 청소부들이 그곳의 창문을 자주 놓칩니다.
>
> 문의 사항이 있으시면, 전화해 주시거나 내일 직원회의에서 제게 문의하셔도 됩니다.
>
> 감사합니다.
>
> 살

어휘 pottery 도자기   frequently 자주

영상 관람 구역: 사막 주간 영화		
187 9월 16일 수요일	〈사막의 색깔〉	오전 10시, 오후 2시
9월 16일 수요일	〈남서부 지역의 예술〉	정오, 오후 4시
9월 17일 목요일	〈리지 맥프리의 그림〉	오전 10시, 오후 2시
188 9월 17일 목요일	〈서부 사막의 천연 보석〉	정오, 오후 4시

어휘 gem 보석

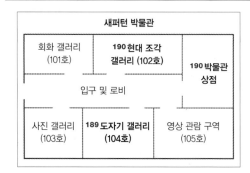

186 노프림 씨는 누구일 것 같은가?

(A) 도예가

(B) 박물관 직원

(C) 청소 전문가

(D) 미술품 수집가

해설 **추론/암시**

노프림 씨가 수신인(To: Harris Nofrim)인 이메일의 첫 문장에서 박물관이 일주일에 한 번 시민들에게 문을 닫는 날 청소 서비스가 방문한다(our cleaning service comes to the museum ~ it is closed to the public)며 9월 15일 오전 8시에 청소부들이 도착하면 그들을 들여보내 주라(When the cleaners come on September 15, please let them in when they arrive at 8:00 a.m.)고 요청하고 있다. 따라서 노프림 씨는 청소 서비스팀을 박물관에 입장시킬 수 있는 권한이 있는 사람임을 알 수 있으므로 (B)가 정답이다.

187 새퍼턴 박물관은 무슨 요일에 문을 닫는가?

(A) 월요일

(B) 화요일

(C) 수요일

(D) 목요일

해설 **연계**

이메일의 첫 문장에서 박물관이 일주일에 한 번 시민들에게 문을 닫는 날 청소 서비스가 방문한다(our cleaning service comes to the museum ~ it is closed to the public)며 9월 15일 오전 8시에 청소부들이 도착하면 그들을 들여보내 주라(When the cleaners come on September 15, please let them in when they arrive at 8:00 a.m.)고 했고, 시간표의 상단에 9월 16일 수요일(Wednesday, Sept. 16)이라고 나와 있다. 따라서 박물관이 문을 닫는 날은 9월 15일 화요일임을 알 수 있으므로 (B)가 정답이다.

188 시간표에 따르면, 9월 17일 정오에 상영되는 영상은 무엇인가?

(A) 〈사막의 색깔〉

(B) 〈남서부 지역의 예술〉

(C) 〈리지 맥프리의 그림〉

(D) 〈서부 사막의 천연 보석〉

해설 **세부 사항**

시간표의 하단에 9월 17일 목요일(Thursday, Sept. 17)에 〈서부 사막의 천연 보석〉(Natural Gems of the Desert West)이 정오와 오후 4시(Noon and 4 P.M.)에 상영된다고 나와 있으므로 정답은 (D)이다.

189 폴레스트로 씨는 몇 호실의 창문이 청소되기를 원하는가?

(A) 102호

(B) 103호

(C) 104호

(D) 105호

해설 **연계**

이메일의 세 번째 문장에서 폴레스트로 씨가 도자기 갤러리의 큰 창문을 청소하도록 해 달라(please make sure they wash the large windows in the pottery gallery)고 했고, 지도에 도자기 갤러리는 104호(Pottery Gallery (Room 104))라고 나와 있다. 따라서 폴레스트로 씨는 도자기 갤러리가 있는 104호의 창문이 청소되기를 원하는 것이므로 (C)가 정답이다.

190 지도에 따르면, 박물관 상점은 어디에 있는가?

(A) 회화 갤러리 옆

(B) 도자기 갤러리와 영상 관람 구역 사이

(C) 현대 조각 갤러리 옆

(D) 사진 갤러리 바로 건너편

해설 **세부 사항**

지도에 따르면 박물관 상점(Museum Store)은 현대 조각 갤러리 (102호)(Modern Sculpture Gallery (Room 102))의 우측에 위치하고 있으므로 (C)가 정답이다.

어휘 adjacent to ~에 인접한

[191-195] 이메일 + 이메일 + 회사 소식지 기사

발신: m.carmen@olive.com
수신: customerservice@valliegrocery.com
195날짜: 4월 1일
제목: 도로변 픽업

발리 식료품점 고객 서비스 관계자분께,

저는 지난달에 랭글리시로 이사를 와서, 귀 매장의 가격이 매우 경쟁력 있다는 것을 알게 되었습니다. 하지만 도로변 픽업이 불가능하다는 것을 알고 놀랐습니다. **191바쁜 직업인으로서 저는 온라인에서 식료품을 선택하고 결제한 다음 퇴근해서 집에 가는 길에 모든 것을 픽업하는 것이 아주 편리할 거라고 생각합니다.** 심지어 이 서비스에 대해 소정의 수수료도 기꺼이 지불할 의향이 있습니다.

192도로변 픽업 서비스 제공을 고려해 보시겠습니까? 그렇게 되면 제가 귀 매장 길 아래쪽에 위치하고 있는 푸드모어 대신 발리 식료품점을 애용할 만한 추가적인 이유가 될 것 같습니다.

메리 카르멘

어휘 curbside 차도 가장자리 competitive 경쟁력 있는
incentive 동기 patronize 애용하다

발신: tenyuu.sakai@valliegrocery.com
수신: lien.cheng@valliegrocery.com
날짜: 6월 15일
제목: 도로변 픽업

청 씨께,

192, 193매주 최소 2~3명의 고객이 우리 매장이 도로변 픽업을 제공하지 않는 이유에 대해 문의한다는 것을 알려 드리고자 글을 씁니다. 저는 우리 직원 수가 너무 적고 웹사이트가 해당 서비스를 할 수 있도록 설계되어 있지 않다고 설명합니다. 저는 몇 년 동안 도로변 픽업을 제공하고 있는 가장 가까운 경쟁업체에 고객을 빼앗기고 있다는 점이 점점 더 걱정됩니다. **193, 194저에게 온라인 주문을 처리할 수 있도록 웹사이트를 업데이트할 기술적 기량이 있으므로 6월 말까지 웹사이트를 업데이트할 수 있으며, 195한 명 이상의 추가 직원을 고용할 경우 우리 매장의 수익과 고객층을 증대할 수 있을 것이라 믿습니다.**

텐유 사카이
고객 서비스 관리자

어휘 competitor 경쟁사 customer base 고객층

발리 식료품점 직원 소식
7월 호

1958월 1일 도로변 픽업 시작
발리 식료품점에서 도로변 픽업 서비스를 시행합니다. 운영 방식은 다음과 같습니다:

1. 고객은 온라인으로 주문하고 결제한다.
2. 팀원이 식료품을 모아 포장한 다음 고객에게 문자를 보낸다.
3. 고객은 지정된 주차 구역에서 대기하며 주차 구역 번호와 함께 문자에 회신한다.
4. 팀원이 고객의 차량으로 식료품을 가져다준다.
이 신규 프로그램이 성공할 수 있도록 함께 노력합시다!

어휘 issue (정기 간행물의) 호 implement 시행하다
bag 봉지에 넣다 designated 지정된

191 첫 번째 이메일에서 카르멘 씨가 암시하는 것은?

(A) 발리 식료품점은 그녀의 집과 직장 사이에 위치한다.
(B) 수년간 랭글리시에 살고 있다.
(C) 푸드모어에서 더 이상 도로변 픽업을 제공하지 않는다.
(D) 푸드모어의 가격이 발리 식료품점의 가격보다 저렴하다.

해설 **추론/암시**

첫 번째 이메일의 세 번째 문장에서 카르멘 씨가 바쁜 직업인으로서 온라인에서 식료품을 선택하고 결제한 다음 퇴근해서 집에 가는 길에 모든 것을 픽업하는 것이 아주 편리할 거라고 생각한다(As a busy professional, I would find it ~ pick everything up on my way home from work)고 한 것으로 보아, 발리 식료품점은 카르멘 씨가 퇴근하여 집으로 가는 경로에 위치해 있음을 짐작할 수 있다. 따라서 (A)가 정답이다.

(Paraphrasing) 지문의 on my way home from work
→ 정답의 between her home and her workplace

192 카르멘 씨에 대해 어떤 결론을 내릴 수 있는가?

(A) 청 씨와 최근에 인터뷰를 했다.
(B) 도로변 픽업을 요청한 많은 쇼핑객 중 한 명이다.
(C) 식품 서비스 산업에 종사하고 있다.
(D) 도로변 픽업이 무료여야 한다고 생각한다.

해설 **연계**

첫 번째 이메일의 두 번째 단락 첫 문장에서 카르멘 씨가 발리 식료품점에 도로변 픽업 서비스 제공을 고려해 보겠느냐(Would you consider offering curbside pickup?)고 묻고 있고, 두 번째 이메일의 첫 문장에서 발리 식료품점의 고객 서비스 관리자인 사카이 씨가 매주 최소 2~3명의 고객이 발리 식료품점은 왜 도로변 픽업을 제공하지 않는지에 대해 문의한다(every week at least two or three customers ask me why our store does not offer curbside pickup)고 알리고 있다. 따라서 카르멘 씨는 발리 식료품점에 도로변 픽업 서비스를 요청한 많은 쇼핑객 중 한 명임을 알 수 있으므로 정답은 (B)이다.

193 두 번째 이메일의 목적은 무엇인가?

(A) 영업 시간 연장 제안 (B) 회의 일정 조율
(C) 신규 서비스 추천 (D) 예상 예산 논의

해설 **주제/목적**

두 번째 이메일은 수신자와 발신자의 도메인이 같은 것으로 보아 발리 식료품점 고객 서비스의 관리자인 사카이 씨가 또 다른 관계자인 청 씨에게 보낸 메일임을 알 수 있다. 두 번째 이메일의 첫 문장에서 매주 최소 2~3명의 고객이 우리 매장

이 도로변 픽업을 제공하지 않는 이유에 대해 문의한다는 것을 알리고자 글을 쓴다(I am writing to let you know ~ why our store does not offer curbside pickup)고 했고, 네 번째 문장에서 자신에게 웹사이트를 업데이트할 기술적 기량이 있어서 6월 말까지 웹사이트를 업데이트할 수 있다(Since I have the technical skills to update our Web site to process online orders, I could update the Web site ~)고 했다. 따라서 고객들의 요구에 부응하여 도로변 픽업 서비스를 새롭게 시행하는 것을 건의하기 위해 글을 쓴 것이므로 (C)가 정답이다.

어휘 projected 예상된

194 두 번째 이메일에서, 사카이 씨는 무엇을 하겠다고 제안하는가?
(A) 매장에 구인 광고판 게시
(B) 일부 팀원 재배치
(C) 고객 불만 부서 확대
(D) 고용주의 웹사이트에 향상된 기능 추가

해설 **세부 사항**
두 번째 이메일의 네 번째 문장에서 사카이 씨가 자신에게 온라인 주문을 처리할 수 있도록 웹사이트를 업데이트할 기술적 기량이 있으므로 6월 말까지 웹사이트를 업데이트할 수 있다(Since I have the technical skills to update our Web site to process online orders, I could update the Web site ~)며 웹사이트에 새로운 서비스 기능을 추가하는 것에 대해 제안하고 있으므로 정답은 (D)이다.

어휘 help-wanted 구인 광고 reassign 재배치하다 enhancement 향상

195 발리 식료품점에 대해 어떤 결론을 내릴 수 있는가?
(A) 배송 서비스에서 예상보다 더 많은 수익을 냈다.
(B) 고객이 자신의 장바구니를 가져와야 한다.
(C) 직원들이 고객으로부터 팁을 받는 것을 허용하지 않는다.
(D) 4월보다 8월에 직원 수가 더 많아질 것이다.

해설 **연계**
첫 번째 이메일의 날짜가 4월 1일(Date: April 1)이고, 두 번째 이메일의 네 번째 문장에서 사카이 씨가 발리 식료품점에 도로변 픽업 서비스를 시작할 것을 제안하며 6월 말까지 웹사이트를 업데이트하고 직원을 추가 고용할 경우 매장의 수익과 고객층을 증대할 수 있을 것이라 믿는다(if we hire one or more additional workers, I believe we could increase our store's profits and customer base)고 했으며, 소식지 기사의 상단에 8월 1일에 도로변 픽업을 시작한다(Curbside pickup to begin on August 1)고 했다. 따라서 발리 식료품점이 사카이 씨의 제안을 받아들였음을 알 수 있으므로 도로변 픽업 서비스를 시작하는 8월에는 직원 수가 늘어날 것임을 알 수 있다. 따라서 (D)가 정답이다.

(Paraphrasing) 지문의 hire one or more additional workers → 정답의 have a larger staff

---

[196-200] 보고서 소개 + 이메일 + 메모

소개: 카카오빈 가공을 위한 대체 기술

우리 연구는 초콜릿을 만들기 위한 카카오빈의 가공에 중점을 두었습니다. **196 전통적인 방법에서는 카카오빈을 수확하여 초콜릿을 만드는 데 사용하기 전에 발효를 위해 며칠 동안 펼쳐서 덮어 둡니다.** 가장 선호되는 덮개는 바나나 껍질입니다. 이 기간 동안 미생물이 작용하여 원두의 쓴맛을 줄여 주고 나중에 초콜릿 소비자가 경험하게 되는 특정한 맛과 향을 더합니다.

198 이 연구에서 우리 팀은 습식 배양이라고 불리는 대체 공정을 평가했습니다. 생 카카오빈을 건조한 다음 특수 액체 속에서 72시간 동안 다시 수분을 공급하며 가열했습니다. 그러고 나서 카카오빈은 다시 건조되어 초콜릿 바를 만드는 데 사용되었습니다. 천연 미생물이 아닌 인공 화학 반응에 의존하는 이 공정은 전통적인 방법보다 상당히 더 빠르고 훨씬 더 예측 가능한 결과를 낳았습니다. 우리 팀은 또한 통제된 상황하에서 좀 더 복잡하고 흥미로운 풍미 특성이 눈에 띄게 증가하는 것을 발견했는데, 배양된 초콜릿에는 다른 과일을 연상시키는 향과 맛을 전달하는 더 높은 수준의 화합물이 있었습니다.

어휘 alternative 대안의 harvest 수확하다 ferment 발효되다 covering 덮개 peel 껍질 microbe 미생물 bitterness 쓴맛 evaluate 평가하다 incubation 배양 rehydrate (건조 식품을) 물을 넣어 원래 상태로 만들다 artificial 인공의 significantly 상당히 notable 눈에 띄는 intriguing 아주 흥미로운 chemical compound 화합물 be suggestive of ~을 연상시키다

수신: 랄프 모건 〈rmorgan@gemstonechocolates.com〉
발신: 아리아나 비노치 〈abinocci@gemstonechocolates.com〉
197 날짜: 3월 12일
제목: 업데이트

모건 씨께,

음식 블로거들이 우리 초콜릿의 독특한 맛과 향에 열광하고 있다는 것을 알게 되면 기쁘실 겁니다. 유럽과 아시아에서 완판된 것으로 보아 대중도 우리 초콜릿을 좋아하는 게 틀림없습니다. 심지어 코코아 함량이 가장 높은 초콜릿만으로 구성된 초콜릿 바인 미드나잇은 대기자 명단도 있습니다. **198 그렇게 카카오빈을 준비할 때 대체 화학 방식을 실행한 것이 젬스톤 초콜릿을 큰 성공의 길에 올려놓았습니다.**

그리고 이제 우리는 그 성공을 바탕으로 더 성장해야 합니다. 네 가지 젬스톤 맛 모두 생산량을 즉시 두 배로 늘려야 합니다. 그러려면 새로운 직원을 고용해 교육하고, 두 번째 근무 교대 조를 편성해야 합니다. 또한 **200 베스퍼 바의 견과류, 트와일라잇 바의 캐러멜, 이벤타이드 바의 천일염 등 바에 사용되는 재료의 조달을 늘려야 합니다.**

197 우리는 내일 구체적인 목표와 관련해 협의를 해야 합니다. 저는 오전에 마케팅 부서와 함께 그들이 준비 중인 대규모 광고 캠페인과 관련해 회의를 할 예정이지만, 오후에는 만날 수 있습니다.

아리아나 비노치
젬스톤 초콜릿 총괄 부사장

어휘 rave 열광하다 plain 아무것도 섞지 않은 consist of ~으로 구성되다 implement 시행하다 output 생산량 establish 설정[설립]하다 procurement 조달 touch base 협의하다 put together ~을 만들다

당신을 위한 선물

유잉 씨께,

한국 여행에서 가져온 젬스톤 초콜릿 바 큰 상자를 동봉합니다. **199휴가 중에 저를 대신해 주신 데 대한 감사를 전하는 좋은 방법인 것 같아서요. 200제가 가장 좋아하는 것은 천일염이 들어간 것이지만** 당신이 견과류를 얼마나 좋아하는지 알고 있어요. 다른 직원들을 위한 선물로 이것들을 더 많이 사고 싶었는데, 제가 갔던 매장은 고객 한 명당 점보 버라이어티 팩 한 개만 허용했고 다른 가게들은 품절되었습니다. 아마 그들과 조금 나눠야 할 것 같습니다.

당신의 친구이자 동료,

폴렛 권

어휘 enclosed 동봉된   fill in for ~을 대신하다

196 카카오빈의 전통적인 가공 방법에 대하여 보고서 소개에 명시된 것은?

(A) **바나나 식물의 일부를 이용한다.**
(B) 완료하는 데 하루도 걸리지 않는다.
(C) 카카오빈 건조가 포함된다.
(D) 카카오빈에 쓴맛을 더해 준다.

해설 Not/True

보고서 소개의 두 번째 문장에서 전통적인 방법에서는 카카오빈을 수확하여 초콜릿을 만드는 데 사용하기 전에 발효를 위해 며칠 동안 펼쳐서 덮어 둔다(In the traditional method, cocoa beans are harvested and, ~ spread out and covered for a few days to ferment)며, 가장 선호되는 덮개는 바나나 껍질(The covering most favored is banana peels)이라고 했다. 따라서 (A)가 정답이다.

Paraphrasing 지문의 banana peels → 정답의 parts from banana plants

197 비노치 씨는 3월 13일 오전에 누구를 만날 예정인가?

(A) 초콜릿 소매업체를 대표하는 대리인
(B) 원료를 공급하는 도급업체
(C) **제품 홍보를 이해하는 전문가**
(D) 신제품 조리법을 개발하는 요리사

해설 세부 사항

이메일이 작성된 날짜가 3월 12일(Date: March 12)이고, 이메일의 마지막 단락에서 비노치 씨가 모건 씨에게 내일 목표와 관련해 협의를 하자(We ~ tomorrow regarding specific targets)고 한 뒤, 오전에 마케팅 부서와 그들이 준비 중인 광고 캠페인에 관한 회의를 할 예정이라며 오후에는 만날 수 있다(In the morning, I am scheduled to meet with the marketing department about the big advertising ~ we could meet in the afternoon)고 했다. 따라서 비노치 씨는 내일, 즉 13일 오전에 제품 홍보가 주 업무인 마케팅부와 만날 예정이므로 (C)가 정답이다.

어휘 agent 대리인, 중개상   represent 대표하다   contractor 도급업자   supply 공급하다

Paraphrasing 지문의 the marketing department → 정답의 Specialists ~ product promotion

198 최근 젬스톤 초콜릿 성공의 원인일 것 같은 것은 무엇인가?

(A) 새로운 직원 채용으로 생산성 2배 향상
(B) **습식 배양 과정 적용**
(C) 창의적인 포장 디자인 도입
(D) 공장 직원 교육 수정

해설 연계

보고서 소개의 두 번째 단락 첫 문장에서 이 연구에서 우리 팀은 습식 배양이라고 불리는 대체 공정을 평가했다(In this research, our team evaluated an alternative process called moist incubation)고 했고, 이메일의 첫 단락 마지막 문장에서 그렇게 카카오빈을 준비할 때 대체 화학 방식을 실행한 것이 젬스톤 초콜릿을 큰 성공의 길에 올려 놓았다(So, implementing the alternative chemical method ~ on the path to a major success)고 했다. 따라서 젬스톤 초콜릿이 최근 큰 성공을 거둔 것은 연구에서 평가했던 습식 배양 과정을 공정에 적용한 덕분임을 알 수 있으므로 (B)가 정답이다.

어휘 productivity 생산성   adopt 채택하다   imaginative 창의적인   revise 수정하다

199 유잉 씨에 대해 메모에 명시된 것은?

(A) 팀원들을 위해 선물을 샀다.
(B) **권 씨가 없는 동안 일을 대신했다.**
(C) 출장에서 막 돌아왔다.
(D) 곧 휴가를 떠난다.

해설 Not/True

메모의 두 번째 문장에서 권 씨가 유잉 씨에게 휴가 중에 자리를 대신해 준 것에 대한 감사를 전하는 좋은 방법인 것 같았다(They seem like a lovely way to thank you for filling in for me while I was on vacation)고 한 것으로 보아 권 씨가 휴가를 떠나 있는 동안 유잉 씨가 권 씨의 업무를 대신해 주었음을 알 수 있다. 따라서 (B)가 정답이다.

어휘 treat 선물

200 권 씨가 가장 좋아하는 젬스톤 초콜릿 바는 무엇일 것 같은가?

(A) 미드나잇   (B) 베스퍼
(C) 트와일라잇   (D) **이벤타이드**

해설 연계

이메일의 두 번째 단락 마지막 문장에서 베스퍼 바의 견과류, 트와일라잇 바의 캐러멜, 이벤타이드 바의 천일염 등 바에 사용되는 재료의 조달을 늘려야 한다(We also must increase the procurement of the ingredients used in the bars ~ sea salt for the Eventide bar)고 했고, 메모의 세 번째 문장에서 권 씨가 자신이 가장 좋아하는 것은 천일염이 들어간 것(My favorite is the one with sea salt)이라고 했다. 따라서 권 씨가 가장 좋아하는 초콜릿 바는 천일염이 들어 있는 이벤타이드 바라는 것을 알 수 있으므로 (D)가 정답이다.

ETS 기출 모의고사 2회

LISTENING TEST

1 (B)	2 (B)	3 (C)	4 (A)	5 (D)
6 (B)	7 (B)	8 (B)	9 (A)	10 (A)
11 (A)	12 (C)	13 (B)	14 (C)	15 (A)
16 (C)	17 (A)	18 (C)	19 (A)	20 (B)
21 (C)	22 (B)	23 (C)	24 (A)	25 (B)
26 (A)	27 (B)	28 (A)	29 (A)	30 (C)
31 (B)	32 (C)	33 (A)	34 (C)	35 (A)
36 (C)	37 (D)	38 (D)	39 (D)	40 (C)
41 (B)	42 (C)	43 (A)	44 (D)	45 (D)
46 (A)	47 (B)	48 (C)	49 (D)	50 (D)
51 (D)	52 (B)	53 (A)	54 (D)	55 (B)
56 (A)	57 (B)	58 (C)	59 (C)	60 (A)
61 (B)	62 (B)	63 (D)	64 (B)	65 (A)
66 (B)	67 (D)	68 (C)	69 (A)	70 (C)
71 (B)	72 (D)	73 (C)	74 (C)	75 (B)
76 (A)	77 (A)	78 (B)	79 (D)	80 (B)
81 (C)	82 (B)	83 (A)	84 (A)	85 (C)
86 (C)	87 (B)	88 (A)	89 (D)	90 (B)
91 (B)	92 (C)	93 (C)	94 (D)	95 (D)
96 (B)	97 (A)	98 (C)	99 (B)	100 (A)

READING TEST

101 (A)	102 (C)	103 (B)	104 (B)	105 (C)
106 (C)	107 (D)	108 (A)	109 (B)	110 (C)
111 (D)	112 (D)	113 (A)	114 (A)	115 (C)
116 (B)	117 (D)	118 (B)	119 (D)	120 (C)
121 (B)	122 (D)	123 (C)	124 (D)	125 (A)
126 (B)	127 (A)	128 (A)	129 (C)	130 (B)
131 (D)	132 (A)	133 (D)	134 (C)	135 (B)
136 (D)	137 (D)	138 (D)	139 (D)	140 (D)
141 (D)	142 (A)	143 (D)	144 (C)	145 (B)
146 (C)	147 (C)	148 (B)	149 (A)	150 (D)
151 (C)	152 (B)	153 (A)	154 (D)	155 (B)
156 (D)	157 (C)	158 (C)	159 (A)	160 (C)
161 (D)	162 (D)	163 (C)	164 (B)	165 (D)
166 (C)	167 (B)	168 (B)	169 (A)	170 (C)
171 (A)	172 (A)	173 (D)	174 (D)	175 (C)
176 (C)	177 (C)	178 (D)	179 (D)	180 (D)
181 (C)	182 (C)	183 (D)	184 (A)	185 (B)
186 (B)	187 (A)	188 (D)	189 (C)	190 (D)
191 (A)	192 (D)	193 (A)	194 (C)	195 (B)
196 (B)	197 (C)	198 (D)	199 (B)	200 (C)

PART 1

1 W-Am

(A) He's changing a flat tire.
(B) He's standing next to a car.
(C) He's placing a cup on top of a car.
(D) He's stacking boxes on the ground.

(A) 남자가 펑크 난 타이어를 교체하고 있다.
(B) 남자가 차 옆에 서 있다.
(C) 남자가 차 위에 컵을 올려놓고 있다.
(D) 남자가 바닥에 상자를 쌓고 있다.

해설 **인물 중심 사진**
(A) **동작 묘사 오답:** 남자가 펑크 난 타이어를 교체하고 있는 (is changing) 모습이 아니다.
(B) **정답:** 남자가 차 옆에 서 있는(is standing) 모습이므로 정답이다.
(C) **동작 묘사 오답:** 남자가 차 위에 컵을 올려놓고 있는(is placing) 모습이 아니다.
(D) **사진에 없는 명사를 이용한 오답:** 사진에 상자(boxes)가 보이지 않는다.

어휘 flat (tire) 펑크 난 타이어   place 놓다   stack 쌓다

2 M-Cn

(A) One of the people is reaching for some soap.
(B) One of the people is pouring a drink into a glass.
(C) The people are mopping a kitchen floor.
(D) The people are shaking hands.

(A) 사람들 중 한 명이 비누를 향해 손을 뻗고 있다.
(B) 사람들 중 한 명이 잔에 음료를 따르고 있다.
(C) 사람들이 부엌 바닥을 걸레질하고 있다.
(D) 사람들이 악수를 하고 있다.

해설 **인물 중심 사진**
(A) **동작 묘사 오답:** 사람들 중 한 명이 비누를 향해 손을 뻗고 있는(is reaching for) 모습이 아니다.
(B) **정답:** 사람들 중 한 명이 잔에 음료를 따르고 있는(is pouring) 모습이므로 정답이다.
(C) **동작 묘사 오답:** 사람들이 부엌 바닥을 걸레질하고 있는 (are mopping) 모습이 아니다.
(D) **동작 묘사 오답:** 사람들이 악수를 하고 있는(are shaking hands) 모습이 아니다.

어휘 reach for ~을 향해 손을 뻗다, 내밀다   pour 붓다
mop 대걸레로 닦다; 대걸레

3 W-Br

(A) The door to a building has been left open.
(B) Some chairs have been set in a line.
(C) A plastic bin is on top of a work area.
(D) Some tools are attached to a wall.

(A) 건물로 들어가는 문이 열려 있다.
(B) 의자들이 일렬로 놓여 있다.
(C) 플라스틱 통이 작업 공간 위에 있다.
(D) 도구들이 벽에 부착되어 있다.

해설 **사물 사진**

(A) **상태 묘사 오답**: 건물로 들어가는 문이 열려 있는(has been left open) 상태가 아니다.
(B) **사진에 없는 명사를 이용한 오답**: 사진에 의자들(chairs)이 보이지 않는다.
(C) **정답**: 플라스틱 통이 작업 공간 위에 있는(is on top of a work area) 모습이므로 정답이다.
(D) **상태 묘사 오답**: 도구들이 벽에 부착되어 있는(are attached to a wall) 상태가 아니다.

어휘 bin 용기   attach 부착하다

4 M-Au

(A) Some trees line a pedestrian walkway.
(B) Some workers are pruning trees.
(C) A person is riding a bike down a street.
(D) There's a water fountain in a courtyard.

(A) 나무들이 보행자 통로를 따라 늘어서 있다.
(B) 작업자들이 나무를 가지치기하고 있다.
(C) 한 사람이 길을 따라 자전거를 타고 있다.
(D) 뜰에 식수대가 있다.

해설 **인물/사물 혼합 사진**

(A) **정답**: 나무들이 보행자 통로를 따라 늘어서 있는(line a pedestrian walkway) 모습이므로 정답이다.
(B) **사진에 없는 명사를 이용한 오답**: 사진에 작업자들(Some workers)이 보이지 않는다.
(C) **사진에 없는 명사를 이용한 오답**: 사진에 자전거(a bike)가 보이지 않는다.
(D) **사진에 없는 명사를 이용한 오답**: 사진에 식수대(a water fountain)가 보이지 않는다.

어휘 pedestrian 보행자   walkway 통로[보도]   prune 가지치기하다   water fountain 식수대   courtyard 뜰[마당]

5 W-Am

(A) A man is changing a lightbulb in a sign.
(B) A tow truck is pulling a bus.
(C) Some people are crossing a street.
(D) A man has been raised above a road.

(A) 남자가 간판의 전구를 교체하고 있다.
(B) 견인차가 버스를 끌고 있다.
(C) 사람들이 길을 건너고 있다.
(D) 남자가 도로 위로 들어올려졌다.

해설 **인물/사물 혼합 사진**

(A) **동작 묘사 오답**: 남자가 간판의 전구를 교체하고 있는(is changing) 모습이 아니다.
(B) **사진에 없는 명사를 이용한 오답**: 사진에 견인차(A tow truck)와 버스(a bus)가 보이지 않는다.
(C) **동작 묘사 오답**: 사람들이 길을 건너고 있는(are crossing) 모습이 아니다.
(D) **정답**: 남자가 도로 위로 들어올려진(has been raised above a road) 모습이므로 정답이다.

어휘 lightbulb 전구   tow truck 견인차   cross (가로질러) 건너다   raise 들어올리다

6 W-Br

(A) A stone pathway leads to a lake.
(B) A wooden structure has been built outdoors.
(C) A nature trail is being cleared of debris.
(D) An outdoor deck is being repaired.

(A) 돌길이 호수로 이어진다.
(B) 나무로 된 구조물이 야외에 지어져 있다.
(C) 자연 산책로에서 쓰레기가 치워지고 있다.
(D) 야외 데크가 수리되고 있다.

해설 **사물/풍경 사진**

(A) **사진에 없는 명사를 이용한 오답**: 사진에 호수(a lake)가 보이지 않는다.
(B) **정답**: 나무로 된 구조물이 야외에 지어져 있는(has been built outdoors) 모습이므로 정답이다.
(C) **진행 상황 묘사 오답**: 자연 산책로에서 쓰레기가 치워지고 있는(is being cleared) 상황이 아니다.
(D) **진행 상황 묘사 오답**: 야외 데크가 수리되고 있는(is being repaired) 상황이 아니다.

어휘 pathway 오솔길   lead to ~으로 이어지다   structure 구조물   trail 산책로   debris 쓰레기, 잔해

PART 2

7 M-Au / W-Am

What kind of cake should we order for the party?

(A) A pastry chef.

(B) Chocolate's always popular.

(C) I'll reserve the large conference room.

파티를 위해 어떤 종류의 케이크를 주문해야 하나요?

(A) 제과사예요.

(B) 초콜릿이 늘 인기가 많죠.

(C) 큰 회의실로 예약할게요.

해설 **주문해야 하는 케이크의 종류를 묻는 What 의문문**

(A) **연상 어휘 오답:** 질문의 cake에서 연상 가능한 pastry chef를 이용한 오답이다.

(B) **정답:** 파티에 어떤 종류의 케이크를 주문해야 하는지 묻는 질문에 초콜릿이 늘 인기가 많다며 우회적으로 초콜릿 케이크를 추천하고 있으므로 정답이다.

(C) **연상 어휘 오답:** 질문의 party에서 연상 가능한 conference room을 이용한 오답이다.

어휘 pastry chef 파티시에   reserve 예약하다

8 W-Br / M-Au

Where can I pick up the order my company placed?

(A) Yes, that's a nice place.

(B) It'll be at the front of the store.

(C) Because I need to go to the airport.

회사에서 주문한 것을 어디에서 수령할 수 있나요?

(A) 네, 거긴 좋은 곳이죠.

(B) 가게 앞에 있을 겁니다.

(C) 공항에 가야 해서요.

해설 주문품 수령 장소를 묻는 Where 의문문

(A) **Yes/No 불가 및 파생어 오답:** Where 의문문에는 Yes/No 응답이 불가능하며 질문의 placed와 파생어 관계인 place를 이용한 오답이다.

(B) **정답:** 회사 주문품 수령 장소를 묻는 질문에 가게 앞에 있다고 구체적인 장소를 언급했으므로 정답이다.

(C) **연상 어휘 오답:** 질문의 pick up에서 연상 가능한 airport를 이용한 오답이다.

9 W-Am / M-Au

What time is the company dinner scheduled to start?

(A) It was canceled.

(B) I'll need more time before I order.

(C) We had a late lunch today.

회식은 몇 시에 시작될 예정인가요?

(A) 취소됐어요.

(B) 주문하기 전에 시간이 더 필요해요.

(C) 우리는 오늘 늦은 점심을 먹었어요.

해설 회식 시작 시간을 묻는 What 의문문

(A) **정답:** 회식이 몇 시에 시작하는지 묻는 질문에 회식이 취소되었다는 정보를 밝히고 있으므로 정답이다.

(B) **어휘 반복 오답:** 질문의 time을 반복 이용한 오답이다.

(C) **연상 어휘 오답:** 질문의 dinner에서 연상 가능한 lunch를 이용한 오답이다.

10 W-Am / M-Cn

Who can tell me where the loading dock is?

(A) Ji-mi would know.

(B) I drove to work this morning.

(C) About ten meters wide.

물류 하역장이 어딘지 알려 주실 분?

(A) 지미가 알 거예요.

(B) 저는 오늘 아침에 차를 타고 출근했어요.

(C) 대략 폭이 10미터 정도 돼요.

해설 물류 하역장의 위치를 알려 줄 사람을 묻는 Who 의문문

(A) **정답:** 물류 하역장이 어디에 있는지 알려 줄 사람을 묻는 질문에 지미가 알 거라며 정보를 가르쳐 줄 사람을 언급하고 있으므로 정답이다.

(B) **질문과 상관없는 오답**

(C) **질문과 상관없는 오답**

어휘 loading dock 물류 하역장

11 W-Br / M-Cn

Why isn't the copier working?

(A) Because a part needs to be replaced.

(B) Fourteen copies for the meeting.

(C) The coffee machine is in the kitchen.

복사기가 왜 작동하지 않죠?

(A) 부품 하나를 교체해야 해서요.

(B) 회의를 위해 14부요.

(C) 커피 머신은 주방에 있어요.

해설 복사기가 작동하지 않는 이유를 묻는 Why 의문문

(A) **정답:** 복사기가 작동하지 않는 이유를 묻는 질문에 부품 하나를 교체해야 한다며 이유를 제시하고 있으므로 정답이다.

(B) **파생어 오답:** 질문의 copier와 파생어 관계인 copies를 이용한 오답이다.

(C) **유사 발음 오답:** 질문의 copier와 부분적으로 발음이 유사한 coffee를 이용한 오답이다.

어휘 copier 복사기   replace 교체하다

12 M-Cn / W-Br

How're our sales doing this quarter?

(A) By two percent.

(B) It's in February.

(C) Better than we expected.

이번 분기 매출은 어떻습니까?

(A) 2퍼센트 차이예요.

(B) 2월이에요.

(C) 우리가 예상했던 것보다 좋아요.

해설 분기 매출을 묻는 **How 의문문**
- (A) **연상 어휘 오답:** 질문의 sales에서 연상 가능한 two percent를 이용한 오답이다.
- (B) **연상 어휘 오답:** 질문의 quarter에서 연상 가능한 February를 이용한 오답이다.
- (C) **정답:** 이번 분기 매출을 묻는 질문에 예상했던 것보다 좋다며 매출 규모를 밝히고 있으므로 정답이다.

어휘 quarter 분기

13 M-Cn / W-Am

Rajeev has an art degree, doesn't he?
- (A) I've been to the market already.
- **(B) Yes, that was on his résumé.**
- (C) It's just down the hall.

라지브는 미술 학위가 있죠, 그렇지 않나요?
- (A) 전 이미 시장에 가 봤어요.
- (B) 네, 그의 이력서에 있었어요.
- (C) 복도를 따라가면 있어요.

해설 학위 여부를 확인하는 **부가 의문문**
- (A) **질문과 상관없는 오답**
- (B) **정답:** 라지브의 미술 학위 여부를 확인하는 질문에 Yes라고 긍정한 뒤 그의 이력서에 있었다며 긍정 답변과 일관된 내용을 덧붙였으므로 정답이다.
- (C) **질문과 상관없는 오답**

어휘 degree 학위   hall 복도

14 M-Au / W-Am

Are you having trouble with the new software?
- (A) My bicycle is old.
- (B) I always wear a hat.
- **(C) No, it's working fine.**

새 소프트웨어를 쓰면서 문제가 있나요?
- (A) 제 자전거는 오래됐어요.
- (B) 저는 항상 모자를 써요.
- (C) 아니요, 잘 작동하고 있어요.

해설 새 소프트웨어 사용에 문제가 있는지 묻는 **일반 의문문**
- (A) **연상 어휘 오답:** 질문의 new에서 연상 가능한 old를 이용한 오답이다.
- (B) **유사 발음 오답:** 질문의 software와 부분적으로 발음이 유사한 wear를 이용한 오답이다.
- (C) **정답:** 새 소프트웨어를 쓰면서 문제가 있는지 묻는 질문에 No라고 대답한 뒤 잘 작동하고 있다며 부정 답변과 일관된 내용을 덧붙였으므로 정답이다.

15 W-Br / M-Au

Where can I see the payroll report?
- **(A) Didn't you get a copy?**
- (B) Thanks, but I had a roll for breakfast.
- (C) A fifteen percent bonus.

급여 명세서는 어디에서 볼 수 있나요?
- (A) 사본 못 받으셨어요?
- (B) 고마워요. 하지만 아침으로 롤빵을 먹었어요.
- (C) 15퍼센트 보너스예요.

해설 급여 명세서를 볼 수 있는 곳을 묻는 **Where 의문문**
- (A) **정답:** 급여 명세서를 볼 수 있는 곳을 묻는 질문에 사본을 못 받았는지 되물으며 사본으로 이미 제공되었음을 우회적으로 표현하고 있으므로 정답이다.
- (B) **유사 발음 오답:** 질문의 payroll과 부분적으로 발음이 유사한 roll을 이용한 오답이다.
- (C) **연상 어휘 오답:** 질문의 payroll에서 연상 가능한 bonus를 이용한 오답이다.

어휘 payroll 급여, 급여 지급 명부

16 W-Am / M-Cn

Don't we still sell beach umbrellas?
- (A) I recently bought a pair of shoes.
- (B) A vacation by the ocean.
- **(C) The supplier went out of business.**

우리 아직 해변 파라솔을 판매하고 있지 않나요?
- (A) 전 최근에 신발 한 켤레를 샀어요.
- (B) 바닷가에서 보내는 휴가예요.
- (C) 납품업체가 폐업했어요.

해설 해변 파라솔의 판매 여부를 확인하는 **부정 의문문**
- (A) **연상 어휘 오답:** 질문의 sell에서 연상 가능한 bought를 이용한 오답이다.
- (B) **연상 어휘 오답:** 질문의 beach에서 연상 가능한 ocean을 이용한 오답이다.
- (C) **정답:** 해변 파라솔을 아직 판매하고 있는지 확인하는 질문에 납품업체가 폐업했다며 판매하지 않음을 간접적으로 밝히고 있으므로 정답이다.

어휘 supplier 납품업체   go out of business 폐업하다

17 M-Cn / W-Br

Why wasn't the article published today?
- **(A) Because Mr. Kim wants to see it first.**
- (B) An arts and crafts magazine.
- (C) Two hundred copies is enough.

왜 기사가 오늘 안 나갔죠?
- (A) 김 씨가 먼저 보고 싶어 하셔서요.
- (B) 미술 공예 잡지예요.
- (C) 200부면 충분해요.

해설 오늘 기사가 나가지 않은 이유를 묻는 **Why 의문문**
- (A) **정답:** 오늘 기사가 나가지 않은 이유를 묻는 질문에 김 씨가 먼저 보고 싶어 한다며 이유를 제시하고 있으므로 정답이다.
- (B) **연상 어휘 오답:** 질문의 article과 published에서 연상 가능한 magazine을 이용한 오답이다.
- (C) **연상 어휘 오답:** 질문의 published에서 연상 가능한 Two hundred copies를 이용한 오답이다.

어휘 publish 게재하다[싣다]   craft 공예

18 W-Br / M-Au

Which travel agency do you recommend?
- (A) I sent it by express mail.
- (B) No, I don't mind.
- **(C) The one on Main Street.**

어떤 여행사를 추천하시나요?
(A) 속달 우편으로 보냈어요.
(B) 아니요, 상관없어요.
(C) 메인 가에 있는 곳이요.

해설 추천 여행사를 묻는 Which 의문문
(A) **연상 어휘 오답:** 질문의 travel에서 연상 가능한 express를 이용한 오답이다.
(B) **Yes/No 불가 오답:** Which 의문문에는 Yes/No로 응답할 수 없다.
(C) **정답:** 추천하는 여행사를 묻는 질문에 메인 가에 있는 곳을 추천하고 있으므로 정답이다.

어휘 travel agency 여행사   express mail 속달 우편

---

19 M-Au / W-Br
Wasn't the shipment supposed to be ready yesterday?
(A) No, it's planned for Thursday.
(B) We've already read the manual.
(C) It's a passenger ship.

어제 배송 준비가 됐어야 하는 거 아니었나요?
(A) 아니요, 목요일로 예정되어 있어요.
(B) 저희는 이미 설명서를 읽었어요.
(C) 여객선입니다.

해설 배송 준비 시점을 확인하는 부정 의문문
(A) **정답:** 배송 준비가 어제였는지 확인하는 질문에 No라고 부정한 뒤 목요일이라고 바로잡고 있으므로 정답이다.
(B) **유사 발음 오답:** 질문의 ready와 부분적으로 발음이 유사한 already를 이용한 오답이다.
(C) **파생어 오답:** 질문의 shipment와 파생어 관계인 ship을 이용한 오답이다.

어휘 shipment 배송(품)   passenger ship 여객선

---

20 M-Cn / W-Br
Would you like to have a break now or after the second session?
(A) I think I just broke that.
(B) Now would be OK.
(C) She won second prize.

지금 쉬고 싶으세요, 아니면 두 번째 세션이 끝난 후에 쉬고 싶으세요?
(A) 제가 방금 깬 것 같아요.
(B) 지금이 좋아요.
(C) 그녀는 2등 상을 받았어요.

해설 선호하는 휴식 시점을 묻는 선택 의문문
(A) **파생어 오답:** 질문의 break과 파생어 관계인 broke를 이용한 오답이다.
(B) **정답:** 선호하는 휴식 시간을 묻는 질문에 전자를 선택해 응답하고 있으므로 정답이다.
(C) **어휘 반복 오답:** 질문의 second를 반복 이용한 오답이다.

---

21 M-Au / W-Am
Could you review my presentation slides today?
(A) Your office has a nice view.
(B) A present for the retirement party.
(C) Of course, I'd be happy to.

오늘 제 프레젠테이션 슬라이드를 검토해 주시겠어요?
(A) 사무실 전망이 멋지네요.
(B) 은퇴 파티를 위한 선물이에요.
(C) 물론이죠, 기꺼이요.

해설 요청하는 의문문
(A) **파생어 오답:** 질문의 review와 파생어 관계인 view를 이용한 오답이다.
(B) **파생어 오답:** 질문의 presentation과 파생어 관계인 present를 이용한 오답이다.
(C) **정답:** 프레젠테이션 슬라이드를 검토해 달라고 요청하는 질문에 Of course라고 대답한 뒤, 기꺼이 하겠다며 긍정 답변과 일관된 내용을 덧붙였으므로 정답이다.

어휘 review 검토하다   retirement 은퇴

---

22 M-Cn / W-Br
Who did the patient see for her last dental cleaning?
(A) I cleaned the floors earlier.
(B) She's a new patient.
(C) Be sure to brush twice daily.

환자가 마지막으로 누구에게 스케일링을 받았죠?
(A) 아까 제가 바닥을 청소했어요.
(B) 새로 온 환자예요.
(C) 매일 두 번씩 꼭 양치질하세요.

해설 환자가 마지막으로 스케일링 받은 사람을 묻는 Who 의문문
(A) **파생어 오답:** 질문의 cleaning과 파생어 관계인 cleaned를 이용한 오답이다.
(B) **정답:** 환자가 마지막으로 스케일링 받은 사람을 묻는 질문에 새로 온 환자라며 이전 진료 내역이 없음을 우회적으로 밝히고 있으므로 정답이다.
(C) **연상 어휘 오답:** 질문의 dental cleaning에서 연상 가능한 brush를 이용한 오답이다.

---

23 M-Au / W-Am
How cold is it outside?
(A) Just some ice water, please.
(B) Look inside those boxes.
(C) I'm bringing a jacket.

밖이 얼마나 추운가요?
(A) 얼음물만 좀 주세요.
(B) 저 상자들 안을 보세요.
(C) 전 재킷을 챙기려고요.

해설 밖이 얼마나 추운지 묻는 How 의문문
(A) **연상 어휘 오답:** 질문의 cold에서 연상 가능한 ice를 이용한 오답이다.
(B) **연상 어휘 오답:** 질문의 outside에서 연상 가능한 inside를 이용한 오답이다.

(C) **정답:** 밖이 얼마나 추운지 묻는 질문에 자신은 재킷을 챙기려고 한다며 날씨가 춥다는 것을 우회적으로 밝히고 있으므로 정답이다.

24 W-Am / M-Cn

We'd appreciate your feedback on our new mobile application.
(A) I have some time tomorrow.
(B) We already ate.
(C) A job opening.

새로운 모바일 애플리케이션에 대한 의견을 주시면 감사하겠습니다.
(A) 내일 시간이 있어요.
(B) 우리는 벌써 먹었어요.
(C) 일자리예요.

해설 **요청하는 평서문**
(A) **정답:** 새로운 모바일 애플리케이션에 대한 의견을 달라는 평서문에 내일 시간이 있다며 지금은 요청을 들어줄 수 없음을 간접적으로 밝히고 있으므로 정답이다.
(B) **단어 반복 및 유사 발음 오답:** 평서문의 We를 반복하였고, 평서문의 appreciate와 부분적으로 발음이 유사한 ate를 이용한 오답이다.
(C) **연상 어휘 오답:** 평서문의 application을 '지원서'로 잘못 이해했을 때 연상 가능한 job opening을 이용한 오답이다.

어휘 appreciate 고마워하다   job opening (직장의) 공석

25 M-Cn / M-Au

All the concert tickets are sold out.
(A) Yes, I enjoyed it.
(B) Have you checked online?
(C) A jazz band.

콘서트 티켓이 매진됐어요.
(A) 네, 즐거웠어요.
(B) 온라인은 확인해 보셨나요?
(C) 재즈 밴드예요.

해설 **정보를 전달하는 평서문**
(A) **연상 어휘 오답:** 평서문의 concert에서 연상 가능한 enjoyed를 이용한 오답이다.
(B) **정답:** 콘서트 티켓이 매진되었다는 평서문에 온라인은 확인해 봤는지 되묻고 있으므로 정답이다.
(C) **연상 어휘 오답:** 평서문의 concert에서 연상 가능한 jazz band를 이용한 오답이다.

26 W-Am / M-Cn

I'd like to add some outdoor seating for the coffee shop.
(A) The weather is getting nicer.
(B) Do you take sugar in your coffee?
(C) At a traffic intersection.

커피숍에 야외 좌석을 추가하고 싶어요.
(A) 날씨가 점점 좋아지고 있죠.
(B) 커피에 설탕 넣으시나요?
(C) 교차로에서요.

해설 **의견을 제시하는 평서문**
(A) **정답:** 커피숍에 야외 좌석을 추가하고 싶다는 평서문에 날씨가 점점 좋아지고 있다며 호응하고 있으므로 정답이다.
(B) **단어 반복 오답:** 평서문의 coffee를 반복 이용한 오답이다.
(C) **질문과 상관없는 오답**

어휘 seating 좌석   intersection 교차로

27 M-Cn / W-Br

The executive director called a special meeting for ten A.M. tomorrow.
(A) No, it's in the process directions.
(B) I'll reschedule our factory visit.
(C) A conference room in the west wing.

상무님께서 내일 오전 10시에 특별 회의를 소집하셨어요.
(A) 아니요, 공정 안내서에 있어요.
(B) 공장 방문 일정을 변경할게요.
(C) 서쪽 별관에 있는 회의실이에요.

해설 **정보를 전달하는 평서문**
(A) **파생어 오답:** 평서문의 director와 파생어 관계인 directions를 이용한 오답이다.
(B) **정답:** 상무님이 내일 오전 10시에 특별 회의를 소집했다는 평서문에 공장 방문 일정을 변경하겠다며 대책을 마련하고 있으므로 정답이다.
(C) **연상 어휘 오답:** 평서문의 meeting에서 연상 가능한 conference를 이용한 오답이다.

어휘 executive director 상무   directions 지침서. 사용법
wing 부속 건물

28 W-Br / M-Au

Should we take the bus or the train to the trade show?
(A) I just called a car service.
(B) Yes, he was trained last week.
(C) At the ticket counter.

무역 박람회에 갈 때 버스를 탈까요, 아니면 기차를 탈까요?
(A) 방금 차량 서비스에 전화했어요.
(B) 네, 그는 지난주에 훈련받았어요.
(C) 매표소에서요.

해설 **교통수단을 묻는 선택 의문문**
(A) **정답:** 무역 박람회에 가는 교통수단을 묻자 차량 서비스에 전화했다며 교통편을 이미 마련했음을 우회적으로 밝히고 있으므로 정답이다.
(B) **Yes/No 불가 및 유사 발음 오답:** 문장과 문장을 연결하는 경우를 제외하고는 선택 의문문에는 Yes/No로 응답할 수 없고, 질문의 train과 부분적으로 발음이 유사한 trained를 이용한 오답이다.
(C) **연상 어휘 오답:** 질문의 bus와 train에서 연상 가능한 ticket을 이용한 오답이다.

29 M-Au / W-Am

Will the budget be revised in time for our four o'clock conference call?
(A) Yes, I think I can finish it.
(B) It's the second room in that hall.
(C) No, the December product launch.

4시 전화 회의에 맞춰 예산이 수정될까요?
(A) 네, 끝낼 수 있을 것 같아요.
(B) 거기 홀에 있는 두 번째 방이에요.
(C) 아니요, 12월 제품 출시예요.

해설 **예산 수정 시점을 묻는 일반 의문문**
(A) **정답:** 전화 회의에 맞춰 예산이 수정될지 묻는 질문에 그렇다(Yes)고 긍정한 뒤 끝낼 수 있다며 긍정 답변과 일관된 내용을 덧붙이고 있으므로 정답이다.
(B) **연상 어휘 오답:** 질문의 conference에서 연상 가능한 hall을 이용한 오답이다.
(C) **질문과 상관없는 오답**

어휘 budget 예산 revise 수정하다 launch 출시

30 W-Br / M-Au

Why don't we take our clients out to lunch?
(A) The recycling's been taken out.
(B) No, we hired at least two.
(C) I'll call Nemo's Restaurant.

고객들을 데리고 나가서 점심을 먹는 게 어때요?
(A) 재활용품은 내다 버렸어요.
(B) 아니요, 최소 2명을 채용했어요.
(C) 니모즈 레스토랑에 전화할게요.

해설 **제안하는 의문문**
(A) **파생어 오답:** 질문의 take와 파생어 관계인 taken을 이용한 오답이다.
(B) **단어 반복 오답:** 질문의 we를 반복 이용한 오답이다.
(C) **정답:** 고객들을 데리고 나가서 점심을 먹자고 제안하는 질문에 니모즈 레스토랑에 전화하겠다며 제안을 우회적으로 수용하고 있으므로 정답이다.

31 W-Am / M-Cn

The proposal you've submitted is quite impressive.
(A) This sink needs to be repaired.
(B) There are several people on my team.
(C) I counted five of them.

제출하신 제안서가 무척 훌륭하네요.
(A) 이 싱크대는 수리해야 해요.
(B) 팀에 여러 명이 있어요.
(C) 다섯 개를 세어봤습니다.

해설 **의견을 제시하는 평서문**
(A) **질문과 상관없는 오답**
(B) **정답:** 제출한 제안서가 무척 훌륭하다는 평서문에 팀에 여러 명이 있다며 공을 다른 사람들에게도 돌리고 있으므로 정답이다.
(C) **질문과 상관없는 오답**

어휘 proposal 제안(서) impressive 인상적인

PART 3

[32-34] M-Cn / W-Br

M Hello, Ms. Lambert. **32 Marcel Bertrand has just arrived and is waiting in the reception area.** He says he has an appointment with you at ten A.M.

W Mr. Bertrand? **33 There must be some mistake. That meeting is scheduled for tomorrow.**

M Should I ask him if he can return then?

W Well, he's here now, and I'd hate to waste his time. I can rearrange my calendar, but I'll need a few minutes to prepare.

M OK. **34 I'll ask Mr. Bertrand if he wants any tea or coffee** and tell him you'll be down in a few minutes.

남 안녕하세요, 램버트 씨. **32 마르셀 버트런드 씨가 방금 도착해서 안내실에서 기다리고 있어요.** 오전 10시에 약속했다고 말씀하십니다.
여 버트런드 씨? **33 뭔가 착오가 있는 것 같네요. 그 회의는 내일로 잡혀 있어요.**
남 그때 다시 오실 수 있는지 여쭤볼까요?
여 음, 지금 오셨으니 시간을 허비하게 만들고 싶지는 않네요. 제 일정을 다시 조정할 수는 있는데 준비하려면 몇 분 필요해요.
남 알겠습니다. **34 버트런드 씨에게 차나 커피를 마실지 여쭤보고** 몇 분 후에 내려오신다고 말씀드릴게요.

어휘 reception area 안내실, 로비 rearrange 재조정하다

32 남자는 왜 여자에게 전화하고 있는가?
(A) 약속을 취소하려고
(B) 실수에 대해 사과하려고
(C) 방문자가 있다고 알리려고
(D) 서명을 요청하려고

해설 **전화의 목적**
남자가 첫 대사에서 마르셀 버트런드 씨가 방금 도착해서 안내실에서 기다리고 있다(Marcel Bertrand has just arrived and is waiting in the reception area)고 했으므로 (C)가 정답이다.

33 여자는 어떤 문제를 언급하는가?
(A) 일정에 착오가 있었다.
(B) 서류가 제출되지 않았다.
(C) 장치가 오작동하고 있다.
(D) 더 이상 회의실을 사용할 수 없다.

해설 **여자가 언급한 문제**
여자가 첫 대사에서 뭔가 착오가 있는 것 같다(There must be some mistake)며 회의는 내일로 잡혀 있다(That meeting is scheduled for tomorrow)고 했으므로 (A)가 정답이다.

어휘 misunderstanding 착오, 오해 paperwork 서류 malfunction 오작동하다

Paraphrasing 대화의 some mistake
→ 정답의 misunderstanding

34 남자는 버트런드 씨에게 무엇을 제공할 것인가?
(A) 사과   (B) 할인가
(C) 음료수   (D) 읽을거리

해설 **남자가 버트런드 씨에게 제공하는 것**
남자가 마지막 대사에서 버트런드 씨에게 차나 커피를 마실지 여쭤보겠다(I'll ask Mr. Bertrand if he wants any tea or coffee)고 했으므로 (C)가 정답이다.

Paraphrasing 대화의 any tea or coffee
→ 정답의 A beverage

[35-37] M-Au / W-Am / M-Cn   **3인 대화**

> M1 Good morning. **35 I'd like to put in a work order for some repairs in my apartment.**
> W OK, **35 thank you for coming to the leasing office.** Kyle is our maintenance supervisor.
> M2 Pleasure to meet you. What seems to be the problem?
> M1 **36 I can't access my outdoor patio because both the handle and the lock on the door to the patio are broken.**
> W Well, we'll take a look as soon as possible. Kyle, are you free now?
> M2 **37 Actually, I'm waiting for the delivery of a shipment of air-conditioning filters. Could you sign for them when they come in?**
> W **37 Sure, I can do that.**

> 남1 안녕하세요. **35** 아파트 수리를 위해서 작업 요청서를 제출하고 싶은데요.
> 여 네. **35** 임대 사무소를 찾아 주셔서 감사합니다. 카일은 유지 보수 관리자예요.
> 남2 만나서 반갑습니다. 무슨 문제인가요?
> 남1 **36** 테라스 문 손잡이와 잠금장치가 모두 고장 나서 야외 테라스를 이용할 수가 없어요.
> 여 가능한 한 빨리 살펴보겠습니다. 카일, 지금 시간 되시나요?
> 남2 **37** 실은 에어컨 필터 배송을 기다리고 있어요. 오면 서명 좀 해 주시겠어요?
> 여 **37** 그럼요, 제가 할게요.

> **어휘** work order 작업 요청서   leasing office 임대 사무소
> maintenance 유지 보수   access 이용[접근]하다   patio
> 테라스

35 대화는 어디에서 이루어지고 있는 것 같은가?
(A) 부동산 관리 사무소   (B) 기차역
(C) 커뮤니티 센터   (D) 철물점

해설 **대화의 장소**
첫 번째 남자가 첫 대사에서 아파트 수리를 위해서 작업 요청서를 제출하고 싶다(I'd like to put in a work order for some repairs in my apartment)고 했고, 여자가 임대

사무소를 찾아 줘서 고맙다(thank you for coming to the leasing office)고 응답했으므로 (A)가 정답이다.

어휘 property 부동산   hardware 철물

Paraphrasing 대화의 leasing office
→ 정답의 property management office

36 어떤 문제가 논의되고 있는가?
(A) 전기실이 잠겨 있다.
(B) 주방 배관에서 물이 새고 있다.
(C) 테라스 문이 고장 났다.
(D) 통로를 수리해야 한다.

해설 **논의되는 문제**
첫 번째 남자가 두 번째 대사에서 테라스 문 손잡이와 잠금장치가 모두 고장 나서 야외 테라스를 이용할 수가 없다(I can't access my outdoor patio because both the handle and the lock on the door to the patio are broken)고 했으므로 (C)가 정답이다.

어휘 electrical 전기의   leak 새다

37 여자는 무엇을 하기로 동의하는가?
(A) 동영상 녹화   (B) 작업 일정 변경
(C) 기술자 호출   **(D) 배송품 수령 확인 서명**

해설 **여자가 동의하는 것**
두 번째 남자가 두 번째 대사에서 에어컨 필터 배송을 기다리고 있다(I'm waiting for the delivery of a shipment ~ filters)면서 오면 서명 좀 해 달라(Could you sign for them when they come in?)고 요청하자 여자가 본인이 하겠다(Sure, I can do that)고 했으므로 (D)가 정답이다.

어휘 technician 기술자

[38-40] M-Cn / W-Am

> M Thanks for taking on this project. **38 My family has owned this restaurant for many years, and it definitely needs updates to the exterior.**
> W **38 My pleasure. 39 I know you mentioned wanting to cover the outside with wood siding. The problem is, the afternoon sun is harsh here, so it'd need resealing every year.**
> M Good point. What would you suggest instead?
> W I'd consider using an inexpensive vinyl or concrete panels. **40 I'll send you some estimates for different options tonight.**

> 남 이 프로젝트를 맡아 주셔서 감사합니다. **38** 저희 가족은 이 식당을 수년간 소유해 왔는데 확실히 외관을 개선할 필요가 있어요.
> 여 **38** 천만에요. **39** 제가 알기로는 외부를 목재 외장재로 덮고 싶다고 말씀하셨는데요. 문제는 이곳의 오후 햇살이 따가워서 매년 재시공을 해야 합니다.

남 좋은 지적입니다. 대신 어떤 걸 제안하시나요?

여 저렴한 비닐이나 콘크리트 패널 사용을 고려하고 싶군요. **40오늘 밤 다양한 옵션에 대한 견적을 보내 드릴게요.**

어휘 take on ~을 맡다　exterior 외관　siding (건물) 외장재　harsh 혹독한　inexpensive 저렴한　estimate 견적(서)

38 화자들은 주로 무엇에 대해 논의하고 있는가?
(A) 식당 메뉴 재구성　　(B) 조경 서비스 제공
(C) 가구 구매　　**(D) 건물 개조**

해설 **대화의 주제**
남자가 첫 대사에서 이 프로젝트를 맡아 줘서 고맙다고 한 뒤, 우리 가족은 이 식당을 수년간 소유해 왔는데 확실히 외관을 개선할 필요가 있다(My family has owned this restaurant for many years, and it definitely needs updates to the exterior)고 했다. 이어서 여자가 천만에요(My pleasure)라고 응답하면서 관련 내용을 상의하고 있으므로 (D)가 정답이다.

어휘 landscape 조경하다　renovate 개조하다

(Paraphrasing) 대화의 updates to the exterior
→ 정답의 Renovating a building

39 여자는 무엇에 관해 주의를 주는가?
(A) 특정 자재 사용　　(B) 미숙련 직원 채용
(C) 예산 초과　　(D) 주문 처리 지연

해설 **여자가 주의를 주는 것**
여자가 첫 대사에서 의뢰인이 외부를 목재 외장재로 덮고 싶다고 했지만(I know you mentioned wanting to cover the outside with wood siding) 이곳은 오후 햇살이 따가워서 해마다 재시공을 해야 하는 것이 문제(The problem is, the afternoon sun is harsh here, so it'd need resealing every year)라고 했으므로 (A)가 정답이다.

어휘 particular 특정한　unskilled 서투른　exceed 초과하다

(Paraphrasing) 대화의 cover the outside with wood siding → 정답의 Using a particular material

40 여자는 남자에게 무엇을 보낼 것인가?
(A) 사진　　(B) 제품 견본
(C) 비용 견적　　(D) 판매업체명

해설 **여자가 남자에게 보낼 것**
여자가 마지막 대사에서 오늘 밤 다양한 옵션에 대한 견적을 보내 주겠다(I'll send you some estimates for different options tonight)고 했으므로 (C)가 정답이다.

(Paraphrasing) 대화의 some estimates
→ 정답의 Cost estimates

어휘 vendor 판매업체

[41-43] W-Br / M-Cn

W Mr. Bora, **41,42 I was just reviewing a patient's file—the information from her last appointment is missing.** Do you know what happened?

M **42 I do, Dr. Patel. When we converted the paper patient files to digital versions last week, the most recent entries seem to have been lost.**

W I see. Well, I do need that information. What can we do to fix this problem?

M Don't worry, we still have the paper files— you can use those for now. **43 A database technician will be coming at two o'clock this afternoon to retrieve the missing data.** She said this is a common database issue that she can fix quickly.

여 보라 씨, **41,42방금 어떤 환자의 파일을 검토하고 있었는데, 저번 진료 정보가 없네요.** 어떻게 된 일인지 아세요?

남 **42네, 파텔 박사님.** 지난주에 서면 환자 파일을 디지털 버전으로 변환했을 때 가장 최근에 입력한 내용들이 사라진 것 같아요.

여 그렇군요. 음, 그 정보가 꼭 필요해요. 이 문제를 해결하려면 어떻게 해야 하죠?

남 걱정 마세요. 아직 서면 파일이 있으니 지금은 그것을 사용하시면 됩니다. **43오늘 오후 2시에 데이터베이스 기술자가 손실된 데이터를 복구하러 옵니다.** 기술자가 금방 고칠 수 있는 흔한 데이터베이스 오류라고 했어요.

어휘 convert 전환하다　entry 기재 사항　technician 기술자　retrieve 복구하다

41 화자들은 어디에 있는가?
(A) 자동차 정비소　　**(B) 병원**
(C) 컴퓨터 매장　　(D) 인쇄소

해설 **대화의 장소**
여자가 첫 대사에서 방금 어떤 환자의 파일을 검토하고 있었는데, 저번 진료 정보가 없다(I was just reviewing a patient's file—the information from her last appointment is missing)면서 환자 파일에 관한 이야기가 이어지고 있으므로 (B)가 정답이다.

42 화자들은 무엇에 대해 논의하고 있는가?
(A) 배송 지연　　(B) 취소된 약속
(C) 누락된 정보　　(D) 엉뚱한 라벨이 붙은 품목

해설 **대화의 주제**
여자가 첫 대사에서 방금 어떤 환자의 파일을 검토하고 있었는데, 저번 진료 정보가 없다(I was just reviewing a patient's file—the information from her last appointment is missing)면서 어떻게 된 일인지 물어보니 남자가 안다(I do, Dr. Patel)면서 지난주에 서면 환자 파일을 디지털 버전으로 변환했을 때 가장 최근에 입력한 내용들이 사라졌다(When we converted the paper

patient files to digital versions last week, the most recent entries seem to have been lost)며 누락된 정보에 대한 내용을 이어가고 있으므로 (C)가 정답이다.

어휘 mislabel 엉뚱한 라벨을 붙이다

43 오후에 무슨 일이 일어날 것인가?
(A) 기술자가 도착한다.   (B) 교육이 진행된다.
(C) 동료가 일찍 퇴근한다.   (D) 계약이 마무리된다.

해설 **오후에 일어날 일**
남자가 마지막 대사에서 오늘 오후 2시에 데이터베이스 기술자가 손실된 데이터를 복구하러 올 것(A database technician will be coming at two o'clock this afternoon to retrieve the missing data)이라고 했으므로 (A)가 정답이다.

어휘 contract 계약(서)   finalize 마무리하다

(Paraphrasing) 대화의 A database technician will be coming → 정답의 A technician will arrive.

[44-46] M-Au / W-Br

> M   Sushmita, **44 I have an idea for a new TV show we could produce.** How about basing it on the young-adult novel *Mountain Trek*?
>
> W   Well, that book used to be popular, but I don't think it's been selling well recently.
>
> M   **45 It's making a comeback, actually, probably because readers have been posting good reviews on social media sites.**
>
> W   In that case, we should look into getting the rights to the book. We can start by connecting with the publisher. **46 Could you e-mail them, please?**
>
> 남   스쉬미타, **44** 우리가 제작할 수 있는 새 TV 프로그램에 대한 아이디어가 있어요. 청소년 소설 〈마운틴 트렉〉을 바탕으로 해 보는 건 어떨까요?
>
> 여   음. 그 책은 예전에는 인기가 있었지만 최근에는 잘 안 팔리는 것 같은데요.
>
> 남   **45** 실은 독자들이 소셜 미디어 사이트에 좋다는 후기를 올리고 있어서 그런지 다시 인기를 얻고 있어요.
>
> 여   그렇다면 판권을 확보할 방법을 알아봐야겠네요. 먼저 출판사에 연락부터 하죠. **46** 그쪽에 이메일 좀 보내 주실래요?
>
> **어휘** base 기반하다   make a comeback 재기하다
> rights 판권   publisher 출판사

44 주로 무엇에 관한 대화인가?
(A) 도서전 장소
(B) 입사 지원자 면접
(C) 회의 강연자
(D) **새 프로그램을 위한 아이디어**

해설 **대화의 주제**
남자가 첫 대사에서 우리가 제작할 수 있는 새 TV 프로그램에 대한 아이디어가 있다(I have an idea for a new TV

show we could produce)고 한 뒤, 관련 내용이 이어지므로 (D)가 정답이다.

어휘 fair 박람회   applicant 지원자

45 남자에 따르면, 무엇이 제품을 인기 있게 만들었는가?
(A) 할인가   (B) 판촉 행사
(C) 유명인의 홍보   (D) **긍정적인 평가**

해설 **제품의 인기 이유**
남자가 두 번째 대사에서 독자들이 소셜 미디어 사이트에 좋다는 후기를 올리고 있어서 그런지 다시 인기를 얻고 있다(It's making a comeback, actually, probably because readers have been posting good reviews on social media sites)고 했으므로 (D)가 정답이다.

어휘 promotional 판촉의   endorsement 홍보, 지지

(Paraphrasing) 대화의 good reviews
→ 정답의 Positive reviews

46 여자는 남자에게 무엇을 해 달라고 요청하는가?
(A) **이메일 보내기**   (B) 수치 재확인하기
(C) 세미나 일정 잡기   (D) 설문지 만들기

해설 **여자의 요청 사항**
여자가 마지막 대사에서 그쪽에 이메일 좀 보내 달라(Could you e-mail them, please?)고 했으므로 (A)가 정답이다.

어휘 figures 수치   questionnaire 설문지

(Paraphrasing) 대화의 e-mail → 정답의 Send an e-mail

[47-49] W-Am / M-Cn

> W   Hello, Luis. **47 You worked on the advertising campaign for the local car dealership, right?**
>
> M   **47 I've been working on that account for a month.** Why do you ask?
>
> W   I just reviewed the proposal, and **48,49 I noticed that some of the rates you quoted for advertisements were outdated.**
>
> M   Really? Which ones?
>
> W   The rates for some of the radio ads.
>
> M   **49 Well, let me follow up with the studio representative I talked to and see what's going on.**
>
> W   That would be great. This hasn't been sent to the client yet.
>
> 여   안녕하세요, 루이스. **47** 지역 자동차 대리점을 위해 광고 캠페인을 진행하셨죠?
>
> 남   **47** 한 달 전부터 그 고객을 위해 일하고 있죠. 왜 물어보세요?
>
> 여   방금 제안서를 검토했는데 **48,49** 광고 견적을 낸 가격 일부가 오래되어서 안 맞네요.
>
> 남   정말요? 어떤 거죠?

여 라디오 광고비예요.

남 49음, 제가 이야기를 나눴던 스튜디오 담당자와 후속 조치를 하고 상황을 파악해 볼게요.

여 그게 좋겠네요. 이건 아직 고객에게 보내지 않았어요.

어휘 car dealership 자동차 대리점 account 고객 proposal 제안(서) quote 견적을 내다 outdated 해묵은 follow up ~에 후속 조치를 하다 representative 담당자

---

47 화자들은 어디에서 일하는 것 같은가?

(A) 아트 스튜디오　　　**(B) 광고 대행사**

(C) 은행　　　(D) 자동차 정비소

해설　화자들의 근무지

여자가 첫 대사에서 지역 자동차 대리점을 위해 광고 캠페인을 진행했는지(You worked on the advertising campaign for the local car dealership, right?) 물었고 남자가 한 달 전부터 그 고객을 위해 일하고 있다(I've been working on that account for a month)고 했으므로 (B)가 정답이다.

48 여자는 어떤 문제를 언급하는가?

(A) 고객이 불만이다.

(B) 대출이 승인되지 않았다.

(C) 일부 정보가 오래되었다.

(D) 일부 직원이 시간이 없다.

해설　여자가 언급한 문제

여자가 두 번째 대사에서 광고 견적을 낸 가격 일부가 오래되어서 안 맞다(I noticed that some of the rates you quoted for advertisements were outdated)고 했으므로 (C)가 정답이다.

어휘 loan 대출 approve 승인하다 unavailable 시간이 없는

(Paraphrasing) 대화의 some of the rates you quoted for advertisements ➡ 정답의 Some information

49 여자가 "이건 아직 고객에게 보내지 않았어요"라고 말할 때 무엇을 의미하는가?

(A) 기한을 놓쳤다.

(B) 배송 서비스가 지연되고 있다.

(C) 프로젝트가 취소되었다.

(D) 수정이 가능하다.

해설　화자의 의도

여자가 두 번째 대사에서 광고 견적을 낸 가격 일부가 오래되어서 안 맞다(I noticed that some of the rates ~ were outdated)고 문제점을 언급했고 남자가 이야기를 나눴던 스튜디오 담당자와 후속 조치를 하고 상황을 파악해 보겠다(Well, let me follow up with the studio representative I talked to and see what's going on)고 했다. 이후에 여자가 인용문을 언급했으므로 (D)가 정답이다.

[50-52] W-Br / M-Cn

W Lorenzo, thanks for coming. **50 I looked at the designs for our new line of humorous birthday cards. I don't think they'll stand out** from all the other greeting cards being sold.

M **50 I agree. 51 I wonder about contracting a well-known visual artist for the line—** someone whose artwork is instantly recognizable. Maybe someone like Kelly Taylor?

W Oh, I like that idea. **52 But we're operating on a short timeline.** How quickly do you think Kelly can get the artwork done? These need to be printed by October.

M You'd be surprised at how quickly she works. She has a team of assistants who help her with big projects.

여 로렌조, 와 줘서 고마워요. **50 익살스러운 생일 카드 신제품군의 디자인을 살펴봤어요.** 판매되는 온갖 다른 축하 카드들 사이에서 **50 그다지 눈에 띄지 않을 것 같은데요.**

남 **50 동의해요. 51 해당 제품군을 위해 유명한 시각 예술가와 계약하면 어떨까 해요.** 보면 바로 작품을 알아볼 수 있는 그런 사람이요. 켈리 테일러 같은 사람?

여 오, 아이디어 마음에 드네요. **52 하지만 일정이 촉박하게 돌아가고 있어요.** 켈리 씨가 얼마나 빨리 작품을 완성할 수 있을까요? 이것들은 10월까지 인쇄되어야 해요.

남 켈리 씨가 얼마나 빨리 작업하는지 알면 놀라실 거예요. 그녀에게는 대형 프로젝트를 도와주는 조수 팀이 있어요.

어휘 stand out 눈에 띄다 contract 계약하다 instantly 바로, 즉시 recognizable (쉽게) 알아볼 수 있는 operate 일하다 assistant 조수

---

50 대화의 목적은 무엇인가?

(A) 웹사이트 디자인 완성　　(B) 기념일 확정

(C) 매장 개장 계획　　**(D) 신제품군 논의**

해설　대화의 목적

여자가 첫 대사에서 익살스러운 생일 카드 신제품군의 디자인을 살펴봤다(I looked at the designs for our new line ~ cards)면서 그다지 눈에 띄지 않을 것 같다(I don't think they'll stand out)고 우려하자 남자가 동의한다(I agree)고 한 뒤, 아이디어를 제시하고 있으므로 (D)가 정답이다.

(Paraphrasing) 대화의 our new line of humorous birthday cards ➡ 정답의 a new product line

51 남자는 무엇을 하자고 제안하는가?

(A) 소셜 미디어에서 캠페인 시작

(B) 마케팅 전문가와 상담

(C) 대량 주문 시 가격 협상

(D) 유명 아티스트 고용

해설 **남자의 제안 사항**
남자가 첫 대사에서 해당 제품군을 위해 유명한 시각 예술가와 계약하면 어떨지(I wonder about contracting a well-known visual artist for the line) 제안하고 있으므로 (D)가 정답이다.

어휘 consult 상담하다   negotiate 협상하다

(Paraphrasing) 대화의 contracting a well-known visual artist → 정답의 Hiring a well-known artist

52 여자는 왜 걱정하는가?
(A) 디자인은 승인이 필요하다.
(B) 마감 기한이 빨리 다가오고 있다.
(C) 재료가 비싸다.
(D) 경쟁사가 인기를 얻고 있다.

해설 **여자가 걱정하는 이유**
여자가 마지막 대사에서 일정이 촉박하게 돌아가고 있다(But we're operating on a short timeline)고 했으므로 (B)가 정답이다.

어휘 approach 다가오다   competitor 경쟁사

(Paraphrasing) 대화의 operating on a short timeline → 정답의 A deadline is approaching quickly.

[53-55] M-Au / W-Br

M Junko, the leadership team has given us a new assignment. **53 They want us to prepare a media statement about changes the airline will make next quarter.**

W Oh, yes—passengers should be pleased with the airline's new meal options.

M That's right. And the best part is that **54 Claudia Silvestri—the popular celebrity chef—created the new menu.**

W Wonderful! OK, so besides preparing the media statements for news outlets, **55 we should also come up with some creative ideas for announcing this news on our social media pages.**

M Definitely. **55 Do you want to meet this afternoon?**

W Sounds good. One P.M.?

남 준코, 리더십 팀에서 새로운 업무를 맡겼어요. **53 다음 분기에 항공사가 변경할 사항에 대해 언론 성명서를 준비하라고 하네요.**

여 아, 네. 승객들이 항공사의 새로운 식사 옵션에 만족할 겁니다.

남 그럼요. 그리고 가장 좋은 점은 **54 인기 있는 유명 요리사인 클라우디아 실베스트리가 신메뉴를 만들었다는 거죠.**

여 멋져요! 자, 그러니까 뉴스 매체를 위한 언론 발표자료도 준비해야 하지만 **55 소셜 미디어 페이지에 이 소식을 알리기 위한 창의적인 아이디어도 생각해 내야 해요.**

남 물론이죠. **55 오늘 오후에 만날래요?**

여 좋아요. 오후 1시요?

어휘 assignment 업무   statement 성명서   outlet 매체

53 화자들은 어떤 부서에서 일하는 것 같은가?
(A) 홍보   (B) 재무
(C) 인사   (D) 연구개발

해설 **화자들의 근무 부서**
남자가 첫 대사에서 리더십 팀에서 새로운 업무를 맡겼는데, 다음 분기에 항공사가 변경할 사항에 대해 언론 발표자료를 준비하는 것(They want us to prepare a media statement about changes the airline will make next quarter)이라고 했으므로 (A)가 정답이다.

어휘 public relations 홍보   finance 재무[재정]

54 클라우디아 실베스트리는 무엇을 했는가?
(A) 비행기를 디자인했다.   (B) 기사를 썼다.
(C) 소프트웨어를 개발했다.   **(D) 메뉴를 만들었다.**

해설 **클라우디아 실베스트리가 한 일**
남자가 두 번째 대사에서 인기 있는 유명 요리사인 클라우디아 실베스트리가 신메뉴를 만들었다(Claudia Silvestri—the popular celebrity chef—created the new menu)고 했으므로 (D)가 정답이다.

55 화자들은 왜 오늘 오후에 만날 것인가?
(A) 의견을 분석하려고   **(B) 아이디어를 내려고**
(C) 워크숍을 이끌려고   (D) 시설을 둘러보려고

해설 **오후에 화자들이 만나는 이유**
여자가 두 번째 대사에서 뉴스 매체를 위한 언론 발표자료도 준비해야 하지만 소셜 미디어 페이지에 이 소식을 알리기 위한 창의적인 아이디어도 생각해 내야 한다(we should also come up with some creative ideas ~)고 하자 남자가 동의하며 오늘 오후에 만나자(Do you want to meet this afternoon?)고 제안했으므로 (B)가 정답이다.

어휘 analyze 분석하다   generate 생산하다   facility 시설

(Paraphrasing) 대화의 come up with some creative ideas → 정답의 generate some ideas

[56-58] M-Au / W-Am / W-Br   3인 대화

M   Hi. **56 I'm just stopping by to ask about bringing in my boat for some basic maintenance.** I've used your services before.

W1 Sure. We have availability this afternoon, if you could bring your boat by then. Are you just looking for a tune-up?

M   Yes. **57 But also my canvas cover has a rip in it.** Could the fabric be mended?

W1 Well, Carmen's our upholsterer. **58 Carmen, do you have time to repair a canvas cover this afternoon?**

W2 **58 I'm fully booked with other requests today,** but I could get to it first thing Monday morning.

| 남 | 안녕하세요. 56 기본 유지 보수를 위해 보트를 가져오는 것에 대해 문의하려고 들렀어요. 전에 여기 서비스를 이용한 적이 있습니다. |

남 안녕하세요. 56 기본 유지 보수를 위해 보트를 가져오는 것에 대해 문의하려고 들렀어요. 전에 여기 서비스를 이용한 적이 있습니다.

여1 그렇군요. 오늘 오후까지 보트를 가져올 수 있으시면 시간이 있어요. 그냥 점검만 하실 건가요?

남 네. 57 그런데 캔버스 덮개에 찢어진 부분도 있어요. 천도 수선 가능한가요?

여1 어, 카르멘이 이곳의 직공이에요. 58 카르멘, 오늘 오후에 캔버스 덮개를 수선할 시간 되시나요?

여2 58 오늘은 다른 요청들로 예약이 꽉 찼지만, 월요일 아침에 가장 먼저 처리할 수 있어요.

어휘 stop by 잠깐 들르다 maintenance 유지 보수 tune-up (차량이나 보트 등의) 점검, 정비 rip 찢어진 곳 mend 수선하다 upholsterer 직공

---

56 화자들은 무엇에 대해 논의하고 있는가?
(A) 보트 유지 보수 (B) 실내 장식
(C) 퍼레이드 준비 (D) 차량 대여

해설 **대화의 주제**
남자가 첫 대사에서 기본 유지 보수를 위해 보트를 가져오는 것에 대해 문의하려고 들렀다(I'm just stopping by to ask about bringing in my boat for some basic maintenance)고 한 뒤, 관련 내용에 관한 대화가 이어지므로 (A)가 정답이다.

57 남자는 어떤 구체적인 문제를 언급하는가?
(A) 송장이 잘못되었다. (B) **직물이 찢어졌다.**
(C) 악천후가 예상된다. (D) 열쇠가 없어졌다.

해설 **남자가 언급한 문제점**
남자가 마지막 대사에서 캔버스 덮개에 찢어진 부분도 있다(But also my canvas cover has a rip in it)며 문제를 언급했으므로 (B)가 정답이다.

어휘 invoice 송장 torn 찢어진(tear - tore - torn)
predict 예상하다

(Paraphrasing) 대화의 my canvas cover has a rip
→ 정답의 Some material is torn.

58 카르멘은 왜 오늘 오후에 남자를 돕지 못하는가?
(A) 관리자의 통보를 기다리고 있다.
(B) 오전 근무만 한다.
(C) **다른 할 일이 있다.**
(D) 치과 예약이 있다.

해설 **카르멘이 남자를 돕지 못하는 이유**
첫 번째 여자가 두 번째 여자를 카르멘이라고 부르며 오늘 오후에 캔버스 덮개를 수선할 시간이 되는지(Carmen, do you have time to repair a canvas cover this afternoon?)묻자 두 번째 여자가 오늘은 다른 요청들로 예약이 꽉 찼다(I'm fully booked with other requests today)고 했으므로 (C)가 정답이다.

어휘 supervisor 관리자 shift (교대) 근무

(Paraphrasing) 대화의 I'm fully booked with other requests → 정답의 She has other work to do.

M 59 The workers have cleared out all the exhibits from the Hall of Chinese Sculptures. The top museum donors will sit at a table at the head of the room. 60 Can you help me with the rest of the seating chart for the appreciation dinner?

W 59 I'm on my way to give a tour now.

M OK. When you're done, let's discuss what else is left to do.

W Sure. Oh, I just remembered that 61 we need to print the name tags for everyone so that they're ready when the guests arrive. Could you take care of that?

남 59 직원들이 중국 조각 전시실에 있는 전시품을 전부 치웠어요. 박물관에 기부를 가장 많이 한 사람들이 맨 앞에 있는 탁자에 앉을 겁니다. 60 감사 만찬을 위한 좌석 배치도에서 나머지 부분 좀 도와주실 수 있나요?

여 59 지금 관람객을 안내하러 가는 길이에요.

남 그렇군요. 끝나면 남은 일에 대해 논의해 봅시다.

여 그래요. 아, 방금 생각났는데 61 손님들이 도착했을 때 준비되도록 명찰을 인쇄해야 해요. 처리해 주실 수 있나요?

어휘 exhibit 전시품 donor 기부자 appreciation 감사

---

59 화자들은 어디에서 일하는 것 같은가?
(A) 공장 (B) 대학교
(C) **박물관** (D) 여행사

해설 **화자들의 근무 장소**
남자가 첫 대사에서 직원들이 중국 조각 전시실에 있는 전시품을 전부 치웠다(The workers have cleared out all the exhibits from the Hall of Chinese Sculptures)면서 박물관에 기부를 가장 많이 한 사람들이 맨 앞에 있는 탁자에 앉을 것(The top museum donors will sit at a table at the head of the room)이라고 한 뒤, 여자에게 도움을 요청하는 말에 여자가 지금 관람객을 안내하러 가는 길(I'm on my way to give a tour now)이라고 대답했으므로 (C)가 정답이다.

60 여자가 "지금 관람객을 안내하러 가는 길이에요"라고 말할 때 무엇을 의미하는가?
(A) **일을 도울 수 없다.**
(B) 늦게 도착하는 것을 용납할 수 없다.
(C) 최근에 훈련을 마쳤다.
(D) 남자가 투어에 참여했으면 한다.

해설 **화자의 의도**
남자가 첫 대사에서 감사 만찬을 위한 좌석 배치도에서 나머지 부분 좀 도와줄 수 있는지(Can you help me with the rest of the seating chart for the appreciation dinner?) 물었고 이에 대한 응답으로 여자가 인용문을 언급했으므로 (A)가 정답이다.

---

61 여자는 남자에게 무엇을 해 달라고 요청하는가?

(A) 케이터링 업체에 전화　　**(B) 명찰 인쇄**

(C) 손님 교통편 준비　　(D) 소책자 검토

해설 **여자의 요청 사항**

여자가 마지막 대사에서 손님들이 도착했을 때 준비되도록 명찰을 인쇄해야 한다(we need to print the name tags for everyone so that they're ready when the guests arrive)면서 처리해 줄 수 있는지(Could you take care of that?) 물었으므로 (B)가 정답이다.

어휘 arrange 준비하다　brochure 소책자

[62-64] W-Am / M-Au　　　　　**평면도**

W	Hello, Ivan. **62 I'm so glad you and your crew are available today to load my furniture and boxes onto your truck.** I can't wait to get settled in my new apartment.
M	**62 Thanks for hiring us.** We'll be careful not to scratch or damage anything. Where should we start?
W	Please start with the antique table. It's the heaviest thing I own. **63 Just go straight down to the end of this hallway. See the window on the end? There's a door right next to it. It's in that room.**
M	Sure. We'll start with the table.
W	**64 Also, I've left some refreshments out for you.** Please help yourselves while you're working.

여	안녕하세요, 아이반. **62 사장님과 직원들이 오늘 제 가구와 상자들을 트럭에 실어 주실 수 있어서 천만다행이에요.** 얼른 새 아파트에 자리 잡고 싶어요.
남	**62 저희 업체를 이용해 주셔서 감사합니다.** 하나도 긁히거나 손상되지 않도록 주의하겠습니다. 어디부터 시작할까요?
여	골동품 탁자부터 시작해 주세요. 제가 가진 것 중에 가장 무거워요. **63 이 복도를 따라 끝까지 쭉 가세요. 끝에 창문 보이세요? 창문 바로 옆에 문이 있어요. 그 방 안에 있어요.**
남	알겠습니다. 탁자부터 시작하겠습니다.
여	**64 그리고 여러분을 위해 다과도 좀 놓아두었어요.** 일하시는 동안 마음껏 드세요.

어휘 settle 정착하다　antique 골동품의　refreshments 다과

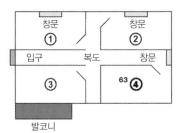

62 남자는 누구인 것 같은가?

(A) 건축가　　(B) 이삿짐 운송업자

(C) 부동산 중개업자　　(D) 건물 관리인

해설 **남자의 직업**

여자가 첫 대사에서 사장님과 직원들이 오늘 제 가구와 상자들을 트럭에 실을 수 있어서 천만다행(I'm so glad you and your crew are available today to load my furniture and boxes onto your truck)이라고 하자 남자가 우리 업체를 이용해 줘서 고맙다(Thanks for hiring us)고 했으므로 (B)가 정답이다.

63 시각 정보에 따르면, 여자는 어느 방을 가리키는가?

(A) 1호실　　(B) 2호실

(C) 3호실　　**(D) 4호실**

해설 **시각 정보 연계**

여자가 두 번째 대사에서 이 복도를 따라 끝까지 쭉 가면 끝에 창문이 보인다(Just go straight down to the end of this hallway. See the window on the end?)고 하면서 창문 바로 옆에 문이 있는데(There's a door right next to it) 그 방 안에 있다(It's in that room)고 했다. 평면도를 보면 복도 끝 창문 옆에 문이 있는 방은 4호실이므로 (D)가 정답이다.

64 여자는 무엇을 제공하는가?

(A) 보너스　　**(B) 다과**

(C) 전동 공구　　(D) 계약

해설 **여자가 제공하는 것**

여자가 마지막 대사에서 여러분을 위해 다과도 좀 놓아두었다(Also, I've left some refreshments out for you)고 했으므로 (B)가 정답이다.

어휘 power tool 전동 공구

[65-67] W-Br / M-Cn　　　　　**웹 드롭다운 메뉴**

W	Hi. **65 I'm here to pick up a cake.** My name is Nanping Wei.
M	Oh, sorry. I don't see a cake here for you. When did you order it?
W	I ordered it online last week. It's for a graduation party tomorrow.
M	Let me check the system. When you placed your order, you chose your pickup location from the drop-down menu. According to the system, you chose our downtown store. **66 This is the Walnut Street store.**
W	Oh, I don't have time to go downtown to get the cake.
M	**67 I'll give them a call. They should be able to deliver the cake here within an hour.** You can come back and pick it up.

여	안녕하세요. **65** 케이크 찾으러 왔어요. 제 이름은 난핑 웨이입니다.
남	죄송합니다. 여기는 손님 케이크가 없네요. 언제 주문하셨나요?
여	지난주에 인터넷으로 주문했어요. 내일 졸업 파티에 쓸 건데요.
남	시스템을 확인해 볼게요. 주문하실 때 드롭다운 메뉴에서 찾을 장소를 선택하셨네요. 시스템에 따르면 시내 매장을 선택하셨고요. **66** 여기는 월넛 가 매장입니다.
여	저런, 케이크를 가지러 시내에 갈 시간이 없는데요.
남	**67** 제가 그쪽에 전화할게요. 1시간 내에 여기까지 케이크를 배달할 수 있을 겁니다. 다시 와서 찾아가세요.

어휘 place an order 주문하다

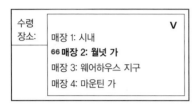

65 남자는 어떤 종류의 업체에서 일하는가?
(A) 제과점
(B) 가구점
(C) 미술용품점
(D) 호텔

해설 **화자가 일하는 업체의 종류**
여자가 첫 대사에서 케이크를 찾으러 왔다(I'm here to pick up a cake)고 했고 이후 주문한 케이크에 관한 대화가 이어지므로 (A)가 정답이다.

66 시각 정보에 따르면, 대화는 어느 매장에서 이루어지고 있는가?
(A) 매장 1
(B) 매장 2
(C) 매장 3
(D) 매장 4

해설 **시각 정보 연계**
남자가 두 번째 대사에서 시스템에 따르면 손님은 시내 매장을 선택했는데 여기는 월넛 가 매장(This is the Walnut Street store)이라고 알려 주고 있다. 웹 드롭다운 메뉴를 보면 월넛 가 매장은 매장 2이므로 (B)가 정답이다.

67 남자는 무엇을 하겠다고 말하는가?
(A) 송장 조회하기
(B) 구매품 환불하기
(C) 대체 품목 제공하기
(D) 배송 일정 잡기

해설 **남자가 하겠다고 하는 일**
여자가 마지막 대사에서 케이크를 가지러 시내에 갈 시간이 없다고 하자 남자가 그쪽에 전화하겠다(I'll give them a call)면서 1시간 내에 여기까지 케이크를 배달할 수 있다(They should be able to deliver the cake here within an hour)고 했으므로 (D)가 정답이다.

어휘 replacement 대체(품)

[68-70] W-Am / M-Cn 요금표

W	**68** Manor Hotel. How can I help you?
M	Hi. Do you have a room available for next Saturday?
W	We do! And you're in luck: **68** we've teamed up with Woodworth Gardens to offer package deals including admission to the gardens this weekend.
M	Really? Even for a one-night stay? **69** I'll only be in town for one night. My store is open on Sundays, and I need to be there to work the register.
W	Yes, we charge daily rates with and without admission to the gardens. **70** So, you'd like a single, right?
M	**70** That's right—and I'll definitely be visiting the gardens. I have a garden shop, and I'd love to get some inspiration!
여	**68** 매너 호텔입니다. 무엇을 도와드릴까요?
남	안녕하세요. 다음 주 토요일에 빈방 있나요?
여	있어요! 운이 좋으시네요. **68** 이번 주말에 우드워스 가든과 협력해 정원 입장을 포함한 패키지 상품을 제공해요.
남	정말요? 1박도요? **69** 저는 시내에서 하룻밤만 묵어요. 제 가게가 일요일마다 문을 여는데 계산대에서 일하려면 거기 있어야 하거든요.
여	네, 저희는 정원 입장이 포함된 경우, 포함되지 않은 경우 따로 요금을 부과해요. **70** 그럼 싱글로 하시는 거죠?
남	**70** 맞아요. 그리고 꼭 정원을 방문할 겁니다. 정원용품 가게를 하고 있는 데 영감을 얻고 싶거든요!

어휘 team up with ~와 협력하다   register 계산대
charge 요금을 부과하다   inspiration 영감

매너 호텔 주말 요금		
객실(1박)	정원 입장 미포함	**70** 정원 입장 포함
70 싱글	70달러	**70** 90달러
더블	80달러	100달러

68 매너 호텔은 이번 주말에 무엇을 하는가?
(A) 부지 개선
(B) 무료 조식 제공
(C) 현지 업체와 제휴
(D) 연례 축제 개최

해설 **호텔이 이번 주말에 할 일**
여자가 첫 대사에서 매너 호텔(Manor Hotel)이라고 전화를 받은 뒤에 두 번째 대사에서 이번 주말에 우드워스 가든과 협력해 정원 입장을 포함한 패키지 상품을 제공한다(we've teamed up with Woodworth Gardens to offer package deals including admission to the gardens this weekend)고 했으므로 (C)가 정답이다.

(Paraphrasing) 대화의 teamed up with Woodworth Gardens → 정답의 Partnering with a local business

69 남자는 왜 하룻밤만 묵을 수 있다고 말하는가?

(A) 남자의 사업체가 일요일마다 문을 연다.
(B) 예산이 한정되어 있다.
(C) 이른 시간에 회의가 있다.
(D) 일요일에 파티에 참석한다.

해설 **남자가 하루만 묵을 수 있는 이유**
남자가 두 번째 대사에서 시내에서 하룻밤만 묵는다(I'll only be in town for one night)면서 가게가 일요일마다 문을 여는데 계산대에서 일하려면 거기 있어야 한다(My store is open on Sundays, and I need to be there to work the register)고 했으므로 (A)가 정답이다.

(Paraphrasing) 대화의 My store is open on Sundays → 정답의 His business is open on Sundays.

70 시각 정보에 따르면, 남자는 얼마를 지불할 것인가?

(A) 70달러   (B) 80달러
(C) 90달러   (D) 100달러

해설 **시각 정보 연계**
여자가 마지막 대사에서 싱글로 하는 건지(So, you'd like a single, right?) 물어보자 남자가 맞다(That's right)고 한 뒤, 꼭 정원을 방문하겠다(I'll definitely be visiting the gardens)고 했다. 요금표를 보면 정원 입장이 포함된 싱글 요금은 90달러이므로 (C)가 정답이다.

PART 4

[71-73] 여행 정보

> W-Br I hope you're enjoying the scenic views on our bus tour so far. We're approaching the town of Littleton. **71 Littleton is famous for its bread and cakes.** We'll be stopping there for two hours, which is plenty of time to have a piece of cake and take a ferry ride on Lake Ashmore. And remember—**72 it may be warm and sunny, but out on the lake, it gets chilly, so bring a jacket. 73 If you mention that you're with our tour company at the ferryboat office, you'll receive a reduced rate on your ticket.**
>
> 지금까지 버스 투어에서 경치를 즐기고 계시길 바랍니다. 우리는 리틀턴 마을에 가까워지고 있는데요. 71 리틀턴은 빵과 케이크로 유명하죠. 그곳에 2시간 동안 머물 예정인데, 케이크 한 조각 먹고 애쉬모어 호수에서 배를 타기에 넉넉한 시간입니다. 그리고 명심하세요. 72 날씨가 따뜻하고 화창할 수도 있지만 호수로 나가면 쌀쌀하니 재킷을 챙기세요. 73 연락선 사무실에 저희 여행사에서 왔다고 이야기하시면 티켓 요금을 할인 받을 수 있습니다.
>
> 어휘 scenic 경치가 좋은   approach 다가가다
> chilly 쌀쌀한   ferryboat 연락선   rate 요금

71 화자에 따르면, 리틀턴은 무엇으로 유명한가?

(A) 도자기   (B) 빵류
(C) 역사 건축물   (D) 등산로

해설 **리틀턴에서 유명한 것**
초반부에서 리틀턴은 빵과 케이크로 유명하다(Littleton is famous for its bread and cakes)고 했으므로 (B)가 정답이다.

어휘 porcelain pottery 도자기   architecture 건축물
trail 등산로

(Paraphrasing) 담화의 bread and cakes → 정답의 Baked goods

72 화자는 청자에게 무엇을 하도록 상기시키는가?

(A) 무리에서 떨어지지 않기   (B) 제시간에 버스로 돌아오기
(C) 사진 찍기   (D) 따뜻한 옷 가지고 가기

해설 **화자가 청자들에게 상기시키는 것**
후반부에 날씨가 따뜻하고 화창할 수도 있지만 호수로 나가면 쌀쌀하니 재킷을 챙기라(it may be warm and sunny, but out on the lake, it gets chilly, so bring a jacket)고 했으므로 (D)가 정답이다.

(Paraphrasing) 담화의 bring a jacket
→ 정답의 Bring warm clothing

73 청자들은 어떻게 할인을 받을 수 있는가?

(A) 메일 목록에 등록해서   (B) 온라인에 후기를 올려서
(C) 여행사 이름을 언급해서   (D) 쿠폰을 사용해서

해설 **청자들이 할인 받는 방법**
후반부에 연락선 사무실에 우리 여행사에서 왔다고 이야기하면 티켓 요금을 할인 받을 수 있다(If you mention that you're with our tour company at the ferryboat office, you'll receive a reduced rate on your ticket)고 했으므로 (C)가 정답이다.

(Paraphrasing) 담화의 mention that you're with our tour company → 정답의 mentioning a tour company name
담화의 a reduced rate → 질문의 a discount

[74-76] 광고

> W-Am Centerville Apartments are now available for rent. **74 These beautiful two- and three-bedroom apartments are conveniently located near the city's main train station.** That makes it easy to live without a car! **75 Plus, we've recently renovated every apartment to be more energy efficient.** We added extra insulation and energy-efficient heating and cooling systems to help you keep your utility costs down. **76 And if you sign a lease by the end of April, we'll give you a ten percent discount on your first month's rent.** Call Centerville Real Estate at 555-1212 today to schedule a viewing.
>
> 센터빌 아파트는 이제 임대가 가능합니다. 74 침실이 두세 개인 멋진 아파트는 도시의 주요 기차역 근처 편리한 위치에 있습니다.

따라서 차 없이도 편리하게 생활할 수 있습니다! **75 게다가 최근에 에너지 효율을 높이기 위해 모든 아파트를 개조했습니다.** 공과금을 낮추는 데 도움이 되도록 추가 단열재와 에너지 효율적인 냉난방 시스템을 추가했습니다. **76 또한 4월 말까지 임대 계약을 체결하면 첫 달 임대료에서 10퍼센트 할인해 드립니다.** 오늘 센터빌 부동산 555-1212로 전화해 구경하는 일정을 잡으세요.

> **어휘** conveniently 편리하게 insulation 단열 utility cost 공과금 real estate 부동산

74 화자에 따르면, 아파트 근처에 무엇이 위치하고 있는가?
(A) 도시공원 　　　　　(B) 대학교
(C) 기차역 　　　　　(D) 쇼핑센터

해설 **아파트 근처에 위치한 것**
초반부에 침실이 두세 개인 멋진 아파트는 도시의 주요 기차역 근처 편리한 위치에 있다(These beautiful two- and three-bedroom apartments are conveniently located near the city's main train station)고 했으므로 (C)가 정답이다.

75 화자가 강조하는 건물의 새로운 특징은 무엇인가?
(A) 보안 강화 　　　　　**(B) 에너지 효율**
(C) 지붕이 있는 주차장 　　(D) 부지 내 보관 공간

해설 **화자가 강조하는 건물의 새로운 특징**
중반부에 게다가 최근에 에너지 효율을 높이기 위해 모든 아파트를 개조했다(Plus, we've recently renovated every apartment to be more energy efficient)고 했으므로 (B)가 정답이다.

어휘 emphasize 강조하다 enhance 강화하다

76 4월 말까지 제공되는 특별 혜택은 무엇인가?
(A) 할인된 임대료 　　　(B) 무료 인터넷 접속
(C) 이사 지원 　　　　　(D) 체육관 회원권

해설 **4월 말까지 제공되는 것**
후반부에 4월 말까지 임대 계약을 체결하면 첫 달 임대료에서 10퍼센트 할인해 준다(And if you sign a lease by the end of April, we'll give you a ten percent discount on your first month's rent)고 했으므로 (A)가 정답이다.

어휘 assistance 지원, 보조

[77-79] 전화 메시지

> **M-Au** Hello, Mr. Roberston. This is Vivek Bora, returning your call. **77 You sought legal advice from my firm last week to address your concern that a rival company is using branding very similar to your company's.** **78 Specifically, you had a complaint about the company's logo.** Well, I've looked into the competitor's branding and the similarities are clear. **79 Please let me know when you can meet with me this week to discuss the next steps.**

안녕하세요, 로버스턴 씨. 비벡 보라입니다. 회신 전화 드립니다. **77 지난주에 경쟁사가 귀사와 아주 흡사한 브랜드를 사용하고 있어서 우려를 해결하기 위해 저희 회사에 법률 자문을 구하셨죠. 78 특히 그 회사 로고에 불만이 있으시고요.** 음, 제가 경쟁사의 브랜드를 조사해 봤는데 유사성이 명백합니다. **79 다음 단계에 대해 논의하기 위해 이번 주에 저와 언제 만날 수 있는지 알려 주세요.**

> **어휘** seek 구하다 legal 법적인 firm 기업 address 해결하다 concern 우려

77 화자는 누구인 것 같은가?
(A) 변호사 　　　　　(B) 택배 기사
(C) 광고주 　　　　　(D) 컴퓨터 기술자

해설 **화자의 직업**
초반부에 의뢰인을 상대로 지난주에 경쟁사가 귀사와 아주 흡사한 브랜드를 사용하고 있어서 우려를 해소하기 위해 우리 회사에 법률 자문을 구했다(You sought legal advice from my firm last week ~)고 했으므로 (A)가 정답이다.

어휘 courier 택배 기사, 택배 회사 advertiser 광고주

78 화자가 "유사성이 명백합니다"라고 말할 때 무엇을 의미하는가?
(A) 로고가 효과적이다.
(B) 고소가 타당하다.
(C) 지침이 사용하기 쉽다.
(D) 제품의 품질을 확인해야 한다.

해설 **화자의 의도**
중반부에 의뢰인이 특히 그 회사 로고에 불만이 있었다(Specifically, you had a complaint about the company's logo)고 하면서 자신이 경쟁사의 브랜드를 조사해 봤다(Well, I've looked into the competitor's branding)고 한 뒤, 인용문을 언급했으므로 (B)가 정답이다.

어휘 effective 효과적인 justify 타당성을 입증하다

79 화자는 어떤 정보를 요청하는가?
(A) 회의 일자 　　　　　(B) 연락처 목록
(C) 회의 장소 　　　　　(D) 여행 일정표

해설 **화자가 요청하는 정보**
후반부에 다음 단계에 대해 논의하기 위해 이번 주에 언제 만날 수 있는지 알려 달라(Please let me know when you can meet with me this week to discuss the next steps)고 했으므로 (A)가 정답이다.

어휘 contact 연락처 itinerary 여행 일정표

> (Paraphrasing) 담화의 when you can meet with me
> → 정답의 A meeting date

[80-82] 여행 정보

> **W-Br** **80 Now that you've been to the field and seen where the oregano grows, let's continue our tour inside. This room is where we hang the herbs to dry,** which means the humidity in here has to be kept very low. **81 We have this large**

dehumidifier in the middle of the room that drains all the moisture to the outside. Now — it looks like all these oregano stems are ready for packaging. **82 Who would like some samples to take home?**

80밭에 가서 오레가노가 자라는 곳을 봤으니 실내 투어를 계속하죠. 이 방은 허브를 매달아 말리는 곳인데요. 이곳 습도를 매우 낮게 유지해야 한다는 의미죠. 81방 한가운데에 커다란 제습기가 있어 습기를 전부 빨아들여 밖으로 배출합니다. 자, 오레가노 줄기들이 전부 포장할 상태가 된 것 같군요. 82샘플을 집으로 가져가고 싶으신 분?

어휘 field 밭 humidity 습기 dehumidifier 제습기 drain 배출시키다 moisture 수분 stem 줄기

80 화자의 농장은 무엇을 생산하는가?

(A) 치즈   **(B) 허브**

(C) 커피   (D) 과일

해설 **농장의 생산품**

초반부에 밭에 가서 오레가노가 자라는 곳을 봤으니 실내 투어를 계속하자(Now that you've been to the field and seen where the oregano grows, let's continue our tour inside)며 이 방은 허브를 매달아 말리는 곳(This room is where we hang the herbs to dry)이라고 이어서 소개하고 있으므로 (B)가 정답이다.

81 장치는 무엇을 돕는가?

(A) 기계 리필   (B) 방문자 관찰

(C) 실내 기후 조절   (D) 배송 추적

해설 **장치가 돕는 것**

화자가 중반부에 방 한가운데에 커다란 제습기가 있어 습기를 전부 빨아들여 밖으로 배출한다(We have this large dehumidifier in the middle of the room that drains all the moisture to the outside)고 했으므로 (C)가 정답이다.

어휘 climate 기후 track 추적하다

(Paraphrasing) 담화의 drains all the moisture to the outside → 정답의 Controlling an indoor climate

82 청자들은 무엇을 하도록 권유받았는가?

(A) 향기 맡기   (B) 포장지 디자인하기

(C) 질문하기   **(D) 샘플 가져가기**

해설 **청자가 권유받은 일**

후반부에 샘플을 집으로 가져가고 싶은 사람이 있는지(Who would like some samples to take home?) 물었으므로 (D)가 정답이다.

어휘 fragrance 향기

[83-85] 연설

M-Cn Good morning, everyone. **83 We're approaching the end of our ten-week training**

program that you've been participating in to secure a city bus driver position with our company. **84 We'll be handing out the uniforms next week, so to help ensure we order one that fits you correctly, please select the appropriate size next to your name on the list that I'm passing around.** Thanks. OK, let's start by taking a little time to go over the different fare brackets that passengers will be charged when boarding your vehicle. **85 For example, people who are retired and are carrying special identification are eligible for a discounted fare.**

안녕하세요, 여러분. 83저희 회사에서 시내버스 기사로 일하기 위해 참여해 주신 10주간의 교육 프로그램이 막바지에 이르렀네요. 84다음 주에 유니폼을 배부할 테니 몸에 맞는 유니폼을 주문할 수 있도록 제가 돌리고 있는 목록에서 이름 옆에 적절한 사이즈를 선택해 주세요. 감사합니다. 자, 먼저 승객이 차량에 탑승할 때 부과되는 다양한 요금 체계부터 잠시 살펴보도록 하죠. 85예를 들어 은퇴자와 특수 신분증을 소지한 분들은 할인 요금을 적용 받을 수 있습니다.

어휘 ensure 확실하게 하다 appropriate 적절한 fare 요금 bracket 구간 board 탑승하다 retired 은퇴한 identification 신분증 be eligible for ~할 자격이 있다

83 청자들은 어떤 직책을 위해 교육을 받고 있는가?

(A) 버스 기사   (B) 택시 운전사

(C) 배달 트럭 기사   (D) 자동차 대여업체 직원

해설 **청자들이 교육 받는 직책**

초반부에 우리 회사에서 시내버스 기사로 일하기 위해 참여한 10주간의 교육 프로그램이 막바지에 이르렀다(We're approaching the end of our ten-week training program that you've been participating in to secure a city bus driver position with our company)고 했으므로 (A)가 정답이다.

84 화자는 어떤 정보를 요청하는가?

(A) 일정 가능 여부   **(B) 옷 치수**

(C) 개인 연락처   (D) 이전 운전 경력

해설 **화자가 요청하는 정보**

중반부에 다음 주에 유니폼을 배부한다(We'll be handing out the uniforms next week)면서 몸에 맞는 유니폼을 주문할 수 있도록 돌리고 있는 목록에서 이름 옆에 적절한 사이즈를 선택해 달라(so to help ensure we order one that fits you correctly, please select the appropriate size next to your name on the list that I'm passing around)고 했으므로 (B)가 정답이다.

(Paraphrasing) 담화의 uniforms → 정답의 Clothing

85 화자에 따르면, 누가 할인을 받을 수 있는가?

(A) 대학생   (B) 의료인

(C) 은퇴자   (D) 충성 고객 프로그램 회원

해설 할인을 받을 수 있는 사람

후반부에 은퇴자와 특수 신분증을 소지한 사람은 할인 요금을 적용 받을 수 있다(For example, people who are retired and are carrying special identification are eligible for a discounted fare)고 했으므로 (C)가 정답이다.

어휘 loyalty 충성

(Paraphrasing) 담화의 people who are retired
→ 정답의 Retired individuals

[86-88] 회의 발췌

> **W-Am** We've called tonight's meeting to discuss the proposed closure of a section of Main Street. **86 As government representatives, we all have a responsibility to make decisions that benefit the residents we represent.** The purpose of this street closure would be to create a pedestrian walkway and attract more visitors to the city's shopping district. **87 Before we vote on this matter, however, we'll need input from all high-ranking officials, including Lauren Stewart, the director of transportation.** But as you know, Lauren is at a conference. **88 So instead, tonight we'll go over the proposed budget figures for this project.** Please refer to page ten in your handouts.
>
> 메인 가의 한 구간을 폐쇄하자는 안건에 대해 논의하기 위해 오늘 밤 회의를 소집했습니다. **86** 정부 대표로서 우리 모두는 우리가 대표하는 주민들에게 이익이 되는 결정을 내릴 책임이 있습니다. 이번 도로 폐쇄의 목적은 보행자 통로를 만들고 도시의 쇼핑 지구에 더 많은 방문객을 끌어들이는 것입니다. **87** 그러나 이 문제에 대해 투표하기 전에, 교통국장인 로렌 스튜어트를 비롯한 모든 고위 관리의 의견이 필요할 겁니다. 하지만 알다시피 로렌은 회의에 참석하고 있습니다. **88** 그러니 대신 오늘 밤에는 이 프로젝트의 제안된 예산 수치를 검토하겠습니다. 유인물 10페이지를 참조해 주십시오.
>
> **어휘** propose 제안하다 closure 폐쇄 representative 대표(자) responsibility 책임 official (고위) 관리 refer to ~을 참조하다 handout 유인물

86 청자들은 누구인가?
(A) 건설 노동자　　　　(B) 사업주
(C) 정부 관리　　　　(D) 텔레비전 기자

해설 청자들의 직업

초반부에서 정부 대표로서 우리 모두는 우리가 대표하는 주민들에게 이익이 되는 결정을 내릴 책임이 있다(As government representatives, we all have a responsibility to make decisions that benefit the residents we represent)고 했으므로 (C)가 정답이다.

(Paraphrasing) 담화의 government representatives
→ 정답의 Government officials

87 화자가 "로렌은 회의에 참석하고 있습니다"라고 말할 때 무엇을 의미하는가?
(A) 자원봉사자가 필요할 것이다.
(B) 결정은 다른 시간에 할 것이다.
(C) 회의 내용을 기록해야 한다.
(D) 회의는 일찍 끝날 것이다.

해설 화자의 의도

중반부에 이 문제에 대해 투표하기 전에, 교통국장인 로렌 스튜어트를 비롯한 모든 고위 관리의 의견이 필요하다(Before we vote on this matter, however, we'll need input from all high-ranking officials, including Lauren Stewart, the director of transportation)고 한 뒤, 인용문을 언급했으므로 (B)가 정답이다.

88 청자들은 다음에 무엇을 할 것인가?
(A) 제안된 예산 검토하기　　(B) 건설 현장 견학하기
(C) 건축 투시도 살펴보기　　(D) 시민 불만 사항 해결하기

해설 청자들이 다음에 할 일

후반부에 로렌이 회의 중이므로 투표 대신 오늘 밤에는 이 프로젝트의 제안된 예산 수치를 검토하겠다(So instead, tonight we'll go over the proposed budget figures for this project)고 했으므로 (A)가 정답이다.

어휘 architectural 건축의 rendering 투시도

(Paraphrasing) 담화의 go over → 정답의 Review

[89-91] 담화

> **W-Br** Welcome to our site for this archaeological dig. A few preliminaries before we get started. **89 If you haven't already read our safety guide, please read through it tonight.** Also, at our last dig, a lot of tools went missing. To avoid losing anything this year, I've prepared these checklists that we'll use every day to keep track of who has what. **90 You'll report which tools you're taking and returning to Narumi every morning and evening. 91 Now, a project of this size normally takes a few months.** We have enough funding for six weeks.
>
> 이번 고고학 발굴 현장에 오신 것을 환영합니다. 시작하기 전에 몇 가지 사전 준비 사항이 있어요. **89** 아직 안전 지침을 읽지 않으셨다면 오늘 밤에 읽어 보시기 바랍니다. 그리고 지난번 발굴 과정에서 도구가 많이 사라졌어요. 올해는 하나라도 분실하는 일이 없도록 매일 누가 무엇을 가지고 있는지 추적하는 데 사용할 점검 목록을 준비했습니다. **90** 여러분은 매일 아침과 저녁에 어떤 도구를 가져가고, 반납하는지를 나루미에게 보고하게 됩니다. **91** 자, 이 정도 규모의 프로젝트는 보통 몇 달이 걸리는데요. 우리에겐 6주 치 자금이 있습니다.
>
> **어휘** archaeological 고고학의 dig 발굴 preliminary 사전 준비 avoid 피하다 keep track of ~을 추적하다 funding 자금

89 화자는 청자들에게 무엇을 읽으라고 요청하는가?
(A) 재고 목록
(B) 신문 기사
(C) 계약서
(D) 안전 지침

해설 **청자들이 읽어야 할 것**
초반부에 아직 안전 지침을 읽지 않았다면 오늘 밤에 읽어 보라(If you haven't already read our safety guide, please read through it tonight)고 했으므로 (D)가 정답이다.

어휘 inventory 재고   contract 계약(서)

90 나루미가 맡은 책임은 무엇인가?
(A) 식비 상환하기
(B) 도구 사용 내역 추적하기
(C) 작업 할당하기
(D) 기자들과 이야기하기

해설 **나루미가 맡은 책임**
중반부에 매일 아침과 저녁에 어떤 도구를 가져가고, 반납하는지를 나루미에게 보고하게 된다(You'll report which tools you're taking and returning to Narumi every morning and evening)고 했으므로 (B)가 정답이다.

어휘 reimburse 상환하다   expense 비용   distribute 분배하다   assignment 배정, 할당

91 화자가 "우리에겐 6주 치 자금이 있습니다"라고 말할 때 무엇을 의미하는가?
(A) 청자들은 일정을 조정해야 한다.
(B) 청자들은 빨리 작업해야 한다.
(C) 장비를 더 주문해야 한다.
(D) 조수들이 고용될 예정이다.

해설 **화자의 의도**
후반부에 이 정도 규모의 프로젝트는 보통 몇 달이 걸린다(Now, a project of this size normally takes a few months)고 한 뒤, 인용문을 언급했으므로 (B)가 정답이다.

어휘 adjust 조정하다   assistant 조수, 보조

[92-94] 방송

M-Au This is WKLO radio in Clarksville with an interesting story in today's community news segment! **92 Last month, local musician Lolade Iyanda needed a couch. After finding a used one listed online, she purchased it from the owners.** It fit perfectly in her apartment. This week, when removing the seat covers to place them in the washing machine, **93 she was surprised to find 1,000 dollars inside the cushions.** She immediately returned the money. Well, the thankful sellers have contacted our radio station hoping to generate free publicity for Ms. Iyanda's upcoming piano recital at Bryant Hall. She's a talented pianist, **94 so everyone please stop by on Friday at seven o'clock to support her!**

클락스빌에 있는 WKLO 라디오입니다. 오늘의 지역 뉴스 코너에 흥미진진한 이야기가 있습니다! **92지난달 지역 음악가 롤레이드 이얀다는 소파가 필요했죠.** 온라인에 올라온 중고 소파를 발견하고 주인들에게 샀고요. 이얀다 씨 아파트에 딱 맞았죠. 이번 주 이얀다 씨는 세탁기에 넣으려고 시트커버를 벗겼는데 **93쿠션 안에서 1,000달러를 발견하고는 깜짝 놀랐어요.** 이얀다 씨는 즉시 돈을 돌려줬습니다. 고마웠던 판매자들은 라디오 방송국에 연락해 브라이언트 홀에서 곧 열리는 이얀다 씨의 피아노 연주회를 무료로 홍보해 달라고 희망했죠. 이얀다 씨는 재능 있는 피아니스트이므로 **94모두 금요일 7시에 들러 응원해 주세요!**

어휘 segment 부분   couch 소파   publicity 홍보   upcoming 다가오는   stop by 들르다

92 이얀다 씨는 지난달에 무엇을 했는가?
(A) 새로운 일을 시작했다.
(B) 아파트를 임차했다.
(C) 가구를 구입했다.
(D) 멀리 이사했다.

해설 **이얀다가 지난달에 한 일**
초반부에 지난달 지역 음악가 롤레이드 이얀다는 소파가 필요했다(Last month, local musician Lolade Iyanda needed a couch)고 한 뒤, 온라인에 올라온 중고 소파를 발견하고 주인들에게 샀다(After finding a used one listed online, she purchased it from the owners)고 했으므로 (C)가 정답이다.

(Paraphrasing) 담화의 a couch → 정답의 some furniture

93 이얀다 씨는 왜 놀랐는가?
(A) 대회에서 우승했다.
(B) 옛날 친구와 다시 연락이 닿았다.
(C) 현금을 발견했다.
(D) 유난히 수도 요금이 많이 나온 고지서를 받았다.

해설 **이얀다가 놀란 이유**
중반부에 이얀다 씨가 쿠션 안에서 1,000달러를 발견하고는 깜짝 놀랐다(she was surprised to find 1,000 dollars inside the cushions)고 했으므로 (C)가 정답이다.

어휘 reconnect 다시 연락이 닿다   bill 고지서

(Paraphrasing) 담화의 1,000 dollars → 정답의 some cash

94 화자는 청자들에게 무엇을 하라고 권장하는가?
(A) 곡 신청
(B) 악기 기부
(C) 광고란 구입
(D) 공연 참석

해설 **화자가 청자들에게 권장하는 것**
후반부에 이얀다 씨의 공연을 홍보하는 이유를 언급하며 모두 금요일 7시에 들러 응원해 달라(so everyone please stop by on Friday at seven o'clock to support her!)고 했으므로 (D)가 정답이다.

어휘 donate 기부하다   instrument 악기

(Paraphrasing) 담화의 piano recital
→ 정답의 a performance

[95-97] 담화 + 그래프

M-Cn At our last board meeting, **95 I talked about an initiative to help reduce waste by packaging our cereal in smaller boxes.** We conducted a pilot this past month and found that **96 the cereal selected for the tryout yielded our worst-performing sales.** We believe that our consumers might think they're getting less product. Right now, we're working with an outside advertising firm to help spread the word that the product weight remains the same. **97 Our new ads will start running in two weeks,** so I expect to have more positive data to share at our next quarterly meeting.

지난번 이사회에서 **95 저는 시리얼을 더 작은 상자에 포장해 폐기물 감소에 도움이 되는 계획에 대해 이야기했는데요.** 지난달에 시범 운영을 해보니 **96 시험해 보려고 선택한 시리얼이 최악의 매출 실적을 냈어요.** 소비자들은 양이 더 적은 제품을 받는다고 생각하는 듯합니다. 저희는 지금 제품 무게가 그대로라는 사실을 퍼뜨리기 위해 외부 광고 회사와 협력하고 있습니다. **97 새 광고가 2주 후에 방영될 예정이니** 다음 분기 회의에서 더 많은 긍정적인 데이터를 공유하리라 기대합니다.

어휘 board 이사회 initiative 계획 conduct 수행하다 pilot 시범 tryout 시험 yield (수익을) 내다 spread 퍼뜨리다 remain 남아 있다 quarterly 분기의

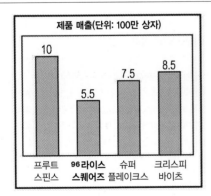
제품 매출(단위: 100만 상자)

95 화자는 주로 무엇에 대해 이야기하는가?
(A) 가격 인상 (B) 신제품 라인
(C) 성분 변경 **(D) 포장 변경**

해설 **담화의 주제**
초반부에 지난번 이사회에서 시리얼을 더 작은 상자에 포장해 폐기물 감소에 도움이 되는 계획에 대해 이야기했다(I talked about an initiative to help reduce waste by packaging our cereal in smaller boxes)고 말한 뒤 관련 내용을 이어가고 있으므로 (D)가 정답이다.

어휘 ingredient 성분, 재료 modification 변경

96 시각 정보에 따르면, 어떤 시리얼이 시범 프로젝트에 사용되었는가?
(A) 프루트 스핀스 **(B) 라이스 스퀘어즈**
(C) 슈퍼 플레이크스 (D) 크리스피 바이츠

해설 **시각 정보 연계**
초반부에 지난달에 시험해 보려고 선택한 시리얼이 최악의 매출 실적을 냈다(the cereal selected for the tryout yielded our worst-performing sales)고 했다. 그래프에서 매출이 가장 낮은 제품은 라이스 스퀘어즈이므로 (B)가 정답이다.

97 2주 후에 무슨 일이 일어날 것인가?
(A) 광고 캠페인이 시작된다.
(B) 임원이 퇴직한다.
(C) 생산 시설이 다시 문을 연다.
(D) 제품 라인이 단종된다.

해설 **2주 후에 있을 일**
후반부에 새 광고가 2주 후에 방영될 예정(Our new ads will start running in two weeks)이라고 했으므로 (A)가 정답이다.

어휘 executive 임원 discontinue 중단되다

(Paraphrasing) 담화의 new ads will start running
→ 정답의 An advertising campaign will start.

[98-100] 전화 메세지 + 삽화

W-Am Hi, it's Sung-Hee. Just some quick updates. My janitorial team cleaned the filters on the new vacuum cleaners. It was relatively easy, **98 but it took longer than expected for the filters to dry.** We had to leave them outside for a full day. **99 Murat had a good idea about spraying an air freshener on the filter.** It'll leave a nice smell in the room when we're done cleaning. We're going to try it on our next assignment. Oh, and **100 I'll be submitting an extra expense report this week.** We helped another team clean and had to refuel the company van an extra time.

안녕하세요. 성희예요. 몇 가지 간단한 새 소식입니다. 청소팀이 새 진공청소기 필터를 세척했습니다. 비교적 쉬웠지만 **98 필터가 마르는 데 예상보다 오래 걸렸어요.** 하루 종일 외부에 놔둬야 했죠. **99 무라트가 필터에 방향제를 뿌리는 좋은 아이디어를 생각해 냈어요.** 청소가 끝나면 방에 좋은 냄새가 남을 거예요. 다음 임무 때 한번 시도해 보려고요. 아, 그리고 **100 이번 주에 추가 경비 보고서를 제출하려 합니다.** 다른 팀의 청소를 도왔고 회사 밴에 주유를 한 번 더 해야 했어요.

어휘 janitorial 청소의 relatively 비교적 air freshener 방향제 refuel 재급유하다 reinstall 재설치하다

140

1단계: 제거하세요.	2단계: 비누와 온수로 씻으세요.
98 3단계: 4시간 동안 말리세요.	4단계: 다시 설치하세요.

98 시각 정보에 따르면, 어느 단계가 예상대로 진행되지
않았는가?

(A) 1단계   (B) 2단계
(C) 3단계   (D) 4단계

해설 시각 정보 연계

초반부에 필터가 마르는 데 예상보다 오래 걸렸다(but it took longer than expected for the filters to dry)고 했다. 삽화를 보면 말리는 단계는 3단계이므로 (C)가 정답이다.

99 무라트는 무엇을 하자고 제안했는가?

(A) 연장된 보증 구매
(B) 향기 나는 제품 사용
(C) 차량 청소
(D) 잠재 고객에게 엽서 보내기

해설 무라트의 제안 사항

중반부에 무라트가 필터에 방향제를 뿌리는 좋은 아이디어를 생각해 냈다(Murat had a good idea about spraying an air freshener on the filter)고 했으므로 (B)가 정답이다.

어휘 warranty 보증(서)   scented 향기가 나는   potential 잠재적인

(Paraphrasing) 담화의 spraying an air freshener
→ 정답의 Using a scented product

100 화자는 이번 주에 어떤 서류를 추가로 제출할 예정인가?

(A) 경비 보고서   (B) 시간표
(C) 재고 보고서   (D) 안전 점검표

해설 추가로 제출할 서류

후반부에 이번 주에 추가 경비 보고서를 제출하려 한다(I'll be submitting an extra expense report this week)고 했으므로 (A)가 정답이다.

(Paraphrasing) 담화의 an extra expense report
→ 질문의 additional document

PART 5

101 명사 자리_동사의 목적어

번역 오델 씨는 내일 새 팀장에 대한 결정을 내릴 것이라고 말했다.

해설 빈칸은 동사 make의 목적어 역할을 하며 소유격 대명사 her의 수식을 받는 자리이다. 따라서 '결정'을 뜻하는 명사 (A) decision이 정답이다. (B) decides는 동사, (C) decisive는 형용사, (D) decisively는 부사로 품사상 빈칸에 들어갈 수 없다.

어휘 decisive 결정적인

102 접속사 자리_등위접속사

번역 주차장 이용은 매장 직원과 건물 주민에 한합니다.

해설 전치사 to의 목적어 역할을 하는 명사구 store employees와 building residents를 연결해 줄 등위접속사가 필요하다. '매장 직원과 건물 주민에 한정된다'는 내용이므로 등위접속사 (C) and가 정답이다. 등위접속사로 쓰일 때 (A) so와 (B) for는 절과 절만을 연결하고, (D) until은 전치사로서 명사구를 연결할 수는 있지만 의미상 적절하지 않다.

103 인칭대명사의 격_소유격

번역 아이워수 씨의 팀원들은 그의 강력한 리더십 능력을 높이 평가한다.

해설 빈칸은 「형용사 + 복합명사」로 이루어진 명사구 strong leadership skills를 한정 수식하는 자리이다. 따라서 명사구 앞에서 수식할 수 있는 소유격 인칭대명사인 (B) his가 정답이다.

어휘 appreciate 진가를 알아보다[인정하다]

104 부사 어휘

번역 바닥 닦는 기구를 다 사용하고 나면 청소 도구장에 다시 넣어 주세요.

해설 동사 put을 수식하여 '바닥 닦는 기구를 청소 도구장에 다시 넣어 달라'는 내용이 되어야 자연스러우므로 '(이전 장소로) 다시'라는 의미의 부사 (B) back이 정답이다. (A) easy와 (D) already는 문맥상 어울리지 않고, (C) very는 형용사나 부사 바로 앞에서 의미를 강조할 때 쓰인다.

어휘 polisher 닦는 기구   maintenance 유지 (관리)

105 명사 어휘

번역 많은 회사들이 직원들의 소셜 미디어 사용에 관한 정책을 업데이트하고 있다.

해설 빈칸은 동사 are updating의 목적어 자리이므로 회사에서 업데이트하는 대상이면서 동시에 빈칸 뒤 전치사구의 수식을 받아 '직원들의 소셜 미디어 사용에 관련된' 것이어야 한다. 따라서 '정책, 방침'을 뜻하는 (C) policies가 정답이다. (A) supplies는 '물품', (B)의 design은 '설계, 디자인', (D)의 occasion은 '경우'라는 의미이다.

어휘 regarding ~에 관하여

106 과거분사

번역 오늘 밤 자정 전에 주문된 모든 은 제품은 무료 배송됩니다.

해설 문장의 동사 will be shipped가 있으므로 빈칸은 주어 All silverware orders를 수식하는 자리이다. 빈칸 뒤에 목적어가 없고 전치사구 before midnight tonight과 함께 '오늘 밤 자정 전에 주문된 모든 은 제품'이라는 의미가 되어야 하므로 과거분사 (C) placed가 정답이다. 다른 보기는 모두 동사로 빈칸에 적절하지 않다.

어휘 silverware 은 제품   free of charge 무료로

107 부사 자리_동사 수식

번역 주민들은 실외 공용 공간을 이용할 때 소음 수준을 낮게 유지할 것을 정중히 요청받는다.

해설 빈칸은 be동사와 과거분사 asked 사이에서 동사구를 수식하는 부사 자리이므로, '공손하게, 정중하게'라는 의미의 부사 (D) respectfully가 정답이다. (A) respect는 명사/동사, (B) respectful은 형용사, (C) respective는 형용사이므로 품사상 빈칸에 들어갈 수 없다.

어휘 respective 각각의

108 형용사 자리_명사 수식

번역 리노는 기술 회사들이 본사를 설립하는 인기 있는 장소가 되고 있다.

해설 빈칸 앞에 부정관사 a, 뒤에 명사 place가 있으므로 명사를 수식하는 형용사 자리이다. 따라서 '인기 있는'을 뜻하는 형용사 (A) popular가 정답이다. (B) popularity는 명사로 place와 복합명사를 이루기에 부적절하고 (C) popularly는 부사, (D) popularize는 동사로 품사상 답이 될 수 없다.

어휘 establish 설립하다   headquarters 본사

109 동사 어휘

번역 블릭시안 컴퍼니의 조사로 많은 직원들이 장거리 출퇴근을 한다는 것을 알게 되었다.

해설 빈칸 뒤의 that절을 목적어로 취해 적절한 문맥을 만드는 동사 어휘를 고르는 문제이다. '직원들의 출퇴근 시간이 길다는 것을 알게 되었다'는 내용이 되어야 적절하므로 '발견하다, 알게 되다'를 뜻하는 find의 과거형 (B) found가 정답이다.

어휘 commute 통근하다; 통근(거리)

110 전치사 어휘

번역 이력서와 자기소개서를 제출하기 전에 지원 지침을 주의 깊게 읽으세요.

해설 동명사구 submitting your résumé and cover letter를 목적어로 취해 '이력서와 자기소개서를 제출하기 전에'라는 내용이 되어야 자연스러우므로 '전에'라는 뜻의 전치사 (C) before가 정답이다.

어휘 application 지원   cover letter 자기소개서

111 형용사 어휘

번역 예산이 너무 빠듯해서 콘퍼런스 기획자들은 참석자들을 위해 간단하고 저렴한 환영 행사를 계획했다.

해설 빈칸은 주어 the budget의 보어 자리이므로, budget을 수식하기에 적절한 형용사를 골라야 한다. 또한 빈칸 뒤에서 '간단하고 저렴한 행사를 계획했다'고 했으므로 그 이유가 되기에 적절하려면 '예산이 빠듯해서'라는 내용이 되어야 한다. 따라서 '빠듯한'이라는 뜻의 (D) tight가 정답이다.

어휘 coordinator 진행 담당자   low-cost 값싼

112 명사절 접속사

번역 귀사의 웹사이트에서 다음 번 구매 시 제가 할인을 받을 수 있는지 알려 주십시오.

해설 빈칸에는 let의 목적격 보어 자리에 들어간 동사 know의 목적어 역할을 하는 명사절을 이끄는 접속사가 필요하다. 따라서 '~인지 아닌지'라는 의미로 완전한 절을 이끄는 명사절 접속사 (D) whether가 정답이다. (A) then과 (B) often은 부사, (C) except는 전치사/부사절 접속사이므로 명사절을 이끌 수 없다.

어휘 be eligible to ~할 자격이 있다

113 형용사 자리_목적격 보어

번역 몽코 은행은 귀하의 개인 정보를 안전하게 지키기 위해 특별한 조치를 취하고 있습니다.

해설 빈칸은 to부정사 to keep의 목적격 보어 자리이다. to keep의 목적어 역할을 하는 명사 your personal information을 수식하여 '당신의 개인 정보를 안전하게 지킨다'는 내용이 되어야 하므로 '안전한'을 뜻하는 형용사 (A) safe가 정답이다. 명사인 (B) safety(안전)와 (C) saving(절약, 저금)도 보어 역할을 할 수는 있지만 personal information과 동격이 아니므로 빈칸에 적절하지 않다

어휘 extraordinary 특별한

114 명사절 접속사

번역 제품 마케팅 책임자는 동부 지역의 브랜드 인지도가 지속적으로 높아질 것이라고 확신한다.

해설 빈칸은 감정을 나타내는 형용사 confident 뒤에 완전한 절을 연결하는 자리이고, '브랜드 인지도가 계속 높아질 것이라고 확신한다'는 내용이 되어야 하므로 명사절 접속사 (A) that이 정답이다. (B) also는 부사, (C) about과 (D) of는 전치사이므로 빈칸 뒤의 절을 연결할 수 없다.

어휘 brand awareness 브랜드 인지도   region 지역

115 부사 어휘

번역 높은 배송 수요를 충족시키기 위해서는 모든 생산 팀에 초과 근무가 고르게 요구됩니다.

해설 be동사와 과거분사 required 사이에서 동사구를 수식하여 '초과 근무가 모든 생산 팀에 고르게 요구된다'는 의미가 되어야 적절하므로 '고르게'라는 뜻의 (C) evenly가 정답이다. (A) hardly는 '거의 ~않다', (B) eagerly는 '열렬하게', (D)

deeply는 '깊게'라는 의미이다.

어휘 demand 수요   overtime 초과 근무

116 동사 자리

번역 리스틀리 스마트워치는 심박수를 정확하게 측정하지만 48시간마다 재충전해야 합니다.

해설 빈칸은 주어 The Wristly smartwatch의 동사 자리이고, 빈칸 뒤에 목적어 heart rate가 있으므로 능동태가 와야 한다. 따라서 (B) tracks가 정답이다. (A) will be tracked는 수동태이므로 빈칸 뒤에 목적어가 없어야 하고, (C) tracking은 동명사/현재분사, (D) to track은 to부정사로 동사 자리에 들어갈 수 없다.

어휘 heart rate 심박수   recharge 재충전하다

117 명사 어휘

번역 파라즈 안타르는 뉴스 리포터로서 방송계에서 경력을 쌓기를 희망한다.

해설 빈칸은 to부정사 to pursue의 목적어 자리로 전치사구 in broadcasting as a news reporter의 수식을 받아 '뉴스 리포터로서 방송계에서의 경력'이라는 의미가 되어야 적절하다. 따라서 '경력, 직업'을 뜻하는 (D) career가 정답이다. (A) trail은 '자취, 자국', (B) view는 '견해', (C) purpose는 '목적'을 뜻한다.

어휘 pursue 추구하다, 계속하다   broadcasting 방송업

118 명사 어휘

번역 시상식 연회 메뉴에 대한 수정 사항은 수석 주방장인 델미로 로이스의 승인을 받아야 한다.

해설 전치사구 to the awards banquet menu의 수식을 받고 있으므로 시상식 연회 메뉴에 관한 것이고, 문장 뒤 내용으로 보아 수석 주방장의 승인을 받아야 하는 대상이어야 한다. '메뉴에 대한 수정 사항을 승인받아야 한다'는 내용이 되어야 적절하므로 '수정'을 뜻하는 (B) modifications가 정답이다. (A)의 reaction은 '반응', (C)의 administration은 '운영, 관리', (D)의 portion은 '부분, (음식의) 1 인분'이라는 의미이다.

어휘 awards banquet 시상식 연회

119 전치사 어휘

번역 어번 파이낸셜은 계좌 간 송금에 대해 수수료를 부과하지 않습니다.

해설 빈칸 뒤의 명사 accounts를 목적어로 취해 '계좌들 사이에 돈을 이체하는 것'이라는 내용이 되어야 적절하므로 '~ 사이에'를 뜻하는 (D) between이 정답이다.

어휘 charge 부과하다   transfer 이체하다   account 계좌

120 부정대명사

번역 지난달 3번가에 새로운 빵집이 문을 열기 전까지 아나스 브레드 컴퍼니는 스프링필드의 유일한 빵집이었다.

해설 until이 이끄는 부사절의 주어 역할을 하는 동시에 주절에 언급된 단수명사 bakery를 대신하면서 부정관사 a와 형용사 new의 수식을 받아 '새로운 곳(빵집)'을 의미하는 부정대명사가 필요하므로 (C) one이 정답이다. 재귀대명사인 (A) itself는 주어 역할을 하지 않고, (B) whose와 (D) another는 관사나 형용사의 수식을 받지 않는다.

121 부사 어휘

번역 책이 상자에 너무 빽빽하게 포장되면 강한 압력으로 제본이 변형될 수 있다.

해설 부사 too와 함께 동사구 are packed를 수식하여 '너무 빽빽하게 포장되면'이라는 의미가 되어야 자연스러우므로 '빽빽하게'를 뜻하는 (B) closely가 정답이다. (A) keenly는 '예리하게', (C) patiently는 '참을성 있게', (D) greatly는 '대단히'라는 의미이다.

어휘 pressure 압력   deform 변형시키다   binding 제본

122 동사 자리

번역 관객들에게 최상의 경험을 주기 위해 콘서트홀의 음향 설계가 조정되고 있다.

해설 문장에 동사가 보이지 않으므로 빈칸은 동사 자리이다. 주어 The concert hall's acoustical design은 3인칭 단수이고 빈칸 뒤에 목적어가 없으므로 단수동사 수동태가 들어가야 한다. 따라서 정답은 (D) is being adjusted이다. (A) adjustment와 (C) adjuster는 명사로 품사상 들어갈 수 없고, (B) were adjusting은 복수동사 능동태이므로 답이 될 수 없다.

어휘 acoustical 음향의

123 형용사 어휘

번역 접객업에서 경쟁력을 갖기 위해 많은 호텔이 손님들에게 푸짐한 아침 식사를 제공한다.

해설 경쟁 우위를 차지하기 위해 호텔에서 손님들에게 제공하는 아침 식사 breakfast를 수식하기에 적절한 형용사를 골라야 한다. 따라서 '푸짐한 아침 식사'라는 의미가 되어야 적절하므로 '(식사가) 푸짐한'이라는 뜻의 (C) hearty가 정답이다. (A) steady는 '꾸준한', (D) positive는 '긍정적인'이라는 의미로 문맥상 어울리지 않고, 감정을 나타내는 분사 (B) satisfied는 '만족하는'이라는 뜻으로 감정을 느끼는 주체를 수식하므로 답이 될 수 없다.

어휘 competitive 경쟁력 있는   hospitality 접대

124 부사 자리_동사 수식

번역 내일 워크숍 안건을 마무리하기 위해 경영진의 의견을 긴급히 요청합니다.

해설 빈칸은 is와 requested 사이에서 동사를 수식하는 부사 자리이므로 '긴급하게'라는 뜻의 부사 (D) urgently가 정답이다. (A) urged는 동사/과거분사, (B) urgent는 형용사, (C) urgency는 명사이므로 품사상 답이 될 수 없다.

어휘 input 의견, 조언   agenda 안건

125 전치사 어휘

번역 그 안에 포함된 민감한 정보 때문에 작성된 양식을 이메일로 보내서는 안 된다.

해설 빈칸은 완전한 절에 명사구 the sensitive information을 연결하는 자리로 전치사가 들어가야 한다. 문맥상 '민감한 정보 때문에'라는 내용이 되어야 하므로 '~ 때문에'를 뜻하는 전치사 (A) On account of가 정답이다. (B) Such as는 '~ 같은', (C) Rather than은 '~보다는'이라는 뜻으로 의미상 적합하지 않고, (D) As though는 부사절 접속사로 뒤에 절이 와야 한다.

어휘 sensitive 민감한   contain ~이 들어 있다

126 명사 자리_동사의 목적어

번역 우리 컨설턴트들은 초기의 대폭 할인이 고객들이 쇼핑 클럽에 가입하는 충분한 동기를 제공할 것이라는 데 동의한다.

해설 빈칸은 동사 provide의 목적어 자리이고 형용사 enough의 수식을 받고 있으므로 명사가 들어가야 한다. 따라서 명사인 (B) motivation과 (D) motivator 중에 선택해야 한다. 빈칸 앞에 관사나 소유격이 없어 가산 단수명사인 (D) motivator(동기 요인)는 들어갈 수 없으므로 '동기, 계기'를 뜻하는 불가산명사 (B) motivation이 정답이다. (A) motivate와 (C) motivates는 동사로 품사상 답이 될 수 없다.

어휘 steep 급격한   initial 초기의

127 형용사 어휘

번역 최 씨의 고용은 일시적이었지만, 우리 회사에 대한 그녀의 기여는 지속적인 영향을 미쳤다.

해설 앞 문장에서 '최 씨의 고용은 일시적이었음에도 불구하고'라고 했으므로 뒤에는 반대되는 내용이 와야 한다. 따라서 명사 effect를 수식하여 '지속적인 영향'이라는 의미가 되어야 적절하므로 '지속적인'을 뜻하는 (A) lasting이 정답이다. (B) presenting은 '제시하는', (C) falling은 '떨어지는', (D) covering은 '덮는'이라는 뜻으로 문맥상 어울리지 않는다.

어휘 temporary 일시적인   contribution 기여

128 부정대명사

번역 인턴들은 금요일 오후 2시에 업무를 마칠 수 있는 선택권을 받았지만, 그렇게 하기로 선택한 사람은 거의 없었다.

해설 등위접속사 but이 이끄는 절의 주어 역할을 하는 동시에 주절에 언급된 The interns 중 일부를 대신할 수 있는 대명사가 필요하다. 빈칸 뒤에 복수동사 have가 이어지고 있으므로 복수 취급하는 부정대명사 (A) few가 정답이다. (B) nobody, (C) such, (D) anyone은 모두 단수 취급하므로 단수동사가 와야 한다.

129 동사 어휘

번역 하니니 패션즈는 분기마다 가장 많은 판매 전화를 한 직원에게 포상한다.

해설 가장 많은 판매 전화를 한 직원을 목적어로 취해 적절한 문맥을 이루는 동사를 골라야 한다. 문맥상 '직원에게 포상한다'는 의미가 되어야 자연스러우므로 '(상 등을) 수여하다'를 뜻하는 (C) honors가 정답이다. (A)의 remind는 '상기시키다', (B)의 offer는 '제공하다', (D)의 admit은 '인정하다'라는 뜻이다.

130 전치사 자리

번역 눈이 오는 날씨의 경우, 시내버스 운행이 지연되거나 취소될 수 있습니다.

해설 빈칸은 콤마 뒤의 완전한 절에 명사구 snowy weather를 연결하는 자리이므로 전치사가 들어가야 한다. 또한 '눈이 오는 날씨의 경우에는'이라는 의미가 되어야 하므로 '~인 경우'를 뜻하는 (B) In the event of가 정답이다. (A) As much as는 명사구를 연결할 수는 있지만 '~만큼'이라는 의미로 문맥상 부적합하고, (C) In order that과 (D) Even though는 부사절 접속사이므로 답이 될 수 없다.

PART 6

[131-134] 정보

> 브랜트머 B10 토스터 오븐을 구입하신 것을 축하드립니다. 기기를 작동시키기 전에 설명서를 주의 깊게 읽어 주십시오. 이 **131 기기**는 실내 사용 전용으로 제작된 것에 유의해 주십시오. **132 이것은** 실외 또는 사용자가 없는 상태에서 절대 작동해서는 안 됩니다. 브랜트머에 의해 제조된 모든 토스터는 출고하기 전 엄격한 검사와 테스트 과정을 거칩니다. B10 모델은 제조상 결함이 있을 경우 브랜트머가 무상으로 기기를 교체해 줄 것을 명시한 1년 보증서에 **133 의해** 보장됩니다. **134 부적절한 사용의 증거는 이 보증을 무효화합니다.**

> **어휘** unit (상품의) 한 개   intend 의도하다   setting 환경   undergo 겪다   rigorous 엄격한   inspection 검사   back 뒷받침하다   warranty 보증(서)   state 명시하다

131 명사 어휘

해설 앞 문장에서 브랜트머 B10 토스터 오븐(the Brantmerr B10 toaster oven)을 구입하신 것을 축하드린다며 기기(the unit)를 작동시키기 전에 설명서를 주의 깊게 읽으라고 한 것으로 보아, 빈칸이 있는 문장은 브랜트머 B10 토스터 오븐에 대해 설명하는 내용임을 알 수 있다. 따라서 빈칸에는 토스터 오븐을 대신할 수 있는 명사가 들어가야 하므로 '(가정용) 기기'를 뜻하는 (D) appliance가 정답이다. (A) part는 '부품', (B) material은 '재료', (C) furniture는 '가구'라는 의미이다.

132 대명사 어휘

해설 빈칸은 동사 should never be operated의 주어 자리이므로 주격 대명사가 들어가야 한다. 또한 실외 또는 사용자가 없는 상태에서 작동되어서는 안 된다는 내용으로 보아, 앞 문장에서 언급된 브랜트머 B10 토스터 오븐(the Brantmerr B10 toaster oven)에 대해 추가로 설명하는 문장임을 알

수 있다. 따라서 토스터 오븐, 기기를 대신 받는 대명사가 들어가야 하므로 (A) It이 정답이다. (B) Any는 '아무(것)'을 뜻하는 부정대명사이므로 정해진 명사를 받을 수 없고, (C) What은 명사절 접속사, (D) We는 단수 사물명사를 대신할 수 없으므로 답이 될 수 없다.

133 전치사 어휘

해설 수동태 is backed 뒤에 연결되는 전치사로, 빈칸 뒤의 명사구 a one-year warranty를 목적어로 취해 '1년 보증서에 의해 보장된다'는 의미가 되어야 한다. 따라서 '~에 의해'라는 의미의 (A) by가 정답이다.

134 문맥에 맞는 문장 고르기

번역 (A) 저희는 이제 자사 공장을 견학할 수 있도록 고객들을 초대합니다.
(B) 제품 디자인에 대한 사소한 변경은 매년 이루어집니다.
(C) 부적절한 사용의 증거는 이 보증을 무효화합니다.
(D) 브랜트머는 모든 전자제품에 대해 재활용 프로그램을 지원할 예정입니다.

해설 빈칸 앞에서 B10 모델은 제조상 결함이 있을 경우 무상으로 기기를 교체해 줄 것을 명시한 1년 보증서에 의해 보장된다(The B10 model is backed by a one-year warranty ~ if there are any manufacturing defects)고 했으므로, 빈칸에는 제품 보증과 관련된 내용이 이어져야 일관성 있는 문맥이 완성된다. 따라서 부적절하게 사용한 증거가 있을 경우 보증이 무효가 된다며 제품을 보증 받기 위한 요건에 대해 추가로 안내하고 있는 (C)가 정답이다.

어휘 minor 사소한 alteration 변경 improper 부적절한 usage 사용 void 무효로 하다 guarantee 보증, 보장

[135-138] 회람

> **회람**
> 수신: 전 직원
> 발신: 서비스 혁신팀
> 날짜: 9월 26일
> 제목: 성사 되었습니다!
>
> 좋은 소식입니다! 정부 당국에서 새해 첫날부터 자사 놈벡스 전자 창고에서 드론으로 부품을 배송할 수 있는 허가를 내주었습니다. 각각의 드론은 왕복 비행 거리가 16킬로미터입니다. 이로써 우리는 무려 20곳이나 되는 지역 제조업체 및 기관에 **135 도달할** 수 있게 됩니다. 드론은 **136 완전히** 자동입니다. 드론은 GPS, 탑재 컴퓨터, 인공 지능을 이용하여 목적지까지 길을 찾아가고 스스로 돌아옵니다. **137 그것들은 특정 무게와 크기 이하의 짐만 운반할 수 있습니다.** 너무 크거나 무거운 배송물은 당사의 택배 트럭 서비스로 배송됩니다.
>
> 드론이 실제로 작동하는 것을 보고 싶은 직원들은 이번 주 금요일 오후 3시에 서쪽 주차장에서 열리는 **138 시연회**에 참석할 수 있습니다.

어휘 be a go 가능하다, 성사되다 government official 정부 관리, 공무원 grant 승인하다 component 부품 warehouse 창고 round-trip 왕복의 enable 가능하게 하다 institution 기관 automated 자동인 onboard 탑재된 artificial intelligence 인공 지능 on one's own 스스로 courier 택배 (회사)

135 동사 어휘

해설 앞 문장에서 정부 당국에서 우리 창고에서 드론으로 부품을 배달할 수 있는 허가(permission to deliver components)를 내주었다면서 드론의 왕복 거리가 16킬로미터(a round-trip range of 16 kilometers)라고 했으므로, '이로써 업체 및 기관 20곳에 드론으로 도달할 수 있다'는 내용이 되어야 적합하다. 따라서 '~에 이르다, 도달하다'라는 뜻의 (B) reach가 정답이다. (A) invoice는 '청구서를 보내다', (C) attract는 '끌어들이다', (D) call은 '전화하다'라는 의미이다.

136 부사 자리_동사 수식

해설 수동태 동사구인 be동사 are와 과거분사 automated 사이에서 동사를 수식하는 부사 자리이므로 '완전히'라는 의미의 부사 (D) fully가 정답이다. (A) full은 형용사. (B) fullest는 형용사 full의 최상급. (C) fullness는 명사이므로 품사상 답이 될 수 없다.

137 문맥에 맞는 문장 고르기

번역 (A) 우리 엔지니어링 부서에서도 여러 특허를 출원했습니다.
(B) 수중 드론은 해저 탐험에 사용되고 있습니다.
(C) 그것들은 특정 무게와 크기 이하의 짐만 운반할 수 있습니다.
(D) 당사의 연례 세일은 같은 기간 동안 열립니다.

해설 빈칸 뒤에서 너무 크거나 무거운 배송물은 택배 트럭 서비스로 배송된다(Shipments that are too big or heavy will be delivered by our courier truck service)고 했으므로, 빈칸에는 드론이 배송할 수 있는 배송물의 크기 및 무게와 관련된 내용이 들어가야 앞뒤 문맥의 연결이 자연스럽다. 따라서 드론(They)은 특정 무게와 크기 이하의 짐만 운반할 수 있다고 언급하는 (C)가 정답이다.

어휘 patent 특허(권) load 짐 period 기간, 시기

138 명사 자리_동사의 목적어

해설 빈칸은 동사 may attend의 목적어 자리이고 빈칸 앞에 부정관사가 있으므로 명사가 들어가야 한다. 명사 보기인 (A) demonstration과 (B) demonstrator 중, 문맥상 '시연회에 참석할 수 있다'는 의미가 되어야 하므로 '시연'을 뜻하는 (A) demonstration이 정답이다. (B) demonstrator는 '시연자'를 뜻하므로 attend의 목적어로 적합하지 않고, (C) demonstrated는 동사/과거분사, (D) demonstrate는 동사로 품사상 들어갈 수 없다.

[139-142] 이메일

수신: karl.blankenship@myrtlemail.net
발신: phyllis_casares@rochestercity.gov
날짜: 6월 8일
제목: 답장: 엘름 가

블랭켄십 씨께:

38번 주간 고속도로의 혼잡을 피하고자 엘름 가를 이용하는 운전자의 수가 증가했음을 알리는 메시지를 보내 주셔서 감사합니다. **139귀하의 몇몇 이웃들도 의견을 제출해 주셨습니다.** 이 상황은 **140일시적인** 것임을 유념해 주십시오. 건설 작업자들이 도로 포장 작업을 완료하는 동안 고속도로가 단일 북행 차선으로 축소되었습니다. 공사는 향후 4일 이내에 완료될 예정입니다. **141그동안**, 경찰이 해당 지역을 순찰하도록 할 것입니다. 교통량을 **142모니터링하기 위해** 레이더 속도 감지기를 설치할 예정입니다. 이러한 조치들로 교통 흐름과 지역 안전이 개선되기를 바랍니다.

필리스 카사레스, 부국장
도시 교통국

어휘 motorist 운전자   congestion 혼잡   interstate 주간(州間) 고속도로   northbound 북행의   lane 차선   paving (도로) 포장   patrol 순찰하다   detector 감지기   measure 조치

139 문맥에 맞는 문장 고르기

번역 (A) 귀하께서 다음 회의에 참석하시는 것을 환영합니다.
(B) 그들은 정기적으로 우리의 대중교통 시스템을 이용합니다.
(C) 우리는 그것이 성장한 속도에 감명받았습니다.
(D) 귀하의 몇몇 이웃들도 의견을 제출해 주셨습니다.

해설 빈칸 앞에서 38번 고속도로의 혼잡을 피하고자 엘름 가를 이용하는 운전자 수가 증가했음을 알리는 메시지를 보내 주셔서 감사하다(Thank you for your message reporting the increased number of motorists using Elm Avenue to avoid the congestion on Interstate 38)고 했으므로, 빈칸에는 교통 혼잡과 관련된 신고가 접수되고 있는 상황에 대한 내용이 들어가야 일관성 있는 문맥이 완성될 수 있다. 따라서 귀하의 몇몇 이웃들도 의견을 제출하였다고 유사한 상황을 추가로 언급하고 있는 (D)가 정답이다.

어휘 regularly 정기적으로   rate 속도   submit 제출하다

140 형용사 어휘

해설 빈칸 뒤 문장에서 도로포장 작업을 완료하는 동안(while the construction crew completes some paving work) 고속도로가 1차선으로 축소되었고 공사가 향후 4일 이내에 완료될 것(scheduled to be completed within the next four days)이라고 했으므로 '이 상황은 일시적인 것'이라는 내용이 되어야 적합하다. 따라서 '일시적인'을 뜻하는 (B) temporary가 정답이다. (A) identical은 '동일한', (C) impossible은 '불가능한', (D) doubtful은 '의심스러운'이라는 의미이다.

141 접속부사

해설 앞 문장에는 공사는 향후 4일 이내에 완료된다(completed within the next four days)고 했고, 빈칸 뒤에는 경찰이 그 지역을 순찰하도록 할 것이라며 공사 기간에 이루어질 조치에 대해 안내하고 있다. 따라서 앞에서 언급된 '공사가 완료되는 동안'을 한마디로 표현해 줄 수 있는 '그동안'이라는 의미의 (D) In the meantime이 정답이다. (A) If so는 '만약 그렇다면', (B) After all은 '결국에는', (C) On the contrary는 '그와는 반대로'라는 뜻이다.

142 to부정사_부사적 용법

해설 빈칸 앞에 완전한 절이 있고 빈칸 뒤에 명사구가 왔으므로, 빈칸에는 앞에 나온 완전한 절을 수식하면서 뒤에 온 명사구를 목적어로 취할 수 있는 to부정사가 와야 한다. 따라서 정답은 (A) to monitor이다.

[143-146] 편지

시어도어 뉴컴
에드먼턴 백화점
900 35번가 웨스트
에드먼턴, 앨버타주 T5J 2R4

9월 16일

뉴컴 씨께,

지난주에 저의 오래된 직립형 진공청소기의 대체품을 찾으러 귀하의 매장을 방문했습니다. 귀하의 직원인 사라이 제브린이 저에게 무선 모델을 **143고려해** 볼 것을 제안했습니다. 저는 제브린 씨에게 무선 진공청소기가 매력적인 것은 알겠지만 두 가지 걱정거리가 있다고 말했습니다. **144저는 무선 청소기가 너무 비쌀까 봐 걱정했습니다.** 또한 무선 모델이 제가 필요한 만큼 충분히 강력할지 회의적이었습니다. **145그녀는** 귀사에 제 가격선에 맞는 강력한 무선 청소기가 있다고 장담했습니다. 저는 그런 청소기가 있을 것이라 생각하지 않았습니다. 하지만 제브린 씨는 놀라울 정도로 성능이 좋은 몇 가지 모델을 시연해 주었습니다. 저는 더트 지니 진공청소기를 구입했고 기기의 성능에 매우 만족합니다. **146마찬가지로** 제브린 씨로부터 받은 서비스도 만족스러웠습니다!

레오라 황

어휘 upright 직립형의   vacuum (cleaner) 진공청소기   cordless 무선의   appealing 매력적인   skeptical 회의적인   assure 보장하다   demonstrate 시연하다

143 동사 어휘

해설 앞 문장에서 오래된 진공청소기를 대체할 제품을 찾으러 귀하의 매장을 방문했다(visited your store to find a replacement)고 했으므로, 빈칸이 있는 문장은 매장 직원이 제품을 추천하는 내용이 되어야 적합하다. 따라서 '직원이 저에게 무선 모델을 고려해 볼 것을 제안했다'는 의미가 되어야 하므로 '고려하다'를 뜻하는 (D) consider가 정답이다. (A) return은 '반납하다', (B) design은 '설계하다', (C) borrow는 '빌리다'라는 의미이다.

144 문맥에 맞는 문장 고르기

번역 (A) 에드먼턴 백화점에서 진공청소기 먼지 봉투를 샀다.
(B) 무선 진공청소기는 운반이 용이합니다.
(C) 저는 무선 청소기가 너무 비쌀까 봐 걱정했습니다.
(D) 진공청소기를 내려놓았을 때 조리대가 더러웠습니다.

해설 빈칸 앞에서 직원에게 무선 진공청소기가 매력적인 것은 알겠지만 두 가지 걱정거리가 있다고 말했다(I told ~ I had two concerns)고 했고, 빈칸 뒤에서 또한(also) 무선 모델이 충분히 강력할지 회의적이었다고 했으므로, 빈칸에는 두 가지 걱정거리 중 뒤 문장에 언급된 걱정거리를 제외한 나머지 하나에 대한 내용이 들어가야 자연스럽다. 따라서 무선 청소기가 너무 비쌀까 봐 걱정했다고 언급하고 있는 (C)가 정답이다.

어휘 countertop 조리대 drop off ~을 내려놓다

145 대명사 어휘

해설 빈칸은 동사 assured의 주어 자리이다. 빈칸 앞 내용에서 직원인 사라이 제브린(Sarai Jebreen)이 제품 모델을 제안했다고 했으므로, 작성자(me)에게 맞는 무선 청소기가 있다고 장담한 사람도 그 직원임을 알 수 있다. 따라서 Ms. Jebreen을 대신하는 인칭대명사인 (B) She가 정답이다.

146 부사 어휘

해설 앞 문장에서 자신이 진공청소기를 구입했고 기기의 성능에 매우 만족한다(I am delighted)고 했고, 빈칸이 있는 문장에서는 제브린 씨로부터 받은 서비스도 만족스럽다(I am pleased)고 했다. 따라서 앞뒤 문장 모두 만족 사항에 대해 언급하며 비슷한 내용이 연결되고 있으므로 '마찬가지로'라는 뜻의 (C) likewise가 정답이다.

PART 7

[147-148] 공지

타털리 호텔

날짜: 12월 7일
시간: 오후 8시 12분
객실 번호: 394
투숙객 성명: 조지아 할페린

할페린 씨께,

147 귀하의 문에서 '방해 금지' 표지판을 보았기 때문에 아래의 서비스를 할 수 없었습니다.

☐ 매일 청소 서비스 제공
☐ 보고된 유지 관리 문제 해결
☒ **147세탁 및 다림질한 옷 배달**
☐ 추가 세면도구 또는 수건 배달

고객님의 요청에 대한 지원을 받을 준비가 되시면 주야간 언제든 0번으로 프런트 데스크에 전화 주시거나 오전 8시부터 오후 7시 사이에 **148 메인 로비에 있는 게스트 서비스 데스크로 방문해 주십시오.**

즐거운 숙박 되시길 바랍니다!

어휘 address 해결하다 toiletries 세면도구 dial 전화를 걸다

---

147 할페린 씨는 호텔에 무엇을 요청했는가?

(A) 객실 청소 (B) 텔레비전 수리
(C) 세탁 서비스 (D) 여분의 비누

해설 **세부 사항**
첫 문장에서 할페린 씨에게 귀하의 문에서 '방해금지' 표지판을 보았기 때문에 아래의 서비스를 할 수 없었다(Because we saw a "Do Not Disturb" sign on your door, we were unable to do the following)고 했고, 두 번째 단락에 나열된 서비스 항목 중 세탁 및 다림질한 옷 배달(Deliver your washed and ironed clothing)에 표시가 되어 있다. 따라서 할페린 씨는 호텔에 세탁 서비스를 요청했다는 것을 알 수 있으므로 (C)가 정답이다.

(Paraphrasing) 지문의 washed and ironed clothing → 정답의 Laundry

148 게스트 서비스 데스크에 대해 언급된 것은?

(A) 24시간 운영된다.
(B) 메인 로비에 위치한다.
(C) 할페린 씨의 객실 열쇠를 가지고 있다.
(D) 할페린 씨에게 오전 8시에 전화할 예정이다.

해설 **Not/True**
세 번째 단락에서 메인 로비에 있는 게스트 서비스 데스크로 방문해 달라(visit the Guest Services desk in the main lobby)고 했으므로 게스트 서비스 데스크는 메인 로비에 있다는 것을 알 수 있다. 따라서 (B)가 정답이다.

[149-150] 광고

심플 뱅크의 역대 최고 혜택

12월 31일까지 심플 뱅크 신용카드에 가입하시고 100달러 보너스를 받으세요! **149 심플 뱅크의 신용카드는** Everyday-Consumers.com에서 올해 1위를 차지했고, 〈파이낸셜 뷰〉 잡지는 3년 연속 최고의 캐시백 카드로 선정했습니다. 모든 카드 소지자들은 아래의 혜택을 누립니다.

- **150 모든 매장 및 온라인 구매 시 3퍼센트 캐시백**
- 호텔 및 레스토랑 최대 5퍼센트 할인
- 버스, 기차, 경전철 요금 최대 10퍼센트 할인
- 연회비 없음

지금 www.simplebank.com/creditcard로 방문하셔서 가입하시고 보너스를 받으세요! 카드 소지자가 되기 위해 심플 뱅크에 당좌 예금이나 보통 예금 계좌는 없어도 됩니다.

어휘 name 지명하다 cardholder 카드 소지자 light-rail 경전철 fare 요금 checking account 당좌 예금 savings account 보통 예금

149 심플 뱅크 신용카드에 대해 명시된 것은?

(A) 금융 전문가들로부터 높은 평가를 받았다.

(B) 은행 계좌와 연결되어야 한다.

(C) 카드 소지자에게 연회비를 청구한다.

(D) 캐시백 및 기프트 카드 보상을 모두 제공한다.

해설 **Not/True**

첫 단락의 두 번째 문장에서 심플 뱅크의 신용카드는 Everyday-Consumers.com에서 올해 1위를 차지했고 〈파이낸셜 뷰〉 잡지는 3년 연속 최고의 캐시백 카드로 선정했다(Simple Bank's credit card received the top ranking this year from Everyday-Consumers. com, and *Financial View* magazine has named it the best cash-back card for three years in a row)고 했으므로 금융계에서 우수한 평가를 받고 있음을 알 수 있다. 따라서 정답은 (A)이다.

어휘 rate 평가하다 professional 전문가

Paraphrasing 지문의 received the top ranking, named it the best → 정답의 highly rated

150 가장 큰 할인을 받는 구매의 종류는 무엇인가?

(A) 레스토랑 식사   (B) 잡지 구독

(C) 호텔 숙박   (D) 교통 승차권

해설 **세부 사항**

혜택 항목에 모든 매장 및 온라인 구매 시 3퍼센트 캐시백(3% cash back on every in-store and online purchase), 호텔 및 레스토랑 최대 5퍼센트 할인(Up to a 5% discount on hotels and restaurants), 버스, 기차, 경전철 요금 최대 10퍼센트 할인(Up to a 10% discount on bus, train, and light-rail fares)이라고 나와 있으므로, 교통 요금에 적용되는 10퍼센트가 가장 높은 할인율임을 알 수 있다. 따라서 정답은 (D)이다.

어휘 subscription 구독 accommodation 숙박 시설

Paraphrasing 지문의 bus, train, and light-rail fares → 정답의 Transportation tickets

[151-152] 박물관 전시 공지

라다크 다르는 인도에서 가장 존경 받는 그래픽 소설가 중 한 명으로 남아 있는 다작 삽화가였습니다. 이 전시는 초기 스케치와 일지 일부를 포함한 그의 작품들을 전시합니다. **151 다르의 그래픽 소설이 다채롭고 환상적인 풍경을 묘사하지만, 많은 학자들은 그의 이야기가 그의 실제 삶에서 일어난 사건들에 어느 정도 기반을 두고 있다고 보고 있습니다.** 다르의 스케치와 일지는 이 이론을 뒷받침합니다. **152 다르의 일지는 또한 프로젝트별로 진행 과정을 기록한 별도의 일지를 두는 그의 꼼꼼한 기록 관리를 보여줍니다.** 다르의 근면함과 직업의식은 그가 어떻게 그런 엄청난 양의 작품을 제작할 수 있었는지를 설명해 줍니다.

어휘 prolific 다작하는 revered 존경 받는 depict 묘사하다 landscape 풍경 scholar 학자 loosely 대략 lend (지지 등을) 제공하다 reveal 드러내다 meticulous 꼼꼼한 progress 진전 diligence 근면 work ethic 직업의식[윤리] tremendous 엄청난 volume 양

151 공지에서 다르 씨의 그래픽 소설에 대해 암시하는 것은?

(A) 매장에서 구입할 수 없다.

(B) 많은 영화에 영감을 주었다.

(C) 완전히 허구는 아니다.

(D) 컴퓨터 그래픽을 이용해 제작되었다.

해설 **추론/암시**

세 번째 문장에서 다르의 그래픽 소설이 다채롭고 환상적인 풍경을 묘사하지만, 많은 학자들은 그의 이야기가 그의 실제 삶에서 일어난 사건들에 어느 정도 기반을 두고 있다고 보고 있다(While Dhar's graphic novels ~ his stories are loosely based on actual events from his life)고 한 것으로 보아 다르 씨의 작품이 허구로만 이루어진 것은 아님을 짐작할 수 있다. 따라서 정답은 (C)이다.

어휘 fictional 허구적인

152 공지에서 다르 씨의 일지에 대해 언급하는 것은?

(A) 몇 년 동안 비밀로 유지되었다.

(B) 그가 얼마나 체계적이었는지 보여준다.

(C) 다루기에 너무 섬세하다.

(D) 인도의 한 도서관에 기증되었다.

해설 **Not/True**

다섯 번째 문장에서 다르의 일지는 또한 프로젝트별로 진행 과정을 기록한 별도의 일지를 두는 그의 꼼꼼한 기록 관리를 보여준다(Dhar's journals also reveal his meticulous record keeping, with separate journals to track his progress on each project)고 했으므로 다르가 얼마나 체계적으로 일을 진행했는지를 알 수 있다. 따라서 정답은 (B)이다.

어휘 organized 체계적인, 조직적인 delicate 섬세한

[153-154] 문자 메시지

닝 수 [오전 10시 14분]

지금 건설 현장에 있는데 오늘 작업자들이 수도관을 설치할 겁니다. 그것들을 감쌀 단열재가 필요해요. 툴리빌 자재의 평소 연락 담당에게 전화했는데 곧장 음성 사서함으로 연결되네요. 툴리빌의 대표 번호가 있으세요? 우리가 지난번에 단열재가 필요했을 때 툴리빌에서 아주 빨리 배달해 줬거든요.

데이지 게라 [오전 10시 15분]

153 툴리빌이 우리가 미클린 프로젝트에 이용했던 공급업체 맞죠?

닝 수 (오전 10시 16분)

바로 거기예요.

데이지 게라 [오전 10시 17분]

분명히 어딘가에 대표 사무실 번호가 기재된 구매 주문서가 있을 거예요. 제가 찾는 대로 문자로 보내 드릴게요.

닝 수 [오전 10시 18분]

그러면 큰 도움이 될 것 같습니다. **154 그동안 저는 정확히 얼마나 요청해야 할지 알 수 있도록 단열재가 없는 파이프 치수를 다시 재 보겠습니다.**

어휘 insulation 단열재 materials 자재 vendor 판매사 remeasure 다시 재다 piping 관

153 오전 10시 16분에 수 씨가 "바로 거기예요"라고 쓴 의도는 무엇인가?

(A) 툴리빌 자재가 이전 건설 프로젝트를 도왔다.
(B) 툴리빌 자재는 현재 건설 현장과 가깝다.
(C) 게라 씨가 필요한 단열재의 종류를 확인했다.
(D) 게라 씨가 분실되었던 문서를 찾았다.

해설 의도 파악

10시 15분에 게라 씨가 툴리빌이 미클린 프로젝트에 이용한 공급업체가 맞는지(Tullyville is the vendor we used for the Micklin project, right?)를 묻자, 10시 16분에 수 씨가 바로 거기(That's the one)라고 답했다. 따라서 수 씨는 툴리빌이 과거 프로젝트를 도왔던 업체임을 확인해 주려는 의도로 한 말임을 알 수 있으므로 (A)가 정답이다

어휘 identify 확인하다 misplace 제자리에 두지 않다

154 수 씨는 다음에 무엇을 할 것 같은가?

(A) 추가 배관 주문하기
(B) 구매 주문서 읽기
(C) 미클린 프로젝트 현장 방문하기
(D) 치수 측정하기

해설 추론/암시

10시 18분에 수 씨가 그동안 자신은 정확히 얼마나 요청해야 할지 알 수 있도록 단열재가 없는 파이프 치수를 다시 재겠다(In the meantime, I'll go ahead and remeasure the uncovered piping ~)고 했으므로 정답은 (D)이다.

(Paraphrasing) 지문의 remeasure → 정답의 Take some measurements

[155-157] 기사

새로운 전기 페리 출시

오슬로 (8월 10일) — 드라멘 시스템즈가 월요일에 세 번째 순수 전기 페리를 출시했다. **155악셀레르 3은 영국 하리치와 네덜란드 로테르담 사이를 매일 두 번 운항할 예정이다.**

155이 네 시간짜리 페리 항로는 현재 전동 선박에 의해 운행되는 최장 항로가 될 것이다. 악셀레르 3의 출시는 전동 선박에 있어 중요한 순간이다. 이전에, 순수 전기 선박이 운항하는 최장 항로는 에욀란피오르를 가로지르는 30분짜리 항로였다.

오슬로에 본사를 둔 드라멘 시스템즈의 엔지니어들은 이 결실이 10년의 노력을 보여준다고 말했다. 그들은 페리가 장거리 항로를 운행할 수 있도록 혁신적인 배터리 시스템을 설계했다. **156이 페리는 이탈리아 제노바의 아피다빌 조선소에서 건조되었다.**

배터리는 이동 경로 양쪽에서 **157충전되어야** 한다. 이 페리는 향후 10년 안에 순수 전기 선단으로 전환할 것으로 예상되는 포메라 시라이더 서비스에서 운영하게 된다.

"이 항로의 전기 페리 전환은 배기가스를 크게 줄일 것으로 예상됩니다."라고 포메라 시라이더 서비스의 대변인 아가타 C. 바커가 말했다.

어휘 electric-powered 전동의 vessel 선박 mark ~임을 보여주다 innovative 혁신적인 shipyard 조선소 charge 충전하다 transition 전환하다; 전환 fleet 선단(船團) emission 배기가스, 배출물 spokesperson 대변인

155 기사에 따르면, 악셀레르 3에 관하여 중요한 점은 무엇인가?

(A) 기록적인 시간 안에 개발되었다.
(B) 전동 페리 중 최장 항로를 이동한다.
(C) 대단히 높은 속도로 이동한다.
(D) 드라멘 시스템즈가 설계한 최초의 선박이다.

해설 세부 사항

첫 번째 단락 두 번째 문장에서 악셀레르 3은 영국 하리치와 네덜란드 로테르담 사이를 매일 두 번 운항할 예정(The Akselere 3 will travel twice daily between ~)이라고 했고, 두 번째 단락 첫 문장에서 이 네 시간짜리 페리 항로는 현재 전동 선박에 의해 운행되는 최장 항로가 될 것(The four-hour ferry route will be the longest route currently served by an electric-powered vessel)이라고 했다. 따라서 악셀레르 3은 전동 페리 중 가장 긴 항로를 운행하게 될 것이므로 (B)가 정답이다.

어휘 record 기록적인 unusually 대단히

(Paraphrasing) 지문의 vessel → 정답의 ferry

156 악셀레르 3은 어디에서 건조되었는가?

(A) 하리치   (B) 로테르담
(C) 오슬로   (D) 제노바

해설 세부 사항

세 번째 단락의 세 번째 문장에서 이 페리는 이탈리아 제노바의 아피다빌 조선소에 의해 건조되었다(The ferry was constructed by Affidabile Shipyard in Genoa, Italy)고 했으므로 정답은 (D)이다.

157 네 번째 단락 1행의 "charged"와 의미가 가장 가까운 단어는?

(A) 지휘되다   (B) 동력이 공급되다
(C) 위탁되다   (D) 접근되다

해설 동의어 찾기

의미상 배터리는 '충전되어야' 한다는 뜻으로 쓰였으므로 '동력이 공급되다'를 뜻하는 (B) energized가 정답이다.

[158-160] 공지

침실 2개짜리 아파트 공실

몬태나주 빌링스 잭슨 가 3034

침실 2개, 욕실 1개로 구성된 이 매력적인 110제곱미터 넓이의 주거 공간은 12세대 아파트의 3층에 있습니다. 최신 식기세척기, 오븐, 냉장고가 있는 리모델링된 부엌이 특징입니다. 침실마다 대형 벽장이 있습니다.

158빌링스 시 중심부에 있는 잭슨 가와 풀먼 가의 교차로에 위치한 160이 건물은 트라이던트 나이트라이프 지구와 카스텐 대학교에서 도보 거리에 있습니다. 식료품점과 주말 농산물 시장도 인근에 있습니다. 8번과 15번 버스 노선을 통해 도시 전역으로 편리한 대중교통 이용이 가능합니다.

월세는 1,300달러입니다. 임대차 기간은 12개월이며 **159첫 번째 달과 마지막 달의 임차료에 상응하는 보증금을 지불해야 합니다.** 직접 둘러볼 일정을 잡으시려면 부동산 관리자 조안 라이트에게 406-555-0122로 연락하세요.

158 아파트에 대해 명시된 것은?

(A) 도시 중심부에 있다.
(B) 한때 학생 숙소로 사용되었다.
(C) 입주민을 위한 무료 주차가 제공된다.
(D) 건물의 12층에 있다.

해설 **Not / True**
두 번째 단락의 첫 문장에서 이 건물은 빌링스 시 중심부에 있
는 잭슨 가와 풀먼 가의 교차로에 위치한다(Located at the
intersection of Jackson and Pullman Avenues in
the heart of the city of Billings)고 했다. 따라서 아파
트가 도시 중심부에 있음을 알 수 있으므로 (A)가 정답이다.

(Paraphrasing) 지문의 in the heart of the city
→ 정답의 in the central part of the city

159 임차인에 대해 명시된 요구 사항은 무엇인가?

(A) 신원 보증인 제시
(B) 24개월 임대차 계약
(C) 보증금으로 2개월 치 임차료 납부
(D) 현재 고용 상태 증명 제시

해설 **Not / True**
세 번째 단락의 두 번째 문장에서 첫 번째 달과 마지막 달
의 임차료에 상응하는 보증금을 지불해야 한다(payment
of a security deposit equal to the first and last
month's rent is required)고 했으므로 임차인은 두 달 치
임차료를 보증금으로 지불해야 한다는 것을 알 수 있다. 따라
서 (C)가 정답이다.

어휘 reference 신원 보증인

(Paraphrasing) 지문의 the first and last month's rent
→ 정답의 two months' rent

160 [1], [2], [3], [4]로 표시된 곳 중에서 다음 문장이 들어가기에
가장 적합한 위치는?

"식료품점과 주말 농산물 시장도 인근에 있습니다."

(A) [1]　　　　　　(B) [2]
(C) [3]　　　　　　(D) [4]

해설 **문장 삽입**
주어진 문장에서 식료품점과 시장 또한(also) 가까이 있다
고 했으므로, 주어진 문장 앞에는 건물의 주변 상권이나 입지
에 대해 설명하는 내용이 있어야 한다. 따라서 이 건물은 트
라이던트 나이트라이프 지구와 카스텐 대학에서 도보 거리
에 있다(the building is within walking distance ~
Karsten College)며 건물의 위치에 대해 언급한 문장 뒤
[3]에 들어가는 것이 글의 흐름상 자연스러우므로 (C)가 정답
이다.

[161-163] 설명서

161 센드 플루투스는 세계 최고의 국제 송금 서비스입니다. 저희는
숨겨진 수수료 없이 최상의 환율로 귀하의 돈을 안전하게 송금해
드립니다. 저희는 개인 또는 사업 목적을 위한 크고 작은 거래에 해
결책을 가지고 있습니다. **162** 전적으로 온라인으로 운영되므로 언
제 어디서나 송금을 시작하실 수 있습니다!

이 쉬운 단계를 따라 전 세계 거의 모든 곳으로 귀하의 돈을 송금
하세요.

1. **무료 계좌를 만드세요.** 온라인으로 가입하시거나 무료 휴대폰
앱을 사용하세요.
2. **송금할 금액을 입력하세요.** 원하는 송금 금액을 표시하세요.
3. **수취인 정보를 입력하세요.** 수취인의 은행 계좌 정보를 제시하
세요.
4. **신원을 확인해 주세요.** 문자 메시지나 이메일로 발송되는 개인
식별 번호를 입력하세요.
5. **163** 송금 비용을 지불하세요. 은행 계좌로부터 직접 이체, 전신
송금, 또는 신용카드를 이용하여 돈을 보내고 수수료를 지불하
세요.
6. **완료되었습니다!**

지금 www.sendplutus.com을 방문해 가입하세요.

161 센드 플루투스는 어떤 서비스를 제공하는가?

(A) 포괄적인 온라인 뱅킹　　(B) 금융 투자 자문
(C) 은행 보안 상담　　　　　**(D) 국제 송금**

해설 **세부 사항**
첫 문장에서 센드 플루투스는 세계 최고의 국제 송금 서비
스(Send Plutus is the world's top-rated service for
transferring funds internationally)라고 소개하고 있으
므로 (D)가 정답이다.

어휘 investment 투자 consultation 상담

(Paraphrasing) 지문의 transferring funds
internationally → 정답의 International money
transfers

162 센드 플루투스에 대해 설명서에 암시된 것은?

(A) 비교적 새로운 서비스이다.
(B) 다수의 해외 사무소가 있다.
(C) 기업 전용으로 고안되었다.
(D) 디지털 기술을 이용해야 한다.

해설 **추론 / 암시**
첫 단락의 네 번째 문장에서 센드 플루투스는 전적으로 온라
인으로 운영되므로 언제 어디서나 송금을 시작할 수 있다(We
operate entirely online, so you can start your
transfer anytime, anywhere!)고 한 것으로 보아 온라인
으로 서비스를 이용할 수 있다는 것을 알 수 있다. 따라서 정
답은 (D)이다.

어휘 relatively 비교적 multiple 다수의 solely 오로지

Paraphrasing 지문의 operate entirely online
→ 정답의 requires the use of digital technology

163 고객이 센드 플루토스의 서비스 비용을 지불할 수 있는
방법으로 언급된 것이 아닌 것은?

(A) 신용카드 지불하기

(B) 전신 송금

(C) 센드 플루토스로 수표 발송

(D) 은행 계좌에서 돈 인출

해설 **Not / True**

설명서의 다섯 번째 단계에서 송금 비용을 지불하라(Pay for
your transfer)면서 은행 계좌로부터 직접 이체, 전신 송
금, 또는 신용카드를 이용하여 돈을 보내고 수수료를 지불
하라(Send your money and pay the fee using a
direct transfer from your bank account, a wire
transfer, or a credit card)고 했다. 수표를 발송하는 방
법을 언급하지 않았으므로 (C)가 정답이다.

어휘 charge 신용카드로 결제하다   draw 인출하다

Paraphrasing 지문의 transfer → 보기 (D)의 Drawing
money

[164-167] 기사

판매 부진에 대응하는 레규리안

레규리안의 장기 고객들은 다음 달 회사의 가을 카탈로그를 볼 때
뭔가 달라진 점을 알 수 있을 것이다. **164 이 브랜드의 유명한 크고
튼튼한 여행 가방 대신, 카탈로그는 서류 가방과 숄더백 같은 작은
품목들을 선보일 예정이다.** 이 변화는 한때 레규리안 여행 가방 하
나에 옷장에 있는 모든 것을 담을 수 있다고 자랑하는 광고를 했던
회사의 극적인 변화를 보여준다.

레규리안의 전략 변화는 최신 패션 잡지 트렌드보다는 변화하는 여
행 패턴에 기인한다.

"간단히 말해서, **165 사람들은 장기 여행은 덜 하고 단기 여행은 더
많이 하고 있습니다.**"라고 레규리안의 최고경영자인 제나 모렐리가
말했다. "사람들은 이제 직장에서 휴가를 며칠씩 더 쉽게 낼 수 있
어서 현재 제공되고 있는 저가 항공을 이용할 것입니다."

"기술 덕분에 더 이상 가족을 보기 위해 여행할 필요가 없어져서
사람들은 관광객으로서 더 많은 여행을 하고 있습니다."라고 그녀
는 덧붙였다. "2주 여행이 점점 더 드물어지면서 큰 여행 가방에 대
한 수요도 줄어들고 있습니다."

몇 년 전, 업계 전문가들은 높은 항공 수하물 수수료가 여행 용품
의 판매를 **166 위축시킬** 것이라고 예측했다. 하지만 그 예측은 틀
린 것으로 판명되었다. 대신, 고객들은 비용보다는 편리함에 더 영
향을 받는 것으로 보인다.

"우리의 새 페랄타 숄더백은 고객이 원하는 것이 무엇인지를 보여
주는 좋은 예입니다."라고 모렐리 씨는 말했다. "이 가방은 세련되
고 현대적인 디자인에 여러 작은 수납공간으로 구성되어 있습니다.
하지만 **167 사람들이 정말 좋아하는 점은 가볍고 인체 공학적인 어
깨끈이 있다는 사실입니다.** 그들은 가방을 메고 온종일 편하게 걸
어다닐 수 있습니다."

어휘 lagging 뒤떨어지는   heavy-duty 튼튼한   shift
변화   boast 자랑하다   simply put 간단히 말해서   take
advantage of ~을 이용하다   predict 예측하다   depress
부진하게 만들다   accessories 부대용품   sleek 세련된
compartment (수납) 칸   ergonomic 인체 공학의

164 기사에서 레규리안에 대해 암시된 것은?

(A) 더 이상 대형 수하물 가방을 전문으로 하지 않는다.

(B) 이제 옷장 보관 시스템을 생산한다.

(C) 직원들이 여행할 수 있도록 휴가를 제공한다.

(D) 올해는 가을 카탈로그를 발행하지 않는다.

해설 **추론 / 암시**

첫 번째 단락의 두 번째 문장에서 이 브랜드의 유명한 크고
튼튼한 여행 가방 대신 카탈로그는 서류 가방과 숄더백 같은
작은 품목들을 선보일 예정(Instead of the big heavy-
duty suitcases that the brand is known for,
the catalog will feature smaller items, such as
briefcases and shoulder bags)이라고 했다. 따라서 레
규리안이 기존의 주력 상품인 크고 튼튼한 여행 가방에서 벗
어나 소형 가방으로 제품군을 확장하는 변화를 꾀하고 있다는
것을 알 수 있으므로 (A)가 정답이다.

어휘 specialize in ~을 전문으로 하다   time off 휴가

165 기사에서 언급된 트렌드는 무엇인가?

(A) 올해 여행 비용이 크게 증가했다.

(B) 패션 잡지에서 더 다양한 스타일을 홍보하고 있다.

(C) 다양한 브랜드를 시도하는 데 소비자들의 관심이
증가하고 있다.

(D) 여행자들이 더 짧은 기간 동안 더 많은 여행을 한다.

해설 **Not / True**

세 번째 단락의 첫 문장에서 사람들은 장기 여행은 덜 하고 단
기 여행은 더 많이 하고 있다(people are taking fewer
long trips, but more short trips)고 언급하였으므로 정
답은 (D)이다.

어휘 significantly 상당히   promote 홍보하다

166 다섯 번째 단락 3행의 "depress"와 의미가 가장 가까운
단어는?

(A) 거절하다   (B) 슬프게 하다

(C) 줄이다   (D) 강요하다

해설 **동의어 찾기**

의미상 판매를 '위축시킨다'는 뜻으로 쓰였으므로 '줄이다'를
뜻하는 (C) reduce가 정답이다.

167 모렐리 씨에 따르면, 고객들이 페랄타 가방의 어떤 점을 가장
좋아하는가?

(A) 가격이 저렴하다.   **(B) 휴대하기 편하다.**

(C) 시각적으로 매력적이다.   (D) 주머니가 여러 개 있다.

해설 **세부 사항**

마지막 단락의 세 번째 문장에서 모렐리 씨가 페랄타 가방
에 대해 사람들이 정말 좋아하는 점은 가볍고 인체 공학적인

ETS 기출

모의고사 2회

151

어깨끈이 있다는 사실(what people really love is the fact that it's lightweight and has an ergonomic shoulder strap)이라고 한 뒤, 그들은 가방을 메고 온종일 편하게 걸어다닐 수 있다(They can walk around with it all day in complete comfort)고 했다. 따라서 모렐리 씨는 고객들이 페랄타 가방이 들고 다니기 편하다는 점을 가장 좋아한다고 언급하고 있으므로 (B)가 정답이다.

어휘　visually 시각적으로　contain 들어 있다

(Paraphrasing)　지문의 walk around with it
→ 정답의 carry

[168-171] 이메일

수신: 전 직원
발신: 수니타 달
날짜: 4월 15일
제목: 중요한 정보

직원 여러분께,

169우리 회사는 창립 이래로 5년간 크게 성장했고, 171현재 사무 공간은 더 이상 우리의 요구를 충족시키지 못합니다. 현재 많은 직원들이 한 사람을 위한 사무 공간을 공유하고 있습니다. 따라서 168울레인 테크놀로지는 6월에 시내에 있는 골드만 풀 빌딩으로 본사를 이전할 예정입니다. 새 사무실은 모두가 개별적인 업무 공간을 가질 수 있을 만큼 충분히 크면서, 여전히 회사가 확장할 수 있는 공간이 남습니다. 이 일을 원활하게 진행하기 위해 모든 부서 관리자를 대상으로 매주 이사 업데이트 회의를 할 예정입니다.

가구와 상자에 포장된 자료의 운반은 이사 전문업체가 담당하겠지만 노트북과 기밀 자료는 직원들이 직접 새 사무실로 가져가야 합니다. 1705월 15일, 우리 홍보부는 업계 간행물에 보도 자료를 발행하고 사업 협력사와 주요 고객들에게 우리가 곧 이전한다는 것을 발표하는 서신과 이메일을 발송할 예정입니다. 그때 여러분의 고객 및 주요 연락처에 우리의 새 주소를 알려 주세요. 여러분의 전화 내선 번호를 포함한 기타 모든 연락 정보는 그대로 유지됩니다.

수니타 달, 사무장 / 이사 진행 담당자

어휘　founding 창립　facilitate 가능[용이]하게 하다
undertaking (맡은) 일　confidential 기밀의　issue 발행하다　press release 보도 자료　extension number 내선 번호　coordinator 진행 담당자

168 이메일의 목적은 무엇인가?
(A) 회의 일정 잡기　　(B) 곧 있을 변화 설명하기
(C) 신규 고객 맞이하기　(D) 신제품 발표하기

해설　**주제/목적**
세 번째 문장에서 울레인 테크놀로지는 6월에 시내에 있는 골드만 풀 빌딩으로 본사를 이전할 예정(Urlane Technology will move its headquarters ~ downtown)이라고 안내하며 이메일 전체에 걸쳐 회사 이전과 관련된 사항에 대해 설명하고 있으므로 정답은 (B)이다.

(Paraphrasing)　지문의 move its headquarters
→ 정답의 upcoming change

169 울레인 테크놀로지에 대해 명시된 것은?
(A) 사업을 한 지 5년이 되었다.
(B) 두 곳 이상의 도시에 사무실이 있다.
(C) 100명 미만의 직원을 고용하고 있다.
(D) 최근에 새로운 노트북을 구입했다.

해설　**Not/True**
첫 문장에서 우리 회사는 창립 이래로 5년간 크게 성장했다(Our company has grown significantly in the five years since its founding)고 했으므로 정답은 (A)이다.

170 이메일에 따르면, 홍보부는 5월 15일에 무슨 일을 할 것인가?
(A) 부서 관리자 회의 개최
(B) 상자에 포장된 자료를 다른 장소로 운반
(C) 회사 사업 협력사들과 정보 공유
(D) 고객에게 업데이트된 전화 내선 번호 목록 전송

해설　**세부 사항**
두 번째 단락의 두 번째 문장에서 5월 15일에 우리 홍보부는 업계 간행물에 보도 자료를 발행하고 사업 협력사와 주요 고객들에게 우리가 곧 이전한다는 것을 발표하는 서신과 이메일을 발송할 예정(On May 15, our public relations department will ~ e-mails to our business partners and key customers announcing our upcoming move)이라고 했으므로 정답은 (C)이다.

171 [1], [2], [3], [4]로 표시된 곳 중에서 다음 문장이 들어가기에 가장 적합한 위치는?
"현재 많은 직원들이 한 사람을 위한 사무 공간을 공유하고 있습니다."
(A) [1]　　　　　　　(B) [2]
(C) [3]　　　　　　　(D) [4]

해설　**문장 삽입**
주어진 문장에서 현재 많은 직원들이 한 사람을 위한 사무 공간을 같이 쓰고 있다고 했으므로, 주어진 문장 주변에는 사무 공간이 직원들 수에 비해 충분하지 못하다는 내용이 있어야 적절하다. 따라서 현재 사무 공간은 더 이상 우리의 요구를 충족시키지 못한다(office space no longer meets our needs)며 사무 공간의 부족을 언급한 문장 뒤 [1]에 들어가는 것이 글의 흐름상 자연스러우므로 (A)가 정답이다.

[172-175] 온라인 채팅

사쿠라 미야케 [오전 9시 30분] 모두들 안녕하세요. 공지가 늦어서 죄송합니다만, 172저는 지금 내일 오후 5시에 제프 쿠리를 위한 작은 깜짝 파티를 준비 중입니다.

에두아르 펠러린 [오전 9시 31분] 12월에 있을 그의 은퇴를 축하하려고요?

사쿠라 미야케 [오전 9시 32분] 아니요. 172그가 퍼치 푸즈를 고객사로 잡았습니다! 오늘 오후 2시 직원회의에서 공식적으로 발표될 거예요.

조 바에즈 [오전 9시 33분] 엄청난 소식이네요! 그들이 우리에게서 광고를 제작하도록 설득하기 위해 수년간 노력해 왔잖아요.

사쿠라 미야케 [오전 9시 34분] 제가 버그만스에서 케이크를 픽업해 올 거고, 스탠이 음료를 맡기로 했어요.

일라이자 해블록 [오전 9시 35분] 저는 뭘 하면 될까요?

사쿠라 미야케 [오전 9시 36분] 내일 4시쯤 시간이 되면 회의실 꾸미는 걸 도와주시면 좋겠습니다.

일라이자 해블록 [오전 9시 37분] 알겠습니다.

에두아르 펠러린 [오전 9시 38분] 173지난달 라토야의 기념 파티에서 남은 풍선이랑 색 테이프가 조금 있어요. 창고에 있습니다. 173제가 챙길게요.

사쿠라 미야케 [오전 9시 39분] 고맙습니다! 휴게실에 있는 수납장도 확인해 주세요. 거기에 종이 접시, 냅킨, 플라스틱 포크가 있을 거예요.

조 바에즈 [오전 9시 40분] 174,175저는 내일 오후 4시부터 5시 30분까지 새로운 그래픽 아트 디자인 소프트웨어 교육을 받습니다. 175그 후에 가면 너무 늦을까요?

사쿠라 미야케 [오전 9시 41분] 전혀요. 그리고 제프는 분명 퍼치 푸즈 로고를 재디자인하는 것에 대한 그의 아이디어를 당신에게 알려 주고 싶어 할 거예요.

어휘 land 잡다, 획득하다 account 고객 formally 공식적으로 streamer (장식용) 색 테이프

---

172 미야케 씨는 왜 쿠리 씨를 위해 파티를 준비하는가?

(A) 신규 고객 영입을 축하하려고
(B) 퍼치 푸즈에서 새 직책을 맡게 된 것을 축하하려고
(C) 곧 있을 그의 은퇴를 기념하려고
(D) 그의 근무 기념일을 축하하려고

해설 **세부 사항**

9시 30분에 미야케 씨가 지금 내일 오후 5시에 제프 쿠리를 위한 작은 깜짝 파티를 준비 중(I'm organizing a small surprise party for Jeff Koury ~)이라고 한 뒤, 9시 32분에 그가 퍼치 푸즈를 고객으로 잡았다(He landed the Perch Foods account!)는 소식을 전하고 있다. 따라서 미야케 씨는 쿠리 씨가 새로운 고객사를 확보한 일을 축하하기 위해 파티를 준비하고 있음을 알 수 있으므로 정답은 (A)이다.

어휘 recruitment 모집 observe 축하[기념]하다

(Paraphrasing) 지문의 He landed ~ account → 정답의 his recruitment of a new client

173 펠러린 씨는 무엇을 하겠다고 말하는가?

(A) 오후 2시 직원회의 진행하기
(B) 파티용품 챙기기
(C) 케이크 주문하기
(D) 탄산음료 픽업하기

해설 **세부 사항**

9시 38분에 펠러린 씨가 지난달 라토야의 기념 파티에서 남은 풍선이랑 색 테이프가 조금 있다(There are some balloons and streamers left over ~)면서 자신이 챙기겠다(I'll grab them)고 했다. 따라서 (B)가 정답이다.

(Paraphrasing) 지문의 grab → 정답의 Gather
지문의 balloons and streamers → 정답의 party

---

suppplies

174 바에즈 씨에 대해 암시된 것은?

(A) 회사의 교육을 감독한다.
(B) 해블록 씨와 사무실을 같이 쓴다.
(C) 빵집 근처에 산다.
(D) 그래픽 아티스트이다.

해설 **추론 / 암시**

9시 40분에 바에즈 씨가 내일 오후 4시부터 5시 30분까지 새로운 그래픽 아트 디자인 소프트웨어 교육을 받는다(I'm getting trained on the new graphic arts design software tomorrow ~)고 한 것으로 보아 바에즈 씨는 그래픽 아트 디자인 업무를 하는 사람임을 짐작할 수 있다. 따라서 정답은 (D)이다.

어휘 oversee 감독하다

175 오전 9시 41분에 미야케 씨가 "전혀요"라고 쓴 의도는 무엇인가?

(A) 예산을 확인하는 것을 개의치 않는다.
(B) 쿠리 씨에게 파티에 대해 말하지 않을 것이다.
(C) 오후 5시 30분 이후에도 파티가 계속될 것이다.
(D) 새 소프트웨어 프로그램은 배우기 쉽다.

해설 **의도 파악**

9시 40분에 바에즈 씨가 내일 오후 4시부터 5시 30분까지 새로운 그래픽 아트 디자인 소프트웨어 교육을 받는다(I'm getting trained ~ from 4:00 to 5:30 P.M.)면서 그 후에 가면 너무 늦을지(Would it be too late if I come after that?)를 묻자 9시 41분에 미야케 씨가 전혀요(Not at all)라고 대답했다. 따라서 미야케 씨는 바에즈 씨에게 교육이 끝나는 5시 30분 이후에도 파티가 계속되어 참석할 수 있다는 점을 강조하려는 의도로 한 말임을 알 수 있으므로 (C)가 정답이다.

[176-180] 기사 + 후기

현지 예술과 고급 풍미가 어우러진 쿠치나 이탈리아나
176알렉스 싱 작성

마이애미 비치 (6월 12일) – 많은 기대를 모았던 새로운 레스토랑 쿠치나 이탈리아나의 177개점이 7월 1일로 정해졌다. 178소유주이자 셰프인 에밀리아 카라파노가 뉴욕 브루클린에서 그 지역의 이탈리안 푸드 트럭 운영을 시작했을 때, 그것은 순식간에 센세이션을 일으켰다. 사업이 성장함에 따라 그녀는 보다 영구적인 공간으로 사업을 이전하여 다양하고 대표적인 이탈리아 요리를 현대적인 버전으로 제공하는 아늑한 음식점을 만들었다. 음식 잡지의 극찬하는 평론과 인기 요리 프로그램에 출연한 카파라노의 프로필에 힘입어 쿠치나 이탈리아나 본점은 지속적인 인기를 누리며 전국적인 명성을 얻게 되었다. 180이제 마이애미 비치에 이 호평 받는 레스토랑의 자체 지점이 생길 예정이다.

훌륭한 요리 외에, 쿠치나 이탈리아나 본점은 또한 현지 예술가들의 작품을 특징으로 한다 "저희 뉴욕 레스토랑에서는 음식과 예술이 함께합니다."라고 카라파노 씨는 말했다. "저는 더 널리 알려질 자격이 있는 예술가들이 꿈을 실현할 수 있도록 돕고 싶었습니다. 제가 그렇게 할 수 있었던 것처럼요." 이 가치 있는 사명을 이어가

기 위해 **180 새로운 레스토랑은 플로리다에 기반을 둔 예술가들의 작품을 전시할 예정이다.**

> **어휘** anticipated 기대하던　regional 지역의　sensation 선풍적인 관심　operation 사업체　permanent 영구적인　cozy 아늑한　eatery 음식점　contemporary 현대의　catapult (~으로) 급격히 높이다　prominence 명성　glowing 극찬하는　acclaimed 호평 받는　cuisine 요리　go hand in hand 함께 가다　worthy 가치 있는

---

https://www.customerreviewsite.com/restaurants

180 쿠치나 이탈리아나ー마이애미 비치 (별 4개)

제 여동생과 저는 주말에 방문하려고 했고, 개점한 지 일주일 만에 쿠치나 이탈리아나에 예약을 할 수 있었을 때 매우 신났습니다. 정말 멋진 경험이었습니다! **180 전시되어 있는 아름다운 예술 작품은 매력적인 분위기를 자아냈고** 서비스는 신속하고 전문적이었으며 음식은 훌륭했습니다. 훈제 연어 라비올리는 맛있었고 디저트로 주문한 카놀리는 우리가 먹어본 것 중 최고였습니다. 하지만 안타깝게도 **179 레스토랑은 사람들로 붐비고 매우 시끄러웠습니다. 서로 대화하는 소리가 잘 들리지 않아 즐거움이 일부 반감되었습니다.** 그것 말고는 근사한 저녁이었습니다.

ー 바바라 오, 올랜도

> **어휘** thrilled 아주 신이 난　atmosphere 분위기　prompt 신속한　take away ~을 빼앗다, 없애다

176 싱 씨의 직업은 무엇일 것 같은가?

(A) 레스토랑 지배인　　(B) 예술가 에이전트
(C) 신문 기자　　　　(D) 예술 평론가

해설　추론/암시
기사의 상단 제목 아래에 알렉스 싱 작성(By Alex Singh)이라고 나와 있는 것으로 보아 싱 씨는 신문 기자라는 것을 알 수 있다. 따라서 정답은 (C)이다.

> **어휘** profession 직업　critic 평론가

177 기사의 첫 번째 단락 2행의 "opening"과 의미가 가장 가까운 단어는?

(A) 빈 공간　　　　　(B) 공석
(C) 개시　　　　　(D) 첫 공연

해설　동의어 찾기
의미상 새로운 레스토랑의 기다리던 '개점'이라는 뜻으로 쓰였으므로 '개시, 시작'을 뜻하는 (C) launch가 정답이다.

178 기사에 따르면, 쿠치나 이탈리아나 본점에 대해 명시된 것은?

(A) 두 자매가 설립했다.　　(B) 처음에는 인기가 없었다.
(C) 다큐멘터리에 나왔다.　**(D) 푸드 트럭으로 시작했다.**

해설　Not/True
기사의 두 번째 문장에서 소유주이자 셰프인 에밀리아 카라파노가 뉴욕 브루클린에서 그 지역의 이탈리안 푸드 트럭 운영을 시작했다(owner-Chef Emilia Carafano began operating her regional Italian food truck in Brooklyn, New York)고 언급하고 있으므로, 쿠치나 이

탈리아나가 푸드 트럭에서 시작된 것임을 알 수 있다. 따라서 (D)가 정답이다.

179 후기에 따르면, 오 씨가 새로운 쿠치나 이탈리아나에 대해 불만스러웠던 점은 무엇인가?

(A) 소음　　　　　(B) 위치
(C) 가격　　　　　　(D) 서비스

해설　세부 사항
후기의 다섯 번째 문장에서 오 씨가 레스토랑은 사람들로 붐비고 매우 시끄러웠다(the restaurant was crowded and very loud)고 했고, 서로 대화하는 소리가 잘 들리지 않아 즐거움이 일부 반감되었다(It was hard for us to hear each other talk, so that took away some of our enjoyment)고 했다. 따라서 오 씨는 레스토랑의 소음에 대해 불평하는 것이므로 정답은 (A)이다.

> **Paraphrasing** 지문의 took away some of our enjoyment → 질문의 dislike

180 오 씨가 새로운 쿠치나 이탈리아나에서 본 예술 작품에 대해 어떤 결론을 내릴 수 있는가?

(A) 일주일 동안만 전시되었다.
(B) 카라파노 씨가 그렸다.
(C) 고전과 현대 양식의 조합이었다.
(D) 플로리다 출신의 예술가들이 제작했다.

해설　연계
기사의 첫 단락 마지막 문장에서 이제 마이애미 비치에 이 호평 받는 레스토랑의 자체 지점이 생길 예정(Now Miami Beach will have its own branch of the acclaimed restaurant)이며 두 번째 단락 마지막 문장에서 새로운 레스토랑은 플로리다에 기반을 둔 예술가들의 작품을 전시할 예정(the new restaurant will display the works of Florida-based artists)이라고 했다. 또한 후기의 제목이 쿠치나 이탈리아나 마이애미 비치(Cucina Italianaー Miami Beach)이고 세 번째 문장에서 전시되어 있는 아름다운 예술 작품은 매력적인 분위기를 자아냈다(The beautiful artwork displayed created a lovely atmosphere)고 했다. 따라서 오 씨가 방문했으며 새로 문을 연 쿠치나 이탈리아나 마이애미 비치점은 플로리다 예술가들의 작품을 전시하고 있음을 알 수 있으므로 정답은 (D)이다.

> **Paraphrasing** 지문의 Florida-based artists → 정답의 artists from Florida

[181-185] 일정표 + 이메일

11월 직업 교육 과정

181 렌브룩 코퍼레이션은 직원들이 매년 최소 두 개의 직업 교육 과정에 등록할 것을 권장합니다. 다음은 11월 한 달 동안 제공되는 강좌입니다. 등록을 고려 중이라면 먼저 상사와 이야기하여 강좌가 적합한지 확인하세요. 모든 수업은 90분이며 11월 오전 4회에 걸쳐 진행됩니다. 문의 사항이 있으면 jtnan@renbrookcorporation.com으로 지태 난에게 연락하세요.

강좌 번호	강좌명 및 설명	요일 및 시간	강의실
N22-01	비즈니스 분석 입문: 업무 절차를 더 잘 이해하고 개선하기 위한 기본 데이터 분석 적용 방법	월요일 오전 8시 30분	본관, 회의실
182 N22-12	**182** 비즈니스 분석: 데이터 분석을 위한 고급 응용 (입문 과정 수료가 필수 사항임을 유의하세요.)	수요일 오전 8시 30분	본관, 교육 강의실
185 N22-03	자신 있게 협상하기: 사업 협상 준비 및 결과 극대화를 위한 전략 채택 방법	**185** 화요일 오전 11시	팔린관, 3호실
184 N22-44	**184** 데이터 보안: 고객 기밀 유지 및 회사 데이터 보안	금요일 오전 11시	팔린관, 3호실

어휘 analytics 분석 fundamental 기본적인 advance 고급의 application 적용 completion 수료 introductory 입문자를 위한 prerequisite 필수 조건 negotiate 협상하다 adopt 채택하다 strategy 전략 maximize 극대화하다 confidentiality 기밀

수신: 지태 난
발신: 앤더스 윌슨
날짜: 10월 7일
제목: 제 수업

안녕하세요, 지태 씨,

183 저는 11월에 N22-44 강좌를 진행하기로 예정되어 있습니다. 안타깝게도, 방금 그 기간 동안 컴퓨터 교육을 담당하라는 요청을 받았습니다. 직원들에게 새로운 컴퓨터 시스템을 소개하는 일은 회사의 최우선 과제입니다. **184** N22-44를 가르칠 다른 사람을 찾을 수 있기를 바라며 저의 부하 직원 수잔 로건을 추천하고 싶습니다. **185** 또 다른 방안은 N22-03을 가르치기로 되어 있는 강사와 수업 배정을 맞바꾸는 것인데, 제가 그 과정을 가르친 경험이 있고 제가 가능한 시간에 일정이 잡혀 있기 때문입니다.

불편을 드려 죄송합니다.

앤더스 윌슨
내선 번호 3944

어휘 take charge of ~을 맡다 corporate 기업의 priority 우선 사항 assignment 배정, 배치

181 일정에 암시된 것은?
(A) 일부 과정은 1년에 두 번 진행된다.
(B) 일부 과정은 처음으로 제공된다.
(C) 직원들은 매년 2개 이상의 과정을 수강할 수 있다.
(D) 강좌를 수강하는 직원은 업무 경감을 요청할 수 있다.

해설 추론/암시
일정의 첫 문장에서 렌브룩 코퍼레이션은 직원들이 매년 최소

두 개의 직무 교육 과정에 등록할 것을 권장한다(Renbrook Corporation expects employees to register for a minimum of two professional education courses each year)고 했으므로 랜브룩 코퍼레이션의 직원들은 매년 두 개 이상의 교육 과정을 들을 수 있다는 것을 알 수 있다. 따라서 정답은 (C)이다.

(Paraphrasing) 지문의 register for a minimum of two ~ courses → 정답의 take more than two courses

182 N22-12 강좌에 대해 언급된 것은?
(A) 부서 관리자에 한한다.
(B) 3호실에서 진행한다.
(C) 입문 과정의 다음 과정이다.
(D) 난 씨가 가르칠 것이다.

해설 Not/True
일정표의 두 번째 칸에 있는 N22-12는 비즈니스 분석: 데이터 분석을 위한 고급 응용(Business Analytics: Advance applications for data analysis) 과정이며, 입문 과정 수료가 필수 사항임을 유의하라(Please note that completion of the introductory-level course is a prerequisite)는 주의 사항이 언급되어 있다. 따라서 N22-12는 입문 수업 수강 후에 듣는 상위 과정임을 알 수 있으므로 정답은 (C)이다.

183 이메일의 목적은 무엇인가?
(A) 신입사원 소개   (B) 강의 등록 방법 문의
(C) 신규 강좌 추천   **(D) 일정 충돌 논의**

해설 주제/목적
이메일의 첫 문장에서 윌슨 씨가 11월에 N22-44 강좌를 진행하기로 예정되어 있다(I have been scheduled to lead the N22-44 course in November)고 한 뒤, 방금 그 기간 동안 컴퓨터 교육을 담당하라는 요청을 받았다(I have just been asked to take charge of computer training during that time)고 덧붙였다. 따라서 강의 일정이 다른 업무 일정과 겹치는 문제에 대해 논의하려고 이메일을 쓴 것이므로 정답은 (D)이다.

184 로건 씨는 어떤 주제에 관해 잘 알 것 같은가?
(A) 데이터 보안   (B) 직장 내 의사소통
(C) 고객 협상   (D) 비즈니스 분석

해설 연계
이메일의 네 번째 문장에서 윌슨 씨는 N22-44를 가르칠 다른 사람을 찾을 수 있기를 바라며 자신의 부하 직원인 수잔 로건을 추천하고 싶다(I hope ~ and would like to suggest my assistant, Susan Logan)고 했다. 또한 일정표 마지막에 있는 N22-44는 데이터 보안: 고객 기밀 유지 및 회사 데이터 보안(Data Privacy: Maintaining client confidentiality and the security of company data)에 관한 과정이라고 나와 있다. 윌슨 씨가 데이터 보안 수업의 강사로 로건 씨를 추천하고 있으므로 정답은 (A)이다.

185 윌슨 씨는 11월에 언제 강의를 할 시간이 되는가?

(A) 월요일   **(B) 화요일**

(C) 수요일   (D) 금요일

해설 **연계**

이메일의 마지막 문장에서 윌슨 씨가 또 다른 방안은 N22-03을 가르치기로 되어 있는 강사와 수업 배정을 맞바꾸는 것인데 자신이 가능한 시간에 일정이 잡혀 있기 때문(Another option might be to switch course assignments with the instructor assigned to teach N22-03, as ~ it is scheduled for a time when I am available)이라고 했다. 일정표의 세 번째에 있는 N22-03의 강의 요일 및 시간은 화요일 오전 11시(Tuesdays 11:00 AM)로 나와 있다. 따라서 윌슨 씨가 강의할 수 있는 때는 화요일임을 알 수 있으므로 정답은 (B)이다.

[186-190] 기사 + 웹페이지 + 이메일

> ### 186 건축물 논평: 드림 피크
> 커스틴 블레이클리 작성
>
> 멜버른 (8월 2일) – 186,188우리 시의 새로운 컨벤션 센터인 드림 피크가 2주 후 개장할 예정이며 시의 접객 산업에 도움이 될 것으로 기대되고 있다. 187지난주 마무리 작업이 이루어지는 동안 살짝 들여다볼 수 있었다. 한 마디로, 건물은 장관이었다!
>
> 메이플 가와 오크 가 사이의 메인 대로에 위치한 드림 피크에는 통풍이 잘되고 햇볕이 잘 드는 2,000제곱미터의 반짝이는 그랜드 홀이 자리잡고 있다. 또한 900석의 강당과 전용 전시장이 있고 3개 층에 걸쳐 다양한 크고 작은 회의실이 펼쳐져 있다. 모든 회의실은 최첨단 시청각 기술과 고속 와이파이를 갖추고 있다. 올해 예정된 행사에는 3개의 무역 박람회와 퍼즐 컨벤션, 관광업 콘퍼런스가 있다.
>
> 현재 8월 17일로 예정된 그랜드 오프닝은 라이브 음악, 가벼운 다과, 제니퍼 레인 부시장이 주도하는 개관식으로 구성된다. 행사는 일반 시민에게 공개된다.
>
> **어휘** boon 이익, 혜택   hospitality 접객   sneak peek 살짝 엿보기, 예고편   spectacular 장관을 이루는   airy 바람이 잘 통하는   sun-drenched 햇빛이 잘 드는   auditorium 강당   dedicated 전용의   venue 장소   state-of-the-art 최첨단의   audiovisual 시청각의   refreshments 다과   deputy mayor 부시장

---

https://www.internationalwordpuzzlefans.org/events

행사	등록	소개	회원

놓치지 마세요!

188,190올해 국제 단어 퍼즐 컨벤션이 11월 3일부터 5일까지 호주 멜버른의 드림 피크 컨벤션 센터에서 개최됩니다. 다시 한번, 하리 차우다리가 사회자를 맡습니다. 189수많은 퍼즐 책의 저자인 차우다리 씨는 〈런던 아나운서〉 신문의 주간 퍼즐 섹션을 편집합니다. 컨벤션 참석을 위해서는 사전 등록이 요구됩니다. 국제 단어 퍼즐 팬 회원은 등록비에서 10퍼센트 할인을 받습니다. 등록 페이지를 방문하셔서 작성 양식 및 인근 호텔의 특별 요금에 관한 정보를 확인하세요.

어휘 master of ceremonies 사회자   advance 사전의

수신: 하리 차우다리 〈hchaudhari@londonannouncer.co.uk〉

발신: 레이카 오카다 〈rokada@okinawacommunityfm.co.jp〉

날짜: 11월 20일

제목: 게스트 출연

첨부: 쇼 정보

차우다리 씨께,

19011월 4일 컨벤션에서 만나 뵙게 되어 기뻤습니다. 1월 13일 일본 표준 시간(GMT +9)으로 오후 7시부터 8시까지 저희 생방송 라디오 쇼 〈후스 토킹 나우〉에 게스트가 되어 주시는 데 동의해 주셔서 정말 흥분됩니다. 쇼에 대한 설명을 첨부했습니다.

안정적인 전화 연결을 보장하기 위해 1월 13일 방송 시간 10분 전에 81-980-76-6459로 저희 방송국에 전화해 주십시오. 또한 가급적 빠른 시일 내에, 가장 자랑스럽게 생각하시는 저서를 포함한 귀하의 약력과 청취자들에게 귀하를 소개할 때 제가 언급하기를 원하시는 기타 정보를 보내 주십시오. 귀하와의 대화가 기대됩니다!

레이카 오카다

오키나와 커뮤니티 FM

어휘 appearance 출연   delightful 정말 기쁜   description 설명   reliable 안정적인   biography 전기

---

186 기사의 주요 주제는 무엇인가?

(A) 컨벤션 센터가 그 이름을 얻게 된 계기

(B) 컨벤션 센터의 특징

(C) 멜버른의 인기 관광 명소

(D) 정부 관계자의 최근 활동

해설 **주제/목적**

기사의 제목이 드림 피크 건축물에 대한 논평(Architecture Review: Dream Peak)이고, 첫 문장에서 우리 시의 새로운 컨벤션 센터인 드림 피크가 2주 후 개장할 예정이며 시의 접객 산업에 도움이 될 것으로 기대되고 있다(The city's new convention centre, Dream Peak, is scheduled to open ~ to the city's hospitality industry)는 내용을 시작으로 새로 개관할 컨벤션 센터의 특징에 대해 열거하고 있으므로 정답은 (B)이다.

어휘 feature 특징   tourist attraction 관광 명소

187 기사에 따르면, 블레이클리 씨는 지난주에 무엇을 했는가?

(A) 건물 한 곳을 둘러보았다.

(B) 런던으로 여행을 갔다.

(C) 회의 공간을 예약했다.

(D) 장기 프로젝트를 완료했다.

해설 **세부 사항**

기사의 첫 번째 문장에서 새롭게 개장하는 컨벤션 센터를 설명한 뒤, 두 번째 문장에서 지난주 마무리 작업이 이루어지는 동안 살짝 들여다볼 수 있었다(I was given a sneak peek last week ~)고 했다. 따라서 블레이클리 씨는 지난주에 새로운 컨벤션 센터를 미리 둘러보았다는 것을 알 수 있으므로 정답은 (A)이다.

어휘 book 예약하다   long-term 장기의

Paraphrasing 지문의 was given a sneak peek
→ 정답의 toured

188 국제 단어 퍼즐 컨벤션에 대해 명시된 것은?

(A) 회원에게만 공개된다.

(B) 등록비를 인상했다.

(C) 10년 동안 매년 개최되었다.

(D) 신축 장소에서 개최될 예정이다.

해설 연계

기사의 첫 문장에서 우리 시의 새로운 컨벤션 센터인 드림 피크가 2주 후 개장할 예정(The city's new convention centre, Dream Peak, is scheduled to open in two weeks)이라고 했고, 웹페이지의 첫 문장에서 올해 국제 단어 퍼즐 컨벤션이 11월 3일부터 5일까지 호주 멜버른의 드림 피크 컨벤션 센터에서 개최된다(This year's International Word Puzzle Convention will take place ~ at the Dream Peak Convention Centre)고 했다. 따라서 국제 단어 퍼즐 컨벤션이 신축 컨벤션 센터에서 열릴 예정임을 알 수 있으므로 (D)가 정답이다.

Paraphrasing 지문의 new convention centre
→ 정답의 newly constructed venue

189 웹페이지에서 차우다리 씨에 대해 언급하는 것은?

(A) 높은 평가를 받는 신문을 소유하고 있다.

(B) 행사에 참석할 수 없다.

(C) 여러 권의 책을 썼다.

(D) 오키나와에서 살고 있다.

해설 세부 사항

웹페이지의 세 번째 문장에서 수많은 퍼즐 책의 저자인 차우다리 씨(The author of numerous puzzle books, Mr. Chaudhari)라고 소개하고 있으므로 정답은 (C)이다.

어휘 respected 높이 평가되는

Paraphrasing 지문의 numerous → 정답의 multiple

190 오카다 씨에 대해 암시된 것은?

(A) 부시장 레인을 인터뷰했다.

(B) 한때 차우다리 씨를 위해 일했다.

(C) 차우다리 씨의 전기를 쓰고 있다.

(D) 최근에 멜버른에 있었다.

해설 연계

웹페이지의 첫 문장에서 올해 국제 단어 퍼즐 컨벤션이 11월 3일부터 5일까지 호주 멜버른의 드림 피크 컨벤션 센터에서 개최된다(This year's International Word Puzzle Convention will take place in Melbourne, Australia, from 3 to 5 November at the Dream Peak Convention Centre)고 했고, 이메일의 첫 문장에서 오카다 씨가 차우다리 씨에게 11월 4일 컨벤션에서 만나 뵙게 되어 기뻤다(It was delightful meeting you at the convention on 4 November)고 했다. 따라서 오카다 씨가 멜버른에서 열린 국제 단어 퍼즐 컨벤션에서 차우다리 씨를 만났다는 것을 알 수 있으므로 정답은 (D)이다.

[191-195] 여행 일정표 + 이메일 + 이메일

크레스트몬트 도보 여행 일정표
크레스트몬트 방문자 센터 후원
6월 5일 수요일

오전 8시 15분	노앵크 가 214번지 **191 설리번 공원 정문 입구**에서 만납니다.
오전 8시 30분	**설리번 공원** 화원을 거닐며 산책을 즐기세요. 매년 이맘때 장미와 백일홍이 장관입니다!
195 오전 9시 30분	**195 에드워즈 홀** 크레스트몬트에 남아 있는 가장 오래된 건물인 에드워즈 홀은 현재 크레스트몬트 역사 학회의 본거지입니다. 현재 전시회는 〈도시는 성장한다: 크레스트몬트 창립 가족들의 초상〉입니다.
오전 10시 30분	**구 기차역** 기차는 더 이상 크레스트몬트에 정차하지 않지만, 왕년의 기차역은 예술가를 위한 활기찬 장소로 탈바꿈했습니다. 간단한 식사를 위해 런치 바스켓 카페에 들르기 전에 몇몇 스튜디오와 갤러리를 방문합니다.
오전 11시 30분	**192 밴더워터 가구 회사** 100년도 더 전에 설립되어 오늘날에도 여전히 운영되고 있는 이 회사는 **192 세계적인 명작으로 인정받는 상징적인 밴더워터 안락의자를 세상에 내놓았습니다. 공장 일부가 방문객에게 개방됩니다.
오후 12시 30분	**193 넬리스 코너** 엽서, 티셔츠 및 기타 기념품을 구입할 수 있는 크레스트몬트의 가장 사랑받는 기념품 가게 중 한 곳에서 투어를 마무리합니다.

어휘 itinerary 여행 일정표 sponsor 후원하다 stroll 산책
zinnia 백일홍 portrait 초상화 convert 전환시키다 lively 활기 넘치는 iconic 상징적인 armchair 안락의자
wrap up ~을 마무리 짓다 memorabilia 기념품

발신: 줄리 셰스 <jhuli.sheth@crestmontvisitorcenter.org>
수신: 6월 5일 투어 그룹
날짜: 6월 3일
제목: 투어 알림 및 업데이트

여러분께,

수요일 도보 여행을 기대하고 계시길 바랍니다! 이전에 받으셨던 투어 일정에 한 가지 변경 사항이 있습니다. **193 넬리스 코너가 보수 공사로 임시 휴업 중이어서 대신 인근에 매우 유사한 장소인 캔들웍스(영화관 옆)로 갈 예정입니다.**

여러분 중 몇 분께서 투어에 다른 인원을 추가하는 것에 대해 문의하셨습니다. 아쉽게도 15명의 인원 제한이 찼지만, **194 금요일 투어(6월 7일)는 아직 자리가 남아 있습니다.** 티켓을 구입하시려면 555-0153으로 전화주세요. 곧 뵙겠습니다!

줄리 셰스
크레스트몬트 방문자 센터

어휘 reminder 상기시키는 것 temporarily 일시적으로

발신: 홍슈 권 〈hkwon@jaspermail.com〉
수신: 줄리 세스 〈jhuli.sheth@crestmontvisitorcenter.org〉
날짜: 6월 4일
제목: 투어 알림 및 업데이트

세스 씨께,

제가 내일 투어에 조금 늦는다는 것을 알려 드리려고 글을 씁니다. 오전에 중요한 업무 전화가 있어서 **195오전 9시 30분 방문지에서 투어에 합류할 계획입니다.**

홍슈 권

191 6월 5일 투어에 대해 여행 일정표에 명시된 것은?
 (A) 공원 입구에서 시작한다.
 (B) 크레스트몬트 시청에 들른다.
 (C) 우천 시 취소될 것이다.
 (D) 무료 단체 사진이 포함되어 있다.

해설 **Not / True**
 여행 일정표의 첫 일정에서 설리번 공원 정문 입구에서 만난다(Meet at the front entrance of Sullivan Park)고 안내하고 있으므로 정답은 (A)이다.

192 여행 일정표에 따르면, 무엇이 크레스트몬트시에 국제적인 명성을 가져다 주었는가?
 (A) 미술관 (B) 화원
 (C) 초상화 컬렉션 **(D) 가구 제작**

해설 **세부 사항**
 여행 일정표의 다섯 번째 일정인 밴더워터 가구 회사(The Vanderwater Furniture Company)는 세계적인 명작으로 인정받는 상징적인 밴더워터 안락의자를 세상에 내놓았다(introduced the iconic Vanderwater armchair, recognized worldwide as a classic)고 설명하고 있다. 따라서 크레스트몬트시는 밴더워터 가구회사에서 제작한 안락의자로 국제적으로 유명해졌다는 것을 알 수 있으므로 정답은 (D)이다.

193 캔들윅스에서 투어 참가자들은 무엇을 할 수 있을 것 같은가?
 (A) 기념품 쇼핑
 (B) 기차 관련 영화 시청
 (C) 현지 예술가의 강좌 수강
 (D) 크레스트몬트 원주민에 관한 학습

해설 **연계**
 첫 번째 이메일의 세 번째 문장에서 넬리스 코너가 보수 공사로 임시 휴업 중이어서 대신 인근에 매우 유사한 장소인 캔들윅스로 갈 예정(Because Nellie's Corner is temporarily closed for renovations, we will go instead to nearby Candlewick's ~ a very similar place)이라고 했고, 여행 일정표의 마지막에 있는 넬리스 코너(Nellie's Corner) 투어 일정에서 엽서, 티셔츠 및 기타 기념품을 구입할 수 있는 크레스트몬트의 가장 사랑받는 기념품 가게 중 한 곳에서 투어를 마무리한다(We will wrap up the tour ~ where you can buy postcards, T-shirts, and other memorabilia)고 안내하고 있다. 따라서 캔들윅스는 넬리스 코너와 같은 기념품 가게라는 것을

알 수 있으므로 정답은 (A)이다.

(Paraphrasing) 지문의 buy ~ memorabilia → 정답의 Shop for souvenirs

194 사람들이 6월 7일 투어 티켓을 구매할 수 있는 방법은 무엇인가?
 (A) 웹사이트 방문 (B) 세스 씨에게 이메일 발송
 (C) 전화번호로 연락 (D) 투어 가이드에게 얘기

해설 **세부 사항**
 첫 번째 이메일의 두 번째 단락 두 번째 문장에서 금요일 투어(6월 7일)는 아직 자리가 남아 있다(there are ~ Friday's tour (June 7))며 티켓을 구입하려면 555-0153으로 전화하라(To purchase tickets, please call us at 555-0153)고 했으므로 정답은 (C)이다.

195 권 씨는 어디에서 투어 그룹과 만날 것 같은가?
 (A) 설리번 공원 **(B) 에드워즈 홀**
 (C) 구 기차역 (D) 밴더워터 가구 회사

해설 **연계**
 두 번째 이메일의 마지막 문장에서 권 씨가 오전 9시 30분 방문지에서 투어에 합류할 계획(I plan to meet up with the tour at the 9:30 A.M. stop)이라고 했고, 여행 일정표에 오전 9시 30분(9:30 A.M.) 방문지는 에드워즈 홀(Edwards Hall)이라고 나와 있다. 따라서 정답은 (B)이다.

[196-200] 이메일 + 웹페이지 + 회람

수신: 반힐 주민
발신: 반힐 폐기물 관리부
날짜: 3월 1일
제목: 재활용 서비스

주민 여러분께:

기억하시겠지만, **1971월 5일** 반힐 시의회는 올해 시 예산을 감축하기로 표결했습니다. 이 감축에 영향을 받는 서비스 중에는 지역 사회 내 가정을 위한 재활용 수거 서비스가 있습니다. **1963월 12일** 금요일이 도로변 재활용 수거의 마지막 날이 될 예정입니다. **1993월 15일** 월요일부터는 종이, 판지, 플라스틱 제품, 알루미늄 캔, 유리병 및 병을 셸번 로의 시립 폐기물 관리 센터로 가져오십시오. 라벨이 명확하게 부착되어 있으니 알맞은 통에 재활용품을 분류해 주십시오.

원하실 경우, 우리 지역에서 유료 도로변 재활용 수거 서비스를 제공하는 민간 폐기물 관리 회사 중 한 곳과 계약하실 수도 있습니다. 회사의 목록은 www.barnhillcity.ie에서 확인하실 수 있습니다.

셸번 로 시설에서는 앞으로도 중고 엔진 및 식용유, 배터리, 라텍스 페인트 등을 주기적으로 수거할 예정입니다.

협조해 주셔서 감사합니다.

시무스 코너, 반힐 폐기물 관리부 담당자

어휘 waste 폐기물 council 의회 vote 표결하다 reduction 삭감 household 가정 curbside 도로변 cardboard 판지 sort 분류하다 periodic 주기적인

https://www.ecolandrecycling.ie/households

198에코랜드 리사이클링의 가정용 표준 배출통 서비스 가격은 월 6유로입니다. 재활용품은 매주 수거됩니다. 우리는 알루미늄 캔, 종이, 판지, 유리병, 병을 수거합니다. **199플라스틱으로 만든 제품은 수거하지 않습니다.**

요금에는 바퀴 달린 대형 배출통 2개가 포함되어 있습니다. 추가 배출통은 하나당 2유로의 비용으로 주문하실 수 있습니다.

200신규 고객들을 위해 특별 혜택을 제공 중이오니 서비스 첫 해 요금을 미리 결제하시고 할인을 받으십시오. 자세한 내용은 020-912-0314로 전화해 주십시오.

어휘 wheelie bin 바퀴 달린 쓰레기통

회람

수신: 전 재활용 담당팀
발신: 어윈 미타니, 영업부
날짜: 4월 10일
답장: 3구역의 신규 반힐 고객

에코랜드 리사이클링은 반힐에 거주하는 고객들을 계속 받고 있습니다. **2003구역의 목요일 정기 순회 구역에 아래 4개의 주소를 추가해 주세요. 전부 1년 치 전액 결제되었습니다.**

제프리 무엘레안스, 메인 가 29
다이애나 스퍼버, 센터 로 661
오티스 라야노, 풀턴 가 97
패트리샤 첸, 타로우 로 1300

---

196 이메일의 목적은 무엇인가?

(A) 도시의 새로운 폐기물 관리 담당자를 소개
(B) 시민들에게 시의 서비스가 중단될 예정임을 공지
(C) 시민들에게 일회용 용기의 사용을 줄여 줄 것을 요청
(D) 시민들에게 재활용 요구 사항에 대한 설문 조사 작성 요청

해설 **주제/목적**
이메일의 세 번째 문장에서 3월 12일 금요일이 도로변 재활용 수거의 마지막 날이 될 예정(Friday. 12 March, will be the last day of curbside recycling pickup)이라고 한 것으로 보아 주민들에게 재활용 수거 서비스가 종료됨을 알리는 이메일임을 알 수 있다. 따라서 정답은 (B)이다.

어휘 discontinue 중단하다 disposable 일회용의

197 이메일에서 반힐 시의회에 대해 명시된 것은?

(A) 향후 재활용 수거를 재개할 수 있다.
(B) 쓰레기 수거 비용을 인상할 것이다.
(C) 돈을 절약할 방법을 몇 가지 찾아냈다.
(D) 셸번 로 시설을 확장하기로 표결했다.

해설 **Not/True**
이메일의 첫 문장에서 반힐 시의회는 올해 시 예산을 감축하기로 표결했다(the Barnhill City Council voted to reduce the city budget)고 한 뒤, 이 감축에 영향을 받는 서비스 중에는 지역 사회 내 가정을 위한 재활용 수거 서비스가 있다(Among the services affected ~ in the community)고 했다. 따라서 반힐 시의회는 예산 감축을 위

한 방안을 몇 가지 찾아냈다는 것을 알 수 있으므로 정답은 (C)이다.

어휘 resume 재개하다 identify 찾다

198 웹페이지에서 에코랜드 리사이클링의 표준 서비스에 대해 명시하는 것은?

(A) 다른 서비스보다 저렴하다.
(B) 일주일에 2회 수거가 포함되어 있다.
(C) 기업을 대상으로 한다.
(D) 한 달에 6유로이다.

해설 **Not/True**
웹페이지의 첫 문장에서 에코랜드 리사이클링의 가정용 표준 배출통 서비스 가격은 월 6유로(Ecoland Recycling's standard bin service for households is priced at €6 per month)라고 명시하고 있으므로 (D)가 정답이다.

(Paraphrasing) 지문의 is priced at → 정답의 costs

199 에코랜드 리사이클링의 반힐 고객은 왜 셸번 로 시설을 방문할 것인가?

(A) 추가 배출통을 얻으려고
(B) 플라스틱 제품을 재활용하려고
(C) 도로변 수거 서비스에 등록하려고
(D) 민간 재활용 업체에 대해 알아보려고

해설 **연계**
이메일의 네 번째 문장에서 3월 15일 월요일부터는 종이, 판지, 플라스틱 제품, 알루미늄 캔, 유리병 및 병을 셸번 로의 시립 폐기물 관리 센터로 가져오라(you may deliver ~ to the city's waste management centre on Shelburne Road)고 했고, 웹페이지의 네 번째 문장에서 에코랜드 리사이클링은 플라스틱으로 만든 제품은 수거하지 않는다(Objects made of plastic are not accepted)고 했다. 따라서 반힐 고객은 플라스틱 제품을 재활용하려고 폐기물 센터를 방문할 것임을 알 수 있으므로 정답은 (B)이다.

200 에코랜드 리사이클링의 3구역 신규 고객에 대해 암시된 것은?

(A) 자기 소유 재활용 배출통을 제공해야 한다.
(B) 이전에 다른 재활용 업체와 계약을 했다.
(C) 재활용 계약에 대한 할인을 받았다.
(D) 동네 주택 소유자 협회에 속해 있다.

해설 **연계**
웹페이지의 세 번째 단락 첫 문장에서 신규 고객들을 위해 특별 혜택을 제공 중이니 서비스 첫 해 요금을 미리 결제하고 할인을 받으라(Pay in advance ~ and receive a reduced price)고 했고, 회람의 두 번째 문장에서 3구역의 목요일 정기 순회 구역에 아래 4개의 주소를 추가하라(Please add the following four addresses ~ in Zone 3)고 한 뒤, 전부 1년 치 전액 결제되었다(All are fully paid up for the year)고 했다. 따라서 에코랜드 리사이클링에 새로 가입한 3구역 고객들은 모두 1년 치 요금을 결제하고 할인 받았다는 것을 알 수 있으므로 정답은 (C)이다.

(Paraphrasing) 지문의 a reduced price
→ 정답의 a discount

PART 1

1　W-Br

(A) The man is moving a vehicle.
(B) The man is holding on to a doorknob.
(C) The man is sweeping the stairs.
(D) The man is carrying a large box.

(A) 남자가 차량을 이동하고 있다.
(B) 남자가 문고리를 붙잡고 있다.
(C) 남자가 계단을 쓸고 있다.
(D) 남자가 큰 상자를 나르고 있다.

해설　**인물 중심 사진**
(A) **사진에 없는 명사를 이용한 오답:** 사진에 차량(a vehicle)이 보이지 않는다.
(B) **동작 묘사 오답:** 남자가 문고리를 붙잡고 있는(is holding on) 모습이 아니다.
(C) **동작 묘사 오답:** 남자가 계단을 쓸고 있는(is sweeping) 모습이 아니다.
(D) **정답:** 남자가 큰 상자를 나르고 있는(is carrying) 모습이므로 정답이다.

어휘　vehicle 차량　doorknob 문고리　sweep (빗자루로) 쓸다

2　M-Au

(A) One of the women is walking down a ramp.
(B) One of the women is looking into a bag.
(C) A bicycle is chained to a handrail.
(D) Some poles are lying on a dock.

(A) 여자들 중 한 명이 경사로를 걸어 내려오고 있다.
(B) 여자들 중 한 명이 가방 속을 들여다보고 있다.
(C) 자전거 한 대가 난간에 묶여 있다.
(D) 기둥들이 부두 위에 놓여 있다.

해설　**인물/사물 혼합 사진**
(A) **정답:** 여자들 중 한 명이 경사로를 걸어 내려오고 있는(is walking down) 모습이므로 정답이다.
(B) **동작 묘사 오답:** 여자들 중 한 명이 가방 속을 들여다보고 있는(is looking into) 모습이 아니다.
(C) **상태 묘사 오답:** 자전거가 난간에 묶여 있는(is chained to a handrail) 상태가 아니다.
(D) **상태 묘사 오답:** 기둥들이 부두 위에 놓여 있는(are lying on a dock) 상태가 아니다.

어휘　ramp 경사로　handrail 난간　pole 기둥　lie 놓여 있다　dock 부두

3 W-Am

(A) The man is leading a tour.
(B) The man is hanging a painting on a wall.
(C) The man is standing in front of a painting.
(D) The man is painting a window frame.

(A) 남자가 투어를 인솔하고 있다.
(B) 남자가 벽에 그림을 걸고 있다.
(C) 남자가 그림 앞에 서 있다.
(D) 남자가 창틀을 칠하고 있다.

해설 **인물 중심 사진**
(A) **동작 묘사 오답:** 남자가 투어를 인솔하고 있는(is leading) 모습이 아니다.
(B) **동작 묘사 오답:** 남자가 그림을 벽에 걸고 있는(is hanging) 모습이 아니다.
(C) **정답:** 남자가 그림 앞에 서 있는(is standing) 모습이므로 정답이다.
(D) **사진에 없는 명사를 이용한 오답:** 사진에 창틀(a window frame)이 보이지 않는다

4 M-Au

(A) Wooden boards have been propped up against a fence.
(B) Baskets have been stacked on a wooden crate.
(C) Flowers are being repotted.
(D) An umbrella is being closed.

(A) 널빤지들이 울타리에 받쳐져 있다.
(B) 바구니들이 나무 상자 위에 쌓여 있다
(C) 꽃을 다른 화분에 옮겨 심고 있다.
(D) 파라솔이 접히고 있다.

해설 **사물 사진**
(A) **상태 묘사 오답:** 널빤지들이 울타리에 받쳐져 있는(have been propped up against) 상태가 아니다.
(B) **정답:** 바구니들이 나무 상자 위에 쌓여 있는(have been stacked on a wooden crate) 모습이므로 정답이다.
(C) **진행 상황 묘사 오답:** 꽃을 다른 화분에 옮겨 심고 있는(are being repotted) 상황이 아니다.
(D) **진행 상황 묘사 오답:** 파라솔이 접히고 있는(is being closed) 상황이 아니다.

어휘 wooden board 널빤지 prop 받치다 stack 쌓다
crate (나무) 상자 repot 다른 화분에 옮겨 심다

5 M-Cn

(A) Tools have been hung from a shelving unit.
(B) A ladder has been left in the corner of a warehouse.
(C) Products have been stocked on shelves.
(D) Some boxes have been loaded onto a conveyor belt.

(A) 공구들이 선반에 걸려 있다.
(B) 사다리가 창고 구석에 놓여 있다.
(C) 제품들이 선반틀에 채워져 있다.
(D) 상자들이 컨베이어 벨트 위에 적재되어 있다.

해설 **사물 사진**
(A) **사진에 없는 명사를 이용한 오답:** 사진에 공구들(Tools)이 보이지 않는다.
(B) **사진에 없는 명사를 이용한 오답:** 사진에 사다리(A ladder)가 보이지 않는다.
(C) **정답:** 제품들이 선반에 채워져 있는(have been stocked on shelves) 모습이므로 정답이다.
(D) **사진에 없는 명사를 이용한 오답:** 사진에 컨베이어 벨트(a conveyor belt)가 보이지 않는다.

어휘 shelving unit 선반 warehouse 창고 stock 채우다
load 적재하다

6 W-Am

(A) A picnic area has been set up near some trees.
(B) A picnic basket has been left on a bench.
(C) A tent is sheltering a picnic area.
(D) There's a cooking grill next to a fence.

(A) 피크닉장이 나무들 근처에 마련되어 있다.
(B) 피크닉 바구니가 벤치 위에 놓여 있다.
(C) 천막이 피크닉장을 덮고 있다.
(D) 울타리 옆에 요리용 그릴이 있다.

해설 **사물/풍경 사진**
(A) **정답:** 피크닉장이 나무들 근처에 마련되어 있는(has been set up near some trees) 모습이므로 정답이다.
(B) **사진에 없는 명사를 이용한 오답:** 사진에 피크닉 바구니(A picnic basket)가 보이지 않는다.
(C) **사진에 없는 명사를 이용한 오답:** 사진에 천막(A tent)이 보이지 않는다.
(D) **사진에 없는 명사를 이용한 오답:** 사진에 요리용 그릴(a cooking grill)이 보이지 않는다.

어휘 set up ~을 설치하다 shelter 막아 주다

PART 2

질문에 Yes라고 긍정한 뒤 방금 이야기했다며 긍정 답변과 일관된 내용을 덧붙였으므로 정답이다.

(C) **연상 어휘 오답:** 질문의 chef에서 연상 가능한 restaurant's dessert menu를 이용한 오답이다.

---

7 W-Am / M-Au

When's the health conference?
(A) At the end of the month.
(B) Because registration fees increased.
(C) I feel much better today.

보건 콘퍼런스가 언제죠?
(A) 이번 달 말이요.
(B) 등록비가 올라서요.
(C) 오늘은 훨씬 나아졌어요.

해설 **콘퍼런스 일정을 묻는 When 의문문**
(A) **정답:** 학회가 열리는 시기를 묻는 질문에 이번 달 말이라고 구체적인 시점을 알려 주고 있으므로 정답이다.
(B) **연상 어휘 오답:** 질문의 conference에서 연상 가능한 registration fees를 이용한 오답이다.
(C) **연상 어휘 오답:** 질문의 health에서 연상 가능한 feel much better를 이용한 오답이다.

---

8 M-Cn / W-Am

Why are we using a different caterer this year?
(A) Around eleven o'clock, I think.
(B) Because we have a smaller budget.
(C) No, I haven't used that software yet.

올해는 왜 다른 케이터링 업체를 이용하나요?
(A) 11시쯤인 것 같아요.
(B) 예산이 줄어들었기 때문이에요.
(C) 아니요, 아직 그 소프트웨어를 써보지 않았어요.

해설 **올해 다른 케이터링 업체를 이용하는 이유를 묻는 Why 의문문**
(A) 질문과 상관없는 오답
(B) **정답:** 올해 다른 케이터링 업체를 이용하는 이유를 묻는 질문에 예산이 줄었다며 구체적인 이유를 밝히고 있으므로 정답이다.
(C) **Yes/No 불가 오답:** Why 의문문에는 Yes/No로 응답할 수 없다.

어휘 budget 예산

---

9 W-Am / M-Au

Did you let the chef know about the customer's complaint?
(A) Interesting. I didn't know that.
(B) Yes, I just spoke to her.
(C) The restaurant's dessert menu.

주방장에게 고객의 불만 사항에 대해 알려 주셨나요?
(A) 흥미롭군요. 몰랐네요.
(B) 네, 방금 이야기했어요.
(C) 식당의 디저트 메뉴예요.

해설 **주방장에게 고객의 불만 사항을 알려 주었는지 확인하는 일반 의문문**
(A) **어휘 반복 오답:** 질문의 know를 반복 이용한 오답이다.
(B) **정답:** 주방장에게 고객의 불만 사항을 알려 주었는지 묻는

---

10 M-Cn / W-Am

Where did you meet Mr. Raj?
(A) He's an excellent speaker.
(B) At the community center.
(C) Have you eaten yet?

어디에서 라즈 씨를 만났나요?
(A) 그는 훌륭한 연설가예요.
(B) 커뮤니티 센터에서요.
(C) 식사하셨어요?

해설 **라즈 씨를 만난 장소를 묻는 Where 의문문**
(A) **연상 어휘 오답:** 질문의 Mr. Raj에서 연상 가능한 He를 이용한 오답이다.
(B) **정답:** 라즈 씨를 만난 장소를 묻는 질문에 커뮤니티 센터라고 구체적인 장소를 밝히고 있으므로 정답이다.
(C) 질문과 상관없는 오답

---

11 W-Am / M-Au

You should call technical support if you have any problems.
(A) Thanks. I will.
(B) Because we're busy.
(C) Put a support beam here.

문제가 있으면 기술 지원팀에 전화해야 됩니다.
(A) 고마워요. 그럴게요.
(B) 저희는 바빠서요.
(C) 지지대를 여기에 놓으세요.

해설 **정보를 전달하는 평서문**
(A) **정답:** 문제가 있으면 기술 지원팀에 전화하라는 평서문에 고맙다며 그렇게 하겠다고 응답하고 있으므로 정답이다.
(B) 평서문과 상관없는 오답
(C) **어휘 반복 오답:** 평서문의 support를 반복 이용한 오답이다.

어휘 technical support 기술 지원 beam 기둥

---

12 M-Cn / M-Au

How often does the restaurant have to replace its serving dishes?
(A) Table twelve needs service.
(B) Be careful. That plate is hot.
(C) Usually twice a year.

식당은 서빙 접시들을 얼마나 자주 교체해야 하나요?
(A) 12번 테이블에 서비스가 필요해요.
(B) 조심하세요. 저 접시는 뜨거워요.
(C) 보통 일 년에 두 번이에요.

해설 **식당이 서빙 접시를 교체해야 하는 빈도를 묻는 How often 의문문**
(A) **연상 어휘 및 파생어 오답:** 질문의 restaurant에서 연상 가능한 Table twelve를 이용했고, 질문의 serving과

파생어 관계인 service를 이용한 오답이다.

(B) **연상 어휘 오답:** 질문의 dishes에서 연상 가능한 plate를 이용한 오답이다.

(C) **정답:** 서빙 접시의 교체 빈도를 묻는 질문에 일 년에 두 번이라고 구체적인 빈도를 알려 주고 있으므로 정답이다.

어휘 replace 교체하다 plate 접시

13 W-Br / M-Cn

Can you bring me Ms. Campbell's medical records?
(A) Sure—just one second.
(B) I've never heard of that pharmacy.
(C) Two shuttle buses.

캠벨 씨의 의료 기록 좀 가져다 주실 수 있나요?
(A) 그러죠. 잠시만요.
(B) 그 약국에 대해 들어본 적이 없어요.
(C) 셔틀버스 두 대예요.

해설 요청하는 의문문

(A) **정답:** 캠벨 씨의 의료 기록을 가져다 달라는 요청에 Sure이라 긍정한 뒤 긍정 답변과 일관된 내용을 덧붙였으므로 정답이다.

(B) **연상 어휘 오답:** 질문의 medical records에서 연상 가능한 pharmacy를 이용한 오답이다.

(C) **질문과 상관없는 오답**

어휘 medical records 의료 기록 pharmacy 약국

14 M-Cn / W-Am

Why was the staff meeting canceled?
(A) Because Ms. Ishikawa is out of the office.
(B) Since last week.
(C) Let's meet at the theater.

직원회의가 왜 취소됐나요?
(A) 이시카와 씨가 사무실을 비워서요.
(B) 지난주부터요.
(C) 극장에서 만나요.

해설 직원회의의 취소 사유를 묻는 Why 의문문

(A) **정답:** 직원회의가 취소된 이유를 묻는 질문에 이시카와 씨가 사무실을 비웠다고 이유를 밝히고 있으므로 정답이다.

(B) **질문과 상관없는 오답:** When 의문문에 적합한 응답이다.

(C) **파생어 오답:** 질문의 meeting과 파생어 관계인 meet를 이용한 오답이다.

15 M-Au / W-Br

Melissa is doing a factory visit this morning, isn't she?
(A) The plastics manufacturing industry.
(B) Right, so she'll be late to the meeting.
(C) I bought them at the hardware store.

오늘 오전에 멜리사가 공장을 방문하죠, 그렇지 않나요?
(A) 플라스틱 제조업이에요.
(B) 맞아요. 그래서 그녀는 회의에 늦을 겁니다.
(C) 철물점에서 샀어요.

해설 멜리사의 공장 방문 여부를 확인하는 부가 의문문

(A) **연상 어휘 오답:** 질문의 factory에서 연상 가능한 manufacturing industry를 이용한 오답이다.

(B) **정답:** 멜리사의 공장 방문 여부를 확인하는 질문에 Right이라고 긍정한 뒤 그래서 그녀가 회의에 늦는다며 긍정 답변과 일관된 내용을 덧붙이고 있으므로 정답이다.

(C) **연상 어휘 오답:** 질문의 factory에서 연상 가능한 hardware를 이용한 오답이다.

어휘 manufacturing 제조업 hardware 철물; (컴퓨터의) 하드웨어

16 M-Au / W-Am

What kind of appliance should we buy for the office?
(A) A new coffeemaker.
(B) Sure, I was going there anyway.
(C) An application process.

사무실에 어떤 가전제품을 사야 하나요?
(A) 새 커피 메이커요.
(B) 그럼요. 어차피 저도 거기로 가던 참이었어요.
(C) 신청 절차예요.

해설 사무실에 구입할 가전제품을 묻는 What 의문문

(A) **정답:** 사무실에 어떤 가전제품을 구입해야 하는지 묻는 질문에 새 커피 메이커라고 구체적으로 밝히고 있으므로 정답이다.

(B) **Yes/No 불가 오답:** What 의문문에는 Yes/No 응답이 불가능한데, Sure도 일종의 Yes 응답이라고 볼 수 있으므로 오답이다.

(C) **파생어 오답:** 질문의 appliance와 파생어 관계인 application을 이용한 오답이다.

어휘 appliance 가전제품 application 신청(서)

17 W-Br / M-Cn

How often does the gym offer a discount on membership?
(A) Sorry. I don't know.
(B) It's next to the post office.
(C) Remember to bring your own towel.

헬스장은 얼마나 자주 회원 할인을 제공하나요?
(A) 죄송해요. 모르겠어요.
(B) 우체국 옆에 있어요.
(C) 잊지 말고 본인 수건을 가져오세요.

해설 헬스장의 회원 할인 제공 빈도를 묻는 How often 의문문

(A) **정답:** 헬스장의 회원 할인 제공 빈도를 묻는 질문에 Sorry라고 한 뒤, 모른다며 정보를 제공할 수 없음을 밝히고 있으므로 정답이다.

(B) **유사 발음 오답:** 질문의 offer와 부분적으로 발음이 유사한 office를 이용한 오답이다.

(C) **연상 어휘 오답:** 질문의 gym에서 연상 가능한 towel을 이용한 오답이다.

18 W-Br / M-Cn

Is the shipment going to be transported by truck or by train?

(A) It's coming by truck.

(B) I can sign the invoice.

(C) Road construction.

화물은 트럭으로 운송되나요, 아니면 기차로 운송되나요?

(A) 트럭으로 오고 있어요.

(B) 제가 송장에 서명할게요.

(C) 도로 공사예요.

해설　화물의 운송 방식을 묻는 선택 의문문

(A) **정답:** 화물의 운송 방식을 묻는 질문에 전자를 선택해 응답하고 있으므로 정답이다.

(B) **연상 어휘 오답:** 질문의 shipment에서 연상 가능한 invoice를 이용한 오답이다.

(C) **연상 어휘 오답:** 질문의 transported by truck에서 연상 가능한 Road construction을 이용한 오답이다

어휘　transport 운송하다　invoice 청구서　construction 공사

19 M-Au / M-Cn

Could I ride with you to the company retreat?

(A) Yes, it was very interesting.

(B) I'll be on vacation at that time.

(C) We had a lot of fun.

회사 야유회에 갈 때 저도 좀 태워 주실래요?

(A) 네, 매우 흥미진진했어요.

(B) 그때 저는 휴가예요.

(C) 정말 재미있었어요.

해설　요청하는 의문문

(A) **연상 어휘 오답:** 질문의 company retreat에서 연상 가능한 interesting을 이용한 오답이다.

(B) **정답:** 회사 야유회에 갈 때 태워 달라는 요청에 그때 휴가라며 태워 줄 수 없음을 우회적으로 밝히고 있으므로 정답이다.

(C) **연상 어휘 오답:** 질문의 company retreat에서 연상 가능한 a lot of fun을 이용한 오답이다.

어휘　retreat 야유회

20 W-Am / M-Au

I think I'm going to exchange this shirt.

(A) Let's change meeting rooms.

(B) Is something wrong with it?

(C) Turn left at the lights.

이 셔츠를 교환해야 할 것 같아요.

(A) 회의실을 바꿉시다.

(B) 무슨 문제라도 있나요?

(C) 신호등에서 좌회전하세요.

해설　의견을 제시하는 평서문

(A) **파생어 오답:** 평서문의 exchange와 파생어 관계인 change를 이용한 오답이다.

(B) **정답:** 셔츠를 교환해야 할 것 같다는 평서문에 무슨 문제가 있는지 교환을 생각하는 이유를 되묻고 있으므로 정답

이다.

(C) 평서문과 상관없는 오답

21 W-Br / M-Cn

When will the caterers begin setting up for the party?

(A) An hour from now.

(B) At the back of the building.

(C) Mostly Indian food.

케이터링 업체는 언제 파티 준비를 시작하죠?

(A) 지금부터 한 시간 뒤예요.

(B) 건물 뒤에서요.

(C) 대부분 인도 음식이에요.

해설　케이터링 업체의 파티 준비 시점을 묻는 When 의문문

(A) **정답:** 케이터링 업체의 파티 준비 시점을 묻는 질문에 한 시간 뒤라고 구체적인 시점을 밝히고 있으므로 정답이다.

(B) **질문과 상관없는 오답:** Where 의문문에 적합한 응답이다.

(C) **연상 어휘 오답:** 질문의 caterers에서 연상 가능한 Indian food를 이용한 오답이다.

22 M-Au / W-Br

Who will be the keynote speaker at the conference?

(A) At the downtown conference center.

(B) The agenda hasn't been posted yet.

(C) What an impressive speech!

회의의 기조 연설자가 누구죠?

(A) 시내 회의장에서요.

(B) 안건이 아직 게시되지 않았어요.

(C) 정말 감동적인 연설이에요!

해설　회의의 기조 연설자를 묻는 Who 의문문

(A) **어휘 반복 오답:** 질문의 conference를 반복 이용한 오답이다.

(B) **정답:** 회의의 기조 연설자를 묻는 질문에 안건이 아직 게시되지 않았다며 모른다는 것을 우회적으로 밝히고 있으므로 정답이다.

(C) **파생어 오답:** 질문의 speaker와 파생어 관계인 speech를 이용한 오답이다.

어휘　keynote speaker 기조 연설자　agenda 안건 impressive 감동적인, 인상적인

23 M-Au / W-Am

Aren't you going to enter a photo in the contest?

(A) I don't take portraits.

(B) Here's your confirmation number.

(C) You can take a sample home with you.

공모전에 사진 제출 안 하시나요?

(A) 저는 인물 사진은 안 찍어요.

(B) 여기 예약 확인 번호예요.

(C) 샘플을 집에 갖고 가셔도 돼요.

해설 **공모전에 사진을 제출할지 묻는 부정 의문문**
(A) **정답:** 공모전에 사진을 제출할지 묻는 질문에 인물 사진은 안 찍는다며 공모전에 참가하지 않음을 우회적으로 밝히고 있으므로 정답이다.
(B) 질문과 상관없는 오답
(C) **연상 어휘 오답:** 질문의 photo에서 연상 가능한 take를 이용한 오답이다.

어휘 portrait 인물 사진, 초상화   confirmation 확인

24 M-Cn / W-Am
Mohini, don't you go to that café around the corner?
(A) No, usually around lunchtime.
(B) Yes, it's a nice place to sit and get coffee.
(C) I went to see that movie yesterday.

모히니, 모퉁이에 있는 카페에 가지 않나요?
(A) 아니요, 보통 점심시간쯤에요.
(B) 네, 앉아서 커피 마시기 좋은 곳이에요.
(C) 저는 어제 그 영화를 보러 갔어요.

해설 **카페 방문 여부를 묻는 부정 의문문**
(A) **어휘 반복 및 연상 어휘 오답:** 질문의 around를 반복 이용하고 질문의 café에서 연상 가능한 lunchtime을 이용한 오답이다.
(B) **정답:** 모퉁이에 있는 카페에 가는지 묻는 질문에 Yes라고 긍정한 뒤, 긍정 답변과 일관된 내용을 덧붙이고 있으므로 정답이다.
(C) **파생어 오답:** 질문의 go와 파생어 관계인 went를 이용한 오답이다.

25 W-Am / W-Br
How often will the workshops be held?
(A) I'll see if he's working yet.
(B) Nisreen would be able to tell you.
(C) Let me hold on to it for you.

워크숍은 얼마나 자주 열리나요?
(A) 그가 아직 일하고 있는지 확인해 볼게요.
(B) 니스린이 알려 줄 수 있을 거예요.
(C) 제가 맡아 드릴게요.

해설 **워크숍 개최 빈도를 묻는 How often 의문문**
(A) **유사 발음 오답:** 질문의 workshops와 부분적으로 발음이 유사한 working을 이용한 오답이다.
(B) **정답:** 워크숍 개최 빈도를 묻는 질문에 나스린이 알려 줄 수 있다며 관련 정보를 아는 사람을 알려 주고 있으므로 정답이다.
(C) **파생어 오답:** 질문의 held와 파생어 관계인 hold를 이용한 오답이다.

어휘 hold on to ~을 맡아 주다

26 M-Cn / W-Am
We're almost out of printer paper.
(A) A front-page article.
(B) Either way is fine.
(C) There's an office supply store nearby.

프린터 용지가 거의 떨어졌어요.
(A) 기사 1면이에요.
(B) 어느 쪽이든 괜찮아요.
(C) 근처에 사무용품점이 있어요.

해설 **상황을 설명하는 평서문**
(A) **연상 어휘 오답:** 평서문의 paper에서 연상 가능한 front-page를 이용한 오답이다.
(B) 평서문과 상관없는 오답
(C) **정답:** 프린터 용지가 거의 떨어졌다는 평서문에 근처에 사무용품점이 있다며 해결 방안을 알려 주고 있으므로 정답이다.

어휘 article 기사   office supply 사무용품

27 M-Cn / W-Br
Where should we plant the daffodils and tulips?
(A) How much sun do they need?
(B) We're taking a holiday in November.
(C) The key is under the doormat.

수선화와 튤립을 어디에 심어야 할까요?
(A) 햇볕이 얼마나 필요한가요?
(B) 우린 11월에 휴가를 가려고요.
(C) 열쇠는 현관 깔개 밑에 있어요.

해설 **꽃을 심을 장소를 묻는 Where 의문문**
(A) **정답:** 수선화와 튤립을 심을 장소를 묻는 질문에 햇볕이 얼마나 필요한지 심을 장소와 관련된 정보를 되묻고 있으므로 정답이다.
(B) **어휘 반복 오답:** 질문의 we를 반복 이용한 오답이다.
(C) 질문과 상관없는 오답

어휘 daffodil 수선화

28 W-Am / W-Br
Aren't the machines for the new assembly line being delivered soon?
(A) It was a much faster production method.
(B) We just started setting them up.
(C) The team we've assembled is highly qualified.

새 조립 라인 기계들이 곧 배송되지 않나요?
(A) 그게 훨씬 빠른 생산 방식이었어요.
(B) 이제 막 설치를 시작했어요.
(C) 우리가 구성한 팀은 아주 유능해요.

해설 **새 조립 라인 기계들의 배송 일정을 묻는 부정 의문문**
(A) **연상 어휘 오답:** 질문의 machines, assembly line에서 연상 가능한 production method를 이용한 오답이다.
(B) **정답:** 새 조립 라인의 기계들이 곧 배송되는지를 묻는 질문에 막 설치를 시작했다며 이미 도착했음을 우회적으로 밝히고 있으므로 정답이다.
(C) **파생어 오답:** 질문의 assembly와 파생어 관계인 assembled를 이용한 오답이다.

어휘 assembly 조립   production 생산   assemble 구성하다   qualified 자질을 갖춘

29 M-Cn / W-Br

Are you aware of the new procedure for ordering supplies?
(A) I've been out of the office.
(B) A box of printer paper.
(C) It's a new branch location.

새로운 비품 주문 절차에 대해 아시나요?
(A) 전 사무실에 없었어요.
(B) 프린터 용지 한 상자요.
(C) 신규 지점 위치예요.

해설 **새로운 비품 주문 절차에 대해 묻는 일반 의문문**
(A) **정답:** 새로운 비품 주문 절차를 알고 있는지 묻는 질문에 사무실에 없었다며 모른다는 것을 우회적으로 밝히고 있으므로 정답이다.
(B) **연상 어휘 오답:** 질문의 supplies에서 연상 가능한 printer paper를 이용한 오답이다.
(C) **어휘 반복 오답:** 질문의 new를 반복 이용한 오답이다.

어휘 be aware of ~을 알다 procedure 절차 branch 분점

30 W-Br / M-Au

A new logo might help our business stand out more.
(A) I like the one we have now.
(B) A few of them are standing outside.
(C) Here, let me help you lift that.

새로운 로고는 우리 회사가 더 돋보이는 데 도움이 될 것 같습니다.
(A) 저는 지금 있는 게 마음에 들어요.
(B) 그들 중 몇 명은 밖에 서 있어요.
(C) 자, 그거 들어 올리는 것 도와 드릴게요.

해설 **의견을 제시하는 평서문**
(A) **정답:** 새로운 로고는 우리 회사가 더 돋보이는 데 도움이 될 것 같다는 평서문에 지금 로고가 마음에 든다며 반대되는 의견을 제시하고 있으므로 정답이다.
(B) **파생어 오답:** 평서문의 stand와 파생어 관계인 standing을 이용한 오답이다.
(C) **어휘 반복 오답:** 평서문의 help를 반복 이용한 오답이다.

어휘 stand out 돋보이다 lift 들어 올리다

31 M-Au / W-Br

Which lightbulbs are we supposed to replace?
(A) My jacket's hanging in the closet.
(B) If you two can finish the report soon.
(C) I replaced them all last week.

어떤 전구를 교체해야 하나요?
(A) 제 재킷은 옷장에 걸려 있어요.
(B) 두 분이 곧 보고서를 끝낼 수 있다면요.
(C) 지난주에 제가 전부 교체했어요.

해설 **교체해야 할 전구를 묻는 Which 의문문**
(A) **질문과 상관없는 오답**
(B) **유사 발음 오답:** 질문의 replace와 부분적으로 발음이 유사한 report를 이용한 오답이다.

(C) **정답:** 교체해야 할 전구를 묻는 질문에 지난주에 자신이 전부 교체했다며 교체할 필요가 없다는 것을 우회적으로 밝히고 있으므로 정답이다.

PART 3

[32-34] M-Cn / W-Am

> M 32,33 I'm calling to ask if you'll be hiring any interns this summer. 32 I'm in my first year of law school. I'd like to get some practical experience.
>
> W 32 I think applications for the internship program open soon. 33 You'll have to apply through our Web site. Then you'll hear from Rajesh Patel. He coordinates the program.
>
> M OK. Thank you. 34 If I'm hired, will the costs of commuting to the office be reimbursed?
>
> W 34 I'm sorry, no. We don't do that.

> 남 32,33 이번 여름에 인턴을 채용하는지 문의하려고 전화했습니다. 32 저는 로스쿨 1학년이에요. 실무 경험을 쌓고 싶어요.
>
> 여 32 인턴십 프로그램 지원이 곧 시작될 것 같아요. 33 저희 웹사이트를 통해 지원하셔야 해요. 그러면 라제시 파텔 씨로부터 연락을 받게 될 겁니다. 그가 프로그램을 총괄하거든요.
>
> 남 알겠습니다. 감사합니다. 34 제가 채용되면 사무실 통근 비용이 상환되나요?
>
> 여 34 죄송하지만 아니에요. 그렇게 하지는 않습니다.

어휘 practical 실무적인 apply 지원하다 coordinate 총괄하다 commute 통근하다 reimburse 상환하다

32 여자는 어디에서 일하는 것 같은가?
(A) 여행사
(B) 인터넷 서비스 제공업체
(C) 법률 사무소
(D) 부동산 중개소

해설 **여자의 근무 장소**
남자가 첫 대사에서 이번 여름에 인턴을 채용하는지 문의하려고 전화했다(I'm calling to ask if you'll be hiring any interns this summer)면서 자신이 로스쿨 1학년 (I'm in my first year of law school)이라고 소개하며 실무 경험을 쌓고 싶다(I'd like to get some practical experience)고 말했다. 여자가 응답으로 인턴십 프로그램 지원이 곧 시작될 것 같다(I think applications for the internship program open soon)고 했으므로 (C)가 정답이다.

어휘 firm 회사 real estate 부동산

33 남자는 웹사이트에서 무엇을 할 수 있는가?
(A) 티켓 구매
(B) 입사 지원
(C) 서비스 취소
(D) 고객 계정 개설

해설 **남자가 웹사이트에서 할 수 있는 것**
남자가 첫 대사에서 이번 여름에 인턴을 채용할 예정인지

문의하려고 전화했다(I'm calling to ask if you'll be hiring any interns this summer)고 했고 여자가 웹사이트를 통해 지원해야 한다(You'll have to apply through our Web site)고 했으므로 (B)가 정답이다.

어휘 account 계좌, 계정

34 여자는 왜 사과하는가?
(A) 동료가 시간이 없다.
(B) 웹페이지가 작동하지 않는다.
(C) 지원서가 처리되지 않았다.
(D) 비용이 상환되지 않을 것이다.

해설 **여자가 사과하는 이유**
남자가 마지막 대사에서 채용되면 사무실 통근 비용이 상환되는지(If I'm hired, will the costs of commuting to the office be reimbursed?) 묻자 여자가 미안하다며 아니다(I'm sorry, no)라고 말했으므로 (D)가 정답이다.

어휘 process 처리하다   expense 비용

(Paraphrasing) 대화의 the costs of commuting to the office → 정답의 An expense

[35-37] W-Br / M-Cn

> W **35 Mr. Jeong, I have some questions about the Becker account. I want to be sure that my calculations are correct before I finalize an invoice for the work that our company did.**
> M That was a complex building renovation. How can I help?
> W I'm looking at the expenses from the month of September. It looks like some details are missing. **36 Can you send me the receipts for the materials we purchased back then?**
> M Yes, I can e-mail those to you.
> W Great. Could you do it right away? **37 I'm expecting a call from Mr. Becker at three.**
> M Sure.
>
> 여 **35**정 씨, 베커 씨 거래에 대해 몇 가지 질문이 있어요. 우리 회사가 수행한 작업에 대한 청구서를 마무리하기 전에 제 계산이 정확한지 확인하고 싶어요.
> 남 복잡한 건물 보수 작업이었죠. 어떻게 도와드릴까요?
> 여 9월달 경비를 보고 있는데요. 몇 가지 세부 사항이 누락된 것 같아요. **36**그때 구매한 자재 영수증을 보내 주실 수 있나요?
> 남 네, 이메일로 보내 드릴게요.
> 여 좋습니다. 바로 가능할까요? **37**3시에 베커 씨한테 전화가 올 거예요.
> 남 물론이죠.
>
> **어휘** calculations 계산   materials 자재

35 여자의 직업은 무엇인 것 같은가?
(A) 건축가   (B) 연구원
(C) 마케팅 전문가   **(D) 회계사**

해설 **여자의 직업**
여자가 첫 대사에서 베커 씨 거래에 대해 몇 가지 질문이 있다(Mr. Jeong, I have some questions about the Becker account)면서 회사가 수행한 작업에 대한 청구서를 마무리하기 전에 계산이 정확한지 확인하고 싶다(I want to be sure that my calculations are correct before I finalize an invoice ~)고 했으므로 (D)가 정답이다.

어휘 architect 건축가   accountant 회계사

36 여자는 무엇을 요청하는가?
(A) 영수증   (B) 공급업체 주소
(C) 전자 파일 위치   (D) 배송 일정

해설 **여자의 요청 사항**
여자가 두 번째 대사에서 당시 구매한 자재 영수증을 보내 달라(Can you send me the receipts for the materials we purchased back then?)고 했으므로 (A)가 정답이다.

37 3시에 어떤 일이 일어날 것인가?
(A) 제품 시연   (B) 기자 회견
(C) 고객 전화   (D) 소프트웨어 업그레이드

해설 **3시에 일어날 일**
여자가 마지막 대사에서 3시에 베커 씨한테 전화가 올 것이다(I'm expecting a call from Mr. Becker at three)라고 했으므로 (C)가 정답이다.

어휘 demonstration 시연   press conference 기자 회견

[38-40] M-Au / W-Br

> M **38 Those eyeglass frames are a good choice for you. Now, about the lenses for your new glasses**—you mentioned that your eyes hurt after a long day working at your computer. Have you considered blue-light lenses?
> W Oh, yes—someone at work said those lenses could help with eyestrain. **39 Are they much more expensive than standard lenses?**
> M They're about 50 dollars more, **40 but we'll be running a promotion next week—if you wait until then, they'll be cheaper.**
>
> 남 **38**안경테는 잘 선택하셨어요. 자, 새 안경 렌즈는 컴퓨터로 오래 일하고 나면 눈이 아프다고 하셨죠. 블루라이트 렌즈는 고려해 보셨나요?
> 여 아, 네. 직장 동료가 그 렌즈가 눈 피로에 도움이 된다고 그러더군요. **39**일반 렌즈보다 훨씬 더 비싼가요?
> 남 50달러 정도 더 비싸요. **40**하지만 다음 주에 판촉 행사를 진행할 예정입니다. 그때까지 기다리시면 더 저렴해질 겁니다.
>
> **어휘** eyestrain 눈의 피로   promotion 판촉 행사

38 남자는 무엇을 팔 것 같은가?
- (A) 사진 액자
- (B) 컴퓨터
- (C) 옥외 조명
- (D) 안경

해설 **남자가 파는 물건**
남자가 첫 대사에서 안경테를 잘 선택했다(Those eyeglass frames are a good choice for you)고 말한 뒤 새 안경 렌즈(Now, about the lenses for your new glasses)에 관한 이야기를 이어가고 있으므로 (D)가 정답이다.

39 여자는 무엇에 대해 묻는가?
- (A) 제품 가격
- (B) 제품 색상
- (C) 배송일
- (D) 품질 보증

해설 **여자가 묻는 것**
여자가 마지막 대사에서 일반 렌즈보다 훨씬 비싼지(Are they much more expensive than standard lenses?) 물었으므로 (A)가 정답이다.

어휘 warranty 보증(서)

40 남자는 다음 주에 어떤 일이 일어날 것이라고 말하는가?
- (A) 직책 하나가 충원된다.
- (B) 수리가 완료된다.
- (C) 상품이 할인된다.
- (D) 배송품이 도착한다.

해설 **남자가 다음 주에 일어날 것이라고 말하는 일**
남자가 마지막 대사에서 다음 주에 판촉 행사를 진행한다(we'll be running a promotion next week)면서 그 때까지 기다리면 더 저렴해진다(if you wait until then, they'll be cheaper)고 했으므로 (C)가 정답이다.

(Paraphrasing) 대화의 they'll be cheaper
→ 정답의 A product will be discounted.

[41-43] M-Cn / W-Am

> M **41 My article about upcoming summer events in Plainsville was just published.**
>
> W That's wonderful news! **41 I'm still working on my article about the new botanical garden.** What events are coming up in June?
>
> M There are many, but **42 the highlight event will take place at the end of June. It's a food festival**—with a total of 50 vendors. There'll be restaurants, food trucks, and gourmet market stalls.
>
> W That sounds great! **43 Why don't I post a link to the article on all our social media outlets?** That will help reach a wider audience. **43 I can do that right now.**
>
> 남 **41 플레인스빌에서 곧 있을 여름 행사에 대한 제 기사가 방금 게시되었어요.**
>
> 여 정말 좋은 소식이네요! **41 저는 새로 생긴 식물원에 관한 기사를 아직도 쓰고 있어요.** 6월에는 어떤 행사가 열리죠?
>
> 남 많이 있지만, **42 주요 행사는 6월 말에 열려요. 음식 축제인데** 총 50개의 판매업체가 참여해요. 식당, 푸드 트럭, 고급 음식 가판대가 있을 거예요.

여 굉장하네요! **43 제가 소셜 미디어 매체마다 전부 기사 링크를 게시하면 어떨까요?** 그러면 더 많은 사람들에게 기사가 도달하는 데 도움이 될 텐데요. **지금 당장 할 수 있어요.**

어휘 upcoming 곧 있을 publish 게재하다
botanical garden 식물원 gourmet 고급 음식
stall 가판대, 좌판 outlet 매체

41 화자들은 누구인 것 같은가?
- (A) 여행사 직원
- (B) 행사 기획자
- (C) 식당 요리사
- (D) 잡지사 기자

해설 **화자들의 직업**
남자가 첫 대사에서 플레인스빌에서 곧 있을 여름 행사에 대한 자신의 기사가 방금 게시되었다(My article about upcoming summer events in Plainsville was just published)고 하자 여자가 첫 대사에서 자신은 새로 생긴 식물원에 관한 기사를 아직도 쓰고 있다(I'm still working on my article about the new botanical garden)고 했으므로 (D)가 정답이다.

어휘 journalist 기자

42 남자가 강조하는 구체적인 행사는 무엇인가?
- (A) 음악 공연
- (B) 도서전
- (C) 음식 축제
- (D) 미술 전시회

해설 **남자가 강조하는 행사**
남자가 두 번째 대사에서 주요 행사는 6월 말에 열린다(the highlight event will take place at the end of June)면서 음식 축제(It's a food festival)라고 했으므로 (C)가 정답이다.

어휘 fair 박람회 exhibition 전시회

43 여자는 다음에 무엇을 하겠다고 말하는가?
- (A) 고객에게 샘플 제공
- (B) 소셜 미디어에 링크 게시
- (C) 이력서 검토
- (D) 유인물 인쇄

해설 **여자가 다음에 하겠다고 말하는 것**
여자가 마지막 대사에서 소셜 미디어 매체마다 전부 기사 링크를 게시하면 어떨지(Why don't I post a link to the article on all our social media outlets) 의견을 묻고 이어서 지금 당장 할 수 있다(I can do that right now)고 했으므로 (B)가 정답이다.

어휘 review 검토하다 handout 유인물

[44-46] W-Br / W-Am / M-Au   3인 대화

> W1 **44 We're glad you came in to interview for this position, Mr. Romero. Our lead graphic designer just retired, and we've had a hard time finding his replacement.**
>
> W2 That's right. Your résumé is very impressive. How did you find out about the position?

M **45I saw the company's recruitment video on television**, which made me interested in seeking a position with your company.

W1 Great. **46What we like to do before we start discussing your job history is to have you walk us through your portfolio of work.** You can describe each work sample as you go.

M **46Sure. I have it right here.**

여 44로메로 씨, 이 직책을 위한 면접에 참여해 주셔서 기쁩니다. 저희 수석 그래픽 디자이너가 얼마 전에 은퇴했는데 후임자를 찾느라 애를 먹고 있어요.

여2 맞습니다. 이력서가 아주 인상적이네요. 이 직책에 대해서는 어떻게 알게 되셨나요?

남 45텔레비전에서 회사의 채용 영상을 보고, 귀사에서 일자리를 구하는 데 관심이 생겼습니다.

여1 좋습니다. 46경력에 대해 논의하기 전에 작업 포트폴리오에 대해 저희에게 자세히 설명해 주셨으면 합니다. 진행하시면서 각 작업 샘플에 대해 설명해 주시면 됩니다.

남 46네, 여기 있습니다.

어휘 position 직책 retire 은퇴하다 recruitment 채용
walk ~ through ~에게 자세히 설명하다 describe 설명하다

---

44 남자는 어떤 직업을 위해 면접을 보고 있는가?
(A) 회계사 (B) 건축가
(C) 그래픽 디자이너 (D) 소프트웨어 엔지니어

해설 **남자가 면접을 보는 직업**
첫 번째 여자가 첫 대사에서 남자에게 면접에 참여해 줘서 기쁘다(We're glad you came in to interview for this position, Mr. Romero)고 하면서 수석 그래픽 디자이너가 얼마 전에 은퇴했는데 후임자를 찾느라 애를 먹고 있다(Our lead graphic designer just retired, and we've had a hard time finding his replacement)고 했으므로 (C)가 정답이다.

45 남자는 어디에서 구인 광고를 보았는가?
(A) 소셜 미디어 (B) 텔레비전
(C) 옥외 광고판 (D) 신문

해설 **남자가 구인 광고를 본 곳**
남자가 첫 대사에서 텔레비전에서 회사의 채용 영상을 봤다고(I saw the company's recruitment video on television) 했으므로 (B)가 정답이다.

어휘 billboard 옥외 광고판

46 남자는 다음에 무엇을 할 것 같은가?
(A) 경비실로 이동하기
(B) 다른 동료 만나기
(C) 포트폴리오 제시하기
(D) 회사 정책에 대해 질문하기

해설 **남자가 다음에 할 일**
첫 번째 여자가 마지막 대사에서 경력에 대해 논의하기 전에 작업 포트폴리오에 대해 자세히 설명해 달라(What we like to do ~ is to have you walk us through your

---

portfolio of work)고 요청하자 남자가 네(Sure)라며 여기 있다(I have it right here)고 했으므로 (C)가 정답이다.

어휘 colleague (직장) 동료 policy 정책

[47-49] M-Au / W-Am

M Hi, Carmen. Thanks for agreeing to help me prepare to run a five-kilometer race. This will be my first race!

W No problem. **47I've helped lots of people train to run long distances. I'll create an exercise program that starts off slowly.** It'll be safe and fun!

M Great. **48I'm leaving on a business trip next week, though. I'd like to wait until I get back so my training isn't interrupted.**

W Actually, the exercises at this stage are simple. You can do them in a hotel room. **49I'll upload your program onto a mobile application. You can mark your progress there.** I'll forward that app to you.

남 안녕하세요, 카르멘. 5킬로미터 경주 준비를 도와주셔서 고마워요. 이번이 제 첫 번째 경주예요!

여 별말씀을요. 47많은 사람들이 장거리를 달릴 수 있도록 제가 훈련을 도왔죠. 천천히 시작하는 운동 프로그램을 짜려고 해요. 안전하고 재미있을 거예요!

남 좋은데요. 48그런데 제가 다음 주에 출장을 떠나요. 훈련이 중단되지 않도록 돌아올 때까지 기다리고 싶어요.

여 사실 이 단계에서 하는 운동은 간단해요. 호텔 방에서도 할 수 있거든요. 49제가 모바일 애플리케이션에 프로그램을 올릴게요. 거기에 진행 상황을 표시하시면 돼요. 그 앱을 보내 드릴게요.

어휘 interrupt 중단하다 mark 표시하다 progress 진행
forward 보내다

---

47 여자는 누구인 것 같은가?
(A) 컴퓨터 기술자 (B) 호텔 접수 담당자
(C) 행사 주최자 (D) 헬스 트레이너

해설 **여자의 직업**
여자가 첫 대사에서 많은 사람들이 장거리를 달릴 수 있도록 훈련을 도왔다(I've helped lots of people train to run long distances)면서 천천히 시작하는 운동 프로그램을 짜려고 한다(I'll create an exercise program that starts off slowly)고 했으므로 (D)가 정답이다.

어휘 receptionist 접수 담당자

48 남자는 왜 프로그램을 미루고 싶어하는가?
(A) 자금이 없다.
(B) 출장을 떠난다.
(C) 준비가 되지 않았다고 생각한다.
(D) 더 많은 참가자를 기다리고 있다.

해설 남자가 프로그램을 미루고 싶은 이유

남자가 마지막 대사에서 다음 주에 출장을 떠난다(I'm leaving on a business trip next week)며 훈련이 중단되지 않도록 돌아올 때까지 기다리고 싶다(I'd like to wait until I get back so my training isn't interrupted)고 했으므로 (B)가 정답이다.

어휘 funding 자금

---

49 여자는 무엇을 제안하는가?
(A) 모바일 애플리케이션 사용 (B) 사전 등록
(C) 예약 시간 변경 (D) 정기 모임

해설 여자가 제안하는 것

여자가 마지막 대사에서 모바일 애플리케이션에 프로그램을 올리겠다(I'll upload your program onto a mobile application)면서 거기에 진행 상황을 표시하라(You can mark your progress there)고 했으므로 (A)가 정답이다.

어휘 in advance 사전에 **regularly** 정기적으로

[50-52] W-Br / M-Au

W Kota! What a surprise to see you here in Newark. I haven't seen you since flight school.

M Oh, hi, Junko. Yes, **50 I was just hired by Sand Airlines last month. And they have me flying the Springfield to Newark route.**

W **50 I used to fly that route. 51 If you ever have a long layover in Springfield, you should go to Jim's Restaurant downtown.** It has great food.

M Thanks for the recommendation. **52 Oh, I see my crew lining up to go through security, so you'll have to excuse me.**

여 코타! 여기 뉴어크에서 뵙다니 정말 놀랍네요. 비행 학교 이후로는 만나지 못했잖아요.

남 오, 안녕하세요, 준코. 네, **50 지난달에 샌드 항공에 취직했는데 스프링필드에서 뉴어크까지의 노선을 운항하는 일을 맡게 되었어요.**

여 **50 저도 그 항로로 자주 비행했어요. 51 스프링필드에 오래 경유하게 되면 시내에 있는 짐스 레스토랑에 가 보세요.** 음식이 아주 맛있어요.

남 추천해 줘서 고마워요. **52 아, 승무원들이 보안 검색을 받느라 줄을 서 있네요. 먼저 가 볼게요.**

어휘 layover (비행기) 경유지 **recommendation** 추천

---

50 화자들은 누구인 것 같은가?
(A) 수하물 처리 직원 (B) 여행사 직원
(C) 항공기 조종사 (D) 공항 보안 직원

해설 화자들의 직업

남자가 첫 대사에서 지난달에 샌드 항공에 취직했고(I was just hired by Sand Airlines last month) 스프링필드에서 뉴어크까지의 노선을 운항하는 일을 맡게 되었다(And they have me flying the Springfield to Newark

---

route)고 말하자 여자가 자신도 그 항로로 자주 비행했다(I used to fly that route)고 했으므로 (C)가 정답이다.

어휘 handler 처리[취급]하는 사람

---

51 여자는 남자에게 무엇을 하라고 권하는가?
(A) 일찍 출근
(B) 레스토랑 방문
(C) 웹사이트에서 최신 소식 확인
(D) 도시 관광

해설 여자가 남자에게 권하는 것

여자가 마지막 대사에서 스프링필드에 오래 경유하게 되면 시내에 있는 짐스 레스토랑에 가 보라(If you ever have a long layover in Springfield, you should go to Jim's Restaurant downtown)고 권하고 있으므로 (B)가 정답이다.

(Paraphrasing) 대화의 go to Jim's Restaurant
→ 정답의 Visit a restaurant

---

52 남자는 다음에 무엇을 할 것 같은가?
(A) 유니폼 세탁 맡기기 (B) 근무 일정 확인하기
(C) 식사 구입하기 (D) 보안 검색대 통과하기

해설 남자가 다음에 할 일

남자가 마지막 대사에서 승무원들이 보안 검색을 받느라 줄을 서 있다(I see my crew lining up to go through security)며 먼저 가 보겠다(you'll have to excuse me)고 했으므로 (D)가 정답이다.

어휘 checkpoint 검색대

[53-55] W-Br / M-Au / M-Cn   3인 대화

W Klaus and Artem, **53 I'm sure you heard the unfortunate news that one of our biggest clients, ALD Corporation, did not renew its contract.** It's switching to another advertising agency.

M1 Well, I spoke to the director at ALD Corp. **54 She told me the main reason was because we weren't responding to e-mails fast enough.**

W **54 That's something we need to focus on. We really need to be sure that we're communicating regularly with our clients. 55 Artem, what do you think?**

M2 Let's discuss this with our entire team. **55 I'll organize a meeting so that we can make a list of ways we can improve.**

여 클라우스, 아르템. **53 우리의 최대 고객사 중 하나인 ALD 사가 재계약을 하지 않았다는 안타까운 소식을 들으셨을 겁니다.** 다른 광고 대행사로 바꾼다고 하네요.

남1 음, 제가 ALD 사 이사와 이야기했는데요. **54 우리가 이메일에 충분히 빠르게 응답하지 않은 것이 주된 이유라고 하더군요.**

여 **54 그 점이 우리가 집중해야 할 부분이에요. 고객과

170

정기적으로 소통해야 할 필요가 있어요. **55** 아르템, 어떻게 생각하세요?

남2 팀 전체와 이 문제를 상의해 봅시다. **55** 회의를 잡아서 개선 방안을 목록으로 작성하도록 합시다.

> **어휘** unfortunate 안타까운 renew 갱신[연장]하다 contract 계약(서) switch 바꾸다 respond to ~에 응답하다 entire 전체의 improve 개선하다

53 화자들의 회사에서 최근에 무슨 일이 있었는가?

(A) 고객이 계약을 종료했다.
(B) 한 부서에서 컨설턴트를 고용했다.
(C) 본사를 이전했다.
(D) 기업 대출이 거절되었다.

해설 **화자들의 회사에서 최근에 생긴 일**
여자가 첫 대사에서 우리의 최대 고객사 중 하나인 ALD 사가 재계약을 하지 않았다는 안타까운 소식을 들었을 것이다(I'm sure you heard the unfortunate news that one of our biggest clients, ALD Corporation, did not renew its contract)라고 했으므로 (A)가 정답이다.

어휘 relocate 이전하다 reject 거절하다

> (Paraphrasing) 대화의 did not renew its contract → 정답의 ended a contract

54 여자는 회사가 무엇에 집중해야 한다고 말하는가?

(A) 기술 개선 (B) 업계 콘퍼런스 참석
(C) 팀워크 활동 조직 **(D) 더 나은 소통 유지**

해설 **여자가 집중해야 한다고 말하는 것**
남자가 첫 대사에서 우리가 이메일에 충분히 빠르게 응답하지 않은 것이 주된 이유(She told me the main reason was because we weren't responding to e-mails fast enough)라고 하자 여자가 그 점이 우리가 집중해야 할 부분(That's something we need to focus on)이라며 고객과 정기적으로 소통해야 할 필요가 있다(We really need to be sure that we're communicating regularly with our clients)고 했다. 따라서 (D)가 정답이다.

어휘 maintain 유지하다

> (Paraphrasing) 대화의 communicating regularly with our clients → 정답의 Maintaining better communication

55 아르템은 왜 회의 일정을 잡겠다고 말하는가?

(A) 행사를 계획하려고
(B) 새 직원을 맞이하려고
(C) 소프트웨어를 배우려고
(D) 아이디어를 생각해 내려고

해설 **아르템이 회의 일정을 잡는 이유**
여자가 마지막 대사에서 아르템 씨에게 어떻게 생각하느냐(Artem, what do you think?)고 물었고 이어 남자가 회의를 잡아서 개선 방안을 목록으로 작성합시다(I'll organize

a meeting so that we can make a list of ways we can improve)라고 했으므로 (D)가 정답이다.

> (Paraphrasing) 대화의 make a list of ways we can improve → 정답의 To brainstorm some ideas

[56-58] W-Am / M-Cn

W Mr. Cho, **56** the finance team finished the budget for constructing the Strausburg Shopping Center. Since you're the project manager, I need your approval.

M We're hoping to break ground at the end of the year, so I appreciate your team's fast work.

W It's an exciting project—**57** it'll be the biggest shopping center our company's ever built, right?

M There's the York Shopping Center in Glenville.

W **57** I forgot about that.

M OK, let's see. **58** Wow—it's going to cost a lot more than I expected.

W Well, the price of building materials has gone up this year.

M In that case, **58** I'm going to need some time to think about this.

여 조 씨, **56** 재무팀이 스트라우스버그 쇼핑센터 건설 예산 편성을 마쳤어요. 프로젝트 관리자인 당신의 승인이 필요해요.

남 연말에 착공할 수 있었으면 하고 바라고 있는데 그쪽 팀에서 빠르게 작업해 줘서 고마워요.

여 기대되는 프로젝트예요. **57** 우리 회사가 지은 쇼핑센터 중에 최대 규모가 되겠죠, 그렇죠?

남 글렌빌에 요크 쇼핑센터가 있어요.

여 **57** 그건 잊고 있었네요.

남 그래요. 봅시다. **58** 와, 제가 예상했던 것보다 비용이 훨씬 많이 드네요.

여 음, 올해 건축 자재 가격이 올랐어요.

남 그렇다면 **58** 이 건은 생각할 시간이 좀 필요하겠어요.

> **어휘** construct 건설하다 approval 승인 break ground 착공하다 appreciate 고맙게 생각하다

56 화자들은 주로 무엇에 대해 논의하고 있는가?

(A) 쇼핑 (B) 투자 대상 행사
(C) 건설 공사 (D) 직원 설문 조사

해설 **대화의 주제**
여자가 첫 대사에서 재무팀이 스트라우스버그 쇼핑센터 건설 예산 편성을 마쳤다(the finance team finished the budget for constructing the Strausburg Shopping Center)며 프로젝트 관리자인 남자의 승인이 필요하다(Since you're the project manager, I need your approval)고 했고 이후 공사 프로젝트 관련 내용이 이어지므로 (C)가 정답이다.

어휘 investor 투자자

57 남자는 왜 "글렌빌에 요크 쇼핑센터가 있어요"라고 말하는가?

    (A) 추천하려고

    (B) 추측을 바로잡으려고

    (C) 계획을 승인한다는 의사를 표시하려고

    (D) 초대장을 보내려고

해설 **화자의 의도**

여자가 두 번째 대사에서 우리 회사가 지은 쇼핑센터 중에 최대 규모가 아닌지(it'll be the biggest shopping center our company's ever built, right?) 묻자 남자가 인용문을 언급했고 여자가 그건 잊고 있었다(I forgot about that)고 자신의 추측이 틀렸음을 인정하므로 (B)가 정답이다.

어휘 assumption 추측   extend (초대장을) 보내다

58 남자는 문서를 검토하는 데 왜 시간이 더 필요한가?

    (A) 일부 정보가 누락되었다.

    (B) 다른 업무가 더 시급하다.

    (C) 제안서가 여러 페이지로 이루어져 있다.

    (D) 비용이 예상보다 비싸다.

해설 **남자가 문서를 검토하는 데 시간이 더 필요한 이유**

남자가 세 번째 대사에서 예상보다 비용이 훨씬 많이 든다(Wow—it's going to cost a lot more than I expected)고 하자 여자가 올해 건축 자재 가격이 올랐다고 했고 이에 남자가 이 건은 생각할 시간이 필요하다(I'm going to need some time to think about this)고 했으므로 (D)가 정답이다.

어휘 urgent 시급한

(Paraphrasing) 대화의 cost a lot more than I expected → 정답의 A cost is higher than expected.

[59-61] M-Cn / W-Am

> M　Hello. **59 I'm calling because I'd like your laboratory to do some soil testing for me.**
> W　**59 Sure. What kind of test do you need done?**
> M　**60 Well, I'm a farmer, and I'm considering buying land in Springfield.** But I'd like to test the soil for nutrient levels first.
> W　We can do that for you. How soon do you need the results?
> M　**61 I need the results within a few days. Would that be possible?**
> W　Actually, I'll be in that area tomorrow. And reports are e-mailed within 24 hours.
> M　Great. What are your fees?
> 남　59 안녕하세요. 연구실에서 토양 검사를 해 주셨으면 해서 전화드렸습니다.
> 여　59 물론이죠. 어떤 검사가 필요하신가요?

> 남　60 저는 농부인데 스프링필드에 있는 땅을 사려고 고민하고 있어요. 하지만 먼저 토양의 양분 수준부터 검사하고 싶어요.
> 여　저희가 해 드릴 수 있습니다. 얼마나 빨리 결과가 필요하신가요?
> 남　61 며칠 내로 결과가 필요한데 가능할까요?
> 여　실은 제가 내일 그 지역에 갑니다. 그리고 보고서는 24시간 이내에 이메일로 보내 드립니다.
> 남　좋습니다. 비용은 어떻게 되나요?

어휘 laboratory 연구실   nutrient 영양분

59 여자의 직업은 무엇인 것 같은가?

    (A) 변호사   (B) 재무 분석가

    (C) 과학자   (D) 공인중개사

해설 **여자의 직업**

남자가 첫 대사에서 연구실에서 토양 검사를 해 주셨으면 해서 전화했다(I'm calling because I'd like your laboratory to do some soil testing for me)고 했고 이어서 여자가 물론(Sure)이라고 긍정하며 어떤 검사가 필요한지(What kind of test do you need done?) 물었으므로 (C)가 정답이다.

어휘 financial analyst 재무 분석가

60 남자는 스프링필드에 대해 무엇이라고 말하는가?

    (A) 최근에 그곳의 시장으로 선출되었다.

    (B) 그곳의 농지 매입에 관심이 있다.

    (C) 그가 쓰고 있는 기사의 주제다.

    (D) 그가 자란 도시다.

해설 **남자가 스프링필드에 대해 말하는 것**

남자가 두 번째 대사에서 자신은 농부인데 스프링필드에 있는 땅을 사려고 고민하고 있다(I'm considering buying land in Springfield)고 했으므로 (B)가 정답이다.

어휘 elect 선출하다   mayor 시장   farmland 농지   subject 주제

(Paraphrasing) 대화의 considering buying land → 정답의 interested in buying farmland

61 여자는 왜 "제가 내일 그 지역에 갑니다"라고 말하는가?

    (A) 과중한 업무량에 대해 불평하려고

    (B) 초청을 거절한 이유를 설명하려고

    (C) 작업을 제시간에 완료할 수 있음을 밝히려고

    (D) 남자를 태워 주겠다고 제안하려고

해설 **화자의 의도**

남자가 세 번째 대사에서 며칠 내로 결과가 필요한데(I need the results within a few days) 가능할지(Would that be possible?) 물었고 이에 대한 응답으로 여자가 인용문을 언급했으므로 (C)가 정답이다.

어휘 workload 업무량   turn down ~을 거절하다
on time 시간을 어기지 않고

M　Hey, Sakura. **62 I was thinking of getting a dessert to bring to Jin-Ah's retirement party.** Have you ever tried anything from Gladstone's Bakery?

W　No, I haven't. But I have heard great reviews about Gladstone's.

M　**63 A lot of people in the office like chocolate cake.**

W　**63 OK, why don't you get that? 64 I'd be happy to give you some money toward paying for it.**

M　Oh, that won't be necessary. But thanks!

남　안녕, 사쿠라. 62진아 씨 은퇴 파티에 가져갈 디저트를 살까 생각하고 있었어요. 글래드스톤 베이커리에서 뭐 먹어본 적 있어요?

여　아니요, 못 먹어 봤어요. 그래도 듣자 하니 글래드스톤은 평이 아주 좋던데요.

남　63사무실에 초콜릿 케이크를 좋아하는 사람이 많아요.

여　63좋은데요. 그걸로 사세요. 64비용을 지불하는 데 저도 기꺼이 돈을 보탤게요.

남　그럴 필요 없어요. 아무튼 고마워요!

62 화자들은 어떤 유형의 행사에 참석할 것인가?
(A) 연극 공연　　　　(B) 은퇴 기념 파티
(C) 기업 만찬　　　　(D) 미술 전시회 개막식

해설　화자들이 참석할 행사의 종류
남자가 첫 대사에서 진아 씨 은퇴 파티에 가져갈 디저트를 살까 생각하고 있었다(I was thinking of getting a dessert to bring to Jin-Ah's retirement party)고 했고 은퇴 파티에 쓸 케이크에 대한 대화가 이어지므로 (B)가 정답이다.

어휘　corporate 기업　**banquet** 연회

63 시각 정보에 따르면, 남자는 물품에 얼마를 지불하겠는가?
(A) 12달러　　　　(B) 15달러
(C) 18달러　　　　(D) 11달러

해설　시각 정보 연계
남자가 두 번째 대사에서 사무실에 초콜릿 케이크를 좋아하는 사람이 많다(A lot of people in the office like

chocolate cake)고 했고 여자가 좋다(OK)고 하며 그걸로 사라(why don't you get that?)고 제안했다. 가격표를 보면 초콜릿 케이크는 18달러이므로 (C)가 정답이다.

64 여자는 무엇을 하겠다고 제안하는가?
(A) 사진 찍기　　　　(B) 회의실 준비하기
(C) 비품 가져오기　　(D) 돈 보태기

해설　여자의 제안 사항
여자가 마지막 대사에서 비용을 지불하는 데 기꺼이 돈을 보태겠다(I'd be happy to give you some money toward paying for it)고 했으므로 (D)가 정답이다.

어휘　contribute 기여하다

(Paraphrasing)　대화의 give you some money
→ 정답의 Contribute some money

W　Welcome to the ticket counter for Ace Airlines. How can I help you?

M　**65 I'd like to change the reservation for my return flight.** I see there's a nine A.M. flight on Monday, and I'd like to take that one. Here's my ticket information.

W　Certainly. I'll take care of that. There's a fee of 100 dollars for the change.

M　That's fine. Here's my credit card. I'm glad it was so easy—**66 I decided I'd like to stay at the conference I'm attending for another day.**

W　I understand. By the way, if you need transportation into the city, the sign over there will tell you where to go.

M　**67 I'm planning to take the hotel's courtesy shuttle,** so thanks for the tip!

여　어서 오세요. 에이스 항공 발권 창구입니다. 무엇을 도와드릴까요?

남　65돌아오는 항공편 예약을 변경하고 싶어요. 월요일 오전 9시 항공편이 있는데, 그 항공편을 이용하고 싶어요. 이건 제 항공권 정보예요.

여　물론입니다. 처리해 드릴게요. 변경 시 수수료 100달러가 붙습니다.

남　괜찮습니다. 제 신용카드예요. 수월해서 다행이에요. 66참석하고 있는 콘퍼런스에 하루 더 참여하기로 결정했거든요.

여　그렇군요. 참, 시내로 가는 교통편이 필요하시면 저쪽에 있는 표지판에 어디로 가야 할지 나와 있어요.

남　67호텔 무료 셔틀을 탈 계획이예요. 알려 줘서 고마워요!

어휘　transportation 교통(편)　**courtesy** 무료로 제공되는

교통수단		
1	주차장 셔틀	
2	택시	
67 3	**호텔 셔틀**	
4	버스	

65 남자는 여자에게 무엇을 해 달라고 요청하는가?

(A) 보상 프로그램 가입　(B) 수하물 검사

(C) 예약 변경　(D) 티켓 환불

해설　남자가 여자에게 요청하는 것

남자가 첫 대사에서 돌아오는 항공편 예약을 변경하고 싶다 (I'd like to change the reservation for my return flight)고 했으므로 (C)가 정답이다.

어휘　enroll 가입시키다　rewards program 보상 프로그램 luggage 수하물　refund 환불하다

66 남자는 왜 여행하고 있는가?

(A) 주택을 구입하려고　**(B) 회의에 참석하려고**

(C) 인터뷰를 진행하려고　(D) 관광을 하려고

해설　남자가 여행하는 이유

남자가 두 번째 대사에서 참석하고 있는 콘퍼런스에 하루 더 참여하기로 했다(I decided I'd like to stay at the conference I'm attending for another day)고 했으므로 (B)가 정답이다.

어휘　conduct 수행하다　sightseeing 관광

67 시각 정보에 따르면, 남자는 다음에 어디로 갈 것 같은가?

(A) 1구역　(B) 2구역

(C) 3구역　(D) 4구역

해설　시각 정보 연계

남자가 마지막 대사에서 호텔 무료 셔틀을 탈 계획이다(I'm planning to take the hotel's courtesy shuttle)라고 했다. 표지판을 보면 호텔 셔틀은 3구역이므로 (C)가 정답이다.

[68-70] M-Cn / W-Am　　　　　**임대 옵션**

M　Thanks for showing me the apartment yesterday, Ms. Gao. **68 I was really impressed with the big windows—you can see the whole city from the living room.**

W　Yes, it's great. Are you ready to sign a lease?

M　I am. But I remember you said there were several lease options?

W　That's right. The rent depends on the duration of the lease. Most tenants choose the two-year lease.

M　**69 Well, I may have to move next year if my company relocates. So, the one-year lease is better for me.**

W　OK. You'll just need to let me know your move-in date. **70 That way I can have the apartment professionally cleaned before you move in.**

남　가오 씨, 어제 아파트를 보여 주셔서 감사합니다. 68 커다란 창문이 인상 깊었어요. 거실에서 도시 전체를 볼 수 있더군요.

여　맞아요, 멋지죠. 임대 계약을 하시겠어요?

남　네. 하지만 몇 가지 임대 옵션이 있다고 하신 걸로 기억하는데요?

여　맞습니다. 임대 기간에 따라 임대료가 다릅니다. 세입자 대다수는 2년 임대를 선택해요.

남　69 음, 회사가 이전하면 내년에 이사를 해야 할 수도 있어요. 그래서 전 1년 임대가 나아요.

여　알겠습니다. 입주 날짜만 알려 주세요. 70 그러면 입주하시기 전에 전문 청소 서비스를 이용해 아파트를 청소해 두겠습니다.

어휘　lease 임대차 계약　depend on ~에 따라 다르다 duration 기간　tenant 세입자　professionally 전문적으로

임대 옵션	
기간	월 임대료
2년	1,300달러
69 1년	**1,350달러**
6개월	1,450달러
1개월	1,500달러

68 남자는 아파트의 어떤 특징을 좋아하는가?

(A) 나무 바닥재　(B) 신형 가전제품

(C) 부엌 크기　**(D) 거실에서 보이는 전망**

해설　남자가 좋아하는 아파트의 특징

남자가 첫 대사에서 커다란 창문이 인상 깊었다(I was really impressed with the big windows)면서 거실에서 도시 전체를 볼 수 있다(you can see the whole city from the living room)고 했으므로 (D)가 정답이다.

어휘　flooring 바닥재　appliance 가전제품

69 시각 정보에 따르면, 남자는 얼마를 지불하겠는가?

(A) 1,300달러　**(B) 1,350달러**

(C) 1,450달러　(D) 1,500달러

해설　시각 정보 연계

남자가 마지막 대사에서 회사가 이전하면 내년에 이사를 해야 할 수도 있다(I may have to move next year if my company relocates)고 하면서 자신에게는 1년 임대가 낫다(the one-year lease is better for me)고 했다. 임대 옵션을 보면 1년 계약 월 임대료는 1,350달러이므로 (B)가 정답이다.

70 여자는 무엇을 하겠다고 말하는가?

(A) 전문 청소 서비스 의뢰　(B) 열쇠 한 세트 제작

(C) 주차 공간 지정　(D) 헬스장 이용권 제공

해설 **여자가 하겠다고 말하는 일**

여자가 마지막 대사에서 입주하기 전에 전문 청소 서비스를 이용해 아파트를 청소해 두겠다(That way I can have the apartment professionally cleaned before you move in)고 했으므로 (A)가 정답이다.

(Paraphrasing) 대화의 have the apartment professionally cleaned → 정답의 Arrange for a professional cleaning

PART 4

[71-73] 회의 발췌

M-Cn Good morning. **71 I'm Kevin Williams— co-owner of this apparel business.** I'd like to welcome you as new employees to High Point Style. This is a family business. My father started selling business suits twenty years ago, and we're proud to provide finely fashioned business attire for the working professional. We're committed to maintaining a loyal customer base, and **72 so our number one goal is to make sure we provide quality customer service at all times.** Now, recently, **73 I installed a security alarm, so I'll give you the code to enter.**

안녕하세요. **71 저는 이 의류 사업체의 공동 소유주인 케빈 윌리엄스**입니다. 하이 포인트 스타일의 신입 사원이 되신 여러분을 환영합니다. 저희는 가족 사업체입니다. 제 아버지께서 20년 전에 정장을 판매하기 시작하셨죠. 저희는 직장인을 위해 고급 비즈니스 의상을 제공한다는 점에 자부심을 가지고 있습니다. 저희는 충성도 높은 고객층을 유지하기 위해 전념하고 있으며, **72 최우선 목표는 항상 양질의 고객 서비스를 제공하는 것입니다.** 자, 최근에 **73 보안 경보기를 설치했으니 출입 코드를 알려 드리겠습니다.**

어휘 apparel 의류 finely 고급의 fashioned ~식의 attire 의복 be committed to ~에 전념하다 customer base 고객층 install 설치하다

71 화자는 어디에서 일하는가?

(A) 섬유 공장 (B) 사진 액자 가게
(C) 의류점 (D) 인테리어 디자인 회사

해설 **화자의 근무 장소**

도입부에서 화자가 이 의류 사업체의 공동 소유주인 케빈 윌리엄스(I'm Kevin Williams—co-owner of this apparel business)라고 자신을 소개하고 있으므로 (C)가 정답이다.

어휘 textile 섬유

(Paraphrasing) 담화의 apparel business → 정답의 clothing store

72 화자는 어떤 목표를 언급하는가?

(A) 비용 절감 (B) 경쟁사보다 더 많이 판매
(C) 다른 지점 개설 **(D) 우수한 고객 서비스 제공**

해설 **화자가 언급하는 목표**

담화 후반부에서 최우선 목표는 항상 양질의 고객 서비스를 제공하는 것(so our number one goal is to make sure we provide quality customer service at all times)이라고 했으므로 (D)가 정답이다.

어휘 competitor 경쟁사 location 지점

(Paraphrasing) 담화의 quality customer service → 정답의 excellent customer service

73 화자는 청자들에게 무엇을 주겠다고 말하는가?

(A) 근무 일정 (B) 유니폼
(C) 연락처 목록 **(D) 경보 코드**

해설 **화자가 청자들에게 주겠다고 말하는 것**

후반부에서 화자가 보안 경보기를 설치했으니 출입 코드를 알려 주겠다(I installed a security alarm, so I'll give you the code to enter)고 했으므로 (D)가 정답이다.

[74-76] 설명

W-Am Welcome to Data Analysis 101. **74 Today, we'll learn the basics of our company's preferred tool for analyzing data.** As a reminder, **75 if you complete this training webinar, you'll receive a gift card to the coffee shop in our lobby.** So, the first thing to do is open up the program, as you can see on my screen. For practice, we'll be assigning codes to data so that it can be analyzed. Open your sample spreadsheet. **76 Next, you'll adjust any column titles in your spreadsheet so that they're one-word titles, like "Year" or "Income."**

데이터 분석 101에 오신 것을 환영합니다. **74 오늘은 우리 회사가 선호하는 데이터 분석 도구의 기본에 대해 알아보겠습니다.** 확인 차원에서 말씀드리지만 **75 이번 교육 웨비나를 완료하면 로비에 있는 커피숍 기프트 카드를 받습니다.** 그럼, 먼저 하실 일은 제 화면에서 볼 수 있듯이 프로그램을 여는 겁니다. 연습을 위해 데이터 분석이 가능하도록 데이터에 코드를 할당하겠습니다. 샘플 스프레드시트를 여세요. **76 다음으로 스프레드시트의 열 제목을 '연도'나 '소득'처럼 한 단어 제목이 되도록 조정하세요.**

어휘 analyze 분석하다 reminder 상기시키는 것 assign 할당하다 adjust 조정하다 column 열, 세로줄

74 청자들은 무엇을 배우고 있는가?

(A) 컴퓨터 프로그램 사용법
(B) 월별 재고 조사 완료하는 방법
(C) 비품 주문 방법
(D) 판매 송장 작성법

해설 **청자들이 배우고 있는 것**
도입부에 오늘은 우리 회사가 선호하는 데이터 분석 도구의 기본에 대해 알아보겠다(Today, we'll learn the basics of our company's preferred tool for analyzing data)고 했으므로 (A)가 정답이다.

어휘 inventory 재고 조사

75 청자들은 웨비나를 완료하면 무엇을 받게 되는가?
(A) 추가 휴가 일수   (B) 기프트 카드
(C) 수료증   (D) 지역 축제 티켓

해설 **청자들이 웨비나를 완료하면 받게 되는 것**
초반부에서 이번 교육 웨비나를 완료하면 로비에 있는 커피숍 기프트 카드를 받는다(if you complete this training webinar, you'll receive a gift card to the coffee shop in our lobby)고 했으므로 (B)가 정답이다.

어휘 certificate 증명서, 자격증

76 화자에 따르면, 청자들은 다음에 무엇을 할 것인가?
(A) 사번 입력   (B) 재고 목록 확인
(C) 가격 정보 갱신   (D) 세로줄 제목 변경

해설 **청자들이 다음에 할 일**
후반부에 다음으로 스프레드시트의 열 제목을 '연도'나 '소득'처럼 한 단어 제목이 되도록 조정하라(Next, you'll adjust any column titles in your spreadsheet so that they're one-word titles, like "Year" or "Income.")고 했으므로 (D)가 정답이다.

어휘 identification 신분증

(Paraphrasing) 담화의 adjust any column titles → 대화의 Change column titles

[77-79] 전화 메시지

M-Au Hi, Pablo. My name is Ivan, and like you, I'm a flight instructor at Barton Airport. **⁷⁷ On March seventh, I have a lesson scheduled with a student who needs to log some time in the CRS 1000 aircraft.** Well, the schedule shows that you've reserved that aircraft for that date. And the only other aircraft available is the Pello 2. **⁷⁸ The thing is the CRS 1000 has a navigation system that my student needs to master to qualify for his pilot's license. ⁷⁹ Would you be willing to fly the Pello 2 that day so that I can take the CRS 1000?**

안녕하세요, 파블로. 제 이름은 이반인데요. 선생님과 마찬가지로 바튼 공항의 비행 강사입니다. ⁷⁷제가 3월 7일에 CRS 1000 항공기로 비행 시간을 기록해야 하는 학생과 수업이 예정되어 있어요. 일정에 보니 선생님이 그 날짜에 해당 항공기를 예약하셨네요. 그리고 이용할 수 있는 다른 항공기는 펠로 2가 유일하고요. ⁷⁸문제는 CRS 1000에는 제 학생이 조종사 면허를 취득하기 위해 숙달해야 하는 내비게이션 시스템이 있다는 겁니다. ⁷⁹제가 CRS 1000을 탈 수 있도록 그날 펠로 2를 조종하실 수 있을까요?

어휘 instructor 강사   log 비행[운항]하다   aircraft 항공기
reserve 예약하다   qualify for ~의 자격을 얻다

77 화자는 3월 7일에 무엇을 할 예정인가?
(A) 해외 여행 가기   (B) 비행 수업하기
(C) 공항 둘러보기   (D) 항공기 구입하기

해설 **3월 7일에 예정된 일**
화자가 초반부에 3월 7일에 CRS 1000 항공기로 비행 시간을 기록해야 하는 학생과 수업이 예정되어 있다(On March seventh, I have a lesson scheduled with a student who needs to log some time in the CRS 1000 aircraft)고 했으므로 (B)가 정답이다.

(Paraphrasing) 담화의 have a lesson scheduled with a student who needs to log some time in the CRS 1000 aircraft → 정답의 Give a flying lesson

78 화자는 왜 특정 항공기를 선호하는가?
(A) 특별한 네비게이션 시스템이 있다.
(B) 평판이 아주 좋다.
(C) 여분의 화물 공간이 있다.
(D) 매우 빠른 속도에 도달할 수 있다.

해설 **화자가 특정 항공기를 선호하는 이유**
화자가 후반부에 문제는 CRS 1000에는 학생이 조종사 면허를 취득하기 위해 숙달해야 하는 내비게이션 시스템이 있다(The thing is the CRS 1000 has a navigation system that my student needs to master to qualify for his pilot's license)고 했으므로 (A)가 정답이다.

어휘 reputation 평판   cargo 화물

(Paraphrasing) 담화의 a navigation system that my student needs to master to qualify for his pilot's license → 정답의 a special navigation system

79 화자는 청자에게 무엇을 요청하는가?
(A) 비행기에 동승   (B) 몇 가지 서류 제공
(C) 다른 비행기 이용   (D) 추천

해설 **화자가 청자에게 요청하는 것**
후반부에 자신이 CRS 1000을 탈 수 있도록 그날 펠로 2를 조종할 수 있는지(Would you be willing to fly the Pello 2 that day so that I can take the CRS 1000?) 물었으므로 (C)가 정답이다.

어휘 accompany 동행하다   documentation 서류

[80-82] 회의 발췌

W-Am **⁸⁰ Just a reminder that we'll be having several corporate executives visit our factory this afternoon.** So I'd like to provide you shift supervisors the latest company updates. As you know, during each of our three daily production shifts, one car is removed from the production line, so that an inspector can assess any flaws that are appearing. **81 Last month, I'm pleased to report that the total number of flaws decreased. 82 Also, our goal by year's end is to transition one part of our assembly line—section 4—so that it can be entirely operated by robots.** In that section, robotic arms will weld the cars' exterior metal body parts together.

80 혹시나 해서 다시 말씀드립니다. 오늘 오후에 회사 경영진 몇 분이 우리 공장을 방문합니다. 그래서 교대 근무 감독자인 여러분에게 최근 회사 상황에 대해 알려 드리고자 합니다. 알다시피 매일 세 번의 생산 교대 시간마다 검사관이 보이는 결함을 진단할 수 있도록 자동차 한 대가 생산 라인에서 빠집니다. 81 지난달에 전체 결함 건수가 감소했다고 보고를 드리게 돼 흐뭇하죠. 82 또한 연말까지 우리 목표는 조립 라인 한 부분인 섹션 4를 전적으로 로봇에 의해 운영되도록 전환하는 것입니다. 해당 섹션에서는 로봇 팔이 자동차의 외부 금속 차체 부분을 용접합니다.

어휘 corporate 기업의   executive 경영진, 임원   shift 교대 (근무)   supervisor 관리자   inspector 검사관   assess 진단하다   flaw 결함   transition 전환하다; 전환   weld 용접하다   exterior 외부의

80 화자는 청자들에게 무엇을 상기시키는가?
(A) 보안 코드 변경
(B) 예정된 교육 세션
(C) 회사 방침
(D) 경영진 방문

해설 화자가 청자들에게 상기시키는 것
도입부에 혹시나 해서 다시 말씀드리는데 오늘 오후에 회사 경영진 몇 분이 우리 공장을 방문한다(Just a reminder that we'll be having several corporate executives visit our factory this afternoon)고 했으므로 (D)가 정답이다.

81 화자는 지난달에 무슨 일이 있었다고 말하는가?
(A) 매출이 증가했다.
(B) 제품 결함이 감소했다.
(C) 교대 근무가 추가되었다.
(D) 신차 모델이 생산을 시작했다.

해설 지난달에 있었던 일
중반부에 지난달에 전체 결함 건수가 감소했다고 보고를 하게 되어 흐뭇하다(Last month, I'm pleased to report that the total number of flaws decreased)고 했으므로 (B)가 정답이다.

어휘 defect 결함   decline 감소하다

(Paraphrasing) 담화의 the total number of flaws decreased → 정답의 Product defects declined.

82 어떤 목표가 논의되는가?
(A) 고객 서비스 개선
(B) 경쟁사와의 합병
(C) 생산 기술 개선
(D) 해외로 사업 확장

해설 논의되는 목표
후반부에 연말까지 우리 목표는 조립 라인 한 부분인 섹션 4를 전적으로 로봇에 의해 운영되도록 전환하는 것(Also, our goal by year's end is to transition one part of

our assembly line—section 4—so that it can be entirely operated by robots)이라고 했으므로 (C)가 정답이다.

어휘 merge 합병하다

(Paraphrasing) 담화의 to transition one part of our assembly line—section 4—so that it can be entirely operated by robots → 정답의 Updating production technology

[83-85] 전화 메시지

M-Au **83 This is Juan Ramirez in apartment 14C. I'm calling about the maintenance request I submitted last week. 84 The paint around my windowsill has been peeling and it needs to be repainted. I just received a notice that someone will come do it tomorrow, but I'm leaving on a business trip tonight. So please call me back about that. 85 Also, I've realized that I would like to rent one of the parking spaces in the tenant garage if there's still one available. I know it'll be an additional 100 dollars per month, and that's fine.**

83 14C 아파트에 사는 후안 라미레즈예요. 지난주에 제출했던 유지 보수 요청 건 때문에 전화드립니다. 84 창턱 주변 페인트가 벗겨지고 있어서 새로 칠해야 합니다. 방금 그 일을 하러 내일 누가 온다는 통지를 받았어요. 그런데 제가 오늘 밤에 출장을 떠납니다. 그러니 그 건에 대해서는 다시 전화해 주세요. 85 또 생각났는데 세입자 차고에 아직 주차 공간 하나가 남아 있다면 임대하고 싶어요. 한 달에 100달러가 추가되는 것으로 알고 있는데 괜찮습니다.

어휘 maintenance 유지 보수   windowsill 창턱   peel 벗겨지다   tenant 세입자   garage 주차장   additional 추가의

83 화자는 누구에게 전화하고 있는가?
(A) 여행사 직원
(B) 건축가
(C) 건물 관리자
(D) 셔틀 운전기사

해설 화자가 전화하고 있는 사람
화자가 도입부에서 14C 아파트에 사는 후안 라미레즈(This is Juan Ramirez in apartment 14C)라고 자신을 소개한 뒤 지난주에 제출했던 유지 보수 요청 건 때문에 전화한다(I'm calling about the maintenance request I submitted last week)고 했으므로 (C)가 정답이다.

84 화자가 "제가 오늘 밤에 출장을 떠납니다"라고 말할 때 무엇을 의미하는가?
(A) 공항까지 교통편이 필요하다.
(B) 서류 작업을 완료할 수 없다.
(C) 여행 일정이 갑자기 변경되었다.
(D) 약속을 다시 잡아야 한다.

해설 화자의 의도
초반부에 창턱 주변 페인트가 벗겨지고 있어서 새로 칠해야

한다(The paint around my windowsill has been peeling and it needs to be repainted)고 하면서 방금 그 일을 하러 내일 누가 온다는 통지를 받았다(I just received a notice that someone will come do it tomorrow)고 했다. 이후에 인용문을 언급하며 내일 페인트칠을 받지 못한다는 것을 알리고 있으므로 (D)가 정답이다.

어휘 paperwork 서류 작업 itinerary 여행 일정

85 화자는 무엇을 위해 추가 비용을 지불하겠다고 말하는가?
(A) 익일 배송 **(B) 주차 공간**
(C) 더 큰 건물 (D) 경치 좋은 전망

해설 **추가 비용을 지불하겠다고 말하는 대상**
후반부에 세입자 차고에 아직 주차 공간 하나가 남아 있다면 임대하고 싶다(Also, I've realized that I would like to rent one of the parking spaces in the tenant garage if there's still one available)면서 한 달에 100달러가 추가되는 것으로 알고 있는데 괜찮다(I know it'll be an additional 100 dollars per month, and that's fine)고 했으므로 (B)가 정답이다.

어휘 overnight 밤사이에 property 건물 scenic 경치가 좋은

[86-88] 여행 정보

W-Br Welcome to the *Faces in Time* exhibit of the Anderson Art Museum. **86 The exhibit features portraits carved out of tree trunks by artists from various countries, including Nigeria, the Philippines, Brazil, and France. 87 I'd like to remind you that these carvings are on loan to us, and pictures cannot be taken in these temporary galleries.** The other galleries in this museum are permanent. **88 If you'd like a set of headphones to listen to the different artists describe their work, please come up to the front now.**

앤더슨 미술관의 전시회 〈시간 속 얼굴들〉에 오신 것을 환영합니다. 86 이 전시회는 나이지리아, 필리핀, 브라질, 프랑스를 포함한 다양한 국가의 예술가들이 나무 줄기로 조각한 흉상들을 전시하고 있습니다. 87 이 조각품들은 우리가 대여한 것들이며 단기 전시 갤러리에서는 사진을 찍을 수 없다는 점 알려 드립니다. 이 미술관의 다른 갤러리들은 상설 전시입니다. 88 다양한 예술가들이 해 주는 작품 설명을 헤드폰으로 듣고 싶으시면 지금 앞으로 나오세요.

어휘 feature 특징을 이루다 portrait 흉상, 인물상 carve 조각하다 trunk 줄기 loan (작품을) 대여하다 temporary 임시의 permanent 상설의, 영구적인 describe 설명하다

86 전시회에는 어떤 종류의 작품이 전시되는가?
(A) 유화 (B) 직조 바구니
(C) 점토 도자기 **(D) 나무 조각**

해설 **전시회에 전시되는 작품의 종류**
초반부에서 이 전시회는 나이지리아, 필리핀, 브라질, 프랑스를 포함한 다양한 국가의 예술가들이 나무 줄기로 조각한 흉

상들을 전시하고 있다(The exhibit features portraits carved out of tree trunks by artists from various countries, ~ and France)고 했으므로 (D)가 정답이다.

어휘 weave 엮다(weave - wove - woven) clay 점토 pottery 도자기 carving 조각품

(Paraphrasing) 담화의 portraits carved out of tree trunks ➡ 정답의 Wooden carvings

87 화자가 "이 미술관의 다른 갤러리들은 상설 전시입니다"라고 말할 때 무엇을 의미하는가?
(A) 지도를 이용할 수 있다. (B) 어린이를 환영한다.
(C) 사진 촬영이 가능하다. (D) 입장료가 무료다.

해설 **화자의 의도**
화자가 중반부에 이 조각품들은 우리가 대여한 것들이며 단기 전시 갤러리에서는 사진을 찍을 수 없다(I'd like to remind you that these carvings are on loan to us, and pictures cannot be taken in these temporary galleries)고 했다. 이후 다른 갤러리는 상설 전시라는 점을 인용문에서 언급했으므로 (C)가 정답이다.

88 화자는 청자들에게 무엇을 제공하는가?
(A) 아트 프린트 (B) 팸플릿
(C) 헤드폰 (D) 생수

해설 **화자가 청자들에게 제공하는 것**
화자가 후반부에 다양한 예술가들이 해 주는 작품 설명을 헤드폰으로 듣고 싶으면 지금 앞으로 나오라(If you'd like a set of headphones to listen ~ come up to the front now)고 했으므로 (C)가 정답이다.

[89-91] 광고

M-Cn **89 Want to transform your favorite photograph into a beautiful canvas art piece?** Go to laza.com, where you can instantly upload a photo, choose your canvas, and place your order, and we'll handle the rest. **90 Our system has built-in software that will help you choose the best canvas size for your image's resolution, whether large or small. 91 And with our no-questions-asked money-back guarantee, you can rest assured that you'll be satisfied with your purchase. That's an offer no other services like ours can match!**

89 여러분이 가장 좋아하는 사진을 아름다운 캔버스 예술 작품으로 바꾸고 싶으신가요? laza.com에 접속해 사진을 즉시 업로드하고 캔버스를 선택한 후 주문해 주시면 나머지는 저희가 알아서 처리해 드립니다. 90 저희 시스템에는 이미지가 크건 작건 간에 그것의 해상도에 최적화된 캔버스 크기를 선택하는 데 도움이 되는 소프트웨어가 내장되어 있습니다. 91 그리고 조건 없는 환불 보장 정책이 있으니 구매하시면 만족하실 테니 안심하세요. 이것은 동종업계의 다른 서비스 업체에서는 찾아볼 수 없는 혜택입니다!

어휘 transform 바꾸다 instantly 즉시 rest 나머지
built-in 내장된 resolution 해상도 money-back
guarantee 환불 보장 정책 rest assured 안심하다
be satisfied with ~에 만족하다 offer 혜택 match
필적하다

89 회사는 무엇을 전문으로 하는가?

(A) 디지털 미술관 제작

(B) 캔버스에 사진 인쇄

(C) 상업용 사진 촬영 기획

(D) 첨부 파일 이미지 압축

해설 **회사의 전문 분야**

도입부에 가장 좋아하는 사진을 아름다운 캔버스 예술 작품
으로 바꾸고 싶은지(Want to transform your favorite
photograph into a beautiful canvas art piece?)
물었으므로 (B)가 정답이다.

어휘 specialize in ~을 전문으로 하다 commercial 상업적인
compress 압축하다 attachment 첨부

(Paraphrasing) 담화의 transform your favorite
photograph into a beautiful canvas art piece
→ 정답의 Printing photographs on canvases

90 화자는 소프트웨어가 무엇에 도움이 된다고 말하는가?

(A) 한 번에 여러 파일 불러오기

(B) 카테고리로 이미지 라벨링 하기

(C) 사진 위에 텍스트 덧씌우기

(D) 적절한 사이즈 선택하기

해설 **소프트웨어가 도움이 되는 것**

중반부에 우리 시스템에는 이미지가 크건 작건 간에 그것
의 해상도에 최적화된 캔버스 크기를 선택하는 데 도움이 되
는 소프트웨어가 내장되어 있다(Our system has built-
in software that will help you choose the best
canvas size for your image's resolution, whether
large or small)고 했으므로 (D)가 정답이다.

어휘 import 불러오다 in batch 대량으로 overlay 덧씌우다

(Paraphrasing) 담화의 choose the best canvas size
→ 정답의 Selecting the appropriate size

91 화자에 따르면, 회사는 경쟁사에 비해 어떤 강점이 있는가?

(A) 저렴한 구독 요금제가 있다.

(B) 업계 전문가들이 선호한다.

(C) 쉬운 환불을 제공한다.

(D) 더 신속한 고객 지원을 제공한다.

해설 **경쟁사들 대비 강점**

후반부에 조건 없는 환불 보장 정책이 있으니 구매하면 만족
할 것(And with our no-questions-asked money-
back guarantee, ~ you'll be satisfied with your
purchase)이라고 장담한 뒤 이것은 동종업계의 다른 서비
스 업체에서는 찾아볼 수 없는 혜택(That's an offer no
other services like ours can match!)이라고 했으므로
(C)가 정답이다.

(Paraphrasing) 담화의 no-questions-asked money-
back guarantee → 정답의 easy refunds

[92-94] 회의 발췌

W-Am **92 We opened our small storefront six
years ago selling only women's shoes.** We've
gradually added some men's and children's
shoes, but we just don't have the floor space to
provide the selection we want. **93 So, I'm happy
to announce that I've acquired a new, much
larger space for us.** I know some of you might
be worried about losing customers, but the
location's just down the street. **94 With all the
space, there'll even be enough room to have
an in-house repair shop.** I've just hired two
experienced individuals who will be quite
skilled at doing that specialized work.

92우리는 6년 전에 여성용 신발만 파는 작은 가게를 열었습니다.
점차 남성용과 아동용 신발을 추가해 왔지만, 원하는 다양한 제품
을 제공하기에는 매장 공간이 부족했습니다. 93그래서 훨씬 더 넓
은 새 공간을 얻었다는 소식을 알리게 되어 기쁩니다. 고객을 잃을
까 걱정하는 분들도 있겠지만, 길을 따라 조금만 가면 되는 위치입
니다. 94전체 공간을 고려하면 매장 내에 수리점을 둘 공간도 충분
할 거예요. 방금 이런 전문적인 작업을 능숙하게 해 줄 노련한 직원
두 사람을 고용했어요.

어휘 storefront 가게 gradually 점차 acquire 얻다
in-house 내부의 individual 개인 skilled at ~에 능숙한

92 담화는 어디에서 진행되고 있는가?

(A) 미용실　　　　　　(B) 귀금속상

(C) 자동차 대리점　　　**(D) 신발 가게**

해설 **대화의 장소**

도입부에 우리는 6년 전에 여성용 신발만 파는 작은 가게를
열었다(We opened our small storefront six years
ago selling only women's shoes)고 하며 신발 가게
확장 이전에 관한 내용이 이어지므로 (D)가 정답이다.

어휘 automobile dealership 자동차 대리점

93 화자는 왜 "길을 따라 조금만 가면 되는 위치입니다"라고
말하는가?

(A) 청자들이 운전하지 못하게 하려고

(B) 변화에 대해 청자들을 안심시키려고

(C) 잠깐 휴식을 취할 것을 권유하려고

(D) 결정에 대한 실망감을 표현하려고

해설 **화자의 의도**

중반부에 훨씬 더 넓은 새 공간을 얻었다(So, I'm happy
to announce that I've acquired a new, much
larger space for us)고 알리며 고객을 잃을까 걱정하
는 사람들도 있겠다(I know some of you might be
worried about losing customers)고 한 뒤 인용문을
언급했으므로 (B)가 정답이다.

어휘 discourage 단념하게 하다 reassure 안심시키다
disappointment 실망

94 새로운 직원들은 무엇을 할 것인가?
(A) 제품 광고하기 (B) 재무 상태 처리하기
(C) 예약 일정 잡기 **(D) 물품 수리하기**

해설 **새로운 직원들이 할 일**
후반부에 전체 공간을 고려하면 매장 내에 수리점을 둘 공
간도 충분하다(With all the space, there'll even be
enough room to have an in-house repair shop)고
한 뒤 방금 이런 전문적인 작업을 능숙하게 해 줄 노련한 직원
두 사람을 고용했다(I've just hired two experienced
individuals who will be quite skilled at doing
that specialized work)고 했으므로 (D)가 정답이다.

[95-97] 회의 발췌 + 지도

M-Cn Before we get our staff meeting started,
I have exciting news. **95 As you know, our
company takes environmental sustainability
seriously. As part of this, we've just installed
an electric-vehicle charging area with eight
new charging stations on our corporate
campus. 96 This means that employees with
electric cars will be able to use this amenity to
recharge their car's battery during the workday.
You'll find these charging stations outside
the building's east entrance. 97 If anyone
has additional ideas for how we can further
promote environmental practices, please use
the link included in our company newsletter to
submit suggestions.**

직원회의를 시작하기 전에, 신나는 소식이 있어요. **95** 알다시피 자
사는 환경 지속 가능성을 중요하게 생각하죠. 그 일환으로 회사 부
지에 8개의 새 충전소를 갖춘 전기 자동차 충전 구역을 설치했습니
다. **96** 그러니까 전기 자동차가 있는 직원은 근무 시간 동안 이 편의
시설을 이용해 차 배터리를 충전할 수 있어요. 건물 동쪽 출입구 밖
에 이 충전소가 있습니다. **97** 환경에 이로운 관행을 더욱 장려할 수
있는 방법에 대한 추가적인 아이디어가 있으신 분이 계시다면 회사
소식지에 포함된 링크를 활용해 제안을 제출해 주세요.

어휘 environmental sustainability 환경 지속 가능성
campus 부지 amenity 편의 시설 promote 장려하다
practice 관행, 습관

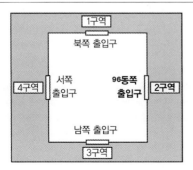

95 담화는 주로 무엇에 관한 것인가?
(A) 연례 회사 행사 (B) 휴대폰 방침
(C) 직원 설문 조사 **(D) 지속 가능성 계획**

해설 **담화의 주제**
초반부에 알다시피 자사는 환경 지속 가능성을 중요하
게 생각한다(As you know, our company takes
environmental sustainability seriously)고 운을 떼
며 그 일환으로 회사 부지에 8개의 새 충전소를 갖춘 전기 자
동차 충전 구역을 설치했다(As part of this, we've just
installed an electric-vehicle charging area ~ on
our corporate campus)고 한 뒤 관련 내용이 이어지므
로 (D)가 정답이다.

어휘 annual 연례의 initiative 계획

96 시각 정보에 따르면, 화자는 편의 시설이 어디에 있다고
말하는가?
(A) 1구역 (B) 2구역
(C) 3구역 (D) 4구역

해설 **시각 정보 연계**
중반부에 전기 자동차가 있는 직원은 근무 시간 동안 이 편
의 시설을 이용해 차 배터리를 충전할 수 있다(This means
that employees with electric cars will be able to
use this amenity to recharge their car's battery
during the workday)고 한 뒤 건물 동쪽 입구 밖에 충
전소가 있다(You'll find these charging stations
outside the building's east entrance)고 했다. 지도
를 보면 동쪽 출입구는 2구역이므로 (B)가 정답이다.

97 화자에 따르면, 청자들은 어떻게 의견을 제출할 수 있는가?
(A) 링크를 이용해서 (B) 이메일을 보내서
(C) 관리자와 대화해서 (D) 회의 일정을 잡아서

해설 **청자들이 의견을 제출하는 방법**
후반부에 환경에 이로운 관행을 더욱 장려할 수 있는 방법에
대한 추가적인 아이디어가 있으신 분이 계시다면 회사 소식지
에 포함된 링크를 활용해 제안을 제출하라(If anyone has
additional ideas for how we can further promote
environmental practices, please use the link
included in our company newsletter to submit
suggestions)고 했으므로 (A)가 정답이다.

(Paraphrasing) 담화의 suggestions
→ 질문의 recommendations

[98-100] 방송 + 일정표

W-Br Welcome, everyone! I'm Marion Clement,
and **98** I'm excited to be hosting today's episode
of *Food Bites* while your regular host is on
vacation. Today I'll be talking to Jyoti Mehta. For
those of you who don't know, Ms. Mehta started
a local restaurant chain that serves vegetarian
cuisine. **99** I'll be asking her about the process

of creating a successful business and what she's learned along the way. **100** But first, I'd like to thank our sponsor, Mattress Pod. Mattress Pod uses cutting-edge technology to ensure that you stay cool while you sleep.

어서 오세요, 여러분! 저는 마리온 클레멘트입니다. **98** 정규 진행자가 휴가를 간 사이 제가 오늘의 〈푸드 바이츠〉 에피소드를 진행하게 되어 설레네요. 오늘 저는 죠티 메타와 이야기를 나누려고 합니다. 모르시는 분들을 위해 알려 드리면 메타 씨는 채식 요리를 제공하는 지역 레스토랑 체인을 시작했습니다. **99** 메타 씨에게 성공적인 사업체를 만드는 과정과 그 과정에서 배운 것에 대해 여쭤보려고 합니다. **100** 하지만 먼저 우리 후원 업체인 매트리스 팟에게 감사하고 싶습니다. 매트리스 팟은 최첨단 기술을 활용해 잠자는 동안 시원함을 유지할 수 있도록 해 줍니다.

어휘 host 주최하다; 진행자 regular 정규의 cuisine 요리 sponsor 후원 업체 cutting-edge 최첨단의

라디오 쇼	방송 시간	진행자
〈테크 챗〉	11:00	사빈 클라인
〈지역 뉴스〉	12:00	조종규
98 〈푸드 바이츠〉	1:00	**시오리 아주마**
〈가든 블룸즈〉	2:00	베아트리즈 플로레스

98 시각 정보에 따르면, 화자는 누구를 대신하는가?
(A) 사빈 클라인   (B) 조종규
(C) 시오리 아주마   (D) 베아트리즈 플로레스

해설 **시각 정보 연계**
초반부에 정규 진행자가 휴가를 간 사이 자신이 오늘의 〈푸드 바이츠〉 에피소드를 진행하게 되어 설렌다(I'm excited to be hosting today's episode of Food Bites while your regular host is on vacation)고 했다. 일정표를 보면 〈푸드 바이츠〉 진행자는 시오리 아주마이므로 (C)가 정답이다.

어휘 substitute for ~을 대체하다

99 화자에 따르면, 인터뷰의 초점은 무엇인가?
(A) 환경친화적인 방법 사용하기
(B) 베스트셀러 저술하기
(C) 지역 사회에서 자원봉사 하기
(D) 성공적인 사업체 만들기

해설 **인터뷰의 주제**
화자가 중반부에 메타 씨에게 성공적인 사업체를 만드는 과정과 그 과정에서 배운 것에 대해 물어보려고 한다(I'll be asking her about the process of creating a successful business and what she's learned along the way)고 했으므로 (D)가 정답이다.

(Paraphrasing) 담화의 creating a successful business → 정답의 Developing a successful business

100 화자는 누구에게 감사를 표하는가?
(A) 쇼의 청취자   (B) 제작진
(C) 쇼의 후원 업체   (D) 방송국 사장

해설 **화자가 감사를 표하는 사람**
후반부에 먼저 우리 후원 업체인 매트리스 팟에게 감사하고 싶다(But first, I'd like to thank our sponsor, Mattress Pod)고 했으므로 (C)가 정답이다.

어휘 production 제작 station 방송국

PART 5

101 전치사 어휘

번역 하비슨 앤 컴퍼니는 5월 14일에 25주년을 기념할 것이다.

해설 빈칸 뒤에 날짜를 나타내는 명사구 May 14가 있고, '5월 14일에 25주년을 기념할 것이다'라는 내용이 되어야 하므로 요일이나 날짜 앞에서 '~에'를 나타내는 시간 전치사 (C) on이 정답이다.

어휘 mark 기념[축하]하다

102 동사 자리

번역 패션트랙 애슬레틱웨어는 전 세계 소매점에서 수천 명의 직원을 고용한다.

해설 Fashiontrack Athleticwear가 주어인 문장에 동사가 보이지 않으므로 빈칸은 동사 자리이다. 따라서 '고용하다'라는 뜻의 동사인 (A) employs가 정답이다. (B) employer는 명사, (C) employable은 형용사, (D) employing은 현재분사/동명사로 품사상 답이 될 수 없다.

103 등위접속사

번역 노에 씨는 오디오 북 듣는 것을 즐겨서, 장거리 통근을 개의치 않는다.

해설 빈칸은 앞뒤에 있는 절과 절을 연결하는 자리이고, '오디오 북을 듣는 것을 즐겨서 장거리 통근을 개의치 않는다'라는 내용이 되어야 자연스러우므로 '그래서'라는 뜻으로 인과 관계를 나타내는 등위접속사 (C) so가 정답이다. (A) for는 '왜냐하면'이라는 의미의 등위접속사로 쓰일 수 있지만 인과 관계가 어색하고, (B) but과 (D) or 또한 문맥상 적합하지 않다.

어휘 mind 꺼리다 commute 통근 (거리)

104 부사 자리_동사 수식

번역 만수르 씨는 새로운 커피 제품에 대한 소비자 수요를 정확히 예측했다.

해설 주어 Mr. Mansour와 동사 predicted 사이에서 동사를 수식하는 부사 자리이므로, '정확히'라는 의미의 부사 (D) correctly가 정답이다. (A) correct는 형용사/동사, (B) correcting은 동명사/현재분사/명사, (C) corrects는 동사이므로 품사상 답이 될 수 없다.

어휘 predict 예측하다 consumer 소비자 demand 수요

105 부사 어휘

번역 커넥트 넷은 먼로 카운티의 약 40퍼센트에 인터넷 서비스를 제공한다.

해설 빈칸 뒤 수사 40을 수식하기에 적절한 부사를 고르는 문제이다. 문맥상 '약 40퍼센트'라는 의미가 되어야 자연스러우므로, 숫자 앞에서 부사로 쓰여 '약, ~쯤'이라는 뜻을 나타내는 (B) about이 정답이다.

106 형용사 자리_주격 보어

번역 양식은 자사 웹사이트에서 이용하실 수 있으며 편하실 때 다운로드하실 수 있습니다.

해설 빈칸은 be동사 뒤 주격 보어 자리이므로 형용사나 분사, 또는 명사가 들어갈 수 있다. '양식은 웹사이트에서 이용할 수 있다'는 내용이 되어야 하므로 '이용할 수 있는'을 뜻하는 형용사 (A) available이 정답이다. (B) availability, (C) availabilities, (D) availableness는 모두 명사로 주어인 The forms와 동격이 아니므로 답이 될 수 없다.

어휘 at one's convenience 편할 때   availability 이용도

107 형용사 어휘

번역 정제 공장은 최대 용량으로 가동될 때 매일 3만 리터의 올리브유를 가공할 수 있다.

해설 빈칸 뒤의 명사 capacity를 수식하기에 적절한 형용사를 고르는 문제이다. 빈칸 뒤에서 공장에서 하루에 가공할 수 있는 올리브유의 양에 대해 이야기하고 있으므로 공장이 '최대 용량으로 가동될 때'라는 내용이 되어야 자연스럽다. 따라서 '최대의, 가득한'이라는 의미의 (A) full이 정답이다.

어휘 capacity 용량   refinery 정제 공장   process 가공하다

108 명사 자리_to부정사의 목적어

번역 직원들은 일정 충돌을 피하기 위해 공유 달력에 약속을 업데이트할 것을 권장합니다.

해설 빈칸은 to부정사 to update의 목적어 역할을 하는 명사 자리이다. 따라서 '약속'을 뜻하는 명사 (B) appointments가 정답이다. 동명사인 (A) appointing은 명사 자리에 들어갈 수는 있지만 뒤에 목적어가 필요하고, (C) appointed는 동사/과거분사, (D) appoint는 동사로 품사상 답이 될 수 없다.

어휘 scheduling conflict 일정 충돌, 겹치는 일정

109 명사 어휘

번역 고위 경영진은 다음 주 월요일 오후 2시 30분에 효과적인 회의를 이끄는 방법에 대한 워크숍을 실시할 예정이다.

해설 빈칸에 들어갈 명사는 경영진에서 수행하는(conduct) 활동에 관한 것이면서, 빈칸 뒤에서 수식하는 전치사구와 어울려야 한다. '효과적 회의를 이끄는 방법에 대한 워크숍을 실시하다'는 내용이 되어야 자연스러우므로, '워크숍, 연수회'를 뜻하는 (B) workshop이 정답이다. (A) search는 '검색', (C) manual은 '설명서', (D) decision은 '결정'이라는 뜻이다.

어휘 conduct (특정 활동을) 하다

110 형용사 자리_명사 수식

번역 코니스 접착제는 우수한 자동차용 다목적 접착제를 제조하는 것으로 가장 잘 알려져 있다.

해설 빈칸은 동명사 manufacturing의 목적어 역할을 하는 명사구 multipurpose glues를 수식하는 자리이고, '우수한 다목적 접착제'라는 의미가 되어야 하므로 '훌륭한, 우수한'을 뜻하는 형용사 (B) excellent가 정답이다. (A) excel과 (D) excels는 동사, (C) excelled는 동사/과거분사로 빈칸에 들어갈 수 없다.

어휘 adhesive 접착제   multipurpose 다목적   automotive 자동차의   excel 능가하다

111 동사 어휘

번역 온라인 구매 후 화면에 표시된 지시에 따라 간단한 설문 조사에 참여해 주세요.

해설 주어가 없이 please로 시작하는 명령문에 들어갈 동사 어휘를 고르는 문제이다. '지시에 따라 설문 조사를 해 달라'는 내용이 되어야 하므로 '따르다'는 의미의 (C) follow가 정답이다. (A) guide는 '안내하다', (B) chase는 '뒤쫓다', (D) uphold는 '지지하다'라는 의미이므로 문맥상 어울리지 않는다.

어휘 on-screen 화면의

112 재귀대명사

번역 IT 기술자들이 소프트웨어 전환을 실행하는 데 두 달이 소요될 것이다.

해설 빈칸은 동사 will give의 목적어 역할을 하는 자리이고, 주어인 The IT technicians를 대신하여 'IT 기술자들이 스스로에게 두 달을 줄 것이다'라는 의미가 되어야 하므로 목적격 재귀대명사인 (A) themselves가 정답이다.

어휘 execute 실행하다   transition 전환

113 전치사 어휘

번역 직원들은 이사 일로부터 10일 이내에 주소 변경에 대해 인사부에 통지해야 한다.

해설 빈칸 뒤에 기간을 나타내는 명사구 ten days가 있고, 문맥상 '10일 이내에'라는 내용이 되어야 하므로 기간 표현과 함께 쓰여 '~ 이내에'를 뜻하는 전치사 (D) within이 정답이다. 참고로 since는 완료 동사와 함께 쓰이며 뒤에 과거 시점을 나타내는 명사구가 온다. before는 뒤에 시점을 나타내는 명사구가 와야 하며, '이사하기 10일 전'을 의미하려면 '10 days before moving'의 형태로 써야 한다.

어휘 notify 통지하다

114 명사 자리_복합명사

번역 프리미엄 가입자는 에듀톤 아카데미의 온라인 학습 플랫폼에 있는 강좌를 평생 이용할 수 있습니다.

해설 동사 have의 목적어 역할을 하는 명사 자리로, 빈칸 앞의 명사 lifetime과 함께 쓰여 '평생 이용[입장]'이라는 의미의 복합명사를 만들 수 있는 '입장, 접근[이용]'이라는 뜻의 (B) access가 정답이다. (A) accessible은 형용사, (D)

accessed는 동사/과거분사로 품사상 적절하지 않고, (C) accessing은 타동사 access의 동명사로 목적어 자리에 들어갈 수는 있지만 목적어를 동반해야 하므로 답이 될 수 없다.

115 동사 어휘

번역 이 조리법에서는 재료가 잘 섞이도록 하기 위해 최소 3분 동안 반죽을 섞을 것을 권장합니다.

해설 동사 recommends의 목적어 역할을 하며 동명사 형태로 들어갈 동사 어휘를 고르는 문제이다. 빈칸 뒤에서 '재료가 잘 섞이도록 하기 위해서'라는 목적에 대해 언급하고 있으므로 '반죽을 섞을 것을 권장한다'는 내용이 되어야 적절하다. 따라서 '섞다'라는 뜻의 (D) mixing이 정답이다. (A)의 measure는 '측량하다', (B)의 check는 '확인하다', (C)의 pour는 '붓다'라는 의미이다.

어휘 batter 반죽   ingredient 재료   combine 결합하다

116 부정대명사

번역 히코리 크리크는 페어뷰에서 멀지 않아 하루 안에 두 군데 모두 쉽게 방문할 수 있다.

해설 빈칸은 동사 can visit의 목적어 자리이고, 앞에서 언급한 히코리 크리크와 페어뷰라는 두 곳의 장소를 대신하여 '두 군데 모두 방문할 수 있다'는 의미가 되어야 하므로 '둘 다'를 뜻하는 부정대명사인 (B) both가 정답이다. (A) which는 관계대명사로 뒤에 절이 와야 하고, (C) none은 '아무[하나]도 ~않다', (D) fewer는 '더 적은 사람[것]들'이라는 뜻으로 의미상 어울리지 않는다.

117 형용사 어휘

번역 한 씨는 작성이 끝난 대출 서류를 봉투에 담아 올리버 씨의 책상 위에 놓고 갔다.

해설 빈칸은 명사구 loan documents를 수식하는 형용사 자리이다. '작성된 서류를 놓고 갔다'는 의미가 되어야하므로 '작성된, 완료된'을 뜻하는 (C) completed가 정답이다. (A) accomplished는 '기량이 뛰어난', (B) satisfied는 '만족한', (D) inhabited는 '서식하는'이라는 뜻으로 모두 document를 수식하기에는 문맥상 적절하지 않다.

어휘 loan 대출   document 서류   envelope 봉투

118 동사 자리_수동태

번역 제빌리즈 트레저 트로브의 반품은 입구 근처에 있는 고객 서비스 데스크에서 처리됩니다.

해설 Returns가 주어인 문장에 동사가 보이지 않으므로 빈칸은 동사 자리이다. 또한 빈칸 뒤에 목적어가 보이지 않고, 반품은 처리(process)의 대상으로 '반품은 처리된다'는 의미가 되어야 하므로 수동태 동사인 (D) are processed가 정답이다. (A) to process는 to부정사, (C) being processed는 동명사/현재분사로 본동사 자리에 들어갈 수 없고, 능동태 동사인 (B) have processed는 답이 될 수 없다.

어휘 treasure trove 매장물   entrance 입구

119 형용사 어휘

번역 워터슬라이드 파크의 계절 한정 근로자들은 해당 시즌이 끝나고 일주일 뒤에 최종 급여를 받는다.

해설 명사 paycheck를 수식하는 형용사를 고르는 문제이다. 계절 한정 근로자에 대해 설명하는 내용이므로 '근무 기간이 끝나고 일주일 뒤 최종 급여를 받는다'는 의미가 되어야 자연스럽다. 따라서 '최종의'라는 뜻의 (A) final이 정답이다. (B) steady는 '꾸준한', (C) absolute는 '완전한', (D) fortunate는 '운 좋은'이라는 의미이다.

어휘 seasonal 특정 계절에 한정된   paycheck 급여

120 접속사 자리

번역 피어스 카드로 구매하실 때마다 거래 금액의 일부가 선택하신 자선 단체에 기부됩니다.

해설 문장 속에 두 개의 완전한 절이 있으므로 두 개의 절을 이어주는 접속사가 필요하다. 빈칸 뒤에 time이 보이고 문맥상 '카드로 구매할 때마다 거래의 일부가 기부된다'는 의미가 되어야 자연스러우므로 time과 함께 쓰여 '~할 때마다'라는 접속사 each time을 이루는 (C) Each가 정답이다. (A) Yet은 '하지만'이라는 등위접속사로 절과 절 사이에서 두 절을 연결하므로 문장 맨 앞에 들어갈 수 없고, (B) Beside는 전치사로 절을 연결할 수 없으며, (D) Until은 '~까지'라는 부사절 접속사로 의미상 적절하지 않다.

어휘 portion 부분[일부]   transaction 거래   donate 기부하다   charity 자선 단체

121 부사 어휘

번역 그리플리 건축은 벨 가에 최첨단 사무실 건물을 짓기 위해 림 건설과 협력하고 있다.

해설 동사 is working과 전치사구 with Lim Construction 사이에서 동사를 수식하여 '림 건설과 협력하여 일하는 중이다'라는 의미가 되어야 적절하므로 '협력하여'라는 뜻의 (C) cooperatively가 정답이다. (A) previously는 '이전에', (B) scarcely는 '거의 ~않다', (D) immensely는 '대단히'라는 의미이다.

어휘 architect 건축가   state-of-the-art 최첨단의

122 형용사 자리_명사 수식

번역 글레이트의 합판 마루는 진짜 목재처럼 보이지만 유지 관리는 훨씬 더 쉽습니다.

해설 전치사 like의 목적어 역할을 하는 명사 wood를 수식하는 형용사 자리이다. '진짜 목재'라는 의미가 되어야 적절하므로 '진품인, 진짜인'이라는 뜻의 형용사 (D) authentic이 정답이다. (A) authentication. (B) authenticity는 명사, (C) authenticate는 동사이므로 품사상 답이 될 수 없다.

어휘 laminate 합판 제품   flooring 마루   authenticate 진짜임을 증명하다

123 접속사 자리_부사절 접속사

번역 권장 사항은 아니지만 용도 변경된 건설 부품 구입이 가능합니다.

해설 빈칸 앞뒤에 두 개의 완전한 절이 있으므로, 빈칸은 접속사 자리이다. 문맥상 '권장하지는 않지만'이라는 내용이 되어야 자연스러우므로 '~이긴 하지만'이라는 뜻의 부사절 접속사 (D) though가 정답이다. (A) then은 부사/명사/형용사, (B) similarly는 부사로 품사상 답이 될 수 없고, (C) because 는 '~ 때문에'라는 뜻으로 문맥상 적합하지 않다.

어휘 repurpose 다른 목적[용도]에 맞게 만들다
component 부품

124 관계대명사

번역 도서관 카드는 카드를 요청하는 마운틴시티 주민 누구에게나 발급됩니다.

해설 빈칸 이하는 선행사 any Mountain City resident를 수식하는 관계절이다. 선행사가 사람이고 빈칸 뒤에 동사 requests가 나오는 것으로 보아 빈칸에는 사람 주격 관계대명사가 들어가야 하므로 (A) who가 정답이다. (B) what은 명사절 접속사, (C) whatever와 (D) whoever는 복합관계대명사로 선행사를 이미 포함하고 있어 선행사를 수식하는 관계사 자리에 들어갈 수 없다.

어휘 issue 발부[지급/교부]하다   resident 주민

125 형용사 자리_명사 수식

번역 가장 가까운 경쟁사에 서버 장애가 발생한 뒤 더 많은 기업이 비리존 웹 호스팅 서비스로 바꿨다.

해설 빈칸은 문장의 주어 역할을 하는 명사 businesses 앞에서 명사를 수식하는 형용사 자리이다. 따라서 '더 많은'을 뜻하는 형용사 (D) More가 정답이다. (A) Despite(~에도 불구하고)는 전치사, (B) Over(~위에)와 (C) Beyond(~너머)는 전치사/부사로 품사상 빈칸에 들어갈 수 없다.

어휘 switch 바꾸다   failure 고장, 정지

126 동사 어휘

번역 3년 동안 같은 임금을 받아온 샤디드 씨는 이번 달에 임금이 인상된다는 것을 알게 되면 안도할 것이다.

해설 빈칸은 콤마 뒤의 절을 수식하는 분사구문에서 Having 뒤에 과거분사로 들어가 빈칸 뒤 목적어인 the same salary와 어울리는 동사 어휘를 고르는 문제이다. 콤마 뒤의 절이 샤디드 씨가 임금 인상을 받을 것을 알면 안도할 것이라는 내용인 것으로 보아, '3년간 같은 임금을 받아온 샤디드 씨'라는 내용이 되어야 적절하므로 '(돈을) 벌다'라는 의미의 (A) earned 가 정답이다. (B)의 offer는 '제공하다', (C)의 need는 '필요로 하다', (D)의 require는 '요구하다'라는 의미이다.

어휘 relieved 안도[안심]한   raise 인상

127 동사 어형_태

번역 모두가 지난주 배포된 직원 명부 사본을 받았어야 한다.

해설 빈칸은 선행사 a copy of the staff directory를 수식하는 관계대명사 that절의 동사 자리이다. 빈칸 뒤에 목적어가 보이지 않고, 직원 명부 사본은 배포의 대상으로 '지난주에 배포된 직원 명부 사본'이라는 내용이 되어야 하므로 수동태 동사인 (C) was distributed가 정답이다. (A) distributed, (D) was distributing은 능동태로 뒤에 목적어가 필요하고, (B) distributing은 동명사/현재분사로 품사상 답이 될 수 없다.

어휘 directory 명부

128 명사 어휘

번역 풍경화 화가 발레리 샘슨은 그림에 대한 영감을 어느 지중해 해안 마을에서 얻었다고 말한다.

해설 동사 says의 목적어 역할을 하는 that이 생략된 명사절의 주어 자리에 들어갈 명사를 고르는 문제이다. '그림에 대한 영감은 지중해 해안 마을이었다'는 내용이 되어야 하므로 '영감'을 뜻하는 (B) inspiration이 정답이다. (A) accessory는 '부속품', (C) hospitality는 '환대', (D) submission은 '제출'이라는 의미이다.

어휘 landscape 풍경화   Mediterranean 지중해의
coastal 해안의

129 부사 어휘

번역 매우 구조적인 토론에 많이 참여한 후, 정치 후보자들은 좀 더 편안한 그룹 회담을 환영했다.

해설 빈칸 뒤 형용사 structured를 수식하기에 적절한 부사를 고르는 문제이다. '짜임새 있는, 체계적으로 구성된'이라는 뜻의 structured를 수식하려면 정도를 나타내는 '매우, 대단히'라는 뜻의 highly가 적합하므로 (C) highly가 정답이다. (A) high와 high의 비교급인 (B) higher는 형용사/부사로 부사 자리에 들어갈 수는 있지만 높낮이를 나타내는 '높이, 높게'라는 뜻이므로 문맥상 적합하지 않다.

어휘 participate in ~에 참여하다   debate 토론   political 정치의   candidate 입후보자   appreciate 환영하다

130 접속부사

번역 그랜저 트랙터의 분기 이익은 실망스러웠고, 그 결과 회사는 재고의 상당 부분을 매각해야 했다.

해설 등위접속사 and로 연결된 두 개의 완전한 절을 의미상 자연스럽게 연결해 줄 부사를 고르는 문제이다. 빈칸 앞의 분기 이익이 실망스러웠다는 내용과 빈칸 뒤의 재고를 매각해야 했다는 내용을 이어주면서 인과 관계를 나타내는 접속부사가 필요하다. 따라서 '그 결과'라는 뜻을 나타내는 (D) as a result가 정답이다. (A) otherwise는 '그렇지 않으면', (B) comparatively는 '비교적', (C) on the contrary는 '그와는 반대로'라는 의미이다.

어휘 quarterly 분기의   profit 이익, 수익   inventory 재고

PART 6

[131-134] 공지

산업부 임시 휴무

게시일: 1월 5일

산업부는 컴퓨터 시스템 종료를 **131 해야 하는** 중요한 소프트웨어 업데이트를 위해 1월 5일인 오늘과 1월 6일인 내일 휴무합니다. 이 기간 **132 동안에는** 온라인으로 자격증 신청을 받을 수 없음을 알려 드립니다. 하지만 직원의 연락을 받으려면 전화를 걸어 음성 메시지를 남겨 주세요. 성명과 **133 유효한** 전화번호를 포함해야 한다는 것을 유의하세요. 회신 전화를 받기 위해서는 두 가지 모두 필요합니다. **134 통화를 지원할 직원을 추가로 배치할 예정입니다.**

어휘 temporarily 일시적으로 post 게시하다 shutdown 폐쇄, 정지 license 면허[자격](증) application 신청 agent (공공 기관의) 직원 phone in 전화를 하다

---

131 현재분사

해설 빈칸 앞에 완전한 절이 있고, 빈칸 이하는 전치사 for의 목적어 역할을 하는 명사구 an important software update를 수식하는 수식어구이다. 빈칸 뒤의 명사구 a shutdown을 목적어로 취해 '컴퓨터 시스템의 종료를 필요로 하는 소프트웨어 업데이트'라는 의미로 빈칸 앞의 명사구를 수식할 수 있어야 하므로 '~을 필요로 하는'을 의미하는 현재분사 (B) necessitating이 정답이다. (A) necessity와 (D) necessities는 명사, (C) necessary는 형용사이다.

132 전치사 어휘

해설 빈칸 뒤에 기간을 나타내는 명사구 this time period가 있고, 앞 문장에서 '소프트웨어 업데이트를 위해 오늘과 내일 산업부가 휴무한다(The Department of Industry will be closed today, January 5, and tomorrow, January 6, ~ update)'고 했으므로 '이 기간 동안 신청을 받을 수 없다'는 내용이 되어야 적절하다. 따라서 '~ 동안'을 의미하는 (D) during이 정답이다.

133 형용사 자리

해설 빈칸은 부정관사 a와 명사구 phone number 사이에서 명사를 수식하는 자리이므로 '유효한'이라는 의미의 형용사 (A) valid가 정답이다. (B) validate와 (C) validates는 동사, (D) validity는 명사이므로 품사상 답이 될 수 없다.

134 문맥에 맞는 문장 고르기

번역 (A) 등록이 성공적으로 갱신되었습니다.
(B) 통화를 지원할 직원을 추가로 배치할 예정입니다.
(C) 사용자는 정기적으로 컴퓨터를 업데이트해야 합니다.
(D) 신분증에 관해서는 직원이 도와드립니다.

해설 빈칸 앞에서 직원의 연락을 받으려면 전화를 걸어 음성 메시지를 남겨 달라(to have an agent contact you, phone in and leave a voice message)며 성명과 전화번호도 함께 알려달라는 당부를 하고 있으므로, 빈칸에는 직원의 전화 연락 서비스와 관련된 내용이 이어져야 일관성

있는 문맥이 완성된다. 따라서 전화 연락 서비스와 관련해 이를 도울 추가 직원을 배치할 예정임을 언급하고 있는 (B)가 정답이다.

어휘 registration 등록 identification card 신분증

[135-138] 편지

5월 3일

실리아 에드가
24 크리스탈 비치 로
미들타운, OH 45055

에드가 씨께,

저희에게 이사 소식을 알려주셔서 감사합니다. **135 매주** 배달되는 우유와 오렌지 주스는 5월 10일부터 고객님의 새로운 주소로 배송될 예정입니다. 배송일이 화요일에서 목요일로 변경되므로 매주 수요일 밤에 빈병을 꺼내 놓는 것을 기억해 주십시오.

배송을 연기해야 하거나 주문 품목 변경을 원하신다면 www.mcgrathdairies.com/customerservice에서 하시면 됩니다. 저희는 유리병에 담긴 신선한 우유**136 뿐만 아니라** 코티지 치즈와 요거트, 달걀을 제공하고 있습니다.

가정 배달의 편리함을 **137 즐기는** 사람이 늘어나고 있는 가운데 고객님을 그중 한 분으로 모시게 되어 기쁩니다. **138 계속해서 서비스를 제공해 드릴 수 있기를** 기대합니다.

프랜시스 부누안
맥그래스 유업 관리자

어휘 count 포함시키다, 계산에 넣다 dairy 유제품 회사

135 형용사 자리_어휘

해설 명사 deliveries를 수식하면서 빈도를 나타내는 형용사를 고르는 문제이다. 빈칸 뒤 문장에서 배송일이 목요일로 변경되므로 매주 수요일 밤(every Wednesday night)마다 빈병을 꺼내 놓을 것을 당부하고 있는 것으로 보아 음료가 매주 배달되고 있음을 알 수 있다. 따라서 '매주 배달되는 우유와 오렌지 주스'라는 의미가 되어야 하므로 '매주, 주 1회의'를 뜻하는 (C) weekly가 정답이다. (A) hourly는 '매시간의', (B) daily는 '매일의', (D) yearly는 '매년 하는'이라는 의미이다.

136 전치사 자리_어휘

해설 빈칸 뒤 명사구 our fresh milk를 연결해 '우유뿐만 아니라 코티지 치즈, 요거트, 달걀을 제공한다'는 문맥이 되어야 자연스러우므로 '~뿐만 아니라'라는 뜻으로 추가의 의미를 나타내는 (C) in addition to가 정답이다. (B) on account of는 '~ 때문에', (D) with regard to는 '~에 관하여'라는 의미이고, (A) as far as는 '~하는 한'이라는 의미의 부사절 접속사이므로 빈칸에 들어갈 수 없다.

137 동사 자리

해설 선행사 the growing number of people을 수식하는 주격 관계대명사 who절의 동사 자리이다. 따라서 '즐기다'라는 뜻의 동사 (D) enjoy가 정답이다. (A) enjoyment는 명사, (B) enjoyable은 형용사, (C) enjoying은 동명사/현재분사이므로 품사상 답이 될 수 없다.

138 문맥에 맞는 문장 고르기

번역 (A) 계속해서 서비스를 제공해 드릴 수 있기를 기대합니다.

(B) 빈병을 재활용하실 것을 권장 드립니다.

(C) 현재 새로운 배달 기사를 채용 중입니다.

(D) 이 서비스를 더 이상 이용하실 수 없게 되어 유감입니다.

해설 빈칸 앞에서 고객으로 모시게 되어 기쁘다(We are pleased to count you among ~)고 했으므로, 그 뒤에서 고객에게 보내는 편지글을 마무리하는 문장으로 고객과의 관계를 지속할 수 있기를 기대한다는 내용이 되어야 적합하다. 따라서 (A)가 정답이다.

어휘 regret 유감스럽게 생각하다

[139-142] 웹페이지

세러벨럼에 관하여

세러벨럼 앱은 다양하고 **139** 흥미로운 훈련들로 수학적이고 분석적인 사고를 자극함으로써 당신의 정신적 예리함을 향상해 줍니다. 소뇌 숙련도 점수(CPS)를 통해 다양한 기술에 대한 여러분의 발전을 확인하세요. 이 **140** 수치는 사용자의 정확도와 응답 시간을 평가하여 결정됩니다. **141** CPS 점수는 앱에 있는 '나의 성과' 섹션에서 찾으실 수 있습니다. 점수는 기술마다 400에서 800점 사이입니다. 자신만의 속도로 훈련하거나 그룹 훈련 기능을 사용해 친구들과 경쟁하세요. 요금제 옵션으로는 매달 5달러 또는 매년 50달러의 회비가 있습니다. **142** 다른 사람들에게 "CPSFRIEND" 프로모션 코드를 이용하여 회원에 가입하도록 권하시고 첫 달 무료 혜택을 받으세요.

어휘 cerebellum 소뇌   acuity 예리함   challenge 자극하다   analytical 분석적인   track 추적하다   progress 진전   proficiency 숙련   determine 결정하다   evaluate 평가하다   accuracy 정확도   range from A to B (범위가) A에서 B까지 이르다   pace 속도   function 기능

139 형용사 자리

해설 빈칸은 전치사 of의 목적어 역할을 하는 명사 exercises를 수식하는 자리이고, 문맥상 '즐거운 훈련들'이라는 의미가 되어야 적절하므로 '흥미로운, 매력적인'이라는 뜻의 분사형 형용사 (D) engaging이 정답이다. (A) engage, (B) engages는 '사로잡다'라는 뜻의 동사로 품사상 오답이고, (C) engaged는 '바쁜'이라는 의미의 형용사로 문맥상 적절하지 않다.

140 명사 어휘

해설 앞 문장에서 소뇌 숙련도 점수를 통해(via your Cerebellum Proficiency Scores) 발전 정도를 확인하라고 했으므로 사용자의 정확도와 응답 시간을 평가하여 결정되는 대상이 '점수(Scores)'라는 것을 알 수 있다. 따라서 점수를 대신할 수 있는 '숫자, 수치'라는 뜻의 명사 (A) numbers가 정답이다. (B)의 amount는 '양, 액수', (C)의 quantity는 '양, 수량', (D)의 conclusion은 '결론'이라는 의미이다.

141 문맥에 맞는 문장 고르기

번역 (A) 추천 보너스는 사용자 1인당 하나로 제한됩니다.

(B) 세러벨럼은 앱을 판매하는 곳이면 어디서든 다운로드하실 수 있습니다.

(C) CPS 점수는 앱에 있는 '나의 성과' 섹션에서 찾으실 수 있습니다.

(D) 사람들은 자신의 지식을 테스트할 수 있는 방법을 찾고 있습니다.

해설 빈칸 앞에서 소뇌 숙련도 점수(your Cerebellum Proficiency Scores)를 통해 여러 기술에 대한 발전 정도를 확인하라면서 정확도와 응답 시간으로 점수(numbers)를 산출한다는 기준에 대해 설명하고 있고, 빈칸 뒤에서 각 항목별로 매겨지는 점수의 범위(from 400 to 800)에 대해 안내하고 있다. 따라서 빈칸에는 점수에 대해 언급하는 내용이 들어가야 문맥이 일관성 있게 연결되므로 CPS 점수를 어디에서 찾을 수 있는지를 안내하고 있는 (C)가 정답이다.

어휘 referral 추천, 소개

142 부정대명사

해설 동사 Encourage의 목적어 자리에 들어갈 적절한 대명사를 고르는 문제이다. 빈칸 뒤에서 첫 달을 무료로 받으라(get your first month free)고 한 것으로 보아 무료 혜택을 받기 위해서는 '다른 사람들에게 프로모션 코드를 이용해 회원에 가입하도록 권하라'라는 내용이 되어야 적합하다. 따라서 '다른 사람들'을 뜻하는 부정대명사 (C) others가 정답이다.

[143-146] 기사

밴쿠버 (4월 6일)—로리스 스위트 트릿츠 아이스크림이 오늘 세계적으로 확장해 나간다고 발표했다. **143** 이 인기 있는 아이스크림 체인은 10년 동안 캐나다의 주요 브랜드였다. 6월에 이 업체는 국경 남쪽의 시애틀에 첫 체인점을 열 예정이다.

"우리는 수년간 미국 시장 진출을 모색해 왔습니다."라고 회사 창립자이자 최고 경영자인 로리 스타우트는 말했다. "이제 마침내 **144** 조건이 딱 들어맞습니다. 경제 상황, 환율—모든 것이 유리합니다."

로리스 스위트 트릿츠 아이스크림은 40가지 맛의 아이스크림으로 구성된 메뉴를 **145** 자랑한다. "우리는 다양한 종류의 맛으로 유명합니다."라고 스타우트 씨는 말했다. "**146** 물론 우리는 초콜릿과 바닐라 같은 전통적인 맛도 제공합니다. 하지만 매우 인기 있는 색다른 맛들도 있습니다."

이 캐나다 회사는 현재 밴쿠버 지역에 14곳의 매장을 운영하고 있다.

어휘 border 국경   founder 창립자   exchange rate 환율   favourable 유리한   range 범위[폭]

143 문맥에 맞는 문장 고르기

번역 (A) 로리스 스위트 트릿츠 아이스크림은 1,000명 이상의 직원을 고용하고 있다.

(B) 아이스크림은 전 세계적으로 즐겨 먹는다.

(C) 이 인기 있는 아이스크림 체인은 10년 동안 캐나다의 주요 브랜드였다.

(D) 밴쿠버에 본사를 둔 이 회사는 최근 새로운 총괄 관리자를 고용했다.

해설 앞 문장에서 로리스 스위트 트릿츠 아이스크림이 세계적으로 사업을 확장해 나간다는 계획을 언급하며 뒤 문장에서 6월에는 국경 남쪽의 시애틀에 첫 체인점을 열 예정이라고 했다. 문맥상 이 아이스크림 체인이 어느 지역에 기반을 두고 있는 기업인지를 설명하는 내용이 들어가야 연결이 자연스러우므로 10년 동안 캐나다의 주요 브랜드였다고 언급하고 있는 (C)가 정답이다.

어휘 staple 주요 상품 based ~에 본사를 둔
general (직급을 나타내어) 총~

144 명사 어휘

해설 빈칸 앞 문장에서 수년간 미국 시장 진출을 모색해 왔다고 했고, 빈칸 뒤 문장에서 드디어 경제 상황, 환율, 모든 것(The economy, the exchange rate—everything)이 좋다고 했다. 따라서 빈칸에는 미국 시장에 진출하기 위해 갖춰져야 할 조건이나 상황, 환경 등을 뜻하는 명사가 들어가야 적절하므로 '상황, 조건'을 뜻하는 명사 (B) conditions가 정답이다. (A)의 tool은 '도구', (C)의 portion은 '부분', (D)의 temperature는 '온도'라는 의미이다.

145 동사 자리

해설 로리스 스위트 트릿츠 아이스크림이 주어인 문장에 동사가 없으므로, 빈칸은 동사 자리이다. 따라서, '자랑하다'라는 뜻의 동사 (A) boasts가 정답이다. (B) boaster는 명사, (C) boasting은 명사/형용사/동명사/현재분사, (D) boastful은 형용사이므로 품사상 답이 될 수 없다.

146 접속부사

해설 빈칸 앞에서 로리스 스위트 트릿츠 아이스크림은 40가지 맛의 아이스크림으로 구성된 메뉴를 자랑한다며 다양한 종류의 맛으로 유명하다고 했는데, 빈칸 뒤에는 초콜릿과 바닐라 같은 전통적인 맛도 제공한다면서 바로 뒤에서 매우 인기 있는 색다른 맛들도 있다고 다시 한번 다양한 메뉴에 대해 강조하고 있다. 다양한 맛에 대해 강조하는 문장들 사이에서 기본 맛에 대한 구색이 갖춰져 있는 것은 당연하다는 내용으로 연결되어야 자연스러우므로 '물론, 당연히'를 의미하는 (D) Of course가 정답이다. (A) There는 '거기서', (B) In fact는 '사실은', (C) Instead는 '대신에'라는 의미이다.

PART 7

[147-149] 광고

에어베스트 항공
편리함, 편안함, 관심
147,148〈국제 비즈니스 여행 잡지〉에서 선정한 최고의 고객 서비스
• 매일 세인트루이스에서 출발하는 항공편 운항
• 신규 유럽 행선지: 프랑크푸르트 및 오슬로

• **147** 이른 아침 및 야간 직항편(24시간 이내에 회의에 참석하고 귀가하세요!)
• 완전히 뒤로 젖혀지는 좌석, 다양한 기내 엔터테인먼트 옵션, **149** 승객이 여행 전 온라인으로 선택할 수 있는 요리사가 준비한 요리 등의 훌륭한 편의 시설

www.airbestairlines.com에서 온라인으로 예약하세요.

어휘 name 선정하다 amenities 편의 시설 reclining (등받이가) 뒤로 젖혀지는 inflight 기내의 cuisine 요리 passenger 승객

147 광고의 대상은 누구일 것 같은가?
　(A) 항공기 조종사　　　(B) 출장 여행자
　(C) 공항 직원　　　　　(D) 관광 가이드

해설 추론/암시
　광고의 상단에 〈국제 비즈니스 여행 잡지〉에서 선정한 최고의 고객 서비스(Named Best Customer Service by *International Business Travel Magazine*)라고 했고, 중반부에 이른 아침 및 야간 직항편(24시간 이내에 회의에 참석하고 귀가하세요!)(Direct flights early in the morning and overnight (Get to meetings and back home within 24 hours!))이라고 홍보하고 있는 것으로 보아 출장 여행자를 대상으로 하는 광고임을 알 수 있다. 따라서 (B)가 정답이다.

148 에어베스트 항공에 대해 명시된 것은?
　(A) 잡지에 언급되었다.
　(B) 오슬로에 본사를 두고 있다.
　(C) 승무원을 채용 중이다.
　(D) 최근에 새 비행기를 구입했다.

해설 Not/True
　광고의 상단에 에어베스트 항공이 〈국제 비즈니스 여행 잡지〉에서 선정한 최고의 고객 서비스(Named Best Customer Service by *International Business Travel Magazine*)라고 했으므로 (A)가 정답이다.

어휘 flight attendant 승무원 acquire 구입하다

149 에어베스트 항공의 편의 시설에 포함된 것은 무엇인가?
　(A) 특히 넓은 좌석
　(B) 다른 곳에서는 이용할 수 없는 엔터테인먼트 옵션
　(C) 무선 인터넷 서비스
　(D) 비행 전에 주문할 수 있는 음식

해설 세부 사항
　광고의 하단에 승객이 여행 전 온라인으로 선택할 수 있는 요리사가 준비한 요리(chef-prepared cuisine that passengers can select online before traveling)를 제공한다고 언급하고 있으므로 (D)가 정답이다.

(Paraphrasing) 지문의 cuisine → 정답의 Food
지문의 traveling → 정답의 a flight

[150-151] 이메일

수신: 제이슨 헤나레 씨
발신: 사라 로테사
답장: 접근 권한
날짜: 8월 8일
첨부: 서명 확인서

헤나레 씨께,

150 푸케코헤 은행은 다른 사람이 고객님의 계좌에 접근하는 것을 승인해 달라는 귀하의 요청을 받았습니다. 진행을 위해서 현재 계좌 소유자와 접근 권한이 필요한 사람 모두 서명 확인서를 작성하셔야 합니다.

151 계좌 소유자로서, 귀하께서는 첨부된 양식을 인쇄하시고 표시된 곳에 서명하셔야 합니다. 마호니 씨의 서명도 받을 책임이 있습니다.

귀하와 마호니 씨께서 양식에 서명하셨으면 우편으로 양식을 반송하시거나 스캔하여 이메일 첨부 파일로 저에게 다시 보내주십시오.

문의 사항이 있으시면 09 555 0109, 내선 번호 513으로 저에게 연락 주십시오.

감사합니다.

사라 로테사, 개인 계좌 관리자
푸케코헤 은행
228 웨슬리 가
푸케코헤, 오클랜드 2120

어휘 authorisation 권한 verification 확인 grant 승인[허락]하다 proceed 진행하다 indicate 표시하다

---

150 이메일의 목적은 무엇인가?

(A) 거래 취소 **(B) 지침 제공**
(C) 오류 수정 (D) 정책 변경 공지

해설 주제/목적

첫 문장에서 푸케코헤 은행에서 다른 사람이 고객의 계좌에 접근하는 것을 승인해 달라는 고객의 요청을 받았다(The Bank of Pukekohe has received your request ~ to your account)며 진행을 위해서 현재 계좌 소유자와 접근 권한이 필요한 사람 모두 서명 확인서를 작성해야 한다(In order to proceed, we require ~ to complete a signature verification form)고 했다. 따라서 고객의 요청에 따른 서비스를 제공하기 위해 고객이 해야 할 일에 대한 지침을 안내하고자 이메일을 쓴 것이므로 (B)가 정답이다.

어휘 transaction 거래 instructions 지침

151 마호니 씨가 할 것으로 예상되는 일은?

(A) 은행 수수료 지불 (B) 이메일 전달
(C) 문서에 서명 (D) 은행 계좌 폐쇄

해설 세부 사항

두 번째 단락의 첫 문장에서 헤나레 씨에게 계좌 소유자로서 첨부된 양식을 인쇄하고 표시된 곳에 서명해야 한다(As the account holder, you will need to print out the attached form and sign where indicated)고 했고, 마호니 씨의 서명도 받을 책임이 있다(You are

also responsible for obtaining Ms. Mahoney's signature)고 했다. 따라서 헤나레 씨가 출력한 양식에 마호니 씨의 서명을 받을 것으로 예상되므로 정답은 (C)이다.

어휘 forward 부치다, 발송하다

[152-153] 공지

파인브룩 매너즈 정책 업데이트: 바비큐 애호가들을 위한 희소식

152 파인브룩 매너즈 주택 소유자 협회는 최근 〈공동 주택 표준 지침서〉 28쪽에 있는 19.3번 항목의 정책을 변경하였습니다. **152,153** 6월 9일부터 주택 소유자는 주택 소유자 협회의 허가 없이 집 뒤쪽의 테라스에서 숯, 가스 또는 프로판 그릴을 사용할 수 있습니다. 하지만 천연가스 선에 그릴을 연결할 계획이라면 설치 전에 협회의 서면 허가가 필요합니다. 사무실에 이 요청을 위한 적절한 양식이 있습니다. 모든 경우에 그릴은 주택으로부터 4피트 이상 떨어진 시멘트 테라스에 설치되어야 합니다.

감사합니다. 안전한 바비큐 파티를 즐기시기 바랍니다!

어휘 manor 저택 association 협회 charcoal 숯 propane 프로판 grill 그릴[석쇠] feet 피트(약 12인치 또는 약 30센티미터)

---

152 공지의 대상은 누구인가?

(A) 건설 회사 근로자 (B) 특정 지역의 사업주
(C) 지역 신문 구독자 **(D) 민영 공동 주택 주민**

해설 세부 사항

첫 문장에서 파인브룩 매너즈 주택 소유자 협회는 최근 〈공동 주택 표준 지침서〉 28쪽에 있는 19.3번 항목의 정책을 변경했다(The Pinebrook Manors Homeowners Association has recently made a policy change to ~ our *Community Standards Guide*)고 알리며, 두 번째 문장에서 6월 9일부터 주택 소유자는 주택 소유자 협회의 허가 없이 집 뒤쪽의 테라스에서 숯, 가스 또는 프로판 그릴을 사용할 수 있다(As of 9 June, homeowners will be permitted to use ~ without approval from the homeowners association)고 했다. 따라서 파인브룩 매너즈 주택의 거주자들을 대상으로 변경된 정책을 알리는 공지문이라는 것을 알 수 있으므로 (D)가 정답이다.

어휘 private 사유의

153 6월 9일부터 허용되는 것은 무엇인가?

(A) 바비큐 그릴 사용 (B) 뒤쪽 테라스 설치
(C) 공용 취사 구역 이용 (D) 천연가스 선 유료 이용

해설 세부 사항

두 번째 문장에서 6월 9일부터 주택 소유자는 주택 소유자 협회의 허가 없이 집 뒤쪽의 테라스에서 숯, 가스 또는 프로판 그릴을 사용할 수 있다(As of 9 June, homeowners will be permitted to use a charcoal, gas, or propane grill on their patios ~ without approval from the homeowners association)고 했으므로 (A)가 정답이다.

[154-155] 후기

호스쿨드 투어스는 아이슬란드 최고의 여행사입니다!

레이캬비크를 방문할 계획이라면 호스쿨드 투어스를 꼭 확인해 보세요. **154세계 곳곳에서 많은 단체 도보 투어를 다녔는데 제가 가본 곳 중 최고의 투어를 제공합니다.** 가이드들은 친절하고 박식합니다. 두 시간 반짜리 코스 동안 합리적인 비용으로 레이캬비크 중심부의 거의 모든 중요한 랜드마크를 보게 됩니다. 투어가 끝난 뒤에는 도시의 고급 레스토랑 중 한 곳에서 식사를 즐길 수 있고 아이슬란드 역사 박물관에서 오후를 보낼 수 있습니다.

155호스쿨드 투어스는 고래 구경을 위한 보트 여행도 제공합니다. 아쉽게도 저는 기회를 놓쳤습니다. 아이슬란드 방문 기간이 더 길었다면 이 여행 중 하나에 갔을 겁니다. 하지만, **155다음 방문에는 꼭 갈 겁니다.**

—엘리스 채

어휘 operator 운영사 knowledgeable 박식한 classy 고급의 excursion (당일치기) 여행

154 채 씨에 대해 암시된 것은?

(A) 경험이 많은 여행자이다.
(B) 레이캬비크에서 일했었다.
(C) 종일 걸리는 도보 투어를 했다.
(D) 레스토랑 식사가 너무 비쌌다고 생각한다.

해설 추론/암시

두 번째 문장에서 채 씨가 세계 곳곳에서 많은 단체 도보 투어를 다녔는데 가본 곳 중 최고의 투어를 제공한다(It offers the best group walking tours I've ever been on- and I have been on many, all over the globe)고 한 것으로 보아 채 씨는 도보 투어를 많이 경험해 본 여행자임을 알 수 있다. 따라서 (A)가 정답이다.

어휘 experienced 경험이 많은 last 지속되다

155 채 씨가 다음 아이슬란드 방문에서 할 계획인 것은 무엇인가?

(A) 박물관 방문
(B) 도시 랜드마크 관람
(C) 고래 구경 가기
(D) 개인 투어 가이드 고용

해설 세부 사항

두 번째 단락의 첫 문장에서 채 씨가 호스쿨드 투어스는 고래 구경을 위한 보트 여행도 제공한다(Hoskuld Tours also offers boat excursions for whale watching)고 했고, 아쉽게도 자신은 기회를 놓쳤다(Unfortunately, I missed my chance)며, 다음 방문 때는 꼭 갈 것(I will definitely do it on my next visit)이라고 했다. 따라서 채 씨는 다음 아이슬란드 방문 때 고래 구경 보트 여행을 할 계획이라는 것을 알 수 있으므로 (C)가 정답이다.

[156-157] 온라인 채팅

미구엘 카날레스 [오전 10시 2분]
156제가 다시 계산을 해 봤습니다. 예산 균형이 맞지 않습니다.

조이 민 [오전 10시 6분]
안타깝네요. 어떻게 해야 할까요?

미구엘 카날레스 [오전 10시 15분]
일치하지 않는 부분 때문에 작년 수입과 지출에 대한 회계 감사를 요청하고 싶습니다. 그냥 미리 알고 계셨으면 했습니다.

조이 민 [오전 10시 17분]
동의합니다. 서류를 작성하면 승인 서명해 드릴게요. **157내부 감사부터 시작하죠. 어떻게 되는지 봅시다. 157필요할 경우 독립된 외부 감사 회사를 고용할 수 있습니다.**

미구엘 카날레스 [오전 10시 18분]
알겠습니다. 감사합니다.

어휘 run the numbers 계산을 하다 discrepancy 불일치 audit 회계 감사 revenue 수입 expenditure 지출 in advance 미리 draw up ~을 작성하다 internal 내부의 external 외부의

156 토론의 주요 주제는 무엇인가?

(A) 예산 삭감
(B) 장부상 문제
(C) 불필요한 서류 작업
(D) 직원 피드백

해설 주제/목적

10시 2분에 카날레스 씨가 자기가 다시 계산을 해 봤다(I ran the numbers again)고 했고, 예산 균형이 맞지 않는다(The budget is still not balanced)며 회계 결산상의 문제를 제기하며 논의를 시작하고 있으므로 (B)가 정답이다.

어휘 budget cut 예산 삭감 bookkeeping 장부, 부기

(Paraphrasing) 지문의 budget is still not balanced
→ 정답의 A bookkeeping issue

157 오전 10시 17분에 민 씨가 "어떻게 되는지 봅시다"라고 쓴 의도는 무엇인가?

(A) 카날레스 씨의 고객들이 곧 도착할 것이라고 생각한다.
(B) 카날레스 씨의 요청을 승인할 것이다.
(C) 조치를 취하기 전에 결과를 기다릴 것이다.
(D) 비용이 증가할 것이라고는 생각하지 않는다.

해설 의도 파악

10시 17분에 민 씨가 내부 감사부터 시작하자(Let's start with an internal audit)면서 어떻게 되는지 보자(We'll see what happens)고 한 뒤, 필요할 경우 독립된 외부 감사 회사를 고용할 수 있다(If we need to, we can then hire an independent external auditing company)고 덧붙였다. 따라서 민 씨는 내부 감사 결과가 나오기를 기다렸다가 그 결과에 따라 외부 감사 업체를 고용할지에 관한 추가 조치 여부를 결정하겠다는 의도로 한 말이므로 (C)가 정답이다.

[158-160] 구인 광고

정보 기술 인프라 관리자

얼팝 비디오 서비시즈: 영국 맨체스터

설명: 당사 IT 시스템의 안전하고 안정적인 운영을 보장하기 위해 기술 팀을 교육하고 감독한다. **158여기에는 네트워크와 서버 인프라, 데이터 통신, 그리고 회사의 전화 시스템을 유지 관리 및 최적화하는 작업이 포함된다.** 인프라 관리자는 또한 하드웨어 및 소프

트웨어 문제를 적시에 해결하기 위해 최종 사용자 고객 서비스를 감독한다.

팀원에게 업무를 배정하고 작업 성과를 평가한다.

159 부서의 정책 및 절차를 결정하고 관리자의 성과를 평가하는 정보 기술 책임자에게 업무를 보고한다.

160 자격: 정보 기술 분야 대학 학위 및 관련 경력 5년 이상.

지원하려면 이력서를 hr@erpopvideoservices.co.uk로 보내세요.

어휘 infrastructure 인프라, 기반 시설 description 설명 supervise 감독하다 secure 안전한, 확실한 stable 안정적인 optimise 최적화하다 oversee 감독하다 end-user 최종 소비자[사용자] resolve 해결하다 in a timely manner 적시에 assign 배정하다 evaluate 평가하다 departmental 부서의 procedure 절차 degree 학위 relevant 관련 있는

---

158 공고된 직무에 대해 명시된 것은?

(A) 캠퍼스 건물의 경비와 관련이 있다.

(B) 승진 가능성을 제공한다.

(C) 전화 시스템의 유지 관리가 요구된다.

(D) 새로 생긴 직책이다.

해설 **Not/True**

두 번째 문장에서 채용 중인 일자리의 직무에는 네트워크와 서버 인프라, 데이터 통신, 회사의 전화 시스템을 유지 관리 및 최적화하는 작업이 포함된다(This includes maintaining and optimising ~ the company's telephone system)고 설명하고 있다. 전화 시스템을 유지 관리하는 작업이 포함된다고 했으므로 (C)가 정답이다.

159 IT 인프라 정책을 설정하는 사람은 누구인가?

(A) 부서 관리자   (B) **부서 책임자**

(C) 인프라 팀원   (D) 사장

해설 **세부 사항**

세 번째 단락에서 IT 부서의 정책 및 절차를 결정하고 관리자의 성과를 평가하는 정보 기술 책임자에게 업무를 보고한다(Reports to the director of Information Technology, who determines departmental policies ~ manager's performance)고 했으므로 IT 인프라 정책을 수립하는 사람은 IT 부서의 책임자임을 알 수 있다. 따라서 (B)가 정답이다.

(Paraphrasing) 지문의 determines → 질문의 sets

160 이 직책에 대해 명시된 요구 사항은 무엇인가?

(A) 재무 행정 경험

(B) 높은 수준의 비밀 정보 사용 허가

(C) 유동적인 근무 시간 확보 가능성

(D) 밀접하게 관련된 직무의 이전 경력

해설 **Not/True**

네 번째 단락에서 자격은 정보 기술 분야 대학 학위 및 관련 경력 5년 이상(Qualifications: University degree in information technology and a minimum of five

years of relevant experience)이라고 명시했으므로 정답은 (D)이다.

어휘 financial administration 재무 행정 security clearance 비밀 정보 사용 허가 flexible 유동적인 related 관련된

(Paraphrasing) 지문의 relevant experience
→ 정답의 Previous work in a closely related role

[161-163] 이메일

수신: 켄드라 클라스니크 〈kendra.klasnik@mailhost.com〉
발신: 마르코 바르가스 〈marco.vargas@buslono.com〉
제목: 다음 주
날짜: 9월 13일

안녕하세요, 켄드라.

161 부슬로노 인더스트리스에 오신 것을 환영합니다! 제 이름은 마르코이고, 당신의 동료 멘토가 될 것입니다. 아마 설명 들으셨겠지만 모든 신입 사원은 입사 첫 6주 동안 동료 멘토와 짝을 이루게 됩니다. 저는 회사 정책 및 문화에 대한 질문에 답하는 것을 도와드리고 새로운 직책에 자리 잡는 것을 돕기 위한 당신의 연락책이 될 겁니다.

162 저는 처음에는 생산 보조원으로, 그리고 현재는 생산 인솔자로서 거의 5년간 부슬로노에서 근무해 왔습니다. 저는 당신이 곧 맡게 될 역할에 대해 실무 지식을 갖고 있습니다.

첫 근무일인 9월 20일에 **163** 가장 먼저 방문할 곳은 인사부로, 그곳에서 스테이시 씨가 서류와 사원증을 준비해 줄 겁니다. 오전 10시 30분에 그녀의 사무실에서 당신과 만나겠습니다. 거기서부터 제가 사무실을 구경시켜 드리고 동료들에게 당신을 소개하겠습니다. 그리고 나서 우리는 모두 구내식당에서 함께 점심을 먹을 것입니다.

월요일에 만나기를 기대합니다.

마르코 바르가스
부슬로노 인더스트리스 생산 인솔자

어휘 peer 동료 hire 신입 사원 pair 짝을 짓다 settled (직장 등에서) 자리를 잡은 firsthand 직접 (체험해서) 얻은 take on (일 등을) 맡다

---

161 바르가스 씨는 왜 클라스니크 씨에게 글을 썼는가?

(A) 일자리를 제안하려고

(B) **자신을 소개하려고**

(C) 직무에 대해 간략하게 설명하려고

(D) 정책에 대한 질문에 답하려고

해설 **주제/목적**

첫 문장에서 바르가스 씨가 클라스니크 씨에게 부슬로노 인더스트리스에 온 것을 환영한다(Welcome to Buslono Industries!)면서 자신은 마르코이고 클라스니크 씨의 동료 멘토가 될 것(My name is Marco, and I will be your peer mentor)이라고 했다. 따라서 바르가스 씨는 신입 사원 클라스니크 씨에게 자신과 자신의 역할에 대해 소개하기 위해 글을 쓴 것임을 알 수 있으므로 (B)가 정답이다.

어휘 outline 개요를 서술하다

162 클라스니크 씨에 대해 암시된 것은?

   (A) 생산 부서에서 근무할 것이다.

   (B) 구내식당의 위치를 알고 있다.

   (C) 이전에 부슬로노 인더스트리스에서 다른 직책을 맡았다.

   (D) 스테이시 씨의 상사가 될 것이다.

해설 **추론/암시**

두 번째 단락의 첫 문장에서 바르가스 씨가 클라스니크 씨에게 자신은 처음에 생산 보조원으로 그리고 현재는 생산 인솔자로서 거의 5년간 부슬로노에서 근무해 왔다(I have been working for Buslono ~ now as a production leader)면서, 클라스니크 씨가 곧 맡게 될 역할에 대해 실무 지식을 갖고 있다(I have firsthand knowledge of the role you're about to take on)고 했다. 따라서 클라스니크 씨는 바르가스 씨와 마찬가지로 생산 부서에서 업무를 맡게 될 것임을 알 수 있으므로 (A)가 정답이다.

163 [1], [2], [3], [4]로 표시된 곳에서 다음 문장이 들어가기에 가장 적합한 위치는?

   "오전 10시 30분에 그녀의 사무실에서 당신과 만나겠습니다."

   (A) [1]   (B) [2]

   (C) [3]   (D) [4]

해설 **문장 삽입**

주어진 문장에서 그녀의 사무실에서 만날 것이라고 했으므로 그녀의 사무실(her office)에서 지칭된 여자와 장소에 대한 내용이 앞에 있어야 한다. [3] 앞에서 가장 먼저 방문할 곳이 인사부(your first stop will be at the HR department)이고 스테이시 씨(Ms. Stacey)가 서류와 사원증을 준비해 줄 것이라고 했으므로, her office 즉, Ms. Stacey와 at the HR department가 언급된 문장 뒤인 [3]에 주어진 문장이 들어가야 자연스럽다. 따라서 (C)가 정답이다.

[164-167] 문자 메시지

산드라 멜렌데즈 [오후 1시 14분] 여러분 중 한 분이 저를 도와주실 수 있기를 바랍니다.

레스터 타바요용 [오후 1시 15분] 제가 해 보겠습니다. 무엇이 필요하신가요?

산드라 멜렌데즈 [오후 1시 16분] 우리가 사무실 창문 청소를 위해 이용하는 회사인 파운틴 오브 클린과 약속을 잡으려고 방금 전화를 했습니다.

다리아 커지크 [오후 1시 17분] **165**확실히 창문 청소가 필요합니다! 옆 건물의 건설 공사로 먼지가 많아졌어요.

산드라 멜렌데즈 [오후 1시 18분] 안타깝게도 파운틴 오브 클린의 전화번호가 끊겼고 웹사이트는 더 이상 이용 불가네요. **166**회사가 폐업한 것 같습니다.

레스터 타바요용 [오후 1시 19분] 유감이네요. **166**항상 일을 잘 해 줬는데요.

산드라 멜렌데즈 [오후 1시 20분] **164**믿을 만한 창문 청소업체를 알고 계신가요? 이전에 근무한 회사에서는 어디를 이용했나요?

레스터 타바요용 [오후 1시 21분] 거기도 파운틴 오브 클린을 이용했던 것 같아요.

다리아 커지크 [오후 1시 22분] 죄송하지만 저는 도움이 안 되네요.

레스터 타바요용 [오후 1시 23분] **167**고티머 씨에게 물어보세요. 예전 회사에서 유지 관리 책임자였어서 방안이 있으실 수도 있어요.

산드라 멜렌데즈 [오후 1시 24분] **167**바로 연락드려 봐야겠어요.

어휘 kick up (먼지를) 일으키다 disconnect (연결을) 끊다
go out of business 폐업하다 get in touch with ~와 연락하다

164 멜렌데즈 씨가 필요로 하는 것은 무엇인가?

   (A) 서비스 공급업체 추천   (B) 회사 안내서

   (C) 고객의 전화번호   (D) 동료의 근무 이력

해설 **세부 사항**

1시 20분에 멜렌데즈 씨가 믿을 만한 창문 청소업체를 알고 있는지(Do you know of any reliable window washers?)와 이전에 근무한 회사에서는 어디를 이용했는지(Who did your last employer use?)를 묻고 있는 것으로 보아 멜렌데즈 씨는 창문 청소업체를 추천 받고자 한다는 것을 알 수 있다. 따라서 (A)가 정답이다.

어휘 handbook 안내서

165 커지크 씨는 왜 건설 공사를 언급하는가?

   (A) 상당한 비용에 대해 해명하려고

   (B) 창문이 유독 더러운 이유를 언급하려고

   (C) 과도한 소음에 대해 불평하려고

   (D) 추가 사무 공간에 대해 감사를 표하려고

해설 **세부 사항**

1시 17분에 커지크 씨가 확실히 창문 청소가 필요하다(The windows could sure use a cleaning!)면서 옆 건물의 건설 공사로 먼지가 많아졌다(The construction project next door has kicked up a lot of dust)고 한 것으로 보아 청소가 필요할 정도로 창문에 먼지가 많이 쌓인 이유가 인근의 공사 때문이라고 말하려는 것임을 알 수 있다. 따라서 (B)가 정답이다.

어휘 justify 해명하다 significant 상당한 expense 비용 excessive 과도한 gratitude 감사

(**Paraphrasing**) 지문의 a lot of dust ➔ 정답의 dirty

166 오후 1시 19분에 타바요용 씨가 "유감이네요"라고 쓴 의도는 무엇인가?

   (A) 작업이 형편없이 되었다고 생각했다.

   (B) 문제에 대해 신경 쓰지 않는다.

   (C) 기밀 출처를 공개할 수 없다.

   (D) 어떠한 정보를 알게 되고는 실망했다.

해설 **의도 파악**

1시 18분에 멜렌데즈 씨가 이용해 오던 창문 청소 업체가 폐업한 것 같다(It seems the company has gone out of business)고 하자, 1시 19분에 타바요용 씨가 유감이다(That's too bad)라고 했고 항상 일을 잘 해 줬다(They always did a good job)며 아쉬워하고 있다. 따라서 타바요용 씨는 그동안 이용하던 업체가 폐업을 한 것 같다는 소식

에 실망스러움을 표현하려는 의도로 한 말임을 알 수 있으므로 (D)가 정답이다.

어휘 disclose 밝히다 confidential 기밀의 source 출처

167 멜렌데즈 씨는 다음으로 무엇을 하겠는가?
(A) 동료에게 연락
(B) 예약
(C) 웹사이트에 로그인
(D) 배송 예약

해설 **세부 사항**
1시 23분에 타바요용 씨가 고티머 씨에게 물어보라(Ask Mr. Gortimer)면서 예전 회사에서 유지 관리 책임자였어서 방안이 있으실 수도 있다(He was the head of maintenance at his old company and might have some ideas)고 제안하자 1시 24분에 멜렌데즈 씨가 바로 연락해 봐야겠다(I'll get in touch with him right away)고 제안을 받아들였다. 따라서 멜렌데즈 씨는 직장 동료인 고티머 씨에게 연락할 것임을 알 수 있으므로 (A)가 정답이다.

(Paraphrasing) 지문의 get in touch with
→ 정답의 Contact

[168-171] 공지

┌───┐
│ **루사카 비즈니스 연합** │
│ **업적 축하 행사** │
│ **로열 너깃 호텔, 6월 12일 토요일 오후 8시~11시** │
│ │
│ 6월 12일, 루사카 비즈니스 연합(LBA)은 여러 지역 사업가들에게 그들의 업적을 인정하기 위한 상을 수여할 예정입니다. 이 행사는 로열 너깃 호텔 연회장에서 개최됩니다. 입장권은 1인당 500콰차입니다. │
│ │
│ 또한 우리는 이번 행사에서 50년 동안 루사카 지역 사회에 공헌한 브렌다 마세보 씨에게 슈프리머시 상을 수여할 예정입니다. 그녀의 매장인 스케치 패스는 40년 동안 가장 다양한 종류의 미술품과 사무용품을 판매하는 곳으로 자리 잡았습니다. 게다가 **168**15년 전 그녀는 루사카 아츠 잼버리를 창설하였고, 이는 수많은 시각 예술가들과 행위 예술가들 그리고 중앙아프리카 전역의 관광객들을 도시로 불러들입니다. 그리고 작년에 마세보 씨는 청소년들을 위한 예술 프로그램을 시작했으며 이 프로그램은 이미 예술과학부로부터 찬사를 **169**끌어냈습니다. │
│ │
│ 우리는 예술품 경매로 저녁을 마무리할 예정입니다. **170**LBA의 웹사이트인 www.lusakabusinessalliance.org.zm에서 경매 물품 확인 및 행사 입장권 구매가 가능합니다. **171**경매에서 모금된 모든 수익금은 지역 청소년을 위한 레크리에이션 기회를 지원하는 것이 사명인 XJK 재단에 도움이 될 것입니다. │
└───┘

어휘 alliance 연합, 동맹 present 수여하다
acknowledge 인정하다 occasion 행사 supremacy 최고 decade 10년 assortment 모음, 종합 initiate 시작하다 draw (반응을) 끌어내다 praise 칭찬 auction 경매 proceeds 수익금 benefit ~에게 도움이 되다
foundation 재단 youth 청소년

168 마세보 씨에 대해 어떤 결론을 내릴 수 있는가?
(A) 최근에 사업을 시작했다.
(B) 다양한 방법으로 예술을 증진시켜 왔다.

(C) 중앙아프리카를 광범위하게 여행했다.
(D) 공무원이었다.

해설 **추론/암시**
두 번째 단락의 세 번째 문장에서 15년 전 그녀(Ms. Brenda Masebo)는 루사카 아츠 잼버리를 창설해 수많은 시각 예술가들과 행위 예술가들 그리고 중앙아프리카 전역의 관광객들을 도시로 불러들인다(15 years ago, she initiated the Lusaka Arts Jamboree, ~ across Central Africa)고 했고, 작년에는 청소년들을 위한 예술 프로그램을 시작했으며 이 프로그램은 이미 예술과학부로부터 찬사를 끌어냈다(And last year, Ms. Masebo began an arts program for teens ~ the Ministry of Arts and Sciences)고 했다. 이러한 점들로 보아 마세보 씨는 여러 방법으로 사람들이 예술을 접할 수 있도록 하고 있다는 것을 알 수 있으므로 (B)가 정답이다.

어휘 promote 촉진[고취]하다 extensively 광범위하게

169 두 번째 단락 7행의 "drawn"과 의미가 가장 가까운 단어는?
(A) 조였다
(B) 표시했다
(C) 불러일으켰다
(D) 삽화를 넣었다

해설 **동의어 찾기**
의미상 예술과학부로부터 찬사를 '끌어냈다'라는 뜻으로 쓰였으므로 '(반응을) 불러일으키다'를 뜻하는 (C) attracted가 정답이다.

170 공지에 따르면, LBA 웹사이트 방문자가 할 수 있는 것은 무엇인가?
(A) 입장권 구입하기
(B) 이메일 업데이트를 받기 위해 등록하기
(C) 현재 회원 명단 보기
(D) 수상 후보로 동료 지명하기

해설 **세부 사항**
마지막 단락의 두 번째 문장에서 LBA의 웹사이트에서 경매 물품 확인 및 행사 입장권 구매가 가능하다(Auction items can be viewed, and tickets for the event can be purchased on the LBA's Web site, www.lusakabusinessalliance.org.zm)고 했으므로 (A)가 정답이다.

어휘 nominate 지명하다

(Paraphrasing) 지문의 purchased → 정답의 Buy

171 행사의 한 가지 목적은 무엇인가?
(A) 조직의 새로운 책임자 소개
(B) 새로운 상의 제정 발표
(C) 매장의 기념일 축하
(D) 대의를 위한 기금 마련

해설 **세부 사항**
마지막 문장에서 경매에서 모금된 모든 수익금은 지역 청소년을 위한 레크리에이션 기회를 지원하는 것이 사명인 XJK 재단에 도움이 될 것(All proceeds raised from the

auction will benefit the XJK Foundation, whose mission is to support recreational opportunities for local youth)이라고 했으므로 (D)가 정답이다.

어휘 raise (자금 등을) 모으다 cause (사회적) 대의, 운동

Paraphrasing 지문의 proceeds → 정답의 money

[172-175] 회람

수신: KL 인터내셔널 홈 굿즈 영업 팀
발신: 알렉스 카딘, 소매 영업 이사
날짜: 10월 29일
제목: 밥솥

중앙 배송 창고에서 재스민 200 밥솥을 전량 판매했다고 통보받았습니다. 재스민 200은 우리의 가장 인기 있는 모델이고 진행 중인 전국 세일 행사의 핵심 제품이 될 것으로 예상되었기 때문에 이 같은 상황은 유감스럽습니다. 175세일에 대한 광고를 본 많은 고객들이 이 제품에 대해 문의할 것이라고 생각합니다. 이 문제는 즉시 해결되어야 합니다.

172재스민 200에 대한 할인은 정가의 15퍼센트였습니다. 172, 173전국적인 세일 사태를 수습하기 위해 본사에서는 우리가 로터스 600 모델을 동일하게 15퍼센트 할인된 가격으로 제공할 수 있도록 허용할 예정입니다. 로터스 600은 최고급 밥솥이기 때문에 많은 고객들이 이 상당한 할인 혜택을 이용해 제품을 구매하고 싶어 할 것이라고 예상합니다.

세일 기간 동안 재스민 200 구매에만 관심 있는 고객들을 위해, 매장 관리자는 할인 가격으로 추후에 구입 가능한 품절 교환권을 제공할 수도 있습니다. 하지만 174관리자들은 고객들에게 해당 모델은 6주에서 8주 정도 대기가 있다는 점을 알려야 합니다.

어휘 retail 소매 warehouse 창고 ongoing 계속 진행 중인 inquire 문의하다 remedy 바로잡다 top-of-the-line 최고급품의 take advantage of ~을 이용하다 substantial 상당한 rain check 품절 교환권

172 회람의 한 가지 주제는 무엇인가?
(A) 이전에 종결된 세일   (B) 새로 출시된 제품
(C) 최근 가격 책정안   (D) 품질 관리 문제

해설 **주제/목적**
두 번째 단락의 첫 문장에서 재스민 200에 대한 할인은 정가의 15퍼센트였다(The discount for the Jasmine 200 was 15 percent off the regular price)고 했고, 전국적인 세일 사태를 수습하기 위해 본사에서는 우리가 로터스 600 모델을 동일하게 15퍼센트 할인된 가격으로 제공할 수 있도록 허용할 것(To remedy the national sale situation, the corporate office will allow us to offer the Lotus 600 model with the same 15 percent discount)이라고 했다. 따라서 할인 행사를 위한 제품의 할인가 책정에 대해 언급하고 있으므로 (C)가 정답이다.

어휘 conclude 끝나다 release 출시하다

173 로터스 600에 대해 암시된 것은?
(A) 처음에는 전국 세일에 포함되지 않았다.
(B) 회사에서 가장 인기 있는 제품이다.
(C) 품절되어 재주문되어야 한다.
(D) 높은 가격으로 인해 판매가 부진하다.

해설 **추론/암시**
두 번째 단락의 두 번째 문장에서 전국적인 세일 사태를 수습하기 위해 본사는 로터스 600 모델을 동일하게 15퍼센트 할인된 가격으로 제공할 수 있도록 허용할 것(To remedy the national sale situation, the corporate office will allow us to offer the Lotus 600 model with the same 15 percent discount)이라고 했다. 따라서 문제 해결을 위해 로터스 600 모델이 할인 목록에 새롭게 추가될 것임을 알 수 있으므로 (A)가 정답이다.

어휘 initially 처음에 out of stock 품절된

174 회람에 따르면, 매장 관리자들이 고객들에게 전달해야 하는 사항은 무엇인가?
(A) 로터스 600의 생산이 곧 중단될 것이다.
(B) 재스민 200 밥솥은 6주에서 8주 동안 구입이 불가능하다.
(C) KL 인터내셔널 홈 굿즈 제품은 이미 대폭 할인되고 있다.
(D) 매장 보수 공사는 완료하는 데 한 달 이상 걸릴 것이다.

해설 **세부 사항**
마지막 문장에서 관리자들은 고객들에게 해당 모델(Jasmine 200)은 6주에서 8주 정도 대기가 있다는 점을 알려야 한다(managers should inform those customers that there will be a six- to eight-week wait for that model)고 했으므로 (B)가 정답이다.

어휘 discontinue 중단하다 heavily 많이

Paraphrasing 지문의 a six- to eight-week wait → 정답의 not be available for six to eight weeks

175 [1], [2], [3], [4]로 표시된 곳 중에서 다음 문장이 들어가기에 가장 적합한 위치는?
"이 문제는 즉시 해결되어야 합니다."
(A) [1]   (B) [2]
(C) [3]   (D) [4]

해설 **문장 삽입**
주어진 문장에서 이 문제는 즉시 해결되어야 한다고 했으므로 이 문제(This problem)라고 부를 수 있는 상황에 대한 내용이 앞에 있어야 한다. [1]이 포함된 단락에서 세일 주력 품목이 품절되어 버린 문제 상황을 언급하고 있으며, 세일 광고를 본 많은 고객들이 이 제품에 대해 문의할 것(many customers who see ads about the sale will inquire about it)이라고 이어질 문제 상황을 언급하고 있다. 따라서 이 문장 뒤인 [1]에 주어진 문장이 들어가야 연결이 자연스러우므로 (A)가 정답이다.

어휘 address 다루다, 해결하다 immediately 즉시

[176-180] 웹페이지 + 웹페이지

https://www.colettesbooks.co.uk/toppicks

콜레츠 북스의 선정 도서

봄이 끝나갈 무렵, 독자들은 여름에 읽을 가치 있는 읽을거리를 찾기 위해 콜레츠 북스를 찾습니다. **176, 177** 매 시즌, 콜레츠는 다섯 권의 신간 베스트를 선정합니다. **177** 그리고 이 다섯 권 중 세 권 이상을 구입한 쇼핑객은 구매가의 15퍼센트를 할인 받습니다.

다음은 올여름을 위한 저희의 추천서입니다.

- **178** 〈구름에 가려진〉, 레이첼 포크 저. 머지않은 미래에 탐험가들이 근처 은하계의 행성에 착륙하고 이미 생명체가 살고 있음을 발견한다.
- **179** 〈바다에서의 10일〉, 이샨 제임스 저. 저자는 19세기 후반 대서양 횡단 여행을 한 그의 조부모의 이야기를 들려준다.
- 〈길에 오르다〉, 페이지 쎄 저. 멀티시티 투어를 위해 밴드에 가입하라는 광고에 응하면서 한 음악가의 삶이 바뀐다.
- 〈내가 여기까지 온 방법〉, 아벨 우메 저. 배우 아벨 우메가 그의 어린 시절과 최종적으로 유명 인사가 되기까지의 과정을 유머러스한 시각으로 돌아본다.
- 〈몇몇 비밀은 지켜지지 않는다〉, 아사미 이시다 저. 아마추어 탐정 에리코 오가와는 일본의 한 작은 마을의 미스터리를 풀기 위해 그녀의 모든 기량을 발휘해야 한다.

www.colettesbooks.co.uk/readercomments에서 온라인 양식을 이용해 의견을 공유하여 이번 시즌 선정 도서에 대한 생각을 저희에게 알려 주시고, www.colettesbooks.co.uk/newsletter에서 저희 소식지 구독 신청을 해주세요.

어휘 pick 선택 turn to (도움 등을 위해) ~에 의지하다 rewarding 가치 있는 read 읽을거리 release 발간 distant (거리가) 먼 land 착륙하다 inhabit 거주하다 recount 이야기하다 eventual 궁극적인 detective 탐정

---

https://www.colettesbooks.co.uk/readercomments

지난달, 한 친구가 콜레츠 북스 선정 도서를 확인해 보라고 권유했는데 전 지금 푹 빠져 있습니다. **180** 여름을 맞아 목록에서 책 세 권을 구입했고 이제 막 첫 번째 책을 완독했습니다. **179** 이샨 제임스의 긴장감 넘치면서도 아주 개인적인 이야기에 생각지도 못한 즐거움을 느꼈습니다. 항해가 그렇게 재미있을 줄 누가 짐작이나 했겠습니까? 이 이야기는 훌륭한 영화가 될 수도 있습니다. **180** 다음 두 달 동안 다른 콜레츠의 여름 선정 도서를 더 읽을 기대감에 차 있습니다.

– 오마르 피타피

어휘 hooked (~에) 빠져 있는 pleasantly 즐겁게 suspenseful 긴장감 넘치는 voyage 항해

176 콜레츠 북스는 얼마나 자주 선정 도서 목록을 만드는가?
(A) 매주 (B) 매달
(C) 매 시즌 (D) 매년

해설 세부 사항
첫 웹페이지의 두 번째 문장에서 매 시즌 콜레츠는 다섯 권의 신간 베스트를 선정한다(Every season, Colette's

selects its top five new releases)고 했으므로 (C)가 정답이다.

177 콜레츠 북스의 고객은 어떻게 할인을 받을 수 있는가?
(A) 독자 클럽에 가입함으로써
(B) 최소 세 권의 추천 도서를 구입함으로써
(C) 웹사이트에 후기를 남김으로써
(D) 주간 소식지를 구독함으로써

해설 세부 사항
첫 번째 웹페이지의 두 번째 문장에서 매 시즌 콜레츠는 다섯 권의 신간 베스트를 선정하고 이 다섯 권 중 세 권 이상을 구입한 쇼핑객은 구매가의 15퍼센트를 할인받는다(Every season, Colette's selects its top five new releases—and shoppers who purchase at least three of the five books receive 15% off their purchase)고 했으므로 (B)가 정답이다.

어휘 review 후기 subscribe to ~을 구독하다

(Paraphrasing) 지문의 purchase → 정답의 buying

178 〈구름에 가려진〉의 독자는 무엇에 관심 있을 것 같은가?
(A) 현대 음악 (B) 탐정 소설
(C) 기상 현상 **(D) 우주여행**

해설 추론/암시
첫 번째 웹페이지의 세 번째 단락에서 레이첼 포크가 쓴 〈구름에 가려진〉(Hidden by Clouds, by Rachel Polk)은 머지않은 미래에 탐험가들이 근처 은하계의 행성에 착륙하고 이미 생명체가 살고 있음을 발견한다(In the not-too-distant future, explorers land on a planet in a nearby galaxy ~ inhabited)는 내용이라고 설명하고 있다. 따라서 〈구름에 가려진〉을 읽는 독자들은 우주 탐험에 관심이 있을 것이라고 짐작할 수 있으므로 (D)가 정답이다.

어휘 contemporary 현대의

(Paraphrasing) 지문의 planet ~ galaxy
→ 정답의 Space

179 피타피 씨가 읽은 책은?
(A) 〈바다에서의 10일〉
(B) 〈길에 오르다〉
(C) 〈내가 여기까지 온 방법〉
(D) 〈몇몇 비밀은 지켜지지 않는다〉

해설 연계
두 번째 웹페이지의 세 번째 문장에서 피타피 씨는 이샨 제임스의 긴장감 넘치면서도 개인적인 이야기에 생각지도 못한 즐거움을 느꼈다(I was pleasantly surprised by Ishan James's ~ story)고 했고, 첫 번째 웹페이지의 추천서 목록 두 번째 항목으로 이샨 제임스가 쓴 〈바다에서의 10일〉(Ten Days at Sea, by Ishan James)이 소개되고 있다. 따라서 피타피 씨가 이샨 제임스의 〈바다에서의 10일〉을 읽었다는 것을 알 수 있으므로 (A)가 정답이다.

180 피타피 씨는 가까운 미래에 무엇을 할 것 같은가?

    (A) 그가 읽은 책을 기반으로 한 영화를 본다.

    (B) 친구가 제안한 책을 찾아본다.

    (C) 좋아하는 작가가 쓴 다른 책을 산다.

    (D) 최근에 구입한 다른 책을 읽는다.

해설 추론/암시

두 번째 웹페이지의 두 번째 문장에서 피타피 씨는 여름을 맞아 목록에서 책 세 권을 구입했고 이제 막 첫 번째 책을 완독했다(For the summer, I purchased three books from the list, and I have just finished the first)고 했고, 마지막 문장에서 다음 두 달 동안 콜레츠의 여름 선정 도서를 더 읽을 기대감에 차 있다(I definitely look forward to reading more of Colette's summer selections ~ months)고 했다. 따라서 피타피 씨는 구입한 세 권 중 나머지 책들을 추가로 읽을 계획이므로 (D)가 정답이다.

[181-185] 정책 + 양식

마르제이 무선 기기 잠금 해제 정책

마르제이 무선에서 구입한 전화기는 당사의 무선 네트워크에 잠기도록 프로그래밍 되어 있어 다른 무선 네트워크에서 작동하지 않습니다. 특정 조건 하에 마르제이 무선은 다른 통신사의 네트워크에서 기기를 사용할 수 있도록 잠금 해제 코드를 제공합니다. 그러나 **181 기술 차이로 인하여 잠금 해제된 마르제이 전화기가 다른 통신사의 네트워크에서 작동하지 않거나, 전화기의 기능이 제한될 수 있습니다.** 마르제이 무선에서 전화기를 잠금 해제하기 위해서는 다음의 요건을 **182 충족해야** 합니다.

1) 기기가 분실 또는 도난 신고되지 않았다.

2) 기기가 다른 계정과 연동되지 않았다.

183 3) 기기가 연체 또는 미납 잔액이 없는 계정과 연동되어 있어야 한다.

4) 기기는 마르제이 무선의 유료 서비스를 최소 60일 이상 사용 중이어야 한다.

잠금 해제 절차를 시작하시려면 마르제이 계정에 로그인하십시오. 먼저 설정을 선택하시고, 그다음은 기기를 선택하셔서 "마르제이 무선 기기 잠금 해제" 양식을 작성하십시오. 617-555-0122로 전화하시면 추가적인 고객 지원을 받으실 수 있습니다. 인근 마르제이 무선 매장을 방문하여 도움을 받으실 수도 있습니다.

어휘 prevent 막다 carrier 통신업체 differing 다른 issued 발급된 functionality 기능 associate 결합시키다 past due 기한 경과 balance 잔액 drop by ~에 잠깐 들르다

마르제이 무선 기기 잠금 해제

계정 소유자 성함	아나 가부로
요청 일자	10월 1일
계정 번호	5902515663
계정 비밀번호	9318
계정 소유자 주소	4069 스타 뷰 웨이 시카고, 일리노이주 60601

마르제이 기기를 잠금 해제하려는 이유를 말씀해 주십시오:	저는 1년 동안 마르제이 고객이었고 서비스에 만족해 왔습니다. 저는 마르제이 가족 요금제를 이용하고 있으며 한 달에 단 100달러에 5회선 제공은 아주 합리적이라고 생각합니다. **183 제가 마르제이에서 구입한 모든 기기에 대한 지불이 거의 끝나갑니다.** 하지만 **184, 185 11월에 캐나다 위니펙으로 이사할 예정인데, 며칠 전 그곳에 방문하고 나서 185 귀사의 서비스 범위가 미국 이외의 지역에는 미치지 않는다는 것을 깨달았습니다.**

어휘 holder 소유자 PIN 비밀번호 plan 요금제 line 전화선 reasonable 합리적인 coverage 서비스 범위 extend 연장하다

181 정책에서 마르제이 무선의 전화기에 대해 언급한 것은?

    (A) 도난당한 경우 즉시 마르제이 무선에 신고해야 한다.

    (B) 할인된 가격에 제공된다.

    (C) 잠금 해제가 되고 나서 다른 네트워크에서 제대로 작동되지 않을 수 있다.

    (D) 마르제이 무선에서 구입한 날로부터 30일 후에 잠금 해제가 가능하다.

해설 Not/True

정책의 첫 번째 단락 세 번째 문장에서 기술 차이로 인하여 잠금 해제된 마르제이 전화기가 다른 통신사의 네트워크에서 작동하지 않을 수 있거나 전화기의 기능이 제한될 수 있다(because of differing technologies, an unlocked Marjay-issued phone may not work on another carrier's network, or the phone may have limited functionality)고 했으므로 (C)가 정답이다.

182 정책의 첫 번째 단락 6행의 "meet"와 의미가 가장 가까운 단어는?

    (A) 가입하다   **(B) 충족시키다**

    (C) 고려하다   (D) 해결하다

해설 동의어 찾기

의미상 요건을 '충족해야' 한다는 뜻으로 쓰였으므로 '충족시키다'라는 의미의 (B) satisfy가 정답이다.

183 가부로 씨가 전화기를 잠금 해제하기 전에 해야 할 일은 무엇일 것 같은가?

    (A) 전화기가 다른 네트워크와 호환되는지 확인한다.

    (B) 전화기를 분실 또는 도난당한 것으로 신고한다.

    (C) 계정에 있는 전화기 비용 결제를 끝낸다.

    (D) 기존 계정을 탈퇴한다.

해설 연계

정책 중반부에 있는 요건의 3번 항목에서 기기가 연체 또는 미납 잔액이 없는 계정과 연결되어 있어야 한다(The device must be associated with an account with no past due or unpaid balances)고 했고, 양식의 오른쪽 마지막 칸의 세 번째 문장에서 가부로 씨는 마르제이에서 구입한 기기에 대한 지불이 거의 끝나간다(I am almost finished paying for all the devices I purchased from Marjay)고 했다. 따라서 가부로 씨는 정책에 따라 잠금 해제를 하기 전에 구입한 기기에 남아 있는 잔액을 지불 완료해야 하므로 (C)가 정답이다.

어휘 compatible 호환이 되는 existing 기존의

184 가부로 씨는 왜 자신의 마르제이 무선 전화기의 잠금을 해제하려고 하는가?
(A) 마르제이 무선이 서비스하지 않는 지역으로 이사를 간다.
(B) 자신의 요금제 가격에 불만이 있다.
(C) 가족 일원에게 자신의 전화기를 줄 생각이다.
(D) 마르제이 무선의 고객 담당자에 불만이 있다.

해설 **세부 사항**
양식 하단에 있는 전화기 잠금 해제 요청에 대한 이유의 마지막 문장에서 가부로 씨는 캐나다 위니펙으로 이사할 예정인데 며칠 전 그곳에 방문하고 나서 마르제이 무선의 서비스 범위가 미국 외 지역에는 미치지 않는다는 것을 깨달았다(I will be relocating to Winnipeg, Canada ~ I realized that your coverage does not extend outside of the United States)고 했으므로 정답은 (A)이다.

어휘 cover 포함시키다 representative 담당자, 직원
(Paraphrasing) 지문의 relocating → 정답의 moving

185 가부로 씨에 대해 명시된 것은?
(A) 5년 동안 마르제이 무선 고객이었다.
(B) 계정 비밀번호를 잊어버렸다.
(C) 마르제이 무선 요금제의 유일한 사용자이다.
(D) 최근에 캐나다로 여행을 갔다.

해설 **Not/True**
양식 하단에 있는 잠금 해제 요청에 대한 이유의 마지막 문장에서 가부로 씨는 캐나다 위니펙으로 이사할 예정인데 며칠 전 그곳에 방문하였다(I will be relocating to Winnipeg, Canada ~ visiting there a few days ago)고 했으므로 가부로 씨는 최근에 캐나다에 다녀왔다는 것을 알 수 있다. 따라서 (D)가 정답이다.

[186-190] 전단 + 편지 + 광고

186 6월 23일에 40여 년 전 처음 문을 연 이래 녹스빌 지역의 랜드마크였던 톰스 푸드 팰리스에 작별을 고하러 오세요! **187** 오후 4시에서 6시 사이에 레스토랑의 주차장에 도착하는 선착순 40분께 무료 기념 티셔츠를 나눠 드립니다.

www.tomsfoodpalace.com에 온라인으로 접속하셔서 선명한 색상의 티셔츠를 구입하실 수도 있습니다. 티셔츠의 앞면에는 "톰스 푸드 팰리스", **186** 뒷면에는 "행복한 은퇴, 톰!"이라고 쓰여 있습니다. **189** 티셔츠 판매 수익금은 톰이 아끼는 자선 단체이자 녹스빌 지역 학교의 어린이 지원 교육 프로그램인 '쿠킹 위드 키즈'에 전달될 예정입니다.

어휘 commemorative 기념하는 retirement 은퇴
proceeds 수익금 charity 자선 단체

〈이스트 테네시 헤럴드〉

편집자님께:

188 저는 어렸을 때부터 아침 식사를 하러 톰 헨슬리의 레스토랑을 방문해 왔습니다. 지난주, 저는 손녀를 데려갔습니다. 제가 가장 좋아하는 종업원인 리타 씨가 놀라운 메시지가 적힌 티셔츠를 입고 있었습니다. 그녀는 헨슬리 씨가 업체를 매각했고 바비큐 레스토랑이 그 자리를 대신할 것이라고 설명했습니다. 바비큐를 좋아하긴 하지만, 특히 아침 식사 시간에 톰스 푸드 팰리스의 따스한 분위기를 대체할 수 있는 곳은 없을 겁니다! **188** 친절한 주인 헨슬리 씨는 테이블마다 커피잔이 항상 가득 차 있는지 확인하면서 늘 아침 손님들에게 인사를 건넵니다.

이 레스토랑을 방문할 기회가 빠르게 줄어들고 있습니다. **187** 어제 저는 레스토랑 밖에서 열린 톰의 은퇴 축하 행사에 참석한 첫 손님들 중 한 명이 되어 영광이었습니다. 귀하의 신문 독자들은 그곳에서 마지막 식사를 즐길 수 있는 시간이 얼마 없다는 것을 알아야 합니다!

티파니 체스터

어휘 display 드러내다 atmosphere 분위기 gracious 인자한 host 주인 customarily 관례적으로 diminish 줄어들다 honored 영광으로 생각하는

브린델즈 바비큐
(구 톰스 푸드 팰리스)

치킨과 갈비 전문점

190 최신 지점 그랜드 오픈:
1192 웨스트 리버 로, 녹스빌

7월 17일 개점
189 개점일 수익금은 '쿠킹 위드 키즈'에 기부됩니다.

이 광고를 언급하시고 아래 지점을 포함한 브린델즈 바비큐 전 지점에서 무료 탄산음료를 받으세요:

2300 파크 서클, 오크 릿지
4049 스웨데스포드몰, 코린턴
5 랜턴 레인, 메리빌

어휘 formerly 예전에 rib 갈비 donate 기부하다

---

186 전단의 목적은 무엇인가?
(A) 새로운 자선 단체에 관심을 불러일으키려고
(B) 은퇴 행사에 사람들을 초대하려고
(C) 기념일 축하 행사에 레스토랑 직원들을 초대하려고
(D) 기업을 위한 마케팅 캠페인을 소개하려고

해설 **주제/목적**
전단의 첫 문장에서 6월 23일에 40여 년 전 처음 문을 연 이래 녹스빌 지역의 랜드마크였던 톰스 푸드 팰리스에 작별을 고하러 오라(Join us on June 23 to say goodbye to Tom's Food Palace ~ since it first opened over 40 years ago!)고 초대하며 두 번째 단락의 두 번째 문장에서 나누어 드리는 티셔츠의 뒷면에는 "행복한 은퇴, 톰!"이라고 쓰여 있다(the back reads "Happy Retirement, Tom!")고 했다. 따라서 전단은 톰스 푸드 팰리스 레스토랑의 톰의 은퇴 행사에 사람들을 초대하기 위한 것이므로 (B)가 정답이다.

어휘 attention 관심 anniversary 기념일

187 체스터 씨에 대해 사실일 것 같은 것은?

(A) 케이터링 업체를 소유하고 있다.

(B) 톰스 푸드 팰리스에서 근무했었다.

(C) 6월 23일에 무료 티셔츠를 받았다.

(D) 행사를 기획했다.

해설 **연계**

전단의 첫 번째 단락 두 번째 문장에서 오후 4시에서 6시 사이에 레스토랑의 주차장에 도착하는 선착순 40명에게 무료 기념 티셔츠를 준다(Free commemorative T-shirts will be given away to the first 40 people who arrive ~ at the restaurant's parking area)고 했고, 편지의 두 번째 단락 두 번째 문장에서 체스터 씨가 어제 레스토랑 밖에서 열린 톰의 은퇴 축하 행사에 참석한 첫 손님들 중한 명이 되어 영광이었다(Yesterday I was honored to be one of the first guests who attended Tom's retirement celebration outside of the restaurant)고 했다. 따라서 체스터 씨는 6월 23에 열린 톰스 푸드 팰리스의 행사에 참석한 첫 40명 중 한 명으로 무료 기념 티셔츠를 받았다는 것을 알 수 있으므로 (C)가 정답이다.

188 편지에서 헨슬리 씨에 대해 암시하는 것은?

(A) 체스터 씨에게 여러 번 인사했다.

(B) 다른 마을로 이사한다.

(C) 레스토랑의 소유권을 가족에게 양도한다.

(D) 체스터 씨와 아침 식사 조리법을 공유했다.

해설 **추론/암시**

편지의 첫 단락 첫 문장에서 체스터 씨가 어렸을 때부터 아침 식사를 하러 톰 헨슬리의 레스토랑을 방문해 왔다(I have been visiting Tom Hensley's restaurant for breakfast since I was a child)고 했고, 같은 단락의 마지막 문장에서 헨슬리 씨는 늘 아침 손님들에게 인사를 건넨다(Mr. Hensley customarily greets his morning guests at each table)고 했다. 따라서 헨슬리 씨는 아침 식사를 하러 온 체스터 씨에게 인사를 한 적이 여러 차례 있었을 것이라고 짐작할 수 있으므로 (A)가 정답이다.

어휘 occasion 경우 transfer 양도하다 ownership 소유권

189 톰스 푸드 팰리스와 브린델즈 바비큐의 공통점은 무엇인가?

(A) 둘 다 교육 프로그램을 지원한다.

(B) 둘 다 온라인으로 선물을 판매한다.

(C) 둘 다 녹스빌에서 설립되었다.

(D) 둘 다 40년 동안 사업을 해왔다.

해설 **연계**

전단의 마지막 문장에서 티셔츠 판매 수익금은 톰이 아끼는 자선 단체이자 녹스빌 지역 학교의 어린이 지원 교육 프로그램인 '쿠킹 위드 키즈'에 전달될 예정(Proceeds from the T-shirt sales will go to Tom's favorite charity, Cooking with Kids, an educational program supporting children in Knoxville schools)이라고 했고, 광고의 중반부에 개점일 수익금은 '쿠킹 위드 키즈'에 기부(Opening-day proceeds will be donated to

Cooking with Kids)한다고 했다. 따라서 톰스 푸드 팰리스와 브린델즈 바비큐 두 곳 모두 '쿠킹 위드 키즈'라는 교육 프로그램에 기부한다는 것을 알 수 있으므로 (A)가 정답이다.

어휘 found 설립하다

190 광고에서 홍보하는 것은 무엇인가?

(A) 웨스트 리버 로 축제   **(B) 신규 사업점 개점**

(C) 할인된 식사 제공   (D) 레스토랑 직원 채용 행사

해설 **세부 사항**

광고의 상단에 최신 지점 그랜드 오픈(Grand opening of our newest location)이라고 홍보하고 있으므로 정답은 (B)이다.

[191-195] 광고 + 이메일 + 프로필

심플레즈 비즈니스 솔루션즈

191 마케팅 관리자가 되는 것은 두 가지 일을 동시에 책임지는 것을 의미합니다. 여러분은 성공적인 마케팅 전략을 세워야 합니다. 동시에, 여러분은 팀원들의 창의력과 생산성을 지지해야 합니다. **192** 우리는 마케팅 관리자를 위한 라이브 온라인 과정을 제공하며 이 과정은 여러분이 이러한 요구의 균형을 맞추는 방법을 이해하고 연구 및 의사소통 기술을 연마하는 데 도움을 줄 것입니다. 우리의 일이 수업에서는 여러분의 성공을 위한 가장 필수적인 기술을 강조합니다. 이 수업의 강사는 베이트솔 인더스트리스의 최고 마케팅 책임자인 애넌스 로이 씨입니다. 각 강좌 날짜마다 등록생 12명으로 참여가 제한됩니다.

온라인 강좌 일자 (택1): 4월 4일, 4월 8일, 4월 13일, 5월 3일

비용:

- **193** 얼리버드 등록 (3월 10일까지): 299달러
- 정규 등록 (3월 25일까지): 349달러

어휘 at once 동시에 productivity 생산성 demand 요구 sharpen (기량 등을) 갈고 닦다 essential 필수적인 instructor 강사 cap 한도를 정하다 registrant 등록자

발신: 마렉 노보트니 〈mnovotny@simplezebusinesssolutions.com〉

수신: 파블로 에스피노자 〈pespinoza@piscesmail.mx〉

193 날짜: 3월 9일

제목: 교육 과정

첨부: 프로필

에스피노자 씨께,

193 오늘 일찍이 등록하신 강좌와 관련하여 글을 씁니다. 안타깝게도 정규 강사인 로이 씨는 일정이 맞지 않아 4월 8일 강좌를 진행할 수 없게 되었습니다. 4월 8일 강좌는 엘레나 자모라가 대신 강의할 예정입니다. **195** 자모라 씨는 마케팅 강좌를 가르친 폭넓은 경험이 있으며 출판 업계에서의 자신의 업무에 대해 주간 팟캐스트를 진행하고 있습니다. 자모라 씨에 대해 더 자세히 알아보실 수 있도록 그녀의 프로필을 첨부했습니다.

로이 씨의 강좌를 선호하신다면 4월 13일에 열리는 수업으로 등록을 변경해 드릴 수 있습니다. 이 옵션이 괜찮으신지 알려주십시오.

마렉 노보트니, 교육 담당자

어휘 extensive 폭넓은 acceptable 받아들일 수 있는

비즈니스 프로필

엘레나 자모라, 기업 교육 강사

자모라 씨는 마케팅 분야의 주요 인사입니다. 웨스턴 메인 대학에서 마케팅 학위를 받은 후, 그녀는 식품 제조사인 엣지웨어 프로덕츠의 분석가로 고용되었습니다. 이후 그녀는 여러 다른 산업 분야에서 최고 마케팅 관리자 직책을 맡았습니다. **194 5년 전, 자모라 씨는 기업 교육 강사로서 자신의 사업을 시작했습니다.** 그녀는 비즈니스 강좌를 열고 있지 않을 때는 **195 자신의 인기 있는 팟캐스트인 〈페이퍼 플레인즈〉를 진행합니다.**

어휘 leading figure 주요 인사, 중진　field 분야　degree 학위　distinct 뚜렷이 다른　facilitate 가능하게 하다

---

191 광고에 따르면, 마케팅 관리자 직책은 왜 유독 어려운가?
(A) 마케팅 팀을 구성하는 것이 어렵다.
(B) 마케팅 캠페인은 장기간 진행된다.
(C) 이 일은 여러 분야의 기술을 필요로 한다.
(D) 마케팅 산업은 끊임없이 변화한다.

해설　세부 사항
광고의 첫 문장에서 마케팅 관리자가 되는 것은 두 가지 일을 동시에 책임지는 것을 의미한다(Being a marketing manager means taking on the responsibilities of two jobs at once)면서, 성공적인 마케팅 전략을 세워야 하는(You must develop a winning marketing strategy) 동시에 팀원들의 창의력과 생산성을 지지해야 한다(At the same time, you must support team members' creativity and productivity)고 했다. 따라서 마케팅 관리자는 동시에 두 분야의 일을 해야 한다고 언급하고 있으므로 (C)가 정답이다.

어휘 assemble 구성하다, 모집하다　constantly 끊임없이

192 광고에서 암시된 것은?
(A) 성공적인 마케팅은 온라인으로 배울 수 없다.
(B) 관리자는 채용 결정에 있어 창의적이어야 한다.
(C) 좋은 마케팅 계획을 수립하는 데는 몇 주가 걸린다.
(D) 효과적인 의사소통 전략을 개발하는 것이 중요하다.

해설　추론/암시
광고의 네 번째 문장에서 우리는 마케팅 관리자를 위한 라이브 온라인 과정을 제공하며 이 과정은 마케팅 관리자가 이러한 요구의 균형을 맞추는 방법을 이해하고 연구 및 의사소통 기술을 연마하는 데 도움을 줄 것(We offer a live online course for marketing managers ~ sharpen your research and communication skills)이라고 강조하고 있다. 따라서 마케팅 관리자에게는 업무의 균형을 잡는 것은 물론 의사소통 기술을 개발하는 것이 중요하다는 것을 짐작할 수 있으므로 (D)가 정답이다.

어휘 effective 효과적인

(Paraphrasing) 지문의 sharpen → 정답의 Developing

---

193 에스피노자 씨가 등록한 과정에 대해 사실인 것은?
(A) 수업에 299달러를 지불했다.
(B) 이미 12명의 등록생이 있다.
(C) 고용주가 그에게 수업을 들을 것을 요구했다.
(D) 비용은 환불 가능하다.

해설　연계
광고의 하단에 얼리버드 등록 (3월 10일까지)은 299달러(Early-bird Registration (by March 10): $299)라고 나와 있고, 작성 날짜가 3월 9일(Date: March 9)인 이메일의 첫 문장에서 노보트니 씨는 오늘 일찍 에스피노자 씨가 등록한 강좌와 관련하여 글을 쓴다(I am writing about the course you registered for earlier today)고 했다. 따라서 에스피노자 씨는 얼리버드 등록 혜택을 받을 수 있는 3월 9일에 등록하였으므로 수업료로 299달러를 지불했을 것이라는 점을 알 수 있다. 따라서 (A)가 정답이다.

194 자모라 씨에 대해 명시된 것은?
(A) 웨스턴 메인 대학에서 가르친다.
(B) 엣지웨어 프로덕츠를 설립했다.
(C) 비행 강사이다.
(D) 자영업자이다.

해설　Not/True
프로필의 네 번째 문장에서 5년 전, 자모라 씨는 기업 교육 강사로서 자신의 사업을 시작했다(Five years ago, Ms. Zamora started her own business as a corporate trainer)고 했으므로 (D)가 정답이다.

어휘 self-employed 자영업을 하는

(Paraphrasing) 지문의 started her own business → 정답의 self-employed

195 〈페이퍼 플레인즈〉의 주제는?
(A) 출판　　　　　(B) 식품업
(C) 기업 교육　　　(D) 여행

해설　연계
프로필의 마지막 문장에서 자모라 씨가 인기 있는 팟캐스트인 〈페이퍼 플레인즈〉를 진행한다(she hosts her popular podcast *Paper Planes*)고 했고, 이메일의 네 번째 문장에서 자모라 씨는 출판 업계에서의 자신의 업무에 대한 주간 팟캐스트를 진행하고 있다(Ms. Zamora ~ has a weekly podcast about her work in the publishing industry)고 했다. 따라서 자모라 씨의 팟캐스트인 〈페이퍼 플레인즈〉는 출판 업계에 대해 주로 다룬다는 것을 알 수 있으므로 (A)가 정답이다.

변화를 겪고 있는 호텔 체인

뉴욕 (7월 6일)—그리스에 본사를 둔 **197 시빌럭스 프로퍼티스**는 호텔을 지속적으로 확장, 재설계 및 개선하고 있다. 몇몇 시빌럭스 호텔은 결혼식과 같은 사적인 행사뿐 아니라 콘퍼런스나 컨벤션을 유치하기 위해 변화를 만들고 있다.

197 시빌럭스 프로퍼티스 최고 운영 책임자인 안젤로 제넬리스는 회사에서 진행 중인 일에 대한 본보기로 자메이카 킹스턴에 있는 자사의 호텔을 꼽는다.

"저희는 최근 행사를 위한 공간을 확장했습니다."라고 제넬리스 씨는 말했다. "게다가, 공간들은 다양한 규모의 고객에 맞춰 쉽게 재구성될 수 있습니다. 저희는 대형 컨벤션을 주최할 수도 있지만 결혼식이나 비즈니스 미팅을 위한 공간도 제공할 수 있습니다."

196 시드니, 밴쿠버, 마이애미를 포함한 세계 각지의 도시에 있는 시빌럭스 호텔 또한 최근 새 단장을 했다.

어휘 undergo 겪다 intend 의도하다 chief operating officer 최고 운영 책임자 point to ~을 가리키다 reconfigure 재구성하다 renovate 개조하다

다가오는 행사

토론토 (7월 25일)—**197 토론토에 본부가 있는 국제 소기업 및 기업가 정신 협회(IASBE)**가 11월 17일부터 24일까지 자메이카 킹스턴의 시빌럭스 호텔에서 제10회 연례 콘퍼런스를 개최한다.

IASBE 콘퍼런스는 전 세계로부터 참가자들을 유치한다. 매일 밤 기조연설자가 등장하며 한 주 동안 수백 개의 회의와 워크숍이 열린다.

모든 컨벤션 행사에 참석하려면 사전 등록이 필요하다. 등록은 www.iasbe.ca/conference를 방문하면 된다. **198 콘퍼런스 참석자를 위해 9월 25일까지 예약되는 모든 객실에 대한 할인 요금이 적용된다.** 컨벤션 프로그램과 출연 연사에 대한 추가 정보가 필요할 경우 다니엘 올니슨에게 dolnisson@iasbe.ca로 연락해야 한다.

어휘 entrepreneurship 기업가 정신 keynote speaker 기조연설자 advanced 사전의 rate 요금 attendee 참석자

수신: 송지와 〈jwsong@songproducts.kr〉
발신: 마틴 넴바드 〈mnembhard@ceebeelux.com〉
198 날짜: 9월 6일
제목: 예약
첨부: IASBE 행사

송 씨께:

이 이메일은 11월 17일부터 24일까지 킹스턴에 있는 저희 시빌럭스 호텔에서의 귀하의 호텔 예약을 확인합니다. **198,199 귀하께서 IASBE 콘퍼런스에 참석하실 예정이라서 제 임의대로 행사 일정 사본을 첨부했습니다.**

저희 호텔은 투숙객들에게 무료 피트니스 수업과 테니스 코트 이용을 제공합니다. 또한 호텔 내에 여러 상점과 레스토랑이 있습니다. 투숙하시는 동안 저희의 모든 편의 시설을 이용하실 수 있습니다.

200 체크인하실 때 신분증을 지참해 주십시오. 저희 호텔에서 만족스러운 숙박을 하시기를 바랍니다.

마틴 넴바드, 예약 관리자

어휘 take the liberty of 마음대로 ~하다 amenities 편의 시설 proof of identity 신분 증명

196 첫 번째 기사에서 시빌럭스 프로퍼티스에 대해 암시된 것은?
(A) 국제적인 사업체이다.
(B) 새로운 최고 운영 책임자를 고용했다.
(C) 최근 본사를 옮겼다.
(D) 다른 호텔 체인과 합병했다.

해설 추론 / 암시

첫 기사의 마지막 문장에서 시드니, 밴쿠버, 마이애미를 포함한 세계 각지의 도시에 있는 시빌럭스 호텔 또한 최근 새 단장을 했다(Ceebeelux hotels in cities around the world, ~ have also been recently renovated)고 한 것으로 보아 시빌럭스 프로퍼티스는 세계적으로 호텔 체인을 운영하는 기업임을 알 수 있다. 따라서 (A)가 정답이다.

어휘 headquarters 본사 merge 합병하다

(Paraphrasing) 지문의 around the world
→ 정답의 international

197 제10회 연례 IASBE 콘퍼런스에 대해 암시된 것은?
(A) 참석 비용이 예년보다 많이 들 것이다.
(B) 새로 단장한 호텔에서 열릴 것이다.
(C) 올니슨 씨가 연사로 출연할 것이다.
(D) 11월 말쯤에는 매진될 것이다.

해설 연계

첫 번째 기사의 첫 문장에서 시빌럭스 프로퍼티스는 호텔을 지속적으로 확장, 재설계 및 개선하고 있다(Greece-based Ceebeelux Properties continues to expand, redesign, and improve its hotels)고 했고 두 번째 단락에서 시빌럭스의 최고 운영 책임자인 안젤로 제넬리스는 회사에서 진행 중인 일에 대한 본보기로 자메이카 킹스턴에 있는 자사의 호텔을 꼽는다(Angelo Genelis ~ points to the company's hotel in Kingston, Jamaica, as a model for what the company is doing)고 했으며, 두 번째 기사의 첫 문장에서 토론토에 본부가 있는 국제 소기업 및 기업가 정신 협회(IASBE)가 11월 17일부터 24일까지 자메이카 킹스턴의 시빌럭스 호텔에서 제10회 연례 콘퍼런스를 개최한다(The ~ (IASBE), based in Toronto, is holding its tenth annual conference ~ at the Ceebeelux Hotel in Kingston, Jamaica)고 했다. 따라서 제10회 연례 IASBE 콘퍼런스는 새롭게 개조된 자메이카 킹스턴 호텔에서 열리는 것임을 알 수 있으므로 (B)가 정답이다.

(Paraphrasing) 지문의 expand, redesign, and improve → 정답의 newly remodeled

198 송 씨에 대해 어떤 결론을 내릴 수 있는가?

(A) 호텔에서 테니스를 칠 계획이다.

(B) 콘퍼런스를 위해 일찍 도착할 계획이다.

(C) 할인된 호텔 요금을 받을 자격이 된다.

(D) 이전에 킹스턴 시빌럭스 호텔에 숙박했다.

해설 **연계**

두 번째 기사의 세 번째 단락 세 번째 문장에서 콘퍼런스 참석자를 위해 9월 25일까지 예약되는 모든 객실에 대한 할인 요금이 적용된다(Discounted rates for conference attendees are available for all rooms booked by 25 September)고 했고, 이메일의 작성 날짜가 9월 6일(Date: 6 September)이고 송 씨가 IASBE 콘퍼런스에 참석할 예정이라(As you will be attending the IASBE conference)고 했다. 따라서 송 씨는 IASBE 콘퍼런스의 참석자로서 9월 25일 이전에 호텔 객실을 예약하여 할인된 요금을 적용받을 수 있으므로 (C)가 정답이다.

어휘 be eligible for ~의 자격이 있다

199 넴바드 씨가 이메일과 함께 보낸 것은 무엇인가?

(A) 피트니스 수업 시간표   (B) 현지 음식점들의 메뉴

(C) 시빌럭스 호텔 가는 길   (D) 콘퍼런스에 대한 정보

해설 **세부 사항**

이메일의 첫 단락 두 번째 문장에서 넴바드 씨가 송 씨에게 IASBE 콘퍼런스에 참석할 예정이라서 임의대로 행사 일정 사본을 첨부했다(As you will be attending the IASBE conference, I have taken the liberty of attaching a copy of the schedule of events)고 했다. 따라서 정답은 (D)이다.

Paraphrasing 지문의 the schedule of events

→ 정답의 Information about a conference

200 넴바드 씨는 송 씨에게 무엇을 해달라고 요청하는가?

(A) 고객 만족도 설문 조사 작성

(B) 매장 쿠폰을 받기 위한 호텔 데스크 방문

(C) 체크인 시 신분증 제시

(D) 예약 날짜 확인

해설 **세부 사항**

이메일의 세 번째 단락 첫 문장에서 넴바드 씨가 송 씨에게 체크인할 때 신분증을 지참해 달라(Please have proof of identity with you when you check in)고 요청하고 있으므로 (C)가 정답이다.

어휘 stop by ~에 들르다   confirm 확인하다

Paraphrasing 지문의 proof of identity

→ 정답의 identification

ETS 토익
단기공략
950+